The quintessential San Francisco transportation, the cable car. See chapter 7. © John Elk III Photography.

In this town, leisure rules. At the top, shooting for the pin at Lincoln Park Municipal Golf Course; and bottom, strolling through the Strybing Arboretum in Golden Gate Park. See chapter 7. Both photos © John Elk III Photography.

The Japanese Tea Garden in Golden Gate Park. See chapter 7. © Robert Holmes Photography.

Left, an overview of the neighborhood of North Beach, home to the City Lights Bookstore and an assortment of funky cafes. Photo opposite © Catherine Karnow; both photos on this page © Robert Holmes Photography.

San Francisco's art scene is not limited to traditional museums—colorful murals abound in the Mission District (top), and can be found elsewhere throughout the city, such as this one (bottom) in the interior of the Coit Tower. See chapter 7. Top photo © Catherine Karnow Photography; bottom photo © John Elk III Photography.

The Age of Aquarius, updated for the millennium—this friendly local sells eggs at the Farmer's Market on the Embarcadero. See chapter 9. © Wolfgang Kaehler Photography.

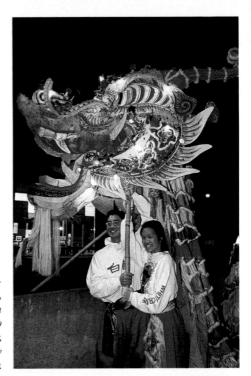

Chinatown is a bustling neighborhood filled with restaurants, shops, and markets—perfect for the urban explorer. See chapter 7. Top photo © John Elk III Photography, bottom photo © Catherine Karnow Photography.

Cars descending Lombard Street, the "crookedest street in the world." See chapter 7. © Jim Corwin / Tony Stone Images.

Night falls over the San Francisco skyline. © Catherine Karnow Photography.

Touristy Fisherman's Wharf attracts millions of visitors every year. See chapter 7. © Tom Tracy / The Stock Market.

Located in the Marina District, the Palace of Fine Arts is home to the Exploratorium. See chapter 7. © John Elk III Photography.

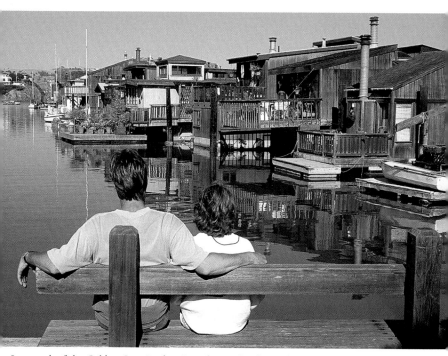

Just north of the Golden Gate Bridge, Sausalito makes for a relaxing day trip from the city. See chapter 11. © Robert Holmes Photography.

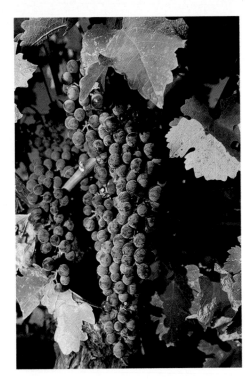

A quick jaunt to the wineries of Napa and Sonoma offers a different taste of Northern California, just about an hour from San Francisco. See chapter 12. Left and both photos opposite © John Elk III Photography; bottom © Jerry Alexander / Tony Stone Worldwide.

*Whether you walk, run, or drive, crossing the Golden Gate Bridge is an unforgettable trip.
See chapter 7. © Andrea Pistolesi Photography.*

When should I travel to get the best airfare?
Where do I go for answers to my travel questions?
What's the best and easiest way to plan and book my trip?

frommers.travelocity.com

Frommer's, the travel guide leader, has teamed up with **Travelocity.com**, the leader in online travel, to bring you an in-depth, easy-to-use resource designed to help you plan and book your trip online.

At **frommers.travelocity.com**, you'll find free online updates about your destination from the experts at Frommer's plus the outstanding travel planning and purchasing features of Travelocity.com. Travelocity.com provides reservations capabilities for 95 percent of all airline seats sold, more than 47,000 hotels, and over 50 car rental companies. In addition, Travelocity.com offers more than 2,000 exciting vacation and cruise packages. Travelocity.com puts you in complete control of your travel planning with these and other great features:

> **Expert travel guidance from Frommer's** - over 150 writers reporting from around the world!

> **Best Fare Finder** - an interactive calendar tells you when to travel to get the best airfare

> **Fare Watcher** - we'll track airfare changes to your favorite destinations

> **Dream Maps** - a mapping feature that suggests travel opportunities based on your budget

> **Shop Safe Guarantee** - 24 hours a day / 7 days a week live customer service, and more!

Whether you're traveling on a tight budget, looking for a quick weekend getaway, or planning the trip of a lifetime, Frommer's guides and Travelocity.com will make your travel dreams a reality. You've bought the book, now book the trip!

Other Great Guides for Your Trip:

Frommer's San Francisco from $60 a Day

Frommer's Portable San Francisco

Unofficial Guide to San Francisco

Frommer's Irreverent Guide to San Francisco

Frommer's Memorable Walks in San Francisco

Wonderful Weekends from San Francisco

Frommer's Portable California Wine Country

Frommer's California

Frommer's California from $60 a Day

The Unofficial Guide to California with Kids

Monks' Guide to California

Frommer's Best-Loved California Driving Tours

Here's what the critics say about Frommer's:

"Amazingly easy to use. Very portable, very complete."
—*Booklist*

♦

"The only mainstream guide to list specific prices. The Walter Cronkite of guidebooks—with all that implies."
—*Travel & Leisure*

♦

"Complete, concise, and filled with useful information."
—*New York Daily News*

♦

"Hotel information is close to encyclopedic."
—*Des Moines Sunday Register*

♦

"Detailed, accurate and easy-to-read information for all price ranges."
—*Glamour Magazine*

Frommer's® 2001

San Francisco

by Erika Lenkert

IDG Books Worldwide, Inc.
An International Data Group Company
Foster City, CA • Chicago, IL • Indianapolis, IN • New York, NY

ABOUT THE AUTHOR

Native San Franciscan **Erika Lenkert** spent the past 4 years seeking adventure, great food, and great accommodations throughout California while celebrating a delightfully wild 3-year stint in Hollywood. She is now full-time in San Francisco, where she is editor-in-chief of WineShopper.com. She also has a restaurant column in *San Francisco Magazine*, and hopes to find time to continue contributing to *Los Angeles, InStyle, Travel & Leisure*, and *Bon Appètit*. And yes, her Siamese cats are still along for the ride.

IDG BOOKS WORLDWIDE, INC.

An International Data Group Company
919 E. Hillsdale Blvd.
Suite 400
Foster City, CA 94404

Find us online at **www.frommers.com**

ISBN 0-7645-6128-6
ISSN 1090-5480

Editor: Marie Morris
Production Editor: Scott Barnes
Photo Editor: Richard Fox
Design by Michele Laseau
Staff Cartographers: John Decamillis, Roberta Stockwell, Elizabeth Puhl
Production by IDG Books Indianapolis Production Department

Front Cover Photo: Gorgeous Golden Gate Bridge

SPECIAL SALES

For general information on IDG Books Worldwide's books in the U.S., please call our Consumer Customer Service Department at 1-800-762-2974. For reseller information, including discounts, bulk sales, customized editions, and premium sales, please call our Reseller Customer Service Department at 1-800-434-3422.

Manufactured in the United States of America.

5   4   3   2   1

Contents

List of Maps

AN INVITATION TO THE READER

In researching this book, we discovered many wonderful places—hotels, restaurants, shops, and more. We're sure you'll find others. Please tell us about them, so we can share the information with your fellow travelers in upcoming editions. If you were disappointed with a recommendation, we'd love to know that, too. Please write to:

Frommer's San Francisco 2001
IDG Books Worldwide, Inc.
909 Third Avenue
New York, NY 10022

AN ADDITIONAL NOTE

Please be advised that travel information is subject to change at any time—and this is especially true of prices. We therefore suggest that you write or call ahead for confirmation when making your travel plans. The authors, editors, and publisher cannot be held responsible for the experiences of readers while traveling. Your safety is important to us, however, so we encourage you to stay alert and be aware of your surroundings. Keep a close eye on cameras, purses, and wallets, all favorite targets of thieves and pickpockets.

WHAT THE SYMBOLS MEAN

✪ Frommer's Favorites

Our favorite places and experiences—outstanding for quality, value, or both.

The following abbreviations are used for credit cards:

AE	American Express	ER	EnRoute
CB	Carte Blanche	JCB	Japan Credit Bank
DC	Diners Club	MC	MasterCard
DISC	Discover	V	Visa

FIND FROMMER'S ONLINE

www.frommers.com offers up-to-the-minute listings on almost 200 cities around the globe—including the latest bargains and candid, personal articles updated daily by Arthur Frommer himself. No other Web site offers such comprehensive and timely coverage of the world of travel.

The Best of San Francisco

From an outsider's perspective, San Francisco is still very much the city it's reputed to be. The restaurant scene is booming, boutiques abound, the Castro is the Castro, liberalism is hip, and all the goings-on in the unique neighborhoods take place against picture-perfect backdrops of famous bridges, bay vistas, cable cars, and colorful only-in-San-Francisco city life. But from an insider's view, the historic City by the Bay is striving to maintain its identity while embracing an evolution spawned by a burgeoning economy, dot-commercialization, and a continuing onslaught of new residents who just don't want to live anywhere else. The result? Out-of-this-universe housing prices, a growing community of 20-something millionaires, and commercial and residential expansion to make room for the deep-pocketed masses.

But that's nothing for you to worry about—so long as you're prepared to pay the high hotel and restaurant prices that come along with the San Francisco's status as the nation's favorite city destination and epicenter of cutting-edge technology. In fact, it makes a visit here even more exciting (minus the traffic, of course).

You'll still encounter classic San Francisco. You'll feel the cool blast of salt air as you stroll across the Golden Gate, stuff yourself on dim sum, browse the Haight for incense and crystals, and walk along the beach. But on the flip side, much is new. As of summer 2000, it was impossible to drive up, down, or around the streets of San Francisco without stumbling on a new happening spot, extensive construction, or whisperings of yet another insider stock tip.

So, what can you expect from the country's most romantic European-style city, which was founded on—and still revels in—the pioneers' boom-or-bust lifestyle? Despite the thick fog bank that blocks out the sun most every summer, the city's stature and future indeed look bright. Like an eternal world's fair, it's all happening in San Francisco, and everyone's invited.

1 Frommer's Favorite San Francisco Experiences

- **A Cafe Hop in North Beach.** One of the most pleasurable smells of San Francisco is the aroma of roasted coffee beans wafting down Columbus Avenue. Start the day with a cup of Viennese at Caffè Trieste (a haven for true San Francisco characters), followed by a walk in and around Washington Square. Continue with lunch at Mario's Bohemian Cigar Store (à la focaccia sandwiches), book browsing at City Lights, more coffee at Caffè Greco, and dinner at L'Osteria del Forno or Moose's. Finish the day with a nightcap as Enrico Caruso plays on the jukebox at Tosca.

- **A Walk Along the Coastal Trail.** Stroll the forested coastal trail from the Cliff House to the Golden Gate Bridge, and you'll see why San Franciscans put up with living on a fault line. Start at the parking lot just above Cliff House and head north. On a clear day you'll have incredible views of the Marin Headlands, but even on foggy days, it's worth the trek to scamper over old bunkers and relish the crisp, cool air. Dress warmly.

- **A Drive to Muir Woods, Stinson Beach, and Point Reyes.** If you have wheels, reserve a day for a trip across the Golden Gate. Take the Stinson Beach exit off Highway 101 and spend a few hours gawking at the monolithic redwoods at Muir Woods (people, I'm telling you, this place is amazing). Continue to Stinson Beach for lunch at the Parkside Café, then head up the coast to the spectacular Point Reyes National Seashore. Rain or shine, it's a day trip you'll never forget.

- **An Adventure at Alcatraz.** Even if you loathe tourist attractions, you'll like Alcatraz. The rangers have done a fantastic job of preserving The Rock—just looking at it is enough to give you the heebie-jeebies—and they give excellent guided tours (highly recommended). Heck, even the boat ride across the bay is worth the price, so don't miss this one.

- **A Stroll Through Chinatown.** Chinatown is a trip. I've been through it at least 100 times, and it's never failed to entertain us. Skip the crummy camera and luggage stores and head straight for the outdoor markets, where a cornucopia of the bizarre, unbelievable, and just plain weird sits in boxes for you to scrutinize (one day I saw an armadillo for sale, and it wasn't meant to be a pet). Better yet, take one of Shirley Fong-Torres's Wok Wiz tours of Chinatown.

- **A Date in the Haight.** Although the flowers of power have wilted, the Haight is still, more or less, the Haight: aging hippies, dazed Dead-heads, skate punks, and an assortment of young panhandlers mix with chi-chi stores that accommodate the new, wealthier alternative residents. Think of it as visiting a people zoo as you walk down the rows of used clothing stores and leather shops, trying hard not to stare at that girl (at least I *think* it's a girl) with the pierced eyebrows and shaved head. End the mystery tour with a plate of mussels at Cha Cha Cha, one of San Francisco's most festive restaurants.

- **An Afternoon at the Marin Headlands.** San Francisco's backyard of sorts, the Marin Headlands are just across the Golden Gate Bridge to the west. They offer not only the best views of the city but also a wealth of outdoor activities. Bird watching, hiking, mountain biking, horseback riding—the list goes on—are all fair game at this glorious national recreation area. Don't miss the Marine Mammal Center, a ward for injured or abandoned seals (cute little buggers) and sea lions.

- **A Walk Across the Golden Gate Bridge.** Don your windbreaker and walking shoes and prepare for a wind-blasted, exhilarating journey across San Francisco's most famous landmark. It's simply one of those things you have to do at least once in your life.

- **A Cruise Through the Castro.** The most populated and festive street in the city is not just for gays and lesbians (although the best cruising in town is right here). While there are some great shops and cafes, it's the people-watching that makes the trip a must. If you have time, catch a flick at the beautiful 1930s Spanish colonial movie palace, the Castro Theatre.

The City Today

Shaken but not stirred by the Loma Prieta earthquake in 1989, San Francisco witnessed a spectacular rebound during the following decade. But the real shake-down originates in the modern gold rush of the Internet industry, which continues to change the face of the city. The seaside Embarcadero, once plagued by a horrendously ugly freeway overpass, has been revitalized by a multimillion-dollar face-lift, complete with palm trees, a new trolley line, wide cobblestoned walkways, a skating, biking, and walking promenade, and new restaurants. SoMa, the once-shady neighborhood south of Market Street, has exploded with new development. It's home to the world-class Museum of Modern Art, the beautiful and attraction-packed Yerba Buena Gardens, a slew of hip new clubs, cafes, and condos, the new baseball stadium, and, most influential, the dominance of dot-commerce companies. In short, San Francisco is hot these days.

Of course, there are typical big-city problems—and then some. Homelessness and panhandling are out of control. Those with enough funds to buy a spacious home in most parts of the U.S. can't afford a one-bedroom condo here. Rental units are practically impossible to find and outrageously expensive, which is quickly changing the city's demographics. Artists, gays, and others seeking an alternative lifestyle can no longer afford to move here and sustain their lifestyle—unless they also happen to have a tech background or an MBA and are willing to join the new corporate forces. Parking's beyond a nightmare even in the outer neighborhoods. Congestion and impatient drivers make cruising the town an anxiety-ridden and very slow ride. And Union Square is looking particularly shabby. (It is, however, slated for renovation.) Thanks to the blessing/curse of the high-tech boom and an influx of new residents, the city's just too darn crowded for its own good.

Some credit mayor Willie Brown for the changes, both good and bad. On some levels, since he was voted into office—and reelected after an interestingly close run-off against openly gay Board of Supervisors president and activist Tom Ammiano—things have been looking up for the city. During his first term, he gave just about every member of former mayor Frank Jordan's administration the boot. Then Brown, the legendary ex-speaker of the house in California's State Assembly, administered steady doses of shock therapy to his proud but oft-troubled city. But has he been effective? Public transportation, always a thorny issue, is still beleaguered, but on the slow road to improvement. Homelessness is no longer a crime, and shelters and work programs are on the rise, although it's hard to stomach the lack of care for street dwellers when so much money is flowing through the city. Meanwhile, in this highly political town, critics still insist that the mayor is nothing more than a show-boater with too many big-business connections who's turning the city into a Hollywood caricature of itself.

As a whole, however, San Francisco is doing just fine. Its symphony is in the black, its convention halls are fully booked, and new Internet companies have spawned legions of young millionaire residents. Even AIDS is on the decline. It's hard to think of a whole city as having ups and down, but after over a decade of getting thumped by the recession and poor management (among other things), San Francisco is all aglitter. It might never relive its heady days as the mecca for progressive Americans, but San Francisco retains its title as Americans' favorite city destination.

- **A Day in Golden Gate Park.** Golden Gate Park is a crucial—and relaxing—part of the San Francisco experience. Its arboreal paths stretch from the Haight all the way to Ocean Beach, offering dozens of fun things to do along the way. Top sights are the Conservatory of Flowers, Japanese Tea Garden, Asian Art Museum, and Steinhart Aquarium. The best time to go is Sunday, when portions of the park are closed to traffic (rent skates or a bike for the full effect). Toward the end of the day, head west to the beach and watch the sunset.
- **A Soul-Stirring Sunday Morning Service at Glide.** Preacher Cecil Williams turns churchgoing into a spiritual party that leaves you feeling elated, hopeful, and unified with the world. All walks of life attend the service, which focuses not on any particular religion, but on what I have in common as people. It's great fun, with plenty of singing and hand clapping.
- **An Early-Morning Cable Car Ride.** Skip the boring California line and take the Powell-Hyde cable car down to Fisherman's Wharf—the ride is worth the wait. When you reach the top of Nob Hill, grab the rail in one hand and hold the camera with the other, because you're about to see a view of the bay that'll make you a believer. Oh, and don't call it a trolley.
- **A Visit to MOMA and Yerba Buena.** Ever since the new MOMA opened in 1995, it's been the best place to go for a quick dose of culture. Start by touring the museum, then head straight for the gift shop (oftentimes more entertaining than the rotating exhibits). Have a light lunch at Caffè Museo, where the food is a vast improvement from most museums' mush. Finish the trip with a stroll through the Yerba Buena Gardens and its slew of new attractions across from the museum.

2 Best Hotel Bets

See chapter 5 for complete reviews.

- **Best for Families:** Kids like the **Westin St. Francis,** 335 Powell St. (☎ 800/ 228-3000 or 415/397-7000), because children under 12 get a Kids Club hat on arrival and special sports bottles and complimentary refills in the restaurants. Those ages 3 to 7 also get coloring books and dinosaur soaps and sponges.
- **Best for Romance:** At the **Sherman House,** 2160 Green St. (☎ 800/424-5777 or 415/563-3600), secure a garden suite with French doors leading out onto a sunken garden terrace with gazebo and pond, or the Paderewski suite, with a fireplace in the bathroom. Honorable mentions include the **Archbishop's Mansion,** 1000 Fulton St. (☎ 800/543-5820 or 415/563-7872), the **Hotel Bohème,** 444 Columbus St. (☎ 415/433-9111), and the **Hotel Majestic,** 1500 Sutter St. ☎ 800/869-8966 or 415/441-1100).
- **Best Public Space in a Historic Hotel:** The **Sheraton Palace Hotel,** 2 New Montgomery St. (☎ 800/325-3535 or 415/392-8600), the extravagant creation of banker Bonanza King Will Ralston in 1875, has one of the grandest rooms in the city: the Garden Court. Running a close second is the magnificent lobby at Nob Hill's **Fairmont Hotel & Tower,** 950 Mason St. (☎ 800/ 527-4727 or 415/772-5000).
- **Best Old World Hotel:** Those who appreciate comfort, beautiful surroundings, absolute privacy, and unobtrusive service choose the **Huntington Hotel,** 1075 California St. (☎ 800/227-4683 or 415/474-5400).
- **Best for Your Budget:** Sure, the rooms at **The San Remo Hotel,** 2237 Mason St. (☎ 800/352-REMO or 415/776-8688), are small, but the North Beach location, friendly staff, and low prices can't be beat. Besides, you're here to see the city, not your hotel room. For overall extra perks, my vote is for the adorable and

super-cheap **Marina Inn,** 3110 Octavia St. (☎ **800/274-1420** or 415/928-1000).

- **Best Moderately Priced Hotel: The Laurel,** 444 Presidio Ave. ☎ **415/567-8467,** may be off the beaten track, but it's the newest affordable and fashionable hotel in the city—with free parking. If you prefer more classically San Francisco surroundings, try the quaint **White Swan Inn,** 845 Bush St. (☎ **800/999-9570** or 415/775-1755).
- **Best Bed-and-Breakfast:** It's a tie between the **Union Street Inn,** 2229 Union St. (☎ **415/346-0424**), and **Bed & Breakfast Inn,** 4 Charlton Court (☎ **415/921-9784**).
- **Best Funky Hotel: The Phoenix Hotel,** 601 Eddy St. (☎ **800/248-9466** or 415/776-1380), wouldn't look out of place in Palm Springs. A favorite with the rock and movie set, including Sinead O'Connor, k.d. lang, and the Red Hot Chili Peppers, it has one of the bluest and most bizarre restaurant/bars in town. It's also one of the only hotels in San Francisco with an outdoor pool.
- **Best Trendy-Chic Hotel:** Check into the **W San Francisco Hotel,** 181 Third St. (☎ **800/877-WHOTEL** or 415/777-5300), and you'll be less than a block from the Museum of Modern Art. But the real visuals are here, where the hottest hotel scene means lots of lookers, fun bar action, and modern surroundings.
- **Best Views:** From the rooms in **The Mandarin Oriental,** 222 Sansome St. (☎ **800/622-0404** or 415/276-9888), all of which are on the 38th to the 48th floors, you'll have a great view of the city and the entire Bay Area, although you'll pay dearly for the vista.
- **Best Service:** The small, luxurious **Campton Place Hotel,** 340 Stockton St. (☎ **800/235-4300** or 415/781-5555); the historic, eager-to-please **Ritz-Carlton,** 600 Stockton St. (☎ **800/241-3333** or 415/296-7465); and the modern, pampering **Mandarin Oriental** (see above) are all tops for service.
- **Best Dining Room:** Never a hotel to do anything second best, **The Ritz-Carlton** (see above) is renowned for pampering its guests as though they were royalty, and the **Dining Room** is no exception. The latest contender? The **Fifth Floor Restaurant** in the **Hotel Palomar,** 12 Fourth St. (☎ **415/348-1111**).

3 Best Dining Bets

See chapter 6 for complete reviews.

- **Best for Cutting a Deal:** Show your business associates you've got class—and deep pockets—by reserving a table at the Financial District's **Aqua,** 252 California St. (☎ **415/956-9662**). It pairs power lunching with excellent seafood and wine.
- **Best Romantic Spot:** Anyone could be seduced at **Fleur de Lys,** 777 Sutter St. (☎ **415/673-7779**), under the rich burgundy-tented canopy that swathes the elegant room in romance. Lots of question-popping here, too.
- **Best for a Celebration:** Great food, a full bar, and a lively atmosphere are the key ingredients that make **Boulevard,** 1 Mission St. (☎ **415/543-6084**), the place to celebrate. Care less about fancy food and more about festive surroundings? Go to **Gordon's House of Fine Eats,** 500 Florida St. (☎ **415/861-8900**), where the menu matches the fun surroundings.
- **Best Decor:** Celeb restaurant designer Pat Kuleto spent a week sketching sea life at the Monterey Bay Aquarium before applying his Midas touch to **Farallon,** 450 Post St. (☎ **415/956-6969**). The result is an orgy of oceanic artwork, from jellyfish lamps to sea urchin chandeliers. It's truly a spectacular achievement in restaurant design.

- **Best Wine List:** Owners of the small **PlumpJack Café,** 3127 Fillmore St. (☎ **415/563-4755**), also operate one of the city's best wine stores. The expertly picked list, which sticks proudly to California wines, offers more than 80 bottles and 33 selections by the glass. And a bonus—it's reasonably priced.
- **Best Pizza:** Has **Pauline's,** 260 Valencia St. (☎ **415/552-2050**), perfected the pizza? Quite possibly. At least it's the best I've ever had. Pauline's does only two things—pizza and salad—and does them better than any other restaurant in the city.
- **Best Desserts:** What a decision! Sweet tooths can be satisfied in a number of spots around town, including **Restaurant Gary Danko,** 800 North Point St. (☎ **415/749-2060**), and **Absinthe,** 398 Hayes St. (☎ **415/551-1590**).
- **Best Value:** No other place in town serves up heaping plates of fresh pasta at penny-pinching prices the way **Pasta Pomodoro,** 655 Union St. (☎ **415/399-0300**), does. It has other locations at 2027 Chestnut St. (☎ **415/474-3400**), 2304 Market St. (☎ **415/558-8123**), 3611 California St. (☎ **415/831-0900**), and 816 Irving St. (☎ **415/566-0900**). Want a little more atmosphere and more sophisticated cooking? Head to **Delfina,** 3621 18th St. (☎ **415/552-4055**), or **The Slanted Door,** 584 Valencia St. (☎ **415/861-8032**).
- **Best Brunch:** The Sunday spread at the **Terrace Restaurant** in the **Ritz-Carlton,** 600 Stockton St. (☎ **415/296-7465**), will set your eyes popping and your feet tapping. Strut around to the lavish buffets featuring sushi, caviar, freshly made blinis, and traditional egg dishes. A jazz trio brings joy to it all.
- **Best Newcomers:** The hottest new places at press time were the **Fifth Floor Restaurant,** 12 Fourth St. (☎ **415/348-1555**), a sexy spot that serves high-end modern French fare, and **Restaurant Gary Danko** (see above), a personal favorite serving "modern classic" cuisine. If you want to hobnob with San Francisco's best, brightest, and most spendy, this is where they are.
- **Best Bistro:** Casual and comfortable, **Fringale Restaurant,** 570 Fourth St. (☎ **415/543-0573**), offers the best moderately priced French food in the city. Start with a scrumptious galette and finish with the vanilla bean crème brûlée. The middle part is up to you.
- **Best Dim Sum:** Downtown and Chinatown dim sum restaurants may be more centrally located, but that's all they've got on **Ton Kiang,** 5821 Geary Blvd. (☎ **415/387-8273**). Carts bring the freshest and most delicious Chinese dumplings and other dim sum delicacies to your table.
- **Best Vegetarian:** For the food, the view of the Golden Gate, and the redwood booths, go to **Greens Restaurant,** Building A, Fort Mason Center (☎ **415/771-6222**). If you want to experience how rich and varied vegetables can taste, sample the extraordinary five-course tasting menu.
- **Best Party Scene:** Throw back a few glasses of sangria with your tapas at **Cha Cha Cha,** 1801 Haight St. (☎ **415/386-5758**), and you'll quickly be swinging with the rest of the crowd.
- **Best Coffee Shop or Cafe:** With all the wonderful coffee shops throughout this cafe town, there can be no one winner. I do, however, love the authentic atmosphere at **Mario's Bohemian Cigar Store,** 566 Columbus Ave. (☎ **415/362-0536**), and **Caffè Trieste,** 601 Vallejo Ave. (☎ **415/392-6739;** see chapter 8, "City Strolls"). If you see one you like, pull up a chair. Just do San Francisco one favor: Stay away from Starbucks and support our unique coffee culture.
- **Funkiest Atmosphere:** San Francisco's most . . . well, *alternative* burger joint is **Hamburger Mary's,** 1582 Folsom St. (☎ **415/626-5767**), a popular hangout for gays, lesbians, and just about everyone else who dances to a different drummer (and you don't even need leather undies to join the party).

Planning Your Trip: The Basics

Regardless of whether you map out your vacation months in advance or travel on a whim, you need to do a little planning to make the most of your stay. This chapter will help you with all the logistics.

1 Visitor Information

Visitors from outside the United States should also see chapter 3, "For Foreign Visitors," for entry requirements and other pertinent information.

The **San Francisco Convention and Visitors Bureau,** 900 Market St. (at Powell Street), Hallidie Plaza, Lower Level, San Francisco, CA 94102 (☎ **415/391-2000;** www.sfvisitor.org), is the best source for specialized information about the city. Even if you don't have a specific question, you might want to send $3 for the 100-page *The San Francisco Book.* It includes a 3-month calendar of events, city history, shopping and dining information, and several good, clear maps, plus a 50-page lodging guide. It's free if you drop by to pick it up. If you simply need specific information faxed to you, you can call ☎ **800/220-5747;** follow the prompts to receive information by fax only. The bureau highlights only members' establishments, so if they don't have what you're looking for, that doesn't mean it's nonexistent.

You can get the latest on San Francisco at the following online addresses (Also see "Planning Your Trip: An Online Directory" following this chapter:

- The *Bay Guardian,* the free weekly's city page: **www.sfbayguardian.com**
- Hotel reservations: **www.hotelres.com/**
- *Q San Francisco,* for gays and lesbians: **www.qsanfrancisco.com/**
- The *SF Gate,* the city's combined *Chronicle* and *Examiner* newspapers: **www.sfgate.com**
- Channel 7, ABC, and KGO's city guide: **www.citysearch7.com**

2 Money

Foreign visitors should also see chapter 3, "For Foreign Visitors," for more information.

All over San Francisco, you'll find **ATMs** linked to a national network that most likely includes your bank at home. Withdrawing cash as you need it is the easiest way to deal with money while you're on the road. **Cirrus** (☎ 800/424-7787; www.mastercard.com/atm/) and **PLUS** (☎ 800/843-7587; www.visa.com/atms) are the two most popular networks. Use the 800 numbers to locate ATMs in your destination. Be sure to check the daily withdrawal limit before you depart, and be prepared for withdrawal fees of $1 to $1.50 if you use another network.

Traveler's checks are something of an anachronism from the days before the ATM made cash accessible at any time. These days, traveler's checks seem less necessary, but you might still prefer the security of knowing you can get a refund or replacement if they're lost or stolen. You can get traveler's checks at almost any bank. **American Express** offers denominations of $10, $20, $50, $100, $500, and $1,000. You'll pay a service charge ranging from 1% to 4%. You can also get American Express traveler's checks over the phone by calling ☎ 800/221-7282; by using this number, Amex gold and platinum card-holders are exempt from the 1% fee. AAA members can get checks without a fee at most AAA offices. **Visa** offers traveler's checks at Citibank locations nationwide, as well as several other banks. The service charge is 1.5% to 2%; checks come in denominations of $20, $50, $100, $500, and $1,000. **MasterCard** also offers traveler's checks. Call ☎ 800/223-9920 for a location near you. If you opt to carry traveler's checks, be sure to keep a record of their serial numbers, separately from the checks, so you're ensured a refund or replacement in case of an emergency.

Credit cards are invaluable when traveling. They are a safe way to carry money and keep a convenient record of your expenses. You can also withdraw cash advances against your credit cards at any bank (although you start paying hefty interest on the advance the moment you get the cash, and you won't get frequent-flyer miles on an airline credit card). At most banks, you don't even need to go to a teller; you can get a cash advance at the ATM if you know your PIN (personal identification number).

Almost every credit card company has an emergency 800 number that you can call if your wallet or purse is stolen. The company may be able to wire you a cash advance off your credit card immediately and, in many places, can deliver an emergency credit card in a day or two. **Citicorp Visa**'s U.S. emergency number is ☎ 800/336-8472. **American Express** cardholders and traveler's check holders should call ☎ 800/221-7282 for all money emergencies. **MasterCard** holders should call ☎ 800/307-7309. Odds are that if your wallet is gone, the police won't be able to recover it for you. However, after you realize that it's gone and you cancel your credit cards, it is still worth informing them. Your credit-card company or insurer might require a police-report number.

3 When to Go

If you're dreaming of convertibles, Frisbee on the beach, and tank-topped evenings, change your reservations and head to Los Angeles. Contrary to California's sunshine-and-bikini image, San Francisco's weather is "mild" (to put it nicely) and can often be downright bone-chilling due to wet foggy air and cool winds—it's nothing like that of southern California. Summer, the most popular time to visit, is often characterized by damp, foggy days, cold, windy nights, and crowded tourist destinations. A good bet is to visit in spring or, better yet, autumn. Every September, right about the time San Franciscans mourn being cheated (or fogged) out of another summer, something wonderful happens: The thermostat rises, the skies clear, and the locals call in sick to work and head for the beach. It's what residents call "Indian summer." The

Even if it's sunny out, don't forget to bring a jacket; the weather can change almost instantly from sunny and warm to windy and cold.

city is also delightful during winter, when the opera and ballet seasons are in full swing, there are fewer tourists, many hotel prices are lower, and downtown bustles with holiday cheer.

CLIMATE

San Francisco's temperate, marine climate usually means relatively mild weather year-round. In summer, chilling fog rolls in most mornings and evenings, and if temperatures top 70°F, we're ready to throw an all-city celebration. Even when autumn's heat occasionally stretches into the 80s and 90s, you should still dress in layers or by early evening you'll learn firsthand why sweatshirt sales are a great business at Fisherman's Wharf. In winter, the mercury seldom falls below freezing and snow is almost unheard of, but that doesn't mean you won't be whimpering if you forget a coat. Still, compared to most of the States' varied weather conditions, San Francisco is consistently pleasant.

That beautifully fluffy, chilly, wet, heavy, sweeping fog makes the city's weather so precarious. A rare combination of water, wind, and topography creates Northern California's summer fog bank. It lies off the coast, and rising air currents pull it in when the land heats up. Held back by coastal mountains along a 600-mile front, the low clouds seek out any passage they can find. The easiest access is the slot where the Pacific Ocean penetrates the continental wall—the Golden Gate.

San Francisco's Average Temperatures (°F) & Rainfall (in.)

	Jan	Feb	Mar	Apr	May	June	July	Aug	Sept	Oct	Nov	Dec
High	56	59	60	61	63	64	64	65	69	68	63	57
Low	46	48	49	49	51	53	53	54	56	55	52	47
Rain	4.5	2.8	2.6	1.5	0.4	0.2	0.1	0.1	0.2	1.1	2.5	3.5

San Francisco Calendar of Events

January

- **San Francisco Sports and Boat Show,** Cow Palace. Draws thousands of boat enthusiasts over a 9-day period. Call the **Cow Palace Box Office** (☎ **415/469-6065**) for details. Mid-January.

February

✪ **Chinese New Year,** Chinatown. In 2001, the year of the serpent, public celebrations will again spill onto every street in Chinatown. Festivities begin with the "Miss Chinatown USA" pageant parade and climax a week later with a celebratory parade of marching bands, rolling floats, barrages of fireworks, and a block-long dragon writhing in and out of the crowds. The revelry runs for several weeks and wraps up with a memorable parade through Chinatown. Arrive early for a good viewing spot on Grant Avenue. Make your hotel reservations early. For dates and information, call ☎ **415/982-3000.**

March

- **St. Patrick's Day Parade.** Almost everyone's honorarily Irish at this festive affair, which starts at 12:45pm at Market and Second streets and continues to City Hall. But the party doesn't stop there. Head down to the Civic Center for the post-party, or venture to Embarcadero's Harrington's bar and celebrate with hundreds of the Irish-for-a-day yuppies as they gallivant around the closed-off streets and numerous pubs. Call ☎ **510/644-1164** for details. Sunday before March 17.

April

- **Cherry Blossom Festival,** Japantown. Meander through the arts-and-crafts and food booths lining the blocked-off streets; watch traditional drumming, flower arranging, origami, or a parade celebrating the cherry blossom and Japanese culture. Call ☎ **415/563-2313** for information. Mid- to late April.

- ✪ **San Francisco International Film Festival,** with screenings at the AMC Kabuki 8 Cinemas, Fillmore and Post streets, and many other locations. Started 44 years ago, this is America's oldest film festival. It features more than 200 films and videos from more than 50 countries, and awards ceremonies where renowned honorees join the festivities. Tickets are relatively inexpensive, and screenings are accessible to the public. Entries include new films by beginning and established directors. For a schedule or information, call ☎ **415/931-FILM.** Mid-April to early May.

May

- **Cinco de Mayo Celebration,** Mission District. The Latino community celebrates the victory of the Mexicans over the French at Puebla in 1862. Mariachi bands, dancers, food, and a parade fill the streets of the Mission. The parade starts at 10am at 24th and Bryant streets and ends at the Civic Center. Sunday before May 5.

- ✪ **Bay to Breakers Foot Race,** Golden Gate Park. Even if you don't participate, you can't avoid this run from downtown to Ocean Beach, which stops morning traffic throughout the city. Around 80,000 entrants gather—many dressed in wacky, innovative, and sometimes X-rated costumes—for the approximately 7$^{1}/_{2}$-mile run. If you're feeling lazy, join the throng of spectators who line the route. Sidewalk parties, bands, and cheerleaders of all ages provide a good dose of true San Francisco fun. The *San Francisco Examiner* (☎ **415/777-7770**) sponsors the event. Third Sunday of May.

- ✪ **Carnival,** Mission Street between 14th and 24th streets, and Harrison Street between 16th and 21st streets. The Mission District's largest annual event is a day of festivities that culminates with a parade on Mission Street on the Sunday of Memorial Day weekend. For one of San Franciscans' favorite events, more than half a million spectators line the route, and samba musicians and dancers continue to entertain on 14th Street, near Harrison, at the end of the march. Just show up, or call the **Mission Economic and Cultural Association** (☎ **415/826-1401**) for complete information.

June

- **Union Street Art Festival,** along Union Street from Fillmore to Gough streets. With a new promotion company leading the way, the Union Street Fair is now the Union Street Art Festival, which intends to celebrate San Francisco with themes, gourmet food booths, music, entertainment, and a juried show with more than 350 artists. No doubt the change won't deter the great-looking yuppie cocktailers from packing every bar and spilling out into the street. Call the Union Street Association (☎ 415/441-7055) or the event promoters (☎ 510/970-3217) for more information. First weekend of June.

- **Haight Street Fair.** Features alternative crafts, ethnic foods, rock bands, and a healthy number of hippies and street kids whooping it up and slamming beers in front of the blaring rock 'n' roll stage. The fair usually extends along Haight between Stanyan and Ashbury streets. For details and the exact date, call ☎ 415/661-8025.

✪ **North Beach Festival,** Grant Avenue, North Beach. In 1999, this party celebrated its 45th anniversary; organizers claim it's the oldest urban street fair in the country. Close to 100,000 city folk meander along Grant Avenue, between Vallejo and Union streets, to eat, drink, and browse the arts-and-crafts booths, poetry readings, swing dancing venue, and *arte di gesso* (sidewalk chalk art). But the most enjoyable part of the event is listening to music and people-watching. Call ☎ 415/989-2220 for details. Usually Father's Day weekend, but call to confirm.

- **San Francisco Lesbian, Gay, Bisexual, Transgender Pride Parade & Celebration,** Market Street. A prideful event drawing up to half a million participants who celebrate all of the above—and then some. The parade's start and finish have been moved around in recent years to accommodate road construction. Regardless of its path, it ends with hundreds of food, art, and information booths and soundstages. Call ☎ 415/864-3733 for information and location. Usually the third or last weekend of June.

✪ **Stern Grove Midsummer Music Festival.** Pack a picnic and head out early to join the thousands who come here to lie in the grass and enjoy classical, jazz, and ethnic music and dance in the Grove, at 19th Avenue and Sloat Boulevard. The free concerts take place every Sunday at 2pm. Show up with a lawn chair or blanket. There are food booths if you forget snacks, but you'll be dying to leave if you don't bring warm clothes—the Sunset District can be one of the coldest parts of the city. Call ☎ 415/252-6252 for listings. Mid-June through August.

July

- **Jazz and All That Art on Fillmore.** The first weekend in July starts with a bang when the upscale portion of Fillmore closes to traffic and several blocks of arts and crafts, gourmet food, and live jazz fill the street. (The blocked-off section is changing, so call for details.) July 7 and 8 from 10am to 6pm. Call ☎ 510/970-3217 for more information.
- **Fourth of July Celebration and Fireworks.** This event can be somewhat of a joke—more often than not, fog, like everyone else, comes into the city to join in the festivities. Sometimes it's almost impossible to view the million-dollar pyrotechnics from Pier 39 on the northern waterfront. Still, it's a party, and if the skies are clear, it's a damn good show.
- **San Francisco Marathon.** One of the largest marathons in the world. For entry information, contact West End Management, the event organizer (☎ 800/698-8699 or 415/284-9492). Usually the second weekend in July.

August

- **Renaissance Pleasure Faire.** An expensive but enjoyable festival takes place north of San Francisco and takes you back to Renaissance times—with games, plays, and arts-and-crafts and food booths. In the past the fair was in Black Point Forest, just east of Novato, but there's talk of a new location. The Faire opens the weekend before Labor Day and runs six to eight weekends and on Labor Day (☎ 800/52-FAIRE).

September

✪ **A La Carte, A La Park,** usually at Sharon Meadow, Golden Gate Park. You probably won't get to go to all the restaurants you'd like while you're visiting the city, but you can get a good sampling at this annual event. Over 40 of the town's favorite restaurants, accompanied by 20 microbreweries and 20 wineries, offer tastings in San Francisco's favorite park. There's entertainment as well, and proceeds benefit the Friends of Recreation & Parks. Admission in 2000 was $9 adults in advance and $10 on site, $8 seniors, free for children under 12. Prices for 2001 were not determined at press time. Call ☎ 415/458-1988 for details. Labor Day weekend.

✪ **Sausalito Art Festival,** Sausalito. A juried exhibit of more than 180 artists. It includes music—provided by Bay Area jazz, rock, and blues performers—and international cuisine, enhanced by wines from some 50 Napa and Sonoma producers. Parking is impossible; take the **Blue & Gold Fleet ferry** (☎ 415/705-5555) from Fisherman's Wharf to the festival site. For more information, call ☎ 415/332-3555. Labor Day weekend.

- **Opera in the Park.** Each year the San Francisco Opera launches its season with a free concert featuring a selection of arias. Usually in Sharon Meadow, Golden Gate Park, on the Sunday after Labor Day; call ☎ 415/861-4008 to confirm the date.

✪ **San Francisco Blues Festival,** on the grounds of Fort Mason. The largest outdoor blues music event on the West Coast will be 29 years old in 2001 and will again feature local and national musicians performing back-to-back during the 3-day extravaganza. You can charge tickets by phone through **BASS Ticketmaster** (☎ 510/762-2277). For schedule information, call ☎ 415/826-6837. Usually in late September.

October

- **Castro Street Fair.** Celebrates life in the city's most famous gay neighborhood. Call ☎ 415/467-3354 or visit www.castrostreetfair.org for information. First Sunday in October.

- **Reggae in the Park,** usually in Sharon Meadow, Golden Gate Park. Going into its 11th year, this event draws thousands to the park to dance and celebrate the soulful sounds. Big-name reggae and world-beat bands play all weekend, and ethnic arts-and-crafts and food booths line the stage's periphery. Tickets are around $15 in advance, $20 on site. Two-day discounted passes are available. Free for children under 12. Call ☎ 415/458-1988 for more details. First weekend in October.

- **Italian Heritage Parade.** The city's Italian community leads the festivities around Fisherman's Wharf celebrating Columbus's landing in America. The festival includes a parade along Columbus Avenue and sporting events, but for the most part, it's just a great excuse to hang out in North Beach and people-watch. For information, call ☎ 415/434-1492. Sunday closest to October 12.

- **Exotic Erotic Halloween Ball.** Thousands come dressed in costume, lingerie, and sometimes even less than that. It's a wild fantasy affair with bands, dancing, and costume contests. *Beware:* It can be somewhat cheesy. Tickets cost approximately $35 per person. For information, call ☎ **415/567-BALL;** for tickets, call ☎ **510/762-BASS.** Friday or Saturday night before Halloween.
- **Halloween.** A huge night in San Francisco. A fantastical parade is organized at Market and Castro, and a mixed gay/straight crowd revels in costumes of extraordinary imagination. October 31.
- **San Francisco Jazz Festival.** This festival presents eclectic programming in an array of fabulous jazz venues throughout the city. With close to 2 weeks of nightly entertainment and dozens of performers, the jazz festival is a hot ticket. Past events have featured Herbie Hancock, Dave Brubeck, the Modern Jazz Quartet, Wayne Shorter, and Bill Frisell. For information, call ☎ **800/850-SFJF** or 415/398-5655. Late October and early November.

December

- *The Nutcracker,* War Memorial Opera House. Performed annually by the **San Francisco Ballet** (☎ **415/865-2000**). Order tickets to this Tchaikovsky tradition well in advance.

4 Tips for Travelers with Special Needs

FOR PEOPLE WITH DISABILITIES

A disability shouldn't stop anyone from traveling. There are more resources out there than ever before.

You can join the **Society for the Advancement of Travel for the Handicapped (SATH),** 347 Fifth Ave., Suite 610, New York, NY 10016 (☎ **212/447-7284;** fax 212/725-8253; www.sath.org), for $45 annually, $30 for seniors and students. Membership includes access to the society's vast network of connections in the travel industry. It provides information sheets on travel destinations and referrals to tour operators who specialize in traveling with disabilities. Its quarterly magazine, *Open World for Disability and Mature Travel,* is full of good information and resources. A year's subscription is $13 ($21 outside the U.S.).

Most of San Francisco's major museums and tourist attractions have wheelchair ramps. Many hotels offer special accommodations and services for wheelchair users and other visitors with disabilities. They include extra-large

Travel Tip

If you suffer from a chronic illness, consult your doctor before your departure. For conditions like epilepsy, diabetes, or heart problems, wear a **Medic Alert Identification Tag** (☎ **800/825-3785;** www.medicalert.org), which immediately alerts doctors to your condition and gives them access to your records through Medic Alert's 24-hour hotline. Membership is $35, plus a $15 annual fee after the first year.

Pack prescription medications in your carry-on luggage. Carry written prescriptions in generic, not brand-name form, and dispense all prescription medications from their original labeled vials. Also bring along copies of your prescriptions in case you lose your pills or run out.

bathrooms, wheelchair ramps, and telecommunication devices for hearing-impaired travelers. The San Francisco Convention and Visitors Bureau (see "Visitor Information," above) has the most up-to-date information.

Travelers in wheelchairs can request special ramped taxis by calling **Yellow Cab** (☎ 415/626-2345), which charges regular rates for the service. Travelers with disabilities can also get a free copy of the *Muni Access Guide,* published by the San Francisco Municipal Railway, Accessible Services Program, Municipal Railway, 949 Presidio Ave., San Francisco, CA 94115 (☎ 415/923-6142), staffed weekdays 8am to 5pm. Many of the major car-rental companies offer hand-controlled cars for drivers with disabilities. **Avis** can provide a vehicle at any of its U.S. locations with 48 hours' advance notice; **Hertz** requires between 24 and 72 hours of advance reservation at most locations. **Wheelchair Getaways** (☎ 800/873-4973; www.blvd.com/wg.htm) rents specialized vans with wheelchair lifts and other features in more than 100 cities across the U.S.

Travelers with disabilities might also want to consider joining a tour that caters specifically to them. One of the best operators is **Flying Wheels Travel,** 143 West Bridge (P.O. Box 382), Owatonna, MN 55060 (☎ 800/535-6790; www.flyingwheels.com). It offers escorted tours and cruises, as well as private tours in minivans with lifts. Other reputable specialized tour operators include **Accessible Journeys** (☎ 800/TINGLES or 610/521-0339), for slow walkers and wheelchair travelers, and **The Guided Tour, Inc.** (☎ 215/782-1370).

Vision-impaired travelers should contact the **American Foundation for the Blind,** 11 Penn Plaza, Suite 300, New York, NY 10001 (☎ 800/232-5463), for information on traveling with guide dogs.

FOR GAYS & LESBIANS

If you head down to the Castro—an area surrounding Castro Street near Market Street—you'll understand why the city is a mecca for gay and lesbian travelers. Since the 1970s, this unique part of town has remained a colorfully festive neighborhood, teeming with "outed" city folk who meander the streets shopping, eating, partying, or cruising. If anyone feels like an outsider in this part of town, it's heterosexuals, who, although warmly welcomed in the community, may feel uncomfortable or downright threatened if they harbor any homophobia or aversion to being "cruised." For many San Franciscans, it's just a fun area (especially on Halloween) with some wonderful shops.

It is estimated that gays and lesbians form one-fourth to one-third of the population of San Francisco, so it's no surprise that clubs and bars catering to them are all over town. Although lesbian interests are concentrated primarily in the East Bay (especially Oakland), a significant community resides in the Mission District, around 16th Street and Valencia.

Several local publications concentrate on in-depth coverage of news, information, and listings of goings-on around town for gay men and lesbians. The *Bay Area Reporter* has the most comprehensive listings, including a weekly calendar of events. Distributed free on Thursdays, it can be found stacked at the corner of 18th and Castro streets and at Ninth and Harrison streets, as well as in bars, bookshops, and stores around town. It may also be available in gay and lesbian bookstores elsewhere in the country.

GUIDES & PUBLICATIONS For accommodations, check the international guides *Odysseus* ($29) and *Inn Places* ($16). These books and others are available by mail from **Giovanni's Room,** 345 S. 12th St., Philadelphia, PA 19107 (☎ 215/923-2960; e-mail: giophilp@netaxs.com), and **A Different**

Light Bookstore, 489 Castro St., San Francisco, CA 94114 (☎ **415/ 431-0891;** www.adlbooks.com). Other locations are in New York City (☎ **212/989-4850**) and Los Angeles (☎ **310/854-6601**).

Our World, 1104 N. Nova Rd., Suite 251, Daytona Beach, FL 32117 (☎ **904/441-5367;** e-mail: info@ourworldmag.com), is a magazine devoted to gay and lesbian travel worldwide. It costs $35 for 10 issues. *Out and About,* 8 W. 19th St., Suite 401, New York, NY 10011 (☎ **800/929-2268;** www.outandabout.com), has been hailed for its "straight" reporting about gay travel. It profiles the best gay or gay-friendly hotels, restaurants, clubs, and other places, with coverage of destinations throughout the world. It costs $49 a year for 10 information-packed issues plus a quarterly calendar. Both of these publications are available at most gay and lesbian bookstores.

ORGANIZATIONS The **International Gay & Lesbian Travel Association (IGLTA),** 4331 N. Federal Hwy., Suite 304, Fort Lauderdale, FL 33308 (☎ **800/448-8550** for a voice mailbox, or 954/776-2626; www.iglta.org), encourages gay and lesbian travel worldwide. It has around 700 travel agency members and offers quarterly newsletters, marketing mailings, and a membership directory that is updated twice a year. Travel agents who are IGLTA members are tied into the organization's vast information resources.

TRAVEL AGENCIES In California, two leading gay-friendly options are **Now Voyager,** 4406 18th St., San Francisco, CA 94114 (☎ **800/255-6951** or 415/626-1169), and **Gunderson Travel Inc.,** 8543 Santa Monica Blvd., Suite 8, West Hollywood, CA 90069 (☎ **800/899-1944** or 310/657-3944; e-mail: gundersontvl@worldnet.att.net).

Also in California is **Skylink Women's Travel,** 1006 Mendocino Ave., Santa Rosa, CA 95401 (☎ **800/225-5759** or 707/546-9888).

General gay and lesbian travel agencies include **Family Abroad** (☎ **800/ 999-5500** or 212/459-1800; gay and lesbian) and **Above and Beyond Tours** (☎ **800/397-2681;** mainly gay men).

FOR WOMEN

Women's services are often lumped together in the lesbian category, but some resources assist women without regard to sexuality. The **Bay Area Women's and Children's Center,** 318 Leavenworth St. (☎ **415/474-2400**), offers specialized services and city information to women and families. The **Women's Building,** 3543 18th St. (☎ **415/431-1180**), is a Mission-area space housing feminist art shows and political events. It offers classes in yoga, aerobics, movement, and tai chi chuan. The **Rape Crisis Hotline** (☎ **415/647-7273** or 415/861-2024) is staffed 24 hours daily.

FOR SENIORS

Don't be shy about asking for discounts—you're entitled to them on public transportation and at many attractions. Always carry some kind of identification, such as a driver's license, that shows your date of birth.

Also, mention that you're a senior citizen when you make your travel reservations. For example, both **Amtrak** (☎ **800/USA-RAIL;** www.amtrak.com) and **Greyhound** (☎ **800/752-4841;** www.greyhound.com) offer discounts to people over 62, as do most airlines. And many hotels offer senior discounts; **Choice Hotels** (Clarion Hotels, Quality Inns, Comfort Inns, Sleep Inns, EconoLodges, Friendship Inns, and Rodeway Inns), for example, give 30% off their published rates to anyone over 50, provided you book your room through their nationwide toll-free reservation numbers (that is, not directly with the hotels or through a travel agent). See appendix B, "Useful Toll-Free Numbers & Web Sites," for a handy list of national numbers.

When making airline reservations, ask about senior discounts, but find out if there's a cheaper promotional fare before committing yourself.

The **Senior Citizen Information Line** (☎ 415/626-1033) offers advice, referrals, and information on city services. The **Friendship Line for the Elderly** (☎ 415/752-3778) is a support, referral, and crisis-intervention service.

Members of the **American Association of Retired Persons (AARP),** 601 E St. NW, Washington, DC 20049 (☎ 800/424-3410 or 202/434-2277; www.aarp.org), get discounts on hotels, airfares, and car rentals. AARP offers members a wide range of special benefits, including *Modern Maturity* magazine and a monthly newsletter.

The **National Council of Senior Citizens,** 8403 Colesville Rd., Suite 1200, Silver Spring, MD 20910 (☎ 301/578-8800), a nonprofit organization, offers a newsletter six times a year (partly devoted to travel tips) and discounts on hotel and auto rentals; annual dues are $13 per person or couple.

The Mature Traveler, a monthly 12-page newsletter, is a valuable resource. It is available by subscription ($30 a year) from GEM Publishing Group, Box 50400, Reno, NV 89513-0400. GEM also publishes *The Book of Deals,* a collection of more than 1,000 senior discounts on airlines, lodging, tours, and attractions around the country; it's available for $9.95 by calling ☎ 800/ 460-6676. Another helpful publication is *101 Tips for the Mature Traveler,* available from **Grand Circle Travel,** 347 Congress St., Suite 3A, Boston, MA 02210 (☎ 800/221-2610 or 617/350-7500; www.gct.com). Grand Circle Travel is also one of the hundreds of travel agencies specializing in vacations for seniors. Many of these packages, however, are of the tour-bus variety, with free trips thrown in for those who organize groups of 10 or more. Seniors seeking more independent travel should probably consult a regular travel agent. **SAGA International Holidays,** 222 Berkeley St., Boston, MA 02116 (☎ 800/ 343-0273; www.sagaholidays.com), offers inclusive tours and cruises for those 50 and older. SAGA also sponsors the more substantial "Road Scholar Tours" (☎ 800/621-2151), which are fun-loving but with an educational bent.

You might also want to peruse *The 50+ Traveler's Guidebook* (St. Martin's Press) or *The Seasoned Traveler* (Country Roads Press). Also check your newsstand for the quarterly magazine *Travel 50 & Beyond.*

FOR FAMILIES

San Francisco is full of sightseeing opportunities and special activities geared toward children. See "Especially for Kids," in chapter 7, for information and ideas for families.

Several books offer tips on travel with kids. *How to Take Great Trips with Your Kids* (The Harvard Common Press) is full of good general advice that can apply to travel anywhere. Another reliable tome with a worldwide focus is *Adventuring with Children* (Foghorn Press).

The Unofficial Guide to California with Kids (IDG Books) is an excellent resource covering the entire state. It rates and ranks attractions for each age group, lists dozens of family-friendly accommodations and restaurants, and suggests lots of beaches and adventures that are great for the whole clan.

Family Travel Times is published six times a year by Travel with Your Children, or TWYCH (☎ 888/822-4388 or 212/477-5524; www. familytraveltimes.com). Subscriptions are $39 a year and include a weekly call-in service for subscribers. A free publication list and a sample issue are available online.

BY PLANE

Dozens of carriers serve San Francisco, including the following major domestic airlines: **Alaska Airlines** (☎ 800/426-0333; www.alaskaair.com), **America West Airlines** (☎ 800/235-9292; www.americawest.com), **American Airlines** (☎ 800/433-7300; www.aa.com), **Continental Airlines** (☎ 800/525-0280; www.flycontinental.com), **Delta Air Lines** (☎ 800/221-1212; www.delta-air.com), **Hawaiian Airlines** (☎ 800/367-5320; www.hawaiianair.com), **Northwest Airlines** (☎ 800/225-2525; www.nwa.com); **Reno Air** (☎ 800/RENO-AIR; www.renoair.com), **Southwest Airlines** (☎ 800/I-FLY-SWA; www.southwestairlines.com), **Tower Air** (☎ 800/34-TOWER outside New York, or 718/553-8500 in New York; www.towerair.com), **TWA** (☎ 800/221-2000; www.twa.com), **United Airlines** (☎ 800/241-6522; www.ual.com), and **US Airways** (☎ 800/428-4322; www.usair.com). **National Airlines** (☎ 888/757-JETS; www.nationalairlines.com) offers flights to San Francisco from Chicago, New York, Dallas, Philadelphia, and Los Angeles through Las Vegas. All passengers can take a free stopover in Las Vegas.

If you're coming from outside the United States, refer to chapter 3, "For Foreign Visitors," which lists the major international carriers.

FLYING FOR LESS: TIPS FOR GETTING THE BEST AIRFARE

- Keep checking your newspaper for **sales.** You almost never see a sale during the peak summer vacation months of July and August or during the Thanksgiving or Christmas holidays, but at slower times, airlines may slash their fares dramatically.
- If your schedule is flexible, ask if you can get a cheaper fare by staying an extra day or by flying midweek. If you stay over a Saturday night, you can usually save. Many airlines won't volunteer this information, so ask lots of questions.
- Formerly known as "bucket shops," **consolidators** (wholesalers who buy tickets in bulk at a discount) today are legitimate and offer some of the best deals around. You can get virtually any flight, on any airline, from them; sometimes their fare is identical to the airline's, but often it's discounted 15% to 50%. The tickets carry the same restrictions the airline imposes on advance and discount fares. Their ads usually run in the Sunday travel section, and many have followed the lead of the major airlines and travel agencies by setting up online reservations systems.

    There are lots of fly-by-night consolidators, though, and problems can range from disputing tickets you never received to finding that you have no seat booked when you get to the airport. Play it safe by going with a reputable business. Here are some suggestions: **1-800-FLY-CHEAP** (www.flycheap.com); **Cheap Seats** (☎ 800/451-7200; www.cheapseatstravel.com); and our favorite, **Cheap Tickets** (☎ 800/377-1000; www.cheaptickets.com). **Council Travel** (☎ 800/226-8624; www.counciltravel.com) and **STA Travel** (☎ 800/781-4040; www.sta.travel.com) cater especially to young travelers, but their bargain prices are available to people of all ages; **Travel Bargains** (☎ 800/AIR-FARE; www.1800airfare.com) was formerly owned by TWA but now offers the deepest discounts on many other airlines, with a 4-day advance purchase.

- Surf the Net for bargains. Start out by consulting "Planning Your Trip: An Online Directory" following this chapter. Among the best sites for finding great deals are **Arthur Frommer's Budget Travel** (www. frommers.com), **Microsoft Expedia** (www.expedia.com), and **Travelocity** (www.travelocity.com). The **Internet Travel Network** (www.itn.net) provides a one-stop shopping destination for air, car, and hotel bookings. Its "Fare Mail" keeps you informed of low-cost deals to any of six locations you request; you can eliminate unwanted messages by specifying, for example, that you want to be notified only when flights from New York to San Francisco drop below $350. **Smarter Living** (www. smarterliving.com) offers a customized weekly e-mail summarizing the discount fares available from your departure city.
- Several major airlines offer a free e-mail service known as **E-Savers,** which allows them to send you their best bargain airfares on a regular basis. It's a service for the spontaneously inclined and travelers looking for a quick getaway. But the fares are cheap, so it's worth a look. Check directly with the individual airlines' Web sites (see above, or appendix B at the end of the book).

BY TRAIN

Traveling by train takes a long time and usually costs as much as, or more than, flying. Still, if you want to take a leisurely ride across America, rail may be a good option.

San Francisco–bound **Amtrak** (☎ **800/872-7245** or 800/USA-RAIL; www.amtrak.com) trains leave from New York and cross the country via Chicago. The journey takes about $3^1/_2$ days and seats sell quickly. At this writing, the lowest round-trip fare costs $314 to $570 from New York and $256 to $464 from Chicago. These heavily restricted tickets are good for 45 to 180 days and allow up to three stops along the way, depending on your ticket.

Round-trip tickets from Los Angeles can cost as little as $92 or as much as $140. Trains arrive in Emeryville, just north of Oakland, and connect with regularly scheduled buses to San Francisco's Ferry Building and CalTrain station in downtown San Francisco.

CalTrain (☎ **800/660-4287** or 415/546-4461) operates train service between San Francisco and the towns of the peninsula. The city depot is at 700 Fourth St., at Townsend Street.

BY CAR

San Francisco is easily accessible by major highways: **Interstate 5,** from the north, and **U.S. 101,** which cuts south-north through the peninsula from San Jose and across the Golden Gate Bridge to points north. If you drive from Los Angeles, you can take the longer coastal route (437 miles and 11 hours) or the inland route (389 miles and 8 hours). From Mendocino, it's 156 miles and 4 hours; from Sacramento, 88 miles and $1^1/_2$ hours; from Yosemite, 210 miles and 4 hours.

Car Rentals

All major car-rental agencies have locations at both airports. You don't need a car to explore San Francisco if you stay in a city hotel. If you decide you need one, tips on car rentals can be found in chapter 4, "Getting to Know San Francisco."

If you are driving and aren't already a member, it's worth joining the **American Automobile Association,** or AAA (☎ **800/922-8228**). It charges $40 to $60 per year (with an additional one-time joining fee), depending on where you join, and provides roadside and other services to motorists. **Amoco Motor Club** (☎ **800/334-3300**) is another recommended choice.

PACKAGE DEALS

Packages combining airfare, accommodations, and perhaps even car rentals or airport transfers are sometimes a good way to go. Although some companies offer escorted tours, others simply buy airline tickets and hotel rooms in bulk, passing on some of the discount to you (you travel independently). Often you pay much less than if you had organized the same trip by booking each component separately. To find out what tours and packages are available, check the ads in the travel section of your newspaper or visit your travel agent.

For information on independent fly-drive packages (no escorted tour groups, just a bulk rate on your airfare, hotel, and possibly rental car), contact **American Airlines Fly AAway Vacations** (☎ **800/321-2121**), **American Express Vacations** (☎ **800/241-1700;** www.leisureweb.com), **Continental Airlines Vacations** (☎ **800/634-5555**), **Delta Vacations** (☎ **800/872-7786**), **TWA Getaway Vacations** (☎ **800/438-2929**), **Southwest Airlines** (☎ **800/I-FLY-SWA;** www.iflyswa.com), or **United Vacations** (☎ **800/328-6877**). Availability varies widely based on season and demand, but it always pays to investigate what the major air carriers are offering.

One of the biggest packagers in the Northeast, **Liberty Travel** (☎ **888/271-1584;** www.libertytravel.com) boasts a full-page ad in many Sunday papers. You won't get much in the way of service, but you get a good deal.

For one-stop shopping on the Web, go to **www.vacationpackager.com**, a search engine that links you to many different package-tour operators offering California vacations, often with a company profile summarizing the basic booking and cancellation terms.

Planning Your Trip: An Online Directory

by Lynne Bairstow

Lynne Bairstow is the editorial director of *e-com* magazine.

Day by day, the Internet becomes more integrated into our lives—including the way we plan and book our travel. By early 2000, 1 in every 10 trips was being booked online, a trend that's sure to accelerate.

The Internet not only provides a wealth of destination information but also gives you the chance to compare experiences with fellow travelers, ask experts for advice, seek out discounted fares once accessible only to travel industry insiders, and stay in touch via e-mail while you're away. The instant communication and storehouse of information has revolutionized the way travel is researched, reserved, and realized.

This Online Directory will help you take better advantage of the travel planning information available online; it's best used along with this book. Part 1 lists general Internet resources that can make any trip easier, such as sites for finding the best possible prices on airline tickets. In Part 2 you'll find some top online guides for San Francisco, organized by category.

Keep in mind this isn't a comprehensive list but a discriminating selection to get you started. Unlike some Web-site rankings, which are based on payment, these listings recognize sites based on their content value and ease of use and aren't paid for. Finally, remember that this is a press-time snapshot of leading Web sites—some undoubtedly will have evolved, changed, or moved by the time you read this.

1 Top Travel Planning Web Sites

While the Internet was once a conglomerate of sites for researching places to visit, several key companies have emerged that offer comprehensive travel planning and booking. In addition to Frommer's Online (see box, below), we list the other top online travel agencies below, along with some more specialized services.

WHY BOOK ONLINE?

Online agencies have come a long way over the past few years. They now provide tips for finding the best fare and give suggested dates or times to travel that yield the lowest price if your plans are flexible. Other sites even allow you to establish the price you're willing to pay, and they check the airlines' willingness to accept it. However, in some cases, these sites may not always yield the best price. Unlike a travel

What You'll Find at the Frommer's Site

We highly recommend **Arthur Frommer's Budget Travel Online (www.frommers.com)** as an excellent travel planning resource. Of course, we're a little biased, but you'll find indispensable travel tips, reviews, monthly vacation giveaways, and online booking. Among the site's most popular features is the regular "Ask the Expert" bulletin boards, which feature one of the Frommer's authors answering your questions in online postings.

Subscribe to Arthur Frommer's Daily Newsletter (**www.frommers.com/newsletters**) to receive the latest travel bargains and inside travel secrets in your e-mailbox every day. You'll read daily headlines and articles from the dean of travel himself, highlighting last-minute deals on airfares, accommodations, cruises, and package vacations. You'll also find great travel advice by checking the Tip of the Day or Hot Spot of the Month.

Search the Destinations archive (**www.frommers.com/ destinations**) of more than 200 domestic and international destinations for great places to stay, tips for traveling there, and what to do while you're there. Once you've researched your trip, the online reservation system (**www.frommers.com/booktravelnow**) takes you to Frommer's favorite sites for booking your vacation at affordable prices.

agent, for example, they may not have access to charter flights offered by wholesalers.

Online booking sites aren't the only places to reserve airline tickets. All major airlines have their own Web sites and often offer incentives—bonus frequent-flyer miles or Net-only discounts, for example—when you buy online or buy an e-ticket.

The new trend is toward conglomerated booking sites. By mid-2000, a consortium of U.S. and European airlines are planning to launch an as-yet-unnamed Web site that will offer fares lower than those available through travel agents. United, Delta, Northwest, and Continental have initiated this effort, based on their success at selling airline seats at their own online sites.

The best of the travel planning sites are now highly personalized; they store your seating preferences, meal preferences, tentative itineraries, and credit-card information, allowing you to quickly plan trips or check agendas.

In many cases, booking your trip online can be better than working with a travel agent. It gives you the widest variety of choices, control, and the 24-hour convenience of planning your trip when you choose. All you need is some time—and often a little patience—and you're likely to find that the fun of online travel research will greatly enhance your trip.

WHO SHOULD BOOK ONLINE?

Online booking is best for travelers who want to know as much as possible about their options, those who have flexibility in their travel dates and are looking for the best price, and bargain hunters driven by a good value who are open-minded about where they travel.

One of the biggest successes in online travel for both passengers and airlines is the offer of last-minute specials, such as American Airlines' weekend deals or other Internet-only fares you must purchase online. Another advantage is that you can cash in on incentives for booking online, such as rebates or bonus frequent-flyer miles.

Business and other frequent travelers also have found numerous benefits in online booking. Advances in mobile technology enable them to check flight status, change plans, or get specific directions from handheld computing devices, mobile phones, and pagers. Some sites will even e-mail or page passengers if their flights are delayed.

Online booking is increasingly able to accommodate complex itineraries, even for international travel. The pace of evolution on the Net is rapid, so you'll probably find additional features and advancements by the time you visit these sites. What the future holds for online travelers is ever-increasing personalization, customization, and reaching out to you.

TRAVEL PLANNING & BOOKING SITES

Below are listings for sites for planning and booking travel. The sites offer domestic and international flight, hotel, and rental-car bookings, plus news, destination information, and deals on cruises and vacation packages. Free (one-time) registration is required for booking.

✪ **Travelocity (incorporates Preview Travel). www.travelocity.com; www.previewtravel.com; www.frommers.travelocity.com**

Travelocity is Frommer's online travel planning/booking partner. Travelocity uses the SABRE system to offer reservations and tickets for more than 400 airlines, plus reservations and purchase capabilities for more than 45,000 hotels and 50 car-rental companies. An exclusive feature of the SABRE system is its **Low Fare Search Engine,** which automatically searches for the three lowest-priced itineraries based on a traveler's criteria. Last-minute deals and consolidator fares are included in the search. If you book with Travelocity, you can select specific seats for your flights with online seat maps and also view diagrams of the most popular commercial aircraft. Its hotel finder provides street-level location maps and photos of selected hotels. With the **Fare Watcher** e-mail feature, you can select up to five routes and receive e-mail notices when the fare changes by $25 or more.

Travelocity's **Destination Guide** includes updated information on some 260 destinations worldwide—supplied by Frommer's.

Note to AOL Users: You can book flights, hotels, rental cars, and cruises on AOL at keyword: Travel. The booking software is provided by Travelocity/Preview Travel and is similar to the Internet site. Use the AOL "Travelers Advantage" program to earn a 5% rebate on flights, hotel rooms, and car rentals.

Online Directory

Staying Secure

More people still look online than book online, partly due to fear of putting their credit card numbers out on the Net. Secure encryption and increasing experience buying online have removed this fear for most travelers. In some cases, however, it's simply easier to buy from a local travel agent who can deliver your tickets to your door (especially if your travel is last minute or you have special requests). You can find a flight online and book it by calling a toll-free number or contacting your travel agent, although this is somewhat less efficient. To be sure you're in secure mode when you book online, look for a little icon of a key or a padlock at the bottom of your Web browser.

Airline Web Sites

Below are the Web sites for the major airlines. These sites offer schedules and flight booking, and most have pages where you can sign up for e-mail alerts for weekend deals and other late-breaking bargains.

Air Canada. www.aircanada.ca
Alaska Airlines. www.alaskaair.com
America West. www.americawest.com
American Airlines. www.aa.com
British Airways. www.british-airways.com
Continental Airlines. www.continental.com
Delta. www.delta-air.com
Northwest Airlines. www.nwa.com
Qantas. www.qantas.com
Southwest. www.southwest.com
TWA. www.twa.com
United Airlines. www.ual.com
US Airways. www.usairways.com
Virgin Atlantic. www.fly.virgin.com

Expedia. expedia.com

Expedia is Travelocity's major competitor. It offers several ways of obtaining the best possible fares: **Flight Price Matcher** service allows your preferred airline to match an available fare with a competitor; a comprehensive **Fare Compare** area shows the differences in fare categories and airlines; and **Fare Calendar** helps you plan your trip around the best possible fares. Its main limitation is that like many online databases, Expedia focuses on the major airlines and hotel chains, so don't expect to find too many budget airlines or one-of-a-kind B&Bs here.

TRIP.com. www.trip.com

TRIP.com began as a site geared toward business travelers, but its innovative features and highly personalized approach have broadened its appeal to leisure travelers as well. It is the leading travel site for those using mobile devices to access Internet travel information.

TRIP.com includes a trip-planning function that provides the average and lowest fare for the route requested, in addition to the current available fare. An on-site "newsstand" features breaking news on airfare sales and other travel specials. Among its most popular features are Flight TRACKER and intelliTRIP. **Flight TRACKER** allows users to track any commercial flight en route to its destination anywhere in the United States., while accessing real-time FAA-based flight monitoring data. **intelliTRIP** is a travel search tool that allows users to identify the best airline, hotel, and rental-car rates in less than 90 seconds.

In addition, the site offers e-mail notification of flight delays, plus city resource guides, currency converters, and a weekly e-mail newsletter of fare updates, travel tips, and traveler forums.

Yahoo! Travel. www.travel.yahoo.com

Yahoo! is currently the most popular of the Internet information portals, and its travel site is a comprehensive mix of online booking, daily travel news, and destination information. The **Best Fares** area offers what it promises, plus provides feedback on refining your search if you have flexibility in travel dates or times. There is also an active section of Message Boards for discussions on travel in general and specific destinations.

SPECIALTY TRAVEL SITES

Although the sites listed above provide the most comprehensive services, some travelers have specialized needs that are best met by a site catering specifically to them.

For adventure travelers, **iExplore (www.iexplore.com)** is a great source for information and booking adventure and experiential travel, as well as related services and products. The site combines secure Internet booking functions with hands-on expertise and 24-hour live customer support by seasoned adventure travelers for those interested in trips off the beaten path. The company is a supporting member of the Ecotourism Society and is committed to environmentally responsible travel worldwide.

Another excellent site for adventure travelers is **Away.com (www.away.com)**, which features unique vacations for challenging the body, mind, and spirit. Trips may include cycling in the Loire Valley, taking an African safari, or assisting in the excavation of a Mayan ruin. For those without the time for such an extended exotic trip, offbeat weekend getaways are also available. Services include a customer service center staffed with experts to answer calls and e-mails, plus a network of over 1,000 prescreened tour operators. Trips are categorized by cultural, adventure, and green travel. Away.com also offers a Daily Escape e-mail newsletter.

GORP (Great Outdoor Recreation Pages; www.gorp.com) has been a standard for adventure travelers since outdoor enthusiasts Diane and Bill Greer founded it in 1995. Tapping their own experiences, they created this Web site, which offers unique travel destinations and encourages active participation by fellow GORP visitors through the sophisticated menu of online forums, contests, and discussions.

For travelers who prefer more unique accommodations, **InnSite (www.innsite.com)** offers listings for inns and B&Bs in all U.S. states and dozens of countries around the globe. Find an inn at your destination, look at images of the rooms, check prices and availability, then send e-mail to the innkeeper if you have further questions. This is an extensive directory of bed-and-breakfast inns but includes listings only if the proprietors submitted one. (*Note:* It's free to get an inn listed.) The descriptions are written by the innkeepers, and many listings link to the inn's own Web sites, where you can find more information and images.

Another good resource for mostly one-of-a-kind places in the U.S. and abroad is **Places to Stay (www.placestostay.com),** which focuses on resort accommodations.

"Have Kids, Still Travel!" is the motto of the **Family Travel Forum (www.familytravelforum.com),** a site dedicated to the ideals, promotion, and support of travel with children. FTF is supported by memberships, which are available in flexible prices from a $2.95 monthly fee to a heftier annual fee for more comprehensive services. Since no advertising is accepted, FTF provides its members with honest, unbiased information, informed advice, and practical tips designed to make traveling with children a healthier, safer, hassle-free experience, not to mention a better value.

TOP VACATION PACKAGE SITES

Both **Expedia** and **Travelocity** (see above) offer excellent selections and searches for complete vacation packages. Travelers can search by destination and desired dates coupled with how much they're willing to spend. Travelocity has a valuable "Cruise Critic" function to help would-be cruisers get first-hand accounts of the quality and details of a cruise from recent passengers.

Travel wholesalers, like **Apple Vacations (www.applevacations.com)** and **Funjet (www.funjet.com)** are good starting points, but they still require that the final booking be handled through a travel agent.

As travel agents tend to be more expert at sorting through the values in vacation packages, you might find **Vacation.com (www.vacation.com)** helpful in previewing packages and finding an appropriate agent to help you book the deal. This site represents a nationwide network of 9,800 local travel agencies that specialize in finding the best values in cruises, vacation packages, tours, and other leisure travel services. To find a Vacation.com member agency, enter your ZIP code and the Vacation.com Agency Finder will locate a nearby office.

LAST-MINUTE DEALS & OTHER ONLINE BARGAINS

There's nothing airlines hate more than flying with lots of empty seats. The Net has enabled them to offer last-minute bargains to entice travelers to fill those seats. Most of these are announced on Tuesday or Wednesday and are valid for travel the following weekend, but some can be booked weeks or months in advance. You can sign up for weekly e-mail alerts at airlines' sites (for their Web sites, see "Airline Web Sites," above) or check sites that compile lists of these bargains, such as **Smarter Living** or **WebFlyer** (see below). To make it easier, visit a site that rounds up all the deals and sends them in one convenient weekly e-mail. Last-minute deals aren't the only online bargains; other sites can help you find value even if you haven't waited until the eleventh hour. Increasingly popular are services that let you name the price you're willing to pay for an air seat or vacation package and travel auction sites.

Bid for Travel. www.bidfortravel.com
Bid for Travel is another of the travel auction sites, similar to Priceline (see below), which are growing in popularity. In addition to airfares, Internet users can place a bid for vacation packages and hotels.

Cheap Tickets. www.cheaptickets.com
Cheap Tickets has exclusive deals that aren't available through more mainstream channels. One caveat about the Cheap Tickets site is that it'll offer fare quotes for a route and later show that this fare isn't valid for your dates of travel—most other Web sites, such as Expedia, consider your dates of travel before showing what fares are available. Despite its problems, Cheap Tickets can be worth the effort because its fares can be lower than those offered by its competitors.

Go4less.com. www.go4less.com
Specializing in last-minute cruise and package deals, Go4less has some excellent offers. The **Hot Deals** section gives an alphabetical listing by destination of super discounted packages.

LastMinuteTravel.com. www.lastminutetravel.com
Suppliers with excess inventory come to this online agency to distribute unsold airline seats, hotel rooms, cruises, and vacation packages. It has great deals, but you have to put up with an excess of advertisements and slow-loading graphics.

Moment's Notice. www.moments-notice.com
As the name suggests, Moment's Notice specializes in last-minute vacation and cruise deals. Browsing is free, but if you want to purchase a trip you have to

join Moment's Notice, which costs $25. Go to **World Wide Hot Deals** for a complete list of special deals in international destinations.

⊙ **1travel.com. www.1travel.com**

Here you'll find deals on domestic and international flights, cruises, hotels, and all-inclusive resorts like Club Med. 1travel.com's **Saving Alert** compiles last-minute air deals so you don't have to scroll through multiple e-mail alerts. A feature called "Drive a little using low-fare airlines" helps map out strategies for using alternate airports to find lower fares. And **Farebeater** searches a database that includes published fares, consolidator bargains, and special deals exclusive to 1travel.com. *Note:* The travel agencies listed by 1travel.com have paid for placement.

⊙ **Priceline.com. http://travel.priceline.com**

Even people who aren't familiar with many Web sites have heard about Priceline.com. Launched in 1998 with a $10 million ad campaign featuring William Shatner, Priceline lets you "name your price" for domestic and international airline tickets and hotel rooms. In other words, you select a route and dates, guarantee with a credit card, and make a bid for what you're willing to pay. If one of the airlines in Priceline's database has a fare lower than your bid, your credit card will automatically be charged for a ticket.

But you can't say when you want to fly—you have to accept any flight leaving between 6am and 10pm on the dates you selected, and you may have to make a stopover. No frequent-flyer miles are awarded, and tickets are nonrefundable and can't be exchanged for another flight. So if your plans change, you're out of luck. Priceline can be good for travelers who have to take off on short notice (and don't qualify for advance-purchase discounts). But be sure to shop around first, because if you overbid, you'll be required to purchase the ticket—and Priceline will pocket the difference between what it paid for the ticket and what you bid.

Priceline says that over 35% of all reasonable offers for domestic flights are being filled on the first try, with much higher fill rates on popular routes (New York to San Francisco, for example). They define "reasonable" as not more than 30% below the lowest generally available advance-purchase fare for the same route.

Smarter Living. www.smarterliving.com

Best known for its e-mail dispatch of weekend deals on 20 airlines, Smarter Living also keeps you posted about last-minute bargains on everything from Windjammer Cruises to flights to Iceland.

SkyAuction.com. www.skyauction.com

This auction site has categories for airfare, travel deals, hotels, and much more.

Know When the Sales Start

While most people learn about last-minute weekend deals from e-mail dispatches, it can be best to find out precisely when these deals become available. Because the deals are limited, they can vanish within hours—sometimes even minutes—so it pays to log on as soon as they're available. Check the pages devoted to these deals on airlines' Web pages to get the info. An example: Southwest's specials are posted Tuesdays at 12:01am (Central time). So if you're looking for a cheap flight, stay up late and check Southwest's site to grab the best new deals.

One of the best sources of travel information is word-of-mouth from some-one who has just been there. Internet discussion groups offer an unprece-dented way for travelers around the globe to connect and share experiences. The **Frommer's Online** site (**www.frommers.com**) offers these message boards and also areas where you can pose questions to the guidebook writ-ers themselves in the section "Ask the Expert." **Yahoo Travel, Expedia,** and **Travelocity** are other good sources of online travel discussion groups.

The granddaddy of specialized discussions on particular topics is **Usenet,** a collection of over 50,000 newsgroups. You'll find a comprehensive listing at **Deja News (www.dejanews.com/usenet/)** or at **www.liszt.com.**

Travelzoo.com. **www.travelzoo.com**
At this Internet portal, over 150 travel companies post special deals. It features a Top 20 list of the best deals on the site, selected by its editorial staff each Wednesday night. The Top 20 is also available via an e-mailing list, free to those who sign up.

WebFlyer. **www.webflyer.com**
A comprehensive online resource for frequent flyers, WebFlyer also has an excellent listing of last-minute air deals. Click on **Deal Watch** for a roundup of weekend deals on flights, hotels, and rental cars from domestic and inter-national suppliers.

ONLINE TRAVELER'S TOOLBOX

Veteran travelers usually carry some essential items to make their trips easier. The following is a selection of online tools to smooth your journey.

ATM Locator: Visa. **www.visa.com/pd/atm/**
ATM Locator: MasterCard. **www.mastercard.com/atm**
Use these sites to find ATMs in hundreds of cities in the U.S. and around the world. Both include maps for some locations and both list airport ATM loca-tions, some with maps. *Tip:* You'll usually get a better exchange rate using ATMs than exchanging traveler's checks at banks, but check in advance to see what kind of fees your bank assesses for using an overseas ATM.

CDC Travel Information. **www.cdc.gov/travel/index.htm**
Health advisories and recommendations for inoculations from the U.S. Cen-ters for Disease Control. The CDC site is good for an overview, but it's best to consult your personal physician to get the latest information on required vaccinations or other health precautions.

✪ Foreign Languages for Travelers. **www.travlang.com**
Here you can learn basic terms in more than 70 languages and click on any underlined phrase to hear what it sounds like. (*Note:* Free audio software and speakers are required.) It also offers hotel and airline finders with excellent prices and a simple system to get the listings you're looking for.

Intellicast. **www.intellicast.com**
Here you'll find weather forecasts for all 50 states and cities around the world. Note that temperatures are in Celsius for many international destinations, so don't think you'll need that winter coat for your next trip to Athens.

Check E-mail at Internet Cafes While Traveling

Until a few years ago, most travelers who checked their e-mail while traveling carried a laptop—an expensive and often technologically troublesome option. Thankfully, Web-based free e-mail programs have made it much easier to check your mail.

Just open an account at one of the numerous "freemail" providers—the original leaders continue to be **Hotmail** (hotmail.com), **Excite** (www.excite.com), and **Yahoo! Mail** (mail.yahoo.com), but many are available. AOL users should check out **AOL Netmail,** and **USA.NET (www.usa.net)** comes highly recommended for functionality and security. You can find hints, tips, and a mile-long list of freemail providers at **www.emailaddresses.com.** Then all you need to check your mail is a Web connection, easily available at Net cafes and copy shops around the world. After logging on, just point the browser to your freemail's Internet address, enter your user name and password, and you'll have access to your mail. From these sites, you can download all your e-mail—even from office accounts—or your local or national Internet Service Provider address. There will be a section (generally called "check other mail") that allows you to add the names of other e-mail servers.

The downside is that most Web-based e-mail sites allow a maximum of only 3MB capacity per mail account, which can fill up quickly. Also, message sending and receiving isn't immediate; some messages may be delayed by several hours or even days.

Internet cafes have become ubiquitous, so for a few dollars an hour you'll be able to check your mail and send messages from virtually anywhere in the world. Interestingly, the cafes tend to be more common in remote areas, where they may offer the best form of access for an entire community, especially if phone lines are difficult to obtain.

✪ **Mapquest. www.mapquest.com**
The best of the mapping sites lets you choose a specific address or destination, and in seconds it returns a map and detailed directions. It really is easier than calling, asking, and writing down directions. The site also links to special travel deals and helpful sites.

Net Cafe Guide. www.netcafeguide.com/mapindex.htm
Stop here to locate Internet cafes at hundreds of locations around the globe. Catch up on your e-mail, log onto the Web, and stay in touch with the home front, usually for just a few dollars per hour.

Tourism Offices Worldwide Directory. www.towd.com
This is an extensive listing of tourism offices, some with links to these offices' Web sites.

Travelers' Tales. www.travelerstales.com
Considered the best in compilations of travel literature, Travelers' Tales are an award-winning series of books grouped by destination (Mexico, Italy, France, China) or by theme (Love & Romance, The Ultimate Journey, Women in the Wild, The Adventure of Food). It's a new kind of travel book that offers a description of a place or type of journey through the experiences of many travelers. It makes for a perfect traveling companion.

The Travelite FAQ. www.travelite.org
Here you'll find tips on packing light, choosing luggage, and selecting appropriate travel wear—helpful if you always tend to pack too much or are a compulsive list maker.

Universal Currency Converter. www.xe.net/currency
Come here to see what your dollar or pound is worth in more than 100 other countries.

U.S. Customs Service Traveler Information.
www.customs.ustreas.gov/travel/index.htm
Wondering what you're allowed to bring into the United States? Check at this thorough site, which includes maximum allowance and duty fees.

U.S. State Department Travel Warnings.
http://travel.state.gov/travel_warnings.html
You'll find reports on places where health concerns or unrest might threaten U.S. travelers. Keep in mind that these warnings can be somewhat dated and conservative. You can also sign up to receive State Department briefings via e-mail.

Web Travel Secrets. www.web-travel-secrets.com
If this list leaves you yearning for more travel-oriented sites, Web Travel Secrets offers one of the best compilations around. One section offers advice and tips on how to find the lowest prices for airlines, hotels, and cruises. The other section provides a comprehensive listing of Web travel links for airfare deals, airlines, booking engines, cars, cruise lines, discount travel and best deals, general travel resources, hotels and hotel discounters, search engines, and travel magazines and newsletters.

2 Top Web Sites for San Francisco

updated by Erika Lenkert

TOP CITY GUIDES

As one of the world's most visited cities, San Francisco has a wide and varied selection of city guides. In addition to the commercial sites, there are many useful, opinionated guides created by individuals.

✪ BayInsider. www.bayinsider.com
Visitors looking for a bar, club, or place to eat should consult the Entertainment section, which contains reviews of the editors' restaurant picks. Check out stories on where to play golf or tennis, ski, windsurf, and more (in the Recreation section). The Travel section suggests nearby trips, including jaunts to the Wine Country, Marin County, and nearby beaches. Also find local news provided by KTVU/Fox2 and the Associated Press, professional sports information, and shopping listings.

Best of the Bay: San Francisco Bay Guardian. www.bestofthebay.com
Edgy, opinionated suggestions on excursions, restaurants, shopping, budget activities, and more are collected by readers and editors of the city's oldest alternative weekly.

✪ City Search San Francisco. http://bayarea.citysearch.com
The substantial articles and listings spend as much time as necessary to communicate all the intricacies of city entertainment highlights. Editors describe and review many museums, bars, performance art, restaurants, hotels, outdoor activities, professional services, and more. Get ideas for day trips to the Wine

Online Directory

Type the keyword "San Francisco" and peruse **Digital City: San Francisco,** AOL's guide for visitors and locals. Here you'll find maps, weather forecasts, and sports articles. The *San Francisco Examiner* provides the news headlines, and Gayot Publishing supplies the restaurant reviews. Much of this is surprisingly impersonal, except some articles on dining by Scott Sax. Digital City is also available on the Web at **digitalcity.aol.com/sanfrancisco.**

Country, Marin County, Half Moon Bay and points south, and a variety of road-trip destinations, such as Monterey and Lake Tahoe. The event calendar links to events throughout the Bay Area. The excellent Visitor and Travel Info section includes tips on getting around and packages all relevant travel information in one place.

Eguide: SF Gate. www.sfgate.com/eguide
The *San Francisco Chronicle* provides much of the content on movies, performance art, dining, nightlife, museums, and galleries.

Gay Global San Francisco. www.gayglobalsf.com
Seeking establishments that cater to gays and lesbians? The descriptions and reviews of accommodations, restaurants, and bars may help you choose. They also highlight neighborhoods, theaters, live music, and other stage venues for drama and spoken word.

North Beach Magazine. www.sfnorthbeach.com
Dedicated to the neighborhood, this guide includes descriptions of restaurants, bars, lodging, and transportation, and parking suggestions. Short articles and photos offer overviews of the area's Italian community and history of the Beat generation.

Q San Francisco. www.qsanfrancisco.com/qsf/guide/contents.html
Get the lowdown on events, bars, restaurants, attractions, tours, gyms, and everything else preferred by editors specializing in gay travel.

San Francisco for Visitors: The Mining Company. http://gosanfran. miningco.com
This Mining Company (about.com) guide, Betsy Malloy, has done a nice job scouring the Net for sites covering lodging, dining, outdoor activities, attractions, nightlife, arts, shopping, sports, and side trips.

San Francisco Underground. www.sftravel.com
This independent guide offers strategies and opinions from readers. It provides reviews of "best" hotels, B&Bs, restaurants, bars, and clubs. Find tips on car rental, parking, public transit, activities, and how to "avoid scams" from airport shuttles.

z San Francisco. www.zpub.com/sf
The Visitor Guide section includes a vast directory of links on attractions, transportation, history, and other information for travelers.

NEWSPAPERS & MAGAZINES

Metroactive. www.metroactive.com
Weekly alternative publication for San Francisco, Sonoma County, Santa Cruz, and Silicon Valley includes listings and reviews of movies, music, performance art, and restaurants. Read human interest stories and features about local issues.

San Francisco Bay Guardian. **www.sfbg.com**
Consult the Guardian's event schedule and guides to dining, shopping, arts, and activities for suggestions.

San Francisco Magazine. **www.sffocus.com**
Monthly magazine targeted at visitors and residents includes dining reviews and ideas for nearby excursions.

✪ SF Gate. **www.sfgate.com**
Read current articles from the *San Francisco Chronicle* and *San Francisco Examiner,* which have joined forces on this site. Local news, international news, and the entertainment guide, Eguide, link from here.

SF Weekly. **www.sfweekly.com**
Read opinionated articles about San Francisco and the Bay Area. The Best of San Francisco section, which links from the home page, highlights the editors' favorite attractions, activities, and restaurants.

DINING GUIDES

CuisineNet. **www.cuisinenet.com/restaurant/san_francisco**
Search by location, cuisine type, and price. The Top Picks section offers frank dining reviews. The rest of the database includes addresses and phone numbers for many restaurants and some reviews from readers.

Daily Diner: San Francisco Bay Area.
   www.dailydiner.com/home.cfm/CID2
Search by location or cuisine to get the address, phone number, and map of each restaurant. Some include reviews by patrons.

✪ OpenTable.com. **www.opentable.com**
A relatively new site, OpenTable takes the hassle out of dinner reservations by offering a broad selection of San Francisco's finest restaurants and a search function that includes price range, area, and availability.

✪ SF Gate: Food. **www.sfgate.com/eguide/food**
See what the *San Francisco Chronicle* restaurant critics have to say about food in the city and around the Bay Area. Search by cuisine and location and check out the sections on Wine, Top 100 Restaurants, Places Open Late, and Best Bargain Restaurants.

TOP ATTRACTIONS

Alcatraz. **www.nps.gov/alcatraz**
The National Park Service posts tour schedules and history of The Rock.

Cable Cars. **www.sfcablecar.com**
In addition to practical maps and fare information, download free Shockwave software for a virtual ride.

Center for the Arts at Yerba Buena Gardens. **www.yerbabuenaarts.org**
The grounds host a variety of traveling lectures and visual and performing arts. Get a calendar of events, descriptions, and ticket purchasing information here.

City Pass. **www.citypass.net/sanfran.htm**
This ticket book will knock off half the admission to the California Legion of Honor, Exploratorium, M.H. de Young Museum, San Francisco Bay Cruises, Museum of Modern Art, and Steinhart Aquarium.

Dirty Harry Tour of San Francisco. **www.movietours.com/harry/intro/**
Clint Eastwood fans enjoy a photo tour of San Francisco spots from the Dirty Harry movies. Go ahead—make a printed version and walk it yourself.

Online Directory

Fisherman's Wharf. www.fishermanswharf.org
Preview the shops, nearby restaurants, hotels, and wax museums of arguably the city's most touristy area. The Tours section outlines ferry and bus services that bring visitors to Alcatraz, Sausalito, Muir Woods, and beyond.

Ghirardelli Square. www.ghirardellisq.com
This old chocolate factory has been transformed into a collection of upscale shops and restaurants. Find descriptions and links to their Web sites.

✪ Golden Gate Bridge. www.goldengate.org
Flip through photos and read facts about this San Francisco landmark. Ferry and bus schedules will help prepare your travel between the city and Marin County.

Pier 39. www.pier39.com
Listen to an audio clip of barking sea lions and watch a slide show of photos from the pier. Consult the maps and directories of shops and restaurants.

SS Jeremiah O'Brien. www.geocities.com/jeremiahobrien
This World War II battleship still cruises in the bay. Get hours and admission prices and check out history, articles, and photos.

TOP MUSEUMS

Asian Art Museum. www.asianart.org
View samples of the permanent collection, from China, India, Iran, Japan, Korea, and Southeast Asia. Read about the visiting exhibitions in the Exhibits section and check hours, admission fees, and directions to the museum.

Exploratorium. www.exploratorium.edu
Especially fun for kids, this hands-on science museum hosts interactive games and puzzles online. Find exhibit information, directions, admission, hours, and a schedule of events.

Legion of Honor. www.thinker.org/legion/index.html
Preview current exhibitions with the slide show, then get directions, an event calendar, admission, and operating hours.

San Francisco Museum of Modern Art. www.sfmoma.org
Brief descriptions with pictures of current and upcoming exhibits show what's happening in the galleries. Get contact information, hours, and admission.

SPORTS & RECREATION

Golden Gate National Recreation Area. www.nps.gov/goga
The National Recreation Area comprises a lot of land and parks around San Francisco. Find basic contact and accessibility information for properties including Fort Funston, Alcatraz, Muir Woods, and the Presidio.

Golden State Warriors (pro basketball). www.nba.com/warriors
The team's official NBA site includes news and ticket and arena information.

Presidio Golf. www.presidiogolf.com
Reserve online to play this public course overlooking the Bay and the city. The Course Layout section includes photos, descriptions, and ratings of each hole.

San Francisco 49ers (pro football). www.sf49ers.com
The team's official site offers game statistics, schedules, and player bios.

✪ San Francisco Giants (pro baseball). www.sfgiants.com
Check schedules, ticket prices, and the stadium seating chart. Read articles about the new stadium, Pacific Bell Park, which opened for the 2000 season.

San Jose Sharks (pro hockey). www.sj-sharks.com
The team's official site includes ticket and arena information as well as player bios and highlights.

Sunshine Daydream. www.sunshinedaydream.com
Adventure-seekers can peruse suggestions about where to go and get equipment to sail, windsurf, paraglide, and more throughout the Bay Area. Download free QuickTime VR software to see 360-degree vistas of Fort Mason, Coit Tower, Ocean Beach, and other favorite San Francisco spots.

GETTING AROUND

If parking in the city starts driving you crazy, consider the train, bus, or ferry.

Bay Area Rapid Transit (BART). www.bart.org
Timetables, prices, and maps for trains that shuttle passengers around San Francisco and across the bay to outlying cities. Purchase tickets online.

Blue and Gold Fleet. www.blueandgoldfleet.com
Ferry schedules and ticket prices for destinations including Angel Island, Alcatraz, Oakland, Tiburon, and Sausalito.

Breeze Net's Car Rental Guide. www.bnm.com/sf.htm
Will it be budget or luxury? Either way, Breeze Net aggregates the details from various rental agencies and lets you reserve online.

Municipal Railway (MUNI). www.ci.sf.ca.us/muni
No-nonsense site posts maps, fares, and schedules for the vast bus and light-rail systems around the city. Also describes accessibility options for people with disabilities.

San Francisco International Airport. www.sfoairport.com
Maps of the terminals and parking lots as well as the ground transportation listings are the most useful information at this basic site.

SIDE TRIPS

Guides published by individuals and companies in Napa and Sonoma's towns offer ideas of places to visit. However, don't miss guides organized by San Francisco publications, such as City Search and Bay Insider. They tend to give the most useful information for visitors arriving from the city. We also recommend such guides for trips into Marin County, down to Half Moon Bay, and beyond.

THE EAST BAY: BERKELEY & OAKLAND

AC Transit. www.actransit.dst.ca.us
No car? Check the bus schedules and fares to get around the East Bay.

East Bay Regional Parks. www.ebparks.org
Use the maps and trail descriptions here to explore the East Bay's woods and wilderness areas, such as Tilden Park and Wildcat Canyon.

OaklandCA.Com. http://oaklandca.com
A basic directory lists contact information for restaurants, lodging, bars, clubs, and attractions. The most useful sections are the city map and event calendar.

✪ Oakland.Com. www.oakland.com
The largest selection of links to attractions, shopping, and the arts around Oakland. The Dining section offers detailed descriptions and some recommendations.

Online Directory

HALF MOON BAY & COASTAL REGION

✪ **Año Nuevo State Reserve. www.anonuevo.org**
If you're in the area between December and March, sign up to watch elephant seals duke it out on the beach for dominance of the harem. Listen to sound files to hear the seals bark online. Get the basics about fees, rules, and reservations, which are essential during the winter because the only way to visit then is on docent-led walks.

Coastside Live. www.coastsidelive.com
Addresses and phone numbers for places to sleep, eat, and shop along the San Mateo County coast.

Half Moon Bay Chamber of Commerce. www.halfmoonbaychamber.org
Useful contact information for outdoor excursions, like exploring beaches, horseback riding, bicycling, and whale watching. The Things To See section includes histories of Half Moon Bay, Princeton-by-the-Sea, Pescadero, Miramar, Montara, and other coastal towns. The Places to Stay section offers decent descriptions of local B&Bs and hotels.

MARIN COUNTY

Angel Island State Park. www.angelisland.org
A ferry shuttles visitors to this island in the bay. Read about the island's natural features and its history as a home to Miwok Indians, military barracks, and an immigration station. See what's going on right now through the live Web cam.

Mount Tamalpais State Park. http://cal-parks.ca.gov/DISTRICTS/marin/mtsp239.htm
Directions, contact information, and natural highlights of Marin County's highest peak.

Muir Woods National Monument. www.nps.gov/muwo
Details on ecology and history accompany photos of the huge coastal redwood trees. The National Park Service posts events, entrance fees, contact information, and a rudimentary map.

Point Reyes National Seashore. www.nps.gov/pore/visit.htm
For a trip just north of the city, read up on the beaches, trails, and history of this protected land. The ranger phone numbers, directions, maps, and other travel information will help you prepare for your excursion.

Town of Tiburon. www.tiburon.org
Basic listings with photos of restaurants are the most useful information here. Link to Web sites of some downtown shops.

WINE COUNTRY

California Wine Country: Vinescape. http://vinescape.com
This directory of Net links leads you to sites of wineries, restaurants, accommodations, and events.

NapaValley.com. www.napavalley.com
Find out about wineries, attractions, shopping, hotels, dining, and more.

Napa & Sonoma Tourist Guide. www.napasonomatourist.com
Navigate the site by choosing a specific town. Detailed descriptions accompany links to hotels, B&Bs, wineries, restaurants, and golf courses in Napa and Sonoma Counties.

Online Directory

Although there's little original content here, if you know where you want to go, the directory of Sonoma County's inns, spas, wineries, restaurants, and outdoor activities offers the necessary contact information.

✪ Wine Country Guide: CitySearch.
www.citysearch7.com/E/F/SFOCA/0000/12/05

This comprehensive guide offers frank dining reviews and lists wineries by location and alphabetically with maps. Some lodging listings have descriptions and reviews; the Places To See section offers details on outdoor activities, such as hiking, whale watching, and tidepooling on the coast. If you really know wine, search by appellation or varietal.

3 For Foreign Visitors

The pervasiveness of American culture around the world may make you feel that you know the USA pretty well, but leaving your own country for the States still requires an additional degree of planning. This chapter will help prepare you for the more common problems (expected and unexpected) you might encounter during your trip to San Francisco.

1 Preparing for Your Trip

ENTRY REQUIREMENTS

Immigration laws are a hot political issue in the United States, and the following requirements may have changed somewhat by the time you plan your trip. Check at any U.S. embassy or consulate for current information and requirements.

DOCUMENT REGULATIONS   The U.S. State Department has a **Visa Waiver Pilot Program** allowing citizens of certain countries to enter the United States without a visa for stays of up to 90 days. At press time, they included Andorra, Argentina, Australia, Austria, Belgium, Brunei, Denmark, Finland, France, Germany, Iceland, Ireland, Italy, Japan, Liechtenstein, Luxembourg, Monaco, the Netherlands, New Zealand, Norway, San Marino, Slovenia, Spain, Sweden, Switzerland, and the United Kingdom. Citizens of these countries need only a valid passport and a round-trip air or cruise ticket in their possession upon arrival. If they first enter the United States, they can then visit Mexico, Canada, Bermuda, and the Caribbean islands and return to the United States without needing a visa. Further information is available from any U.S. embassy or consulate. Canadian citizens can enter the United States without visas; they need only proof of residence.

Citizens of all other countries must have (1) a valid **passport** with an expiration date at least 6 months later than the scheduled end of their visit to the United States; and (2) a **tourist visa,** which can be obtained without charge from the nearest U.S. consulate.

To get a visa, the traveler must submit a completed application form (either in person or by mail) with a $1^1/_2$-inch-square photo, and must demonstrate binding ties to a residence abroad. Usually you can get a visa at once or within 24 hours, but it might take longer during the summer rush from June through August. If you cannot go in person, contact the nearest U.S. embassy or consulate for directions on applying by mail.

Travel Tip

If you have questions about U.S. Immigration policies or laws, call the **Immigration Office** at the San Francisco International Airport (☎ **650/876-2876**). Otherwise, call San Francisco's **INS Ask Immigration System** (☎ **800/375-5283**). Your travel agent or airline office might also be able to give you visa applications and instructions. The U.S. consulate or embassy that issues your visa determines whether you receive a multiple- or single-entry visa and any restrictions on the length of your stay.

British subjects can get up-to-date passport and visa information by calling the **U.S. Embassy Visa Information Line** (☎ **0891/200-290**) or the **London Passport Office** (☎ **0990/210-410** for recorded information).

Foreign driver's licenses are recognized in San Francisco, although you might want to get an international driver's license if your home license is not written in English.

MEDICAL REQUIREMENTS   Unless you're arriving from an area known to be suffering from an epidemic (particularly cholera or yellow fever), no inoculations or vaccinations are required to enter the United States. If you have a disease requiring treatment with medications containing narcotics or drugs requiring a syringe, carry a valid signed prescription from your physician to allay suspicions that you may be smuggling drugs.

For HIV-positive visitors, requirements for entering the United States are somewhat vague and change frequently. According to the latest publication of *HIV and Immigrants: A Manual for AIDS Service Providers,* "although INS doesn't require a medical exam for everyone trying to come into the United States, INS officials may keep out people who they suspect are HIV positive. INS may stop people because they look sick or because they are carrying AIDS/HIV medicine."

It's a confusing situation, so if you're HIV-positive and need advice, contact an AIDS center in your area, or call the Bar Association of San Francisco **Immigration Project** at ☎ **415/982-1600, ext. 767.**

CUSTOMS REQUIREMENTS   Every visitor over 21 years of age can bring in, free of duty, the following: (1) 1 liter of wine or hard liquor; (2) 200 cigarettes (if not U.S.-made), 100 cigars (but not from Cuba), or 4.25 pounds of smoking tobacco; and (3) $100 worth of gifts. These exemptions are offered to travelers who spend at least 72 hours in the United States and who have not claimed them within the preceding 6 months. It is altogether forbidden to bring into the country foodstuffs (particularly fruit, cooked meats, and canned goods) and plants (vegetables, seeds, tropical plants, and the like). Foreign tourists can bring in or take out up to $10,000 in U.S. or foreign currency with no formalities; larger sums must be declared to U.S. Customs on entering or leaving, which includes filing Form CF 4790. For more specific information on U.S. Customs, call your nearest U.S. embassy or consulate.

INSURANCE

Although it's not required of travelers, health insurance is highly recommended. Unlike many European countries, the United States does not usually offer free or low-cost medical care to its citizens or visitors. Doctors and hospitals are expensive and in most cases require advance payment or proof of coverage before they render their services. Policies can cover everything from the loss or theft of your baggage and trip cancellation to the guarantee of bail in case you're arrested. Good policies also cover costs of an accident, repatriation, or death. Automobile clubs, insurance companies, and travel agents sell such packages.

Although lack of health insurance might prevent you from being admitted to a hospital in non-emergencies, don't worry about being left on a street corner to die: The American way is to fix you now and bill the living daylights out of you later.

FOR BRITISH TRAVELERS   Most big travel agents offer their own insurance, and will probably try to sell you their package when you book a holiday. Think before you sign. Britain's Consumers' Association recommends that you insist on seeing the policy and reading the fine print before buying travel insurance. **The Association of British Insurers** (☎ 020/7600-3333) gives advice by phone and publishes the free *Holiday Insurance,* a guide to policy provisions and prices. You might also shop around for better deals: Try **Columbus Travel Insurance Ltd.** (☎ 020/7375-0011) or, for students, **Campus Travel** (☎ 0870/240-1010).

MONEY

CURRENCY   The U.S. monetary system is painfully simple: The most common bills (all ugly, all green) are the $1 (colloquially, a "buck"), $5, $10, and $20 denominations. There are also $2 bills (seldom encountered), $50 bills, and $100 bills (the last two are usually not welcome when paying for small purchases). Note that redesigned bills of denominations over $1 are or will soon be in circulation. Despite rumors to the contrary, the old-style bills are still legal tender.

There are six denominations of coins: 1¢ (1 cent, or a penny); 5¢ (5 cents, or a nickel); 10¢ (10 cents, or a dime); 25¢ (25 cents, or a quarter); 50¢ (50 cents, or a half dollar); and $1. A new gold-colored $1 piece entered circulation in 2000; other versions are the rare silver dollar, prized by collectors, and the quarter-sized Susan B. Anthony coin.

Note: The foreign-exchange bureaus so common in Europe are rare even at airports in the United States, and nonexistent outside major cities. It's best not to change foreign money (or traveler's checks denominated in a currency other than U.S. dollars) at a small-town bank or even a branch in a big city; in fact, leave any currency other than U.S. dollars at home—it might prove a greater nuisance than it's worth.

TRAVELER'S CHECKS   Although traveler's checks are widely accepted, make sure they're denominated in U.S. dollars. Foreign-currency checks are often difficult to exchange. The three brands that are most widely recognized—and least likely to be denied—are Visa, American Express, and Thomas Cook. Be sure to record the numbers of the checks, and keep that information separate should they get lost or stolen. San Francisco businesses are pretty good about taking traveler's checks, but you're better off cashing them in at a bank (in small amounts, of course) and paying in cash. *Remember:* You'll need identification, such as a driver's license or passport, to change a traveler's check. Please see "Money" in Chapter 2 for more information about traveler's checks.

CREDIT CARDS & ATMS   San Francisco's larger hotels accept most major credit cards, and Visa and MasterCard are accepted just about everywhere else. There are, however, a handful of stores and restaurants that do not take credit cards, so be sure to ask in advance. Most businesses display a sticker near their entrance to let you know which cards they accept. (*Note:* Often businesses require a minimum purchase price, usually around $10, to use a credit card.)

Travel Tip

Be sure to keep a copy of all your travel papers separate from your wallet or purse, and leave a copy with someone at home should you need it faxed in an emergency.

It's strongly recommended that you bring at least one major credit card. Hotels, car-rental companies, and airlines usually require a credit-card imprint as a deposit against expenses. In an emergency, a credit card can be priceless.

In downtown San Francisco there's an automated teller machine (ATM) on just about every block. Most accept Visa, MasterCard, and American Express, as well as ATM cards from other U.S. banks. Expect to be charged up to $3 per transaction if you're not using your own bank's ATM. *Tip:* The way around this is to ask for cash back at stores (for example, Safeway) that accept ATM cards and don't charge usage fees. Of course, you have to buy something first.

SAFETY

GENERAL SAFETY TIPS   While most San Francisco tourist areas are generally safe, there are a few neighborhoods you should leave out of your itinerary, such as the Tenderloin and Hunter's Point areas.

Avoid deserted areas, especially at night, and don't go into any of the parks at night unless there's a concert or similar occasion that attracts crowds.

Avoid carrying valuables with you on the street, and don't display expensive cameras or electronic equipment. Hold on to your pocketbook, and place your billfold in an inside pocket. In theaters, restaurants, and other public places, keep your possessions in sight.

Remember also that hotels are open to the public, and in a large hotel, security might not be able to screen everyone entering. Always lock your room door—don't assume that once inside your hotel you are automatically safe and no longer need to be aware of your surroundings.

See "Fast Facts: San Francisco" in chapter 4, "Getting to Know San Francisco," for more city-specific safety tips.

DRIVING SAFETY   Driving safety is important, too, especially given the highly publicized carjackings of foreign tourists in Florida. Question your rental agency about personal safety and ask for a brochure describing safety tips when you pick up your car. Get written directions—or a map with the route clearly marked—from the agency showing how to get to your destination. And, if possible, arrive and depart during daylight hours.

Recently, more and more crime has involved cars and drivers. If you drive off a highway into a doubtful neighborhood, leave the area as quickly as possible. If you have an accident, even on the highway, stay in your car with the doors locked until you assess the situation or until the police arrive. If you're bumped from behind on the street or are involved in a minor accident with no injuries and the situation appears to be suspicious, motion to the other driver to follow you. *Never* get out of your car in such situations. Go directly to the nearest police precinct, well-lit service station, or 24-hour store.

Always try to park in well-lit and well-traveled areas if possible. If you leave your rental car unlocked and empty of your valuables, you're probably safer than if you lock your car with valuables in plain view. Never leave any packages or valuables in sight. If someone attempts to rob you or steal your car, don't try to resist—report the incident to the police department immediately.

2 Getting to the U.S.

Traveling overseas on a budget is something of an oxymoron, but there are ways to knock down the price of a plane ticket by several hundred dollars if you take the time to shop around. For example, travelers from overseas can take advantage of the APEX

(Advance Purchase Excursion) reduced fares offered by all major U.S. and European carriers. For more money-saving airline advice, see "Getting There" in chapter 2, "Planning Your Trip: The Basics."

In addition to the domestic American airlines listed under "Getting There" in chapter 2, a number of international carriers also serve the Bay Area airports. They include, among others: **Aer Lingus** (☎ **01/886-8888** in Dublin; www.aerlingus.ie), **Air Canada** (☎ **800/776-3000;** www.aircanada.ca), **British Airways** (☎ **0345/ 222-111** in the U.K.; www.british-airways.com), **Canadian Airlines** (☎ **800/ 426-7000;** www.cdair.ca), **Japan Airlines** (☎ **0354/89-1111** in Tokyo; www.jal.co.jp), **Qantas** (☎ **13-12-11** in Australia; www.qantas.com.au), and **Virgin Atlantic** (☎ **01293/747-747** in the U.K.; www.fly.virgin.com). British Airways and Virgin Atlantic offer direct flights to San Francisco from London. **Air New Zealand** (☎ **13-2476** in New Zealand; www.airnewzealand.co.nz) flies to Los Angeles and will book you straight through to San Francisco on a partner airline.

Major U.S. carriers, such as **Continental** (☎ **01293/776-464** in the U.K.; www.flycontinental.com), **TWA** (☎ **800/892-4141** in the U.K.; www.twa.com), **United** (☎ **084/584-44777** in the U.K.; www.ual.com), **American** (☎ **020/ 8572-5555** in the U.K.; www.americanair.com), and **Delta** (☎ **0800/414-767** in the U.K.; www.delta-air.com), have service from Europe to the United States. **United** (☎ **02/237-8888** in Sydney, 008/230-322 in the rest of Australia) flies from Sydney to San Francisco.

Visitors arriving by air, no matter what the port of entry, should cultivate patience and resignation before setting foot on U.S. soil. Getting through immigration control can take as long as 2 hours on some days, especially on summer weekends, so be sure to have this guidebook or something else to read. Add the time it takes to clear customs, and you'll see that you should make a generous allowance for delay in planning connections between international and domestic flights—figure on 2 to 3 hours at least.

In contrast, for the traveler arriving by car or rail from Canada, the border-crossing formalities have been streamlined to the vanishing point. Travelers by air from Canada, Bermuda, and some places in the Caribbean can sometimes go through customs and immigration at the point of departure, which is much quicker.

3 Getting Around the U.S.

BY PLANE

Some large airlines (for example, Northwest and Delta) offer travelers on their transatlantic or transpacific flights special discount tickets under the name **Visit USA.** They allow travel between any U.S. destinations at minimum rates. *These discount tickets are not on sale in the United States and must be purchased abroad with your international ticket.* This system is the best, easiest, and fastest way to see the United States at low cost. You should get information well in advance from your travel agent or the office of the airline concerned, because the conditions attached to these discount tickets can change without advance notice.

BY TRAIN

International visitors can buy a **USA Railpass,** good for 15 or 30 days of unlimited travel on Amtrak (☎ **800/USA-RAIL;** www.amtrak.com). The pass is available through many foreign travel agents. Prices in 2000 for a 15-day pass were $295 off-peak adults and $147.50 children 2 to 15, $425 peak; for a 30-day pass, $375 off-peak, $535 peak. With a foreign passport, you can also buy passes at some Amtrak offices in the United States, including locations in San Francisco, Los Angeles, Chicago, New York, Miami, Boston, and Washington, D.C. Reservations are generally required and should be made for each part of your trip as early as possible.

BY BUS

For short hops between cities, the bus is often the most economical form of public transit. However, bus travel in the United States can be both slow and uncomfortable, so this option isn't for everyone—particularly when Amtrak, which is far more luxurious, offers similar rates. **Greyhound/Trailways** (☎ **800/231-2222**), the sole nationwide bus line, offers an Ameripass (☎ **888/454-7277**) for unlimited travel for 7 days at $169, 15 days at $249, 30 days at $349, and 60 days at $479. Passes must be purchased at a Greyhound terminal.

BY CAR

The most cost-effective, convenient, and comfortable way to travel around the United States—especially California—is by car. (In the city of San Francisco, though, you may find a car more of a hassle than a help.) The interstate highway system connects cities and towns all over the country; in addition to these high-speed, limited-access roadways, there's an extensive network of federal, state, and local highways and roads. The national car-rental companies that have offices in San Francisco include **Alamo** (☎ **800/327-9633**), **Avis** (☎ **800/331-1212**), **Budget** (☎ **800/527-0700**), **Dollar** (☎ **800/800-4000**), **Hertz** (☎ **800/654-3131**), **National** (☎ **800/227-7368**), and **Thrifty** (☎ **800/367-2277**).

If you plan to rent a car in the United States, you probably won't need the services of an automobile organization. If you plan to buy or borrow a car, automobile-association membership is recommended. The **American Automobile Association (AAA),** 150 Van Ness Ave., San Francisco, CA 94102 (☎ **800/922-8228;** www.aaa.com), is the country's largest auto club. It supplies its members with maps, insurance, and, most important, emergency road service. The cost of joining runs from $63 for singles to $87 for families, but if you're a member of a foreign auto club with reciprocal arrangements, you can enjoy free AAA service in America. See "Getting There" in chapter 2 for more information.

Fast Facts: For the Foreign Traveler

Business Hours   See "Fast Facts: San Francisco," in chapter 4.

Climate   See "When to Go," in chapter 2.

Currency Exchange   Foreign-exchange bureaus are rare in the United States, and most banks are not equipped to handle currency exchange. San Francisco's money-changing offices include **Bank of America,** 345 Montgomery St. (☎ **415/622-2451**), open Monday to Friday 9am to 6pm, and **Thomas Cook,** 75 Geary St. (☎ **415/362-3452;** www.us.thomascook.com), open Monday to Friday 9am to 5pm and Saturday 10am to 4pm.

Drinking Laws   The legal age for purchase and consumption of alcoholic beverages is 21. Proof of age is required and often requested at bars, nightclubs, and restaurants, so it's always a good idea to bring ID when you go out. In San Francisco, supermarkets and grocery and liquor stores sell liquor daily from 6am to 2am. Licensed restaurants are permitted to sell alcohol during the same hours. Note that many restaurants are licensed only for beer and wine.

A big no-no is having an open container of alcohol in your car or in any public area that isn't zoned for alcohol consumption. The police can, and probably will, fine you on the spot. And nothing will ruin your trip faster than getting a citation for DUI (driving under the influence), so don't even think about driving while intoxicated.

Electricity   U.S. wall outlets give power at 110 to 115 volts, 60 cycles, compared with 220 volts, 50 cycles in most of Europe. In addition to a 100-volt transformer, small foreign appliances, such as hair dryers and shavers, require a plug adapter (available at most hardware stores) with two flat, parallel pins.

Embassies & Consulates   All embassies are located in Washington, D.C. In addition, several major English-speaking countries also have consulates in San Francisco or in Los Angeles.

The embassy of **Australia** is at 1601 Massachusetts Ave. NW, Washington, DC 20036 (☎ 202/797-3000); a consulate-general is at 1 Bush St., Suite 700, San Francisco, CA 94104 (☎ 415/362-6160). The embassy of **Canada** is at 501 Pennsylvania Ave. NW, Washington, DC 20001 (☎ 202/682-1740); the nearest consulate is at 300 S. Grand Ave., 10th Floor, California Plaza, Los Angeles, CA 90071 (☎ 213/346-2700). The embassy of the **Republic of Ireland** is at 2234 Massachusetts Ave. NW, Washington, DC 20008 (☎ 202/462-3939); a consulate is at 44 Montgomery St., Suite 3830, San Francisco, CA 94104 (☎ 415/392-4214). The embassy of **New Zealand** is at 37 Observatory Circle NW, Washington, DC 20008 (☎ 202/328-4800); the nearest consulate is at 12400 Wilshire Blvd., Suite 1150, Los Angeles, CA 90025 (☎ 310/207-1605). The embassy of the **United Kingdom** is at 3100 Massachusetts Ave. NW, Washington, DC 20008 (☎ 202/462-1340); the nearest consulate is at 1 Sansome St., Suite 850, San Francisco, CA 94104 (☎ 415/981-3030). The embassy of **Japan** is at 2520 Massachusetts Ave. NW, Washington, DC 20008 (☎ 202/238-6700); the consulate-general of Japan is at 50 Fremont St., 23rd Floor, San Francisco, CA 94105 (☎ 415/777-3533).

If you are from another country, you can get the telephone number of your embassy by calling information (directory assistance) in Washington, D.C. (☎ 202/555-1212).

Emergencies   You can call the police, an ambulance, or the fire department through the single emergency telephone number ☎ 911 from any phone or pay phone (no coins needed). If that doesn't work, another useful way of reporting an emergency is to call the telephone company operator by dialing 0 (zero, not the letter *O*).

Gasoline (Petrol)   Prices vary, but expect to pay anywhere between $1.35 and $1.95 for 1 U.S. gallon (about 3.8 liters) of "regular" unleaded gasoline (petrol). Higher-octane fuels are also available at most gas stations for slightly higher prices. The printed price includes taxes.

Holidays   On the following legal national holidays, banks, government offices, post offices, and many stores, restaurants, and museums are closed: New Year's Day (January 1), Martin Luther King Day (third Monday in January), Presidents' Day (third Monday in February), Memorial Day (last Monday in May), Independence Day (July 4), Labor Day (first Monday in September), Columbus Day (second Monday in October), Veterans Day (November 11), Thanksgiving Day (fourth Thursday in November), and Christmas Day (December 25). Election Day, for national elections, falls on the Tuesday following the first Monday in November. It's a legal national holiday during a presidential election, which occurs every fourth year (next in 2004).

Mail   If you want to receive mail but aren't sure where you'll be, have it sent to you, in your name, ^c/o **General Delivery** (Poste Restante) at the main post office of the city or region you're visiting. Call ☎ **800/275-8777** for information on the nearest post office. The addressee must pick it up in person and produce proof of identity (driver's license, credit card, passport). Most post offices will hold your mail up to 1 month and are open Monday to Saturday from 8am to 6pm. The local address is **Civic Center Post Office Box Unit,** P.O. Box 429991, San Francisco, CA 94142-9991 (☎ **800/275-8777**). The street address is 101 Hyde St.

Generally found at street intersections, mailboxes are blue and carry the inscription U.S. MAIL. If your mail is addressed to a U.S. destination, don't forget to add the five-digit ZIP code after the two-letter abbreviation of the state to which the mail is addressed (CA for California).

For overseas mail, **postal rates** are as follows: A first-class letter of up to one-half ounce costs 60¢ (48¢ to Canada, 40¢ to Mexico); a first-class postcard costs 55¢ (45¢ to Canada, 40¢ to Mexico); and a preprinted postal aerogramme costs 60¢.

Medical Emergencies   To call an ambulance, dial ☎ **911** from any phone— no coins are needed in pay phones. For hospitals and other emergency information, see "Fast Facts: San Francisco" in chapter 4.

Newspapers & Magazines   Many of San Francisco's newsstands offer a selection of foreign periodicals and newspapers, such as *The Economist, Le Monde,* and *Der Spiegel.* For information on local literature and specific newsstand locations, see "Fast Facts: San Francisco," in chapter 4.

Post Office   See "Mail," above.

Radio & Television   There are five national broadcast television networks: ABC (Channel 7), CBS (Channel 5), NBC (Channel 4), PBS (Channel 9), and Fox (Channel 2). Cable television encompasses the national networks and 50 or so other stations, including the Cable News Network (CNN), ESPN (sports), and MTV. Most hotels offer a dozen cable stations and pay-per-view movies. You'll also find a wide choice of local radio stations. Each broadcasts particular kinds of talk shows, music—classical, country, jazz, rock, pop, gospel—or both, punctuated by news broadcasts and frequent commercials.

Smoking   Heavy smokers are in for a tough time in San Francisco. There is no smoking in public buildings, sports arenas, elevators, theaters, banks, lobbies, restaurants, offices, stores, bed-and-breakfasts, most small hotels, and bars. That's right—as of January 1, 1998, you can't even smoke in a bar in California. The only exception is a bar where drinks are served solely by the owner. You will find, however, that many neighborhood bars turn the other cheek and pass you an ashtray.

Taxes   In the United States there's no value-added tax (VAT) or other direct tax at a national level. Every state, as well as every city, is allowed to levy its own local sales tax on all purchases, including hotel and restaurant checks and airline tickets. Taxes are included in the price of certain goods and services, such as public transportation, cab fares, phone calls, and gasoline. The amount of sales tax varies from 4% to 10%, depending on the state and city, so when you are making major purchases, such as photographic equipment, clothing, or high-fidelity components, it can be a significant part of the cost.

In addition, many cities charge a separate "bed" or room tax on accommodations, above and beyond sales tax.

For information on sales and room taxes in San Francisco, see "Fast Facts: San Francisco," in chapter 4.

Telephone & Fax   Pay phones can be found almost everywhere—at street corners, in bars and restaurants, and in hotels. Outside the metropolitan area, however, public telephones are more difficult to find; stores and gas stations are your best bet.

Phones do not accept pennies and few will take anything larger than a quarter. Some public phones, especially those in airports and large hotels, accept credit cards, such as MasterCard, Visa, and American Express. Credit cards are especially handy for international calls; instructions are printed on the phone.

In San Francisco, **local calls** cost 35¢. To make local calls, dial the seven-digit local number. For domestic long-distance calls or international calls, stock up with a supply of quarters; after you dial the number, a recorded voice instructs you when and in what quantity you should put the coins into the slot. For **domestic long-distance calls,** first dial 1 (the long-distance access code), then the three-digit area code and seven-digit local number. For **direct overseas calls,** dial 011 (the international access code), then the country code (Australia, 61; Republic of Ireland, 353; New Zealand, 64; United Kingdom, 44), followed by the city code, then the local number. To place a call to Canada or the Caribbean, just dial 1, the area code, and the local number.

Before calling from a hotel room, always ask the hotel phone operator if there are any telephone surcharges. They can sometimes be reduced by calling collect or by using a telephone charge card. Hotel charges, which can be exorbitant, can be avoided altogether by using a pay phone in the lobby.

Note that almost all calls to phone numbers in area codes 800, 888, and 877 are toll-free, but your hotel might still charge a fee for making the call.

For **local directory assistance** ("information"), dial ☎ **411;** for **long-distance information** in the United States and Canada, dial 1, then the appropriate area code and 555-1212.

For "collect" (reversed-charge) calls and for "person-to-person" calls, dial 0 (zero, not the letter *O*) followed by the area code and the number you want; an operator or recording then comes on the line. You should specify that you are calling collect or person-to-person, or both. If your operator-assisted call is international, just dial 00 and wait for the operator.

Like the telephone system, **telegraph** services are provided by private corporations, such as ITT, MCI, and above all, **Western Union.** You can bring your telegram to a Western Union office or dictate it over the phone (☎ **800/ 325-6000**). You can also telegraph money, or have it telegraphed to you, very quickly. In San Francisco, there's a Western Union office at 61 Gough St., at Market Street (☎ **415/621-2031**), near the Civic Center. There are several other locations around town, too; call ☎ **800/325-6000** for the one nearest you.

Fax facilities are widely available. They can be found in most hotels and many other establishments. Try Mail Boxes Etc. or any photocopying shop.

Telephone Directory   There are two kinds of telephone directories in the United States. The general directory is the so-called **White Pages,** which lists private and business subscribers in alphabetical order. The inside front cover lists the emergency number for police, fire, and ambulance, and other vital numbers (like the Coast Guard, poison-control center, crime-victims hotline, and so on). The first few pages are devoted to community-service numbers, including a guide to long-distance and international calling, complete with country codes and area codes.

The second directory, printed on yellow paper (hence its name, the **Yellow Pages**), lists local services, businesses, and industries by type of activity, with an index at the back. The listings cover not only such obvious items as automobile repairs by make of car and drugstores (pharmacies), often by geographical location, but also restaurants by type of cuisine and geographical location, bookstores by special subject or language, places of worship by religious denomination, and other information that the tourist might otherwise not readily find. The Yellow Pages also include city plans or detailed maps, often showing postal ZIP codes and public-transportation routes.

Time   The continental United States is divided into four time zones. From east to west, they are eastern time (ET), central time (CT), mountain time (MT), and Pacific time (PT). There are also Alaska time (AT) and Hawaii time (HT). San Francisco is on Pacific standard time, which is 8 hours behind Greenwich mean time. Noon in New York City (ET) is 11am in Chicago (CT), 10am in Denver (MT), 9am in San Francisco (PT), 8am in Anchorage (AT), and 7am in Honolulu (HT).

Daylight saving time is in effect from the first Sunday in April until 2am on the last Sunday in October, except in Arizona, Hawaii, part of Indiana, and Puerto Rico. Daylight saving time moves the clock 1 hour ahead of standard time.

Tipping   Service in America is some of the best in the world and is rarely included in the price of anything. It's part of the American way of life to tip, on the principle that you must expect to pay for any service you get. Many employees receive little direct salary and must depend on tips for their income. In fact, the U.S. federal government imposes income taxes on service personnel based on an estimate of how much they should have earned in tips in relation to their employer's total receipts. In other words, they might have to pay taxes on a tip you didn't give them!

Here are some rules of thumb:

In **hotels,** tip bellhops at least $1 per piece of luggage ($2 to $3 if you have a lot of bags) and tip the chamber staff at least $1 per day (the more expensive the hotel, the bigger the tip). Tip the doorman or concierge only if he or she has provided you with some specific service (for example, calling a cab for you or obtaining difficult-to-get theater tickets). Tip the valet parking attendant at least $2 every time you get your car.

In **restaurants, bars, and nightclubs,** tip service staff 15% to 20% of the check, tip bartenders 10% to 15%, tip checkroom attendants $1 per garment, and tip valet-parking attendants at least $2 per vehicle. Tip the doorman only if he has provided you with some specific service (such as calling a cab for you). Tipping is not expected in cafeterias and fast-food restaurants.

Tip **cab drivers** 15% of the fare.

For **other service personnel,** tip skycaps at airports at least $1 per piece ($2 to $3 if you have a lot of luggage), and tip hairdressers and barbers 15% to 20%.

Tipping gas-station attendants and ushers at movies and theaters is not expected.

Toilets   Public toilets can be hard to find in San Francisco. There are only a handful of fancy new French stalls strategically placed on high-volume streets and few small stores allow you access to their facilities. You can almost always find a toilet in restaurants and bars; note, however, a growing practice in some restaurants and bars of displaying a notice that toilets are for the use of patrons only. You can ignore this sign or, better yet, avoid arguments by paying for a cup of coffee or soft drink, which qualifies you as a patron. Large hotels and fast-food restaurants are probably the best bet for good, clean facilities. Museums, department stores, shopping malls, and, in a pinch, gas stations all have public toilets. If possible, avoid the toilets at parks and beaches, which are a real crap shoot (pun intended) when it comes to cleanliness.

Getting to Know
San Francisco

4

Half the fun of becoming familiar with San Francisco is wandering around and haphazardly stumbling upon great shops, restaurants, and viewpoints that even locals might not know about. You'll find that, although it's metropolitan, San Francisco is a small town, and you won't feel like a stranger for long. If you get disoriented, just remember that downtown is east and the Golden Gate Bridge is north—and even if you do get lost, you probably won't go too far, since water surrounds three sides of the city. The most difficult challenge you'll have, if you're traveling by car, is mastering the maze of one-way streets. This chapter offers useful information on how to become better acquainted with the city.

1 Orientation

ARRIVING
BY PLANE
The Bay Area has two major airports: San Francisco International and Oakland International.

SAN FRANCISCO INTERNATIONAL AIRPORT   Almost four dozen major scheduled carriers serve San Francisco International Airport, 14 miles south of downtown directly on U.S. 101. Travel time to downtown during commuter rush hours is about 40 minutes; at other times, it's about 20 to 25 minutes.

The airport offers a toll-free **hotline** (☎ **800/736-2008**) for information on ground transportation. It's available weekdays from 7am to 5pm local time. During operating hours, a real person answers the line and gives you a rundown of all your options for getting into the city from the airport. Each of the three main terminals has a desk where you can get the same information.

A **cab** from the airport to downtown costs $28 to $32, plus tip.

SFO Airporter buses (☎ **415/495-8404**) depart from outside the lower-level baggage-claim area to downtown San Francisco every 15 to 30 minutes from 6:15am to midnight. They stop at several Union Square–area hotels, including the Grand Hyatt, San Francisco Hilton, San Francisco Marriott, Westin St. Francis, Parc Fifty-Five, Hyatt Regency, and Sheraton Palace. No reservations are needed. For the return trip, SFO Airporter picks up at hotels as early as 5am; make a reservation 24 hours in advance if possible. The cost is $10 each way and children under 2 ride free.

Other private shuttle companies offer door-to-door airport service, in which you share a van with a few other passengers. **SuperShuttle** (☎ **415/558-8500; www.supershuttle.com**) takes you anywhere in the city, charging $11 per person to a hotel, $13 to a residence or business. Add $8 for each additional person. It costs $40 to charter an entire van for up to seven passengers. The shuttle stops every 20 minutes or so and picks up passengers from the marked areas outside the terminals' upper level. Reservations are required for the return trip to the airport only and should be made 1 day before departure. Keep in mind that these shuttles demand they pick you up 2 hours before your domestic flight and 3 hours before for international flights and during holidays.

The San Mateo County Transit system, **SamTrans** (☎ **800/660-4287** within northern California, or 650/508-6200; www.samtrans.com), runs two buses between the airport and the Transbay Terminal at First and Mission streets. The 292 bus costs $2.20 and makes the trip in about 55 minutes. The KX bus costs $3 and takes just 35 minutes but permits only one carry-on bag. Both buses run daily. The 292 starts at 4:46am and the KX starts at 5:30am. Both run frequently until 8pm, then hourly until about midnight.

OAKLAND INTERNATIONAL AIRPORT   About 5 miles south of downtown Oakland, at the Hagenberger Road exit of Calif. 17 (U.S. 880), **Oakland International Airport** (☎ **510/577-4000**) primarily serves passengers with East Bay destinations. Some San Franciscans prefer this less crowded, accessible airport during busy periods.

Taxis from the airport to downtown San Francisco are expensive—approximately $45, plus tip.

Bayporter Express (☎ **415/467-1800**) is a shuttle service that charges $24 for the first person, $10 for each additional person to downtown San Francisco. The fare for outer areas of town is higher. The service accepts advance reservations. To the right of the airport exit, there are usually shuttles that take you to the city for around $20 per person. Keep in mind that they are independently owned, and prices vary.

The cheapest way to reach downtown San Francisco is to take the shuttle bus from the airport to **BART** (Bay Area Rapid Transit; ☎ **510/464-6000**). The AirBART shuttle bus runs about every 15 minutes Monday to Saturday 6am to 11:30pm and Sunday 8:30am to 11:30pm. It stops in front of Terminals 1 and 2 near the ground transportation signs. The cost is $2 for the 10-minute ride to BART's Coliseum terminal. BART fares vary, depending on your destination; the trip to downtown San Francisco costs $2.75 and takes 20 minutes once onboard. The entire excursion should take around 45 minutes.

VISITOR INFORMATION

Once in the city, visit the **San Francisco Visitor Information Center,** on the lower level of Hallidie Plaza, 900 Market St., at Powell Street (☎ **415/391-2000;** fax 415/362-7323). It distributes information, brochures, discount coupons, and advice on restaurants, sights, and events in the city. The staff can provide answers in German, Japanese, French, Italian, and Spanish (as well as English, of course). To find the office, descend the escalator at the cable-car turnaround.

Dial ☎ **415/391-2001** anytime, day or night, for a recorded message about current cultural, theater, music, sports, and other special events. This information is also available in German, French, Japanese, and Spanish.

Keep in mind that this service supports only members of the Convention and Visitors Bureau and is very tourist-oriented. While there's tons of information, it's not representative of all the city has to offer. The office is open Monday to Friday 9am to 5:30pm, Saturday 9am to 3pm, and Sunday 10am to 2pm. It's closed on January 1, Thanksgiving Day, and December 25. You can get a fax with information anytime from the bureau's automated service if you call ☎ **800/220-5747** and follow the prompts.

Pick up a copy of the *Bay Guardian.* The city's free alternative paper lists all city happenings. It has kiosks throughout the city and in most coffee shops.

For specialized information on Chinatown's shops and services, and on the city's Chinese community in general, contact the **Chinese Chamber of Commerce,** 730 Sacramento St., San Francisco, CA 94108 (☎ **415/982-3000**), open daily 9am to 5pm.

The **Visitors Information Center of the Redwood Empire Association,** in The Cannery, 2801 Leavenworth, 2nd floor, San Francisco, CA 94133 (☎ **800/200-8334** or 415/394-5991; www.redwoodempire.com), offers informative brochures and has a knowledgeable desk staff who can plan tours in San Francisco and north of the city. Its annual 48-page *Redwood Empire Visitors' Guide* is available free in person or by mail with up to 6-week delivery. Priority mail in the U.S. costs $5 (check, cash, or money order).; international mail, $5.50. The center offers information on everything from San Francisco hotels and walking tours to museums in northern California. The office is open Monday to Saturday 10am to 5pm.

CITY LAYOUT

San Francisco occupies the tip of a 32-mile-long peninsula between San Francisco Bay and the Pacific Ocean. Its land area measures about 46 square miles. Twin Peaks, in the geographic center of the city, is more than 900 feet high.

San Francisco might seem confusing at first, but it quickly becomes easy to negotiate. The city's downtown streets are arranged in a simple grid pattern, with the exception of Market Street and Columbus Avenue, which cut across the grid at right angles to each other. Hills appear to distort this pattern, however, and can be disorienting. As you learn your way around, the hills will become your landmarks and reference points.

MAIN ARTERIES & STREETS   **Market Street** is San Francisco's main thoroughfare. Most of the city's buses travel this route on their way to the Financial District from the outer neighborhoods to the west and south. The tall office buildings clustered downtown are at the northeast end of Market; 1 block beyond lies the Embarcadero and the bay.

The Embarcadero, an excellent strolling, skating, and biking route (thanks to recent renovations), curves along San Francisco Bay from south of the Bay Bridge to the northeast perimeter of the city. It terminates at Fisherman's Wharf, the famous tourist-oriented pier. Aquatic Park, Fort Mason, and the Golden Gate National Recreation area are on the northernmost point of the peninsula.

From the eastern perimeter of Fort Mason, **Van Ness Avenue** runs due south, back to Market Street. The area just described forms a rough triangle, with Market Street as its southeastern boundary, the waterfront as its northern boundary, and Van Ness Avenue as its western boundary. Within this triangle lie most of the city's main tourist sights.

FINDING AN ADDRESS   Since most of the city's streets are laid out in a grid pattern, finding an address is easy when you know the nearest cross street. Numbers start with 1 at the beginning of the street and proceed at the rate of 100 per block. When asking for directions, find out the nearest cross street and the neighborhood where your destination is located, but be careful not to confuse numerical avenues with numerical streets. Numerical avenues (Third Avenue and so on) are in the Richmond and Sunset districts in the western part of the city. Numerical (Third Street and so on) are south of Market in the east and south parts of town.

Neighborhoods in Brief

Union Square   Union Square is the commercial hub of the city. Most major hotels and department stores are crammed into the area surrounding the actual square, which was named for a series of violent pro-Union mass demonstrations staged here on the eve of the Civil War. A plethora of upscale boutiques, restaurants, and galleries occupy the spaces tucked between the larger buildings. A few blocks west is the **Tenderloin,** a patch of poverty and blight where you should keep your wits about you. The **Theater District** is 3 blocks west of Union Square.

The Financial District   East of Union Square, this area bordered by the Embarcadero, Market, Third, Kearny, and Washington streets is the city's business district and the stomping grounds for many major corporations. The pointy TransAmerica Pyramid, at Montgomery and Clay streets, is one of the district's most conspicuous architectural features. To its east stands the sprawling Embarcadero Center, an $8^1/_2$-acre complex housing offices, shops, and restaurants. Farther east still is the World Trade Center, adjacent to the old Ferry Building, the city's pre-bridge transportation hub. Ferries to Sausalito and Larkspur still leave from this point.

Nob Hill & Russian Hill   Bounded by Bush, Larkin, Pacific, and Stockton streets, Nob Hill is a genteel, well-heeled district, still occupied by the major power brokers and the neighborhood businesses they frequent. Russian Hill extends from Pacific to Bay and from Polk to Mason. It contains steep streets, lush gardens, and high-rises occupied by both the moneyed and the more bohemian.

Chinatown   A large red-and-green gate on Grant Avenue at Bush Street marks the official entrance to Chinatown. Beyond lies a 24-block labyrinth, bordered by Broadway, Bush, Kearny, and Stockton streets, filled with restaurants, markets, temples, shops—and, of course, a substantial percentage of San Francisco's Chinese residents. Chinatown is a great place for exploration all along Stockton, Grant, and Portsmouth Square and the alleys that lead off them, like Ross and Waverly. This area is jam-packed, so don't even think about driving here.

North Beach   The Italian quarter, which stretches from Montgomery and Jackson to Bay Street, is one of the best places in the city to grab a coffee, pull up a cafe chair, and do some serious people-watching. Nightlife is equally happening; restaurants, bars, and clubs along Columbus and Grant avenues attract folks from all over the Bay Area, who fight for a parking place and romp through the festive neighborhood. Down Columbus toward the Financial District are the remains of the city's Beat Generation landmarks, including Ferlinghetti's City Lights Bookstore and Vesuvio's Bar. Broadway—a short strip of sex joints—cuts through the heart of the district. **Telegraph Hill** looms over the east side of North Beach, topped by Coit Tower, one of San Francisco's best vantage points.

Fisherman's Wharf   North Beach runs into Fisherman's Wharf, which was once the busy heart of the city's great harbor and waterfront industries. Today, it is a tacky but interesting tourist area with little, if any, authentic waterfront life, except for recreational boating and some friendly sea lions.

The Marina District   Created on landfill for the Pan Pacific Exposition of 1915, the Marina boasts some of the best views of the Golden Gate, as well as plenty of grassy fields alongside San Francisco Bay. Elegant Mediterranean-style homes and apartments, inhabited by the city's well-to-do singles and wealthy families, line the streets. Here, too, are the Palace of Fine Arts, the Exploratorium, and Fort Mason Center. The main street is Chestnut between Franklin and Lyon, which abounds with shops, cafes, and boutiques. Because of its landfill foundation, the Marina was one of the hardest-hit districts in the 1989 quake.

Cow Hollow   Located west of Van Ness Avenue, between Russian Hill and the Presidio, this flat, grazable area supported 30 dairy farms in 1861. Today, Cow Hollow is largely residential and largely yuppie. Its two primary commercial thoroughfares are Lombard Street, known for its many relatively inexpensive motels, and Union Street, a flourishing shopping sector filled with restaurants, pubs, cafes, and shops.

Pacific Heights   The ultra-elite, such as the Gettys and Danielle Steele—and those lucky enough to buy before the real-estate boom—reside in the mansions and homes here. When the rich meander out of their fortresses, they wander down to Union Street, a long stretch of boutiques, restaurants, cafes, and bars.

Japantown   Bounded by Octavia, Fillmore, California, and Geary, Japantown shelters only about 4% of the city's Japanese population, but exploring these few square blocks and the shops and restaurants within them is still a cultural experience.

Civic Center   Although millions of dollars have gone toward brick sidewalks, ornate lampposts, and elaborate street plantings, the southwestern section of Market Street remains downright dilapidated. The Civic Center, at the "bottom" of Market Street, is an exception. This large complex of buildings includes the domed and newly dapper City Hall, the Opera House, Davies Symphony Hall, and the city's main library. The landscaped plaza connecting the buildings is the staging area for San Francisco's frequent demonstrations for or against just about everything.

SoMa   No part of San Francisco has been more affected by recent development than South of Market (dubbed "SoMa"). The area—until recently, a district of old warehouses and industrial spaces, with a few scattered underground nightclubs, restaurants, and shoddy residential areas—is the hub of dot-commercialization and half-million-dollar-plus lofts. It also houses urban entertainment à la the Museum of Modern Art and Yerba Buena Gardens. The official boundaries are the Embarcadero, Highway 101, and Market Street, with the greatest concentrations of interest around Yerba Buena Center, along Folsom and Harrison streets between Steuart and 6th, and Brannan and Market. Along the waterfront are an array of restaurants and the new and absolutely fab Pacific Bell Park. Farther west, around Folsom between 7th and 11th streets, much of the city's nightclubbing occurs.

Mission District   This is another area greatly affected by the city's new wealth. The Mexican and Latin American populations, with their cuisine, traditions, and art, make the Mission District a vibrant area to visit. Some parts of the neighborhood are still poor and sprinkled with the homeless, gangs, and drug addicts, but more and more young urbanites are infiltrating, moving into the "reasonably" (a relative term) priced rentals and forging the endless oh-so-hot restaurants and bars that stretch from 16th Street and Valencia to 25th and Mission Street. Less adventurous tourists still duck into Mission Dolores, cruise by a few of the 200-plus amazing murals, and head back downtown. But if there ever was a sign that things are a-changin', it's gotta be that President Clinton was recently spotted dining in a Mission Street restaurant (The

San Francisco Neighborhoods

Slanted Door) with Chelsea and friends. Don't be afraid to visit this area, but do use caution at night.

Castro   One of the liveliest streets in town, Castro is practically synonymous with San Francisco's gay community (even though technically it is only a street in the Noe Valley district). Located at the very end of Market Street, between 17th and 18th streets, the Castro supports dozens of shops, restaurants, and bars catering to the gay community. Open-minded straight people are welcome, too.

Haight-Ashbury   Part trendy, part nostalgic, part funky, the Haight, as it's most commonly known, was the soul of the psychedelic, free-loving 1960s and the center of the counterculture movement. Today, the neighborhood straddling upper Haight Street on the eastern border of Golden Gate Park is more gentrified, but the commercial area still harbors all walks of life. Leftover aging hippies mingle with grungy, begging street kids outside Ben and Jerry's ice cream shop (where they might still be talking about Jerry Garcia), nondescript marijuana dealers whisper "Buds" as shoppers pass, and many people walking down the street have Day-Glo hair. But you don't need to be a freak or wear tie-dye to enjoy the Haight—the food, shops, and bars cover all tastes. From Haight, walk south on Cole Street for a more peaceful and quaint neighborhood experience.

Richmond & Sunset Districts   San Francisco's suburbs of sorts, these are the city's largest and most populous neighborhoods, consisting mainly of small (but expensive) homes, shops, and neighborhood restaurants. Although it borders Golden Gate Park and Ocean Beach, few tourists venture into "The Avenues," as this area is referred to locally.

2 Getting Around

BY PUBLIC TRANSPORTATION

The **San Francisco Municipal Railway,** 949 Presidio Ave., better known as "Muni" (☎ **415/673-6864**), operates the city's cable cars, buses, and Metro streetcars. Together, these three services crisscross the entire city. Buses and Metro streetcars cost $1 for adults, 35¢ for seniors over 65 and children 5 to 17. Cable cars, which run 6:30am to 12:30am, cost a whopping $2 for all people over 5 ($1 for seniors 6:30 to 7am and 9pm to midnight). Needless to say, they're packed primarily with tourists. Exact change is required on all vehicles except cable cars. Fares are subject to change.

For detailed route information, phone Muni or consult the bus map at the front of the Yellow Pages. If you plan to use public transportation extensively, you might want to invest in a comprehensive route map ($2), sold at the San Francisco Visitor Information Center (see "Visitor Information" in "Orientation," above) and many downtown retail outlets. Also see "A Money-Saving Tip," below.

BY CABLE CAR   San Francisco's cable cars might not be the most practical means of transport, but the rolling historic landmarks sure are a fun ride. There are only three lines, all condensed in the downtown area. The most scenic, and exciting, is the **Powell-Hyde line,** which follows a zigzag route from the corner of Powell and Market streets, over both Nob Hill and Russian Hill, to a turntable at gaslit Victorian Square in front of Aquatic Park. The **Powell-Mason line** starts at the same intersection and climbs over Nob Hill before descending to Bay Street, just three blocks from Fisherman's Wharf. The least scenic is the **California Street line,** which begins at the foot of Market Street and runs a straight course through Chinatown and over Nob Hill to Van Ness Avenue. All riders must exit at the last stop and wait in line for the return trip. The cable-car system operates approximately 6:30am to 12:30am.

A Money-Saving Tip

Muni discount passes, called **"Passports,"** entitle holders to unlimited rides on buses, Metro streetcars, and cable cars. A Passport costs $6 for 1 day, $10 or $15 for 3 or 7 consecutive days. Muni's **"City Pass,"** which costs $33.25 for adults, $26.25 for seniors 65 and older, and $24.25 for kids 5 to 17, entitles you to unlimited rides for 7 days, plus 50% off admission at 24 of the city's major attractions, including the M. H. De Young Memorial Museum, the Asian Art Museum, the California Academy of Sciences, and the Japanese Tea Garden (all in Golden Gate Park); the Museum of Modern Art; Coit Tower; the Exploratorium; the zoo; and the National Maritime Museum and Historic Ships (where you can visit the USS *Pampanito* and the SS *Jeremiah O'Brien*). You can buy a Passport or City Pass at the San Francisco Visitor Information Center, the Holiday Inn Civic Center, and the TIX Bay Area booth at Union Square, among other outlets.

BY BUS   Buses reach almost every corner of San Francisco and beyond—they travel over the bridges to Marin County and Oakland. Overhead electric cables power some buses; others use conventional gas engines. All are numbered and display their destinations on the front. Signs, curb markings, and yellow bands on adjacent utility poles designate stops, and most bus shelters exhibit Muni's transportation map and schedule. Many buses travel along Market Street or pass near Union Square and run from about 6am to midnight. After midnight, there is infrequent all-night "Owl" service. If you can help it, for safety purposes, avoid taking buses late at night.

Popular tourist routes include bus nos. 5, 7, and 71, all of which run to Golden Gate Park; 41 and 45, which travel along Union Street; and 30, which runs between Union Square and Ghirardelli Square.

BY METRO STREETCAR   Five of Muni's six Metro streetcar lines, designated J, K, L, M, and N, run underground downtown and on the street in the outer neighborhoods. The sleek railcars make the same stops as BART (see below) along Market Street, including Embarcadero Station (in the Financial District), Montgomery and Powell streets (both near Union Square), and the Civic Center (near City Hall). Past the Civic Center, the routes branch off: The J line takes you to Mission Dolores; the K, L, and M lines run to Castro Street; and the N line parallels Golden Gate Park and extends all the way to the Embarcadero. Metros run about every 15 minutes, more frequently during rush hours. They operate Monday to Friday 5am to 12:30am, Saturday 6am to 12:20am, and Sunday 8am to 12:20am. The L and N lines operate 24-7 (all day, all night).

The most recent addition to this system is not a newcomer at all, but is, in fact, San Francisco's beloved rejuvenated 1930s streetcars. The beautiful multicolored F-Market line runs from 17th Street and Castro Street to First and Mission streets; every other car continues to Jones and Beach streets in Fisherman's Wharf. It's a quick and charming way to get up- and downtown without any hassle.

BY BART   BART, an acronym for **Bay Area Rapid Transit** (☎ **650/992-2278**), is a futuristic-looking, high-speed rail network that connects San Francisco with the East Bay—Oakland, Richmond, Concord, and Fremont. Four stations are on Market Street (see "By Metro Streetcar," above). Fares range from $1.10 to $4.30, depending on how far you go. Machines in the stations dispense tickets that are magnetically encoded with a dollar amount. Computerized exits automatically deduct the correct fare. Children 4 and under ride free. Trains run every 15 to 20 minutes, Monday to Friday 4am to midnight, Saturday 6am to midnight, and Sunday 8am to midnight.

San Francisco Mass Transit

IMPORTANT BUS LINES FOR TOURISTS

5 Civic Center, Alamo Square Historic District, Golden Gate Park
21
7 Via Haight & Market to Golden Gate Park, Haight-Ashbury
71
38 Via Geary Blvd. to Japan Center, Richmond District, Lincoln Park
30 North Beach, Union Square, Fisherman's Wharf
15 Via Kearney to North Beach, Chinatown
41 Via Union St. to the Presidio, Pacific Heights
45
32 Via Embarcadero to Fisherman's Wharf, Financial District
42

A $2.5-billion, 33-mile BART extension, currently under construction, includes a southern line that will extend all the way to San Francisco International Airport. It will open, presumably, around the beginning of 2002.

BY TAXI

This isn't New York, so don't expect a taxi to appear whenever you need one—or even close. If you're downtown during rush hour or leaving a major hotel, it won't be hard to hail a cab; just look for the lighted sign on the roof that indicates the vehicle is free. Otherwise, it's a good idea to call one of the following companies to arrange a ride; even then I've had more than one situation when the cab never came. What to do? Call back if your cab is late and insist on attention, but don't expect prompt results on weekends no matter how nicely you ask. The companies: **Veteran's Cab** (☎ 415/552-1300), **Luxor Cabs** (☎ 415/282-4141), **Yellow Cab** (☎ 415/626-2345), and **Pacific** (☎ 415/986-7220). Rates are approximately $2.50 for the first mile and $1.80 for each mile thereafter.

BY CAR

You don't need a car to explore downtown San Francisco. In fact, with the city becoming more crowded by the minute, a car can be your worst nightmare—you're likely to end up stuck in traffic with lots of aggressive and frustrated drivers, pay upward of $25 a day to park, and spend a good portion of your vacation looking for a parking space. If you want to venture outside the city, driving is the best way to go.

Before heading outside the city, especially in winter, call for California **road conditions** (☎ 800/427-7623).

RENTALS   All the major companies operate in the city and have desks at the airports. When we last checked, you could get a compact car for a week for about $170, including all taxes and other charges, but prices change dramatically on a daily basis and depend on which company you rent from.

Some of the national car-rental companies operating in San Francisco include **Alamo** (☎ 800/327-9633), **Avis** (☎ 800/331-1212), **Budget** (☎ 800/527-0700), **Dollar** (☎ 800/800-4000), **Hertz** (☎ 800/654-3131), **National** (☎ 800/227-7368), and **Thrifty** (☎ 800/367-2277).

Car rental rates vary even more than airline fares. Prices depend on the size of the car, where and when you pick it up and drop it off, the length of the rental period, where and how far you drive it, whether you buy insurance, and a host of other factors. A few key questions could save you hundreds of dollars, but you have to ask—reservations agents don't often volunteer money-saving information.

- Are weekend rates lower than weekday rates? Ask if the rate is the same for pick-up Friday morning, for instance, as it is for Thursday night. Reservations agents won't volunteer this information, so don't be shy about asking lots of questions.
- Does the agency assess a drop-off charge if you don't return the car to the same location where you picked it up?
- Are special promotional rates available? If you see an advertised price in your local newspaper, be sure to ask for that specific rate; otherwise, you could be charged the standard cost. Terms change constantly.
- Are discounts available for members of AARP, AAA, frequent-flyer programs, or trade unions? If you belong to any of these organizations, you may be entitled to discounts of up to 30%.
- How much tax will be added to the rental bill? Local tax? State use tax?

Handy Driving Tips

California law requires that both drivers and passengers wear seat belts. You can turn right at a red light (unless otherwise indicated), after yielding to traffic and pedestrians, and after making a complete stop. Cable cars always have the right-of-way, as do pedestrians at intersections and crosswalks. Pay attention to signs and arrows on the streets and roadways or you might suddenly find yourself in a lane that requires exiting or turning when you want to go straight. What's more, San Francisco's many one-way streets can drive you in circles, but most road maps of the city indicate which way traffic flows.

* How much does the rental company charge to refill your gas tank if you return with the tank less than full? Most rental companies claim these prices are "competitive," but fuel is almost always cheaper in town. Try to allow enough time to refuel the car before returning it.

Some companies offer "refueling packages," in which you pay for an entire tank of gas upfront. The cost is usually fairly competitive with local prices, but you don't get credit for any gas remaining in the tank. If a stop at a gas station on the way to the airport will make you miss your plane, then by all means take advantage of the fuel purchase option. Otherwise, skip it.

Most agencies enforce a minimum-age requirement—usually 25. Some also have a maximum-age limit. If you're concerned that these limits might affect you, ask about rental requirements at the time of booking to avoid problems later.

Make sure you're insured. Hasty assumptions about your personal auto insurance or a rental agency's additional coverage could end up costing you tens of thousands of dollars, even if you are involved in an accident that was clearly the fault of another driver.

If you already have your own car insurance, you are most likely covered in the United States for loss of or damage to a rental car and liability in case of injury to any other party involved in an accident. Be sure to check your policy before you spend extra money (usually $10 per day) on the **Collision Damage Waiver (CDW),** which all agencies offer.

Most major credit cards (especially gold cards) provide some degree of coverage as well—if they were used to pay for the rental. Terms vary widely, however, so be sure to call your credit card company directly before you rent and rely on the card for coverage. If you are uninsured, your credit card provides primary coverage as long as you decline the rental agency's insurance. If you already have insurance, your credit card provides secondary coverage, which basically covers your deductible. However, note that *credit cards will not cover liability,* which is the cost of injury to an outside party and/or damage to an outside party's vehicle. If you do not hold an insurance policy, you may seriously want to consider buying additional liability insurance from your rental company, even if you decline the CDW.

PARKING   If you want to have a relaxing vacation, don't even attempt to find street parking in Nob Hill, North Beach, or Chinatown, by Fisherman's Wharf, or on Telegraph Hill. Park in a garage or take a cab or a bus. If you do find street parking, pay attention to street signs that explain when you can park and for how long. Be especially careful not to park in zones that are tow areas during rush hours.

Curb colors also indicate parking regulations. *Red* means no stopping or parking; *blue* is reserved for drivers with disabilities who have a California-issued disabled plate or a placard; *white* means there's a 5-minute limit; *green* indicates a 10-minute limit; and *yellow* and *yellow-and-black* curbs are for commercial vehicles only. Also, don't park at a bus stop or in front of a fire hydrant, and watch out for street-cleaning signs. If you violate the law, you might get a hefty ticket or your car may be towed. To get your car back, you must get a release from the nearest district police department, then go to the towing company to pick up the vehicle.

When parking on a hill, apply the hand brake, put the car in gear, and *curb your wheels*—toward the curb when facing downhill, away from the curb when facing uphill. Curbing your wheels not only prevents a possible "runaway" but also keeps you from getting a ticket—an expensive fine that is aggressively enforced.

BY FERRY

TO/FROM SAUSALITO   The **Golden Gate Ferry Service** fleet (☎ 415/ 923-2000) shuttles passengers daily between the San Francisco Ferry Building, at the foot of Market Street, and downtown Sausalito. Service is frequent, departing at reasonable intervals every day of the year except January 1, Thanksgiving Day, and December 25. Phone for an exact schedule. The ride takes a half hour, and one-way fares are $4.80 for adults and $3.55 for kids 6 to 12. Senior and disabled passengers ride for $2.35; children under 6 ride free. Family rates are available on weekends.

Ferries of the **Blue & Gold Fleet** (☎ 415/773-1188 for recorded info; ☎ 415/ 705-5555 for tickets) also provide round-trip service to downtown Sausalito, leaving from Fisherman's Wharf at Pier 41. The cost is $12 round-trip, half-price for kids 5 to 11. Boats run on a seasonal schedule; phone for departure information.

TO/FROM LARKSPUR   The **Golden Gate Ferry Service** fleet (☎ 415 923-2000) shuttles passengers daily between the San Francisco Ferry Building, at the foot of Market Street, and downtown Larkspur. The Larkspur ferry is primarily a weekday commuter service, with frequent departures around rush hours and limited service on weekends. Boats make the 13-mile trip in about 45 minutes and costs $2.95 for adults, $2.25 for kids 6 to 12, and $1.45 for seniors and passengers with disabilities; on weekends, prices rise to $5, $3.75, and $2.50, respectively.

TO/FROM ANGEL ISLAND & TIBURON   Ferries of the **Blue & Gold Fleet** (☎ 415/773-1188 for recorded info; ☎ 415/705-5555 for tickets) leave from Pier 43^1/$_2$ (Fisherman's Wharf) and travel to both Angel Island and Tiburon. Boats run on a seasonal schedule; phone for departure information. The round-trip fare is $12 to Angel Island, $11 to Tiburon; half-price for kids 5 to 11.

Fast Facts: San Francisco

Airport   See "Getting There," in chapter 2.

American Express   For travel arrangements, traveler's checks, currency exchange, and other member services, there are offices at 560 California St., at Battery Street (☎ 415/536-2686), open Monday to Friday 9am to 5pm, and at 455 Market St., at First Street (☎ 415/536-2600), in the Financial District, open Monday to Friday 8:30am to 5:30pm and Saturday 9am to 2pm. To report lost or stolen traveler's checks, call ☎ 800/221-7282. For American Express Global Assist, call ☎ 800/554-2639.

Area Code   The area code for San Francisco is 415; for Oakland, Berkeley, and much of the East Bay, 510; for the peninsula, generally 650. Most phone numbers in this book are in San Francisco's 415 area code, but there's no need to dial it if you're within city limits.

Baby-sitters   Hotels can often recommend a baby-sitter or child-care service. If yours can't, try **Temporary Tot Tending** (☎ **650/355-7377,** or 650/871-5790 after 6pm), which offers child care by licensed teachers for children 3 to 12. It charges $6.50 an hour, $51 for an entire day, and $150 to $180 for a week, depending on the age of the child. It's open Monday to Friday 6:30am to 6:30pm; weekend service is available only during convention times.

Business Hours   Most banks are open Monday to Friday 9am to 3pm. Several stay open until about 5pm at least 1 day a week. Many banks also have ATMs for 24-hour banking (see "Money," in chapter 2).

Most stores are open Monday to Saturday from 10 or 11am to at least 6pm, with shorter hours on Sunday. But there are exceptions: Stores in Chinatown, Ghirardelli Square, and Pier 39 stay open much later during the tourist season, and large department stores, including Macy's and Nordstrom, keep late hours.

Most restaurants serve lunch from about 11:30am to 2:30pm and dinner from 5:30 to 10pm. They sometimes serve later on weekends. Nightclubs and bars are usually open daily until 2am, when they are legally bound to stop serving alcohol.

Car Rentals   See "Getting Around," earlier in this chapter.

Climate   See "When to Go," in chapter 2.

Dentist   In the event of a dental emergency, see your hotel concierge or contact the **San Francisco Dental Society** (☎ **415/421-1435**) for a referral to a specialist. The **San Francisco Dental Office,** 131 Steuart St. (☎ **415/777-5115**), between Mission and Howard streets, offers emergency service and comprehensive dental care Monday, Tuesday, and Friday 8am to 4:30pm, Wednesday and Thursday 10:30am to 6:30pm.

Doctor   **Saint Francis Memorial Hospital,** 900 Hyde St., between Bush and Pine streets on Nob Hill (☎ **415/353-6000**), provides emergency service 24 hours a day; no appointment is necessary. The hospital also operates a **physician-referral service** (☎ **800/333-1355**).

Driving Rules   See "Getting Around," earlier in this chapter.

Drugstores   There are **Walgreens** pharmacies all over town, including one at 135 Powell St. (☎ **415/391-4433**). The store is open Monday to Saturday 8am to midnight and Sunday 9am to 9pm; the pharmacy is open Monday to Friday 8am to 9pm, Saturday 9am to 5pm, and Sunday 10am to 6pm. The branch on Divisadero Street at Lombard (☎ **415/931-6415**) has a 24-hour pharmacy. **Merrill's** pharmacy, 805 Market St. (☎ **415/431-5466**), is open Monday to Friday 8:30am to 6:30pm, Saturday 9:30am to 5:30pm; the rest of the drugstore is open Monday to Friday 7am to 9pm, Saturday 8am to 7pm, and Sunday 9:30am to 6pm. Both chains accept MasterCard and Visa.

Earthquakes   There will always be earthquakes in California, most of which you'll never notice. However, in case of a significant shaker, there are a few basic precautionary measures you should know. When you are inside a building, seek cover; do not run outside. Stand under a doorway or against a wall and stay away from windows. If you exit a building after a substantial quake, use stairwells, not elevators. If you are in your car, pull over to the side of the road and stop—but not until you are away from bridges, overpasses, telephone poles, and power lines. Stay in your car. If you're out walking, stay outside and away from trees, power lines, and the sides of buildings. If you're in an area with tall buildings, find a doorway in which to stand.

Emergencies Dial ☎ **911** for police, an ambulance, or the fire department; no coins are needed from a public phone. Emergency hotlines include the **Poison Control Center** (☎ **800/523-2222**) and **Rape Crisis** (☎ **415/647-7273**).

Information See "Visitor Information," at the beginning of this chapter.

Liquor Laws Liquor and grocery stores, as well as some drugstores, can sell packaged alcoholic beverages between 6am and 2am. Most restaurants, night-clubs, and bars are licensed to serve alcoholic beverages during the same hours. The legal age for purchase and consumption is 21; proof of age is required.

Maps See "City Layout," earlier in this chapter.

Newspapers & Magazines The city's two main dailies are the *San Francisco Chronicle* and the *San Francisco Examiner;* both are distributed throughout the city. The two papers combine for a massive Sunday edition that includes a pink "Datebook" section—an excellent preview of the week's upcoming events. The free weekly *San Francisco Bay Guardian,* a tabloid of news and listings, is indispensable for nightlife information; it's widely distributed through street-corner kiosks and at city cafes and restaurants.

Of the many free tourist-oriented publications, the most widely read are *Key* and *San Francisco Guide.* Both handbook-sized weeklies contain maps and information on current events. You can find them in most hotels, shops, and restaurants in the major tourist areas.

Pharmacies See "Drugstores," above.

Police For emergencies, dial ☎ **911** from any phone; no coins are needed. For other matters, call ☎ **415/553-0123**.

Post Office There are dozens of post offices around the city. The closest to Union Square is inside Macy's department store, 170 O'Farrell St. (☎ **800/275-8777**). You can pick up mail addressed to you and marked "General Delivery" (Poste Restante) at the **Civic Center Post Office Box Unit,** P.O. Box 429991, San Francisco, CA 94142-9991 (☎ **800/275-8777**). The street address is 101 Hyde St.

Safety San Francisco, like any large city, has its fair share of crime, but most folks don't have firsthand horror stories. There are some areas where you need to exercise extra caution, particularly at night—notably the Tenderloin, the Western Addition (south of Japantown), the Mission District (especially around 16th and Mission streets), the lower Fillmore area (also south of Japantown), around lower Haight Street, and around the Civic Center. In addition, there are a substantial number of homeless people throughout the city with concentrations in and around Union Square, the Theater District (3 blocks west of Union Square), the Tenderloin, and Haight Street, so don't be alarmed if you're approached for spare change. Basically, just use common sense.

For additional crime-prevention information, phone **San Francisco SAFE** (☎ **415/553-1984**).

Smoking If San Francisco is the state's most European city, the comparison stops here. Each year smoking laws become stricter. As of January 1, 1998, smoking was prohibited in restaurants and bars. Although there have been arguments against it, so far the new law has been enforced in most establishments. Hotels are also offering more nonsmoking rooms, which often leaves those who like to puff out in the cold—literally.

Taxes   An 8.5% sales tax is added at the register for all goods and services purchased in San Francisco. The city hotel tax is a whopping 14%. There is no airport tax.

Taxis   See "Getting Around," earlier in this chapter.

Television   In addition to cable stations, available in most hotels, all the major networks and several independent stations are represented. They include Channel 2, KTVU (Fox); Channel 4, KRON (NBC); Channel 5, KPIX (CBS); Channel 7, KGO (ABC); and Channel 9, KQED (PBS).

Time Zone   San Francisco is in the Pacific standard time zone, which is 8 hours behind Greenwich mean time and 3 hours behind eastern time. To find out what time it is, call ☎ **415/767-8900.**

Transit Information   The San Francisco Municipal Railway, better known as **Muni,** operates the city's cable cars, buses, and Metro streetcars. For customer service, call ☎ **415/673-6864** weekdays 7am to 5pm, weekends 9am to 5pm. At other times, recorded information is available.

Useful Telephone Numbers   Tourist information (☎ **415/391-2001**); highway conditions (☎ **800/427-7623**); Movie Phone Line (☎ **415/777-FILM**); Grateful Dead Hotline (☎ **415/457-6388**).

Weather   Call the National Weather Service (☎ **831/656-1725**) to find out when the next fog bank is rolling in.

5 Where to Stay

Whether you want a room with a view or just a room, San Francisco is more than accommodating to its 11 million annual guests. Most of the city's 200-plus hotels cluster near Union Square, but some smaller independent gems are scattered around town.

When reading over your options, keep in mind that the prices listed are "rack" (published) rates. Especially at big, upscale hotels, almost no one actually pays them. Always ask for special discounts or, even better, vacation packages. It's often possible to get the room you want for $100 less than what's quoted here, except in summer when the hotels are packed and bargaining is close to impossible. Use the rates listed here for the big hotels as guidelines for comparison only; prices for inexpensive choices and smaller B&Bs are closer to reality, though.

Hunting for hotels in San Francisco can be a tricky business, particularly if you're not a seasoned traveler. What you don't know—and the reservation agent may not tell you—could very well ruin your vacation, so keep the following pointers in mind when it comes time to book a room:

- Prices listed below do not include state and city taxes, which total 14%. Other hidden extras include parking fees and hefty surcharges—up to $1 per local call—for telephone use.
- San Francisco is Convention City, so if you want a room at a particular hotel during high season, book well in advance.
- Be sure to have a credit card in hand when making a reservation, and don't be surprised if you're asked to pay for at least 1 night in advance (this doesn't happen often, though).
- Hotels usually hold reservations until 6pm. If you don't tell the staff you're arriving late, you might lose your room.
- Almost every hotel in San Francisco requires a credit-card imprint for "incidentals" (and to prevent walkouts). If you don't have a credit card, be sure to make special arrangements with the management before you hang up the phone, and take down names.

The hotels listed below are classified first by area, then by price, using the following categories: **Very Expensive,** more than $200 per night; **Expensive,** $160 to $200 per night; **Moderate,** $100 to $160 per night; and **Inexpensive,** less than $100 per night. These categories reflect the rack rates for an average double room during the high season, which runs approximately from April through September.

When booking a room in a chain hotel, call the hotel's local line and the toll-free number and see where you get the best deal. A hotel makes nothing on a room that stays empty. The clerk who runs the place is more likely to know about vacancies and will often grant deep discounts in order to fill up.

Read the entries carefully: Many hotels also offer rooms at rates above and below the price category that applies to most of the units. If you like the sound of a place that's a bit over your budget, it never hurts to call and ask a few questions. Also note that we do not list single rates. Some hotels, particularly more affordable choices, do charge lower rates for singles, so inquire about them if you are traveling alone.

In general, hotel rates in San Francisco are rather inelastic; they don't vary much because the city is so popular year-round. Still, you should always ask about weekend discounts, corporate rates, and family plans; most larger hotels, and many smaller ones, offer them, but many reservations agents don't mention them unless you ask specifically.

You'll find nonsmoking rooms available in all larger hotels and many smaller hotels; reviews indicate establishments that are entirely nonsmoking. Nowadays, the best advice for smokers is to confirm a smoking-permitted room in advance.

While you'll find most accommodations have an abundance of amenities, don't be alarmed by the lack of air-conditioned guest rooms. San Francisco weather is so mild you'll never miss it.

Most larger hotels can accommodate guests who use wheelchairs or those who have other special needs. Ask when you make a reservation to ensure that your hotel can accommodate your needs, especially if you are interested in a bed-and-breakfast.

HELPING HANDS

Having reservations about your reservations? Leave it up to the pros:

Bed-and-Breakfast California, 12711 McCartysville Place, Saratoga, CA 95070 (☎ **800/872-4500** or 408/867-9662; fax 408/867-0907; www.bbintl.com; e-mail: info@bbintl.com), offers a selection of B&Bs that cost $60 to $140 per night, with a 2-night minimum. Accommodations range from simple rooms in private homes to luxurious, full-service carriage houses, houseboats, and Victorian homes.

San Francisco Reservations, 22 Second St., San Francisco, CA 94105 (☎ **800/ 677-1500** or 415/227-1500; www.hotelres.com), arranges reservations for more than 300 of San Francisco's hotels and often offers discounted rates. The nifty Web site allows Internet users to make reservations online.

1 Union Square

VERY EXPENSIVE

✪ **Campton Place Hotel.** 340 Stockton St. (between Post and Sutter sts.), San Francisco, CA 94108. ☎ **800/235-4300** or 415/781-5555. Fax 415/955-5536. www.camptonplace. com. 110 units. A/C MINIBAR TV TEL. $295–$415 double; from $520 suite. American breakfast $16.50. AE, CB, DC, MC, V. Valet parking $26. Cable car: Powell-Hyde and Powell-Mason lines (1 block west). Bus: 2, 3, 4, 30, or 45.

With a $10 million renovation scheduled for completion in the fall of 2000, this already fabulous luxury boutique hotel is bound to offer some of the best accommodations in town—not to mention the most expensive, because rates are sure to rise. Along with gutting the rooms and replacing the furnishings with limestone, pear

Accommodations Near Union Square & Nob Hill

Sacramento St.

Huntington Park

17

California St.

Legend

Cable Car

0   1/8 mi

0   .125 km

15   16   18   19

Pine St.

23   20

24   22

Bush St.

Mason St.

27   26   25

Burritt Alley

Grant Ave.

21

Kearny St.

28   30   31

29

Sutter St.

Stockton St.

32   33 Tillman Pl.

Campton Pl.

37   36   35   34

Post St.

Powell St.

39   38   42

Union Square

Maiden La.

40   41

Geary St.

43

45

44

46

O'Farrell St.

47   48

52

Third St.

Market St.

Stevenson St.

Cyril Magnin

49

50

Fourth St.

51

Yerba Buena Gardens

wood, and more modern and Asian-influenced decor, management is changing the rooms' layout. Eliminating 17 rooms will make the new 110 units more spacious—a smart move, because they were cramped. You can still expect superlative service, extra-large beds, exquisite bathrooms, bathrobes, top-notch toiletries, and every necessity and whim that's made Campton Place a favored temporary address.

Dining/Diversions: The revered Campton Place Restaurant serves three meals a day. The menu is French to accentuate new chef Laurent Manrique's style. Main courses run $22 to $38.

Amenities: Concierge, 24-hour room service, laundry, valet, complimentary overnight shoeshine, morning newspaper, evening turndown, in-room massage, twice-daily maid service, baby-sitting,· express checkout, video rentals, courtesy car, access to nearby health club, conference rooms. Business services, such as typing, translating, and faxing, available by request at the front desk.

The Clift Hotel. 495 Geary St. (at Taylor St., 2 blocks west of Union Square), San Francisco, CA 94102. ☎ **800/652-5438** in the U.S., or 415/775-4700. Fax 415/441-4621. www.clifthotel.com. 326 units. A/C MINIBAR TV TEL. $255–$305 double; from $360 petite suite; from $405 executive suite. Continental breakfast $12.50. AE, DC, MC, V. Parking $27. Cable car: Powell-Hyde and Powell-Mason lines (2 blocks east). Bus: 2, 3, 4, 30, 38, or 45. Pets accepted.

Ian Schrager, king of such ultra-hip hotels as New York's Royalton and Paramount, L.A.'s Mondrian, and Miami's Delano, began managing this classic old luxury property almost 4 years ago and purchased it last year, but hasn't put his hip spin on the place yet. Meanwhile, he's been charging a small fortune to stay here. While there have been teases of renovation, I found the rooms looking tired during a recent visit, with shabby old Four Seasons robes hanging in the bathrooms. (Four Seasons bailed on the property more than 4 years ago.) The public spaces are classic San Francisco, but the accommodations' furniture, textiles, and bathrooms are rather grim, and some of the mattresses are old and hard—not nearly what you'd expect for the price. That said, the Clift has some wonderful qualities. Situated in the city's Theater District, 2 blocks from Union Square, the location is key. And the Redwood Room bar and French Room dining room are local treasures worth seeking out whether you stay here or not. Extras include padded hangers, individual climate control, two-line telephones, a scale in your dressing room, and complimentary computers and fax in your room on request. Also, the windows open—a nice touch for guests who appreciate fresh air.

The Clift's "Young Travelers Program" provides traveling families with toys and games, diapers, bottles, children's books, and other amenities to help children and their parents feel at home. The hotel also accepts and pampers pets.

Dining/Diversions: Until Schrager's team creates a new venue, the French Room serves breakfast, lunch, and dinner, specializing in seasonal California-French cuisine. The hotel's dramatic Redwood Room, which opened in 1933 and remains one of San Francisco's most opulent piano bars, has beautiful 22-foot-tall fluted redwood columns and is famous for its Gustav Klimt murals. The lobby lounge serves cocktails daily and traditional English tea Monday to Saturday.

Amenities: Concierge, 24-hour room service, children's program, extensive fitness facility, overnight laundry and shoe polishing, 1-hour pressing, evening turndown, twice-daily maid service, 24-hour business center, gift shop.

Hotel Trivia

The Clift Hotel charged a mere $2 per night when it first opened in 1915. The price for a room now? More than $250.

The Donatello. 501 Post St. (at Mason St.), San Francisco, CA 94102. ☎ **800/227-3184** or 415/441-7100. Fax 415/885-8842. 94 units. A/C TV TEL. $194–$240 double; from $350 suite. Extra person $25. Children under 12 free in parents' room. Continental breakfast $9.95. AE, CB, DC, DISC, MC, V. Valet parking $25. Cable car: Powell-Hyde and Powell-Mason lines (2 blocks west). Bus: 2, 3, 4, 30, or 45.

If you're not looking for trendy lodgings or an anonymous business hotel, but want Old World elegance, book a room here. The Donatello is, in a word, dignified. The lobby is classy, with Italian marble and a serious staff. The rooms, which are some of the largest in the city (an average of 425 square feet!), are airy and decorated with traditional dark-wood antiques, tapestries, and original art. Unfortunately, most of the extra-large windows lack great views, and some of the furnishings need to be updated. Still, each room comes with a dish of hard candies and bottled Italian water, as well as guaranteed service from an attentive (though sometimes stuffy) staff. In-room amenities include voicemail, hair dryers, data ports, and terry bathrobes.

Dining/Diversions: Zingari serves Italian cuisine at lunch and dinner; cocktails are available in the lounge.

Amenities: Roof-terrace lounge, mini gym, and spa, which hotel guests share with time-share residents who occupy part of the building; too bad surrounding buildings block much of the view.

Grand Hyatt San Francisco on Union Square. 345 Stockton St. (between Post and Sutter sts.), San Francisco, CA 94108. ☎ **800/233-1234** or 415/398-1234. Fax 415/391-1780. 693 units. A/C MINIBAR TV TEL. $365 double; $410 Regency Club rm. AE, DC, DISC, JCB, MC, V. Valet parking $30. Cable car: Powell-Hyde and Powell-Mason lines (2 blocks west). Bus: 2, 3, 4, 30, 38, or 45.

If the thought of a 10-second walk to Saks Fifth Avenue makes you drool, this high-rise luxury hotel is the place for you. The Grand Hyatt sits amid all the downtown shopping, but it also boasts some of the best views in the area. The lobby is indeed grand, with Chinese artifacts and enormous ceramic vases. Thankfully, the well-kept rooms were recently renovated; they were always upscale corporate digs, but now they're even more luxurious, with new mattresses, bed frames, shower tiles, lounge chairs, desk chairs, and textiles. Rooms have some elbow room and a small desk and sitting area, and the views from most of the 36 floors are truly spectacular. Accommodations include such amenities as TVs in the bathroom, first-run movies, and a telephone with computer-connection capability.

Rates for Regency Club rooms include continental breakfast and evening hors d'oeuvres. Three floors hold Business Plan rooms, which have private fax, telephone with computer hookup, enhanced lighting, coffeemaker, iron and ironing board, and hair dryer. They also include special services—24-hour access to compatible printer, photocopier, and office supplies; free local calls and credit-card phone access; and daily newspaper, all for an additional $45.

Dining/Diversions: Grandviews Restaurant, on the 36th floor, underwent a $2.2 million renovation in 1999. It serves three meals a day, schedules live jazz on selected evenings, and offers great views.

Amenities: Concierge, room service, fitness center, laundry service, newspaper delivery, in-room massage, baby-sitting, free weekday-morning town-car service to the Financial District, fully equipped business center, car-rental desk, tour desk, express checkout.

✪ **Hotel Monaco.** 501 Geary Blvd. (at Taylor St.), San Francisco, CA 94102. ☎ **800/214-4220** or 415/292-0100. Fax 415/292-0111. 201 units. A/C MINIBAR TV TEL. $249–$299 double; from $399–$459 suite. Rates include evening wine hour. Call for discounted rates. AE, DC, DISC, JCB, MC, V. Valet parking $24. Bus: 2, 3, 4, 27, or 38. Pets accepted.

This remodeled 1910 Beaux-Arts building made its debut in June 1995 and is one of the newer divas among Union Square's luxury hotels. For $24 million, the Kimpton Group did this place right—from the cozy main lobby with a two-story French inglenook fireplace to the guest rooms with canopy beds, Chinese-inspired armoires, bamboo writing desks, bold stripes, and vibrant color. Everything is fresh, in the best of taste, and as playful as it is serious, with nifty extras like Web TV and two-line phones. The decor, combined with the breathtaking neighboring restaurant, make this my favorite luxury hotel in the city. The only downside is that many rooms are way too small (especially for the price).

Dining/Diversions: The Grand Cafe restaurant is downtown's best-designed dining room, rivaled only by Farallon. The grand space has sky-high ceilings, elaborate 1920s and 1930s style, and an amazing collection of local art. In the past 2 years, chef Denis Soriano has really settled into his kitchen, making the Grand Cafe one seriously hot dining spot (see chapter 6, "Where to Dine," for complete information).

Amenities: Concierge; room service; health club with steam, sauna, and massage; laundry and dry cleaning; overnight shoeshine; newspaper delivery; in-room massage; twice-daily maid service; baby-sitting; secretarial services; express checkout; courtesy car; nightly wine hour; meeting, business, and banquet facilities.

Hotel Nikko. 222 Mason St. (at O'Farrell St.), San Francisco, CA 94102. ☎ **800/645-5687** or 415/394-1111. Fax 415/394-1106. 523 units. A/C MINIBAR TV TEL. $315–$355 double; $475–$2,000 suite. AE, CB, DISC, DC, JCB, MC, V. Valet parking $27. Cable car: Powell-Hyde and Powell-Mason lines. Bus: 2, 3, 4, 30, 38, or 45.

Part of Japan Airlines' international fleet of super-luxury hotels, the 25-story Hotel Nikko combines the luxuries of Eastern and Western cultures with heavenly results. Work out in the fitness center; take a few laps in the glass-enclosed indoor swimming pool; rest in the Jacuzzi, Japanese sauna, or soaking tub; and top off the morning with a shiatsu massage before starting your day—what more could you ask for?

Ideally located near Union Square and the Theater District, the Nikko has a penchant for pampering that extends to the guest rooms. They feature top-of-the-line amenities such as two-line speaker phones with modem ports, blackout curtains, large windows with city views, and huge marble bathrooms with separate tubs and showers. Suites contain separate sitting areas, stereos with CD players, and entry halls (a Japanese tradition). Although the hotel's decor might be a bit too staid for Western tastes—simple furnishings and beige tones predominate—luxury ultimately prevails.

Dining/Diversions: The delicious restaurant Anzu is where steak house meets sushi for breakfast, lunch, and dinner. On the lobby level is a small sushi bar offering made-to-order sushi, as well as afternoon hors d'oeuvres.

Amenities: Concierge, 24-hour room service, swimming pool, fitness center, sauna, hot tub, shiatsu massage, tanning booth, laundry and valet, twice-daily maid service, baby-sitting, business center, gift and other shops.

The Pan Pacific. 500 Post St. (at Mason St.), San Francisco, CA 94102. ☎ **800/533-6465** or 415/771-8600. Fax 415/398-0267. 329 units. A/C MINIBAR TV TEL. $340–$440 double; from $480 suite. Continental breakfast $8; American breakfast $9. AE, DC, DISC, JCB, MC, V. Valet parking $27. Cable car: Powell-Hyde and Powell-Mason lines. Bus: 2, 3, 4, 30, 38, or 45. Small dogs accepted; $75 charge.

The Pan Pacific is artistically glitzy, enormous, and somehow romantic, all at the same time. If this were a Hollywood set, James Bond might hoodwink a villain here, magically drop down the sky-rise's atrium, and disappear into the night. But all is quiet and intimate in the third-floor lobby, even though the skylight ceiling is another 18 floors up. The lobby's marble fountain with four dancing figures and its player piano set the mood for guests relaxing in front of the fireplace. The rooms underwent a $1.4 million touch-up in 1999 and now are decorated in a swirl of sage and browns in various patterns. They're rather large, immaculate, and well equipped with luxurious extras, including lavish marble bathrooms with mini-TVs at the sink. Other amenities are in-room safes, three touch-tone phones, fax machines, voicemail, and bathrobes. The hotel is conveniently located close to Union Square. Traveling with Fido? No worries, so long as he's small—and you are prepared to pay the additional $50 fee.

Dining/Diversions: The Pacific dining room serves breakfast, lunch, and dinner. It features excellent California cuisine with Asian and French accents.

Amenities: Concierge, 24-hour room service, health club, laundry and valet, newspaper delivery, in-room massage, twice-daily maid service, baby-sitting, secretarial services, express checkout, first-come, first-served complimentary BMW transportation in the city, business center, conference rooms.

✪ **Prescott Hotel.** 545 Post St. (between Mason and Taylor sts.), San Francisco, CA 94102. ☎ **800/283-7322** or 415/563-0303. Fax 415/563-6831. 164 units. MINIBAR TV TEL. $265–$295 double; $275 concierge-level double (including breakfast and evening cocktail reception); from $295 suite. AE, CB, DC, DISC, MC, V. Valet parking $27. Cable car: Powell-Hyde and Powell-Mason lines (1 block east). Bus: 2, 3, 4, 30, 38, or 45.

The Prescott has always been a San Francisco favorite. The staff treats you like royalty, the rooms are beautiful and immaculate, the location (just a block from Union Square) is perfect, and room service is provided by one of the most popular restaurants in the city, Postrio. (In fact, it's not unheard of for visitors to check into the Prescott just to get preferred seating.)

Dark tones of green, plum, and burgundy blend well with the cherrywood furnishings in each of the soundproofed rooms; the view, alas, isn't so pleasant. The very small bathrooms contain terry robes and hair dryers, but only the suites have Jacuzzi bathtubs. Concierge-level guests are pampered with free continental breakfast and evening cocktails.

Dining/Diversions: The hotel provides preferred seating for guests at Postrio (see chapter 6 for complete information). Be sure to make reservations when you book your room.

Amenities: Concierge; room service from Postrio; small gym; same-day valet and laundry service; overnight shoeshine; newspaper delivery; nightly turndown; twice-daily maid service; valet parking; weekday morning limousine service to the Financial District; complimentary morning coffee and tea; evening wine in the living room; gym facilities; conference rooms.

✪ **Westin St. Francis.** 335 Powell St. (between Geary and Post sts.), San Francisco, CA 94102. ☎ **800/228-3000** or 415/397-7000. Fax 415/774-0124. 1,192 units. A/C MINIBAR TV TEL. Main building: $219–$339 double; from $450 suite. Tower: $360–$405 double; from $525 suite. Extra person $30. Continental breakfast $15–$18. AE, DC, DISC, JCB, MC, V. Valet parking $30. Cable car: Powell-Hyde and Powell-Mason lines (direct stop). Bus: 2, 3, 4, 30, 38, 45, or 76. Pets accepted.

At the turn of the 20th century, Charles T. Crocker and a few of his wealthy buddies decided that San Francisco needed a world-class hotel, and up went the St. Francis.

Hotel Trivia

For nearly a century, the most popular place for visitors to rendezvous in San Francisco has been under the magnificent hand-carved grandfather clock in the lobby of the Westin St. Francis hotel.

The Westin St. Francis operates the world's only legal money-laundering operation. In 1938, the hotel's manager ordered that all coinage be sorted, scrubbed, polished, and dried to keep ladies' white gloves from getting dirty, and today the tradition continues.

Since then, hordes of VIPs have hung their hats and hosiery here, including Emperor Hirohito, Queen Elizabeth II, Mother Teresa, King Juan Carlos of Spain, the Shah of Iran, and all the U.S. presidents since Taft. In 1972 the hotel gained the 32-story Tower, doubling the capacity and adding banquet and conference centers. The older rooms of the main building vary in size and have more Old World charm than the newer rooms, but the Tower is remarkable for its great views of the city from above the 18th floor.

Although the St. Francis is too massive to offer the personal service you get at the smaller deluxe hotels on Nob Hill, few other hotels in San Francisco can match its majestic aura. It sounds corny, but the St. Francis is so intertwined with the city's past that it truly is San Francisco: Stroll through the vast, ornate lobby and you can feel 100 years of history oozing from its hand-carved redwood paneling. The hotel did a massive $50 million renovation in 1996 and threw in another $60 million in 1999, replacing the carpeting, furniture, and bedding in every guest room, gussying up the lobby, and restoring the facade. Even if you stay elsewhere, it's worth a visit if only to partake of high tea at the Compass Rose, one of San Francisco's most enduring and enjoyable traditions.

Dining/Diversions: The lobby-level Dewey's, a sports bar, offers a do-it-yourself luncheon buffet, and burgers and pizzas at night. The St. Francis Cafe, also on the lower level, offers a basic breakfast and dinner menu. The Compass Rose is open daily for lunch and afternoon tea (3 to 5pm), with live music, dancing, champagne, cocktails, and caviar tasting in the evening.

Amenities: Concierge, 24-hour room service, laundry, newspaper delivery, in-room massage, twice-daily maid service, baby-sitting referral, Westin Kids Club (great for families), secretarial services, new $2 million fitness center (including gym and spa), business center, tour and car-rental desks, American Airlines ticket office, barber/beauty salon, gift shop.

EXPENSIVE

Handlery Union Square Hotel. 351 Geary St. (between Mason and Powell sts.), San Francisco, CA 94102. ☎ **800/843-4343** or 415/781-7800. Fax 415/781-0269. www. handlery.com. 377 units. A/C TV TEL. $169–$199 double. Club section: from $205 double; from $245 suite. Extra person $10. AE, CB, DC, DISC, JCB, MC, V. Parking $23.50. Cable car: Powell-Hyde and Powell-Mason lines (direct stop). Bus: 2, 3, 4, 30, 38, or 45.

A mere half-block from Union Square, the Handlery covers all bets by offering every amenity you could possibly need, plus lots of extras, to make up for the rather homely rooms. All guest accommodations come with the basic accoutrements, including cable TVs—which are old but have Nintendo and Spectravision movie channels—hair dryers, coffeemakers, and phones with voicemail. But alas, some rooms (especially in the back of the hotel) are rather grim, some mattresses are hard, and furnishings are scuffed and reminiscent of a tired motel. "Club" status includes a complimentary morning newspaper, turndown service, an extra dressing room, bathroom scale, robes, two phones, coffeemaker, refrigerator, and—here's the clincher—an electric shoe polisher. Hipsters can skip this one; the Handlery caters to families and older folks. I recommend the Clarion Bedford over this place; better rooms make it worth the extra blocks to Union Square.

Amenities: Multilingual concierge staff, heated outdoor swimming pool and sauna, access to nearby health club, same-day laundry, baby-sitting, express checkout, conference rooms, barber shop, tour desk, gift shop.

Hilton San Francisco & Towers. 333 O'Farrell St. (between Mason and Taylor sts.), San Francisco, CA 94102. ☎ **800/HILTONS** or 415/771-1400. Fax 415/771-6807. 1,900 units. A/C MINIBAR TV TEL. $189–$309 double; from $425 suite. Children free in parents' room. AE, CB, DC, DISC, MC, V. Parking $28. Cable car: Powell-Hyde and Powell-Mason lines (1 block east). Bus: 2, 3, 4, 7, 9, 21, 27, 30, 38, 45, or 71.

Complete with bustling conventioneers and a line to register that resembles airport check-in, the Hilton's lobby is so enormous and busy that it feels more like a convention hall than a hotel. The three connecting buildings (the original 19-story main structure, a 46-story tower topped by a panoramic restaurant and a 23-story landmark with 386 luxurious rooms and suites) bring the swarms of visitors. Even during quieter times, the sheer enormity of the place makes the Hilton somewhat overwhelming.

After you get past the sweeping grand lobby, jump on an elevator, and wind through endless corridors to your room, you'll find the mystique ends with run-of-the-mill corporate accommodations. Some of the views from the floor-to-ceiling windows in the main tower's rooms might be memorable, but the decor definitely is not. Room size is standard. Unless you're staying in one of the more luxurious units, the feel and decor here are impersonal and plain—perfect for conventioneers, but not for a romantic weekend. Towers-level accommodations offer upgraded services, including a separate registration lounge with complimentary breakfast and hors d'oeuvres and daily newspaper. One bonus: The Hilton is always upgrading somewhere on the property.

Dining/Diversions: Cityscape, on the 46th floor, serves classic American cuisine with a breathtaking 360-degree view; the retractable skylight exposes the night sky in all its grandeur. A coffee shop serves snacks, and the Intermezzo offers Italian-style food to eat in or to go. The Café provides a sidewalk spot for watching the passing parade.

Amenities: Concierge, room service (6am to midnight), laundry, shoeshine, swimming pool, health club ($6 fee), business center, tour desk, shopping arcade.

Hotel Diva. 440 Geary St. (between Mason and Taylor sts.), San Francisco, CA 94102. ☎ **800/553-1900** or 415/885-0200. Fax 415/346-6613. 111 units. A/C TV TEL. $169 double; $189 junior suite; $400 suite. Rates include continental breakfast. AE, DC, DISC, JCB, MC, V. Parking $22. Cable car: Powell-Mason line. Bus: 38 or 38L.

Appropriately named, the Diva is the prima donna of San Francisco's affordable modern hotels. A showbiz darling when it opened in 1985, the sleek, ultramodern Diva won "Best Hotel Design" from *Interiors* magazine. A profusion of curvaceous glass, marble, and steel marks the Euro-tech lobby; the rooms, spotless and neat, are softened with utterly fashionable "Italian modern" furnishings of monochromatic colors, silver, and wood. The enormous headboards, for example, are made of polished stainless steel meant to evoke the bow of a ship. Toys and services abound: VCRs (with a discreet video vending machine), Nintendo, pay-per-view movies, hair dryers, safes, data ports, valet parking, and breakfast delivered to your room. Fitness and business centers complete the package. *Insider tip:* Reserve one of the rooms ending in "09," which have extra-large bathrooms with vanity mirrors and makeup tables. The downside: views that make you want to keep the chic curtains closed.

Hotel Milano. 55 Fifth St. (between Market and Mission sts.), San Francisco, CA 94103. ☎ **800/398-7555** in the U.S., or 415/543-8555. Fax 415/543-5885. 108 units. A/C MINI-BAR TV TEL. $179–$279 double. Extra person $20. AE, CB, DC, DISC, MC, V. Valet parking $24. Bus: All Market St. buses.

Contemporary Italian design, elegantly streamlined rooms, and its central location make Hotel Milano a popular choice for tourists and businesspeople alike. The hotel also has a film-production facility and private screening room to entice media types. Corporate travelers come for the spacious guest rooms, which feature everything an executive could want, from fax/computer modem hookups to a Nintendo game system. Other features include in-room safes and soundproofed windows. Some have spa tubs, bidets, and double lavatories.

Dining/Diversions: M. Point serves breakfast, lunch, and dinner with a fusion and sushi bar menu.

Amenities: Concierge, room service, laundry and valet, fitness center and spa with steam and sauna.

Hotel Rex. 562 Sutter St. (between Powell and Mason sts.), San Francisco, CA 94102. ☎ **800/433-4434** or 415/433-4434. Fax 415/433-3695. 94 units. MINIBAR TV TEL. $195–$255 double; $575–$675 suite. AE, CB, DC, MC, V. Valet parking $25; self-parking $19. Cable car: Powell-Hyde and Powell-Mason lines (1 block east). Bus: 2, 3, 4, 30, 38, or 45.

Joie de Vivre, the most creative hotel group in the city, owns this historic building (formerly the Orchard Hotel), which is near several fine galleries, theaters, and restaurants. The group kept some of the imported furnishings and the European boutique hotel ambience, but gave the lobby and rooms a $2 million face-lift, adding the decorative flair that makes its hotels among the most popular in town. The club-like lobby lounge is modeled after a 1920s library and is, like all the group's properties, cleverly stylish. Joie de Vivre is positioning the Rex as a hotel for the arts and literary community (not unlike the Algonquin Hotel in New York City); in that spirit, an antiquarian bookstore adjoins the lobby.

The renovated rooms, which are above average in size, feature CD players and two-line telephones with voicemail and data port. If you have one of the rooms in the back, you'll look out over a shady, peaceful courtyard (that's something you won't get in New York). Attention to the details makes Hotel Rex one of the better choices in this price range downtown.

Amenities: Concierge; room service; same-day laundry and dry cleaning; complimentary newspaper, coffee, and evening wine hour; morning car service to the Financial District.

✪ **Hotel Triton.** 342 Grant Ave. (at Bush St.), San Francisco, CA 94108. ☎ **800/433-6611** or 415/394-0500. Fax 415/394-0555. www.hotel-tritonsf.com. 140 units. A/C MINIBAR TV TEL. $219–$269 double; $329 suite. AE, DC, DISC, JCB, MC, V. Parking $25. Cable car: Powell-Hyde and Powell-Mason lines (2 blocks west). Pets accepted; $50 charge.

Hotel magnate Bill Kimpton requisitioned a cadre of local artists and designers to "do their thing" to the Hotel Triton. The result was San Francisco's first three-star hotel to break the boring barrier. Described as vogue, chic, retro-futuristic, and even neo-baroque, the Triton begs for attention, from the Dalí-esque lobby to the sumptuous designer suites à la Jerry Garcia, Wyland (the ocean artist), and Joe Boxer. Two dozen environmentally sensitive "EcoRooms"—with biodegradable soaps, filtered water and air, and all-natural linens—were also installed to please the tree-hugger in all of us. A mild caveat: Don't expect perfection; many of the rooms could use a little touching up here and there (stained curtains, chipped furniture), and service isn't as snappy as it could be. However, rooms do come with fax machines, data ports, and coffeemakers.

If you can live with the imperfections and want to inject a little fun and style into your stay, then join Dorothy and Toto for a trip far from Kansas.

Dining/Diversions: Café de la Presse, a European-style newsstand and outdoor cafe, serves breakfast, lunch, and dinner. In the lobby, the hotel serves coffee each morning and wine each evening (included in the room rate).

Amenities: Room service, same-day laundry, exercise room, business center, complimentary house-baked cookies.

Hotel Vintage Court. 650 Bush St. (between Powell and Stockton sts.), San Francisco, CA 94108. ☎ **800/654-1100** or 415/392-4666. Fax 415/392-1889. www.vintagecourt.com. 107 units. A/C MINIBAR TV TEL. $149–$235 double; $300 penthouse suite. Rates include evening wine service. AE, CB, DC, DISC, MC, V. Valet parking $24; self-parking $18. Cable car: Powell-Hyde and Powell-Mason lines (direct stop). Bus: 2, 3, 4, 30, 45, or 76.

Consistent personal service attracts a loyal clientele at this European-style hotel 2 blocks north of Union Square. The lobby, accented with dark wood, deep green, and rose, is welcoming enough to actually spend a little time in, especially when California wines are being poured each evening.

The varietals don't stop at ground level. Each tidy room, renovated in 1995 and scheduled to be completely redone by mid-2000, is named after a winery and mimics a wine-country excursion, with floral bedspreads, matching drapes, and trellised wall-to-wall loop carpeting. Opus One, the deluxe two-room penthouse suite, has an original 1912 stained-glass skylight, wood-burning fireplace, whirlpool tub, complete entertainment center, and panoramic views of the city.

Dining/Diversions: The dining room, Masa's, serves traditional French fare. It is one of the top restaurants in San Francisco (see chapter 6 for complete information). Breakfast is available in the dining room, and the wine service from 5 to 6pm (included in the room rates) features fine California reds and whites.

Amenities: Free morning transportation to the Financial District, tour desk, car-rental service, access to off-premises health club ($10 per day).

The Inn at Union Square. 440 Post St. (between Mason and Powell sts.), San Francisco, CA 94102. ☎ **800/288-4346** or 415/397-3510. Fax 415/989-0529. www.unionsquare.com. 30 units. TV TEL. $165–$350 double. Rates include continental breakfast, afternoon tea, and evening wine and hors d'oeuvres. AE, CB, DC, DISC, JCB, MC, V. Valet parking $24. Cable car: Powell-Hyde and Powell-Mason lines. Bus: 2, 3, 4, 30, 38, or 45.

As narrow as an Amsterdam canal house, the Inn at Union Square is the antithesis of the big, impersonal hotels that surround Union Square. If you need plenty of elbow room, skip this one. But if you're looking for an inn whose staff knows each guest's name and afternoon tea comes with crisp cucumber sandwiches, read on. A half-block west of the square, the seven-story inn makes up for its small stature by spoiling guests with a pile of perks. Mornings start with breakfast served in lounges equipped with the *New York Times,* followed by afternoon tea and evening hors d'oeuvres served in adorable little fireplace lounges at the end of each hall. The handsome rooms, individually decorated with Georgian reproductions and floral fabrics, are smaller than average but infinitely more appreciable than the cookie-cutter rooms of most larger hotels. Smoking is not allowed in the rooms.

Amenities: Complete business services available; use of health club.

The Juliana Hotel. 590 Bush St. (at Stockton St.), San Francisco, CA 94108. ☎ **800/328-3880** or 415/392-2540. Fax 415/391-8447. www.julianahotel.com. 107 units. A/C MINIBAR TV TEL. $169–$199 double; $199–$245 junior suite; $199–$239 executive suite; $359–$559 2-bedroom suite. Continental breakfast $7.95. Special winter packages available. AE, CB, DC, MC, V. Valet parking $25; self-parking $18. Cable car: Powell-Hyde and Powell-Mason lines (1 block west). Bus: 2, 3, 4, 30, 38, or 45.

We love the lobby at this small, European-style hotel. With its rich, homey surroundings, English prints, and comfy couches facing a blazing fire, it feels more like a rich friend's study than the entrance to a hotel. With the addition of daily papers hanging on a wooden rack, the Juliana has created a place that makes me want to kick up my feet and stay awhile. With the coffee here by day and wine by night (included in the room rate), there's no real reason to leave.

The rooms, renovated in 1996, are trendy-bright, with yellow and pale-blue–striped wallpaper, candy-striped yellow and red upholstered chairs, floral patterned bedspreads with matching curtains, and blue carpeting. It's vibrant and cheery, for sure, but not the kind of place where you'd want to nurse a wicked hangover. In-room features include irons and ironing boards, faxes, and coffeemakers. Each bathroom contains a large, well-lit mirror; a hair dryer; and a basket of soap and other toiletries. Rooms can be on the small side, but the junior suites have plenty of space and adorable homey touches.

Dining/Diversions: Oritalia restaurant is attached to the hotel (see chapter 6 for complete information).

Amenities: Room service, laundry and valet, morning transportation to the Financial District, access to off-premises health club.

The Kensington Park Hotel. 450 Post St. (between Powell and Mason sts.), San Francisco, CA 94102. ☎ **800/553-1900** or 415/788-6400. Fax 415/399-9484. 89 units. TV TEL. $175–$205 double; $550 suite. Extra person $10. Rates include continental breakfast; afternoon tea, sherry, and cookies. AE, CB, DC, DISC, MC, V. Valet parking $22. Cable car: Powell-Hyde and Powell-Mason lines ($1/2$ block east).

The Kensington is an old spiffed-up hotel with a cheery, eager-to-please (albeit sometimes shorthanded) staff, tasteful accommodations, and extra efforts that show the hotel really cares about its guests. Large, recently upgraded rooms on the fifth through twelfth floors have handsome furnishings, and the bathrooms, though small, are sweetly appointed in brass and marble. As for the views, ask for an upper corner room and you'll get far more than your money's worth. Coffee and croissants are available on each floor every morning from 7 to 10am; tea, sherry, and cookies are served every afternoon; and there's a complimentary wine hour with piano accompaniment on Thursdays. If you want the full treatment, book the Royal Suite, which contains a canopy bed, fireplace, and Jacuzzi.

Dining/Diversions: Farallon, one of downtown's hottest restaurants, adjoins the hotel (see chapter 6 for complete details).

Amenities: Concierge, room service, same-day laundry, morning newspaper, fax and secretarial services, twice-daily maid service, access to off-premises health club.

✪ **The Maxwell.** 386 Geary St. (at Mason St.), San Francisco, CA 94102. ☎ **888/734-6299** or 415/986-2000. Fax 415/397-2447. 153 units. A/C TV TEL. $155–$215 double; $295–$595 suite. Extra person $15. Corporate discounts available. AE, CB, DC, DISC, MC, V. Parking $19. Cable car: Powell-Hyde and Powell-Mason lines (1 block east). Bus: 2, 3, 4, 30, 38, or 45.

What was once an old, somewhat run-down hotel in an excellent location (1 block from Union Square) is now an incredibly chic-boutique experience that was created in 1997. Rooms blend velvets, brocades, stripes, plaids, rich color, and handcrafted artistic accents into what the management calls "Theatre Deco," fused with Victorian decor (a sort of smoking club/study atmosphere). Rooms come with upholstered chairs, hand-painted bedside lamps, luxurious pillows, and boldly tiled sinks. Each has a writing desk, hair dryer, iron and ironing board, Nintendo, three phones, and data ports. The suites, which are more like personal penthouse apartments, are some of the most stunning in town; unfortunately, from their location you can hear the old elevator kick into gear every time it's beckoned.

Dining/Diversions: Adjoining Max's on the Square Restaurant looks great; its American fare and service are decent but nothing to write home about.

Amenities: Limited room service, concierge, meeting facilities.

Serrano Hotel. 405 Taylor St. (at O'Farrell St.), San Francisco, CA 94102. ☎ **877/294-9709** or 415/885-2500. Fax 415-474-4879. 236 units. A/C MINIBAR TV TEL. From $199 double; from $299 suite. AE, DC, DISC, JCB, MC, V. Valet parking $24. Bus: 2, 3, 4, 27, or 38.

Everything old is new again at the Kimpton Group's landmark hostelry. Los Angeles designer Cheryl Rowley (who also designed the Hotel Monaco) swathed the 17-story 1920s building hotel in her trademark vibrant color and added a dash of Moroccan flair while preserving the building's Spanish revival integrity. Original architectural elements dot the living room-like lobby, with its intricately painted beams, high ceilings, large, ornate fireplace, and dramatic colonnade. Equally colorful guest rooms have oversized windows and high ceilings, cherrywood headboards on new beds, terry robes, and theater-themed artwork. The hotel is in the heart of the Theater District, right off Union Square and 2 blocks from the Powell Street cable car.

Dining/Diversions: Ponzu, named after the citrus-and-soy dipping sauce popular in Japan, blends the flavors of East and West by drawing from a mélange of cuisines: Korea, Vietnam, China, and Japan. It's open for breakfast on weekdays and dinner nightly.

Amenities: Concierge, room service, turndown service available, valet parking, same-day valet and laundry service, complimentary town car service to the Financial District (weekdays 7am to 10am) weekday newspaper delivery, overnight shoeshine service, 24-hour fitness room, complimentary fireside morning coffee and tea service.

Sir Francis Drake. 450 Powell St. (at Sutter St.), San Francisco, CA 94102. ☎ **800/227-5480** or 415/392-7755. Fax 415/391-8719. www.sirfrancisdrake.com. 417 units. A/C MINIBAR TV TEL. $175–$269 double; $500–$850 suite. AE, CB, DC, DISC, MC, V. Parking $25. Cable car: Powell-Hyde and Powell-Mason lines (direct stop). Bus: 2, 3, 4, 45, or 76.

It took a change of ownership and a multimillion-dollar restoration to save the Sir Francis Drake from becoming a Starbucks, but the stately old queen is again housing guests. Granted, the venerable septuagenarian is still showing signs of age—the owners admitted there was more work to be done and threw another $5 million into room renovations in early 1999. But the price of imperfection certainly shows in the room rate: a good $100 less per night than its Nob Hill cousins. The new Sir Francis Drake is a hotel for people who are willing to trade a chipped bathroom tile or oddly matched furniture for the opportunity to vacation in pseudo-grand fashion. Allow Tom Sweeny, the ebullient (and legendary) Beefeater doorman, to handle your bags as you enter the elegant, captivating lobby. Sip cocktails at the superchic Starlight Lounge overlooking the city. Dine at Scala's Bistro, one of the hottest restaurants

Hotel Trivia

Tom Sweeny, the head doorman at the Sir Francis Drake hotel, is San Francisco's living historical monument. Dressed in traditional Beefeaters attire (you can't miss those $1,400 duds), he's been the subject of countless snapshots—an average 200 per day for the past 20 years—and has shaken hands with every president since Jerry Ford.

downtown. In short, live like the king or queen of Union Square without all the pomp, circumstance, and credit-card bills.

Dining/Diversions: Scala's Bistro at the lobby level serves excellent Italian cuisine in a stylish setting (see chapter 6); the Parisian-style Café Expresso does an equally commendable job serving coffees, pastries, and sandwiches daily. The Starlight Room on the 21st floor offers cocktails, entertainment, and dancing nightly with a panoramic view of the city.

Amenities: Concierge, room service, exercise room, business and secretarial services, extensive meeting facilities, laundry, valet, newspaper delivery, in-room massage, baby-sitting, express checkout, courtesy car.

✪ **The White Swan Inn.** 845 Bush St. (between Taylor and Mason sts.), San Francisco, CA 94108. ☎ **800/999-9570** or 415/775-1755. Fax 415/775-5717. 26 units. MINIBAR TV TEL. $165–$185 double; $195 romance suite; $250 2-room suite. Extra person $15. Rates include full breakfast and afternoon wine and hors d'oeuvres. AE, DC, MC, V. Parking $19. Cable car: California St. line (1 block north). Bus: 1, 2, 3, 4, 27, or 45.

From the moment you're buzzed in to this well-secured inn, you'll know you're not in a generic bed-and-breakfast. Close to 50 teddy bears grace the lobby, and if that doesn't cure homesickness, homemade cookies, tea, and coffee will. The romantically homey rooms are warm and cozy—the perfect place to snuggle up with a good book. They're also quite big, with hardwood entryways, rich dark-wood furniture, working fireplaces, and an assortment of books tucked in nooks. The decor is English elegance at its best, if not to excess, with floral prints almost everywhere. Wine and hors d'oeuvres are served daily. The romance suites are not much better than regular rooms, just a little bigger, and feature perks like chocolates, champagne, and a VCR. The inn's location—2^1/$_2$ blocks from Union Square—makes this 1900s building a charming and serene choice, with service and style that will please even the most discriminating traveler. No smoking.

Dining/Diversions: Each morning a generous breakfast is served in a common room just off a tiny garden. Afternoon tea is also served, with hors d'oeuvres, sherry, wine, and home-baked pastries. You can have your sherry in front of the fireplace while you browse through the books in the library.

Amenities: Concierge, laundry, overnight shoeshine, morning newspaper, evening turndown. Guests have access to an off-premises health club ($15 per day).

MODERATE

A few worthy hotel companies operate many properties throughout the city. **Holiday Inn** (☎ **800/465-4329;** www.basshotels.com/holiday-inn) has several strategic locations. **Personality Hotels** (☎ **800/553-1900;** www.personalityhotels.com) spiffs up older buildings in central locales, and **Joie de Vivre** (☎ **800/SF-TRIPS**) has lots of festive options scattered around town.

The Amsterdam Hotel. 749 Taylor St. (between Sutter and Bush sts.), San Francisco, CA 94108. ☎ **800/637-3444** or 415/673-3277. Fax 415/673-0453. 34 units. TV TEL. $109–$149 double. Rates include continental breakfast. AE, MC, V. Parking $13. Bus: 2, 3, 4, or 76.

This small hotel doesn't have the grand feeling of larger properties, but with recently redecorated rooms, it's a very good deal. Rooms are of decent size, and some have Jacuzzi tubs or curiously out-of-place marble or black-lacquer bathrooms, but it's the price that's key. On sunny days, guests head to the small dining patio out back to enjoy breakfast.

The Andrews Hotel. 624 Post St. (between Jones and Taylor sts.), San Francisco, CA 94109. ☎ **800/926-3739** or 415/563-6877. Fax 415/928-6919. www.andrewshotel.com. 48 units (some with shower only). TV TEL. $89–$152 double; $125–$152 petite suite. Rates include continental breakfast and evening wine. AE, DC, JCB, MC, V. Self-parking $15. Cable car: Powell-Hyde and Powell-Mason lines (3 blocks east). Bus: 2, 3, 4, 30, 38, or 45.

Two blocks west of Union Square, the Andrews was a Turkish bath before its conversion in 1981. As is typical in Euro-style hotels, the rooms are small but well maintained and comfortable. They have voicemail, irons, and ironing boards; white lace curtains and fresh flowers in each room add a light touch. Bathrooms tend to be tiny, but for the location and price, the Andrews is a safe bet for an enjoyable stay. A bonus is the adjoining Fino Bar and Ristorante, which offers wine to hotel guests in the evening.

The Beresford Arms. 701 Post St. (at Jones St.), San Francisco, CA 94109. ☎ **800/533-6533** or 415/673-2600. Fax 415/929-1535. 95 units. MINIBAR TV TEL. $129 double; $150 Jacuzzi suite; $185 parlor suite. Extra person $10. Rates include continental breakfast and afternoon wine and tea. Children under 12 free in parents' room. Senior-citizen and AAA discounts available. AE, CB, DC, DISC, MC, V. Valet parking $16; self-parking $13. Cable car: Powell-Hyde line (3 blocks east). Bus: 2, 3, 4, 27, or 38.

The bargain prices are the main reason I recommend this dependable, though a little unfashionable, hotel. On the plus side, many rooms have Jacuzzi whirlpool bathtubs and bidets, and the choice of a wet bar or fully equipped kitchen—an advantage for families. All have VCRs and honor bars, and there's a "Manager's Social Hour" (included in the room rates) with wine and snacks. The downsides are painfully red carpeting in the common areas, a gloomy lobby, and some old mattresses. Modest business services are available. The location, between the Theater District and Union Square in a quieter section of San Francisco, is ideal for visitors without cars. *Tip:* Rooms that face Post Street might be a bit noisier, but they're also larger and sunnier, and some have window seats.

The Beresford Hotel. 635 Sutter St. (near Mason St.), San Francisco, CA 94102. ☎ **800/533-6533** or 415/673-9900. Fax 415/474-0449. 114 units. MINIBAR TV TEL. $109–$129 double. Extra person $10. Rates include continental breakfast. Children under 12 free in parents' room. Senior-citizen and AAA discounts available. Ask for special rates. AE, CB, DC, DISC, MC, V. Self-parking $16. Cable car: Powell-Hyde line (1 block east). Bus: 2, 3, 4, 30, 38, or 45.

Small and friendly, the seven-floor Beresford Hotel is a decent, moderately priced choice near Union Square. Rooms have stocked fridges and a mishmash of furniture; to block out street noise, management recently installed soundproof windows. Everything's well kept, but don't expect much more than a clean place to rest. The White Horse Tavern, an attractive replica of an old English pub, serves breakfast, lunch, and dinner.

The Cartwright Hotel. 524 Sutter St. (at Powell St.), San Francisco, CA 94102. ☎ **800/919-9779** or 415/421-2865. Fax 415/398-6345. 114 units. TV TEL. $149–$269 double or twin; $249–$269 family suite (sleeps 4). AE, CB, DC, DISC, MC, V. Valet parking $24; self-parking $18. Cable car: Powell-Hyde and Powell-Mason lines (direct stop). Bus: 2, 3, 4, 30, or 45.

Diametrically opposed to the hip-hop, happenin' Hotel Triton down the street, the Cartwright Hotel is geared toward the "older, mature traveler" (as hotel marketers like to put it). Management takes pride in its reputation for offering comfortable rooms at fair prices, which explains why most guests have been repeat customers for a long time. Remarkably quiet despite its convenient location near one of the busiest downtown corners, the eight-story hotel looks not unlike it did when it opened some 80 years ago. High-quality antiques collected during its decades of faithful service furnish the lobby and the individually decorated rooms. A nice perk usually reserved for fancier hotels is the fully equipped bathrooms, all of which have tubs, shower massages, thick, fluffy towels, and terry robes. *Tip:* Request a room with a view of the backyard; they're the quietest. Guests have access to a nearby health club. Complimentary wine is served in the small library next to the lobby from 5 to 6pm on Friday and Saturday.

The Clarion Bedford Hotel. 761 Post St. (between Leavenworth and Jones sts.), San Francisco, CA 94109. ☎ **800/252-7466** or 415/673-6040. Fax 415/563-6739. 144 units. MINI-BAR TV TEL. $159–$199 double; from $179 suite. Continental breakfast $8.50. AE, CB, DC, DISC, JCB, MC, V. Valet parking $20. Cable car: Powell-Hyde and Powell-Mason lines (4 blocks east). Bus: 2, 3, 4, or 27.

For the price and location (3 blocks from Union Square), the 17-story Bedford offers a darn good deal. Your hard-earned dollars will get you a large, spotless room with flowery decor that's not exactly *en vogue* but definitely in fine taste, as well as service from an enthusiastic, attentive, and professional staff. Each unit is well furnished with king, queen, or two double beds, writing desk, armchair, in-room coffee, iron and ironing board, Nintendo, and well-stocked honor bar with plenty of munchies. Although closets are big, bathrooms are small. Most rooms are sunny and bright, with priceless views of the city (the higher the floor, the better the view).

The hotel's bistro, Crushed Tomato's, has a small, beautiful mahogany bar opposite the registration desk. There's also room service (breakfast only), dry cleaning, laundry, and secretarial services.

✪ The Commodore International. 825 Sutter St. (at Jones St.), San Francisco, CA 94109. ☎ **800/338-6848** or 415/923-6800. Fax 415/923-6804. www.sftrips.com. 113 units. TV TEL. $99–$149 double. AE, DC, MC, V. Parking $18. Bus: 2, 3, 4, 27, or 76.

If you're looking to pump a little fun and fantasy into your vacation, this is the place. Before its new owners revamped the aging Commodore from top to bottom, it . . . well, okay, it sucked. Then along came San Francisco hotelier Chip Conley, who instantly recognized the dilapidated eyesore's potential, added it to his collection, and let his hip-hop designers do their magic. The result? One groovy hotel. Stealing the show is the Red Room, a Big Apple–style bar and lounge that reflects no other color of the spectrum but ruby red (you gotta see this one). The stylish lobby comes in a close second, followed by the adjoining Titanic Café, a cute little diner serving griddle cakes, Vietnamese tofu sandwiches, and dragon-fire salads. Appealing to the masses, Chip left the first four floors as standard no-frills—though quite comfortable—rooms, while decking out the top two floors in neo-Deco overtones (well worth the extra $10 per night). Rooms are scheduled to undergo renovations in 2000.

The Cornell Hotel. 715 Bush St. (between Powell and Mason sts.), San Francisco, CA 94108. ☎ **800/232-9698** or 415/421-3154. Fax 415/399-1442. 58 units. TV TEL. $110–$145 double. Rates include full breakfast. Package including 7 breakfasts and 5 dinners, $945–$1,015 double per week. AE, CB, DC, MC, V. Parking $13. Cable car: Powell-Hyde and Powell-Mason lines. Bus: 2, 3, 4, 30, or 45.

Its quirks make this hotel more charming than many in its price range. Rameau, the house golden retriever, greets you when you enter the small French-style hotel. Pass the office, where a few faces will glance in your direction and smile, and embark on a ride in the old-fashioned elevator to get to your room. Each floor is dedicated to a French painter and decorated with reproductions. Rooms are all plain and comfortable, with a desk and chairs, and individually decorated in simple, modern style. No smoking is allowed. Breakfast is served in the cavern-like provincial basement dining room, Jeanne d'Arc. Union Square is a few blocks away.

The Fitzgerald. 620 Post St. (between Jones and Taylor sts.), San Francisco, CA 94109. ☎ **800/334-6835** or 415/775-8100. Fax 415/775-1278. www.fitzgeraldhotel.com. 39 units. TV TEL. $79–$189 double. Extra person $10. Rates include continental breakfast. Lower rates in winter. AE, CB, DC, DISC, JCB, MC, V. Self-parking $18. Bus: 2, 3, 4, or 27.

If you think the guy at the front desk looks cramped in his nook of a lobby, wait until you get to your room. The Fitzgerald's guest accommodations may be outfitted with newish furniture, accented with bright bedspreads and patterned carpet, but some of the rooms are really small. (One that I saw had a dresser less than a foot from the bed.) Ask for a larger room. If you can live without a sizable closet, the price, breakfast, and newness of this hotel make it a good value. Families will especially appreciate the two-bedroom suites, which offer one queen- and one full-sized bed. Take heed: The view of the Golden Gate that's printed on the brochure is not actually visible from the hotel.

Breakfast includes home-baked breads, scones, muffins, juice, tea, and coffee. The hotel has a concierge and offers dry cleaning, laundry service, in-room massage, complimentary coffee in the lobby, and free access to a nearby indoor pool and health club.

✪ **King George Hotel.** 334 Mason St. (between Geary and O'Farrell sts.), San Francisco, CA 94102. ☎ **800/288-6005** or 415/781-5050. Fax 415/835-5991. www.kinggeorge.com. 141 units. TV TEL. $160 double; $225 suite. Breakfast $6.50–$8. Special-value packages available seasonally. AE, CB, DC, DISC, JCB, MC, V. Self-parking $19. Cable car: Powell-Hyde and Powell-Mason lines (1 block west). Bus: 2, 3, 4, 30, 38, or 45.

Built in 1914 for the Panama-Pacific Exhibition (when rooms went for $1 per night), the utterly delightful King George has fared well over the years. It continues to draw a mostly European clientele. The location—surrounded by cable-car lines, the Theater District, Union Square, and dozens of restaurants—is superb, and the rooms are surprisingly quiet for such a busy spot. Although rooms can be small, a recent renovation has made the most of the space; there are new mattresses, desks, data ports, Nintendo, voicemail, and a handsome study-like ambience. All units contain hair dryers and lovely amenities. A big hit since it started a few years back is the hotel's English afternoon tea, served above the lobby in the Windsor Tea Room Wednesday to Sunday from 3 to 6:30pm.

The Monticello Inn. 127 Ellis St. (between Mason and Powell sts.), San Francisco, CA 94102. ☎ **800/669-7777** or 415/392-8800. Fax 415/398-2650. 91 units. A/C MINIBAR TV TEL. $149–$159 double; $169–$249 suite. Extra person $15. Rates include continental breakfast, coffee and tea in the lobby, and evening wine. AE, CB, DC, DISC, MC, V. Valet parking $22. Cable car: Powell-Hyde and Powell-Mason lines (direct stop). Muni Metro: All Market St. metros. Bus: All Market St. buses.

Okay, I admit it: I didn't know Monticello was the estate of Thomas Jefferson, and I also didn't know that the Monticello mansion is on the tail side of the nickel (Tom's noggin is on the front). Why the history lesson? In addition to the moniker, Monticello is also the hotel's theme. Federal-style decor, Chippendale furnishings, grandfather clocks, Revolutionary War paintings, a brass-mantled fireplace, and other old stuff scattered around the lobby attempt to create a colonial milieu. Although it makes for a pleasant entrance, the period effect, unfortunately, doesn't quite follow through to the rooms. They're comfortable, spacious, and reasonably attractive, but the stark blue carpets and floral upholstery don't have the same faux-Federal theme (and the homely air conditioners recessed into the walls certainly don't help). If you can live with this, however, you'll be quite content here, especially considering the little extras—umbrellas, voicemail, modem and data port, Nintendo, and a morning ride to the Financial District. The service is wonderful, the downtown location is primo, parking comes with in-out privileges, and there's even access to a great fitness club around the block ($15 fee).

The hotel's restaurant, Puccini & Pinetti, features modern Italian cuisine; it's next door, at the corner of Ellis and Cyril Magnin streets.

○ **Petite Auberge.** 863 Bush St. (between Taylor and Mason sts.), San Francisco, CA 94108. ☎ **415/928-6000**. Fax 415/775-5717. 26 units. TV TEL. $120–$245 double; $245 petite suite. Rates include full breakfast and afternoon tea. AE, DC, MC, V. Parking $19. Cable car: Powell-Hyde and Powell-Mason lines. Bus: 2, 3, 4, 30, 38, or 45.

The Petite Auberge is so pathetically cute I can't stand it. I want to say it's overdone, that any hotel that's filled with teddy bears is absurd, but I can't. Bribed each year with fresh-baked cookies from the never-empty platter, I make rounds through the rooms and ruefully admit that I'm just going to have to use that word I loathe to hear: adorable.

Nobody does French country like the Petite Auberge. Handcrafted armoires, delicate lace curtains, cozy little fireplaces, adorable (there's that word again) little antiques and knickknacks—no hotel in Provence ever had it this good. Honeymooners should splurge on the petite suite, which has a private entrance, deck, and spa tub. The breakfast room, with its mural of a country market scene, terra-cotta tile floors, and gold-yellow tablecloths, opens onto a small garden. California wines, tea, and hors d'oeuvres (included in the room rates) are served each afternoon.

The Savoy Hotel. 580 Geary St. (between Taylor and Jones sts.), San Francisco, CA 94102. ☎ **800/227-4223** or 415/441-2700. Fax 415/441-0124. 83 units. MINIBAR TV TEL. $115–$145 double; from $205 suite. Ask about package, government, senior, and corporate rates. AE, CB, DC, DISC, MC, V. Parking $18. Bus: 2, 3, 4, 27, or 38.

When the Savoy changed hands and underwent renovation in 1989, travelers and *Travel & Leisure* deemed it one of the sweetest affordable options off Union Square. While that's still the case, unfortunately the hotel hasn't kept up with the wear and tear associated with brisk business. However, rooms are still cozy French provincial, with 18th-century period furnishings, featherbeds, and goose-down pillows, plus modern conveniences such as hair dryers. Not all rooms are alike—they can be small, but each has beautiful patterned draperies, triple sheets, full-length mirrors, and two-line telephones. Guests also enjoy concierge service and free overnight shoeshines. Rates include late-afternoon cookies, sherry, and tea, served in the Brasserie Savoy, an excellent seafood restaurant (see chapter 6 for complete details).

Villa Florence. 225 Powell St. (between Geary and O'Farrell sts.), San Francisco, CA 94102. ☎ **800/553-4411** or 415/397-7700. Fax 415/397-1006. 183 units. A/C MINIBAR TV TEL. $119–$199 double; $169–$299 executive king. Rates include evening wine. AE, CB, DC, DISC, MC, V. Valet parking $25. Cable car: Powell-Hyde and Powell-Mason lines (direct stop). Bus: 2, 3, 4, 30, 38, or 45.

Located half a block south of Union Square, fronting the Powell Street cable car line, the seven-story Villa Florence is in one of the liveliest sections of the city (no need to drive, 'cause you're already here). A recent—and sorely needed—renovation brightened up the rooms considerably. Essentially, Villa Florence offers a lower-end replica of the spectacular rooms at the Hotel Monaco (owned by the same company), with lots of bold stripes and vibrant colors. You'll like the large, comfortable bed, CD player, and cable TV; bathrooms contain hand-milled soap and hair dryers. But never mind the rooms: The restaurant is what makes it a worthy contender among Union Square's medium-priced inns—as if the location alone weren't reason enough to book a room. Adjoining the hotel is Kuleto's, one of San Francisco's most popular and stylish Italian restaurants (trust us—you'll want to make a reservation for dinner when you book your room). See chapter 6 for complete information.

The Warwick Regis. 490 Geary St. (between Mason and Taylor sts.), San Francisco, CA 94102. ☎ **800/827-3447** or 415/928-7900. Fax 415/441-8788. 80 units. MINIBAR TV TEL. $159–$169 double; $179–$259 suite. Rates include continental breakfast. AE, CB, DC, DISC, MC, V. Parking $23. Cable car: Powell-Hyde and Powell-Mason lines. Bus: 2, 3, 4, 27, or 38.

Louis XVI might have been a rotten monarch, but he certainly had taste. Fashioned in the style of pre-Revolutionary France, the Warwick is awash with pristine French and English antiques, Italian marble, chandeliers, four-poster beds, hand-carved headboards, and the like. The result is an expensive-looking hotel that, for all its pleasantries and perks, is surprisingly affordable when compared to its Union Square contemporaries (singles are as low as $139). Honeymooners should splurge on the fireplace rooms with canopy beds—ooh la la! Amenities include 24-hour room and concierge service, dry cleaning, laundry, twice-daily maid service, complimentary shoeshine and newspaper (weekdays only), and valet parking. Adjoining the lobby is La Scene Café, a fashionable place to start your day with a latte and end it with a nightcap. There's access to a nearby health club, and a business center and conference rooms are on the premises.

INEXPENSIVE

The Adelaide Inn. 5 Isadora Duncan Court (formerly Adelaide Place, off Taylor St., between Post and Geary sts.), San Francisco, CA 94102. ☎ **415/441-2261.** Fax 415/441-0161. 18 units, all with shared bathroom. TV. $52–$58 double with shared bathroom. Rates include continental breakfast. AE, MC, V. Bus: 2, 3, 4, 27, 38, 76.

San Francisco reputedly is America's most European city, and if you're into the facade, the Adelaide will definitely complete the illusion. The last of the true old-style pensiones, this three-level building tucked in a surprisingly quiet cul-de-sac is bright, cheery, and decorated in long-forgotten style (remember textured wallpaper?). Colors and furniture hark back to the 1960s, not because the owner's gone retro, but probably because he hasn't changed the furnishings since then. But in an inexplicably quaint way, the atmosphere works. Perhaps it's the sunny, funky rooms; the small, bright breakfast room; the stairway skylight; or the shared fridge in the kitchen. It certainly isn't the spongy mattresses or tiny bathrooms or old, wet-smelling showers. Whatever it is, this place does feel a lot like home. Services include morning coffee and rolls and on-the-premises pay phones. *Note:* This place is not for anyone with mobility issues—it has steep stairs and no elevators.

AYH Hostel at Union Square. 312 Mason St. (between Geary and O'Farrell sts.), San Francisco, CA 94102. ☎ **415/788-5604.** Fax 415/788-3023. 260 beds. Hosteling members $17–$19; nonmembers $20–$22. Children under 12 half-price when accompanied by a parent. Maximum stay 14 nights per year. MC, V. Parking $18 in public lot on Mission between 4th and 5th sts. Cable car: Powell-Mason line. Bus: 7B or 38.

For around $20 per night (with a notarized ID), you can relive college-dorm life in an old San Francisco–style building right in the heart of Union Square. Occupying five sparsely decorated floors, rooms here are simple and clean. Each has two or three bunk beds, its own sink, and a closet; best of all, you can lock your door and take the key with you. Although private rooms share hallway bathrooms, a few have private facilities. Suite rooms are reserved for families. Laminated posters adorn the freshly painted hallways, and there are several common rooms, including a reading room, a smoking room, and a large kitchen with lots of tables, chairs, and refrigerator space. There are laundry facilities nearby, and a helpful information desk where you can book tour reservations and sightseeing trips. The hostel is open 24 hours, and reservations are essential during the summer. Persons under 18 may not stay without a parent unless they have a notarized letter, and then must pay the adult rate.

The Golden Gate Hotel. 775 Bush St. (between Powell and Mason sts.), San Francisco, CA 94108. ☎ **800/835-1118** or 415/392-3702. Fax 415/392-6202. www.goldengatehotel. com. 23 units, 14 with bathroom. TV TEL. $78 double without bathroom, $115 double with bathroom. Rates include continental breakfast and afternoon tea. AE, DC, MC, V. Self-parking $12. Cable car: Powell-Hyde and Powell-Mason lines (1 block east). Bus: 2, 3, 4, 30, 38, or 45. Powell & Market BART.

San Francisco's stock of small hotels in historic turn-of-the-century buildings includes some real gems, and the Golden Gate Hotel is one of them. It's 2 blocks north of Union Square and 2 blocks down (literally) from the crest of Nob Hill, with cable-car stops at the corner for easy access to Fisherman's Wharf and Chinatown. The city's theaters and best restaurants are also within walking distance. But the best thing about the Golden Gate Hotel is that it's family run: John and Renate Kenaston are hospitable innkeepers who take obvious pleasure in making their guests comfortable. Each individually decorated room has handsome antique furnishings (plenty of wicker) from the early 1900s, quilted bedspreads, and fresh flowers. Request a room with a claw-foot tub if you enjoy a good, hot soak. Afternoon tea is served daily from 4 to 7pm.

Grant Plaza Hotel. 465 Grant Ave. (at Pine St.), San Francisco, CA 94108. ☎ **800/ 472-6899** or 415/434-3883. Fax 415/434-3886. E-mail: grantplaza@worldnet.att.net. 72 units (most with shower only). TV TEL. $62–$89 double. AE, CB, DC, MC, V. Nearby parking $14.50. Cable car: Powell-Hyde and Powell-Mason lines (2 blocks west).

You won't find any free little bottles of shampoo here. What you will find are cheap rates and basic—and I mean basic—rooms right in the middle of the Union Square–Chinatown action. Many of the small, well-kept rooms in the six-story building overlook Chinatown's main street; all gained new bedspreads, draperies, and hair dryers in 1997. The downsides are minuscule bathrooms and small showers. Corner rooms on higher floors are both larger and brighter. Ask for a room on the top floor—they're the newest and are substantially nicer than the older rooms.

The Sheehan. 620 Sutter St. (near Mason St.), San Francisco, CA 94102. ☎ **800/ 848-1529** or 415/775-6500. Fax 415/775-3271. www.sheehanhotel.com. 65 units, 62 with bathroom. TV TEL. $89–$99 double without bathroom; $99–$169 double with bathroom. Rates include continental breakfast. AE, DISC, JCB, MC, V. Parking $16. Cable car: Powell-Hyde and Powell-Mason lines (2 blocks east). Bus: 2, 3, 4, 30, 38, or 45.

Formerly a YWCA hotel, the Sheehan is dirt-cheap, considering its location 2 blocks from Union Square. Of course, this isn't the Ritz—some walls could use a little paint, and plenty of areas would benefit from a little TLC. Ask for one of the remodeled rooms, and you'll do just fine. Rooms are simply furnished and come with cable TV, and bathrooms are brand-new and contain hair dryers. The hotel has a pleasant lobby and an indoor, heated lap pool and workout area.

2 The Financial District
VERY EXPENSIVE

Hyatt Regency San Francisco. 5 Embarcadero Center, San Francisco, CA 94111. ☎ **800/ 233-1234** or 415/788-1234. Fax 415/398-2567. 805 units. A/C TV TEL. $199–$375 double; $450–$525 suite. Continental breakfast $14. AE, CB, DC, DISC, JCB, MC, V. Valet parking $27. Muni Metro: All Market St. trams. Bus: All Market St. buses.

The Hyatt Regency, a convention favorite, rises from the edge of the Embarcadero Center at the foot of Market Street. The gray concrete structure, with a 1970s, bunker-like facade, is shaped like a vertical triangle, serrated with long rows of jutting balconies. The 17-story atrium lobby, illuminated by museum-quality theater lighting, features flowing water and a simulated environment of California grasslands and wildflowers.

Rooms, which were renovated in 1998, are comfortably furnished. Each has a hair dryer, voicemail, data port, VCR, and coffeemaker. Rooms for "Gold Passport" members, which, along with the suites, underwent a soft-goods renovation in 1999, have tea- and coffee-making facilities, and private fax machines are available free on request. Rooms with two double beds include a sofa or easy chair. The hotel's 16th and 17th floors house the Regency Club, with 102 larger guest rooms, complimentary continental breakfast, and after-dinner cordials.

Dining/Diversions: The Eclipse Café serves breakfast and lunch daily; the Thirteen-Views Bar seats about 200 and is open for morning coffee and evening cocktails. The Equinox is a revolving rooftop restaurant and bar with 360-degree city views.

Amenities: Concierge, laundry, overnight shoeshine, newspaper delivery, express checkout, business center, conference room. Access to health club, off-premises swimming pool, and tennis courts.

✪ The Mandarin Oriental. 222 Sansome St. (between Pine and California sts.), San Francisco, CA 94104. ☎ **800/622-0404** or 415/276-9888. Fax 415/433-0289. www. mandarinoriental.com. 158 units. A/C MINIBAR TV TEL. $415–$485 double; $505–$570 junior suite. Continental breakfast $18. AE, CB, DC, DISC, JCB, MC, V. Valet parking $30. Muni Metro: J, K, L, or M to Montgomery. Bus: All Market St. buses.

If I were seeking respite from researching this guide, I'd probably head straight here, jump into a Jacuzzi, relax, and admire the city from 48 floors up. All the rooms are between the 38th and 48th floors of a downtown high-rise, which affords each of the large accommodations extraordinary panoramic views of the bay and city. Not all rooms have tub-side views, but they do have luxurious marble bathrooms stocked with a natural loofah, a large selection of English toiletries, terry and cotton cloth robes, hair dryer, makeup mirror, and silk slippers. The rooms are less opulent, with a reserved contemporary decor of light colors, Asian accents, and handsome furnishings, which include a spacious desk and sitting area. Because this is mostly a business hotel, additional amenities include three two-line phones with fax hookups, as well as TVs with on-command video access to more than 80 movies.

Dining/Diversions: Silks is a serene dining room, melding California and Asian ingredients, that has won rave reviews.

Amenities: Concierge; 24-hour room service; fitness center with cardio, Nautilus, and free weights; laundry and valet; complimentary newspaper and shoeshine; twice-daily maid service; business center.

The Park Hyatt San Francisco. 333 Battery St. (at Clay St.), San Francisco, CA 94111. ☎ **800/HYATT-CA** or 415/392-1234. Fax 415/421-2433. www.hyatt.com. 360 units. A/C TV TEL. $320–$385 double; $395–$4,000 suite. AE, CB, DC, JCB, MC, V. Parking $28. Cable car: California line. Bus: 12, 15, 41, 42, or 83.

If you're looking for a small luxury business hotel in the heart of the Financial District, stay at the Park Hyatt San Francisco. About half the size of Hyatt's typical mega-hotels, the 26-story Park Hyatt has a rather plain exterior, but is a pleasure to behold from within. The lobby, for example, is lavishly appointed with Australian lacewood paneling, polished Italian granite, handmade custom carpets from China, and opalescent Spanish alabaster chandeliers. A magnificent spiral staircase, encircling a rather

---

Sleeping Seaside

You would think that a city surrounded on three sides by water would have a slew of seaside hotels. Oddly enough, it has only one: the **Seal Rock Inn.** It's about as far from Union Square and Fisherman's Wharf as you can place a hotel in San Francisco, but that just makes it all the more unique. The hotel fronts Sutro Heights park, which faces Ocean Beach. Most rooms in the four-story structure have at least partial views of the ocean; at night, the sound of the surf and distant foghorns lulls guests to sleep. The rooms, although large and spotless, obviously haven't been redecorated since the Nixon administration; a monotone scheme of beige, brown, and gray makes you feel as though you're color-blind. Options range from kitchenettes to two-room suites with wood-burning fireplaces; phones, TVs, covered parking, and free use of the enclosed patio and pool area are standard. Adjacent to the inn is a small cafe serving breakfast and lunch. Golden Gate Park and the Presidio are both nearby, and the Geary bus—which snails its way to Union Square and Market Street—stops right out front.

The Seal Rock Inn (☎ **415/752-8000;** fax 415/752-6034) is at 545 Point Lobos Ave. (at 48th Avenue), in San Francisco. Double rooms range from $98 to $124.

---

phallic bronze sculpture by Italian sculptor Arnaldo Pomodoro, leads to the upper-level restaurant. The guest rooms are a bit more understated, with Italian wood furnishings, large bathrooms, and exceedingly comfortable beds. They have extraordinary views of the city, particularly from the corner suites on the upper floors, which also come with outdoor balconies or a Jacuzzi tub (a tough choice). Ten executive suites have a separate office complete with fax machine and data port hookups. Another nice perk is the complimentary Mercedes-Benz house car service to anywhere in the downtown area.

Dining/Diversions: The Park Grill, open for breakfast, lunch, and dinner, offers upscale American cuisine in an elegant setting; the wine list is excellent. More casual alfresco dining is available at the Outdoor Terrace, which serves lighter fare. There's a full bar on the lobby level.

Amenities: 24-hour room and concierge service, free chauffeur service to the downtown area, laundry, massage, currency exchange, secretarial and business services, library with international newspapers, meeting facilities at the adjacent Federal Reserve Building. Health center; rowing machines and exercise cycles delivered to guest rooms.

✪ **The Sheraton Palace Hotel.** 2 New Montgomery St. (at Market St.), San Francisco, CA 94105. ☎ **800/325-3535** or 415/392-8600. Fax 415/543-0671. 551 units. A/C MINIBAR TV TEL. $300–$390 double; from $450 suite. Extra person $20. Continental breakfast $16; deluxe continental $18. Children under 18 sharing existing bedding free in parents' room. Weekend rates and packages available. AE, DC, DISC, JCB, MC, V. Parking $25. Muni Metro: All Market St. trams. Bus: All Market St. buses.

The original 1875 Palace was one of the world's largest and most luxurious hotels, and every time you walk through the doors, you'll be reminded how incredibly majestic old luxury really is. The hotel was rebuilt after the 1906 quake and renovated in 1991. Its most spectacular attributes remain the regal lobby and the Garden Court, a San Francisco landmark that has been restored to its original 1909 grandeur. A double row of massive Italian-marble Ionic columns flank the court, and 10 huge chandeliers dangle above. The real heart-stopper, however, is the 80,000-pane stained-glass ceiling. Regrettably, the rooms have that standardized, chain-hotel appearance.

Dining/Diversions: On special holidays, the Garden Court serves a $55 brunch that's worth indulging in; a scaled-down version takes place on other weekends. Maxfields's Restaurant, a traditional San Francisco grill, has turn-of-the-century charm and is open daily for lunch and dinner. Kyo-ya is an authentic Japanese restaurant with a separate street entrance. The Pied Piper Bar is named after the $2.5 million Maxfield Parrish mural that dominates the room.

Amenities: Concierge, 24-hour room service, laundry and valet, evening turndown, business service center, lobby-level shops. The fourth-floor health club contains a skylight-covered lap pool, whirlpool, sauna, and exercise room.

3 Nob Hill

VERY EXPENSIVE

The Fairmont Hotel & Tower. 950 Mason St. (at California St.), San Francisco, CA 94108. ☎ **800/527-4727** or 415/772-5000. Fax 415/772-5013. www.fairmont.com. 600 units. A/C MINIBAR TV TEL. Main building $229–$279 double, from $530 suite; Tower $269–$359 double; from $800 suite. Extra person $30. Continental breakfast $14. AE, CB, DC, DISC, MC, V. Parking $30. Cable car: California St. line (direct stop).

The granddaddy of Nob Hill's elite cadre of ritzy hotels, the Fairmont wins top honors for the most jaw-dropping lobby in San Francisco. Even if you're not a guest, it's worth a side trip to gape at its massive, marble Corinthian columns, vaulted ceilings, velvet chairs, gilded mirrors, and spectacular wraparound staircase. Unfortunately, the ostentation doesn't carry over to the guest rooms, which are surprisingly ordinary (aside from the spectacular views from the top floors)—thankfully, they're scheduled for a complete renovation by the end of 2000. In addition to the expected luxuries, guests will appreciate such details as goose-down pillows, electric shoe buffers, bathroom scales, large walk-in closets, and multiline phones with private voicemail.

Dining/Diversions: Masons serves contemporary California cuisine at dinner. The Crown Room offers dinner buffets and Sunday brunch, with a panoramic view of the Bay Area. The Tonga Room offers Chinese and Polynesian specialties in a tropical atmosphere, as well as dancing and a generous happy hour.

Amenities: 24-hour concierge and room service, health club ($15 daily), laundry and valet, complimentary shoeshine, evening turndown, twice-daily maid service, baby-sitting, doctor on call, complimentary morning limousine to the Financial District, business center, barbershop, beauty salon, pharmacy, shopping arcade.

✪ **The Huntington Hotel.** 1075 California St. (between Mason and Taylor sts.), San Francisco, CA 94108. ☎ **800/227-4683** or 415/474-5400. Fax 415/474-6227. www.huntingtonhotel.com. 140 units. A/C MINIBAR TV TEL. $275–$420 double; $475–$990 suite. Continental breakfast $13. Special packages available. AE, CB, DC, DISC, MC, V. Valet parking $19.50. Cable car: California St. line (direct stop). Bus: 1.

One of the kings of Nob Hill, the stately Huntington Hotel has long been a favorite retreat for Hollywood stars and political VIPs who desire privacy and security. Family-owned since 1924—an extreme rarity among large hotels—the Huntington eschews pomp and circumstance; absolute privacy and unobtrusive service are its mainstays. Although the lobby, decorated in grand 19th-century style, is rather petite, the guest rooms are quite large; they feature Brunschwig and Fils fabrics and bed coverings, antique French furnishings, and views of the city. The lavish suites, so opulent that they've been featured in *Architectural Digest,* are individually decorated with custom-made and antique furnishings. Prices are steep, as you would expect, but special offers such as the Romance Package ($285 per couple, including champagne, sherry, and limousine service), make the Huntington worth considering for a special occasion.

Dining/Diversions: The Big Four restaurant offers expensive contemporary American cuisine in one of the city's handsomest dining rooms (see chapter 6 for a full description). Live piano music plays nightly in the lounge.

Amenities: Concierge, room service, laundry, overnight shoeshine, evening turndown, complimentary morning newspaper, twice-daily maid service, complimentary limousine to the Financial District and Union Square, complimentary formal tea or sherry upon arrival. Access to off-premises health club and spa ($20); a spa is scheduled to open by fall 2000.

The Mark Hopkins Intercontinental. 1 Nob Hill (at California and Mason sts.), San Francisco, CA 94108. ☎ **800/327-0200** or 415/392-3434. Fax 415/421-3302. 390 units. A/C MINIBAR TV TEL. $280–$380 double; from $510 suite. Breakfast buffet $20. AE, CB, DC, DISC, MC, V. Valet parking $27. Cable car: California St. line (direct stop). Bus: 1.

Built in 1926 on the spot where railroad millionaire Mark Hopkins's turreted mansion once stood, the 19-story Mark Hopkins gained global fame during World War II when it was *de rigueur* for Pacific-bound servicemen to toast their good-bye to the States in the Top of the Mark cocktail lounge. Nowadays, the hotel caters mostly to convention-bound corporate executives who can afford the high rates. Each neoclassical room comes with all the fancy amenities you'd expect from a world-class hotel, including custom furniture, plush fabrics, sumptuous bathrooms, and extraordinary views of the city. A minor caveat: The hotel has only three guest elevators, making a quick trip to your room difficult during busy periods.

Dining/Diversions: The world-renowned Top of the Mark lounge serves tea from 3 to 5pm, cocktails from 3pm to 1am Monday through Saturday and 4pm to 1am Sunday, and Sunday brunch from 10am to 2:30pm. It offers dancing to live music every night. The plush and decidedly formal Nob Hill Restaurant offers California-French cuisine nightly and a full buffet breakfast each morning. The Nob Hill Terrace, adjacent to the lobby, serves lunch, cocktails, and dinner daily.

Amenities: Concierge, room service, health club, laundry, overnight shoeshine, newspaper delivery, evening turndown on request, in-room massage, twice-daily maid service, baby-sitting, valet parking, courtesy limousine weekday mornings, multilingual guest relations, business center, car-rental desk.

The Renaissance Stanford Court Hotel. 905 California St. (at Powell St.), San Francisco, CA 94108. ☎ **800/468-3571**, 800/622-0957 in CA, or 415/989-3500. Fax 415/391-0513. www.renaissancehotels.com. 393 units. A/C TV TEL. $179–$289 double; from $675 suite. Continental breakfast $15; American breakfast $22.50. AE, DC, DISC, MC, V. Valet parking $29. Cable car: Powell-Hyde and Powell-Mason lines (direct stop). Bus: 1.

The Stanford Court has maintained a long and discreet reputation as one of San Francisco's most exclusive hotels. Keeping company with the Ritz, Fairmont, Mark Hopkins, and Huntington hotels atop Nob Hill, it's frequented mostly by corporate execs. The building was originally the mansion of Leland Stanford, whose legacy lives on in the many portraits and biographies that adorn the rooms. At first, the guest rooms come across as austere and antiquated compared to those at most other top-dollar business hotels, but the quality and comfort of the furnishings are so superior that you're forced to admit there's simply no room for improvement. The Stanford Court also prides itself on its impeccable service; a nice touch is the complimentary tray of tea or coffee placed outside your door on request. The lobby, furnished in 19th-century style with Baccarat chandeliers, French antiques, and a gorgeous stained-glass dome, makes for a grand entrance.

Many of the guest rooms have partially canopied beds; all have writing desks, extremely comfortable beds, and oak armoires that conceal new television sets (with a video-game system and Spectravision movie channels). Bathrooms contain mini-TVs, telephones, hair dryers, heated towel racks, overhead heat lamps, and makeup mirrors.

Dining/Diversions: The award-winning restaurant Fournou's Ovens features contemporary American-Mediterranean cuisine in a romantic multilevel setting.

Amenities: Concierge, 24-hour room service, fitness center, state-of-the-art business center, 24-hour laundry and valet, complimentary overnight shoeshine, complimentary morning newspaper and coffee or tea, baby-sitter on call, complimentary chauffeured car service to downtown destinations, conference rooms, car-rental desk.

✪ **The Ritz-Carlton.** 600 Stockton St. (between Pine and California sts.), San Francisco, CA 94108. ☎ **800/241-3333** or 415/296-7465. Fax 415/986-1268. www.ritzcarlton.com. 336 units. A/C MINIBAR TV TEL. $440 double; $540 club-level double; from $675 suite. Buffet breakfast $18; Sun brunch $55. Weekend discounts and packages available. AE, CB, DC, DISC, MC, V. Parking $30. Cable car: Powell-Hyde and Powell-Mason lines (direct stop).

Ranked among the top hotels in the world (as well as the top hotel in the city) by readers of *Condé Nast Traveler*, the Ritz-Carlton has been the benchmark for San Francisco's luxury hotels since it opened in 1991. A Nob Hill landmark, the former Metropolitan Insurance headquarters stood vacant for years until the Ritz-Carlton company acquired it and embarked on a $4.5 million, four-year renovation. The interior was completely gutted and restored with fine furnishings, fabrics, and artwork, including a pair of Louis XVI blue marble-covered urns with gilt mounts, and 19th-century Waterford candelabras. The guest rooms offer every possible amenity: Italian-marble bathrooms with double sinks, telephone, and name-brand toiletries; plush terry robes; and an in-room safe. The more expensive rooms take advantage of the hotel's location—the south slope of Nob Hill—and have good views of the city. Club rooms, on the seventh, eighth, and ninth floors, have a dedicated concierge, separate elevator-key access, and complimentary meals throughout the day.

Dining/Diversions: The Ritz-Carlton Dining Room, voted among the nation's top restaurants by several magazines, serves dinner Monday to Saturday (see chapter 6 for complete information). The less formal Terrace Restaurant offers contemporary Mediterranean cuisine and outdoor dining in the courtyard. Sunday brunch is easily one of the best in town. The lobby lounge serves afternoon tea, cocktails, and sushi daily, with low-key live entertainment from 3pm to 1am.

Amenities: Outstanding fitness center with pool; concierge; 24-hour room service; same-day laundry and dry cleaning; valet; shoeshine; complimentary morning newspaper; child care; business center; gift boutique.

EXPENSIVE

The Nob Hill Lambourne. 725 Pine St. (between Powell and Stockton sts.), San Francisco, CA 94108. ☎ **800/274-8466** or 415/433-2287. www.nobhilllambourne.com. 20 units. MINIBAR TV TEL. From $210 double; $230 executive; $350 suite. Rates include continental breakfast, evening wine hour. AE, CB, DC, DISC, MC, V. Valet parking $24. Cable car: California St. line (1 block north).

One of San Francisco's top "business boutique" hotels, the Nob Hill Lambourne bills itself as an urban health spa, offering massages, facials, aromatherapy, and yoga lessons

---

Hotel Trivia

The Ritz-Carlton's bar holds claim to one of the country's largest collection of single-malt scotches. Prices range from $7.25 to $66 per glass.

Free Parking: Pass GO, Do Not Pay $200

With parking fees averaging $20 a night at most hotels (talk about a monopoly), you might want to consider staying at one of the lodgings listed below if you're crazy enough to drive the sinister streets of San Francisco. (As one seasoned driver put it, "We separate pedestrians between the quick and the dead.") All offer free parking—some even offer free covered parking—and are moderate- to low-priced:

- **Beck's Motor Lodge,** 2222 Market St. (at 15th Street); ☎ **800/227-4360** or 415/621-8212. See p. 103.
- **Cow Hollow Motor Inn & Suites,** 2190 Lombard St. (between Steiner and Fillmore streets); ☎ **415/921-5800.** See p. 97.
- **Fort Mason Youth Hostel,** Building 240, Fort Mason; ☎ **415/771-7277.** See p. 97.
- **The Laurel,** 444 Presidio Ave. (at Masonic Avenue); ☎ **800/552-8735** or 415/567-8467. See p. 96.
- **The Phoenix Hotel,** 601 Eddy St. (at Larkin Street); ☎ **800/248-9466** or 415/776-1380. See p. 99
- **The Wharf Inn,** 2601 Mason St. (at Beach Street); ☎ **800/548-9918** or 415/673-7411. See p. 92.

---

to ease corporate-level stress. Even without this hook, the Lambourne deserves a top-of-the-class rating. Sporting one of San Francisco's most stylish interiors, the hotel flaunts the comfort and quality of its contemporary French design. Top-quality, hand-sewn mattresses and goose-down comforters complement a host of in-room accoutrements that include laptop computers with Internet access, fax machines, irons and ironing boards, umbrellas, VCRs, CD player/stereos, kitchenettes, and coffeemakers. Bathrooms have oversized tubs, makeup mirrors, and hair dryers. Suites include an additional sitting room, plus a choice of treadmill, Lifecycle, or rowing machine. The wine hour starts at 6pm. Smokers should seek a room elsewhere: This place prohibits puffing.

Amenities: Spa treatments, in-room massage, concierge, dry cleaning, laundry, newspaper delivery, twice-daily maid service, evening turndown, business services.

MODERATE

✪ **The Nob Hill Inn.** 1000 Pine St. (at Taylor St.), San Francisco, CA 94109. ☎ **415/673-6080.** Fax 415/673-6098. 21 units. TV TEL. $109–$179 double; $229–$259 suite. Rates include continental breakfast, afternoon tea, and sherry. AE, CB, DC, DISC, MC, V. Cable car: California St. line. Bus: 1.

Although most of the rooms at the luxurious Nob Hill Inn are well out of budget range, the three "Gramercy" rooms are among the most opulent you will find in the city for under $110. Built in 1907 as a private home, the four-story inn has been masterfully refurbished with Louis XV antiques, expensive fabrics, museum-quality artwork, and a magnificent etched-glass European-style lift. Even the lowest-priced rooms receive equal attention: large bathrooms with marble sinks and claw-foot tubs, antique furnishings, faux-antique phones and discreetly placed televisions, and a comfortable full-sized bed. Granted, the Gramercy rooms are small. But they're so utterly charming that it's tough to complain, especially when you consider that rates include continental breakfast, afternoon tea and sherry, nightly turndown service, and the distinction of being among the city's most prestigious hotels.

4 North Beach/Fisherman's Wharf

EXPENSIVE

The Sheraton Fisherman's Wharf. 2500 Mason St. (between Beach and North Point sts.), San Francisco, CA 94133. ☎ **800/325-3535** or 415/362-5500. Fax 415/956-5275. www.sheratonwharf.com. 525 units. A/C TV TEL. $180–$300 double; from $500 suite. Extra person $20. Continental breakfast $11.50. AE, CB, DC, DISC, MC, V. Parking $24. Cable car: Powell-Mason line (1 block east, 2 blocks south). Bus: 15, 32, or 42.

Built in the mid-1970s, this modern, four-story hotel isn't the most visually appealing (even the brochure doesn't show it from the outside), but it offers the reliable comforts of a Sheraton in San Francisco's most popular tourist area. In 1995, the hotel spent $4 million renovating the rooms and adding a Corporate Floor that caters exclusively to business travelers.

Dining/Diversions: At press time, the restaurant was undergoing renovations, which should be finished in August, 2000. The new name of the restaurant will be Compass Grill.

Amenities: Concierge, 24-hour room service, outdoor heated swimming pool, access to nearby health club, dry cleaning and laundry, newspaper delivery, express checkout, evening turndown, business center, hair salon, car-rental desk.

The Tuscan Inn. 425 North Point St. (at Mason St.), San Francisco, CA 94133. ☎ **800/648-4626** or 415/561-1100. Fax 415/561-1199. www.tuscaninn.com. 221 units. A/C MINI-BAR TV TEL. $188–$268 double; $268–$298 suite. Rates include coffee, tea, and evening fireside wine reception. AE, DC, DISC, MC, V. Parking $20. Cable car: Powell-Mason line. Bus: 15, 32, or 42 .

The Tuscan Inn is, in my opinion, the best hotel at Fisherman's Wharf. Like an island of respectability in a sea of touristy schlock, it exudes a level of style and comfort far beyond its neighboring competitors. Splurge on parking—actually cheaper than the wharf's outrageously priced garages—then saunter toward the plush lobby, warmed by a grand fireplace. Even the rooms are a definite cut above competing Fisherman's Wharf hotels. Most have writing desks and armchairs. The only caveat is the lack of scenic views—a small price to pay for a good hotel in a great location.

Dining/Diversions: The adjoining Cafe Pescatore, open for breakfast, lunch, and dinner, serves standard Italian fare in an airy setting. (See chapter 6 for complete information.)

Amenities: Concierge, room service, laundry service.

MODERATE

✪ **The Hotel Bohème.** 444 Columbus Ave. (between Vallejo and Green sts.), San Francisco, CA 94133. ☎ **415/433-9111.** Fax 415/362-6292. 15 units. TV TEL. $149–$159 double. Rates include afternoon sherry. AE, CB, DISC, DC, JCB, MC, V. Parking $23 at nearby public garage. Cable car: Powell-Mason line. Bus: 12, 15, 30, 41, 45, or 83.

North Beach romance awaits you at the Bohème. Although located on the busiest strip in the neighborhood, the recently renovated hotel sports a style and demeanor reminiscent of a fine home in upscale Nob Hill. The decor recalls the Beat Generation, which flourished here in the 1950s; rooms are small but hopelessly romantic, with gauze-draped canopies and walls artistically accented with lavender, sage green, black, and pumpkin. The staff is ultra-hospitable, and bonuses include hair dryers in the rooms and sherry in the lobby each afternoon. Some of the greatest cafes, restaurants, bars, and shops in the city lie a few steps away, and Chinatown and Union Square are within walking distance. Take note: While the bathrooms are sweet, they're also absolutely tiny. *Tip:* Request a room off the street side; they're quieter.

The Washington Square Inn. 1660 Stockton St. (between Filbert and Union sts.), San Francisco, CA 94133. ☎ **800/388-0220** or 415/981-4220. Fax 415/397-7242. 15 units, 2 with bathroom across the hall. TV TEL. $125–$220 double. Rates include continental breakfast and afternoon tea, wine,and hors d'oeuvres. AE, CB, DC, DISC, MC, V. Valet parking $20. Bus: 15, 30, 41, or 45.

Reminiscent of a traditional English inn—right down to the cucumber sandwiches served during the afternoon tea, wine, and cheese hour—this small, comely bed-and-breakfast is ideal for older couples who prefer a quieter, more subdued environment than the commotion of downtown San Francisco. It's across from Washington Square in North Beach—a coffee-craver's haven—and within walking distance of Fisherman's Wharf and Chinatown. Each room is decorated in English floral fabrics with quality European antique furnishings and plenty of fresh flowers; all have data ports. Faxes and VCRs are available upon request.

The Wharf Inn. 2601 Mason St. (at Beach St.), San Francisco, CA 94133. ☎ **800/548-9918** or 415/673-7411. Fax 415/776-2181. www.wharfinn.com. 51 units. TV TEL. $95–$179 double; penthouse $270–$375. AE, CB, DC, DISC, MC, V. Free parking. Cable car: Powell-Mason line. Bus: 15, 32, or 42.

Our top choice for budget lodging at Fisherman's Wharf, the Wharf Inn offers above-average accommodations at one of the most popular tourist attractions in the world. The recently refurbished rooms, done in handsome tones of forest green, burgundy, and pale yellow, come with all the standard amenities, plus coffee and tea. The main attribute, however, is location—smack-dab in the middle of the wharf, 2 blocks from Pier 39 and the cable-car turnaround, and within walking distance of the Embarcadero and North Beach. The inn is ideal for car-bound families because parking is free (that saves $25 a day right off the bat), and there's no charge for packing along an extra person.

INEXPENSIVE

✪ **The San Remo Hotel.** 2237 Mason St. (at Chestnut St.), San Francisco, CA 94133. ☎ **800/352-REMO** or 415/776-8688. Fax 415/776-2811. www.sanremohotel.com. 62 units, 1 with bathroom. $60–$85 double; $150 suite. AE, CB, DC, MC, V. Parking $10–$12. Cable car: Powell-Mason line. Bus: 15, 22, 30, or 42.

This small, European-style pensione is one of the best budget hotels in San Francisco. In a quiet North Beach neighborhood, within walking distance of Fisherman's Wharf, the San Remo originally served as a boardinghouse for dock workers displaced by the great fire of 1906. As a result, the rooms are small and bathrooms are shared, but all is forgiven when it comes time to pay the bill. Rooms are decorated in cozy country style, with brass and iron beds; oak, maple, or pine armoires; and wicker furnishings. All have ceiling fans. The immaculate shared bathrooms feature claw-foot tubs and brass pull-chain toilets with oak tanks and brass fixtures. If the penthouse is available, book it: You won't find a more romantic place to stay in San Francisco for so little money. It has its own bathroom, TV, fridge, and patio.

5 The Marina/Pacific Heights/Cow Hollow

VERY EXPENSIVE

✪ **El Drisco.** 2901 Pacific Ave. (at Broderick St.), San Francisco, CA 94115. ☎ **800/634-7277** or 415/346-2880. Fax 415/567-5537. www.eldriscohotel.com. 48 units (some with shower only). A/C MINIBAR TV TEL. $150–$220 double; $375–$650 suite. Rates include buffet breakfast and evening wine hour. AE, DC, DISC, MC, V. No parking available. Bus: 3 or 24.

Perched on one of the most coveted blocks of residential property in all of San Francisco, the El Drisco is one of the finest small hotels in the city. The stately six-story structure was built in 1903 as a boardinghouse for the servants who worked in Pacific Heights. After some major refinements by interior designer Glenn Texeira (who also did the Ritz-Carlton in Manila), it now caters to a far more affluent clientele. The guest rooms—swathed in soothing shades of alabaster, celadon, and buttercup yellow—boast superior fabrics, quality antiques, and exceedingly comfortable mattresses. Standard amenities include two-line phones with modem hookup, CD players, and discreetly hidden VCR/TVs. Suites have a couch that unfolds into a bed (although you would never guess from the looks of it), an additional phone and TV, and superior views. The marble-laden bathrooms are quite spacious, and equipped with hair dryers and plush robes. My favorite room is 304A, a corner suite with an extraordinary view of the Pacific Heights mansions and surrounding bay. Guests eat breakfast in one of the hotel's three quiet, comfortable common rooms, where there's 24-hour coffee and tea service. The only things that prevent a top ranking are the service, which is nowhere near the level of the Ritz-Carlton, and the lack of parking.

✪ **Sherman House.** 2160 Green St. (between Webster and Fillmore sts.), San Francisco, CA 94123. ☎ **800/424-5777** or 415/563-3600. Fax 415/563-1882. 14 units. TV TEL. $360–$475 double; $675–$850 suite. Rates include full breakfast and valet parking. AE, DC, MC, V. Cable car: Powell-Hyde line. Bus: 22, 41, or 45.

How expensive is a night at the Sherman House? Put it this way: If you have to ask, you can't afford it. Built in 1876 by philanthropist and music publisher Leander Sherman, this magnificent Pacific Heights Victorian doubled as his home and playhouse for such guest stars as Enrico Caruso, Lillian Russell, and Victor Herbert. After years of neglect, it took 4 years and a small fortune to restore the estate to its original splendor. Today the Sherman House sets the standard in San Francisco for privacy, personal service, and sumptuous furnishings. All rooms are individually decorated with authentic French Second Empire, Biedermeier, or English Jacobean antiques. They contain queen-sized canopy featherbeds, ultra-rich tapestry fabrics, and down comforters; 13 rooms have fireplaces. Rooms also have TVs, VCRs, and stereos, and black granite bathrooms with bathrobes and whirlpool bathtubs. The English-style Hyde Park room offers a fine bay view from its cushioned window seat. The Jacobean-style Paderewski suite was formerly the billiards room, and it retains the dark wainscoting and beamed ceiling. The least expensive room (no. 203) contains a king bed and English antiques, but lacks a fireplace. The most expensive suite is the Thomas Church Garden suite, which consists of two rooms with 1¹/₂ bathrooms, with an adjoining sunken garden terrace with gazebo and pond.

Dining/Diversions: The dining room has a fine reputation, but because of a zoning dispute, it has lost its license to serve food to nonguests; this change might affect the standards. Main courses run about $27 to $40. Although prices are steep, the meal is quite elaborate.

Amenities: Concierge, room service, butler (who will discreetly unpack luggage), dry cleaning and laundry, complimentary newspaper delivery, massage, twice-daily maid service, baby-sitting, secretarial services, personalized shopping, chauffeuring.

EXPENSIVE

Jackson Court. 2198 Jackson St. (at Buchanan St.), San Francisco, CA 94115. ☎ **415/929-7670.** Fax 415/929-1405. 10 units. TV TEL. $150–$215 double. Rates include continental breakfast. AE, MC, V. Parking on street only. Bus: 1, 12, or 22.

The Jackson Court, a stately three-story brownstone Victorian mansion, is in one of San Francisco's most exclusive neighborhoods, Pacific Heights. Its only fault—that it's

Accommodations Around Town

Abigail Hotel **37**
Archbishop's Mansion **13**
Beck's Motor Lodge **18**
Bed & Breakfast Inn **7**
Castillo Inn **15**
Cow Hollow Motor Inn & Suites **3**
Dolores Park Inn **20**
Edward II Inn & Pub **4**
Fort Mason Youth Hostel **1**
Harbor Court **36**
Herb 'n Inn **21**
Hotel Bohème **28**
Hotel Griffon **32**
Hotel Majestic **10**
Hotel Palomar **35**
Hyatt Regency San Francisco **31**
The Inn at the Opera **14**
Inn on Castro **19**
Jackson Court **8**
The Laurel **9**
Mandarin Oriental **30**
Marina Inn **2**
Park Hyatt **29**
The Parker House **17**
Phoenix Hotel **36**
Queen Anne Hotel **10**
Radisson Miyako Hotel **11**
San Remo Hotel **26**
Seal Rock Inn **12**
Sheraton at Fisherman's Wharf **24**
Sheraton Palace Hotel **33**
The Sherman House **6**
Stanyan Park Hotel **22**
Tuscan Inn **25**
24 Henry **16**
Union Street Inn **5**
Washington Square Inn **27**
The Wharf Inn **23**
W Hotel **34**
Willows Bed & Breakfast Inn **6**

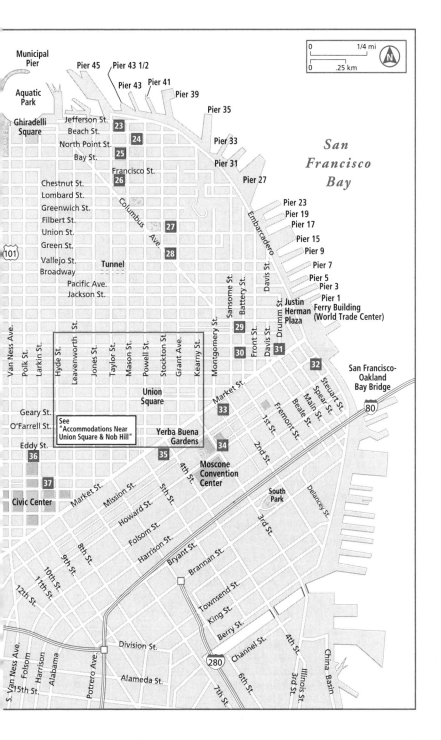

Municipal Pier

Aquatic Park

Ghirardelli Square

Pier 45　Pier 43 1/2

Pier 43　Pier 41

Pier 39

Pier 35

Pier 33

Pier 31

Pier 27

Jefferson St. **23**

Beach St. **24**

North Point St. **25**

Bay St.

Francisco St. **26**

Chestnut St.

Lombard St.

Greenwich St.

Filbert St.

Union St.

Green St.

Vallejo St.

Broadway

Pacific Ave.

Jackson St.

Columbus Ave.

27

28

Tunnel

(101)

San Francisco Bay

Pier 23

Pier 19

Pier 17

Pier 15

Pier 9

Pier 7

Pier 5

Pier 3

Pier 1

Embarcadero

Sansome St.

Battery St.

Davis St.

Drumm St.

Front St.

Davis St.

Justin Herman Plaza

Ferry Building (World Trade Center)

29

30　**31**

32

San Francisco–Oakland Bay Bridge

Van Ness Ave.

Polk St.

Larkin St.

Hyde St.

Leavenworth St.

Jones St.

Taylor St.

Mason St.

Powell St.

Stockton St.

Grant Ave.

Kearny St.

Montgomery St.

Union Square

Geary St.

O'Farrell St.

See "Accommodations Near Union Square & Nob Hill"

Yerba Buena Gardens

Market St. **33**

34

35

Moscone Convention Center

Steuart St.

Spear St.

Main St.

Beale St.

1st St.

Fremont St.

2nd St.

3rd St.

South Park

Delancey St.

(80)

Eddy St. **36**

37

Civic Center

Market St.

Mission St.

Howard St.

Folsom St.

Harrison St.

4th St.

5th St.

8th St.

9th St.

10th St.

11th St.

12th St.

Bryant St.

Brannan St.

Townsend St.

King St.

Berry St.

Channel St.

4th St.

3rd St.

Illinois St.

China Basin

S. Van Ness Ave.

Folsom

Harrison

Alabama

15th St.

Potrero Ave.

Division St.

Alameda St.

(280)

6th St.

7th St.

0　　　1/4 mi

0　　.25 km

far from the action—is also its blessing: If you crave a blissfully quiet vacation in elegant surroundings, this is the place. Each newly renovated room is individually furnished with superior-quality antique furnishings; two have wood-burning fireplaces (*de rigueur* in the winter). The Blue Room features an inviting window seat; the Garden Suite has handcrafted wood paneling and a large picture window looking out on the private garden patio. After breakfast, spend the day browsing the shops along nearby Union and Fillmore streets, and return in time for afternoon tea.

○ **Union Street Inn.** 2229 Union St. (between Fillmore and Steiner sts.), San Francisco, CA 94123. ☎ **415/346-0424.** Fax 415/922-8046. www.unionstreetinn.com. 5 units, 1 cottage. TV TEL. $145–$255 standard double; $255 cottage. Rates include breakfast, hors d'oeuvres, and evening beverages. AE, MC, V. Parking $12. Bus: 22, 28, 41, 45, or 47.

Who would have guessed that one of the most delightful B&Bs in California would be in San Francisco? This two-story Edwardian fronts perpetually busy (and trendy) Union Street, but it's quiet as a church on the inside. The individually decorated rooms are comfortably furnished, and most come with canopied or brass beds with down comforters, fresh flowers, and bay windows (beg for one with a view of the garden). A few even have Jacuzzi tubs. An extended continental breakfast is served in the parlor, in your room, or on an outdoor terrace overlooking a lovely English garden. The ultimate honeymoon retreat is the private carriage house behind the inn, but any room at this warm, friendly inn is guaranteed to please.

MODERATE

○ **Bed & Breakfast Inn.** 4 Charlton Court (off Union St., between Buchanan and Laguna sts.), San Francisco, CA 94123. ☎ **415/921-9784.** Fax 415/921-0544. 13 units, 9 with shared bathroom. $80–$100 double without bathroom, $150 double with bathroom; $250–$300 suite. Rates include continental breakfast. MC, V. Parking $11 at nearby garage. Bus: 41 or 45.

San Francisco's first bed-and-breakfast consists of a trio of Victorian houses all gussied up in English country style, hidden in a cul-de-sac just off Union Street. While it doesn't have quite the casual ambience of neighboring Union Street Inn, the Bed & Breakfast Inn is loaded with charm. Each room is uniquely decorated with family antiques and original art. The Garden Suite—highly recommended for families or groups of four—comes with a fully stocked kitchen, a living room, two bedrooms, two bathrooms (one with a Jacuzzi tub), a study, and French doors leading to the sunroom and garden. Breakfast (freshly baked croissants, fresh fruit, orange juice, and coffee, tea, or cocoa) is either brought to your room with a morning newspaper or served in a sunny Victorian breakfast room with antique china.

The Laurel. 444 Presidio Ave. (at Masonic Ave.), San Francisco, CA 94115. ☎ **800/ 552-8735** or 415/567-8467. Fax: 415/928-1866. www.thelaurelinn.com. 49 units. TV TEL. $119–$149 double. Rates include continental breakfast. AE, MC, V. Free parking. Muni Metro: 1, 43. Pets accepted.

If you don't mind being out of the downtown area, this lovely new hotel is one of the most tranquil, affordable places to rest your head. Tucked just beyond the southern-most tip of the Presidio, the outside is nothing impressive—just another motor inn. And that's what it was until the hotel group Joie de Vivre bought it and breathed new life into the place. Now it serves as a sophisticated spot for the budget-minded traveler. Decor is tres chic and modern, with Zen-like influences. Some rooms have excellent city views; all have CD players, VCRs, cable TV, voicemail, data ports, irons, ironing boards, and spiffy bathrooms. But wait! There's more—concierge services, continental breakfast, 24-hour coffee and tea service, access to nearby fitness facilities, pet-friendly rooms, and, best of all, free parking!

INEXPENSIVE

Cow Hollow Motor Inn & Suites. 2190 Lombard St. (between Steiner and Fillmore sts.), San Francisco, CA 94123. ☎ **415/921-5800.** Fax 415/922-8515. 130 units. A/C TV TEL. $98 double; from $195 suite. Extra person $10. AE, DC, MC, V. Free parking. Bus: 28, 43, or 76.

If you're less interested in being downtown than in playing in and around the beautiful bayfront Marina, check out this modest brick hotel on busy Lombard Street. There's no fancy theme, but each room has cable TV, free local phone calls, free covered parking, and a coffeemaker. All the rooms were renovated in 1996, so you'll be sure to sleep on a firm mattress surrounded by clean, new carpeting and drapes. Families will appreciate the one- and two-bedroom suites, which have full kitchens and dining areas.

✪ **Edward II Inn & Pub.** 3155 Scott St. (at Lombard St.), San Francisco, CA 94123. ☎ **800/473-2846** or 415/922-3000. Fax 415/931-5784. www.citysearch.com/sfo/edwardiiinn. 32 units, 21 with bathroom. TV TEL. $77–$85 double with shared bathroom, $105 double with private bathroom; $175–$235 suite or cottage. Rates include continental breakfast and evening sherry. AE, MC, V. Self-parking $10 across the street. Bus: 28, 43, or 76.

This self-styled three-story "English country" inn has a room for almost anyone's budget, ranging from pensione units with shared bathrooms to luxuriously appointed suites and cottages with living rooms, kitchens, and whirlpool bathtubs. Originally built to house guests who attended the 1915 Pan-Pacific Exposition, it's now run by innkeepers Denise and Bob Holland, who have done a fantastic job maintaining its worldly charm. Regardless of price, all rooms are spotless, comfortably appointed with cozy antique furnishings and plenty of fresh flowers. The only caveat is that its Lombard Street location is usually congested with traffic. Nearby Chestnut and Union Streets offer some of the best shopping and dining in the city. The adjoining pub serves breakfast and evening drinks.

Fort Mason Youth Hostel. Fort Mason, Building 240, San Francisco, CA 94123. ☎ **415/771-7277.** Fax 415/771-1468. 170 beds. $19–$20 per night. Rates include breakfast. MC, V. Free parking. Bus: 28, 30, 42, 47, or 49.

Unbelievable but true—you can get front-row bay views for a mere $19 nightly. The hostel, on national park property, provides dorm-style accommodations and offers easy access to the Marina's shops and restaurants. Rooms sleep 2 to 12 people; communal space includes a fireplace, pool table, kitchen, dining room, coffee bar, and laundry facilities. The breakfast alone practically makes it worth the price. Make reservations well in advance.

✪ **The Marina Inn.** 3110 Octavia St. (at Lombard St.), San Francisco, CA 94123. ☎ **800/274-1420** or 415/928-1000. Fax 415/928-5909. 40 units. TV TEL. Nov–Feb $65–$105 double; Mar–May $75–$115 double; June–Oct $85–$125 double. Rates include continental breakfast. AE, MC, V. Bus: 28, 30, 43, or 76.

The Marina Inn is one of the best low-priced hotels in San Francisco. How it offers so much for so little is mystifying. Each guest room in the 1924 four-story Victorian looks like something from a country furnishings catalog, complete with rustic pinewood furniture, a four-poster bed with silk-soft comforter and new mattress, pretty wallpaper, and soothing tones of rose, hunter green, and pale yellow. You also get new remote-control televisions discreetly hidden in pine cabinetry and nightly turndown service with chocolates on your pillow—all for as little as *$65 a night!* Combine that with continental breakfast, afternoon sherry, friendly service, and an armada of shops and restaurants within easy walking distance, and there you have it: My no. 1 choice for Best Overall Value.

6 Japantown & Environs

EXPENSIVE

The Archbishop's Mansion. 1000 Fulton St. (at Steiner St.), San Francisco, CA 94117. ☎ **800/543-5820** or 415/563-7872. Fax 415/885-3193. 15 units. TV TEL. $159–$419 double. Rates include continental breakfast and evening wine. AE, CB, DC, MC, V. Limited free parking. Bus: 5 or 22.

One thing is certain: The archbishop who built this 1904 belle époque beauty was no Puritan. Drippingly romantic, the Archbishop's Mansion is one of the most opulent and fabulously adorned B&Bs you could possibly imagine. The Don Giovanni suite—larger than most San Francisco houses—holds a huge, cherub-encrusted four-poster bed imported from a French castle, a palatial fireplace, elaborately embroidered linens, and a seven-head shower that you'll never want to leave. Slightly closer to earth is the Carmen suite, which has a deadly romantic combination of a claw-foot bathtub fronting a wood-burning fireplace. In the morning, breakfast is delivered to the guest rooms, and in the evening, wine is served in the elegant parlor.

Amenities: Concierge, limited room service, laundry and valet, complimentary morning newspaper, limousine service.

✪ **The Hotel Majestic.** 1500 Sutter St. (between Octavia and Gough sts.), San Francisco, CA 94109. ☎ **800/869-8966** or 415/441-1100. Fax 415/673-7331. 58 units. TV TEL. $159–$179 double; from $450 suite. Continental breakfast $8.50. Group, government, corporate, and relocation rates available. AE, CB, DC, DISC, MC, V. Valet parking $18. Bus: 2, 4, 42, 47, or 49.

Both tourists and business travelers adore the Majestic because it covers every professional need while retaining the ambience of a luxurious Old World hotel. It was built in 1902, and the lobby alone sweeps guests into another era, with an overabundance of tapestries, tasseled brocades, Corinthian columns, and intricate, lavish detail.

Rooms are furnished with French and English antiques, the centerpiece of many being a large four-poster canopy bed; you'll also find custom-made, mirrored armoires and antique reproductions. All drapes, fabrics, carpet, and bedspreads were replaced in 1997, and half the bathrooms and guest rooms underwent a $2 million renovation in 1999, which ensures you'll rest not only in style, but in fresh surroundings as well. Each room contains a full-sized, well-lit desk and bathrobes; some have fireplaces.

Dining/Diversions: Café Majestic and Bar, which serves California-Asian fare in a romantic setting, attracts a local clientele. The adjacent bar has a French mahogany marble-topped bar and a collection of African butterflies.

Amenities: Concierge, 24-hour room service, valet, dry cleaning, laundry service, complimentary newspaper, in-room massage, baby-sitting, secretarial service, courtesy car on weekdays. Sherry and fresh-baked cookies from 6 to 8pm nightly.

The Radisson Miyako Hotel. 1625 Post St. (at Laguna St.), San Francisco, CA 94115. ☎ **800/533-4557** or 415/922-3200. Fax 415/921-0417. www.miyakosf.com. 218 units. MINIBAR TV TEL. $209–$229 double or twin; from $299 suite. Children under 13 free in parents' rm. AE, CB, DC, DISC, JCB, MC, V. Valet parking $20; self-parking $10. Bus: 2, 3, 4, or 38.

Japantown's Miyako is a tranquil alternative to staying downtown, and it's only about a mile away. The 15-story tower and five-story Garden Wing overlook the Japan Center, which is home to the city's largest complex of Japanese shops and restaurants and a huge movie complex. The hotel manages to maintain a feeling of peace and quiet you'd expect somewhere much more remote. Rooms are Zen-like with East-meets-West decor, plus such amenities as irons and ironing boards, hair dryers, and dual-line data ports. The Western-style (don't think cowboy) rooms are fine, but romantics and adventurers should opt for the traditional-style Japanese rooms with tatami mats and futons, a *tokonoma* (alcove for displaying art), and shoji screens that slide away to frame views of the city. Two futon luxury suites have Japanese rock gardens and deep-tub Japanese bathrooms. A bonus: Fillmore Street's upscale boutiques are a few blocks away.

Dining/Diversions: A new restaurant is scheduled to replace YOYO Bistro in fall 2000.

Amenities: Limited concierge and room service, dry cleaning, newspaper delivery, evening turndown, in-room shiatsu massage, on-call baby-sitting, express checkout, limited exercise room, access to nearby health club, business center, conference rooms.

MODERATE

The Queen Anne Hotel. 1590 Sutter St. (between Gough and Octavia sts.), San Francisco, CA 94109. ☎ **800/227-3970** or 415/441-2828. Fax 415/775-5212. www.queenanne.com. 48 units. TV TEL. $130–$180 double; $185–$295 suite. Extra person $10. Rates include continental breakfast and afternoon tea and sherry. AE, CB, DC, DISC, MC, V. Parking $14. Bus: 2, 3, or 4.

The majestic 1890 Victorian, which was once a grooming school for upper-class young women, is today a stunning hotel. Restored in 1981 and renovated in 1995, the four-story building recalls San Francisco's golden days. Walk under rich, red drapery to the lavish "grand salon" lobby, complete with English oak paneling and period antiques. Rooms contain more antiques—armoires, marble-top dressers, and other Victorian pieces. Some have corner turret bay windows that look out on tree-lined streets, as well as separate parlor areas and wet bars; others have cozy reading nooks and fireplaces. All rooms have a telephone in the bathroom and a computer hookup. Guests can relax in the parlor, with an impressive floor-to-ceiling fireplace, or in the hotel library. The hotel has room service and a concierge, and provides the morning newspaper. There's also access to an off-premises health club with a lap pool. If you don't mind staying outside the downtown area, this hotel comes highly recommended.

7 Civic Center

MODERATE

✪ **The Phoenix Hotel.** 601 Eddy St. (at Larkin St.), San Francisco, CA 94109. ☎ **800/248-9466** or 415/776-1380. Fax 415/885-3109. www.sftrips.com. 44 units. TV TEL. $119–$135 double; $175–$195 suite. Rates include continental breakfast. AE, DC, MC, V. Free parking. Bus: 19, 31, 38, 42, or 47.

If you'd like to tell your friends back home that you've stayed in the same hotel as Linda Ronstadt, Arlo Guthrie, and the Red Hot Chili Peppers, this is the place. *People* described it as the hippest hotel in town. On the fringes of San Francisco's less-than-pleasant Tenderloin District, the retro 1950s-style hotel is a gathering place for visiting rock musicians, writers, and filmmakers who crave a dose of southern California—hence the palm trees and pastel colors. The focal point of the Palm Springs–style hotel is a small, heated outdoor pool adorned with a mural by artist Francis Forlenza and ensconced in a modern-sculpture garden.

The rooms, while far from plush, were upgraded in 1998 and are comfortably equipped with bright, festive furnishings, potted plants, and original local art. In addition to the usual amenities, the inn offers VCRs and movies on request. Services include an on-call massage therapist, concierge, laundry and valet, and—whoo-hoo!—free parking. Adjoining the hotel is Backflip (☎ **415/771-3135**), an oh-so-blue cocktail lounge serving tapas, Caribbean-style appetizers, and a heck of a lot of San Francisco attitude.

INEXPENSIVE

The Abigail Hotel. 246 McAllister St. (between Hyde and Larkin sts.), San Francisco, CA 94102. ☎ **800/243-6510** or 415/861-9728. Fax 415/861-5848. www.theabigail.com. 61 units. TV TEL. $105 standard double; $125 deluxe double; $250 suite. Extra person $10. Rates include continental breakfast. AE, CB, DC, DISC, MC, V. Valet parking $21. Muni Metro: All Market St. trams. Bus: All Market St. buses.

The Abigail is one of San Francisco's rare sleeper hotels: Although it doesn't get much press, it's one of the better affordable lodgings in the city. Built in 1925 to house celebrities performing at the world-renowned Fox Theater, the Abigail more than makes up in charm what it lacks in luxury. The rooms, while on the small side, are cute and comfortably furnished with cozy antiques and down comforters. Morning coffee, pastries, and complimentary newspapers greet you in the beautiful faux-marble lobby designed by Shawn Hall; the vegan restaurant, Millennium (see chapter 6 for complete information), serves dinner.

8 SoMa

VERY EXPENSIVE

The Argent Hotel. 50 Third St. (between Market and Mission sts.), San Francisco, CA 94103. ☎ **800/505-9039** or 415/974-6400. Fax 415/495-6152. www.argenthotel.com. 667 units. A/C MINIBAR TV TEL. $245–$265 double; from $420 suite. AE, DC, DISC, JCB, MC, V. Parking $26. Muni Metro: All Market St. trams. Bus: All Market St. buses.

The large number of rooms and fine location—just a block south of Market Street, and a block from the Moscone Convention Center—make the Argent attractive to both groups and business travelers. Rooms have floor-to-ceiling windows and are well outfitted with three telephones (with voicemail and data ports). Corner suites look across the Bay Bridge and to Candlestick ("3Com") Park. Rates for Executive Level rooms include continental breakfast and evening hors d'oeuvres.

Dining/Diversions: Café Fifty-Three serves three meals daily, plus a special Sunday brunch, and offers garden terrace seating. The adjacent lobby bar serves cocktails, wine, beer, and appetizers.

Amenities: Concierge, room service, laundry and valet, twice-daily maid service, fitness center, business center.

The Harbor Court. 165 Steuart St. (between Mission and Howard sts.), San Francisco, CA 94105. ☎ **800/346-0555** in the U.S., or 415/882-1300. Fax 415/882-1313. 131 units. A/C MINIBAR TV TEL. $175–$325 double. Continental breakfast $12. AE, CB, DC, MC, V. Parking $24. Muni Metro: Embarcadero. Bus: 14, 32, or 80X.

When the Embarcadero Freeway was torn down after the Big One in 1989, one of the major benefactors was the Harbor Court hotel: Its backyard view went from a wall of cement to a dazzling vista of the Bay Bridge (be sure to request a bay-view room, which is $50 extra). Located just off the Embarcadero at the edge of the Financial District, this former YMCA books a lot of corporate travelers, but anyone who seeks stylish, high-quality accommodations—half-canopy beds, large armoires, writing desks, soundproofed windows—with a superb view and lively scene will be perfectly content here. A major bonus for health nuts is the free use of the adjoining fitness club, a top-quality facility with an indoor Olympic-size swimming pool.

Amenities: Concierge, limited room service, dry cleaning, laundry, secretarial services, newspaper delivery, express checkout, valet, courtesy car, access to health club, free refreshments in lobby.

The Hotel Griffon. 155 Steuart St. (between Mission and Howard sts.), San Francisco, CA 94105. ☎ **800/321-2201** or 415/495-2100. Fax 415/495-3522. www.hotelgriffon.com. 62 units. A/C MINIBAR TV TEL. $230–$300 double; $375–$415 suite. Rates include continental breakfast and newspaper. AE, CB, DC, DISC, MC, V. Parking $18. All Market St. buses, BART, and ferries.

After pumping a cool $10 million into a complete rehab in 1989, the Hotel Griffon emerged as a top contender among San Francisco's small hotels. Ideally situated on the historic waterfront, steps from the heart of the Financial District, the Griffon is impeccably outfitted. It boasts contemporary features such as whitewashed brick walls, lofty ceilings, marble vanities, window seats, cherrywood furniture, and art-deco-style lamps (really, this place is smooth). Be sure to request a bay-view room overlooking the Bay Bridge—the added perks and view make it well worth the extra cost.

Dining/Diversions: Red Herring serves creative seafood in its swank dining room complete with a "bait" bar.

Amenities: Concierge, limited room service, laundry and valet, in-room massage, secretarial services, free access to nearby deluxe health center, complimentary town car to the Financial District from 7 to 9am.

San Francisco Marriott. 55 Fourth St. (between Market and Mission sts.), San Francisco, CA 94103. ☎ **800/228-9290** or 415/896-1600. Fax 415/777-2799. 1,500 units. A/C MINIBAR TV TEL. $179–$259 double; $320–$2,700 suite. AE, CB, DC, JCB, MC, V. Parking $27. Cable car: Powell-Hyde and Powell-Mason lines (3 blocks west). Muni Metro: All Market St. trams. Bus: All Market St. buses.

Some call it a masterpiece; others liken it to the world's biggest parking meter. Regardless, the Marriott is one of the largest buildings in the city, making it a popular stop for convention-goers and those looking for a room with a view. Fortunately, the controversy does not extend to the recently renovated rooms, so expect pleasant accommodations, floral patterns, large bathrooms and beds, and exceptional city vistas. Upon arrival, enter from Fourth Street, between Market and Mission, to avoid a long trek to the registration area.

Dining/Diversions: Kinoko, a Japanese teppanyaki restaurant and sushi bar, serves dinner only. The Garden Terrace, facing the hotel's central fountain, has a breakfast bar and two buffets that prepare made-to-order omelets; there is also a varied lunch and dinner menu. There's a lounge in the atrium; the View Lounge (which also serves a light lunch menu) has a panoramic view of the bay and Golden Gate Bridge (assuming there's no fog), as well as live entertainment and a sports bar.

Amenities: Indoor pool and health club, business center, tour desk, car rental, gift shop.

✪ **W San Francisco Hotel.** 181 Third St. (between Mission and Howard sts), San Francisco, CA 94103. ☎ **800/877-WHOTEL** or 415/777-5300. Fax 415/817-7800. 423 units. AC MINIBAR TV TEL. From $399 double; from $900 suite. AE, DC, DISC, JCB, MC, V. Valet parking $33. Muni Metro: J, K, L, or M to Montgomery. Bus: 15, 30, or 45.

Starwood Hotels & Resorts' 31-story property is as modern and hip as its fashionable clientele. Sophisticated, sleek, and stylish, it suits its neighbors, which include the Museum of Modern Art, the Moscone Center, and the Metreon Sony entertainment center. The striking gray granite facade, piped with polished black stone, complements the octagonal three-story glass entrance and lobby. The hip, urban style extends to the guest rooms, which have a residential feel. All contain a "luxury" bed with a pillow-top mattress, goose-down comforters and pillows, an oversized dark wood desk, upholstered chaise lounge, and louvered blinds that open to (usually) great city views.

Each room contains a coffeemaker, bathrobe, safe, iron, ironing board, and hair dryer. The compact media wall comes complete with a Sony CD and video cassette player, an extensive CD library, a 27-inch color TV, and Internet service (with an infrared keyboard). The bath? Supersleek and stocked with Aveda products. All in all, as of 2000 this is the place to be.

Dining/Diversions: The restaurant, XYZ, is deliciously sleek; unfortunately, the food can be less polished. Still, its marble tables, high-backed suede banquettes, high ceilings, and dark-wood accents make for a sexy spot to dine on California cuisine with French influences. It serves three meals daily. Although hanging at hotels is quite a rarity in these parts, the bar has even become a spot for locals to visit.

Amenities: Portable two-line phone with data port, conference calling, and voice-mail; TV with Internet access; fax machine, copier, and printer available; 24-hour concierge and room service. Business amenities and services (including business center), atrium pool and whirlpool, fitness center, outdoor sundeck.

EXPENSIVE

Hotel Palomar. 12 Fourth St. (at Mission St.) San Francisco, CA., 94103. ☎ **877/ 294-9711** or 415/348-1111. Fax 415-348 0302. www.hotelpalomar.com. 198 units. A/C TV TEL. From $170 double; from $325 suite. AE, DC, DISC, JCB, MC, V. Parking: $29. Metro: I5, 30, 8, and all underground Muni and BART.

The Kimpton Group's latest downtown property occupies the top five floors of a refurbished 1907 landmark office building. It's the group's most refined boutique property, with French-inspired interiors designed by Cheryl Rowley. The vibe is all about luxury. Rooms have an updated twist of 1930s modern design, with artful, understated textural elements such as emerald-tone velvets, fine woods, and raffia. The dining room is considered one of the hottest (and most expensive) dining spots of 2000. Tailored lines and rich textures throughout lend a sophisticated, fresh aspect to the overall air of elegance. Rooms contain printers, copiers, faxes, and two-line cordless phones.

Dining/Diversions: Executive chef George Morrone's Fifth Floor Restaurant is one of the hottest tickets in town, so book long before you arrive. It serves modern French cuisine at dinner Monday through Saturday.

Amenities: Concierge, room service, fitness center, complimentary shoeshine and morning paper, valet and laundry, secretarial and business services, safe deposit boxes, and valet parking.

9 The Castro

Everyone is welcome, but most hotels in the Castro cater to a gay and lesbian clientele. Unfortunately, there are few choices, and their amenities don't really compare to those at most of the better hotels in the city.

MODERATE

Dolores Park Inn. c/o Bernie H. Vielwerth, 3641 17th St., San Francisco, CA 94114. ☎/fax **415/621-0482** (call before faxing). 3 units, none with bathroom; 1 kitchenette suite. TV. $129–$229 double; $229 suite. Minimum stay 2 nights for inn, 4 nights for Carriage House. MC, V. Free parking. Muni Metro: F, J, K, L, or M. Bus: 22 or 24.

Conveniently located in the Castro, this inn is within easy walking distance of many shops and clubs and a quick jaunt to downtown. Each room is individually decorated with beautiful antiques and a queen-sized bed. Rumor has it that a few celebrities (Tom Cruise, members of the *Sister Act* cast, Robert Downey, Jr., and others) have stayed here to avoid hype. The owner takes special care in providing a warm, hospitable, and romantic environment with helpful service. The suite has a 20-foot sundeck looking up at Twin Peaks, a kitchen, cable TV/VCR, and four-poster bed. The Carriage House offers a heated marble floor, kitchen, washer/dryer, fireplace, Jacuzzi, and VCR. No smoking.

The Inn on Castro. 321 Castro St. (at Market St.), San Francisco, CA 94114. ☎ **415/ 861-0321.** 8 units (2 with bathroom across the hall). TV TEL. $95–$108 double; $125–$155 suite. Rates include full breakfast and evening brandy. AE, MC, V. Muni Metro: Castro.

One of the better choices in the Castro, half a block from all the action, is this Edwardian-style inn decorated with contemporary furnishings, original modern art, and fresh flowers throughout. Most rooms share a small back patio, and the suite has a private outdoor sitting area. There's also a two-bedroom apartment ($155 to $250).

✪ **The Parker House.** 520 Church St. (between 17th and 18th sts.), San Francisco, CA 94114. ☎ **888/520-PARK** or 415/621-3222. Fax 415/621-4139. www.parkerguesthouse. com. 10 units. TV TEL. $109–$199 double. Rates include continental breakfast. AE, DISC, MC, V. Muni Metro: J Church. Bus: 22, 33. Self-parking $15.

This is the best B&B option in the Castro. The neighborhood's "newest and grandest guesthouse" is a 5,000-square-foot, 1909 Edwardian in a cheery neighborhood a few blocks from the heart of the action and half a block from grassy Dolores Park. The Parker House has a well-decorated common library with fireplace and piano, breakfast room, formal dining room, and garden with patio. There's also a "fern den," fountains, spa, and steam room. Each guest room has voicemail, cable TV, and modem hookups.

INEXPENSIVE

Beck's Motor Lodge. 2222 Market St. (at 15th St.), San Francisco, CA 94114. ☎ **800/ 227-4360** in the U.S., except CA, or 415/621-8212 (from CA, call collect to make reservations). Fax 415/241-0435. 58 units. TV TEL. $85–$135 double. AE, CB, DC, DISC, MC, V. Free parking. Metro: F. Bus: 8 or 37.

In a town where DINK (double income, no kids) tourists happily spend fistfuls of money, you'd think someone would create a gay luxury hotel—or even a moderate hotel, for that matter. But absurdly, the most commercial and modern accommodation in the touristy Castro is this run-of-the-mill motel. Standard but contemporary, the ultra-tidy rooms include coffeemakers, refrigerators, and access to coin-operated washing machines, a sundeck overlooking upper Market Street, and free parking. Unless you're into homey B&Bs, this is really your only choice in the area—fortunately, it's very well maintained.

The Castillo Inn. 48 Henry St., San Francisco, CA 94114. ☎ **800/865-5112** or 415/864-5111. Fax 415/641-1321. 5 units, none with bathroom. $75 double; $160 suite. Rates include continental breakfast. Suite rate negotiable depending on season and number of guests. AE, MC, V. Muni Metro: F, K, L, or M. Bus: 8, 22, 24, or 37.

Just 2 minutes from the heart of the Castro, this charming little house provides a safe, quiet environment. Catering mostly to gay men (although anyone is welcome), the Castillo makes its clientele feel at home. Hardwood floors decorated with throw rugs aid in the warmth. Rooms are small yet cozy; the front desk uses voicemail to collect phone messages. The Castillo also offers the shared use of a large refrigerator and microwave oven in the kitchen. One enormous, two-bedroom suite that sleeps four comfortably has a full kitchen, VCR, parking, and a deck.

24 Henry. 24 Henry St. (at Noe St.), San Francisco, CA 94114. ☎ **800/900-5686** or 415/864-5686. Fax 415/864-0406. E-mail: HenryST24@aol.com. 6 units, 2 with bathroom.

TEL. $80–$95 double; $95 suite. Extra person $25. Rates include continental breakfast. AE, MC, V. Muni Metro: F, J, K, L, M, or N. Bus: 8, 22 or 37.

Its Castro location is not the only thing that makes 24 Henry a good choice for gay travelers. The building, an 1870s Victorian on a serene side street, is quite charming. The five guest rooms have high ceilings, period furniture, and voicemail. Guests tired of tromping around the neighborhood can watch TV or read in the double parlor (where breakfast is served). The apartment suite sleeps three comfortably and has a separate entrance and TV. All rooms are nonsmoking. Under the same management, a house a few blocks away, at 18th Street between Castro and Hartford streets, also offers five rooms, two of which have bathrooms.

The Willows Bed & Breakfast Inn. 710 14th St. (between Church and Market sts.), San Francisco, CA 94114. ☎ **415/431-4770.** Fax 415/431-5295. www.WillowsSF.com. 12 units, none with bathroom. TEL. $92–$120 double; $120–$140 suite. Rates include continental breakfast. AE, DISC, MC, V. Limited on-street parking. Muni Metro: Church St. Station (across the street) or F. Bus: 22 or 37.

Right in the heart of the Castro, the Willows Inn employs a staff eager to greet and attend to visitors. The country and antique willow furnishings don't strictly suit a 1903 Edwardian home, but everything's quite comfortable—especially considering the extras, which include an expanded continental breakfast (fresh fruit, yogurt, baked goods, gourmet coffee, assorted teas, and fresh orange juice), the morning paper, and nightly cocktails. The homey rooms vary in size from large (queen bed) to smaller (double bed) and are priced accordingly.

10 Haight-Ashbury

MODERATE

Stanyan Park Hotel. 750 Stanyan St. (at Waller St.), San Francisco, CA 94117. ☎ **415/ 751-1000.** Fax 415/668-5454. www.stanyanpark.com. 36 units. TV TEL. $115–$170 double; $249–$300 suite. Rates include continental breakfast and afternoon tea service. Rollaway $20; cribs free. AE, CB, DC, DISC, MC, V. Off-site parking $12. Muni Metro: N. Bus: 7, 33, 43, 66, 71, or 73.

The only real hotel on the east end of Golden Gate Park, this small inn is your only non-B&B option in Haight-Ashbury. The Victorian structure has operated as a hotel under a variety of names since 1904 and is on the National Register of Historic Places. It's a charming, three-story establishment decorated with antique furnishings, Victorian wallpaper, and pastel quilts, curtains, and carpets. Bathrooms come complete with massaging showerhead, shampoos, and fancy soaps.

There are six one- and two-bedroom suites. Each has a full kitchen and formal dining and living rooms, and can sleep up to six comfortably; they're ideal for families. There's tea service each afternoon and evening. Continental breakfast is served in a pleasant room off the lobby. All rooms are nonsmoking.

INEXPENSIVE

The Herb 'n Inn. 525 Ashbury St. (between Page and Haight sts.), San Francisco, CA 94117. ☎ **415/553-8542.** Fax 415/553-8541. 4 units. TV (on request). $70–$85 double. Rates include full breakfast. 2-night minimum stay. MC, V. Parking with advance notice. Bus: 6, 7, 33, 43, 66, or 71.

For those of you who want to immerse yourself in the sights and sounds of San Francisco's legendary Haight-Ashbury district without compromising on high-quality (and low-cost) accommodations, there's The Herb 'n Inn. Run by sister-brother duo Pam and Bruce Brennan—who know the history and highlights of the Haight better than anyone—this modernized Victorian inn consists of four attractive guest rooms, a huge country-style kitchen, a sunny back garden, and the beginnings of Bruce's Psychedelic History Museum (a.k.a. the dining room). The Cilantro Room, besides being the largest, has the only private bathroom and a view of the garden—all for only $10 extra per night. The Tarragon Room has two small beds and a private deck (optimal for smokers, who aren't allowed to fire up inside the house); the large Coriander Room faces the near-mythical intersection of Haight and Ashbury streets, where there's always something going on. A hearty breakfast—such as waffles, crêpes, popovers, or potato pancakes—is included, as are office services (including forwarded e-mail), personal city tours à la Bruce, and plenty of free advice on how to spend your day in the city. Kids and gay couples are welcome. *Note:* This place books up months in advance, so plan ahead!

11 Near the Airport

Comfort Suites. 121 E. Grand Ave., South San Francisco, CA 94080. ☎ **800/228-5150** or 650/589-7100. Fax 650/589-7796. 168 units. A/C TV TEL. $139 double. AE, DC, DISC, MC, V.

Two miles north of the airport, well outside the heart of the city, Comfort Suites is a well-appointed option for travelers on the way in or out of town. Each studio-suite has a king bed, queen sleeper sofa (great for the kids), fridge, microwave, coffeemaker, iron and ironing board, and hair dryer. There are enough pay-cable channels to keep you glued to your TV set for an entire day, although you'll have to fight the kids over whether it's the HBO special or another round of Nintendo. Rooms are fine, but the freebies are most attractive: continental breakfast, evening soup-and-bread bar, airport shuttle, and use of the outdoor hot tub.

Embassy Suites. 250 Gateway Blvd., South San Francisco, CA 94080. ☎ **800/362-2779** or 650/589-3400. Fax 650/876-0305. www.embassy-suites.com. 312 units. A/C MINIBAR TV TEL. $119–$209 double. Rates include breakfast. AE, DC, MC, V.

Your best pick of the airport chain hotels—and the most expensive—is Embassy Suites, which does its darnedest to make you forget you're in the middle of drab South San Francisco. The property has an indoor pool, whirlpool, sauna, courtyard with a fountain, palm plants, and bar/restaurant. Each tastefully decorated two-room suite has a wet bar, fridge, microwave, coffeemaker, hair dryer, iron and ironing board, two TVs, and two phones. A cooked-to-order breakfast comes before you're whisked to the airport on the free shuttle.

Holiday Inn. San Francisco International Airport North, 275 S. Airport Blvd. (off Hwy. 101), South San Francisco, CA 94080. ☎ **800/HOLIDAY** or 650/873-3550. Fax 650/873-4524. 224 units. A/C MINIBAR TV TEL. $85–$169 double. AE, CB, DC, DISC, MC, V.

Considering all the free amenities—health spa, movie channels, 24-hour airport shuttle, guest parking—a room at this Holiday Inn is surprisingly reasonable. Granted, there's nary a thing to see or do within a 10-mile radius, but as a stop before a morning flight, the Holiday Inn is always a safe bet: The airport is a mere 5 minutes away on the hotel's complimentary shuttle. The rooms are classic Holiday Inn: large, clean, and inoffensively dull, with the usual amenities such as coffeemakers and hair dryers. To keep you occupied before your flight departs, the hotel has a gym. It also offers full business services, a gift shop, and Rookie's Sports Bar & Grill, which does a brisk bar business most evenings. The smaller City Café serves American-style breakfast, lunch, and dinner.

San Francisco Airport North Travelodge. 326 S. Airport Blvd. (off Hwy. 101), South San Francisco, CA 94080. ☎ **800/578-7878** or 650/583-9600. Fax 650/873-9392. 197 units. A/C TV TEL. $90–$99 double. AE, CB, DC, DISC, MC, V.

The Travelodge is a good choice for families, mainly because of the hotel's large heated pool, which allows the kids to let off some steam while the parents bask in South San Francisco's typically balmy weather. Yes, the rooms are as ordinary as you'd expect from a Travelodge, but they're comfortable and come with Showtime, in-room coffee and tea, voicemail, a copy of *USA Today,* and free toll-free and credit-card calls. The clincher is the 24-hour complimentary shuttle, which makes the 2-mile trip to SFO in 5 minutes. A 24-hour restaurant serving standard American grub is nearby, as is Rookie's Sports Bar & Grill, at the Holiday Inn down the street.

Where to Dine 6

San Francisco's restaurants are so renowned that many people visit just to eat—and with good reason. The city's brilliant chefs, combined with California's abundance of organic produce, seafood, and free-range meats, guarantee some of the world's finest dining, and fierce competition means slackers need not apply to any local kitchen.

Unfortunately, kitchen talent and quality ingredients are costing more and more. Combine that with the onslaught of new millionaire residents to whom foie gras and sweetbreads are as common as bread and butter, and the results are clear: The price of dining in the average San Francisco restaurant has gone up by 30% to 50% in the past 5 years! But there are still bargains to be found, and plenty of places are so good, you might not mind spending $25 to $35 per entree.

It's not all about chi-chi fare. As one of the world's cultural cross-roads, the city is blessed with a cornucopia of cuisines. Afghan, Cajun, Burmese, Jewish, Moroccan, Persian, Cambodian, vegan—whatever you're in the mood for, this town has it covered. So book your reservations and break out the credit cards, because half the fun of visiting San Francisco is the rare opportunity to sample the flavors of the world in one fell swoop.

As you join the locals in their most beloved pastime, there are a few things you should keep in mind:

- If you want a table at the expensive restaurants with the best reputations, you probably need to book 6 to 8 weeks ahead for weekends, and a couple of weeks ahead for weekdays.
- If there's a long wait for a free table, ask if you can order at the bar, which is often faster and more fun.
- Don't leave *anything* valuable in your car while dining, particularly in or near high-crime areas. Give the parking valet only the key to your car, *not* your hotel room or house key.
- Remember: It is against the law to smoke in any restaurant in San Francisco, even if it has a separate bar or lounge area. You're welcome to smoke outside, however.

1 Restaurants by Cuisine

AMERICAN
Beach Chalet Brewery &
   Restaurant (p. *154*)
The Big Four (p. *121*)
Bix (p. *126*)
Boulevard (p. *143*)
Carnelian Room (p. *117*)
Chow (p. *152*)
Doidge's (p. *139*)
Dottie's True Blue Café (p. *116*)
Firewood Café (p. *153*)
Fog City Diner (p. *129*)
Gordon's House of Fine
   Eats (p. *147*)
Hamburger Mary's (p. *146*)
Hard Rock Cafe (p. *125*)
Johnfrank (p. *152*)
Mecca (p. *151*)
Mel's Diner (p. *139*)
Mo's Gourmet Burgers (p. *132*)
Postrio (p. *114*)
Sears Fine Foods (p. *116*)
Tommy's Joynt (p. *142*)
The Waterfront Restaurant &
   Cafe (p. *121*)
Woodward's Garden (p. *148*)

AMERICAN/FRENCH
Universal Café (p. *150*)

ASIAN/ITALIAN
Oritalia (p. *115*)

BREAKFAST
Doidge's (p. *139*)
Home Plate (p. *139*)

CAJUN/CREOLE
The Elite Café (p. *136*)

CALIFORNIA
2223 Restaurant & Bar (p. *151*)
Bix (p. *126*)
Café Flore (p. *152*)
Cliff House (p. *155*)
Gordon Biersch Brewery Restaurant
   (p. *144*)
Hawthorne Lane (p. *143*)

Moose's (p. *128*)
One Market (p. *118*)
Pluto's (p. *140*)

CALIFORNIA/ASIAN
AsiaSF (p. *145*)

CALIFORNIA/EAST-WEST
Cafe Kati (p. *134*)

CALIFORNIA/FRENCH
Brasserie Savoy (p. *114*)
Grand Cafe (p. *111*)
Jardinière (p. *140*)
Ritz-Carlton Dining Room (p. *124*)

CALIFORNIA/FRENCH/
MEDITERRANEAN
PlumpJack Café (p. *137*)

CARIBBEAN
Cha Cha Cha (p. *153*)

CHINESE
Brandy Ho's Hunan Food (p. *126*)
Eliza's (p. *139*)
Great Eastern (p. *126*)
Harbor Village (p. *117*)
House of Nanking (p. *126*)
The Mandarin (p. *133*)
Tommy Toy's (p. *119*)

CHINESE/DIM SUM
Ton Kiang (p. *157*)
Yank Sing (p. *121*)

CRÊPES
Ti Couz (p. *150*)

EAST-WEST FUSION
Eos (p. *153*)

FRENCH
Azie (p. *142*)
Café Claude (p. *116*)
Charles Nob Hill (p. *124*)
Fifth Floor Restaurant (p. *143*)
Fleur de Lys (p. *111*)
Flying Saucer (p. *147*)

Fringale Restaurant (p. *144*)
La Folie (p. *135*)
Lulu (p. *145*)
Masa's (p. *111*)
Rubicon (p. *118*)
South Park Café (p. *145*)

FRENCH BISTRO
Foreign Cinema (p. *147*)

FRENCH/ITALIAN
Florio (p. *136*)
Scala's Bistro (p. *115*)

GREEK
Kokkari (p. *119*)

INDIAN
North India Restaurant (p. *137*)

INTERNATIONAL
World Wrapps (p. *140*)

ITALIAN
A. Sabella's (p. *133*)
Cafe Pescatore (p. *134*)
Caffè Luna Piena (p. *151*)
Caffè Macaroni (p. *131*)
Caffè Sport (p. *128*)
Capp's Corner (p. *131*)
Delfina (p. *149*)
Emporio Armani Cafe (p. *116*)
Firewood Café (p. *153*)
Il Fornaio (p. *129*)
Kuleto's (p. *114*)
L'Osteria del Forno (p. *132*)
Mario's Bohemian Cigar
   Store (p. *132*)
Pane e Vino (p. *137*)
Pasta Pomodoro (p. *132*)
Prego (p. *138*)
Rose Pistola (p. *130*)
Splendido (p. *120*)
Stinking Rose (p. *130*)
Tommaso's (p. *133*)
Zinzino (p. *138*)

ITALIAN/ARGENTINEAN
Il Pollaio (p. *131*)

ITALIAN/VENETIAN
Tavolino (p. *131*)

JAPANESE
Ace Wasabi's Rock 'n' Roll
   Sushi (p. *135*)
Kabuto Sushi (p. *155*)
Kyo-Ya (p. *118*)

MEDITERRANEAN
42 Degrees (p. *148*)
Enrico's (p. *129*)
Moose's (p. *128*)
Zuni Café (p. *142*)

MEXICAN
Andalé Taqueria (p. *138*)
Sweet Heat (p. *154*)
Taquerias La Cumbre (p. *150*)
Zona Rosa (p. *154*)

MODERN CLASSIC
Restaurant Gary Danko (p. *134*)

NOODLES
Long Life Noodle Company &
   Jook Joint (p. *146*)

PERSIAN/MIDDLE EASTERN
Maykadeh (p. *130*)

PIZZA
Marcello's Pizza (p. *153*)
Pauline's (p. *149*)

SAN FRANCISCAN
Black Cat Cafe (p. *128*)

SEAFOOD
A. Sabella's (p. *133*)
Alioto's (p. *133*)
Aqua (p. *117*)
Cliff House (p. *155*)
Farallon (p. *110*)
Hayes Street Grill (p. *141*)
Sam's Grill & Seafood
   Restaurant (p. *120*)
Swan Oyster Depot (p. *125*)
Tadich Grill (p. *120*)

SINGAPOREAN
Straits Café (p. *156*)

SOUTHEAST ASIAN
Betelnut (p. *136*)

SPANISH
Thirsty Bear Brewing
  Company (p. *145*)

STEAK HOUSE
Harris' (p. *135*)

SUSHI
Ace Wasabi's Rock 'n' Roll
  Sushi (p. *135*)
Kabuto Sushi (p. *155*)
Kyo-Ya (p. *118*)

THAI
Khan Toke Thai
  House (p. *155*)

Manora's (p. *146*)
Thep Phanom (p. *154*)

VEGAN
Millennium (p. *141*)

VEGETARIAN
Greens Restaurant, Fort
  Mason (p. *136*)

VIETNAMESE
The Golden Turtle (p. *125*)
Le Colonial (p. *115*)
The Slanted Door (p. *149*)
Tú Lan (p. *146*)

2 Union Square

EXPENSIVE

Farallon. 450 Post St. (between Mason and Powell sts., adjoining the Kensington Park Hotel).
☎ **415/956-6969.** Reservations recommended. Main courses $22—$29. AE, DC, DISC,
MC, V. Mon–Sat 11:30am–2:30pm; Mon–Sat 2:30–5pm (bistro menu); Mon–Wed
5:30–10pm; Thurs–Sat 5:30–10:30pm; Sun 5–9:30pm. Valet parking $12. Bus: 2, 3, 4, or 38.
COASTAL CUISINE/SEAFOOD.

If there is one hot downtown restaurant that's a must-visit, this is it, even if only to
have a cocktail at the exotic bar. The multimillion-dollar attraction is seafood, from
the outrageous decor to the stellar "coastal" cuisine. Hand-blown jellyfish lamps, kelp
bed–like backlit columns, glass clamshells, sea-urchin light fixtures, a sea-life mosaic
floor, and a tentacle-encircled bar set the scene. Thankfully, designer Pat Kuleto's
impressive renovation of the 1924 building left the original Gothic arches intact, making the main dining room one of the most impressive in the city. (The bright, busy
front room and intimate balcony aren't exactly shabby, either.)

  If you think the atmosphere is appealing and lavish, wait until you try the food.
Chef Mark Franz, who opened Stars with Jeremiah Tower, is at the helm of the
$5-million kitchen. He offers starters ranging from the expected (oysters) to the more
ambitious, like iced Atlantic and Pacific shellfish indulgence (a cornucopia of oysters,
clams, crayfish, prawns, mussels, and scallops with horseradish mignonette, for $17.95
per person) and a grand caviar tasting featuring four varieties with traditional accompaniments. While most main courses, such as saffron-poached sablefish and striped
bass "pillows" with prawn mousse, napa cabbage, and foie-gras *coulis,* stick with the
seaside theme, meat and game eaters also get attention. Grilled squab breast stuffed
with mushrooms is served with braised red chard, and grilled veal chop comes with
portabello mushroom galette. The whimsy-meets-sophistication extends only as far as
the food—the service and wine list (more than 300 by the bottle; 24 by the glass)
are seriously professional. This place has been quite the scene since it opened in

Technological Tip

Want to book your reservations online? Go to **www.opentable.com**, where you can
save seats in San Francisco and the Bay Area in real time.

mid-1997, so reserve well in advance. And if it's available, don't miss the huckleberry bombolini, a refreshingly different dessert.

✪ **Fleur de Lys.** 777 Sutter St. (at Jones St.). ☎ **415/673-7779.** Reservations recommended. Main courses $29–$35; 5-course tasting menu $70; 4-course vegetarian menu $58. AE, DC, MC, V. Mon–Thurs 6–9:30pm; Fri–Sat 5:30–10:30pm. Bus: 2, 3, 4, 27, or 38. FRENCH.

Imagine the finest French fare served in a large version of Jeannie's (as in *I Dream of Jeannie*) live-in bottle. Fleur de Lys serves one of the city's most intricate, formal meals in an elegant, recently refurbished dining room draped with 700 yards of rich red, saffron, and parsley-colored floor-to-ceiling hand-painted fabric. Throw in dim French candelabras, an extraordinary sculptural floral centerpiece, and about 20 tables filled with well-dressed diners, and you've got one of the most renowned dining rooms in San Francisco.

Fleur de Lys does everything seriously, from its foie gras starter to its petit fours after dinner. And with chef Hubert Keller (who was President Clinton's first guest chef at the White House) in the kitchen, it's impossible to go wrong. You can order à la carte, from the five-course tasting menu, or from the four-course vegetarian menu. Start with the knockout blue potato chips with cauliflower purée and caviar. Try any of the "symphony" of appetizers, which include oysters and Hudson Valley foie gras, sea scallop cake, and lobster gelée. Venture on to a main course, which might include Atlantic salmon with green onion and ginger, purée of celery root, and applesauce foie gras or lamb loin with parsnip, star anise, and Merlot reduction. Desserts are artistic creations and might feature chocolate tartelette with mandarin oranges and walnuts. A selection of 300 French and California wines makes this an all-around dining fantasy.

Grand Cafe. 501 Geary St. (at Taylor St., adjacent to the Hotel Monaco). ☎ **415/292-0101.** Reservations recommended. Main courses $15–$27. AE, CB, DC, DISC, MC, V. Mon–Sat 7–10:30am; Sun 8–10:30am; daily 11:30am–2:30pm; Mon–Sat 5:30–11pm; Sun 5:30–10pm. Valet parking $7 for 3 hr., $3 each additional half hour. Bus: 2, 3, 4, 27, or 38. CALIFORNIA/FRENCH.

With the exception of Farallon, the Grand Cafe has the most, well, *grand* dining room in San Francisco. The cocktail area is impressive, but the pièce de résistance is the enormous turn-of-the-century grand ballroom, a magnificent combination of old Europe and art nouveau. From every angle you'll see playful sculptures, original murals, and a cadre of dazzling deco chandeliers.

Chef Denis Soriano enjoys the most coveted of clientele: the repeat customer. On a recent visit, seated in a plush booth, my guests and I feasted on decadent polenta soufflé, black mussel ragout in a pastry shell, and endive salad with Roquefort, pears, walnuts, and lemon vinaigrette. Entrees? Expect the likes of Chilean sea bass with white wine, Yukon gold potatoes, and smoked applewood bacon. Service was both friendly and prompt. *Note:* The bar area has its own exhibition kitchen and menu, offering similar dishes for about half the price. The pizzas from the wood-burning oven are excellent.

✪ **Masa's.** In the Hotel Vintage Court, 648 Bush St. (at Stockton St.). ☎ **415/989-7154.** Reservations required; accepted up to 3 weeks in advance. Fixed-price dinner $75–$80. AE, CB, DC, DISC, MC, V. Tues–Sat 6–9:30pm. Closed first 2 weeks in Jan, first week in July. Cable car: Powell-Mason and Powell-Hyde lines. Bus: 2, 3, 4, 30, or 45. Valet parking: $9. FRENCH.

The results are in. Despite the departure of chef Julian Serrano (who headed to Vegas's Bellagio in mid-'98), Chad Callahan, who's been in the kitchen for the past 10 years, is matching the culinary magic of his predecessors. With Callahan, the flawless wine list, and exemplary (even unpretentious) service, Masa's still ranks as one of the top French outposts in the States.

Union Square & Financial District Dining

Legend
Cable Car ▪▪▪▪▪▪

Pacific Ave.

Jackson St.

Washington St.

Powell St.

Stockton St.

Clay St.

Taylor St.

Mason St.

Hyde St.

Golden Ct.

Leroy St.

Jones St.

Sacramento St.

Huntington Park

California St.

Pine St.

Bush St.

Taylor St.

Mason St.

Burritt Alley

Sutter St.

Stockton St.

Cosmo   Pl.

Post St.

Union Square

Jones St.

Geary St.

Hyde St.

Leavenworth St.

O'Farrell St.

Ellis St.

Grant Ave.

Columbus Ave.

Kearny St.

Montgomery St.

🔷21

Jackson Square

Sansome St.

Battery St.

🔷22

Front St.

Davis St.

Drumm St.

🔷20

🔷23

🔷25

🔷26

🔷24

California St.

🔷28 🔷27

🔷19

🔷15

🔷17

🔷18

Claude Ln.

🔷16

Beale St.

Fremont St.

Market St.

1st St.

🔷29

Compton Pl.

Maiden La.

Market St.

New Montgomery St.

🔷30

2nd St.

Mission St.

Howard St.

🔷31

Third St.

🔷32

0   1/8 mi

0   .125 km

Ⓝ

Folsom St.

Dinner is a memorable, expense-be-damned experience from start to finish. If you wish, you can simply leave the decisions up to the kitchen. A typical dinner might begin with foie gras in Madeira truffle sauce, or poached lobster with potatoes, fried leek, and truffle vinaigrette. Main courses might include médaillons of New Zealand fallow deer with zinfandel sauce and caramelized green apples, or Atlantic black bass with saffron sauce. Dessert, as you would imagine, is heavenly.

✪ **Postrio.** In the Prescott Hotel, 545 Post St. (between Mason and Taylor sts.). ☎ **415/ 776-7825.** Reservations recommended. Main courses $6–$16 breakfast; $12–$16 lunch; $24–$36 dinner. AE, CB, DC, DISC, MC, V. Mon–Fri 7–10am; Mon–Sat 11:30am–2pm; Sun brunch 9am–2pm; Sun–Wed 5:30–10pm; Thurs–Sat 5:30–10:30pm. Bar daily 11:30am–2am. Cable car: Powell-Mason and Powell-Hyde lines. Bus: 2, 3, 4, or 38. AMERICAN.

They say the higher you climb, the longer it takes to fall, and that's certainly the case with Wolfgang Puck's Postrio. Over 10 years after launching the trend for large, glamorous downtown dining rooms, it's still a rare night when brother chefs Mitchell and Steven Rosenthal don't perform to a full house. Eating, however, is only half the reason one comes to Postrio. After squeezing through the perpetually swinging bar— which dishes out excellent pizzas from a wood-burning oven in the corner—guests are forced to make a grand entrance down the antebellum staircase to the cavernous dining room below (it's everyone's 15 seconds of fame, so make sure your fly is zipped). Pure Hollywood, for sure, but fun.

The menu combines Italian, Asian, French, and California styles with mixed results. When I last visited Postrio, I had a stellar meal. The time before I was not as lucky. Regardless, the fare's way above par. The menu changes nightly; you might find grilled chicken breast with caramelized onion purée, morels, fava beans, and natural chicken juice, or roasted salmon with porcini mushrooms, artichoke fritters, and garlic aïoli. The desserts, artistically sculpted by pastry chef Susan Brinkley Perez, are always memorable.

MODERATE

Brasserie Savoy. In the Savoy Hotel, 580 Geary St. (at Jones St.). ☎ **415/441-2700.** Reservations recommended. Main courses $16–$19. AE, CB, DC, DISC, MC, V. Daily 5:30– 10:30pm. Bus: 2, 3, 4, 27, or 38. CALIFORNIA/FRENCH.

If you're headed to the theater or are just looking for a good meal and cheery atmosphere downtown, Brasserie Savoy is an excellent option. The atmosphere is French bistro, with a bright, busy dining room and black-and-white marble floors. The food is consistent, affordable, and delicious. Among the appetizers, preferred choices are oysters with champagne sauce, leeks, and Osetra caviar; mussels marinière with shallots, muscadet, and parsley; and freshly made salad. Main-course choices might include bouillabaisse with local seafood and roasted bread, grilled salmon and halibut with veggies and dry vermouth sauce, or grilled rib-eye with pommes frites, watercress, and bordelaise sauce. To finish, try the innovative crème brûlée.

Kuleto's. In the Villa Florence Hotel, 221 Powell St. (between Geary and O'Farrell sts.). ☎ **415/397-7720.** Reservations recommended. Breakfast $5–$10; main courses $10–$20. AE, CB, DC, DISC, MC, V. Mon–Fri 7–10:30am; Sat–Sun 8–10:30am; daily 11:30am–11pm. Cable car: Powell-Mason and Powell-Hyde lines. Muni Metro: Powell. Bus: 2, 3, 4, or 38. ITALIAN.

Kuleto's is a beautiful place filled with beautiful people who are here to see and be seen (don't come underdressed or overdressed). The best plan of action is to skip the wait for a table, muscle a seat at the antipasto bar, and fill up on appetizers, which are often better than the entrees. For a main course, try penne pasta drenched in tangy lamb-sausage marinara sauce, clam linguini (generously overloaded with fresh clams), or any

Impressions

[San Francisco is] the city that knows how.

—Pres. William Howard Taft

[San Francisco is] the city that knows chow.

—Trader Vic, restaurateur

of the fresh-fish specials grilled over hardwoods. If you don't arrive by 6pm, expect to wait—this place fills up fast.

Le Colonial. 20 Cosmo Place (off Taylor St., between Post and Sutter sts). ☎ **415/ 931-3600.** Reservations recommended. Main courses $10–$35. AE, DC, DISC, MC, V. Sun–Tues 5:30–10pm; Wed–Thurs 5:30–11pm; Fri–Sat 5:30pm–midnight. Valet parking $4 first hour, $2 each additional half hour. Bus: 2, 3, 4, or 27. VIETNAMESE.

The first thing we'll say about Le Colonial is it makes some of the best sea bass on earth. Wrapped in banana leaf with glass noodles, ginger, scallions, and cilantro, the buttery fish is genuine bliss. Second, management has done a nice job of transforming Trader Vic's into a sexy 1920s French Vietnamese haven. The long dining room and gloriously secluded front patio celebrate French-Vietnamese colonial decor, with rattan chairs, black-and-white photos, and plantation shutters. In the upstairs lounge (our vote for the sexiest in the city), the cozy couches and seductive surroundings (and, often, live jazz) attract a kicked-back cocktail crowd of swank professionals. Recommended fare includes crispy Vietnamese spring rolls (which I would praise more if Tú Lan hadn't jaded me for life), delicate steamed Vietnamese rice crêpes with chicken, wood-ear mushrooms, and bean sprouts (although the sauce needed a bit more oomph), and delicious wok-seared beef tenderloin (if you make ample use of the ginger soy vinaigrette buried under a watercress onion salad). Alas, the sautéed string beans, though well flavored, can be overcooked, and fried rice with chicken, shrimp, egg, onion, and chili should be skipped entirely—it's a visually unattractive dish with an identity crisis, somewhere between pad Thai and Spanish rice.

Oritalia. In the Juliana Hotel, 586 Bush St. (at Stockton St.). ☎ **415/782-8122.** Reservations recommended. Main courses $17.25–$26.50. AE, DC, MC, V. Daily 5:15–11pm. Bus: 2, 3, 4, 30, 38, or 45. ASIAN/ITALIAN.

If you can't decide between Italian and Asian food, try both. Oritalia (from "Oriental" and "Italian") blends the flavors of Italy, China, Korea, and Southeast Asia to create unique dishes that can be over-the-top or just right. Previously a favorite on upper Fillmore Street, Oritalia moved into bigger and better digs and recently swapped chefs, but still serves the creative Asian-Italian cuisine that made it famous as a food-forward restaurant. The colorful room—with a 19-foot bar, Fortuny silk chandeliers, Oriental rugs, and some booths with curtains for privacy—is in the best of taste, but the real attraction is executive chef Jon Nelson's food. Expect unusual combos like seared day boat scallops with black sesame and sweet dumplings, and Meyer lemon risotto with shao-xing sauce. Pastry chef Francisco Amlaguer's creative desserts may include Valhrona chocolate and raspberry pyramid with primrose sorbet.

Scala's Bistro. In the Sir Francis Drake hotel, 432 Powell St. (at Sutter St.). ☎ **415/ 395-8555.** Reservations recommended. Breakfast $7–$10; lunch and dinner main courses $12–$24. AE, CB, DC, DISC, MC, V. Mon–Fri 7am–midnight; Sat–Sun 8am–midnight. Cable car: Powell-Hyde line. Bus: 2, 3, 4, 30, 45, or 76. FRENCH/ITALIAN.

Firmly entrenched at the base of the refurbished Sir Francis Drake Hotel, this latest venture by husband-and-wife team Giovanni and Donna Scala blends Parisian-bistro and Old World atmosphere. With just the right balance of elegance and informality, it's a perfect place to have some fun (and apparently most people do).

Drawing from her success at Bistro Don Giovanni in Napa, Donna put together a fantastic array of surprisingly inexpensive Italian and French dishes. Start with the "Earth and Surf" calamari appetizer or grilled portabello mushrooms. Golden beet salad and Anchor Steam mussels are also good bets. Generous portions of moist, rich duck-leg confit will satisfy hungry appetites, but if you can order only one thing, make it Scala's signature dish: seared salmon. Resting on a bed of creamy buttermilk mashed potatoes and accented with a tomato, chive, and white-wine sauce, it's truly delish. Finish with creamy Bostini cream pie, a dreamy combo of vanilla custard and orange chiffon cake with a warm chocolate glaze.

INEXPENSIVE

Café Claude. 7 Claude Lane. ☎ **415/392-3515.** www.cafeclaude.com. Reservations recommended. Main courses $7–$13. AE, DC, DISC, MC, V. Mon–Sat 11am–11:30pm. Cable car: Powell-Mason and Powell-Hyde lines. FRENCH.

Euro transplants love Café Claude, a crowded and lively restaurant tucked into a narrow lane near Union Square. Seemingly everything—every table, spoon, salt shaker, and waiter—is imported from France. With prices topping out at about $12 for main courses such as *poussin rôti* (roast Cornish hen with potatoes and aïoli), French shepherd's pie, or *poisson du jour* (fish of the day), Café Claude is a good value. There is live jazz Thursday and Friday from 8pm to 11pm and Saturday from 7 to 10pm. Outdoor seating is available when the weather permits.

Dottie's True Blue Café. In the Pacific Bay Inn, 522 Jones St. (at O'Farrell St.). ☎ **415/885-2767.** Reservations not accepted. Breakfast $5–$9; main courses $4–$8. DISC, MC, V. Thurs–Mon 7:30am–3pm. Cable car: Powell-Mason line. Bus: 2, 3, 4, 27, or 38. AMERICAN.

This family-owned breakfast restaurant is one of my favorite downtown diners. It's the kind of place you'd expect to see off Route 66, where most customers are on a first-name basis with the staff and everyone is welcomed with a hearty hello and steaming mug of coffee. Dottie's serves above-average American morning fare (big portions of French toast, pancakes, bacon and eggs, omelets, and the like) delivered to blue-and-white checkerboard tablecloths on rugged, diner-quality plates. Whatever you order arrives with delicious homemade bread, muffins, or scones, and homemade jelly. There are also daily specials and vegetarian dishes.

Emporio Armani Cafe. 1 Grant Ave. (at O'Farrell St., off Market St.). ☎ **415/677-9010.** Reservations not accepted. Main courses $6–$13. AE, DC, DISC, MC, V. Mon–Sat 11:30am–4:30pm; Sun noon–4:30pm. Bus: All Union Square buses. ITALIAN.

All the hobnobbing of an elite dining club comes cheaply at the Armani Cafe. It's nothing more than a circular counter in the middle of Armani's ever-fashionable (and expensive) clothing store. But the fare and upscale casual atmosphere are enough to lure folks who have only lunch, not a new designer suit, on their minds. Local favorites include the homemade antipasto misto and daily pizza specials. There's also a nice variety of sandwiches and, as always, a large dose of attitude. Although some dishes cost more than $10, you can snack well on a 10-spot here. Outside seating is available in fine weather.

Sears Fine Foods. 439 Powell St. (between Post and Sutter sts.). ☎ **415/986-1160.** Reservations accepted for parties of 6 or more. Breakfast $3–$8; salads and soups $3–$18; main courses $6–$10. No credit cards. Daily 6:30am–2:30pm. Cable car: Powell-Mason and Powell-Hyde lines. Bus: 2, 3, 4, or 38. AMERICAN.

Sears would be the perfect place for breakfast on the way to work, but you can't always guarantee you'll get in the door before 9am. It's not just another pink-tabled diner run by motherly matrons—it's an institution, famous for its crispy, dark-brown waffles, light sourdough French toast, and silver dollar–sized Swedish pancakes. As the story goes, Ben Sears, a retired clown, founded the diner in 1938. His Swedish wife, Hilbur, was responsible for the legendary pancakes, which are still whipped up according to her family's secret recipe. Sears also offers a "healthy-heart menu."

3 The Financial District

EXPENSIVE

✪ **Aqua.** 252 California St. (between Battery and Front sts.). ☎ **415/956-9662.** Reservations required. Main courses $26–$45; 6-course tasting menu $68; vegetarian tasting menu $55. AE, DC, MC, V. Mon–Fri 11:30am–2:15pm; Mon–Sat 5:30–10:30pm. Bus: All Market St. buses. SEAFOOD.

Without question, Aqua remains San Francisco's finest seafood restaurant, light years beyond the genre of shrimp cocktails and lemon-butter sauce. Heralded chef Michael Mina dazzles his customers with a bewildering juxtaposition of earth and sea in his seasonally changing menus. The ahi tartare, for example, is mixed tableside with pears, pine nuts, quail egg, and spices—it's truly divine. The roasted spot prawn with crab stuffing, citrus hollandaise, and hot and sour vinaigrette is deliciously creative. Miso-marinated Chilean sea bass and grilled medallions of ahi tuna with foie gras in Pinot sauce are other show-stoppers. Desserts are equally impressive. Steep prices prevent most people from making a regular appearance, but for special occasions or billable lunches, Aqua is highly recommended.

Carnelian Room. 555 California St. (at Montgomery St.). ☎ **415/433-7500.** Reservations recommended. Main courses $22–$39; Sun brunch $29 adults, $13 children. AE, CB, DC, DISC, MC, V. Daily 6–10pm; Sun brunch 10am–1:30pm. Self-parking $7. Cable car: California St. line. Bus: 1, 9, 15, or 42. CONTEMPORARY AMERICAN.

Soaring 52 stories above the Financial District on the top floor of the Bank of America building, the Carnelian Room is a definite contender for "Best View." Dark oak paneling, brass railings, and huge picture windows positively reek of romance, particularly if you're fortunate enough to get a window table. The upscale menu used to cater to old-style banker's tastes—expensive meat dishes with rich, thick sauces—but the recent trend toward healthier eating has rounded out the menu considerably. You can find numerous fish, fowl, and pasta dishes along with such Carnelian classics as prime rib and thick-cut New York steak, lobster Thermidor, and herb-mustard crusted rack of lamb. A wine cellar of some 36,000 bottles and the restaurant's accomplished sommelier all but guarantee the proper vintage to accompany your meal.

Harbor Village. 4 Embarcadero Center, lobby level (at Drumm St. between Sacramento and Clay sts.). ☎ **415/781-8833.** Reservations recommended. Main courses $10–$32. AE, DC, DISC, JCB, MC, V. Mon–Fri 11am–2:30pm; Sat 10:30am–2:30pm; Sun 10am–2:30pm; daily 5:30–9:30pm. Bus: 15, 45, or 76. CHINESE.

This is one of the city's most upscale Chinese restaurants, serving primarily Cantonese dishes, spicy Szechuan specials, and, during the lunch rush, great dim sum. The courteous staff will guide you through the extensive menu, which includes some 30 seafood dishes, such as striped bass steamed with ginger and scallions. If you've never had shark-fin soup, this is the place to try it. Unique appetizers include shredded spicy chicken and minced squab in lettuce cups. Stir-fried garlic prawns, beggar's chicken cooked in a clay pot, and sizzling beef in black-pepper sauce are excellent main-course choices. Dim sum lunch, served daily, is definitely worth trying. The waitstaff brings trays full of steaming-hot appetizers (and will happily explain what they are), and you choose what you like. Try Shanghai-style steamed pork dumplings flavored with ginger and scallions, rice-paper dumplings filled with sweet shrimp, taro cake, or curried beef wonton.

The restaurant offers validated parking at all the Embarcadero Center garages (at the foot of Clay Street). It'll cost you a few dollars weekdays, but it's free after 5pm Monday to Friday and all day on weekends and holidays.

Kyo-Ya. In the Sheraton Palace Hotel, 2 New Montgomery St. (at Market St.). ☎ **415/ 546-5090.** Reservations recommended. Sushi $4–$16; main courses $25–$30; fixed-price menu $50. AE, CB, DC, DISC, JCB, MC, V. Tues–Fri 11:30am–2pm; Tues–Sat 6–10pm. Muni Metro: All Market St. trams. Bus: All Market St. buses. JAPANESE/SUSHI.

It's anything but cheap, but this restaurant offers an authentic Japanese experience, from the decor to the service to (most assuredly) the stellar food. Specialties feature the freshest sushi and sashimi, as well as grilled and *nabemono* dishes (kettle dishes cooked at the table). To start, try any of the appetizers, and move on to the grilled butter fish with miso sauce. Complete dinners include kobachi, soup, rice, pickles, and dessert. Most consider this—along with Kabuto—the best sushi in the city.

One Market. 1 Market St. (at Steuart St., across from Justin Herman Plaza). ☎ **415/ 777-5577.** Reservations recommended. Main courses $18–$30. AE, DC, MC, V. Mon–Fri 11:30am–2pm; Mon–Thurs 5:30–9:30pm; Fri 5:30–10pm; Sat 5–10pm. Valet parking $8. Bus: All Market St. buses. CALIFORNIA.

The enormous restaurant's decor, both cosmopolitan and folk-artsy, complements the farm-fresh menu. Amid tapestry, banquettes, mahogany, and slate floors, there's seating for 220 in the main dining area. The bar, which features gold walls and sponge-painted mustard columns, displays a prominent colorful mural of a market scene. The menu changes frequently to reflect the freshest local ingredients. Start with a dozen Skookum and Fanny Bay oysters with homemade cocktail sauce and chili malt vinegar dressing, followed by Maine lobster tortellini or seared foie gras with carrot ravioli and cinnamon citrus consommé. Main courses include seared day-boat scallops with spiced pumpkin ravioli, chanterelle mushroom, and pomegranate *jus,* and pan-seared double-cut lamb chops with French green lentils, pearl onions, and lamb *jus.* Whatever you choose, you're bound to find a perfectly accompanying wine from the cellar, which has over 500 selections of American vintages. A corporate crowd convenes from 4 to 6pm weeknights for $2.50 pints and $3 martinis. The room picks up with live jazz nightly.

✪ **Rubicon.** 558 Sacramento St. (between Sansome and Montgomery sts.). ☎ **415/ 434-4100.** Reservations recommended. Main courses $19–$29. AE, DC, MC, V. Mon–Fri 11:30am–2:30pm; Mon–Sat 5:30–10:30pm. Bus: 15 or 41. FRENCH CONTEMPORARY.

Opened in 1994, Rubicon won instant publicity because of its celebrity owners, Francis Ford Coppola and Robert De Niro. Almost 7 years and a change of chefs later, the place still serves some of the best food in town, which allows one to overlook the lacking atmosphere. Named for Coppola's Napa Valley wine, Rubicon features a contemporary and somewhat stiff dining room frequented by big-business power lunchers and an upscale, middle-aged crowd that doesn't mind the steep price of eating very, very well.

Until 1997, renowned chef Traci Des Jardins reigned in the kitchen, but upon departing for Jardiniere she was replaced by Scott Newman, who has made this one of my favorite spots to dine. While the menu changes frequently, favorites among the 10

You Paid What?

47,000 hotels, 700 airlines,
50 rental car companies. And a few
million ways to save money.

Travelocity.com
A Sabre Company

Go Virtually Anywhere.

AOL Keyword: Travel

Will you have enough stories to tell your grandchildren?

Yahoo! Travel

The Sun on Your Face at Belden Place

San Francisco has always been woefully lacking in the alfresco dining department. One exception is Belden Place, an adorable little brick alley in the heart of the Financial District that is open only to foot traffic. When the weather is agreeable, the restaurants that line the alley break out the big umbrellas, tables, and chairs, and voilà—a bit of Paris just off Pine Street.

A handful of adorable cafes line Belden Place and offer a variety of cuisine. There's **Cafe Bastille,** 22 Belden Place (☎ **415/986-5673**), a classic French bistro and fun speakeasy basement serving excellent crêpes, mussels, and French onion soup; it schedules live jazz on weekends. **Cafe Tiramisu,** 28 Belden Place (☎ **415/421-7044**), is a stylish Italian hot spot serving addictive risottos and gnocchi. **Plouf,** 40 Belden Place (☎ **415/986-6491**), specializes in big bowls of mussels slathered in a choice of seven sauces, as well as fresh seafood. **Buddah,** 471 Pine St. (☎ **415/399-9898**), is a chic bistro serving "Italian food with Asian flare." There's also live jazz Thursday through Saturday.

or so appetizers include ahi tuna tartare with soy vinaigrette, out-of-this-world foie gras with caramelized rhubarb compote, and delicate seared scallops with braised endive, sweet onion purée, and truffles. About eight main courses are available daily, and might include peppered New York strip steak with oxtail ravioli and béarnaise or Muscovy duck breast with pears, turnips, and foie gras. Not surprisingly, a stellar wine list accompanies the excellent food.

Tommy Toy's. 655 Montgomery St. (at Columbus Ave. and Washington St.). ☎ **415/ 397-4888.** Reservations recommended. Main courses $16–$28; fixed-price dinner $46.50–$55. AE, DC, DISC, JCB, MC, V. Mon–Fri 11:30am–2:30pm; daily 6–9:30pm. Valet parking (dinner only) $3.50. CHINESE.

If you want romantic, superfancy Chinese, Tommy's is all you: Opulent, dark, unmistakably Asian, and perhaps the only Chinese restaurant where dressing up is apropos. Dimly lit candelabras and ancient paintings accent the $1.5-million dining room, patterned on the 19th-century empress dowager's reading room. Most evenings, the restaurant is crowded with tourists and some locals who come for the six-course fixed-price meal. It usually includes minced squab in lettuce leaves, lobster bisque served in a coconut and topped with puff pastry, a whole lobster sautéed with peanuts and mushrooms, duck served with plum sauce, médaillons of beef, and a light dessert of peach mousse. The à la carte menu flaunts vanilla prawns and other delicacies. On the two occasions I've been here, once the food was very good, the next time it was just okay, and both times the portions were substantial.

MODERATE

✪ **Kokkari.** 200 Jackson St. (at Front St.). ☎ **415/981-0983.** Reservations recommended. Main courses $14.95–$24. AE, DC, MC, V. Mon–Fri 11:30am–2:30pm; Mon–Thurs 5–10pm; Fri–Sat 5–11pm. Valet parking $8. Bus: 12, 15, 41, 42, or 83. GREEK.

Greek food has never been much of a memorable experience for me, but a night at Kokkari changed my mind. The perennially hot restaurant (rated by critic Michael Bauer as one of the best in the States) comforts the crowds in two dining rooms. The first is a beautifully rustic living room with a huge fireplace, oversized furnishings, and a homey air. Past the bar, generally two-deep with yuppies, the other main room is more casual. It has exposed wood beams, pretty standing lamps, and a view of the glass-enclosed private dining room (where, during our dinner, guests attempted a drunken rendition of Greek dancing). Executive chef Jean Alberti gives everyone reason to celebrate with his traditional Aegean dishes. A great way to start is with *Pikilia,* a sampling of traditional Greek spreads served with *dolmathes.* There are excellent soups and salads, too, but try not to fill up on starters. The moussaka (eggplant, lamb, potato, and béchamel) is to die for, and the quail, stuffed with winter greens served on oven-roasted leeks, orzo, and wild rice *pilafi,* is phenomenal.

Sam's Grill & Seafood Restaurant. 374 Bush St. (between Montgomery and Kearny sts.). ☎ **415/421-0594.** Reservations recommended for dinner and for 5 or more at lunch. Main courses $9–$24. AE, CB, DC, MC, V. Mon–Fri 11am–9pm. Bus: 15, 45, or 76. SEAFOOD.

Power lunching at Sam's is a San Francisco tradition, and it has done a brisk business with Financial District types for what seems like forever (since 1967). The entrance, which holds a small mahogany bar, opens onto a main dining room with high-backed booths. It's noisy at midday, but if privacy is your primary concern, choose one of the individually curtained booths that line the corridor to the left of the main dining room. Once you've settled in, consider such favorites as clam chowder, charcoal-broiled fillet of fish, and, for dessert, French pancakes anisette. Shellfish, steak, and veal dishes round out the dinner menu.

Splendido. 4 Embarcadero Center (at Clay and Drumm sts.). ☎ **415/986-3222.** Reservations recommended. Main courses $12–$26. AE, DC, DISC, MC, V. Mon–Fri 11:30am–2:30pm; bar menu daily 2:30–5:30pm; daily 5:30–10pm. Bus: 15, 45, or 76. CONTEMPORARY ITALIAN.

It's not a destination restaurant, but if you're hungry and hanging near the Embarcadero, this beautiful Italian spot will more than do the trick. Warm olive wood, flickering candles, rustic stone walls, hand-painted tiles, and hand-hewn beams create the illusion of an old Mediterranean getaway in the middle of metropolitan Embarcadero Four.

The food is beautifully presented, lovingly prepared, and consistently tasty. Starters might include a light, flavorful Mediterranean seafood soup with toasted country bread. Main courses, served on colorful, individually decorated plates, include a selection of house-made pastas. You might try wonderful pan-seared sea bass with root vegetable purée and citrus *nage* (chicken stock–based broth with lemon and orange zest) or breaded pork chop with Meyer lemon *gremolata* (a sprinkling of a chopped-parsley-and-lemon mix). Dessert is a decadent affair, with such belt-busters as Marsala-and-espresso tiramisu and homemade gelato (sorbets, too). The glass-enclosed atrium is prime territory on sunny days, but you might prefer a seat near the open kitchen. Be sure to glance in the exhibition bakery near the entrance, where you might see chefs rolling fresh pasta.

✪ **Tadich Grill.** 240 California St. (between Battery and Front sts.). ☎ **415/391-1849.** Reservations not accepted. Main courses $12–$18. MC, V. Mon–Fri 11am–9:30pm; Sat 11:30am–9:30pm. Muni Metro: All Market St. trams. BART: Montgomery Station. Bus: All Market St. buses. SEAFOOD.

This venerated California institution arrived with the gold rush in 1849 and claims to be the very first to broil seafood over mesquite charcoal, in the early 1920s. The original mahogany bar extends the length of the restaurant; big plates of sourdough bread top the tables draped in no-nonsense white linen. Power lunchers get one of the seven enclosed private booths.

For a light meal, try one of the delicious seafood salads, such as shrimp or prawn Louis. Hot dishes include baked avocado with shrimp diablo, baked casserole of stuffed turbot with crab and shrimp à la Newburg, and charcoal-broiled petrale sole with butter sauce, a local favorite. Almost everyone orders a side order of big, tasty french fries.

The Waterfront Restaurant & Cafe. Pier 7 (on the Embarcadero near Broadway). ☎ **415/391-2696.** Reservations recommended. Café main courses $14–$21 at lunch, $17–$26 at dinner; dining room main courses $15–$17 at lunch, $23–$28 at dinner. AE, DC, MC, V. Cafe daily 11:30am–10pm; dining room Mon–Fri 11:30am–2:15pm and 5:30–10pm, Sat–Sun 5:30–10pm. Free valet parking. Muni Metro: F. AMERICAN.

Bay Bridge views, a sunny patio, a sleek industrial-chic dining room, and great food have made the Waterfront a hit since its renovation and reopening in late '97. Although renowned executive chef Bruce Hill left and Brian Beach is now in the house, the atmosphere alone (refined upstairs, nautical downstairs) can induce idyllic San Francisco memories. The lunch menu includes a fine selection of appetizers such as Dungeness blue crab cakes and grilled apricot-glazed quail, excellent salads, pizzas, wood-fired grill items, and "house favorites," such as falafel-crusted sea bass and sautéed chicken breast with herbed polenta and rosemary pan sauce. Dinner is more exotic, with such dishes as Sonoma lamb carpaccio, roasted squab with potato and wild rice galette and bing cherry chutney, and Kasu marinated filet of beef with taro gnocchi, tatsoi and shiitake relish, and soy consommé. The wine list is fine and includes many selections starting at $18.

✪ **Yank Sing.** 427 Battery St. (between Clay and Washington sts.). ☎ **415/781-1111.** Dim sum $2.65–$3.40 for 3 to 4 pieces. AE, DC, MC, V. Mon–Fri 11am–3pm; Sat–Sun 10am–4pm. Cable car: California St. line. Bus: 1 or 42. DIM SUM.

Loosely translated as "a delight of the heart," Yank Sing is the best dim sum restaurant in the downtown/Financial District area. Poor quality of ingredients has always been the shortcoming of all but the most expensive Chinese restaurants, but Yank Sing manages to be both affordable and excellent. Confident, experienced servers take the nervousness out of novices—they're good at guessing your gastric threshold. Most dishes are dumplings, filled with tasty concoctions of pork, beef, fish, or vegetables. *Congees* (porridges), spare ribs, stuffed crab claws, scallion pancakes, shrimp balls, pork buns, and other palate-pleasers complete the menu. As at most good dim sum places, you choose the small dishes from a cart continually wheeled around the dining room. While the food is delicious, the location makes this the most popular tourist spot; locals generally head to Ton Kiang (see p. 157). A second location is at 49 Stevenson St., off First Street (☎ **415/541-4949**).

4 Nob Hill/Russian Hill

EXPENSIVE

The Big Four. In the Huntington Hotel, 1075 California St. (between Mason and Taylor sts.). ☎ **415/771-1140.** Reservations recommended. Breakfast from $10.95; lunch main courses $10–$18.50; dinner main courses $19–$34. AE, CB, DC, DISC, MC, V. Mon–Fri 7–10am; Sat–Sun 7–11am; Mon–Fri 11:30am–3pm; daily 5:30–10pm. Valet parking $7. Cable car: California St. line (direct stop). Bus: 1. CONTEMPORARY AMERICAN.

Shining brass, historic California photographs, forest-green leather banquettes, and ram's-horn sconces establish the clubby atmosphere at this Nob Hill restaurant that specializes in seasonal wild game. At dinner, you might find venison chili with black beans, cheddar, and onion crisps to start, then organic ostrich steak with a chive crust and portabello pot pie to follow. If game doesn't interest you, there are plenty of other down-to-earth dishes, including herb-roasted chicken with Yukon gold potatoes, tenderloin of Angus beef, and roasted Atlantic salmon.

Dining Around Town

9th & Irving St.
   Restaurant **24**

42 Degrees **46**

2223 **35**

A. Sabella's **65**

Ace Wasabi's **7**

Alioto's **64**

Alosinthe **26**

Andale Taqueria **5**

Asia SF **68**

Avenue 9 **24**

Azie **54**

Beach Chalet **23**

Betelnut **15**

Boulevard **51**

Café Flore **34**

Cafe Kati **22**

Cafe Pescatore **66**

Caffè Luna Piena **32**

Cha Cha Cha **73**

Chow **30**

Cliff House **19**

Delfina **38**

Doidge's **13**

Ebisu **24**

Elite Café **16**

Eliza's **18**

Eos **71**

Firewood Café **32**

Florio **17**

Flying Saucer **38**

Fog City Diner **68**

Foreign Cinema **40**

Fringale **47**

Gary Danko **63**

Golden Turtle **61**

Gordon Biersch
   Brewery **49**

Gordon's House of
   Fine Eats **41**

Greens Restaurant,
   Fort Mason **1**

Hamburger
   Mary's **44**

Hard Rock Cafe **59**

Harris' **60**

Hawthorn Lane **52**

Hayes Street Grill **26**

Home Plate **6**

House on 9th **24**

Il Fornaio **68**

Jardiniere **25**

Johnfrank **29**

Kabuto Sushi **20**

Khan Toke Thai House **20**

La Folie **62**

Long Life Noodle
   Company **50**

Lulu **54**

Manora's **43**

Marcello's Pizza **33**

Mecca **31**

Mel's Diner **9** & **20**

Millennium **56**

North India Restaurant **10**

Organica the Living
   Cuisine **24**

Pane e Vino **12**

Park Chow **24**

Pauline's Pizza **36**

Plumpjack Café **11**

Pluto's **3**

Prego **20**

The Slanted Door **39**

South Park Café **48**

Straits Café **20**

Swan Oyster Depot **58**

Taquerias La Cumbre **39**

Thep Phanom **28**

Thirsty Bear
   Brewing Company **53**

Ti Couz **39**

Tommy's Joynt **57**

Ton Kiang **21**

Tú Lan **55**

Universal Café **42**

Waterfront **69**

Woodward's Garden **37**

World Wrapps **4**

Zinzino **2**

Zona Rosa **72**

Zuni Café **27**

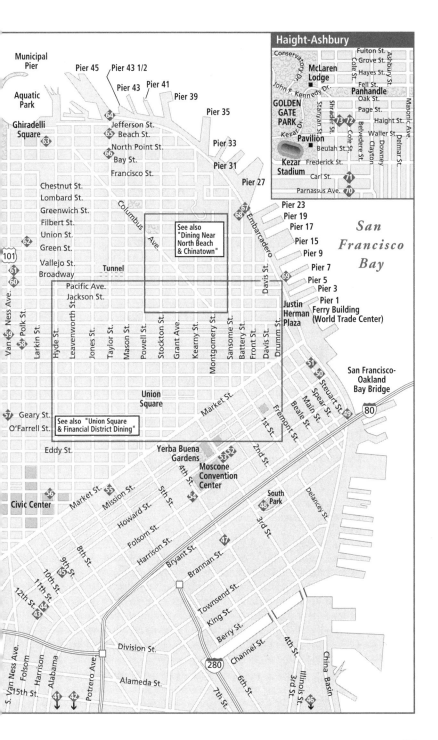

Haight-Ashbury

Conservatory Dr.
Fulton St.
Grove St.
Hayes St.
McLaren Lodge
Fell St.
John F. Kennedy Dr.
Panhandle
Oak St.
GOLDEN GATE PARK
Page St.
Haight St.
Kezar Dr.
Pavilion
Waller St.
Beulah St.
Kezar Stadium
Frederick St.
Carl St.
Parnassus Ave.

Municipal Pier
Pier 45   Pier 43 1/2
Pier 43   Pier 41
Aquatic Park   Pier 39
Pier 35
Ghiradelli Square
Jefferson St.
Beach St.
North Point St.
Bay St.
Francisco St.
Pier 33
Pier 31
Pier 27

Chestnut St.
Lombard St.
Greenwich St.
Filbert St.
Union St.
Green St.
Vallejo St.
Broadway
Columbus Ave.
Tunnel
Pacific Ave.
Jackson St.

See also "Dining Near North Beach & Chinatown"

Pier 23
Pier 19
Pier 17
Pier 15
Pier 9
Pier 7
Pier 5
Pier 3
Pier 1

San Francisco Bay

Embarcadero
Davis St.

Justin Herman Plaza
Ferry Building (World Trade Center)

Van Ness Ave.
Polk St.
Larkin St.
Hyde St.
Leavenworth St.
Jones St.
Taylor St.
Mason St.
Powell St.
Stockton St.
Grant Ave.
Kearny St.
Montgomery St.
Sansome St.
Battery St.
Front St.
Davis St.
Drumm St.

Union Square

Market St.
1st St.
Steuart St.
Spear St.
Main St.
Beale St.
Fremont St.

San Francisco-Oakland Bay Bridge

Geary St.
O'Farrell St.

See also "Union Square & Financial District Dining"

Eddy St.
Yerba Buena Gardens
Moscone Convention Center
2nd St.

Civic Center
Market St.
Mission St.
Howard St.
Folsom St.
Harrison St.
4th St.
5th St.
3rd St.
South Park
Delancey St.

8th St.
9th St.
10th St.
11th St.
12th St.
Bryant St.
Brannan St.

Townsend St.
King St.
Berry St.
4th St.
China Basin

S. Van Ness Ave.
Folsom
Harrison
Alabama
Potrero Ave.
Division St.
Alameda St.
Channel St.
6th St.
7th St.
3rd St.
Illinois St.
15th St.

123

ⓘ Family-Friendly Restaurants

Cliff House *(see p. 155)*   The folks at this oceanfront multiplex of restaurants are used to churning out fast meals for tourists with kids in tow. The best part? If the young-uns get anxious, you can hand over a couple of bucks and send them to the adjoining Musee Mechanique.

Eliza's *(see p. 139)*   Colorful surroundings and a reasonable amount of quiet allow families to gather 'round the table for some of the best Chinese food around. Just don't come starving, because there's usually a wait.

Hard Rock Cafe *(see p. 125)*   Like its affiliates around the world, this loud, nostalgia-laden place offers big portions of decent food, moderate prices, and plenty of blaring music to an almost exclusively tourist clientele.

Mel's Diner *(see p. 139)*   This retro-style burger-slinging joint is not only neat to look at (it was the diner that starred in the movie *American Graffiti*), it also caters to kids. Youngsters get their own color-in menu (crayons are already on the table), and some meals are served in boxes shaped like classic American cars. Juke-boxes at each table will keep the whole family busy figuring out which oldie to select.

Mo's Gourmet Burgers *(see p. 132)*   Head to the second location, near the Metreon, and kill two birds with one stone: Get one of the best burgers in town, then shimmy over to the space-age Metreon shopping and entertainment center for some fun for everyone. If burgers aren't your thing, the Metreon's food court offers affordable gourmet versions of fast food and has plenty of seating.

Pasta Pomodoro *(see p. 132)*   Pasta, pasta, more pasta, plenty of other dishes, plenty of locations, cheery atmosphere, and rock-bottom prices mean you can take the whole family here and let 'em splurge.

✪ **Charles Nob Hill.** 1250 Jones St. (at Clay St.). ☎ **415/771-5400.** Reservations required. Main courses $28–$35; 6-course tasting menu $70. AE, DC, MC, V. Tues–Sun 5:30–10pm. Valet parking $8. Cable car: California St. and Powell-Hyde lines. Bus: 1, 12, 27, or 83. FRENCH.

This utterly refined restaurant serves "classically inspired light French fare" in two dining rooms with velvet banquettes, fresh floral arrangements, and the loud buzz of the older socialite crowd. Although the room is romantic, the atmosphere and noise level are too convivial for real intimacy. Still, the food is great. Start with sautéed Hudson Valley foie gras—a must-try—or the soup of the day. For the main course, you might choose lamb with potato gnocchi and spring vegetables, white bean and artichoke ragout, and thyme-infused lamb reduction, or outstanding pan-seared squab breast with wild mushrooms, savoy cabbage, potato gnocchi, and squab leg confit. Better yet, opt for the $70 six-course tasting menu and let the chef's preference lead you through the meal. Wrap up with dessert, such as apple crêpes with vanilla bean ice cream and caramel glaze; the pastry chef, Steven Durfee, hails from French Laundry, so you can bet it'll be memorable. *Tip:* No matter what, don't drive here unless you plan to use the valet; you might spend over an hour looking for parking.

✪ **Ritz-Carlton Dining Room.** 600 Stockton St. (at California St.). ☎ **415/296-7465.** Reservations recommended. Fixed-price menus $61–$87. AE, CB, DC, DISC, MC, V. Mon–Sat 6–9:30pm. Valet parking $11. Cable car: Powell-Hyde and Powell-Mason lines (direct stop). Bus: 1. CALIFORNIA/FRENCH.

The Ritz-Carlton is renowned for giving guests the royal treatment, and the Dining Room is no exception. On my last visit, no fewer than five tuxedoed staff members surreptitiously attended to my needs (no half-empty water glasses in this joint) as my guests and I fussed over the wine list and joked over the proper pronunciation of "Tatin." The setting is quite regal and sumptuous: crystal chandeliers, rich brocade, elegant table settings, cushy high-backed chairs, and live harp music.

Chef Sylvain Portay might serve roasted glazed Maine lobster in a pressed vegetable broth, or seared salmon with cocoa beans, pequillos peppers, lemon confit, green olives, and balsamic vinegar. The menu changes monthly and offers a choice of three-, four-, and five-course dinners ranging from $61 to $87; the five-course option includes wine pairing per course by French-trained sommelier Stephane La Croix for an additional $45. The Dining Room also features a stunning cheese cart, laden with at least two dozen individually ripened selections.

MODERATE

✪ **Swan Oyster Depot.** 1517 Polk St. (between California and Sacramento sts.). ☎ **415/ 673-1101.** Reservations not accepted. Seafood cocktails $5–$8; clams and oysters on the half shell $6–$7.50 per half dozen. No credit cards. Mon–Sat 8am–5:30pm. Bus: 27. SEAFOOD.

Pushing 90 years of faithful service to Bay Area chowder-heads, the Swan Oyster Depot is classic San Francisco, a unique dining experience you shouldn't miss. Opened in 1912, this tiny hole-in-the-wall run by the city's friendliest servers is little more than a narrow fish market that decided to slap down some bar stools. There are only 20 or so seats, jammed cheek-by-jowl along a long marble bar. Most patrons come for a quick cup of chowder or a plate of oysters on the half-shell that arrive chilling on crushed ice. The menu is limited to fresh crab, shrimp, oyster, and clam cocktails, Maine lobster, and Boston-style clam chowder, all of which are exceedingly fresh. *Note:* Don't let the lunchtime line dissuade you—it moves fast.

INEXPENSIVE

The Golden Turtle. 2211 Van Ness Ave. (between Broadway and Vallejo St.). ☎ **415/ 441-4419.** Reservations recommended. Main courses $8–$14. AE, CB, DISC, MC, V. Tues–Sun 5–11pm. Bus: 38 or 45. VIETNAMESE.

The Golden Turtle is widely regarded as one of the city's finest Vietnamese restaurants, a far cry better than the typical *pho* noodle houses that have recently sprung up all over the place. In a converted Victorian home on a busy stretch of Van Ness, the restaurant's elaborate carved-wood paneling creates a soothing, romantic ambience. Recommended dishes are five-spice roasted chicken; marinated barbecued quail; imperial rolls with minced pork, prawn, and crab; and any of the seasonal crab dishes.

Hard Rock Cafe. 1699 Van Ness Ave. (at Sacramento St.). ☎ **415/885-1699.** Reservations accepted for groups of 15 or more. Main courses $6–$16. AE, DC, DISC, MC, V. Sun–Thurs 11:30am–11pm; Fri–Sat 11:30am–midnight. Valet parking $4.75 for 2 hr. Cable car: California St. line. Bus: 1. AMERICAN.

We hate to plug chains, and this loud, rock-nostalgia–laden place would be no exception if it didn't serve a fine burger and overall decent heaping plates of food at such moderate prices. Music blares to entertain an almost exclusively tourist clientele. For many, the real draw is the merchandise shop, which often has as long a line as the restaurant.

The menu offers burgers, fajitas, baby-back ribs, grilled fish, chicken, salads, and sandwiches. Although it's nothing unique to San Francisco, the Hard Rock is a fine place to bring the kids and grab a bite.

5 Chinatown

INEXPENSIVE

Brandy Ho's Hunan Food. 217 Columbus Ave. (at Pacific Ave.). ☎ **415/788-7527.** Reservations recommended. Main courses $8–$13. AE, DC, DISC, MC, V. Sun–Thurs 11:30am–11pm; Fri–Sat 11:30am–midnight. Bus: 15 or 41. CHINESE.

Fancy black-and-white granite tabletops and a large, open kitchen give you the first clue that the food here is a cut above the usual Hunan fare. Take my advice and start immediately with fried dumplings (in sweet-and-sour sauce) or cold chicken salad. Move on to fish-ball soup with spinach, bamboo shoots, noodles, and other goodies. The best main course is Three Delicacies, a combination of scallops, shrimp, and chicken with onion, bell pepper, and bamboo shoots, seasoned with ginger, garlic, and wine, and served with black-bean sauce. Most dishes are quite hot and spicy, but the kitchen will adjust the level to meet your specifications. There is a small selection of wines and beers, including plum wine and sake.

Great Eastern. 649 Jackson St. (between Kearny St. and Grant Ave.). ☎ **415/986-2500.** Most main courses $8–$13. AE, MC, V. Daily 11am–1am. Bus: 15, 30, 41, or 45. CHINESE.

Great Eastern is famous for fresh and hard-to-find seafood, pulled straight from the myriad tanks that line the walls. Rock cod, steelhead, sea chochs (conchs), sea bass, shrimp, frogs, softshell turtle, abalone—if it's even remotely aquatic and edible, it's on the menu at this hugely popular Hong Kong–style dinner house. The day's catch, sold by the pound, is listed on a board. Both upper- and lower-level dining rooms are rather stylish, with shiny black and emerald furnishings.

House of Nanking. 919 Kearny St. (at Columbus Ave.). ☎ **415/421-1429.** Main courses $5.25–$11.95. MC, V. Mon–Fri 11am–10pm; Sat noon–10pm; Sun 4–10pm. Bus: 9, 12, 15, or 30. CHINESE.

To the unknowing passerby, the House of Nanking has "greasy dive" written all over it. To its legion of fans, however, the wait—sometimes up to an hour—is worth what's on the plate. On the edge of Chinatown, just off Columbus Avenue, this inconspicuous little diner is one of San Francisco's worst-kept secrets. When the line is reasonable, I drop by for a plate of pot stickers and chef-owner Peter Fang's signature shrimp-and-green-onion pancake, served with peanut sauce. Trust the waiter when he recommends a special, or simply point to what looks good on someone else's table. Even with an expansion that doubled the space, seating is tight, so prepare to be bumped around a bit and don't expect good service—it's all part of the Nanking experience.

6 North Beach/Telegraph Hill

EXPENSIVE

Bix. 56 Gold St. (between Sansome and Montgomery sts.). ☎ **415/433-6300.** Reservations recommended. Main courses $7–$14 at lunch; $15–$30 at dinner. AE, CB, DC, DISC, MC, V. Mon–Thurs 11:30am–11pm; Fri 11:30am–midnight; Sat 5:30pm–midnight; Sun 6–10pm. Bus: 15, 30, 41, or 45. CLASSIC AMERICAN/CALIFORNIA.

The martini lifestyle may now be en vogue, but it was never out of style in this sexy and glamorous dining room. Modeled after a 1920s supper club, Bix is utterly stylish, with curving Honduran mahogany, massive silver columns, and art-deco–style lighting, all of which sets the stage for live music and plenty of hobnobbing. While the ultra-sleek setting far overshadows the expensive—and, on one recent occasion, skimpy—food, the legions of diners entranced by the Bix experience don't seem to

Dining Near North Beach & Chinatown

Bix **19**
Black Cat Cafe **14**
Brandy Ho's Hunan Food **16**
Caffè Macaroni **18**
Caffè Sport **8**
Capp's Corner **6**
Enrico's **13**
Great Eastern **20**
House of Nanking **17**
Il Pollaio **5**

L'Osteria del Forno **7**
Mario's Bohemian Cigar Store **3**
Maykedeh **9**
Mo's Gourmet Burgers **10**
Moose's **1**
Pasta Pomodoro **2**
Rose Pistola **4**
Stinking Rose **12**
Tavolino **11**
Tommaso's **14**

care. Chicken hash has been a menu favorite for the past 12 years, but newer main courses—such as New York steak with parmesan potato purée, watercress salad, and walnut–green-peppercorn butter; and seared day-boat scallops with black Périgord truffles, pomme purée, and sauce lie de vin—are as swanky as the room. For the ultimate in luxurious dining, try $118 Beluga caviar on toast.

Caffè Sport. 574 Green St. (between Grant and Columbus aves.). ☎ **415/981-1251.** Reservations accepted only for parties of 2 or more. Main courses $15–$24. No credit cards. Tues–Thurs noon–2pm; Fri–Sat noon–2:30pm; Tues–Thurs 5–10:30pm; Fri–Sat seatings at at 6:30, 8:30, and 10pm. Bus: 15, 30, 41, or 45. ITALIAN.

People either love or hate this stodgy Sicilian eatery. Cluttered with hanging hams, fishnets, decorative plates, dolls, mirrors, and over 2 decades' worth of dust, Caffè Sport was once a culinary landmark. Now it's better known for its surly staff and eclectic ambience than for its good, but cream- and butter-heavy, food. Owner-chef-artiste Antonio Latona serves up hearty portions of attitude along with garlic-laden pasta dishes and is happy to report that this is Senator Dianne Feinstein's favorite North Beach hangout. Lunch is tame in comparison to dinner, when the Sport is mobbed and lively, and strangers might be packed together family-style. Disregard the framed menu that sits on each table and accept the waiter's "suggestions." Whatever arrives— whether calamari, mussels, and shrimp in tomato-garlic sauce, or pasta in pesto sauce—it's bound to be *bene.* Bring a huge appetite, but above all, don't be late if you have a reservation.

Moose's. 1652 Stockton St. (between Filbert and Union sts.). ☎ **415/989-7800** or 800/2 8-MOOSE. www.mooses.com. Reservations recommended. Main courses $13–$26. AE, CB, DC, JCB, MC, V. Mon–Wed 5:30–10pm; Thurs 11:30am–10pm; Fri 11:30am–11:30pm; Sat 10am–11:30pm (bar menu 2:30–5:30pm); Sun 10am–10pm (bar menu 2:30–5pm). Valet parking $6 lunch, $9 dinner for 3 hr. Bus: 15, 30, 41, or 45. MEDITERRANEAN/CALIFORNIA.

You'll see the big blue neon moose out front long before you pass through the doors, and once inside, you'll notice you're in the largest dining room in North Beach. This is where Nob Hill socialites and local politicians come to dine and be seen, but Moose's is not just an image—in fact, the dining room itself is rather sparse and impersonal. The food can be quite good. Appetizers are innovative, fresh, and well balanced (try the Mediterranean fish soup with rouille and croutons that's cooked in the wood-fired oven), and the main courses (especially meats) tend to be lovingly prepared. The menu changes every few months and might include a grilled veal chop with potato galette and a variety of pasta, chicken, and fish dishes.

The bar, separated from the main dining room by a low, frosted-glass partition, remains busy long after the kitchen closes. There's jazz featuring piano and bass nightly and during weekend brunch.

MODERATE

Black Cat Cafe. 501 Broadway (at Kearny St.). ☎ **415/981-2233.** Reservations recommended. Main courses $6–$11 at lunch, $8.75–$25 at dinner. AE, DC, MC, V. Daily 11:30am–4pm and 5:30pm–2am. Valet parking $6 day, $8 night. Bus: 12, 15, 30, or 83. SAN FRANCISCAN.

Reed Hearon's Black Cat mirrors the newly renovated city, with local nostalgia contrived to perfection. The ambience is early 20th-century Parisian brasserie meshed with classic San Francisco. The dining room is designed for optimum people-watching, with high ceilings, bright lighting, low red leather booths, and strategically placed mirrors. The menu features selections honoring North Beach (Italian), Chinatown, Fisherman's Wharf (seafood), and the Barbary Coast (old-fashioned grill). Executive chef Scott Warner presides over the well-organized, extensive menu, which features appetizers such as a savory fritto misto of artichokes and mushrooms. Main courses ranging from rib-eye for four to grilled sea bass with herb butter and french fries (or for the late-night set, perhaps one of the all-day breakfast options). There's also a section highlighting lobster, crab, and shrimp served by the pound and prepared in any of three ways. Wash it all down with a wicked Black Cat Martini (with a sake kick), and slink downstairs to the Blue Bar jazz club, where a limited menu satisfies the lounge lizards. Be warned: They're fun, for sure, but neither is a stop for the serious foodie.

Enrico's. 504 Broadway (at Kearny St.). ☎ **415/982-6223.** Reservations recommended. Main courses $8–$13 at lunch, $13–$19 at dinner. AE, DC, DISC, MC, V. Mon–Thurs 11:30am–11:30pm; Fri–Sat 11:30am–12:30am; bar daily 11:30am–1:30am. Valet parking $7 at lunch, $10 at dinner. Bus: 12, 15, 30, or 83. MEDITERRANEAN.

Enrico's is the hip glitzy sidewalk restaurant/supper club destination on this North Beach strip—it was *the* place to hang out before Broadway took its seedy downward spiral. Families might want to skip this one, but anyone with an appreciation for live jazz (played nightly), late-night noshing, and weirdo-watching from the outdoor patio would be quite content spending an alfresco evening under the heat lamps. Chewy brick-oven pizza, a handful of pastas, zesty tapas, and thick steaks are hot items on the menu, which changes monthly. The best part? No cover charge, and valet parking.

Fog City Diner. 1300 Battery St. (at Lombard St.). ☎ **415/982-2000.** Reservations recommended. Main courses $7.50–$27. CB, DC, DISC, MC, V. Sun–Thurs 11:30am–11pm; Fri–Sat 11:30am–midnight. Bus: 42. AMERICAN.

More popular because of its Visa commercial than its food, Fog City is a tourist destination, with a few locals straggling in for business lunches. The restaurant looks like a genuine American metallic diner—but only from the outside. Inside, dark polished woods, inspired lighting, and a well-stocked raw bar tell you this is no hash-slinger.

Dressed-up dinner dishes include gourmet chili dogs, salads, sandwiches, burgers, cioppino, and pot roast. Fancier fish and meat meals include grilled catches of the day and thick-cut steaks. Lighter eaters can make a meal out of the long list of "small plates," which include crab cakes, and quesadilla with asparagus and chipotle. The food is fine, but if your heart is set on coming here, do so at lunch—you'll be better off elsewhere if you want a special dinner.

Il Fornaio. Levi Plaza, 1265 Battery St. (between Sansome, Battery, Union, and Greenwich sts.). ☎ **415/986-0100.** Reservations recommended. Main courses $9–$18. AE, DC, MC, V. Mon–Fri 7am–10pm; Sat 9am–11pm; Sun 9am–10pm. Valet parking $5. Bus: 12, 32, or 42. ITALIAN.

This trattoria is one of my favorite standbys, producing consistently good Italian fare at decent prices. The large split dining room in Levi Plaza, a few minutes from Pier 39, has a lively atmosphere and smart decor. By day it buzzes with Financial District types and socialites; by night, with couples and gathering friends.

If you don't have a reservation and can't wait to eat, pull up a stool at the marble-topped bar, with its unobstructed view of the open kitchen and dining room. On a sunny day, grab a patio table that looks onto Levi Plaza's fountain. Once you're situated, the first of many delights is the basket of fresh-baked breads, breadsticks, and a dipping dish of olive oil. Complement them with any of the delicious salads or the daily soup (especially if it's carrot), then venture to any of the pastas, pizzas, or main courses. My favorite is rotisserie duck in balsamic vinegar, which Il Fornaio somehow serves without all the fat you'd expect from duck and all the crispy skin you could wish for. Parents especially appreciate the "bambini" menu, which features pint-size fare for under $6. Desserts are decadent and wonderful. Try tiramisu and a glass of rose grappa—a perfect way to end the meal.

Maykadeh. 470 Green St. (between Kearny St. and Grant Ave.). ☎ **415/362-8286.** Reservations recommended. Main courses $10–$22. MC, V. Mon–Thurs 5–10:30pm; Fri–Sat 11:45am–11pm; Sun 11:45am–10pm. Valet parking $6 lunch, $7 dinner. Bus: 15 or 41. PERSIAN/MIDDLE EASTERN.

If you're looking to add a little exotic adventure to your dinner plans, this is the place. Surrounded by a sea of Italian bistros, Maykadeh is one of San Francisco's best and most elegant Persian restaurants. The Middle East might no longer be the culinary capital of the world, but at Maykadeh you can still sample the exotic flavors that characterize Persian cuisine. Of the dozen or so appetizers, some of the best are eggplant with mint garlic sauce, stuffed grape leaves, and lamb tongue with lime juice, sour cream, and saffron (c'mon, live a little). About eight mesquite-grilled items are on the menu, including fillet of lamb marinated in lime, homemade yogurt, saffron, and onions. House specialties include half a dozen vegetarian dishes, such as eggplant braised with saffron, fresh tomato, and dried lime.

Rose Pistola. 532 Columbus Ave. (at Union and Green sts.). ☎ **415/399-0499.** Reservations recommended. Main courses $6.95–$18.50 at lunch; most dishes $9–$24 at dinner. AE, DC, MC, V. Sun–Thurs 11:30am–10:30pm (late-night menu until midnight); Fri–Sat 11:30am–11:30pm (late-night menu until 1am). Valet parking $10. Bus: 15, 30, 41, or 45. ITALIAN.

The hottest restaurant of 1997 is still going strong under the watchful eye of restaurateur extraordinaire Reed Hearon. It's a smart, bustling bistro with divided dining areas and cramped tables next to the bar. Sidewalk seating is pleasant on sunny afternoons, but inside there's plenty to see as chefs crank out the eclectic food from the open kitchen. It's meant to be shared, and, aside from sandwiches, comes à la carte. The appetizer list features a barrage of hot and cold antipasti—prices are reasonable ($3.25 to $7.50), but portions tend to be small. My group was pleased with the innovative and tasty fried chickpeas and bored by the salad.

Along with meats and fowl, the menu includes a variety of fish choices. My party tried mussels in rich tomato broth, which was so flavorful we kept it around to soak up with bread long after the shellfish had been devoured. Our favorite dish was the whole Arctic char, which came crispy, perfectly seasoned, and bathed in fennel and tapenade in a big iron skillet. The "flaming cream" dessert—three fried crème brûlée–type diamonds that arrived afire with a Bacardi-and-apricot sauce—was creative and very tasty, but not worth $7.50.

Stinking Rose. 325 Columbus Ave. (between Vallejo and Broadway). ☎ **415/781-7673.** Reservations recommended. Main courses $12–$18. AE, DC, JCB, MC, V. Sun–Thurs 11am–11pm; Fri–Sat 11am–midnight. Bus: 15, 30, 41, or 45. ITALIAN.

Garlic is the "flower" from which this restaurant gets its name. From soup to ice cream, the supposedly healthful herb is a star ingredient in most every dish. ("We season our garlic with food," exclaims the menu.) From a strictly gourmet point of view, the Stinking Rose is unremarkable. Pizzas, pastas, and meats smothered in simple, overpowering sauces are tasty, but memorable only for their singular garlicky intensity. That said, this is a fun place; the restaurant's lively atmosphere and odoriferous aroma combine for good entertainment. Black-and-white floors, gray marble tables, and large windows overlooking the street help maintain the high energy. The best dishes include garlic-steamed clams and mussels, garlic pizza, and 40-clove garlic chicken (served with garlic mashed potatoes, of course).

Tavolino. 401 Columbus Ave. (at Vallejo St.). ☎ **415/392-1472.** Reservations recommended. Dishes $3.95–$13.50. AE, MC, V. Daily 11:30am–midnight. Bus: 15, 30, 41, 45. ITALIAN/VENETIAN.

This casual, bright restaurant, which opened in May 1998, serves the city's finest (and perhaps only) *cicchetti,* or Venetian tapas. With sidewalk tables surrounding the corner restaurant and most prices topping out at around $10, it's the perfect place for an afternoon drink or snack, but that's not to say dinner is any less enticing. The dining room—a tasteful combination of arches, columns, mahogany, and mosaic tile—is a jovial place. My favorite type of dining is sampling lots of little plates, and that's exactly what you'll do here. Fried olives stuffed with anchovy or almonds are the way to start. Then go with anything from the cold bar (such as delicious oysters, octopus and mussel salad, and chilled shrimp), steamed mussels, soft-shell crab with lemon aïoli, or seafood bolognese with penne pasta. The signature dish is sturgeon *saltimbocca* (pan-fried, wrapped in prosciutto di Parma, and served with fig vinaigrette and crisp-fried sage).

INEXPENSIVE

Caffè Macaroni. 59 Columbus Ave. (at Jackson St.). ☎ **415/956-9737.** Reservations accepted on weekdays—not on weekends. Main courses $6.95–$15.95. No credit cards. Mon–Sat 5–10pm. Bus: 15 or 41. ITALIAN.

You wouldn't know it from the looks (or name) of it, but this tiny, funky restaurant on busy Columbus Avenue is one of the best southern Italian restaurants in the city. It looks as though it can hold only two customers at a time, and if you don't duck your head when entering the upstairs dining room, you might as well ask for one lump or two. Fortunately, the kitchen also packs a wallop, dishing out a large variety of antipasti and excellent pastas. The spinach-and-cheese ravioli with wild-mushroom sauce is outstanding, and the gnocchi is probably the best you'll find outside Italy. The owners and staff are always vivacious and friendly, and young ladies in particular will enjoy the attentions of the charming Italians manning the counter.

Capp's Corner. 1600 Powell St. (at Green St.). ☎ **415/989-2589.** Reservations recommended. Main courses $13–$15. AE, CB, DISC, MC, V. Sun–Fri 10am–midnight; Sat 4–11pm. Bus: 15 or 41. ITALIAN.

Capp's is a place of givens: It's a given that some high-spirited regulars are hunched over the bar; that Frank Sinatra's singing on the jukebox; and that you'll be served huge portions at low prices in a raucous atmosphere that prevails until the wee hours. The waitresses are usually brusque and bossy, but always with a wink. Long tables are set up for family-style dining: bread, soup, salad, choice of main dish (herb-roasted leg of lamb, veal tortellini with sun-dried tomato sauce, osso buco with fresh polenta, fettuccine with rock shrimp), and dessert—all for $15 or so per person, $10 for kids. You might have to wait an hour for a table, but you won't get bored if the old cronies at the bar take a liking to you.

Il Pollaio. 555 Columbus Ave. (between Green and Union sts.). ☎ **415/362-7727.** Reservations not accepted. Main courses $7–$13.50. AE, MC, V. Mon–Sat 11:30am–9pm. Cable car: Powell-Mason line. Bus: 15, 30, 39, or 41. ITALIAN/ARGENTINEAN.

Simple, affordable, and consistently delicious is a winning combination at super-basic Il Pollaio. Order at the counter, be seated in the tiny room, and wait for the fresh-from-the-grill chicken, which is so moist it practically falls off the bone. Each meal comes with a choice of salads, and if you're not in the mood for chicken, you can opt for rabbit, lamb, pork chop, or Italian sausage.

☉ L'Osteria del Forno. 519 Columbus Ave. (between Green and Union sts.). ☎ **415/ 982-1124.** Reservations not accepted. Sandwiches $5.50–$6.50; pizzas $11–$15; main courses $6–$11. No credit cards. Sun–Thurs 11:30am–10pm; Fri–Sat 11:30am–10:30pm. Bus: 15 or 41. ITALIAN.

L'Osteria del Forno might be only slightly larger than a walk-in closet, but it's one of the top three Italian restaurants in North Beach. Peer in the window facing Columbus Avenue, and you'll probably see two Italian women with their hair up, sweating from the heat of the brick-lined oven, which cranks out the best focaccia (and focaccia sandwiches) in the city. There's no pomp or circumstance: Locals come here strictly to eat. The menu features a variety of superb pizzas and fresh pastas, plus a few daily specials (pray for the roast pork braised in milk). Small baskets of warm focaccia keep you going until the arrival of the entrees, which should always be accompanied by a glass of Italian red.

Mario's Bohemian Cigar Store. 566 Columbus Ave. ☎ **415/362-0536.** Sandwiches $6.25–$6.95. No credit cards. Daily 10am–midnight. Closed Dec 24–Jan 1. Bus: 15, 30, 41, or 45. ITALIAN.

Across the street from Washington Square is one of North Beach's most popular neighborhood hangouts. The century-old bar—small, well worn, and perpetually busy—is best known for its focaccia sandwiches, including meatball or eggplant. Wash it all down with an excellent cappuccino or a house Campari as you watch the tourists stroll by. And yes, they do sell cigars.

Note: A newer, larger location that schedules live jazz Wednesday and Sunday nights is at 2209 Polk St., between Green and Vallejo streets (☎ 415/776-8226).

Mo's Gourmet Burgers. 1322 Grant Ave. (Vallejo and Green sts.). ☎ **415/788-3779.** Main courses $4.95–$12.50. MC, V. Mon–Thurs 11am–10:30pm; Fri 11am–11:30pm; Sat 9am–11:30pm; Sun 9am–10:30pm. Bus: 9X, 15, 30, 39, 41, or 45. AMERICAN/BURGERS.

The best—and juiciest—burgers in town are at this simple North Beach diner. Mo's offers a simple but winning combination: big, thick grilled patties of fresh-ground, best-quality, center-cut chuck; fresh french fries; cabbage slaw, sauteed garlic mushrooms, or beans and rice—*voilà*! You've got the city's burger of choice (Zuni Cafe's is a contender, but at almost twice the price). The other food—spicy chicken sandwich; steak with veggies, garlic bread, and potatoes; and token veggie dishes—is also up to snuff, but it's that messy, memorable burger that keeps the carnivores captivated (not to mention the sinisterly sweet shakes). A new location at SoMa's Yerba Buena Gardens, 772 Folsom St., between 3rd and 4th streets (☎ 415/957-3779), is open daily 11am to 9pm.

☉ Pasta Pomodoro. 655 Union St. (at Columbus Ave.). ☎ **415/399-0300.** Reservations not accepted. Main courses $4.60–$8.95. MC, V. Mon–Fri 11am–11pm; Sat noon–midnight; Sun noon–11pm. Cable car: Powell-Mason line. Bus: 15, 30, 41, or 45. ITALIAN.

If you're looking for a good, cheap meal in North Beach—or anywhere else in town, for that matter—this San Francisco chain can't be beat. There's usually a 20-minute wait for a table, but after you're seated you'll be surprised at how promptly you're served. Every dish is fresh and sizable, and, best of all, costs a third of what you'd pay elsewhere. Winners include spaghetti *frutti di mare* made with calamari, mussels, scallops, tomato, garlic and wine; and *cavatappi pollo*, with roast chicken, sun-dried tomatoes, cream, mushrooms, and parmesan—both are under $7.

There are 12 other locations, including 2027 Chestnut St., at Fillmore Street (☎ **415/474-3400**); 2304 Market St., at 16th Street (☎ **415/558-8123**); 3611 California St. (☎ **415/831-0900**); and 816 Irving St., between 9th and 10th streets (☎ **415/566-0900**).

Tommaso's. 1042 Kearny St. (at Broadway). ☎ **415/398-9696.** Reservations not accepted. Pasta and pizza $9–$22; main courses $9–$15. AE, DC, DC, JCB, MC, V. Tues–Sat 5–10:30pm; Sun 4–9:30pm. Closed Dec 15–Jan 15. Bus: 15 or 41. ITALIAN.

From the street, Tommaso's looks wholly unappealing, a drab, windowless brown facade sandwiched between sex shops. Then why are people always waiting in line to get in? Because everyone knows that Tommaso's bakes one of San Francisco's best traditional-style pizzas and has for decades. The center of attention in the downstairs dining room is the chef, who continuously tosses huge hunks of garlic and mozzarella onto pizzas before sliding them into the oak-burning brick oven. Nineteen different toppings make pizza the dish of choice, even though Italian classics such as veal Marsala, chicken cacciatore, superb lasagna, and wonderful calzones are also available. Tommaso's also offers half-bottles of house wines, homemade cannoli, and good Italian coffee. If you can overlook the seedy surroundings, this fun, boisterous restaurant is a great place to take the family.

7 Fisherman's Wharf

EXPENSIVE

A. Sabella's. Fisherman's Wharf, 2766 Taylor St. (at Jefferson St.), 3rd floor. ☎ **415/771-6775.** Reservations recommended. Main courses $12–$47. AE, CB, DC, DISC, MC, V. Daily 11am–11pm. Cable car: Powell-Mason line. 2-hr. validated parking at the Wharf Garage, 350 Beach St. ITALIAN/SEAFOOD.

The Sabella family has been serving seafood in San Francisco since the turn of the century and has operated A. Sabella's restaurant on the wharf continuously since 1920, catering heavily to the tourist trade. The menu offers something for everyone—steak, lamb, seafood, chicken, and pasta, all made from scratch with fresh local ingredients. Where A. Sabella's really shines, however, is in the shellfish department. Its 1,000-gallon saltwater tank allows for fresh crab, abalone, and lobster year-round, which means no restaurant in the city can touch A. Sabella's when it comes to feasting on fresh Dungeness crab and abalone out of season. Of course, such luxuries are anything but cheap.

Alioto's. Fisherman's Wharf (at Taylor St.). ☎ **415/673-0183.** Reservations recommended. Main courses $12–$24 at lunch, $18–$60 at dinner. AE, CB, DC, DISC, MC, V. Daily 11am–11pm. Cable car: Powell-Hyde line. Bus: 30 or 42. SEAFOOD.

One of San Francisco's oldest restaurants, run by one of the city's most prominent families, the Aliotos, this Fisherman's Wharf landmark has a long-standing reputation for serving the Bay's best cioppino. The curbside crab stand, Oysteria Deli, the Steam Kettle Bar, and the new Nonna Rose restaurant are great for a quick, inexpensive dose of San Francisco's finest; for more formal and fancy selections, continue up the carpeted stairs to the multilevel, harbor-view dining room. Don't mess around with the menu: You're after Dungeness crab. Cracked, caked, stuffed, or stewed, it's impossible to get your fill, so bring plenty of money—particularly if you intend to order from Alioto's prodigious (and pricey) wine list. If you happen to be insane and don't care for cracked crab, the griddle-fried sand dabs and rex sole served with tartar sauce are also good.

The Mandarin. At Ghirardelli Square, 900 North Point St. ☎ **415/673-8812.** Reservations recommended. Main courses $15–$45; fixed-price dinners $35–$45. AE, CB, DC, MC, V. Daily 11:30am–11pm. Cable car: Powell-Hyde line. Bus: 19, 30, 42, 47, or 49. CHINESE.

Created by Madame Cecilia Chiang in 1968, The Mandarin is meant to feel like a cultured, northern Chinese home; fine furnishings, silk-covered walls, and good-quality Asian art create one of the most elegant Chinese restaurants in the city. Tables are spaced comfortably apart, and the better of two softly lit dining rooms offers matchless views of the bay.

True to its name, The Mandarin offers exceptional northern Chinese cuisine. Take my advice and start with sesame prawns or minced squab. Follow with smoked tea duck (the house version of Beijing duck, but smoked over burning tea leaves until crispy) or—if you have a party of two or more and call a day in advance—Beggar's Chicken, encased in clay and cooked to slow perfection.

✪ **Restaurant Gary Danko.** 800 North Point St. (at Hyde St.). ☎ **415/749-2060.** www. garydanko.com. Reservations required. 3- to 6-course fixed-price menu $48–$75. AE, DC, MC, V. Daily 5:30–9:30pm. Bus: 42. MODERN CLASSIC.

Gary Danko, who received the James Beard Foundation award for Best Chef in California and made San Francisco's Ritz-Carlton Dining Room the top dining destination during his reign from 1991 to 1996, topped the charts of 1999 openings. Danko and his partner, ex-Ritz team player and renowned maître d' Nick Peyton, have modernized the four-star dining experience with impeccable cuisine and perfectly orchestrated service in an untraditionally unstuffy environment. The three- to six-course fixed-price menu is freestyle, so whether you want a sampling of appetizers or a flight of meat courses, you need only ask. I melted over buttery smooth glazed oysters, which were as creamy as the light accompanying sauce graced with leeks and intricately carved "zucchini pearls." He harmonized the fresh flavors of chanterelle mushrooms, corn, tomato, and tarragon in roast Maine lobster while showcasing the delicate flavor of the crustacean. Seared foie gras with peaches, caramelized onions, and verjus sauce; seared Maine sea scallops with tomato fondue, artichokes, black olives, and spinach; and can you believe an adventurous Moroccan spiced squab with chermoula and orange-cumin carrots? Pure heaven. Diners at the small bar have the option of ordering à la carte. And wine? It's a stellar list, and gracious sommelier Renée-Nicole Kubin tastes each bottle with the customer (and has been known to take back wine that lacked proper characteristics even after the diner volunteered to drink it). If after dinner you have the will to pass on the glorious cheese cart or caramel almond peaches with buttermilk ice cream prepared tableside, a plate of petit fours reminds you that Gary Danko is one sweet and memorable meal.

MODERATE

Cafe Pescatore. 2455 Mason St. (at North Point St., adjoining the Tuscan Inn). ☎ **415/ 561-1111.** Reservations recommended. Main courses $3.95–$8.95 at breakfast, $10–$20 at lunch and dinner. AE, DC, DISC, MC, V. Sun–Thurs 7am–10pm; Fri–Sat 7am–11pm; Sat–Sun 7am–3pm brunch, 3–5pm cafe menu. Cable car: Powell-Mason line. Bus: 15, 39, or 42. ITALIAN.

This cozy trattoria is one of the better bets in Fisherman's Wharf. Two walls of sliding glass doors offer pseudo-sidewalk seating when the weather's warm, although heavy vehicular traffic can detract from the alfresco experience. The consensus is to order anything that's cooked in the open kitchen's wood-fired oven, such as pizzas and roasts. A big hit with tourists is *polenta al forno*—oak-roasted cheese polenta with marinara sauce and fresh pesto. The huge roast chicken is also a safe bet.

8 The Marina/Pacific Heights/Cow Hollow

EXPENSIVE

✪ **Cafe Kati.** 1963 Sutter St. (between Fillmore and Webster sts.). ☎ **415/775-7313.** Reservations recommended. Main courses $19–$29.95. MC, V. Tues–Sun 5:30–10pm. Bus: 2, 3, or 4. CALIFORNIA/EAST-WEST.

Chef Kirk Webber works small wonders in an even smaller kitchen at this diminutive yet distinctive restaurant off Fillmore Street. The menu highlights California-style dishes spiced with a dash of the Orient and Italy, presented in high form, such as the signature Caesar salad sculpted into a towering monument of romaine. The seasonally changing menu offers such cross-cultural creations as miso-marinated Chilean sea bass saddled with tempura kabocha squash and chanterelle mushrooms; and sesame-crusted hamachi with a shiitake mushroom dumpling. When making a reservation, request a table in the front room.

Harris'. 2100 Van Ness Ave. (at Pacific Ave.). ☎ **415/673-1888.** Reservations recommended. Main courses $18–$34. AE, CB, DC, DISC, JCB, MC, V. Mon–Thurs 5:30–9:30pm; Fri 5:30–10:30pm; Sat 5–10:30pm; Sun 5–9:30pm. Bus: 38 or 45. STEAK HOUSE.

Every big city has a great steak restaurant, and in San Francisco it's Harris'—a comfortably elegant establishment where the handsome wood-paneled dining room has curving banquettes and stately waiters. Proprietor Ann Lee Harris knows steaks; she grew up on a cattle ranch and married the owner of the largest feedlot in California. In 1976, the couple opened the Harris Ranch Restaurant on Interstate 5 in central California, where they built a rock-solid reputation up and down the coast. The steaks, which can be seen hanging in a glass-windowed aging room off Pacific Avenue, are cut thick—New York style or T-bone—and are served with a baked potato and seasonal vegetables. Harris' also offers lamb chops, fresh fish, lobster, and roast duckling, as well as venison, buffalo (on occasion), and other seasonal game.

✪ **La Folie.** 2316 Polk St. (between Green and Union sts.). ☎ **415/776-5577.** Reservations recommended. Main courses $34–$48; 5-course tasting menu $75; vegetarian tasting menu $55. AE, CB, DC, DISC, MC, V. Mon–Sat 5:30–10:30pm. Bus: 19, 41, 45, 47, 49, or 76. FRENCH.

My mother and I call this unintimidating, cozy French restaurant "the house of foie gras." Why? Because on our first visit, virtually every dish overflowed with the ultra-rich delicacy. But in truth, there's more to chef Roland Passot's fantastic menu. Like what? Melt-in-your-mouth starters such as roast quail and—drum roll, please—foie gras with salad, wild mushrooms, and roasted garlic. Generous main courses include rôti of quail and squab stuffed with wild mushrooms and wrapped in crispy potato strings, and roast venison with vegetables, quince, and huckleberry sauce. The country French decor is tasteful but not too serious, with whimsical chandeliers and a cloudy sky painted overhead. The staff is friendly, knowledgeable, and accommodating, and the food is outstanding. Best of all, it's served in a relaxed and comfortable environment. Finish with any of the delectable desserts, and when you're done you're sure to loosen your belt a few notches.

MODERATE

Ace Wasabi's Rock 'n' Roll Sushi. 3339 Steiner St. (at Chestnut St.). ☎ **415/567-4903.** Reservations not accepted. Sushi $4–$9. AE, MC, V. Mon–Thurs 5:30–10:30pm; Fri–Sat 5:30–11pm; Sun 5–10pm. Bus: 30. JAPANESE/SUSHI.

Yeah, more sushi, but this time with a twist. What differentiates this Marina hot spot (formerly known as Flying Kamikazes) from the usual sushi spots around town are the unique combinations, the varied menu, and the young, hip atmosphere. The innovative rolls are a nice change for those bored with traditional styles, although they might be too adventurous for some (don't worry, there are plenty of non-seafood and cooked items on the menu). Don't miss the rainbow "Three Amigos" roll or the "Rock and Roll," with cooked eel, avocado, and cucumber. Buckwheat-noodle-and-julienne-vegetable salad is also a treat. The service could be improved—on busy nights you'll wait forever for your server to pour your Sapporo—but the staff is friendly and the atmosphere fun, so nobody seems to mind.

Betelnut. 2030 Union St. (at Buchanan St.). ☎ **415/929-8855.** Reservations recommended. Main courses $9–$16. CB, DC, DISC, MC, V. Sun–Thurs 11:30am–11pm; Fri–Sat 11:30am–midnight. Bus: 22, 41, or 45. SOUTHEAST ASIAN.

While San Francisco is teeming with Asian restaurants, few offer the posh, fashionable environment of this place on upscale Union Street. As the menu explains, the restaurant is an homage to "Pejui Wu," a traditional Asian beer house offering local brews and savory dishes. But with the bamboo paneling, red Formica countertops, and low-hanging lamps, the place feels less like an authentic harbor restaurant and more like a set out of Madonna's movie *Shanghai Surprise*. Still, the atmosphere is en vogue, with dimly lit booths, ringside seating overlooking the bustling stir-fry chefs, sidewalk tables (weather permitting), and body-to-body flirting at the cramped but festive bar. Starters include sashimi and tasty salt-and-pepper whole Gulf prawns; main courses include barbecued lemongrass chicken, Korean char-broiled pork, and Singapore chili crab (seasonal). While prices seem reasonable, the incidentals—such as white rice ($1.60 per person) and tea ($4 per pot)—add up. Whatever you do, order the heavenly signature dessert: a mouth-watering tapioca pudding with sweet red adzuki beans.

The Elite Café. 2049 Fillmore St. (between Pine and California sts.). ☎ **415/346-8668.** Reservations not accepted. Main courses $12–$24. AE, DC, DISC, MC, V. Sun–Mon 5–10pm; Tue–Sat 5–11pm; Sun 10am–3pm. Bus: 22, 41, or 45. CAJUN/CREOLE.

Some habits do indeed die hard, and the Elite is one of them. This place is always bustling with Pacific Heights's beautiful people, who come for fresh oysters, blackened beef filet with Cajun butter, jambalaya, Granddad's chicken and dumplings, and other well-spiced Cajun dishes. The high-backed booths provide more intimate dining than the crowded tables and bar. Brunch is good, too. It includes all kinds of egg dishes—Benedict, sardou, and many more—and such goodies as cornbread, bagels, and lox.

Florio. 1915 Fillmore St. (between Pine and Bush sts.). ☎ **415/775-4300.** Reservations recommended. Most main courses $13–$17. AE, MC, V. Sun–Thurs 5:30–10pm; Fri–Sat 5:30–11pm. Bus: 22, 41, or 45. FRENCH/ITALIAN BISTRO.

When I'm in the mood for a good meal without hoopla, I head directly to bistro-like Florio. Not only because the staff is friendly, or because if they're booked, I can always eat at the bar. Not even because the place is small enough to make me feel that I'm in a restaurant whose number-one goal is not to get as many consumers as possible in and out. The real reason is that I'm addicted to the soft polenta with mushrooms, shrimp and white bean salad, steak frites, and virtually every other little comfort dish that makes its way to the table. The wines by the glass (and by the bottle) always disappoint, but I don't care. I pull up a chair, make myself at home, and enjoy casual and cozy surroundings and consistently satisfying food. I suggest you do the same.

Greens Restaurant, Fort Mason. Building A, Fort Mason Center (enter Fort Mason opposite the Safeway at Buchanan and Marina sts.). ☎ **415/771-6222.** Reservations recommended 2 weeks in advance. Main courses $8–$13 at lunch, $13–$18 at dinner; fixed-priced dinner $45; brunch $8–$12. DISC, MC, V. Tues–Fri 11:30am–2pm; Sat 11:30am–2:30pm; Sun 10am–2pm; Mon–Fri 5:30–9:30pm; Sat 5:30–9pm. Greens To Go Mon–Fri 8am–9:30pm; Sat 8am–4:30pm; Sun 9am–3:30pm. Bus: 28 or 30. VEGETARIAN.

Knowledgeable locals swear by Greens, where executive chef Annie Somerville (author of *Fields of Greens*) cooks with the seasons, using produce from Green Gulch Farm and other local organic farms. In an old warehouse, with enormous windows overlooking the bridge and the bay, the restaurant is both a pioneer and a legend. A weeknight dinner might feature such appetizers as tomato, white-bean, and sorrel soup, or grilled asparagus with lemon, parmesan, and watercress. Follow with spring-vegetable risotto with asparagus, peas, shiitake and cremini mushrooms, and parmesan cheese; or Sri

Lankan curry of new potatoes, cauliflower, carrots, peppers, and snap peas stewed with tomatoes, coconut milk, ginger, and spices. A special four-course dinner is served on Saturday only. A recent example began with grilled asparagus, yellowfin potatoes, and peppers with blood-orange beurre blanc, followed by shiitake and cremini mushroom lasagna with leeks and mushroom port sauce. Desserts are equally adventuresome— try chocolate pave with mint crème anglaise or espresso ice cream with chocolate sauce (*Insider tip:* A "Late Evening Dessert" is served Monday to Saturday from 9:30 to 11pm). Lunch and brunch are somewhat simpler, but equally inventive.

Like the restaurant, the adjacent Greens To Go bakery is operated by the Zen Center. It sells homemade breads, sandwiches, soups, salads, pastries.

North India Restaurant. 3131 Webster St. (at Lombard St.). ☎ **415/931-1556.** Reservations recommended. Main courses $14.50–$19.95; fixed-price dinner (5–7pm) $12.95. AE, DC, MC, V. Mon–Fri 11:30am–2:30pm; daily 5–10:30pm. Bus: 41 or 45. INDIAN.

Although many Indian restaurants lack atmosphere, chef Parvesh Sahi's presides over a plush, dimly lit dining room, providing the perfect ambience for an intimate evening out with some ethnic flair. As you settle into a maroon velvet chair and browse the menu, soft Indian music reminds you what part of the world your taste buds will venture to. Start by ordering a cup of sweet and spicy chai and oversized, moist samosas (spiced potatoes and green peas served in a crisp pocket). Venture onward with any of the tandoori specials, such as the mixed seafood dish, with sea bass, jumbo prawns, and calamari. There are plenty of vegetarian dishes, ranging from *aloo gobi* (cauliflower and potatoes in curry sauce) to *baingan aloo masala* (eggplant, potatoes, tomatoes, ginger, garlic, green onions, and spices). Bottomless pots of delicious mango chutney and cucumber-dill sauce accompany your tasty feast. Anything you order will be fresh, well prepared, and served by courteous waiters wearing vests adorned with Indian-style mirrors and gold embroidery. Although expensive for Indian food, it's worth the extra bucks if you want to be ensured good quality and atmosphere.

✪ **Pane e Vino.** 3011 Steiner St. (at Union St.). ☎ **415/346-2111.** Reservations recommended. Main courses $8.50–$19.95. AE, MC, V. Mon–Thurs 11:30am–2:30pm and 5–10:30pm; Fri–Sat 11:30am–10:30pm; Sun 5–10pm. Valet parking (Mon–Sat evenings only) $8. Bus: 41 or 45. ITALIAN.

Pane e Vino is one of San Francisco's most authentic Italian restaurants. The food is consistently good—be careful not to fill up on the outstanding breads—the prices reasonable, and the mostly Italian-accented staff always smooth and efficient under pressure (you'll see). The two small dining rooms, separated by an open kitchen that emanates heavenly aromas, offer only limited seating, so expect a wait even if you have a reservation. The menu offers a wide selection of appetizers, including a fine carpaccio, *vitello tonnato* (sliced roasted veal and capers in lemony tuna sauce), and the hugely popular chilled artichoke stuffed with bread and tomatoes and served with vinaigrette. The antipasti of mixed grilled vegetables always spurs a fork fight. The broad selection of pastas includes flavorful *pennette alla boscaiola* with porcini mushrooms and pancetta in tomato cream sauce. Other specialties are grilled fish and meat dishes, including chicken breast marinated in lime juice and herbs. Top dessert picks are any of the Italian ice creams, crème caramel, and (but of course) creamy tiramisu.

✪ **PlumpJack Café.** 3127 Fillmore St. (between Filbert and Greenwich sts.). ☎ **415/563-4755.** www.plumpjackcafe.com. Reservations recommended. Main courses $15–$25. AE, DC, DISC, MC, V. Mon–Fri 11:30am–2pm; Mon–Sat 5:30–10pm. Valet parking $8. Bus: 41 or 45. CALIFORNIA/FRENCH/MEDITERRANEAN.

Wildly popular among San Francisco's style-setters, this small Cow Hollow restaurant is one of the neighborhood's most "in" places to dine. That's partly because it's run by one of the Getty clan (as in J. Paul), and because everything old is new again since chef Keith Luce took over the kitchen.

Appetizers might include crispy duckling confit on shallot marmalade with frisée and banyula vinaigrette. Main dishes might include parmesan breaded breast of capon stuffed with basil and prosciutto and drizzled with crushed tomato-almond sauce. Top it off with lime-leaf–scented panna cotta with fresh strawberries and rhubarb syrup. The extraordinarily extensive California wine list—gleaned from the Plump-Jack wine shop down the street—is sold at next to retail, with many wines available by the glass.

Prego. 2000 Union St. (at Buchanan St.). ☎ **415/563-3305.** Reservations recommended. Pasta and pizza $9–$13; main courses $13–$20. AE, DC, MC, V. Daily 11:30am–midnight. Bus: 22, 41, or 45. ITALIAN.

A light and airy trattoria with an upscale clientele, Prego is a place to be seen or people-watch as you dine behind the windows facing Union Street. Specialties include thin-crust, oak-fired pizzas, pasta, and grilled fish and meats. Spit-roasted, free-range chicken is prepared on a rotisserie and served with potatoes and vegetables. A good selection of wine is available by the glass or bottle.

✪ **Zinzino.** 2355 Chestnut St. (at Divisadero St.). ☎ **415/346-6623.** Reservations recommended. Main courses $9.50–$18.50. AE, DC, MC, V. Tues–Thurs 6–10pm; Fri–Sat 5:30–11pm; Sun 5:30–9:30pm. Bus: 22 or 30. ITALIAN.

Owner Ken Zankel and Spago alumna Andrea Rappaport have combined forces to create one of the city's top Italian restaurants. Zinzino might look like a tiny trattoria from the outside, but you could fit a small nuclear sub in the space from the sun-drenched facade to the shaded back patio of this former Laundromat.

Start with crispy calamari with a choice of herbed aïoli or tomato sauces (second in quality only to Scala's Earth and Surf), roasted jumbo prawns wrapped in crisp pancetta and bathed in tangy balsamic-reduction sauce, or peculiar-tasting shaved-fennel-and-mint salad—or try them all. Rappaport is giving Zuni Café a run for its money with her version of roasted half chicken, one of the most tender birds I can recall ("It's all the wood-fired oven," she admits). The accompanying goat-cheese salad and potato frisée were also superb.

INEXPENSIVE

✪ **Andalé Taqueria.** 2150 Chestnut St. (between Steiner and Pierce sts.). ☎ **415/749-0506.** Reservations not acepted. Most dishes $5.25–$9.50. AE, MC, V. Mon–Thurs 11am–10pm; Fri–Sat 11am–11pm; Sun 11am–9pm. Bus: 22, 28, 30, 30X, 43, 76, or 82X. MEXICAN.

I love this place. Andalé (Spanish for "hurry up") offers incredible high-end fast food for the health-conscious and the just plain hungry. As the long menu explains, this small California chain prides itself on its fresh ingredients and low-cal options. It uses no lard, preservatives, or canned items; salad dressings made with cholesterol-free double virgin olive oil; whole vegetarian beans (not refried); skinless chicken; salsas and aguas frescas made from fresh fruits and veggies; and mesquite-grilled meats. Add the location (on a sunny shopping stretch), sophisticated decor, full bar, and check-me-out patio seating (complete with corner fireplace), and it's no wonder the good-looking, fitness-fanatic Marina District considers this place home. Cafeteria-style service keeps prices low. *Bargain tips:* No one can complain about a quarter of a mesquite-roasted chicken with potatoes, salsa, and tortillas for $5.95. If you want to go traditional, stick with the giant burritos or the fantastic $2.75 tacos—a nibbler's dream.

✪ **Doidge's.** 2217 Union St. (between Fillmore and Steiner sts.). ☎ **415/921-2149.** Reservations essential on weekends. Breakfast $6–$10; lunch $5.25–$10. MC, V. Mon–Fri 8am–1:45pm; Sat–Sun 8am–2:45pm. Bus: 22 or 45. AMERICAN/BREAKFAST.

Doidge's, sweet, small, and always packed, has served one of the better breakfasts in San Francisco since 1971. The restaurant's fame rests on eggs Benedict; eggs Florentine, prepared with thinly sliced Motherlode ham, runs a close second. Invariably, the menu includes a gourmet omelet packed with luscious combinations; to delight the kid in you, hot chocolate comes in your very own teapot. Lunch also puts a gourmet spin on such favorites as Cobb salad, a lean ground chuck burger, and the good ol' BLT. The six seats at the original mahogany counter are most coveted by locals.

✪ **Eliza's.** 2877 California St. (at Broderick St.). ☎ **415/621-4819.** Reservations not accepted. Main courses $4.50–$5.15 at lunch, $5.25–$9 at dinner. MC, V ($10 minimum). Mon–Fri 11am–3pm and 5–9:45pm; Sat 11am–9:45pm. Bus: 6, 7, 21, 66, or 71. HUNAN/MANDARIN.

Eliza's is one of my very favorite restaurants—I eat here at least once a week. Despite the humorous train-wreck–like design of modern architecture, glass art, and color, this perennially packed neighborhood haunt serves some of the freshest, best-tasting, cheap Chinese in town. Unlike most comparable options, here the atmosphere (albeit unintentionally funky) and presentation parallel the food. The fantastically fresh soups, salads, seafood, pork, chicken, duck, and such specials as spicy eggplant are outstanding and served on beautiful Italian plates. (Get the sea bass with black bean sauce and go straight to heaven!) I often come at midday and order the wonderful kung-pao chicken lunch special: a mixture of tender chicken, peanuts, chili peppers, subtly hot sauce, and perfectly crunchy vegetables. It's one of 21 main-course choices that come with rice and soup for around $5. The place is also jumping at night, so prepare to stand in line.

Home Plate. 2274 Lombard St. (at Pierce St.). ☎ **415/922-HOME.** Reservations not accepted. Main courses $3.75–$6.50. MC, V. Daily 7am–4pm. Bus: 28, 30, 43, or 76. BREAKFAST.

Dollar for dollar, Home Plate just might be the best breakfast place in San Francisco. Many Marina residents kick off their hectic weekends by carbo-loading on big piles of buttermilk pancakes and waffles smothered with fresh fruit, or hefty omelets stuffed with everything from applewood-smoked ham to spinach. The first dish to arrive is a coveted plate of freshly baked scones, best eaten with a bit of butter and a dab of jam. Be sure to look over the daily specials scrawled on the little green chalkboard before you order. As every fan of this tiny cafe knows, it's best to call ahead and ask to have your name put on the waiting list before you slide into Home Plate.

Mel's Diner. 2165 Lombard St. (at Fillmore St.). ☎ **415/921-3039.** Reservations accepted. Main courses $4–$5.50 at breakfast, $6–$8 at lunch, $8–$12 at dinner. No credit cards. Sun–Wed 6am–2am; Thurs 6am–3am; Fri–Sat 24-hr. Bus: 22, 30, or 43. AMERICAN.

Sure, it's contrived, touristy, and nowhere near healthy, but when you get that urge for a chocolate shake and banana cream pie at the stroke of midnight—or when you want to entertain the kids—no other place in the city comes through like Mel's Diner. Modeled after a classic 1950s diner, right down to the nickel jukebox at each table, Mel's harks back to the halcyon days when cholesterol and fried foods didn't jab your guilty conscience with every greasy, wonderful bite. Too bad the prices don't reflect the '50s; a burger with fries and a Coke runs about $8.

    There's another Mel's at 3355 Geary St., at Stanyan Street (☎ **415/387-2244**); it's open 6am to 3am Thursday through Saturday.

Pluto's. 3258 Scott St. (at Chestnut St.). ☎ **415/7-PLUTOS.** Reservations not accepted. Main courses $3.50–$5.75. MC, V. Mon–Thurs 11:30am–10pm; Fri 11:30am–11pm; Sat 9:30am–11pm; Sun 9:30am–10pm. Bus: 28, 30, 42, or 76. CALIFORNIA.

Catering to the Marina District's underpaid and overworked DINKs (double income, no kids), Pluto's combines assembly-line efficiency with high quality. The result is cheap, fresh fare: huge salads with a dozen choices of toppings, oven-roasted poultry and grilled meats (the flank steak is great), sandwiches, and a wide array of sides like crispy garlic potato rings, seasonal veggies, and barbecued chicken wings. Pluto's serves cappuccinos, tea, sodas, bottled brews, and Napa wines, as well as homemade desserts. The ordering system is bewildering to newcomers; grab a checklist, then hand it to the servers who check off your order and relay it to the cashier. Seating is limited during the rush, but the turnover is fairly fast. A second location is at 627 Irving St., at 7th Avenue (☎ **415/753-8867**).

World Wrapps. 2257 Chestnut St. (between Pierce and Scott sts.). ☎ **415/563-9727.** Reservations not accepted. Wraps $2.95–$7. MC, V. Daily 11am–11pm. Bus: 22, 28, 30, 43, or 76. INTERNATIONAL.

There are hardly any tables here and plenty of other eateries nearby, so what's the big deal? It's yet another version of San Franciscans' beloved burrito, only this time it's not Mexican-influenced. These are tortillas filled with your choice of cuisine from around the world (hence the name). Fresh ingredients, cheap prices, and the love affair Marina residents have with hanging out on this street make World Wrapps the place to grab a bite. A second location is at 2227 Polk St., between Green and Vallejo streets (☎ **415/931-9727**).

9 Civic Center

EXPENSIVE

Jardinière. 300 Grove St. (at Franklin St.). ☎ **415/861-5555.** Reservations recommended. Main courses $21–$29; 6-course tasting menu $75. AE, CB, DC, DISC, MC, V. Daily 5:30–10:30pm; late menu Tues–Sun 10:30–midnight. Valet parking $8. Bus: 19 or 21. FRENCH/CALIFORNIA.

Jardinière is a pre- and post-symphony favorite, but it also happens to be the perfect setting for a cocktail. A culinary dream team runs the sexy dining room: owner-chef Traci Des Jardins, who packed up her pots and pans at Rubicon to go solo; owner-designer Pat Kuleto, who created the swank ambience; and general manager Doug Washington, whose good looks and unswerving charm won him local fame in the restaurant circuit. On most evenings the two-story brick structure is abuzz with an older crowd (including Mayor Brown, a regular) that sips cocktails at the centerpiece mahogany bar or watches the scene discreetly from the circular balcony. The restaurant's champagne theme extends to twinkling lights and fun ice buckets built into the balcony railing, making the atmosphere conducive to throwing back a few in the best of style—especially when there's live jazz (at 7pm nightly).

Actually, cocktailing is my preferred reason to visit Jardinière. True, the daily changing menu is lovely; it might include seared scallops with truffled potatoes and truffle reduction, the famed truffled chicken pot pie, or venison with celery root, red wine, braised cabbage, and juniper sauce. But the atmosphere just doesn't have enough warmth for me. Still, anyone in search of a quality meal will not be disappointed. Late diners can also come here for the limited menu served Tuesdays through Sundays from 10:30pm to midnight. I also have to give kudos to the great wine selection—many by the glass, and over 300 bottles.

MODERATE

Absinthe. 398 Hayes St. (at Gough St.). ☎ **415/551-1590.** Reservations recommended.
Breakfast $6–$12; most main courses $8.50–$18 at lunch, $9–$20 at dinner. AE, DC, DISC,
MC, V. Tues–Fri 7:30am–1am (bar menu 3pm–1am); Sat 10:30am–1am (brunch until 3pm,
bar menu 3pm–1am); Sun 10:30am–10:30pm (brunch until 3pm, bar menu 3pm–10:30pm).
Valet parking (Tues–Sat) $6 with dinner, $18 without. Bus: 21. SOUTHERN FRENCH.

A sexy, fun, *and* reasonably priced restaurant preferred by everyone from the theater-
going crowd to the young and chic is this Hayes Valley hot spot. Decor is scrumptious
brasserie, with French rattan cafe chairs, copper-topped tables, pressed-tin ceiling, soft
lighting, period art, and a rich use of color and fabric, including leather and mohair
banquettes. Fare is fun—from the specialty cocktails (ever had a "Ginger Rogers,"
made with gin, mint, lemon juice, ginger ale, and a squeeze of lime?) and good wine
list to the slew of seafood starters, including oysters and cold seafood platters. Appetizers range from classic (Caesar salad, French onion soup) to modern luxe (perhaps
grilled asparagus with black-truffled mayonnaise, or lamb's lettuce with pickled beets
and walnuts). Main courses are equally satisfying, from coq au vin to grilled salmon
with beet vinaigrette, dried fig and walnut crostini, and grilled vegetables to an excellent burger to inventive vegetarian dishes. Don't forget the fine cheese menu or the
noteworthy desserts. Stopping for breakfast? Anticipate creamy polenta with mascarpone, maple syrup, bananas, and toasted walnuts; soft-boiled eggs with sage croutons;
and the usual suspects.

Hayes Street Grill. 320 Hayes St. (near Franklin St.). ☎ 415/863-5545. Reservations rec-
ommended. Main courses $9.25–$18.75. AE, DC, DISC, MC, V. Mon–Fri 11:30am–2pm;
Mon–Thurs 5–9:30pm; Fri 5–10:30pm; Sat 5:30–10:30pm; Sun 5–8:30pm. Bus: 19, 31, or 38.
SEAFOOD.

For well over a decade this small, no-nonsense seafood restaurant owned and operated
by revered food writer and chef Patricia Unterman has maintained a solid reputation
among San Francisco's picky epicureans for its impeccably fresh and straightforwardly
prepared fish. Choices ranging from Hawaiian swordfish to Puget Sound salmon—
cooked to perfection, naturally—are matched with your sauce of choice (Szechuan
peanut, tomatillo salsa, shallot butter) and a side of signature french fries. Fancier
seafood specials, such as paella with clams, mussels, scallops, calamari, chorizo, and
saffron rice, are available, as well as an impressive selection of garden-fresh salads and
local grilled meats. Finish with the outstanding crème brûlée.

Millennium. In the Abigail Hotel, 246 McAllister St. (between Hyde and Larkin sts.).
☎ 415/487-9800. Reservations recommended. Main courses $13–$18. DC, MC, V. Daily
5–9:30pm. Bus: 5, 9, or 71. VEGAN.

Banking on the trend toward lighter, healthier cooking, chef Eric Tucker and his band
of merry waiters set out to prove that a meatless menu doesn't mean you have to sac-
rifice taste. In a narrow, handsome Parisian-style dining room with checkered tile
flooring, French windows, and sponge-painted walls, Millennium has had nothing but
favorable reviews for its egg-, butter-, and dairy-free creations since the day it opened.
Granted, it can be a hit-or-miss experience for nonvegans like me, but I've also had
some fantastic dishes (particularly soups). Favorites include sweet and spicy plantain
torte served over a wonderful papaya and black-bean salsa appetizer, and main courses
such as the filo purse filled with a ragout of wild mushrooms, leeks, and butternut
squash, or the warm Yukon Gold potato salad with sauteed portabello mushrooms.
Even the wine-and-beer list has a good selection of organic labels.

✪ **Zuni Café.** 1658 Market St. (at Franklin St.). ☎ **415/552-2522.** Reservations recommended. Main courses $15–$22.50. AE, MC, V. Tues–Sat 11:30am–midnight; Sun 11am–11pm. Valet parking $5. Muni Metro: All Market St. trams. Bus: 6, 7, 71, or 75. MEDITERRANEAN.

Even factoring in the sometimes-snotty waitstaff, Zuni Café a favorite place to have lunch. Its expanse of windows and prime Market Street location guarantee good people-watching—a favorite San Francisco pastime—and chef Judy Rodgers's Mediterranean-influenced menu is wonderfully diverse and satisfying. For the full effect, sit at the bustling, copper-topped bar and peruse the foot-long oyster menu (a dozen or so varieties are on hand at all times); you can also sit in the stylish exposed-brick dining room or on the outdoor patio. Although the changing menu always includes meat (such as New York steak with Belgian endive gratin) and fish (grilled or braised in the kitchen's brick oven), the proven winners are Rodgers's brick-oven-roasted chicken for two with Tuscan-style bread salad, the polenta appetizer with mascarpone, and the hamburger on grilled rosemary focaccia bread (a strong contender for the city's best burger). Whatever you decide, be sure to order a side of shoestring potatoes.

INEXPENSIVE

Tommy's Joynt. 1109 Geary St. (at Van Ness Ave.). ☎ **415/775-4216.** Reservations not accepted. Main courses $4–$7. No credit cards. Daily 10am–2am. Bus: 2, 3, 4, or 38. AMERICAN.

With its colorful mural exterior, Tommy's Joynt is hard to miss. It's a late-night favorite for those in search of a cheap and hearty meal. The interior looks like a Buffalo Bill museum that imploded—a wild collage of stuffed birds, a mounted buffalo head, an ancient piano, rusty firearms, fading prints, a beer-guzzling lion, and Santa Claus masks. The Hofbrau-style buffet offers a cornucopia of rib-clinging à la carte dishes such as the signature buffalo stew, ham sandwiches, sloppy joes, oxtails, corned beef, meatballs, and mashed potatoes. There's plenty of seating and almost 100 varieties of beer.

10 SoMa

EXPENSIVE

✪ **Azie.** 826 Folsom St (at 4th St.). ☎ **415/538-9444.** Reservations recommended. Main courses $22–$29. AE, DC, MC, V. Sun–Thurs 5:30–10:30pm; Fri–Sat 5:30–11:30pm. Valet parking $10. Bus: 15, 30, 32, 42, or 45. ASIAN-INSPIRED FRENCH.

Eschewing the same old same old, this ultraswank SoMa spot is a breath of fresh, hip, sexy air—in both food and atmosphere. Fashionable from the salt and pepper shakers to the DJ who spins unobtrusive jazzy grooves on the first-floor turntable, this deliciously dim dining room celebrates a "modernist interpretation of Pacific Rim." The rich red-and-brown split-level room contains fun light fixtures, 22-foot ceilings intimated by columns, translucent paneling, curtained booths (on the first floor), and an exhibition kitchen. Equally sexy, is executive chef and partner Jody Denton's innovative and beautifully presented cuisine. Denton, one of the city's rising talents, offers various must-try dishes: "poker chips and dice"—sashimi four ways with cubed sticky rice and wasabi-tobiko dipping sauce; "nine bites," a slew of adorable mini appetizers I order every time I set foot in the door; and tuna sashimi roll—especially if you like truffle oil, because the truffle ponzu dipping sauce scents the entire table. Main courses are delightful—inventive, generous, and, following the trend of 2000, luxurious. How so? How about lobster and sweetbread pot au feu with truffles, fingerling potatoes, turnips, and fennel. My favorite? Whole crispy fish. The ambitious wine list features 300 to 400 selections. Desserts include cheeses, perhaps triple chocolate cream napoleon, and almond cardamom panna cotta.

✪ **Boulevard.** 1 Mission St. (at Embarcadero and Steuart St.). ☎ **415/543-6084.** Reservations recommended. Main courses $19–$30. AE, CB, DC, DISC, MC, V. Mon–Fri 11:30am–2:15pm; Sun–Wed 5:30–10pm; Thurs–Sat 5:30–10:30pm. Valet parking $9. Bus: 15, 30, 32, 42, or 45. AMERICAN.

Master restaurant designer Pat Kuleto and chef Nancy Oaks teamed up to create one of San Francisco's most exciting restaurants, and although it made its debut in 1993, it's still one of my—and the city's—all-time favorites.

The dramatically artistic belle époque interior, with vaulted brick ceilings, floral banquettes, a mosaic floor, and tulip-shaped lamps, is the setting for Oaks's equally impressive sculptural and mouth-watering dishes. Starters alone could make a perfect meal, especially if you indulge in sweetbreads wrapped in prosciutto on watercress and Lola Rose lettuce, with garlic croutons and whole-grain mustard vinaigrette; Sonoma foie gras with elderberry syrup, toast, and Bosc pear salad; or Maine sea scallops on garlic mashed potato croustade with truffle and portabello mushroom relish. The nine or so main courses are equally creative and might include pan-roasted miso-glazed sea bass with asparagus salad, Japanese rice, and shiitake mushroom broth, or spit-roasted cider-cured pork loin with sweet potato–swirled mashed potatoes and sauteed baby red chard. Vegetarian items, such as wild-mushroom risotto with fresh chanterelles and parmesan, are also offered. Three levels of formality—bar, open kitchen, and main dining room—keep things from getting too snobby. Although steep prices prevent most from making Boulevard a regular gig, you'd be hard-pressed to find a better place for a special, fun-filled occasion. Cocktailers: Do ask the bartender about the special martinis—they're some of the best in town.

✪ **Fifth Floor Restaurant.** In the Hotel Palomar, 12 Fourth St. (at Market St). ☎ **415/348-1555.** Reservations required. Main courses: $24–$39. AE, DC, DISC, MC, V. Mon–Thurs 5:30–10pm; Fri–Sat 5:30–11pm. Valet parking: $8 per hour up to $24. Bus: All Market St. buses. MODERN FRENCH.

Two white-hot restaurants opened in late 1999, and this is one of them (Restaurant Gary Danko is the other). For a brief moment, skeptics wondered whether locals would head downtown to the fifth floor of a hotel and pay more than $30 per entree. It's no mystery now. Since its opening, executive chef George Morrone (who opened Aqua and has reigned at L.A.'s Hotel Bel-Air and San Francisco's Campton Place), has enjoyed a month-long waiting list. Like the decor—rich colors and fabrics, red leather and velvet banquettes, Frette linens, zebra-striped carpeting, and a club-like atmosphere—his menu features all things luxurious. You'll see Kobe beef, foie gras, sea urchin (accompanied by salmon paillard, Belon oyster, and diver scallop), caviar, the signature "tuna foie gras," suckling pig à l'orange, milk-fed veal steak with Madeira glazed sweetbreads, curry oil, and jasmine rice—the list goes on. While giving a nod to the classics, the kitchen goes one step further—into a world of pure modern indulgence. Some say it's the best food in town. Me? The jury's still out. But if you want a memorable meal and can afford to pay through the nose for it, this is your place. Sommelier Rajat Parr is big on little wineries and specialties from Burgundy; the outstanding wine list offers 250-plus selections.

Hawthorne Lane. 22 Hawthorne Lane (at Howard St. between Second and Third sts.). ☎ **415/777-9779.** Reservations recommended. Jacket appropriate but not required. Main courses $10–$14 at lunch, $20–$34 at dinner. CB, DC, DISC, JCB, MC, V. Mon–Fri 11:30am–2pm; Sun–Thurs 5:30–10pm; Fri–Sat 5:30–10:30pm. Bar menu Mon–Thurs

2:30–10pm; Fri–Sat 5:30–10:30pm; Sun 5:30–10pm. BART: Montgomery Station. Muni Metro: F, J, K, L, M, or N. Bus: 12, 30, 45, or 76. CALIFORNIA.

David Gingrass, who with his then-wife Anne launched the famed Postrio, presides over the kitchen at Hawthorne Lane. Menus change with the seasons and reflect the Asian and European influences that made the team famous under Wolfgang Puck. The bar area is comfortable and inviting, with both cocktail tables and bar seating. In the dining room, earthquake reinforcement beams divide the space in a way that is not only functional, but also decorative. The room is not too fancy or pretentious, but well lit and adorned with bright artwork, fresh floral arrangements, and a leaf motif throughout.

Meals here haven't been mind-blowing of late, but they are certainly above par. Each dish is beautifully presented without being too contrived, but usually with a whimsical accent, such as a leaf-shaped pastry or a bird made of a carrot sliver. Dishes tend to be well balanced, and accompaniments are often more exciting than the main course. If it's on the menu, don't pass up the black-cod appetizer served with a miso glaze. Main courses might include roasted Sonoma lamb with wild mushroom risotto, warm escarole salad, and pomegranate sauce. Desserts are as good to look at as they are to eat.

MODERATE

○ **Fringale Restaurant.** 570 Fourth St. (between Brannan and Bryant sts.). ☎ 415/ **543-0573.** Reservations recommended. Main courses $4–$12 at lunch; $11–$21 at dinner. AE, MC, V. Mon–Fri 11:30am–3pm; Mon–Sat 5:30–10:30pm. Bus: 30 or 45. FRENCH.

One of San Francisco's best restaurants for the money, Fringale—colloquial French for "sudden urge to eat"—has enjoyed a weeklong waiting list since the day chef and co-owner Gerald Hirigoyen opened this small bistro. Sponged, eggshell-blue walls and other muted sand and earth tones provide a serene dining environment, which is all but shattered when the 18-table room fills with Hirigoyen's fans. For starters, try steamed mussels with fried garlic vinaigrette, or the sheep's-milk cheese and prosciutto terrine with figs and greens. Among the dozen or so main courses on the seasonally changing menu, you might find rack of lamb with potato gratin or pork tenderloin confit with onion and apple marmalade. Desserts are worth savoring, too, particularly the Gateau Basque (which has won me many culinary friends since I began preparing it myself with the help of Hirigoyen's cookbook). The mostly French waiters provide charming service, and prices are surprisingly reasonable for such high-quality cuisine.

Gordon Biersch Brewery Restaurant. 2 Harrison St. (on the Embarcadero). ☎ 415/ **243-8246.** Reservations recommended. Main courses $7.50–$17. AE, DC, DISC, MC, V. Mon–Fri 11:30am–3pm; Sat–Sun 11:30am–4pm; Sun–Mon 5–9pm; Tues–Thurs 5–10pm; Fri–Sat 5–10:30pm (bar closes later). Bus: 32. CALIFORNIA.

Popular with the young Republican crowd (loose ties and tight skirts predominate), this modern, two-tiered brewery and restaurant eschews traditional brew-pub fare— no spicy chicken wings on this menu—in an attempt to attract a more upscale clientele. And it works. The baby-back ribs with garlic fries are the best-seller, followed by the lemon-roasted half chicken with garlic mashed potatoes. Start with the delicate and crunchy calamari fritti appetizer or, if you're garlic hounds, the tangy Caesar salad. Most dishes can be paired with one of the brewery's lagers. Couples bent on a quiet, romantic dinner can skip this one; when the lower-level bar fills up, you practically have to shout to be heard. But beer-lovers who want to pair their suds with decent grub will be quite content.

Lulu. 816 Folsom St. (at Fourth St.). ☎ **415/495-5775.** Reservations recommended. Main courses $7–$13 at lunch; $10–$18 at dinner. AE, DC, MC, V. Sun–Thurs 11:30am–10:30pm; Fri–Sat 11:30am–11pm. Valet parking $10. Bus: 15, 30, 32, 42, or 45. FRENCH PROVINCAL.

Famed chef Reed Hearon put this place on the map, but long after his departure, Lulu is still an excellent place for a San Francisco dining experience. Energy radiates throughout the enormous dining room as the cadre of cooks, communicating with headsets, slide bubbling plates of pizza and shellfish in and out of the open kitchen's wood-fired ovens. Watching the carefully orchestrated chaos makes dining here something of an event. The main room seats 170 and has a crowded bar that overlooks the cavernous room, but even amid a sea of stylish diners, the room somehow feels warm and convivial. Then there's the food, which is consistently good. Locals return again and again for roasted mussels piled high on an iron skillet; pork loin with fennel, garlic, and olive oil; and any of the other wonderful dishes. Everything is served family style and is meant to be shared. Save room for dessert; opt for the gooey, oozing chocolate cake with a side of melting ice cream.

South Park Café. 108 South Park (between Second and Third sts. and Brannan and Bryant sts.). ☎ **415/495-7275.** Reservations recommended for dinner. Main courses $12.50–$18. AE, MC, V. Mon–Fri 7:30am–10pm; Sat 6–10pm. Bus: 15, 30, 32, 42, 45, or 76. FRENCH.

Want to immerse yourself in the dot-community? Head to lunch at casual-chic South Park Café, where the chat is of IPOs, ISPs, and B-to-B and C-to-C markets in between bites of white-wine mussels or roasted duck breast with lavender sauce. The restaurant is in one of the most cutting-edge parts of town. On a sunny day, you can watch the young and the hopelessly hip lunch at the adjoining park.

Thirsty Bear Brewing Company. 661 Howard St. (1 block east of the Moscone Center). ☎ **415/974-0905.** Reservations recommended. Main courses $12–$18. AE, DC, MC, V. Mon–Fri 11:30am–11pm; Sat noon–11pm; Sun 4:30–11pm. Bus: 12, 15, 30, 45, or 76. SPANISH.

Despite the dumb name, the Thirsty Bear Brewing Company is a favorite of the Financial District/SoMa crowd, who come for the excellent house-made brews and Spanish food. Paella Valenciana—a sizzling combo of chicken, shrimp, sausage, shellfish, and saffron-laden rice served in a cast-iron skillet—is a must. Upscale pub grub includes a variety of hot and cold tapas, a few winners being *escalivada* (roasted vegetables—spicy caramelized onions are outstanding—served at room temperature) and *espinacas à la catalana* (spinach sautéed with garlic, pine nuts, and raisins). Ask the waiter which brews best accompany the dishes. The house's signature dessert is La Sagrada Familia—twin towers of sugar cones (fans of Gaudí will recognize them immediately) filled with chocolate mousse that rest on a bed of Chantilly cream and fresh berries. Almost as impressive as the food is the costly conversion from a high-ceilinged brick warehouse to a two-level industrial-chic brew pub complete with pool tables and dartboards.

INEXPENSIVE

✪ **AsiaSF.** 201 9th St. (at Howard St.). ☎ **415/255-8889.** Reservations recommended. Main courses $7–$17. AE, DC, MC, V ($20 minimum). Daily 5–10pm. Bus: 9, 12, 42, or 47. CALIFORNIA/ASIAN.

At AsiaSF you'll be entertained by Asian men—dressed as women—who lip-sync show tunes as they dish out an excellent grilled shrimp and herb salad, Asian-influenced hamburger, pot stickers, duck quesadillas, and chicken sate. Fortunately, the food and the atmosphere are as colorful as the staff, which means a night here is more than a meal—it's a very happening event.

Hamburger Mary's. 1582 Folsom St. (at 12th St.). ☎ **415/626-5767.** Reservations recommended. Breakfast $5–$9; main courses $6–$10. AE, DC, DISC, MC, V. Tues–Thurs 11:30am–10:30pm (bar closes at 1am); Fri 11:30am–midnight (bar closes at 2am); Sat 10am–midnight (bar closes at 2am); Sun 10am–10:30pm (bar closes at 1am). Bus: 9, 12, 42, or 47. AMERICAN.

It's not the hamburgers but the wildly alternative clientele that keeps Hamburger Mary's popular with gays, lesbians, and just about everyone else who's a little left of center. The kitschy decor includes thrift-shop floral wallpaper, family photos, garage-sale prints, stained glass, religious drawings, and Oriental screens. You'll get to know the bar well—it's where you'll stand with the tattooed masses while you wait for a table. Don't despair: They mix a good drink, and people-watching is what you're here for anyway. Sandwiches, salads, and vegetarian dishes provide an alternative to the famous greasy burgers, served on healthful nine-grain bread (like it makes a difference). *Tip:* Go with the home fries over the french fries. In the morning, Hamburger Mary's doubles as a breakfast joint, a good stop for a three-egg omelet or French toast.

Long Life Noodle Company & Jook Joint. 139 Steuart St. (near Mission St.). ☎ **415/281-3818.** Reservations recommended. Main courses $5.50–$8.50. MC, V. Mon–Thurs 11:30am–10pm; Fri 11:30am–11pm; Sat 5pm–11am. Bus: 15, 30, 32, 42, or 45. NOODLES.

Asian noodles are all the rage, so it comes as no surprise that big-time restaurateurs such as George Chen of Betelnut are willing to invest big bucks in what has traditionally been a small-change business. The concept at Long Life is to offer a wide range of unfamiliar noodle dishes from China, Korea, Japan, and other Asian lands and serve them in a familiar Westernized setting (in this case, a sleek, super-modern space with lots of neon and Plexiglas). The problem is choosing from the 30 or so noodle dishes, all of which are wildly different. Do you go with Buddha's Bliss (ramen noodles in miso broth with smoked trout, tofu, and endoki mushrooms) or Enchanted Heat (a "Chinese hangover cure" composed of whole-wheat noodles, lily pods, tree ears, and secret healing ginseng herbs)? I recommend the Ghengis' Buns, crisp sesame biscuits filled with Chinese roast beef, cucumber, cilantro, and hoisin sauce; wash it all down with Cool Cucumber Juice or Ginseng Ginger Ale.

✪ **Manora's.** 1600 Folsom St. (at 12th St.). ☎ **415/861-6224.** Reservations not accepted. Main courses $6.95–$11.95. MC, V. Mon–Fri 11:30am–2:30pm; Mon–Sat 5:30–10:30pm; Sun 5–10pm. Bus: 9, 12, or 47. THAI.

Manora's cranks out some of the best Thai in town and is well worth a jaunt to SoMa. But this is no relaxed affair. It's perpetually packed (unless you come early), and you'll be seated sardine-like at one of the cramped but well-appointed tables. During the dinner rush, the noise level can make conversation among larger parties almost impossible, but the food is so darn good, you'll probably prefer to turn toward your plate and stuff your face. Start with a Thai iced tea or coffee and tangy soup or chicken satay, which comes with decadent peanut sauce. Follow with any of the wonderful dinner dishes—which should be shared—and a side of rice. There are endless options, including a vast array of vegetarian plates. Every remarkably flavorful dish arrives seemingly seconds after you order it, which is great if you're hungry, a bummer if you were planning a long, leisurely dinner. Come before 7pm or after 9pm if you don't want a loud, rushed meal.

✪ **Tú Lan.** 8 Sixth St. (at Market St.). ☎ **415/626-0927.** Reservations not accepted. Main courses $3.50–$7. No credit cards. Mon–Sat 11am–9pm. Bus: 6, 7, 27, 31, 66, or 71. Cable car: Powell-Mason and Powell-Hyde lines. Muni Metro: F, J, K, L, M, N. VIETNAMESE.

You'll have to brave the winos, weirdos, and street stench to get to this total dive bordering Union Square and SoMa, but I do it happily to get my hands on the best imperial rolls on the planet. Daily crowds and even Julia Child (whose face graces the greasy old menus) have been known to pull up a chair at this down-and-dirty shack of a restaurant. They feast on such goodies as out-of-this-world imperial rolls on a bed of rice noodles, lettuce, peanuts, and mint (under $5), and other regional dishes.

11 The Mission District

EXPENSIVE

Flying Saucer. 1000 Guerrero St. (at 22nd St.). ☎ **415/641-9955.** Reservations recommended. Main courses $19–$36. AE, MC, V. Mon–Sat 5:30–10pm. BART: 24th St. Station. Bus: 14 or 26. FRENCH.

Outrageously yet artfully presented food is the hallmark of this Mission District fixture. Peering into the glass-walled kitchen, diners can catch the kitchen staff leaning over plates, carefully standing a jumbo prawn on its head atop a baked column of potato polenta. Fish, beef, and fowl dishes are competently grilled, baked, or flamed before being surrounded by a flurry of sauces and garnishes. While the pricey food is certainly intense and flavorful, the overwhelming sensation at this bistro is visual. The party extends from the plate to the decor, where plastic flying saucers mingle with colorful murals and creative lighting. The menu changes frequently, and there are almost always specials. If you ask your waiter to bring you the chef's most flamboyant-looking offering, chances are you won't be disappointed. Reservations are essential, as is a blind eye to the sometimes infuriatingly snotty service.

MODERATE

✪ **Foreign Cinema.** 2534 Mission St. (between 21st and 22nd sts.). ☎ **415/648-7600.** www.foreigncinema.com. Reservations recommended. Main courses $12–$19. MC, V. Sun–Wed 5:30–10pm; Thurs–Sat 5:30–11pm; late-night menu until 1am. Valet parking $8. Bus: 14, 14L, 49. FRENCH BISTRO.

This place is so chic that it's hard to believe it's a San Francisco restaurant, and so well hidden on Mission Street that it eludes me every time I seek the valet. The ultratrendy vibe carries through the long, mysterious entry hall and alternative-cool hosts at the end of it to the doorway and beyond. An indoor seat is a lovely place to watch San Francisco's most fashionable; outdoors (heated, partially covered, but still chilly), the enormous foreign film showing on the side of an adjoining building steals the show. (Although the purpose is not to actually watch the film, it's still a bummer for those facing away from it.) Thing is, the food has been uneven. Not surprising since this newbie seats and serves up to 200. Still, it's a drag when sweetbreads or foie gras appetizers come tired and cold. On occasions that they don't, the food surpasses "good enough" and even can be classified as enjoyable. It might also include asparagus salad with truffle vinaigrette, frogs' legs, herb-crusted chicken breast with garlic mashed potatoes, roasted duck breast with black mission figs, rosemary marinated lamb loin with potato gratin, and lobster and monkfish bouillabaisse with coral aïoli. But truth be told, even if the food sucked I'd come here. It's just that cool.

Gordon's House of Fine Eats. 500 Florida St. (at 18th St). ☎ **415/861-8900.** Reservations recommended. Main courses $8.25–$28. AE, MC, V. Mon–Fri 11:30am–4:30pm; Sun–Mon 5:30–10pm; Tues–Wed 5:30–11pm; Thurs–Sat 5:30pm–midnight . Bus: 27. AMERICAN.

This is one of my favorite spots for a fun night out with friends. The food is fine, not noteworthy on the serious foodie scale, but all is good once you submerge yourself in the jovial scene. In the 110-seat color-and-concrete warehouse space, San Francisco's funky-fashionable and everyday dot-commers cluster around mahogany tables beneath a 20-foot open-beam ceiling. A long dining counter faces the open kitchen

Hidden Treasures

Okay, so I couldn't find a neat category in which to place these two restaurants, but since they're among the city's best, it would be a crime to leave them out. If you're not familiar with the streets of San Francisco, be sure to call first to get directions; otherwise, you'll spend more time driving than dining.

✪ **42 Degrees,** 235 16th St., at Illinois Street, 1 block off Third Street (☎ 415/777-5558), tucked behind the Esprit Outlet in an industrial area, is an oh-so-chic supper club. A jazz trio sets the mood in the warehouse-like, velvet-soft two-story dining room. Sleek cocktailers crowd the dark bar area, which specializes in scotches, cognacs, and a selection of small vintners' wines. The dining mezzanine has a men's smoking-club feel with a great view of the Bay Bridge; downstairs is all 1940s sophistication, from the red velvet curtains that frame 22-foot windows right down to the waitstaff and clientele. There's also a dining patio that's a perfect spot for a sunny luncheon. Dishes are Mediterranean-influenced and rather expensive. The menu changes weekly but usually includes house favorites such as hearts of romaine salad with Caesar dressing, marrow bones with toast, Atlantic salmon, and Niman meats. It's easier to book a table at lunch, but the time to come is for dinner, when the chi-chi vibe is full-force; reservations are definitely recommended. Prices for main courses run $19 to $27. Lunch is served in the summer only, Monday to Friday 11:30am to 3pm. Dinner is Wednesday through Sunday 6 to 10:30pm. Take bus 22. American Express, MasterCard, and Visa are accepted. If you find yourself parking along a dank industrial street where no decent restaurant would dare to set up shop, you're in the right place.

Woodward's Garden, 1700 Mission St., at Duboce Avenue (☎ 415/621-7122), named after a turn-of-the-century amusement center in the same location, is the kind of gem many San Franciscans don't even know about. And good thing: There are only nine tables. Local foodies will mention Woodward's as if everyone should know about it, but its location (under a freeway on-ramp in SoMa), simple exterior, and unobtrusive sign keep this upscale, modestly priced restaurant under wraps. Still, the intimate (okay, tiny) environment makes for sincerely romantic dining. But it's not just the stealthy hype that keeps the place popular: The limited, but ambitious, menu makes Woodward's an all-around winner. The five or so entrees might include sauteed salmon with fava beans, spring leeks, baby carrots, mashed potatoes, and beurre blanc, or pan-fried truffled chicken breast with hedgehog mushrooms, baby artichokes, white beans, frisée, and radicchio. To top it off, with so few tables and both the kitchen (formerly of Postrio and Greens) and the waitstaff so attentive, you'll feel they opened their doors just for you. Don't traipse down here without reservations—or a car, for that matter. Main courses run $16.50 to $28. There are seatings from Tuesday to Sunday at 6, 6:30, 8, and 8:30pm. MasterCard and Visa are accepted.

for stoveside seating. Eclectic live music drifts through the room almost nightly from the band quietly jamming on the understated mezzanine. At least partial credit for the festive vibe must go to owner-chef Gordon Drysdale, previously of San Francisco's Bix and Caffè Museo at the Museum of Modern Art, who bounces through the dining room almost every evening. The menu sections include the likes of "healthful," "comfort," "local showcase," and "luxury." The ultra-rich appetizer coquille St. Jacques—scallop shells bubbling with mushroom cream sauce beneath seared scallops—is luxurious. Moist and decadent pork osso buco towering over a heap of brown butter spaetzle is indeed comfort at its most comfortable. Grilled king salmon with salt-roasted beet vinaigrette might be one of the night's tributes to local showcase. Healthful? A selection ranging from a veggie burger to fava bean ravioli with morels and artichoke chips. Do what you will, but don't skip dessert. Go directly for the baked s'more Alaskan, a masterpiece of chocolate graham cracker, crème anglaise, and ice cream.

INEXPENSIVE

✪ **Delfina.** 3621 18th St. (between Dolores and Guererro sts.). ☎ **415/552-4055.** Reservations required. Main courses $9–$15. MC, V. Daily 5:30–10pm. Bus: 26, 33; Metro: J. SEASONAL ITALIAN.

Delfina was the darling of late 1998, and it remains the standard-setter for neighborhood restaurants of the millennium. Why? Because it eschews bells, whistles, big-time design, and fancy preparations for something that used to be utterly San Francisco: straightforward simplicity and a small-business feel. Unpretentious atmosphere, unreasonably reasonable prices, and chef and co-owner Craig Stoll's ultrafresh seasonal Italian cuisine mean you're in for a painless and delicious experience from the minute you're seated by Craig's fiancée, Ann Spencer, to the time you receive your surprisingly low (by local standards) bill. The recipe for success has been so rewarding for Delfina that it was forced to expand to accommodate frustrated diners begging for reservations. The menu features Neiman Ranch flat-iron steak with French fries; roasted chicken with Yukon gold mashed potatoes and shiitake mushrooms; and Alaskan halibut roasted on a fig leaf with yellow wax beans and tarragon butter. The only downside: It's impossible to find parking, and there's no valet.

✪ **Pauline's.** 260 Valencia St. (between 14th St. and Duboce Ave.). ☎ **415/552-2050.** Reservations recommended. Main courses $10.50–$21.50. MC, V. Tues–Sat 5–10pm. Bus: 14, 26, or 49. PIZZA.

Housed in a cheery yellow double-decker building that stands out like a beacon in a somewhat seedy neighborhood, Pauline's does only two things—pizzas and salads—but does them better than any other restaurant in the city. It's worth running the gauntlet of panhandlers for a slice of Italian sausage pizza on handmade thin-crust dough. The eclectic toppings include house-spiced chicken, French goat cheese, roasted eggplant, Danish fontina cheese, and tasso (spiced pork shoulder). The salads are equally amazing: certified organic, handpicked by California growers, and topped with fresh and dried herbs (including edible flowers) from Pauline's own gardens in Berkeley. The wine list offers a smart selection of low-priced wines, and service is excellent. Yes, prices are a bit steep (small pizzas start at $11.75), but what a paltry price to pay for perfection.

✪ **The Slanted Door.** 584 Valencia St. (at 17th St.). ☎ **415/861-8032.** Reservations recommended. Lunch main courses $6.50–$15.50; most dinner dishes $7–$18.50. MC, V. Tues–Sun 11:30am–3pm; Sun–Thurs 5:30–10pm; Fri–Sat 5:30–10:30pm. Valet parking $7. Bus: 22, 26, 33, 49, or 53. BART: 16th St. Station. VIETNAMESE.

This place is so hip that Mick Jagger and President Clinton made stopovers last time they hit town. Why? Despite the sometimes-aloof staff, the colorful industrial-chic warehouse of a dining room serves incredibly fresh and flavorful Vietnamese food at excellent prices (not that Mick and Bill cared about price). Pull up a modern, color-washed chair and order anything from clay-pot catfish or amazing green papaya salad to one of the inexpensive lunch rice dishes, which come in a large ceramic bowl and are topped with such options as grilled shrimp or stir-fried eggplant. Dinner items, which change seasonally, might include steamed chicken with black-bean sauce, long beans with shrimp, or vegetarian noodles sauteed with mushrooms, lily buds, tofu, bamboo, and shiitake mushrooms. Whatever you order, it's bound to be wholesome, but flavorful and outstanding. There's also an eclectic collection of teas, which come by the pot for $3 to $5.

✪ **Taquerias La Cumbre.** 515 Valencia St. (between 16th and 17th sts.). ☎ **415/ 863-8205.** Reservations not accepted. Tacos and burritos $2–$4.25; dinner plates $5–$7. DISC, MC, V. Mon–Sat 11am–10pm; Sun noon–9pm. BART: Mission. Bus: 14, 22, 33, 49, or 53. MEXICAN.

If San Francisco commissioned a flag honoring its favorite food, we'd probably all be waving a banner of the Golden Gate Bridge bolstering a giant burrito—that's how much we love the mammoth tortilla-wrapped meals. And while most restaurants gussy up their gastronomic goods with million-dollar decor and glamorous gimmicks, the burrito needs only to be craftily constructed. Use fresh pork, steak, chicken, or vegetables, plus cheese, beans, rice, salsa, and maybe a dash of guacamole or sour cream, and practically the whole town will drive to the remotest corners to taste it. In this case, the fact that it's served in a cafeteria-like brick-lined room with overly shellacked tables and chairs is all the better: There's no mistaking the attraction here.

Ti Couz. 3108 16th St. (at Valencia St.). ☎ **415/252-7373.** Reservations not accepted. Crêpes $1.95–$8.25. MC, V. Mon–Thurs 11am–11pm; Fri–Sat 10am–1am; Sun 10am–10pm. BART: 16th & Mission. Bus: 14, 22, 33, 49, or 53. CRÊPES.

At Ti Couz (say "Tee Cooz"), one of the most architecturally stylish and popular restaurants in the Mission, the headliner is simple: the delicate, paper-thin crêpe. While the fillings aren't exactly original, they're well executed and infinite in their combinations. The menu advises how to enjoy these wraps: Order a light crêpe as an appetizer, a heftier one as a main course, and a drippingly sweet one for dessert. Recommended combinations are listed, but you can build your own from the 15 main-course selections (such as smoked salmon, mushrooms, sausage, ham, scallops, and onions) and 19 dessert options (caramel, fruit, chocolate, Nutella, and more). Soups and salads are equally stellar; the sensational seafood salad, for example, is a compilation of shrimp, scallops, and ahi tuna with veggies and five kinds of lettuce. Ciders and beer complement the cuisine.

✪ **Universal Café.** 2814 19th St. (at Bryant St.). ☎ **415/821-4608.** Reservations recommended for dinner. Main courses $2–$8 at breakfast (full on weekends, continental on weekdays), $5–$12 at lunch, $8–$20 at dinner. AE, MC, V. Tues–Fri 11:30am–2:30pm; Sat–Sun 9am–2:30pm; Tues–Thurs 6–10pm; Fri–Sat 6–11pm; Sun 5:30–10pm. Bus: 27. AMERICAN/FRENCH.

It was love at first sight (and bite) at this small restaurant in the middle of an up-and-coming part of inner Mission. Not only does the place look good—suave and stylish, with thick floor-to-ceiling windows and a profusion of sculptured metal and marble—it also attracts a nightly gaggle of locals. They come for phenomenal focaccia sandwiches (such as moist and memorable salmon), inventive thin-crust pizzas, and gourmet salads at lunch. Superb dinner dishes include braised duck leg on a bed of creamy polenta; sea bass served with risotto, spinach, and caramelized onions; and hearty pot roast with lumpy mashed potatoes and fresh veggies. Granted, it's on the way to nowhere, but if you're near the Mission and have a few minutes to spare, it's well worth the detour.

Get Away For Less.

Avis features GM cars.

With great offers and services from Avis, you'll get more out of your vacation! And now you can **save $20 on a weekly rental**. All the information you need is on the coupon below. Plus most rentals come with free unlimited mileage to save you even more.

As an added touch you can count on our famous "We try harder." service for a fast, hassle-free rental. Because speed and personal service is what everyone at Avis is dedicated to delivering.

For more information and reservations, call your travel agent or Avis toll free at **1-800-831-8000**.

AVIS

We try harder.

For You.

Save $20 On A Weekly Rental

Reserve an Avis Intermediate through Full Size 4-Door car for a minimum of five consecutive days. At time of rental, present this coupon at the Avis counter and you can save $20. **An advance reservation is required.** Subject to complete Terms and Conditions below. Rental must begin by 06/30/01.

For reservations and information, call your travel consultant or Avis toll free at **1-800-831-8000**.

Terms and Conditions: Coupon valid on an Intermediate (Group C) through a Full Size 4-Door (Group E) car. Dollars off applies to the cost of the total rental with a minimum of 5 days. A Saturday night overstay is required. Coupon must be surrendered at time of rental; one per rental. Coupon valid at Avis participating locations in the U.S. An advance reservation is required. Cars subject to availability. Taxes, local government surcharges, vehicle licensing and an airport recruitment fee at some locations, optional items such as LDW, additional driver fee and refueling fee are extra. Renter must meet Avis driver and credit requirements. Minimum age is 25 but may vary by location. Rental must begin by 6/30/01.

Coupon #: **MUNA002**

Rental Sales Agent Instructions
At checkout:
In AWD, enter AWD number.
In CPN, enter **MUNA002**.
Complete this information:
RA # _____
Rental location _____
Attach to COUPON tape.

AVIS

www.avis.com

11/99 DTPP

It's a Whole New World with

Frommer's

12 The Castro

Although you see gay and lesbian singles and couples at almost any restaurant in San Francisco, the following spots cater particularly to the gay community—but being gay is certainly not a requirement for enjoying them.

EXPENSIVE

✪ **Mecca.** 2029 Market St. (between 14th and Church sts.). ☎ **415/621-7000.** www.sfmecca.com. Reservations recommended. Main courses $15–$25. AE, DC, MC, V. Mon–Wed 6–11pm; Thurs–Fri 6pm–midnight; Sun 5–10pm. Valet parking $8. Muni Metro: F, K, L, or M. Bus: 8, 22, 24, or 37. AMERICAN.

In 1996, Mecca entered the scene in a decadent swirl of chocolate-brown velvet, stainless steel, cement, and brown Naugahyde—industrial-chic supper club that makes you want to order a martini just so you'll match the ambience. The eclectic city clientele (with a heavy dash of same-sex couples) mingles at the oval centerpiece bar. A night here promises a live DJ spinning hot grooves (or live entertainment on Mondays) and a fine California meal, served at tables tucked into several nooks. Menu options include such classic starters as Osetra caviar, oysters on the half shell, and Caesar salad, as well as more creative dishes, such as stir-fried clams with garlic and minced pork in black-bean sauce. Main courses include shrimp and lemongrass-crusted Chilean sea bass, rosemary-grilled rack of lamb, and soft-shell crabs with white-corn salsa and Creole mustard vinaigrette. The food is very good, but it's that only-in–San Francisco vibe that makes this place the smokin' hot spot in the Castro.

MODERATE

Caffè Luna Piena. 558 Castro St. (between 18th and 19th sts.). ☎ **415/621-2566.** Reservations recommended for brunch. Main courses $9–$17. AE, DC, DISC, MC, V. Daily 9am–3pm; Tues–Sun 5:30–10pm. Muni Metro: F, K, L, or M. Bus: 24, 35, or 37. ITALIAN.

This is one of the Castro's warmest and most sophisticated dining environments, complete with rich yellow walls adorned with local artwork. The room stretches back to the outdoor dining patio (yes, there are heat lamps) and a lush Japanese garden. The fare is contemporary American with Italian and Mediterranean influences. Lunch options include soups, salads, and sandwiches (with a choice of garlic fries or a green salad), such as grilled eggplant with roasted red pepper and smoked mozzarella on *pane integrale.* Main lunch courses might include blanched vegetables and lemon-caper vinaigrette. Dinner features such dishes as grilled black-pepper filet mignon with herb blue cheese–cabernet butter and caramelized red onions, and roasted vegetable lasagna with sweet-potato sauce. Counter diners can watch chefs at work in the partially open kitchen. If you come for Saturday or Sunday brunch, reserve in advance or be prepared to wait in line. The menu includes salmon hash with poached eggs and tomato coulis, almond French toast with fruit compote and mascarpone cream, and other breakfast treats.

Johnfrank. 2100 Market St. (at 14th St). ☎ **415/503-0333.** Reservations recommended. Main courses $14–$19.75. AE, MC, V. Sat–Sun 11am–3pm; Sun–Thurs 5:30–11pm; Fri–Sat 5pm–midnight. Limited parking. Muni Metro: F, K, L, or M. Bus: 8, 22, 24, or 37. MODERN AMERICAN BRASSERIE.

This sleek, bustling hot spot has upped the dining-quality ante in the ever-vibrant Castro, while keeping prices reasonable. All walks of San Francisco life happily crowd the long bar, in a rather loud room with low ceilings, a bamboo floor, and modern artwork. Sure, they're here because it's a top contender in the Castro, but they're also here to enjoy the culinary consequences of a partnership between local restaurant veterans Frank Everett and John Hurley. What's on the menu? Endive and citrus salad with blue cheese and orange-coriander vinaigrette; beef tongue with baby greens, green shallots, and Madeira vinaigrette; sauteed sweetbreads; and sour-cherry–stuffed quail. And that's just a few of the appetizers! Dinner might include oven-roasted Atlantic salmon with house-made mushroom spaetzle; grilled lamb with minted onion relish, mashed potatoes, grilled treviso, and juniper berry *jus;* pan-roasted half chicken; grilled center-cut pork chop; or vegetarian specials. The wine list is both affordable and approachable.

2223 Restaurant & Bar. 2223 Market St. (between Sanchez and Noe sts.). ☎ **415/ 431-0692.** Reservations recommended. Main courses $12.95–$19.95. AE, DC, MC, V. Sat–Sun 10am–2pm; Sun–Thurs 5:30–10pm; Fri–Sat 5:30–11pm. Muni Metro: F, L, K, or M. Bus: 8, 22, 24, or 37. CALIFORNIA.

Surrounded by hardwood floors, candles, streamlined modern light fixtures, and loud music, festive gays and straights come here for heavy-handed specialty drinks and grilled pork chops or ever-popular roasted chicken with garlic mashed potatoes. Along with Mecca, this is currently the dining and schmoozing spot in the area.

INEXPENSIVE
Café Flore. 2298 Market St. (at Noe St.). ☎ **415/621-8579.** Reservations not accepted. American breakfast $5.95; main courses $4.50–$10. No credit cards. Sun–Thurs 7am–11:30pm; Fri–Sat 7am–midnight. Muni Metro: F. Bus: 8. CALIFORNIA.

Sheathed with glass on three sides, overlooking Market Street, Noe Street, and a verdant patio in back, Café Flore attracts young, bright, and articulate members of the gay (mostly male) community. Local wits refer to it as a place where body piercing is encouraged but not mandatory, but that kind of exhibitionism tends to be more prevalent in the evening than during the day.

Many dishes rely on organic ingredients; they include a succulent version of roasted (sometimes free-range) chicken, soups, pastas, and steaks. Café latte costs $2 a cup. Plan on hearing a lot of noise and possibly seeing a handsome young man sending not-particularly-furtive glances your way. Those with late-night munchies, take heed: Although the restaurant stays open later, the kitchen closes at 10pm.

Chow. 215 Church St. (near Market St.). ☎ **415/552-2469.** Reservations not accepted. Main courses $4.95–$7.50. MC, V. Sun–Thurs 11am–11pm; Fri–Sat 11am–midnight. Muni Metro: F, J, K, L, or M. Bus: 8 or 37. AMERICAN.

Chow claims to serve American cuisine, but the management must be thinking of today's America, because the menu is not exactly baseball and apple pie. And that's just fine. If I can't decide between a burger, Italian, or Asian-influenced fare, I just come here. Mixed with the expected Cobb salad are fresh fish and grilled rosemary-lemon chicken. Exotic twists include noodles with peanut sauce, Fuji apples, and cucumber, and an array of other innovative pastas. More traditional are the budget-wise daily sandwich specials, which range from scrambled egg, ham, Cheddar, and asparagus (Sunday) to chicken salad with bleu cheese, bacon, and apple (Thursday); both come with salad, soup, or fries for less than $7. While the food and prices alone would be a good argument for coming here, beer on tap, a great inexpensive wine selection, and the fun, tavern-like environment clinch the deal. If you're on the run, you can grab a pizza slice ($1.50) and other quick bits for a mere pittance. A second location, Park Chow, is at 1240 Ninth Ave. (☎ **415/665-9912**).

✪ **Firewood Café.** 4248 18th St. (at Diamond St.). ☎ **415/252-0999.** Reservations not accepted. Main courses $6.25–$8.95. MC, V. Daily 11am–11pm. Muni Metro: F, K, L, or M. Bus: 8, 33, 35, or 37. ITALIAN/AMERICAN.

One of the sharpest rooms in the neighborhood, the colorful Firewood put its money in the essentials and eliminated extra overhead. There are no waiters or waitresses; everyone orders at the counter, then relaxes at the single family-style table, one of the small tables facing the huge street-side windows, or in the cheery back dining room. Management didn't skimp on the cozy-chic atmosphere and inspired but limited menu: The fresh salads ($6.75) come with a choice of three "fixin's" ranging from caramelized onions to spiced walnuts, and three gourmet dressing options. Then there's the pastas—three tortellini selections, such as roasted chicken and mortadella—and gourmet pizzas; calamari with lemon-garlic aïoli is a winner. Or how about herb-roasted half or whole chicken ($6.25 or $12.50, respectively) with roasted new potatoes? Wines cost $3.95 to $4.95 by the glass and a reasonable $16.95 to $19.95 per bottle. Draft and bottled beers are also available, and desserts top off at $2.95. (Thank goodness someone realized that $7 for an after-dinner treat is bordering on ridiculous.)

Marcello's Pizza. 420 Castro St. (at Market St.). ☎ **415/863-3900.** Reservations not accepted. Pizza slices $1.90–$2.80; pies $9.20–$21.50. No credit cards. Sun–Thurs 11am–1am; Fri–Sat 11am–2am. Muni Metro: L, M, or N to Castro St. Station. PIZZA.

Marcello's isn't a fancy place, just a traditional pizza joint with a couple of tables, tasty pizza by the slice, and a few other basic dishes. Weekend nights there's a line out the door of drunk and/or stoned Castro Street partyers with the late-night munchies.

13 Haight-Ashbury
MODERATE
✪ **Eos.** 901 Cole (at Carl St.). ☎ **415/566-3063.** Reservations recommended. Main courses $18–$28. AE, MC, V. Mon–Sat 5:30–11pm; Sun 5–11pm. Muni Metro: N. Bus: 6, 33, or 43. EAST-WEST FUSION.

Named after the Greek goddess of dawn, Eos is certainly basking in the spotlight, thanks to chef-proprietor Arnold Wong, a master of texture and taste who perfected his craft while working at Masa's and Silks. With a twinge of guilt, you dig in and mar the artistic presentation of each dish, such as the albacore tuna Tetaki tower, which comes seared with cracked black pepper, sprouts, white miso sauce, and black tobiko caviar. For starters, try tea-smoked salmon and mango spring rolls with wasabi–honey mustard dipping sauce. Unfortunately, the stark, industrial-deco decor does little to dampen the decibels, making a romantic outing nearly impossible unless you're into shouting. Around the corner is a less noisy, casual wine bar (with the same name) that stocks more than 400 vintages from around the globe.

INEXPENSIVE
✪ **Cha Cha Cha.** 1801 Haight St. (at Shrader St.). ☎ **415/386-5758.** Reservations not accepted. Tapas $4.50–$7.75; main courses $9–$13. MC, V. Daily 11:30am–4pm; Sun–Thurs 5–11pm; Fri–Sat 5–11:30pm. Muni Metro: N. Bus: 6, 7, 66, 71, or 73. CARIBBEAN.

This is one of my all-time favorite places to get festive, but it's not for everybody. Cha Cha Cha is not a meal; it's an experience. Put your name on the mile-long list, crowd into the minuscule bar, and sip sangria while you wait (try not to spill when you get bumped by all the young, attractive patrons who are also waiting). When you do finally get seated (it usually takes at least an hour), you'll dine in a loud—and I mean *loud*—dining room with Santeria altars, banana trees, and plastic tropical tablecloths. The best thing to do is order from the tapas menu and share the dishes family-style. Fried calamari, fried new potatoes, Cajun shrimp, and mussels in saffron broth are all bursting with flavor and accompanied by rich, luscious sauces—but whatever you choose, you can't go wrong. This is the kind of place where you take friends in a party-ing mood, let your hair down, and make an evening of it. If you want all the flavor without the festivities, come during lunch. There's a second, larger location in the Mission at 2327 Mission St., between 19th and 20th streets (☎ 415/648-0504).

Sweet Heat. 1725 Haight St. ☎ **415/387-8845.** www.citysearch.com. Reservations not accepted. All entrees under $9. MC, V. Daily 11:30am–11pm. MEXICAN.

If you're looking for a flavorful light lunch, check out this casual place offering "healthy Mexican food to die for." Far from traditional Mexican food, Sweet Heat has capitalized on California's love affair with old-style food prepared in new ways, and the results are impressive. Prices are low—$4.50 for a veggie burrito with grilled zucchini, red pepper, and roasted corn; $5.95 for a tasty scallop burrito with green chili chut-ney. The other location, at 2141 Polk St. (☎ **415/775-1055**), is equally popular and delicious. Both locations have a tequila bar with 40 variations.

✪ **Thep Phanom.** 400 Waller St. (at Fillmore St.). ☎ **415/431-2526.** Reservations rec-ommended. Main courses $7.95–$11.95. AE, CB, DC, DISC, MC, V. Daily 5:30–10:30pm. Bus: 6, 7, 22, 66, or 71. THAI.

By successfully incorporating flavors from India, China, Burma, Malaysia, and more recently the West, Thep Phanom rose through the ranks to become one of the best Thai restaurants in San Francisco. Case in point: There's almost always a line out the front door. Start with the signature dish, *ped swan*—boneless duck in a light honey sauce served on a bed of spinach. *Larb ped* (minced duck salad), velvety basil-spiked seafood curry served on banana leaves, and spicy *yum plamuk* (calamari salad) are also recommended. The Haight location attracts an eclectic crowd; the atmosphere is informal, and the decor quite tasteful. Don't leave anything even remotely valuable in your car.

Zona Rosa. 1797 Haight St. (at Shrader St.). ☎ **415/668-7717.** Reservations not accept-ed. Burritos $4.50–$5.75. No credit cards. Mon–Thurs 11am–10pm; Fri–Sat 11am–10:30pm. Muni Metro: N. Bus: 6, 7, 66, 71, or 73. MEXICAN.

This is a great place to stop and get a cheap (and healthful) bite. The most popular items are the burritos, which are made to order and include your choice of beans (refried, whole pinto, or black), meats, or vegetarian ingredients. You can sit on a stool at the window and watch the Haight Street freaks strolling by, relax at one of five col-orful interior tables, or take it to go and head to Golden Gate Park (just 2 blocks away). Zona Rosa is one of the best burrito stores around.

14 Richmond/Sunset Districts

MODERATE

Beach Chalet Brewery & Restaurant. 1000 Great Hwy. (at west end of Golden Gate Park, near Fulton St.). ☎ **415/386-8439.** Reservations accepted. Main courses $8–$20 at lunch, $12.50–$20 at dinner. MC, V. Mon–Thurs 11:30am–10pm; Fri–Sat 11:30am–11pm; Sun 10am–10pm. Bistro menu Mon–Sat 3–5:30pm; bar open until midnight Sun–Thurs, 2am Fri–Sat. Muni Metro: N. Bus: 18, 31, or 38. AMERICAN.

Since reopening on New Year's Eve 1996, the Beach Chalet has been one of the most popular reasons to make it out to the breakers. The restaurant occupies the upper floor of a historic public lounge that originally opened in 1900, was rebuilt in 1925, and, after being closed for more than 15 years, was recently renovated. Today, the main floor's wonderful restored WPA frescoes and historical displays on the area are enough to lure tourists and locals, but upstairs is something altogether different. The only thing harking back to yesteryear is the timeless view of the Pacific Ocean. While the place is bright and cheery, I agree with the critics: The restaurant should have been more reminiscent of its heritage.

Dinner is pricey and the view disappears with the sun, so come for lunch or bistro snacks, when you can eat your Niman-Schell burger, rock shrimp quesadilla, or chopped vegetable and romaine salad with one of the best vistas around. After dinner, it's a more local thing, especially on Tuesday, Friday, and Saturday when live blues accompanies the cocktails and house-made brews. *Note:* Be careful getting into the parking lot (accessible only from the northbound side of the highway); it's a quick, sandy turn.

Cliff House. 1090 Point Lobos (at Merrie Way). ☎ **415/386-3330.** Reservations recommended for upstairs and brunch only. Upstairs main courses $7–$12 at breakfast, $7–$16 at lunch, $15–$29 at dinner. Main room main courses $9–$22 at lunch, $17–$25 at dinner. AE, DC, MC, V. Upstairs Mon–Fri 9am–3:30pm; Sat–Sun 8:30am–4pm; daily 5–10pm. Main room Mon–Thurs 11am–10:30pm; Fri–Sat 11am–11pm; Sun 9am–2pm and 3:30–10:30pm. Bus: 18 or 38. SEAFOOD/CALIFORNIA.

In the old days (we're talking way back), the Cliff House was the place to go for a romantic night on the town. Nowadays, the aging San Francisco landmark caters mostly to tourists who arrive by the busload to gander at the Sutro Bath remains next door.

Three restaurants in the main two-story building give diners a choice of how much they want to spend. **Phineas T. Barnacle** is the least expensive; it serves sandwiches, salads, soups, and such Hofbrau-style across from the elaborate saloon-style bar. Afterward, you can seat yourself at the window-side tables overlooking the shore, or beside the fireplace if you're chilled. A step up from the P.T.B. (literally) is **Upstairs at the Cliff House,** a slightly more formal setting that's best known for its breakfast omelets. The main room, known as the **Seafood and Beverage Co.,** is the fanciest of the lot. Refurbished to recall its glory days near the turn of the century, it offers superb ocean views, particularly at sunset, when the fog lets up; unfortunately, the food is a distant second to the scenery. The best M.O. is to arrive before dusk, request a window seat, order a few appetizers and cocktails, and enjoy the view. Or opt for the elaborate Sunday brunch served from 10am to 3pm in the newly renovated Terrace Room.

Kabuto Sushi. 5116 Geary Blvd. (at 15th Ave.). ☎ **415/752-5652.** Reservations recommended. Sushi $3–$10; main courses $11–$18. MC, V. Tues–Sat 5:30–11pm; Sun 5:30–10pm. Bus: 2, 28, or 38. JAPANESE/SUSHI.

In a town overflowing with seafood and pretentious taste buds, you'd think it'd be easier to find great sushi. But the truth is, finding an outstanding sushi restaurant in San Francisco is more challenging than spotting a parking space in Nob Hill. Still, chopsticking these fish-and-rice delicacies is one of the most joyous and adventurous ways to dine, and Kabuto is one of the best (and most expensive) places to do it. Chef Sachio Kojima, who presides over the small, crowded sushi bar, constructs each dish with smooth, lightning-fast movements known only to master chefs. If you're big on wasabi, ask for the stronger stuff Kojima serves on request.

Khan Toke Thai House. 5937 Geary Blvd. ☎ **415/668-6654.** Reservations recommended. Main courses $6–$12; fixed-price dinner $17.95. AE, MC, V. Daily 5–10pm. Bus: 38. THAI.

Khan Toke Thai is so traditional, you're asked to remove your shoes before being seated. Popular for special occasions, this Richmond Distinct fixture is easily the prettiest

Lunching Near Golden Gate Park

Curiously (and happily), there are no restaurants other than museum cafes in Golden Gate Park, but that doesn't mean your choices are limited to the hot dog cart. The newly chic neighborhood of Inner Sunset boasts a handful of excellent moderately priced restaurants. All serve lunch and are a block outside the park along Ninth Avenue.

One of my favorites is **Park Chow,** 1240 Ninth Ave., between Lincoln and Irving (☎ **415/665-9912**). Its rambling wood-frame house and roof garden are a casual venue for Italian-inspired eclectic fare such as burgers, Asian noodles, grills, and roasts—all at serious bargain prices for such high-quality dining. Brunch goes until 2:30pm on weekends.

Bare-bones traditional **Ebisu,** 1283 Ninth Ave., between Lincoln and Irving (☎ **415/556-1770**), a neighborhood favorite for 17 years, serves some of the city's best sushi, sashimi, and Japanese fare. The absolutely delightful **Avenue 9,** 1243 Ninth Ave. (☎ **415/664-6999**), is a colorful retro-modern setting for the creative kitchen. It cooks fabulous gourmet cheeseburgers, flat-iron steaks, fries, spinach and prawn salad, Yukon gold potato latkes with house-cured salmon, and poached eggs with hollandaise sauce. Brunch is offered on Sunday from 10am to 3pm. Another design-conscious restaurant, **House on 9th,** 1269 Ninth Ave. (☎ **415/682-3898**), serves great noodle dishes and curries in an architecturally playful room. It's open for lunch Tuesday through Friday and is also worth a visit at dinner (Tuesday through Sunday).

For something totally different, head to **Organica The Living Cuisine,** 1224 Ninth Ave. (☎ **415/665-6519**), an entirely raw, organic, vegan restaurant that's critically acclaimed and worlds more creative than you could possibly imagine. It's open daily. (Chef-owner-wild man Juliano recently published a fab cookbook.)

Thai restaurant in the city; lavishly carved teak interiors evoke the ambience of a Thai temple.

To start, order the *tom yam gong* lemongrass shrimp with mushroom, tomato, and cilantro soup. Follow with such well-flavored dishes as ground pork with fresh ginger, green onion, peanuts, and lemon juice; prawns with hot chiles, mint leaves, lime juice, lemongrass, and onions; or chicken with cashew nuts, crispy chiles, and onions. For a real treat, have the deep-fried pompano topped with sauteed ginger, onions, peppers, pickled garlic, and yellow-bean sauce, or deep-fried red snapper with "three-flavors" sauce and hot basil leaves. A complete dinner including appetizer, soup, salad, two main courses, dessert, and coffee is a great value.

Straits Café. 3300 Geary Blvd. (at Parker St.). ☎ **415/668-1783.** Reservations recommended. Main courses $8.25–$21.95. AE, DC, MC, V. Sun–Thurs 11:30am–3pm and 5–10pm; Fri–Sat 11:30am–11pm. Bus: 2, 3, 4, or 38. SINGAPOREAN.

Straits Café is what I like to call "adventure dining," because you never know quite what you're going to get. Burlap palm trees, pastel-painted trompe l'oeil houses, faux balconies, and clotheslines strung across the walls evoke a surreal image of a Singaporean village in the Richmond District. The cuisine, however, is the real thing. Among chef Chris Yeo's spicy Malaysian-Indian-Chinese offerings are *murtabak* (stuffed Indian bread), chili crab, basil chicken, *nonya daging rendang* (beef simmered in lime leaves), *ikan pangang* (fish stuffed with chili paste), and, hottest of all, *sambal udang* (prawns sauteed in chili-shallot sambal sauce). For dessert, try the sago pudding.

INEXPENSIVE

✪ **Ton Kiang.** 5821 Geary Blvd. (between 22nd and 23rd aves.). ☎ **415/387-8273.** Reservations accepted for parties of 8 or more. Dim sum $1.80–$4.50. AE, MC, V. Daily 10:30am–10pm. Bus: 38. CHINESE/DIM SUM.

Ton Kiang is the number one place in the city to do dim sum. Wait in the never-ending line (which is out the door anytime between 11am and 1:30pm), get a table on the first or second floor, and be ready to party with your palate. From stuffed crab claws, roast Peking duck, and a gazillion dumpling selections (including scallop and vegetable, shrimp, and beef) to the delicious and hard-to-find *doa miu* (snow pea sprouts flash-sauteed with garlic and peanut oil), shark-fin soup, and a mesmerizing mango pudding, every tray of morsels coming from the kitchen is an absolute delight. This is definitely one of my favorite places to do lunch, and it happens to have an unusually friendly staff.

7

Exploring San Francisco

San Francisco's parks, museums, tours, and landmarks are favorites for travelers the world over and offer an array of activities to suit every visitor. But no particular activity or place makes the city one of the most popular destinations in the world. It's San Francisco itself—its charm, its atmosphere, its perfect blend of big metropolis with small-town hospitality. No matter what you do while you're here—whether you spend all your time in central areas like Union Square or North Beach, or explore the outer neighborhoods—you're bound to collect a treasure trove of vacation memories that can only be found in this culturally rich, strikingly beautiful City by the Bay.

1 Famous San Francisco Sights

✪ **Alcatraz Island.** Pier 41, near Fisherman's Wharf. ☎ **415/773-1188** (info only). Admission (includes ferry trip and audio tour) $12.25 adults with headset, $8.75 without; $10.50 seniors 62 and older with headset, $7 without; $7 children 5–11 with headset, $5.50 without. Winter daily 9:30am–2:15pm; summer daily 9:15am–4:15pm. Advance purchase advised. Ferries depart at 15 and 45 min. after the hour. Arrive at least 20 min. before sailing time.

Visible from Fisherman's Wharf, Alcatraz Island (a.k.a. "The Rock") has seen a checkered history. Juan Manuel Ayala discovered it in 1775 and named it after the many pelicans that nested on the island. From the 1850s to 1933, when the army vacated the island, it served as a military post, protecting the bay shoreline. In 1934, the government converted the buildings of the military outpost into a maximum-security prison. Given the sheer cliffs, treacherous tides and currents, and frigid water temperatures, it was believed to be a totally escape-proof prison. Among the famous gangsters who occupied cell blocks A through D were Al Capone, Robert Stroud, the so-called Birdman of Alcatraz (because he was an expert in ornithological diseases), Machine Gun Kelly, and Alvin Karpis. It cost a fortune to keep them imprisoned here because all supplies, including water, had to be shipped in. In 1963, after an apparent escape in which no bodies were recovered, the government closed the prison, and in 1972 it became part of the Golden Gate National Recreation Area. The wildlife that was driven away during the military and prison years has begun to return—the black-crested night heron and other seabirds are nesting here again—and a new trail passes through the island's nature areas.

Funky Favorites at Fisherman's Wharf

The following sights cluster on or near Fisherman's Wharf. To reach the area by cable car, take the Powell-Mason line to the last stop and walk to the wharf; by bus, take no. 30, 32, or 42. If you're arriving by car, park on adjacent streets or on the wharf between Taylor and Jones streets.

The popular battle-scarred World War II fleet submarine **USS *Pampanito,*** Pier 45, Fisherman's Wharf (☎ **415/775-1943**), saw plenty of action in the Pacific. It has been completely restored, and visitors are free to crawl around inside. Admission includes an audio tour. It runs $6 for adults 13 to 61, $4 for children 6 to 12, and free for seniors and children under 6; the family pass (two adults, up to four kids) costs $20. The *Pampanito* is open daily 9am to 8pm.

Ripley's Believe It or Not! Museum, 175 Jefferson St. (☎ **415/771-6188;** www.ripleysf.com), has drawn curious spectators through its doors for over 30 years. Inside, you'll experience the extraordinary world of improbabilities: a one-third-scale matchstick cable car, a shrunken human torso once owned by Ernest Hemingway, a dinosaur made from car bumpers, a walk through a kaleidoscope tunnel, and video displays and illusions. Robert LeRoy Ripley's infamous arsenal may lead you to ponder whether truth is, in fact, stranger than fiction. Admission is $8.95 for adults, $7 for seniors over 60, $5.95 for children 5 to 12, free for children under 5. From June 15 through Labor Day, it is open Sunday to Thursday 9am to 11pm, until midnight on Friday and Saturday; the rest of the year, Sunday to Thursday 10am to 9:30pm, until midnight on Friday and Saturday. Call for special hours on major holidays.

Conceived and executed in the Madame Tussaud mold, San Francisco's **Wax Museum,** 145 Jefferson St. (☎ **415/202-0400**), has long been a kitschy harborside tourist trap. In 1999, with the closing of the adjoining Haunted Goldmine, the museum expanded, undergoing a $15-million tear-down and renovation. It should be open by fall 2000 as a huge complex that includes national retail and restaurant chains. (Not any less of a tourist trap, mind you, only a newer, slicker one.) Surely the overhaul will spiff up the museum's 250 lifelike figures, including singer Michael Jackson, Marilyn Monroe, John Wayne, former president George Bush, and "Feared Leaders," such as Fidel Castro. The Chamber of Horrors, which features Dracula, Frankenstein, and a werewolf, along with bloody victims hanging from meat hooks, will reopen. But the clinchers will be the addition of pop icons such as Leonardo DiCaprio and Will Smith. Admission is likely to change with the reopening, but before the renovations, prices were $12.95 for adults, $9.95 for teens 12 to 17, $10.95 for seniors over 60, $6.95 for children 4 to 11, and free for children under 6. Call for the reopening schedule and new hours.

Tours, including an audio tour of the prison block and a slide show, are given by the park's rangers, who entertain their guests with interesting anecdotes.

It's a popular excursion and space is limited, so purchase tickets as far in advance as possible. **Blue & Gold Fleet** (☎ **415/705-5555**) operates the tour; it accepts American Express, MasterCard, and Visa, and there's a $2.25 per ticket service charge on phone orders. You can also buy tickets in advance from the Blue & Gold ticket office on Pier 41.

Major San Francisco Sights

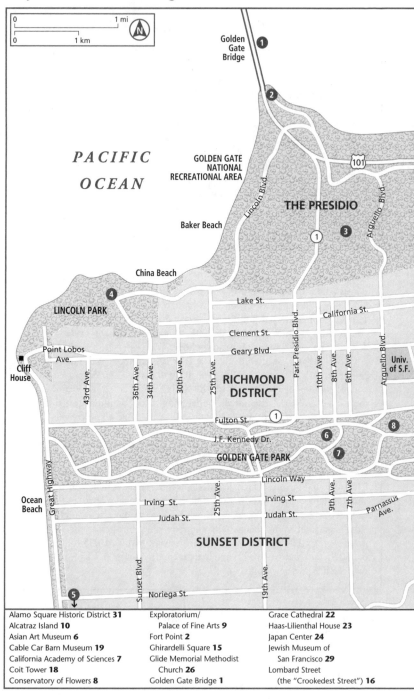

PACIFIC
OCEAN

Golden Gate Bridge ➊

Fort Point ➋

GOLDEN GATE NATIONAL RECREATIONAL AREA

THE PRESIDIO

101

Baker Beach

➌

Arguello Blvd.

China Beach

➍

LINCOLN PARK

Lake St.

California St.

Clement St.

Point Lobos Ave.

Geary Blvd.

Cliff House

43rd Ave.

36th Ave.

34th Ave.

30th Ave.

25th Ave.

RICHMOND DISTRICT

Park Presidio Blvd.

10th Ave.

8th Ave.

6th Ave.

Arguello Blvd.

Univ. of S.F.

Fulton St.

➑

J.F. Kennedy Dr.

➏

GOLDEN GATE PARK

➐

Lincoln Way

Ocean Beach

Great Highway

Irving St.

25th Ave.

Irving St.

9th Ave.

7th Ave.

Parnassus Ave.

Judah St.

Judah St.

SUNSET DISTRICT

Sunset Blvd.

19th Ave.

➎

Noriega St.

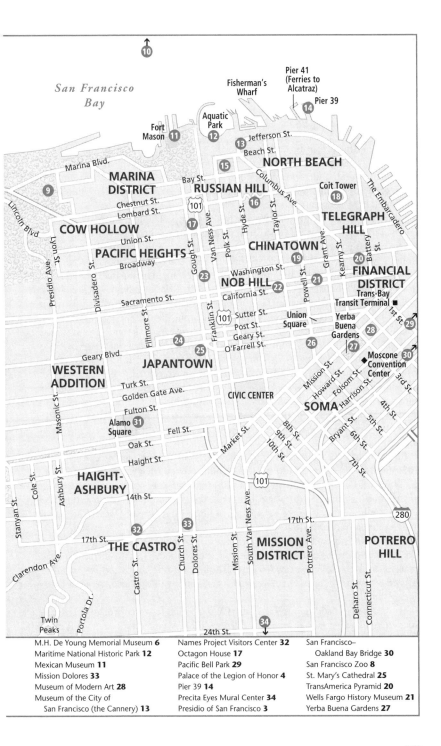

San Francisco
Bay

Pier 41
(Ferries to
Alcatraz)

Fisherman's
Wharf

Pier 39

Fort
Mason **11**

Aquatic
Park **12**

14

Jefferson St.

Beach St. **13**

15

NORTH BEACH

Marina Blvd.

**MARINA
DISTRICT**

Bay St.

RUSSIAN HILL

Columbus Ave.

Coit Tower **18**

9

Chestnut St.
Lombard St.

101

16

**TELEGRAPH
HILL**

Lincoln Blvd

COW HOLLOW

17

Hyde St.

Taylor St.

20

Battery St.

Union St.

CHINATOWN

PACIFIC HEIGHTS

Van Ness Ave.

Polk St.

19

Grant Ave.

Kearny St.

**FINANCIAL
DISTRICT**

Broadway

Gough St.

23

Washington St.

21

Trans-Bay
Transit Terminal ■

Presidio Ave.

Divisadero St.

Sacramento St.

Fillmore St.

NOB HILL **22**

California St.

Powell St.

29

Franklin St.

101

Sutter St.

Union
Square

Yerba
Buena
Gardens **28**

1st St.

Post St.

24

Geary St.

26

27

Geary Blvd.

25

O'Farrell St.

Moscone
Convention
Center **30**

**WESTERN
ADDITION**

JAPANTOWN

Mission St.

Howard St.

Folsom St.

3rd St.

Masonic St.

Turk St.

Golden Gate Ave.

CIVIC CENTER

Harrison St.

Fulton St.

SOMA

4th St.

Alamo
Square **31**

Fell St.

8th St.

Bryant St.

5th St.

6th St.

Oak St.

9th St.

7th St.

Haight St.

10th St.

101

**HAIGHT-
ASHBURY**

14th St.

Stanyan St.

Cole St.

Ashbury St.

Market St.

South Van Ness Ave.

17th St.

280

32

33

17th St.

**POTRERO
HILL**

17th St.

THE CASTRO

Church St.

Dolores St.

Mission St.

**MISSION
DISTRICT**

Potrero Ave.

Clarendon Ave.

Castro St.

Portola Dr.

Deharo St.

Connecticut St.

Twin
Peaks

24th St.

34

10

M.H. De Young Memorial Museum **6**	Names Project Visitors Center **32**	San Francisco–
Maritime National Historic Park **12**	Octagon House **17**	Oakland Bay Bridge **30**
Mexican Museum **11**	Pacific Bell Park **29**	San Francisco Zoo **8**
Mission Dolores **33**	Palace of the Legion of Honor **4**	St. Mary's Cathedral **25**
Museum of Modern Art **28**	Pier 39 **14**	TransAmerica Pyramid **20**
Museum of the City of	Precita Eyes Mural Center **34**	Wells Fargo History Museum **21**
San Francisco (the Cannery) **13**	Presidio of San Francisco **3**	Yerba Buena Gardens **27**

Allow about 2¹/₂ hours for the round-trip and the tour. Wear comfortable shoes and take a heavy sweater or windbreaker, because even when the sun's out, it's cold. The National Park Service also notes that there are a lot of hills to climb on the tour.

For those who want to get a closer look at Alcatraz without going ashore, two boat-tour operators offer short circumnavigations of the island (see "Self-Guided & Organized Tours," below, for complete information).

Fisherman's Wharf & Pier 39.

Few cities in America are as adept at wholesaling their historical sites as San Francisco, which has converted Fisherman's Wharf into one of the most popular tourist attractions in the world. Unless you come really early in the morning, you won't find any traces of the traditional waterfront life that once existed here; the only fishing going on around here is for tourists' dollars.

Originally called Meigg's Wharf, this bustling strip of waterfront got its present moniker from generations of fishers who used to base their boats here. Today, the bay has become so polluted with toxins that bright yellow placards warn against eating fish from the waters. A small fleet of fewer than 30 boats still operates from here, but basically Fisherman's Wharf has been converted into one long shopping mall that stretches from Ghirardelli Square at the west end to Pier 39 at the east. Some people love it, others can't get far enough away from it, but most agree that Fisherman's Wharf, for better or for worse, has to be seen at least once in your life.

Ghirardelli Square, 900 North Point St., between Polk and Larkin streets (☎ 415/775-5500), dates from 1864, when it served as a factory making Civil War uniforms. It's best known as the former chocolate and spice factory of Domingo Ghirardelli (say "Gear-a-deli"). The factory has been converted into a 10-level mall containing 50-plus stores and 11 dining establishments. Scheduled street performers entertain regularly in the West Plaza. The stores generally stay open from 10am to 9pm in the summer and until 6 or 7pm in the winter. Incidentally, the Ghirardelli Chocolate Company still makes chocolate, but its factory is in a lower-rent district in the East Bay.

Pier 39, on the waterfront at the Embarcadero and Beach Street (☎ 415/705-5500), is a 4¹/₂-acre, multilevel waterfront complex a few blocks east of Fisherman's Wharf. Constructed on an abandoned cargo pier, it is, ostensibly, a re-creation of a turn-of-the-century street scene, but don't expect a slice of old-time maritime life. This is the busiest mall of the lot and, according to the *London Observer,* the third most visited attraction in the world, behind Disney World and Disneyland. It has more than 100 stores, 10 bay-view restaurants (including the Bubba Gump Shrimp Co., an over-buttered spin-off from the *Forrest Gump* movie), a two-tiered Venetian carousel, and a new big-screen Cinemax Theater showing the *Great San Francisco Adventure.* Shops are open daily 10:30am to 8:30pm, with extended weekend hours during the summer.

The latest major addition to Fisherman's Wharf is **Underwater World,** a $38 million, 707,000-gallon marine attraction filled with sharks, stingrays, and more. A moving footpath transports visitors through clear acrylic tunnels.

Accommodating a total of 350 boats, two marinas flank the pier and house the **Blue & Gold bay sightseeing fleet.** In recent years, some 600 California **sea lions** have taken up residence on the adjacent floating docks. Until they abandon their new playground, which seems more and more unlikely, these playful, noisy creatures (some nights you can hear them all the way from Washington Square) create one of the best free attractions on the wharf. Docent-led programs, offered at Pier 39 on weekends

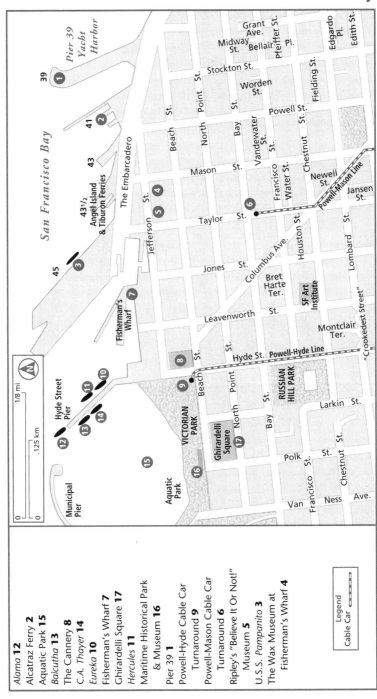

Pier 39 Yacht Harbor

San Francisco Bay

Grant Ave.
Midway St.
Bellair
Pfeiffer Pl.
Edgardo Pl.
Edith St.

Stockton St.

Worden St.

Powell St.

St.

Point

St.

St.

Vandewater St.

Chestnut

Fielding St.

Powell-Mason Line

Beach

North

Bay

Newell St.

Jansen St.

Mason St.

Francisco St.

Water St.

Houston St.

The Embercadero

43½
Angel Island
& Tiburon Ferries

Taylor St.

Jefferson St.

Columbus Ave.

Lombard

Jones St.

Bret Harte Ter.

SF Art Institute

Montclair Ter.

Leavenworth St.

"Crookedest Street"

Fisherman's Wharf

Hyde St. Powell-Hyde Line

Hyde Street Pier

Beach St.

North Point

RUSSIAN HILL PARK

Larkin St.

VICTORIAN PARK

Beach

Bay

Municipal Pier

Aquatic Park

Ghirardelli Square

North

Polk St.

Chestnut St.

St.

Francisco St.

Van Ness Ave.

1/8 mi
.125 km
0

Legend
Cable Car

from 11am to 5pm, teach visitors about the range, habitat, and adaptability of the California sea lion.

✪ **Cable Cars.** Powell-Hyde and Powell-Mason lines begin at the base of Powell and Market sts.; California St. line begins at the foot of Market St.

Although they may not be San Francisco's most practical means of transportation, cable cars are certainly the best loved. Designated official historic landmarks by the National Park Service in 1964, they clank up and down the city's steep hills like mobile museum pieces, tirelessly hauling thousands of tourists each day to nowhere in particular.

London-born engineer Andrew Hallidie invented San Francisco's cable cars in 1869. He got the idea by way of serendipity. As the story goes, Hallidie was watching a team of overworked horses haul a heavily laden carriage up a steep San Francisco slope. As he watched, one horse slipped and the car rolled back, dragging the other tired beasts with it. At that moment Hallidie resolved that he would invent a mechanical contraption to replace such horses, and just 4 years later, in 1873, the first cable car made its maiden run from the top of Clay Street. Promptly ridiculed as "Hallidie's Folly," the cars were slow to gain acceptance. One early onlooker voiced the general opinion by exclaiming, "I don't believe it—the damned thing works!"

Even today, many visitors have difficulty believing that these vehicles, which have no engines, actually work. The cars, each weighing about 6 tons, run along a steel cable, enclosed under the street in a center rail. You can't see the cable unless you peer straight down into the crack, but you'll hear its characteristic clickity-clanking sound whenever you're nearby. The cars move when the gripper (not the driver) pulls back a lever that closes a pincerlike "grip" on the cable. The speed of the car, therefore, is determined by the speed of the cable, which is a constant $9^1/_2$ miles per hour—never more, never less.

The two types of cable cars in use hold a maximum of 90 and 100 passengers, and the limits are rigidly enforced. The best views are from the outer running boards, where you have to hold on tightly when taking curves. Everyone, it seems, prefers to ride on the running boards.

Hallidie's cable cars have been imitated and used throughout the world, but all have been replaced by more efficient means of transportation. San Francisco planned to do so, too, but the proposal met with so much opposition that the cable cars' perpetuation was actually written into the city charter in 1955. The mandate cannot be revoked without the approval of a majority of the city's voters—a distant and doubtful prospect.

San Francisco's three existing lines form the world's only surviving system of cable cars, which you can experience for yourself should you choose to wait in the endless boarding line (up to a 2-hour wait in summer). For more information on riding them, see "Getting Around" in chapter 4, "Getting to Know San Francisco."

The Cannery. 2801 Leavenworth St. ☎ **415/771-3112.** www.thecannery.com.

The Cannery was built in 1894 as a fruit-canning plant and converted into a mall in the 1960s. It contains 50-plus shops, a paint-it-yourself ceramic studio, a comedy club, and several restaurants and galleries, including **Jack's Cannery Bar** (☎ **415/931-6400**), which features 110 beers on tap (the most anywhere in the country). Vendors' stalls and sidewalk cafes occupy the courtyard amid a grove of century-old olive trees, and on summer weekends, street performers are out in force entertaining tourists.

Coit Tower. Telegraph Hill. ☎ **415/362-0808.** Admission to the top $3.75 adults, $2.50 seniors, $1.50 children 6–12. Daily 10am–6pm. Bus: 39 ("Coit").

In a city known for its great views and vantage points, Coit Tower is tops. Located atop Telegraph Hill, just east of North Beach, the round stone tower offers panoramic views of the city and the bay.

Completed in 1933, the tower is the legacy of Lillie Hitchcock Coit, a wealthy eccentric who left San Francisco a $125,000 bequest "for the purpose of adding beauty to the city I have always loved" and as a memorial to its volunteer firemen. She had been saved from a fire as a child and held the city's firefighters in particularly high esteem.

Inside the base of the tower are impressive **murals** titled *Life in California, 1934,* which were completed under the WPA during the New Deal. They are the work of more than 25 artists, many of whom had studied under Mexican muralist Diego Rivera.

✪ **Golden Gate Bridge.** Bridge-bound Golden Gate Transit buses (☎ **415/923-2000**) depart every 30 to 60 min. during the day for Marin County, starting from the Transbay Terminal (Mission and First sts.) and stopping at Market and Seventh sts., at the Civic Center, and along Van Ness Ave. and Lombard St.

The year 2001 marks the 65th birthday of possibly the most beautiful, and certainly the most photographed, bridge in the world. Often half-veiled by the city's trademark rolling fog, San Francisco's Golden Gate Bridge spans tidal currents, ocean waves, and battering winds to connect the City by the Bay with the Redwood Empire to the north.

With its gracefully swung single span, spidery bracing cables, and zooming twin towers, the bridge looks more like a work of abstract art than one of the 20th century's greatest practical engineering feats. Construction began in May 1937 and was completed at the then-colossal cost of $35 million.

The mile-long steel link (longer if you factor in the approach), which reaches a height of 746 feet above the water, is an awesome bridge to cross. Traffic usually moves quickly, so crossing by car won't give you too much time to see the sights. If you drive ($3 toll, payable southbound) from the city, park in the lot at the foot of the bridge on the city side and make the crossing by foot. Back in your car, continue to Marin's Vista Point, at the bridge's northern end. Look back and you'll be rewarded with one of the greatest views of San Francisco.

Millions of pedestrians walk or bike across each year, gazing up at the tall red towers, out at the vistas of San Francisco and Marin County, and down into the stacks of oceangoing liners. You can walk out onto the span from either end, but be prepared— it's usually windy and cold, and the bridge vibrates. Still, walking even a short distance is one of the best ways to experience the immense scale of the structure.

Lombard Street. Between Hyde and Leavenworth sts.

Known as the "crookedest street in the world," this whimsically winding block of Lombard Street draws thousands of visitors each year (much to the chagrin of neighborhood residents, most of whom would prefer to block off the street to tourists). The angle of the street is so steep that the road has to snake back and forth to make a descent possible. The brick-lined street zigzags around the residences' bright flower gardens, which explode with color during warmer months. This short stretch of Lombard Street is one way, downhill, and fun to drive. Take the curves slowly and in low gear, and expect a wait during the weekend. Save your film for the bottom, where, if you're lucky, you can find a parking space and take a few snapshots of the silly spectacle. You can also take staircases (without curves) up or down on either side of the street.

2 Museums

For information on museums in Golden Gate Park, see section 4, "Golden Gate Park," later in this chapter.

Cable Car Barn Museum. Washington and Mason sts. ☎ **415/474-1887.** Free admission. Apr–Oct daily 10am–6pm; Nov–Mar daily 10am–5pm. Cable car: Both Powell St. lines.

If you've ever wondered how cable cars work, this nifty museum explains (and demonstrates!) it all. Yes, this is a museum, but the Cable Car Barn is no stuffed shirt. It's the living powerhouse, repair shop, and storage place of the cable-car system and is in full operation. Built for the Ferries and Cliff House Railway in 1887, the building underwent an $18 million reconstruction to restore its original gaslight-era look, install an amazing spectators' gallery, and add a museum of San Francisco transit history.

The exposed machinery, which pulls the cables under San Francisco's streets, looks like a Rube Goldberg invention. Stand in the mezzanine gallery and become mesmerized by the massive groaning and vibrating winches as they thread the cable that hauls the cars through a huge figure-eight and back into the system using slack-absorbing tension wheels. For a better view, move to the lower-level viewing room, where you can see the massive pulleys and gears operating underground.

Also on display here is one of the first grip cars developed by Andrew S. Hallidie, operated for the first time on Clay Street on August 2, 1873. Other displays include an antique grip car and trailer that operated on Pacific Avenue until 1929, and dozens of exact-scale models of cars used on the various city lines. There's also a shop where you can buy a variety of cable car gifts.

✪ **California Palace of the Legion of Honor.** In Lincoln Park (34th Ave. and Clement St.). ☎ **415/750-3600** or 415/863-3330 (recorded information). Admission (including the Asian Art Museum and M. H. De Young Memorial Museum) $8 adults, $6 seniors 65 and over, $5 youths 12–17, free for children under 12. Fees may be higher for special exhibitions. Free to all second Wed of each month (9:30am–8:45pm). Tues–Sun 9:30am–5pm. Bus: 18 or 38.

Designed as a memorial to California's World War I casualties, the neoclassical structure is an exact replica of the Legion of Honor Palace in Paris, right down to the inscription HONNEUR ET PATRIE above the portal.

The Legion of Honor reopened in late 1995 after a 2-year, $34.6 million renovation and seismic upgrading that was stalled by the discovery of almost 300 turn-of-the-century coffins. The exterior's grassy expanses, cliff-side paths, and incredible view of the Golden Gate make this an absolute must-visit attraction before you even get in the door. But the inside is equally impressive. The museum's permanent collection covers 4,000 years of art and includes paintings, sculpture, and decorative arts from Europe, as well as international tapestries, prints, and drawings. The chronological display of more than 800 years of European art includes one of the world's finest collections of Rodin's sculptures.

✪ **The Exploratorium.** 3601 Lyon St., in the Palace of Fine Arts (at Marina Blvd.). ☎ **415/563-7337** or 415/561-0360 (recorded information). Admission $9 adults, $7 seniors and college students with ID, $5 children 6–17, $2.50 children 3–5, free for children under 3. Free to all first Wed of each month. AE, MC, V. Summer (Memorial Day–Labor Day) and holidays, Mon–Tues and Thurs–Sun 10am–6pm; Wed 10am–9pm. Rest of the year Tues and Thurs–Sun 10am–5pm; Wed 10am–9pm. Closed Thanksgiving, Dec 25. Free parking. Bus: 30 from Stockton St. to the Marina stop.

Scientific American magazine rates the Exploratorium as "the best science museum in the world"—pretty heady stuff for this exciting hands-on science fair. It contains more than 650 permanent exhibits that explore everything from giant bubble blowing to

Einstein's theory of relativity. It's like a mad scientist's penny arcade, an educational fun house, and an experimental laboratory all rolled into one. Touch a tornado, shape a glowing electrical current, finger-paint using a computer, or take a sensory journey in total darkness in the Tactile Dome—you could spend all day here and still not see everything. Every exhibit at the Exploratorium is designed to be interactive, educational, safe, and, most important, fun. And don't think it's just for kids; parents inevitably end up being the most reluctant to leave. On the way out, be sure to stop in the wonderful gift store, which is chock-full of affordable brain candy.

The museum is in the Marina District at the beautiful Palace of Fine Arts, the only building left standing from the Panama-Pacific Exposition of 1915, which celebrated the opening of the Panama Canal. The adjoining park and lagoon—the perfect place for an afternoon picnic—is home to ducks, swans, seagulls, and grouchy geese, so bring bread.

Haas-Lilienthal House. 2007 Franklin St. (at Washington St.). ☎ **415/441-3004.** Guided tour $5 adults, $3 seniors and children 6–12. Wed noon–3:15pm; Sun 11am–4:15pm. Cable car: California St. line. Bus: 1, 12, 19, 27, 42, 47, 49, 83.

Of the city's many gingerbread Victorians, this handsome Queen Anne house is one of the most flamboyant. The 1886 structure features all the architectural frills of the period, including dormer windows, flying cupolas, ornate trim, and winsome turrets. The elaborately styled house is now a museum, its rooms fully furnished with period pieces. The Foundation for San Francisco's Architectural Heritage maintains the house and offers docent-led tours. The 1-hour tours (the only way to see the house) start every 20 to 30 minutes. A new Costume Exhibit features such themes as Ragtime-era costumes, artifacts, and accessories.

The Jewish Museum San Francisco. 121 Steuart St. (between Mission and Howard sts.). ☎ **415/543-8880.** Admission $5 adults, $3 students and seniors. Free to all Thurs 6–8pm, first Mon of each month. Sun–Wed 11am–5pm; Thurs 11am–8pm. Closed Fri–Sat. Bus: 14, 32.

The Jewish Museum San Francisco was inaugurated in 1984 to educate the community about Jewish history, traditions, and values. The museum mounts a variety of shows that concentrate on the themes of immigration, assimilation, and identity of the Jewish community in the United States and around the world. They are illustrated by paintings, sculptures, and photographs, as well as educational programs involving nonsectarian schools and summer camps. In 2000 renovations began on a new location at Jesse Street and Mission Street, but the move isn't scheduled until 2002.

Mexican Museum. Building D, Fort Mason, Marina Blvd. (at Laguna St.). ☎ **415/202-9700.** Admission $3 adults, $2 children. Free to all first Wed of the month. Wed–Fri noon–5pm; Sat–Sun 11am–5pm. Bus: 28 or 76.

The first museum in the nation dedicated to the work of Mexican and other Latino artists, the Mexican Museum maintains an impressive collection of art covering pre-Hispanic, colonial, folk, Mexican fine art, and Chicano/Mexican-American art. Revolving shows range from the art of New Mexican women to such subjects as Mexican surrealism. *Note:* The museum is expected to relocate to the Yerba Buena neighborhood at the end of 2000.

Octagon House. 2645 Gough St. (at Union St.). ☎ **415/441-7512.** Free admission; donation suggested. Feb–Dec second Sun and second and fourth Thurs of each month noon–3pm. Closed Jan and holidays. Bus: 41 or 45.

This unusual, eight-sided, cupola-topped house dates from 1861 and is maintained by the National Society of Colonial Dames of America. The architectural features are extraordinary, and from the second floor it is possible to look up into the cupola, which is illuminated at night. In the small museum, you'll find Early American furniture, portraits, silver, pewter, looking glasses, and English and Chinese ceramics. There are also some historic documents, including signatures of 54 of the 56 signers of the Declaration of Independence. Even if you're not able to visit the inside, this strange structure is worth a look.

San Francisco Maritime National Historical Park. At the foot of Polk St. (near Fisherman's Wharf). ☎ **415/556-3002.** Museum free; ships $5 adults, $3 seniors over 62 and children 11–17. Museum daily 10am–5pm. Ships on Hyde St. Pier May 15–Sept 15 daily 9:30am–5:30pm; Sept 16–May 14 daily 9:30am–5pm. Closed Jan 1, Thanksgiving, Dec 25. Cable car: Powell-Hyde St. line to the last stop. Bus: 19, 30, 32, 42, or 47.

Shaped like an art deco ship, the Maritime Museum is filled with sailing, whaling, and fishing lore. Remarkably good exhibits include intricate model craft and scrimshaw. The collection of shipwreck photographs and historic marine scenes includes an 1851 snapshot of hundreds of abandoned ships, deserted en masse by crews dashing off to participate in the gold rush. Beautifully carved, brightly painted wooden figureheads from old windjammers line the walls.

Two blocks east, at the park's Hyde Street Pier, are several historic ships, now moored and open to the public.

The *Balclutha,* one of the last surviving square-riggers and the handsomest vessel in San Francisco Bay, was built in Glasgow, Scotland, in 1886 and used to carry grain from California at a near-record speed of 300 miles a day. The ship is now completely restored. Visitors are invited to spin the wheel, squint at the compass, and imagine they're weathering a mighty storm. Kids can climb into the bunking quarters, visit the "slop chest" ("galley" to you, matey), and read the sea chanteys (clean ones only) that decorate the walls.

The 1890 *Eureka* still carries a cargo of nostalgia for San Franciscans. It was the last of 50 paddle-wheel ferries that regularly plied the bay; it made its final trip in 1957. Restored to its original splendor at the height of the ferryboat era, the side-wheeler is loaded with deck cargo, including antique cars and trucks.

The black-hulled, three-masted *C. A. Thayer,* built in 1895, was crafted for the lumber trade and carried logs felled in the Pacific Northwest to the carpentry shops of California.

Other historic ships docked here include the tiny two-masted *Alma,* one of the last scow schooners to bring hay to the horses of San Francisco; the *Hercules,* a huge 1907 oceangoing steam tug; and the *Eppleton Hall,* a side-wheel tugboat built in England in 1914 to operate on London's River Thames.

At the pier's small-boat shop, visitors can follow the restoration progress of historic boats from the museum's collection. It's behind the maritime bookstore on your right as you approach the ships.

✪ **San Francisco Museum of Modern Art (MOMA).** 151 Third St. (2 blocks south of Market St., across from Yerba Buena Gardens). ☎ **415/357-4000.** Admission $9 adults, $6 seniors, $5 students over 12 with ID, free for children under 13. Half-price for all Thurs 6–9pm; free to all first Tues of each month. Labor Day–Memorial Day Thurs 11am–9pm; Fri–Tues 11am–6pm. Memorial Day–Labor Day Thurs 10am–9pm; Fri–Tues 10am–6pm. Closed Wed and major holidays. Muni Metro: J, K, L, or M to Montgomery Station. Bus: 15, 30, or 45.

Swiss architect Mario Botta, in association with Hellmuth, Obata, and Kassabaum, designed the $62 million museum, which opened in SoMa in January 1995. The building is the most welcomed new development in years and has made SoMa one of the more popular areas to visit for tourists and residents alike. The museum's collection consists of more than 15,000 works, including close to 5,000 paintings and sculptures by artists such as Henri Matisse, Jackson Pollock, and Willem de Kooning. Other artists represented include Diego Rivera, Georgia O'Keeffe, Paul Klee, the Fauvists, and exceptional holdings of Richard Diebenkorn. MOMA was also one of the first to recognize photography as a major art form; its extensive collection includes more than 9,000 photographs by such notables as Ansel Adams, Alfred Stieglitz, Edward Weston, and Henri Cartier-Bresson. Docent-led tours take place daily. Times are posted at the admission desk. Phone for current details of upcoming special events.

The Caffè Museo, to the right of the museum entrance, sets a new precedent for museum food with flavorful and fresh soups, sandwiches, and salads as respectable as those served in many local restaurants.

No matter what, don't miss the Museum Store, which carries a wonderful array of architectural gifts, books, and trinkets. It's one of the best stores in town.

Wells Fargo History Museum. 420 Montgomery St. (at California St.). ☎ **415/ 396-2619.** Free admission. Mon–Fri 9am–5pm. Closed bank holidays. Muni Metro: Montgomery St. Bus: Any to Market St. Cable car: California St. line.

Wells Fargo, one of California's largest banks, got its start in the Wild West. Its history museum, at the bank's head office, houses hundreds of genuine relics from the company's whip-and-six-shooter days, including pistols, photographs, early banking articles, posters, and mining equipment.

✪ **Yerba Buena Center for the Arts/Yerba Buena Gardens.** 701 Mission St. ☎ **415/ 978-2700** or 415/978-ARTS (box office). www.yerbabuenaarts.org. Admission $5 adults, $3 seniors and students. Free to all first Thurs of each month 5–8pm. Tues–Wed and Sat–Sun 11am–6pm; Thurs–Fri 11am–8pm. Muni Metro: Powell or Montgomery. Bus: 30, 45, or 9X.

The Yerba Buena Center, which opened in 1993, is the city's cultural facility, similar to New York's Lincoln Center. It stands on top of the northern extension of the underground Moscone Convention Center. The center's two buildings present music, theater, dance, and visual arts. James Stewart Polshek designed the 755-seat theater, and Fumihiko Maki designed by the Galleries and Arts Forum, which features three galleries and a space designed especially for dance.

Cutting-edge computer art, multimedia shows, traditional exhibitions, and performances occupy the center's high-tech galleries. A recent exhibition, "Surf Trip: Surf Culture Art and Artifacts," featured a colorful look at the sport and the most influential surf films, including *The Endless Summer* and *Free Ride.*

The 5-acre **Yerba Buena Gardens** feature several artworks. The most dramatic outdoor piece is an emotional mixed-media memorial to Martin Luther King, Jr. Created by sculptor Houston Conwill, poet Estella Majozo, and architect Joseph de Pace, it features 12 panels, each inscribed with quotations from King, sheltered behind a 50-foot-high waterfall.

The new children's addition, **Zeum** (☎ **415/777-2800**), includes a cafe, interactive cultural center, ice-skating rink, fabulous 1906 carousel, and interactive play and learning garden. Sony's new Metreon Entertainment Center (☎ **415/537-3400**) is a 350,000-square-foot complex housing movie theaters, an IMAX Theatre, great fast-food restaurants, interactive attractions (including one that features Maurice Sendak's *Where the Wild Things Are*), and shops. Also in the Yerba Buena Center are a bowling alley, child-care center, and ice-skating rink. As part of the plan to develop this area as the city's cultural hub, the California Historical Society opened at 678 Mission St. in 1995, and the Mexican Museum will relocate in the area in late 2000.

3 Neighborhoods Worth a Visit

To really get to know San Francisco, break out of the downtown and Fisherman's Wharf areas to explore the ethnically and culturally diverse neighborhoods. Walk the streets, browse the shops, grab a bite at a local restaurant—you'll find that San Francisco's beauty and charm is around every corner, not just at the popular tourist destinations.

Note: For information on Fisherman's Wharf, see "Famous San Francisco Sights," earlier in this chapter. For information on other San Francisco neighborhoods and districts that aren't discussed here, see the "Neighborhoods in Brief" section in chapter 4.

NOB HILL

When the cable car started operating in 1873, this hill became the city's exclusive residential area. The "Big Four" and the "Comstock Bonanza kings" built their mansions here, but they were all destroyed by the earthquake and fire in 1906. The only two surviving buildings were the Flood Mansion, which serves today as the Pacific Union Club, and the Fairmont Hotel, which was under construction when the earthquake struck. Today the burned-out sites of former mansions hold the city's luxury hotels—the **Mark Hopkins,** the **Stanford Court,** the **Fairmont,** and the **Huntington**—as well as spectacular **Grace Cathedral,** which stands on the Crocker mansion site. Nob Hill is worth a visit if only to stroll around **Huntington Park,** attend a Sunday service at the cathedral, or ooh and aah your way around the Fairmont's spectacular lobby.

SOUTH OF MARKET (SOMA)

From Market Street to Townsend and the Embarcadero to Division Street, SoMa has become the city's newest cultural and multimedia center. The process started when alternative clubs began opening in the old warehouses in the area nearly a decade ago.

A wave of entrepreneurs followed, seeking to start new businesses in what was once an extremely low-rent area compared to the neighboring Financial District. Today, gentrification and high rents hold sway, spurred by a building boom that started with the **Moscone Convention Center** and continued with the **Center for the Arts at Yerba Buena Gardens** and the **San Francisco Museum of Modern Art.** Other institutions, businesses, and museums move into the area daily. A substantial portion of the city's nightlife takes place in warehouse spaces throughout the district.

NORTH BEACH

In the late 1800s, an enormous influx of Italian immigrants to North Beach firmly established this aromatic area as San Francisco's "Little Italy." Dozens of Italian restaurants and coffeehouses continue to flourish in what is still the center of the city's Italian community. Walk down **Columbus Avenue** on any given morning and you're bound to be bombarded with the wonderful aromas of roasting coffee and savory pasta sauces. Although there are some interesting shops and bookstores in the area, it's the dozens of eclectic little cafes, delis, bakeries, and coffee shops that give North Beach its Italian-bohemian character.

For a proper perspective, follow the detailed walking tour in chapter 8, "City Strolls," or sign up for a guided Javawalk with coffee nut Elaine Sosa (see "Walking Tours," later in this chapter).

✪ CHINATOWN

The first Chinese came to San Francisco in the early 1800s to work as servants. By 1851, 25,000 Chinese were working in California, and most had settled in San Francisco's Chinatown. Fleeing famine and the Opium Wars, they had come seeking the promise of good fortune in the "Gold Mountain" of California, hoping to return with wealth to their families in China. For the majority, the reality of life in California did not live up to the promise. First employed as workers in the gold mines during the gold rush, they were later used to build the railroads, working as little more than slaves and facing constant prejudice. Yet the community, segregated in the Chinatown ghetto, thrived. Growing prejudice led to the Chinese Exclusion Act of 1882, which halted all Chinese immigration for 10 years and severely limited it thereafter; the Chinese Exclusion Act was not repealed until 1943. The Chinese were also denied the opportunity to buy homes outside the Chinatown ghetto until the 1950s.

Today San Francisco has the second-largest community of Chinese in the United States (about 33% of the city's population is Chinese). More than 80,000 people live in Chinatown, but the majority of Chinese have moved out into newer areas like the Richmond and Sunset districts. Although frequented by tourists, the area continues to cater to Chinese shoppers, who crowd the vegetable and herbal markets, restaurants, and shops. Tradition runs deep here, and if you're lucky, through an open window you might hear women mixing mahjong tiles as they play the century-old game.

The gateway at Grant Avenue and Bush Street marks the entry to Chinatown. The heart of the neighborhood is at Portsmouth Square, where you'll find locals playing board games (often gambling) or just sitting quietly.

The **Chinese Historical Society of America,** 644 Broadway (☎ **415/391-1188**), has a small but interesting collection relating to the Chinese in San Francisco. It's open Monday and Wednesday through Friday from 10:30am to 4pm, Tuesday 1 to 4pm. Admission is free.

On Waverly Place, a street where the Chinese celebratory colors of red, yellow, and green are much in evidence, you'll find three **temples:** Jeng Sen at no. 146, Tien Hou at no. 125, and Norras at no. 109.

A block west of Grant Avenue, **Stockton Street** from 1000 to 1200 is the community's main shopping street, lined with grocers, fishmongers, tea sellers, herbalists, noodle parlors, and restaurants. Here, too, is the Kon Chow Temple at no. 855, above the Chinatown post office. Explore at your leisure. A Chinatown walking tour is outlined in chapter 8.

JAPANTOWN

More than 12,000 citizens of Japanese descent live in San Francisco, or Soko, as it is often called by the Japanese who first emigrated here. Initially, they settled in Chinatown and south of Market along Stevenson and Jessie streets from Fourth to Seventh. After the earthquake in 1906, SoMa became a light industrial and warehouse area and the largest Japanese concentration took root in the Western Addition between Van Ness Avenue and Fillmore Street, the site of today's Japantown. By 1940 it covered 30 blocks.

In 1913 the Alien Land Law was passed, depriving Japanese Americans of the right to buy land. From 1924 to 1952 the United States banned Japanese immigration. During World War II, the U.S. government froze Japanese bank accounts, interned community leaders, and removed 112,000 Japanese Americans—two-thirds of them citizens—to camps in California, Utah, and Idaho. Japantown was emptied of Japanese, and war workers took their place. Upon their release in 1945, the Japanese found their old neighborhood occupied. Most of them resettled in the Richmond and Sunset districts; some did return to Japantown, but it had shrunk to a mere 6 or so blocks. Among the community's notable sights are the **Buddhist Church of San Francisco,** 1881 Pine St. (at Octavia Street); the **Konko Church of San Francisco,** 1909 Bush St. (at Laguna Street); the **Sokoji-Soto Zen Buddhist Temple,** 1691 Laguna St. (at Sutter Street); **Nihonmachi Mall,** 1700 block of Buchanan Street between Sutter and Post streets, which contains two steel fountains by Ruth Asawa; and the Japan Center.

The **Japan Center** is an Asian-oriented shopping mall occupying 3 square blocks bounded by Post, Geary, Laguna, and Fillmore streets. At its center stands the five-tiered **Peace Pagoda,** designed by world-famous Japanese architect Yoshiro Taniguchi "to convey the friendship and goodwill of the Japanese to the people of the United States." Surrounding the pagoda, in a network of arcades, squares, and bridges, are dozens of shops and showrooms featuring everything from TVs and tansu chests to pearls, bonsai (dwarf trees), and kimonos. When it opened in 1968, the complex seemed as modern as a jumbo jet. Today, the concrete structure seems less impressive, but it still holds some interesting surprises. The **Kabuki Springs & Spa** (see box, "Urban Renewal") is the center's most famous tenant. The Japan Center houses numerous restaurants, teahouses, and shops, and the Asian-inspired 14-story Radisson Miyako Hotel (see chapter 5, "Where to Stay," for complete information).

There is often live entertainment on summer weekends, including Japanese music and dance performances, tea ceremonies, flower-arranging demonstrations, martial-arts presentations, and other cultural events. The Japan Center is open Monday to Friday 10am to 10pm, and Saturday and Sunday 9am to 10pm. To get there, take bus no. 2, 3, or 4 (exit at Buchanan and Sutter streets), or no. 22 or 38 (exit at the northeast corner of Geary Boulevard and Fillmore Street).

HAIGHT-ASHBURY

Few of San Francisco's neighborhoods are as varied—or as famous—as Haight-Ashbury. Walk along Haight Street and you'll encounter everything from drug-dazed drifters begging for change to an armada of the city's most countercultural (read: cool) shops, clubs, and cafes. Yet, turn anywhere off Haight, and instantly you're among the

Urban Renewal

The **Kabuki Springs & Spa,** 1750 Geary Blvd. (☎ **415/922-6002**), the Japan Center's most famous tenant, was once an authentic, traditional Japanese bath-house. The Joie de Vivre hotel group bought and renovated it, and it's now more of a pan-Asian spa with a focus on wellness. The deep ceramic communal tubs, private baths, and shiatsu massages remain; joining them are an array of massages and ayurvedic treatments, body scrubs, wraps, and facials.

Spa Radiance, 3061 Fillmore St. (☎ **415/346-6281;** www.sparadiance.com), is an utterly San Francisco spa experience. No, I'm not talking groovy, hippie-like treatments. This is an unassuming Victorian where Sharon Stone reportedly has come for rejuvenation, from wonderfully luxurious treatments such as facials (14 kinds!), body treatments, massages, manicures, pedicures, and waxing.

clean-cut, young urban professionals who are the only ones who can afford the steep rents in this hip 'hood. The result is an interesting mix of well-to-do and well-screw-you, aging flower children, former Dead-heads, homeless people, and throngs of tourists who try not to stare as they wander through this most human of zoos. Some find it depressing, others find it fascinating, but everyone agrees that it ain't what it was in the free-lovin' psychedelic Summer of Love. Is it still worth a visit? Absolutely, if only to enjoy a cone of Cherry Garcia at the now-famous Ben & Jerry's ice cream shop on the corner of Haight and Ashbury streets, then wander and gawk at the area's exotic people.

THE CASTRO

Castro Street, between Market and 18th, is the center of the city's gay community, as well as a lovely neighborhood teeming with shops, restaurants, bars, and other insti-tutions that cater to the area's colorful residents. Among the landmarks are **Harvey Milk Plaza,** the **Names Project quilt,** and the **Castro Theatre,** a 1930s movie palace with a Wurlitzer. The gay community began to move here in the late 1960s and early 1970s from a neighborhood called Polk Gulch, which still has a number of gay-oriented bars and stores. Castro is one of the liveliest streets in the city and the perfect place to shop for gifts and revel in how free-spirited this town is.

THE MISSION DISTRICT

Once inhabited almost entirely by Irish immigrants, the Mission District is now the center of the city's Latino community. It's an oblong area stretching roughly from 14th to 30th streets between Potrero Avenue on the east and Dolores on the west. In the outer areas many of the city's finest Victorians still stand, although many seem strange-ly out of place in the mostly lower-income neighborhoods. The heart of the commu-nity lies along 24th Street between Van Ness and Potrero, where dozens of excellent ethnic restaurants, bakeries, bars, and specialty stores attract people from all over the city. The area surrounding 16th Street and Valencia is a hotbed for impressive—and impressively cheap—restaurants and bars catering to the city's hip crowd. The Mission District at night isn't exactly the safest place, and walking around the area should be done with caution, but it's usually quite safe during the day, and highly recommended.

For an even better insight into the community, go to the **Precita Eyes Mural Arts Center,** 2981 24th St., between Harrison and Alabama streets (☎ **415/285-2287**), and take one of the $1^3/_4$ -hour tours conducted on Saturday and Sunday at 11am and 1:30pm. They cost $10 for adults, $8 for students with ID, $5 for seniors, $2 for

The Castro & the Haight

children under 18. You'll see 85 murals in an 8-block walk. Every year during Mural Awareness Month (usually May), tours are given daily. All tours leave from the center's other location, 2981 24th St., at Harrison Street (☎ 415/285-2287). Other signs of cultural life include a number of progressive theaters—Eureka, Theater Rhinoceros, and Theater Artaud, to name only a few.

At 16th and Dolores is the **Mission San Francisco de Assisi,** better known as Mission Dolores. It's the city's oldest surviving building (see the separate listing in "Here's the Church & Here's the Steeple . . .," below) and the district's namesake.

4 Golden Gate Park

Everybody loves Golden Gate Park—people, dogs, birds, frogs, turtles, bison, trees, bushes, and flowers. Literally everything feels unified here in San Francisco's enormous arboreal front yard, but this great city landmark wasn't always a favorite place to convene. It was conceived in the 1860s and 1870s, and took its current shape in the 1880s and 1890s thanks to the skill and effort of John McClaren, a Scot who arrived in 1887 and began landscaping the park. Totaling 1,017 acres, the park is a narrow strip that stretches from the Pacific coast inland. No one had thought about the challenge the sand dunes and wind would present to any landscape artist. McClaren developed a new strain of grass called "sea bent," which he had planted to hold the sandy soil along the Firth of Forth, and he used it to anchor the soil here, too. He also built the two windmills that stand on the western edge of the park to pump water for irrigation. Every year the ocean eroded the western fringe of the park, and ultimately he solved this problem, too. It took him 40 years to build a natural wall, putting out bundles of sticks that the tides covered with sand. Under his brilliant eye, the park took shape.

Today's Golden Gate Park is a truly magical place. Spend one sunny day stretched out on the grass along JFK Drive, have a good read in Shakespeare Garden, or stroll around Stow Lake and you too will understand the allure. It's an interactive botanical symphony, and everyone is invited to play in the orchestra.

The park consists of hundreds of gardens and attractions attached by wooded paths and paved roads. While many worthy sites are clearly visible, there are infinite hidden treasures, so pick up information if you want to find the more obscure, quaint spots. For information on the park, head first to the **McClaren Lodge and Park Headquarters** (☎ 415/831-2700), which is open daily. Of the dozens of special gardens in the park, most recognized are the **Rhododendron Dell,** the **Rose Garden,** the **Strybing Arboretum,** and, at the western edge of the park, a springtime array of thousands of tulips and daffodils around the **Dutch windmill.**

In addition to the highlights below, the park contains lots of recreational facilities: tennis courts; baseball, soccer, and polo fields; a golf course; riding stables; and fly-casting pools. The Strawberry Hill boathouse handles boat rentals. The park is also the home of three major museums: the M. H. De Young Memorial Museum, the Asian Art Museum, and the California Academy of Sciences (see separate listings below). *Note:* There's talk of moving the De Young to an undetermined location, and the Asian Art Museum is moving to the old Main Library site in the Civic Center around 2001.

For further information, call ☎ **415/391-2000.** Enter the park at Kezar Drive, an extension of Fell Street. Bus: 5, 6, 7, 16AX, BX, 66, or 71.

MUSEUMS INSIDE THE PARK

Asian Art Museum. In Golden Gate Park, near 10th Ave. and Fulton St. ☎ **415/379-8800** or 415/752-2635 for the hearing impaired. Admission (including the M. H. De Young Memorial Museum and California Palace of the Legion of Honor) $7 adults, $5 seniors 65 and over, $4 youths 12–17, free for children under 12. Fees may be higher for special exhibitions. Free to all first Wed of each month. Tues–Sun 9:30am–4:45pm; first Wed of each month 9:30am–8:45pm. Bus: 5, 21, 44, or 71.

Adjacent to the M. H. De Young Museum and the Japanese Tea Garden, this exhibition space, opened in 1966, can display only about 1,800 pieces from the museum's vast collection of 12,000. About half of the works on exhibit are in the ground-floor

---

Handy Tip

If you plan to visit all the park's attractions, consider buying the Culture Pass, which enables you to visit the three museums and the Japanese Tea Garden for $12. Passes are available at each site and at the **San Francisco Visitor Information Center,** on the lower level of Hallidie Plaza, 900 Market St., at Powell Street (☎ **415/391-2000**; fax 415/362-7323).

Golden Gate Park

Japanese Tea Garden **7**
McLaren Memorial Rhododendron Dell **2**
M.H. De Young Memorial Museum and
Asian Art Museum **3**
Music Concourse **4**
Riding Stables **10**
Stow Lake **8**
Strybing Arboretum & Botanical Gardens **6**

Beach Chalet **14**
Boat House **9**
Buffalo Paddock **11**
California Academy of Sciences,
Steinhart Aquarium, and
Morrison Planetarium **5**
Conservatory of Flowers **1**
Dutch Windmill **13**
Golden Gate Golf Course **12**

Chinese and Korean galleries; they include world-class sculptures, paintings, bronzes, ceramics, jades, and decorative objects spanning 6,000 years of history. The wide range of exhibits from Pakistan, India, Tibet, Japan, Southeast Asia, and many more regions includes the world's oldest-known "dated" Chinese Buddha. The free daily guided tours are highly informative and recommended. Call for times.

California Academy of Sciences. On the Music Concourse of Golden Gate Park. ☎ **415/ 750-7145** for recorded information. Admission (aquarium and Natural History Museum) $8.50 adults, $5.50 seniors 65 and over and students 12–17, $2 children 4–11, free for children under 4. Free to all first Wed of each month. Planetarium shows $2.50 adults, $1.25 seniors 65 and over and children under 18. Labor Day–Memorial Day daily 10am–5pm; Memorial Day–Labor Day daily 9am–6pm; first Wed of each month 10am–9pm. Muni Metro: N to Golden Gate Park. Bus: 5, 44, or 71.

Clustered around the Music Concourse in Golden Gate Park are three outstanding museums and exhibitions guaranteed to entertain every member of the family. The **Steinhart Aquarium** is the most diverse aquarium in the world, housing some 14,000 specimens, including amphibians, reptiles, marine mammals, penguins, and much more, in 189 displays. A huge hit with the youngsters is the California tide pool and a "hands-on" area where children can touch starfish and sea urchins. The living coral reef is the largest display of its kind in the country and the only one in the West. In the Fish Roundabout, fast-swimming schools of fish in a 100,000-gallon tank surround visitors.

The **Morrison Planetarium** presents sky shows as well as laser-light shows. Sky shows offer guided tours through the universe projected onto a 65-foot domed ceiling. Approximately four major exhibits, with titles such as "Star Death: The Birth of Black Holes" and "The Universe Unveiled," are presented each year. Related cosmos exhibits are in the adjacent Earth and Space Hall. Sky shows begin at 2pm on weekdays and hourly every weekend and holiday (call ☎ **415/750-7141** for more information). **Laserium laser-light shows** take place in the planetarium Saturday and Sunday at 5pm (call ☎ **415/750-7138** for more information).

The **Natural History Museum** includes several halls displaying classic dioramas of fauna in their habitats. The Wattis Hall of Human Cultures traces the evolution of different human cultures and the way they adapted to their natural environment. The "Wild California" exhibition in Meyer Hall includes a 14,000-gallon aquarium and seabird rookery, life-sized battling elephant seals, and two larger-than-life views of microscopic life forms. In McBean-Peterson Hall, visitors can walk through an exhibit tracing the course of $3\frac{1}{2}$ billion years of evolution, from the earliest life forms to the present day. The Hohfeld Earth and Space Hall allows visitors to experience a simulation of two of San Francisco's biggest earthquakes, determine what their weight would be on other planets, see a real moon rock, and learn about the rotation of the planet at a replica of Foucault's pendulum (the real one is in Paris).

M. H. De Young Memorial Museum. In Golden Gate Park (near 10th Ave. and Fulton St.). ☎ **415/750-3600** or 415/863-3330 (recorded information). Admission (including the Asian Art Museum and California Palace of the Legion of Honor) $7 adults, $5 seniors over 65, $4 youths 13–17, free for children under 13. Fees may be higher for special exhibitions. Free to all first Wed of each month. Tues–Sun 9:30am–5pm; first Wed of each month 9:30am–8:45pm. Bus: 5, 44, or 71.

One of the city's oldest museums, the De Young is best known for its American art dating from colonial times to the 20th century. The collection includes paintings, sculptures, furniture, and decorative arts by Paul Revere, Winslow Homer, John Singer Sargent, and Georgia O'Keeffe. Take special note of the American landscapes, as well as the fun trompe l'oeil and still-life works from the turn of the century.

Named after the late 19th-century publisher of the *San Francisco Chronicle,* the museum also possesses an important textile collection, with primary emphasis on rugs from central Asia and the Near East. Other collections on view include decorative art from Africa, Oceania, and the Americas. Major traveling exhibitions are equally eclectic, including everything from ancient rugs to great Dutch paintings. Call the museum to find out what's on. Tours are offered daily; call for times.

The museum's Café De Young is exceptional, serving daily specials that might include Peruvian stew, Chinese chicken salad, and Italian vegetables in tomato-basil sauce. In summer, visitors can dine in the garden among bronze statuary. The cafe is open Wednesday to Sunday 10am to 4pm.

OTHER HIGHLIGHTS

CONSERVATORY OF FLOWERS (1878)   Built for the 1894 Midwinter Exposition, this striking assemblage of glass architecture usually exhibits a rotating display of plants and shrubs at all times of the year. Unfortunately, in recent years rough weather has damaged the already delicate structure. Renovations aren't scheduled to be finished until 2004. Still, the exterior, which is modeled on the famous glass house at Kew Gardens in London, is indeed grand.

JAPANESE TEA GARDEN (1894)   McClaren hired the Hagiwara family to care for this garden developed for the 1894 Midwinter Exposition. It's a quiet place with cherry trees, shrubs, and bonsai crisscrossed by winding paths and high-arched bridges crossing over pools of water. Focal points and places for contemplation include the massive bronze Buddha (cast in Japan in 1790 and donated by the Gump family), the Shinto wooden pagoda, and the Wishing Bridge, which, reflected in the water, looks as though it completes a circle. The garden is open daily November through February 8:30am to 5pm (teahouse 10am to 4:30pm), March through October 8:30am to 6pm (teahouse 10am to 5:30pm). For **information** on admissions, call ☎ **415/752-4227.** For the **teahouse**, call ☎ **415/752-1171.**

✪ STRAWBERRY HILL/STOW LAKE   Rent a paddleboat, rowboat, or motorboat and cruise around the circular lake as painters create still lifes and joggers pass along the grassy shoreline. Ducks waddle around waiting to be fed, and turtles bathe on rocks and logs. Strawberry Hill, the 430-foot-high artificial island that lies at the center of Stow Lake, is a perfect picnic spot and boasts a bird's-eye view of San Francisco and the bay. It also has a waterfall and peace pagoda. For the **boathouse**, call ☎ **415/752-0347.** Boat rentals are available daily from 9am to 4pm.

STRYBING ARBORETUM & BOTANICAL GARDENS   Six thousand plant species grow here, among them some ancient plants in a special "primitive garden," rare species, and a grove of California redwoods. Docent tours begin at 1pm daily. Open Monday to Friday 8am to 4:30pm, and Saturday and Sunday 10am to 5pm. For more information, call ☎ **415/753-7090.**

5 The Presidio & Golden Gate National Recreation Area

THE PRESIDIO

In October 1994, the Presidio passed from the U.S. Army to the National Park Service and became one of a handful of urban national parks that combines historical, architectural, and natural elements into one giant arboreal expanse. (It also contains a previously private golf course and a home for George Lucas's production company.) The 1,480-acre area incorporates a variety of terrain—coastal scrub, dunes, and prairie grasslands that shelter many rare plants and more than 150 species of birds, some of which nest here.

This military outpost has a 220-year history, from its founding in September 1776 by the Spanish under José Joaquin Moraga to its closure in 1995. From 1822 to 1835, the property was in Mexican hands.

During the war with Mexico, American forces occupied the fort, and in 1848, when California became part of the Union, it was formally transferred to the United States. When San Francisco suddenly became an important urban area during the gold rush, the U.S. government installed battalions of soldiers and built Fort Point to protect the entry to the harbor. It expanded the post during the Civil War and during the Indian Wars of the 1870s and 1880s. By the 1890s, it was no longer a frontier post but a major base for American expansion into the Pacific. During the war with Spain in 1898, thousands of troops camped in tent cities awaiting shipment to the Philippines, and the Army General Hospital treated the sick and wounded. By 1905, 12 coastal defense batteries were built along the headlands. In 1914, troops under the command of Gen. John Pershing left here to pursue Pancho Villa and his men. The Presidio expanded during the 1920s when Crissy Army Airfield (the first airfield on the West Coast) was established, but the major action was seen during World War II after the attack on Pearl Harbor. Soldiers dug foxholes along nearby beaches, and the Presidio became the headquarters for the Western Defense Command. Some 1.6 million men shipped out from nearby Fort Mason to fight in the Pacific; many returned to the hospital, whose capacity peaked one year at 72,000 patients. In the 1950s, the Presidio served as the headquarters for the Sixth U.S. Army and a missile defense post, but its role slowly shrank. In 1972, it was included in new legislation establishing the Golden Gate National Recreation Area; in 1989, the Pentagon decided to close the post and transfer it to the National Park Service.

Today, the area encompasses more than 510 historic buildings, a scenic golf course, a national cemetery, and a variety of terrain and natural habitats. The National Park Service offers a variety of walking and biking tours around the Presidio; reservations are suggested. At press time the **Presidio Museum** was moving to new digs at 102 Montgomery St. on the parade grounds (open Wednesday to Sunday noon to 5pm). Here you can find the Presidio story told in dioramas, exhibitions, and photographs. For more information, call the **Visitor Information Center** at ☎ **415/561-4323.** Take the 28, 76, or 82X bus.

San Francisco Zoo & Children's Zoo. Sloat Blvd. and 45th Ave. ☎ **415/753-7080.** www.sfzoo.org. Admission to main zoo and children's zoo $9 adults, $6.50 seniors and youths 12–17, $3 children 3–11, free for children under 3 accompanied by an adult. Free to all first Wed of each month. Carousel $2. Main zoo daily 10am–5pm. Children's Zoo Mon–Fri 11am–4pm; Sat–Sun 10:30am–4:30pm. Muni Metro: L from downtown Market St. to the end of the line.

Located between the Pacific Ocean and Lake Merced, in the southwest corner of the city, the San Francisco Zoo is among America's highest-rated animal parks. Begun in 1889 with a grizzly bear named Monarch donated by the *San Francisco Examiner,* the zoo now sprawls over 65 acres and is growing. It attracts up to a million visitors each year. Most of the 1,000-plus inhabitants are in landscaped enclosures guarded by concealed moats. The innovative Primate Discovery Center is particularly noteworthy for its many rare and endangered species. Expansive outdoor atriums, sprawling meadows, and a midnight world for exotic nocturnal primates house such species as the owl-faced macaque, ruffed-tailed lemur, black-and-white colobus monkeys, patas monkeys, and emperor tamarins—pint-sized primates distinguished by their long, majestic mustaches.

Golden Gate National Recreation Area

Other highlights include Koala Crossing, which connects to the Australian Walk About exhibit with its kangaroos, emus, and wallaroos; Gorilla World, one of the world's largest exhibits of the gentle giants; and Penguin Island, home to a large breeding colony of Magellanic penguins. The new Feline Conservation Center is a wooded sanctuary and breeding facility for the zoo's endangered snow leopards, Persian leopards, and other jungle cats. Musk Ox Meadow is a 2½-acre habitat for a herd of rare white-fronted musk oxen brought from Alaska. The Otter River exhibit features waterfalls, logs, and boulders for North American otters to climb. And the Lion House is home to rare Sumatran and Siberian tigers, Prince Charles (a rare white Bengal tiger), and the African lions (you can watch them being fed at 2pm Tuesday to Sunday).

The Children's Zoo, adjacent to the main park, allows both kids and adults to get close to animals. The barnyard is alive with strokable domestic animals, such as sheep, goats, ponies, and a llama. Also of interest is the Insect Zoo, which showcases a multitude of species, including the hissing cockroach and walking sticks.

A free, informal walking tour of the zoo is available on weekends at 11am. The Zebra Zephyr train tour takes visitors on a 30-minute "safari" daily (only on weekends in winter). The tour is $2.50 for adults, $1.50 for seniors and children under 16.

GOLDEN GATE NATIONAL RECREATION AREA

The largest urban park in the world, the GGNRA makes New York's Central Park look like a putting green, covering three counties along 28 miles of stunning, condo-free shoreline. Run by the National Park Service, the Recreation Area wraps around the northern and western edges of the city, and just about all of it is open to the public with no access fees. The Muni bus system provides transportation to the more popular sites, including Aquatic Park, the Cliff House, Fort Mason, and Ocean Beach. For more information, contact the **National Park Service** (☎ **415/556-0560**). For more detailed information on particular sites, see the "Staying Active" section near the end of this chapter.

Here is a brief rundown of the salient features of the park's peninsula section, starting at the northern section and moving westward around the coastline:

Aquatic Park, adjacent to the Hyde Street Pier, has a small swimming beach, although it's not that appealing (and darn cold). Far more entertaining is a visit to the ship-shaped museum across the lawn that's part of the San Francisco Maritime National Historical Park (see "Museums," above, for more information).

Fort Mason Center, from Bay Street to the shoreline, consists of several buildings and piers used during World War II. Today they hold a variety of museums, theaters, and organizations, and Greens vegetarian restaurant, which affords views of the Golden Gate Bridge (see chapter 6, "Where to Dine," for more information). For information about Fort Mason events, call ☎ **415/441-5706.** The park headquarters is also at Fort Mason.

Farther west along the bay at the northern end of Laguna Street is **Marina Green,** a favorite local spot for kite-flying, jogging, and walking along the Promenade. The St. Francis Yacht Club is also here.

Next comes the 3½-mile paved **Golden Gate Promenade,** San Francisco's best and most scenic biking, jogging, and walking path. It runs along the shore past Crissy Field (be sure to stop and watch the gonzo windsurfers) and ends at Fort Point under the Golden Gate Bridge.

Fort Point (☎ 415/556-1693) was built in 1853 to protect the narrow entrance to the harbor. It was designed to house 500 soldiers manning 126 muzzle-loading cannons. By 1900, the fort's soldiers and obsolete guns had been removed, but the formidable brick edifice remains. Fort Point is open daily from 10am to 5pm, and guided tours and cannon demonstrations are given at the site once or twice daily, depending on the time of year.

Lincoln Boulevard sweeps around the western edge of the bay to Baker Beach, where the waves roll ashore—a fine spot for sunbathing, walking, or fishing. Hikers can follow the Coastal Trail from Fort Point along this part of the coastline all the way to Lands End.

A short distance from Baker Beach, **China Beach** is a small cove where swimming is permitted. Changing rooms, showers, a sundeck, and rest rooms are available.

A little farther around the coast is **Lands End,** looking out to Pyramid Rock. A lower and an upper trail offer hiking amid windswept cypresses and pines on the cliffs above the Pacific.

Still farther along the coast lie **Point Lobos,** the **Sutro Baths,** and the **Cliff House.** The Cliff House has been serving refreshments to visitors since 1863 and providing views of Seal Rocks, home to a colony of sea lions and many marine birds. There's an **information center** (open daily from 10am to 5pm; ☎ 415/556-8642) as well as the incredible Musée Mecanique, an authentic old-fashioned arcade with 150 coin-operated amusement machines. Northeast of the Cliff House, only traces of the Sutro Baths remain. The swimming facility, a major summer attraction that could accommodate up to 24,000 people, burned down in 1966.

A little farther inland at the western end of California Street is **Lincoln Park,** which contains a golf course and the spectacular Palace of the Legion of Honor museum.

At the southern end of Ocean Beach, 4 miles down the coast, is another area of the park around Fort Funston, where there's an easy loop trail across the cliffs (ranger office: ☎ 415/239-2366). Here you can watch hang gliders taking advantage of the high cliffs and strong winds.

Farther south along route 280, **Sweeney Ridge,** accessible only by car, affords sweeping views of the coastline from the many trails that crisscross its 1,000 acres. From here the expedition led by Don Gaspar de Portolá first saw San Francisco Bay in 1769. It's in Pacifica; take Sneath Lane off Route 35 (Skyline Boulevard) in San Bruno.

The GGNRA extends into Marin County, where it encompasses the Marin Headlands, Muir Woods National Monument, and the Olema Valley behind the Point Reyes National Seashore. See chapter 11, "Side Trips from San Francisco," for information on these areas.

6 Here's the Church & Here's the Steeple . . .

Some of San Francisco's churches and religious buildings are worth checking out.

✪ **Glide Memorial United Methodist Church.** 330 Ellis St. (west of Union Square.). ☎ 415/771-6300. Services Sun at 9 and 11am. Muni Metro: Powell. Bus: 37.

There would be nothing special about this Tenderloin-area church if it weren't for its exhilarating pastor, Cecil Williams. Reverend Williams's enthusiastic and uplifting preaching and singing with homeless and poor people of the neighborhood has

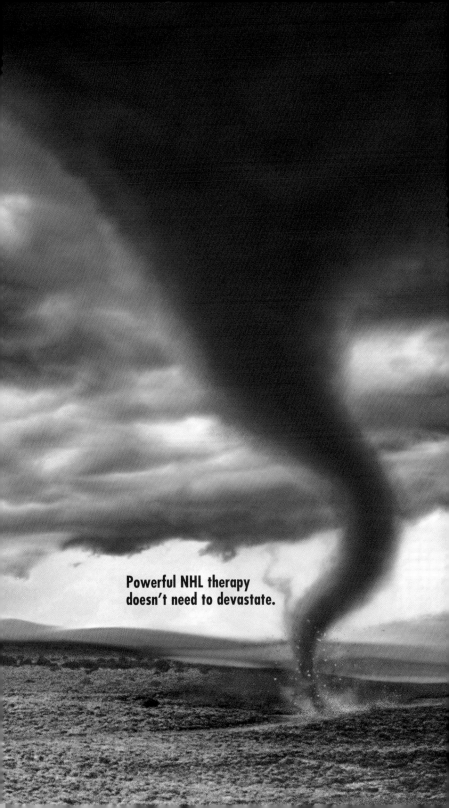

**Powerful NHL therapy
doesn't need to devastate.**

Powerful therapy,
targeted precisely.

For relapsed or refractory low-grade or follicular, CD20+, B-cell non-Hodgkin's lymphoma (NHL)

Impressive response rates

- Overall response rate of 48% (80/166) in a large, multicenter clinical trial[1]
- Median duration of response 11.2 months[2]
- To date, an estimated 38,000 US patients have been treated in postmarketing use[3]

Keeps downstream treatment options open

- Myelosuppression was uncommon in controlled clinical trials: severe neutropenia, thrombocytopenia, and anemia occurred in 1.9%, 1.3%, and 1% of patients, respectively*[1]
- Immune reactivity was uncommon: less than 1% (3/355) of patients in clinical trials developed detectable human antichimeric antibodies (HACA); no human antimurine antibodies (HAMA) were observed in 67 patients evaluated[1]

Rapidly depletes B cells with no apparent increase in infection

- Median B-cell levels return to baseline within 6 to 12 months of treatment[1]

The most common adverse events are part of an infusion-related symptom complex, primarily fever and chills/rigors, and are limited to the duration of infusion. These symptoms are generally mild to moderate, reversible, and occur predominantly during the first infusion. Some patients have experienced more severe (Grade 3/4) events, including hypotension and bronchospasm (1.0% each), and angioedema (0.3%). Recurrence of angina or arrhythmia has occurred in patients with pre-existing cardiac disease[1]

*Safety data, except where indicated, are based on 315 patients treated in five single-agent studies of Rituxan. These include NHL patients with bulky disease (lesions >10 cm), those who have received more than one course of Rituxan, and NHL patients receiving 375 mg/m² for eight doses.[1]

References: 1. Rituxan full Prescribing Information, July 1999. **2.** Data on file, IDEC Pharmaceuticals Corp. **3.** Data on file, Genentech, Inc.

WARNINGS

Infusion-related reactions: Infusion-related deaths (death within 24 hours of infusion) have been reported at a rate of approximately 0.04–0.07% (4–7 per 10,000 patients treated). These events appear as manifestations of an infusion-related complex and include hypoxia, pulmonary infiltrates, adult respiratory distress syndrome, myocardial infarction, ventricular fibrillation or cardiogenic shock. Nearly all fatal infusion-related events occurred in association with the first infusion. In the reported cases, the following factors were more frequently associated with fatal outcomes: women, patients with pulmonary infiltrates, and patients with CLL or mantle cell lymphoma (see WARNINGS section in brief summary of full prescribing information).

Regarding the management of infusion-related reactions:

- Patients who develop clinically significant cardiopulmonary events should have RITUXAN infusion discontinued and receive medical treatment.
- Patients with pre-existing cardiac and pulmonary conditions or those with prior clinically significant cardiopulmonary adverse events should be monitored during and after subsequent infusions of RITUXAN.
- Patients with high numbers of circulating malignant cells (≥25,000/mm³) with or without other evidence of high tumor burden should be more closely monitored for infusion reactions and tumor lysis syndrome.

Tumor Lysis Syndrome (TLS): Acute renal failure requiring dialysis with instances of fatal outcome has been reported in the setting of TLS. Assessment of serum electrolytes and renal function is indicated in patients with rapid decreases in tumor volume (see WARNINGS section in brief summary of full prescribing information).

Please see brief summary of full prescribing information on adjacent page.

Rituxan®

R i t u x i m a b

Power with Precision.

Rituxan®
R i t u x i m a b

BRIEF SUMMARY
The following is a brief summary. Before prescribing, please consult full prescribing information.

WARNINGS

Infusion-related reactions: Infusion-related deaths (death within 24 hours of infusion) have been reported at a rate of approximately 0.04–0.07% (4–7 per 10,000 patients treated). These events appear as manifestations of an infusion-related complex and include hypoxia, pulmonary infiltrates, adult respiratory distress syndrome, myocardial infarction, ventricular fibrillation or cardiogenic shock. Nearly all fatal infusion-related events occurred in association with the first infusion. In the reported cases, the following factors were more frequently associated with fatal outcomes: women, patients with pulmonary infiltrates, and patients with CLL or mantle cell lymphoma (see WARNINGS).

Regarding the management of infusion-related reactions:

- Patients who develop clinically significant cardiopulmonary events should have RITUXAN infusion discontinued and receive medical treatment.
- Patients with pre-existing cardiac and pulmonary conditions or those with prior clinically significant cardiopulmonary adverse events should be monitored during and after subsequent infusions of RITUXAN.
- Patients with high numbers of circulating malignant cells (≥25,000/mm³) with or without other evidence of high tumor burden should be more closely monitored for infusion reactions and tumor lysis syndrome.

Tumor Lysis Syndrome (TLS): Acute renal failure requiring dialysis with instances of fatal outcome has been reported in the setting of TLS. Assessment of serum electrolytes and renal function is indicated in patients with rapid decreases in tumor volume (see WARNINGS).

INDICATIONS AND USAGE
RITUXAN is indicated for the treatment of patients with relapsed or refractory low-grade or follicular, CD20 positive, B-cell non-Hodgkin's lymphoma.

CONTRAINDICATIONS
RITUXAN is contraindicated in patients with known Type I hypersensitivity or anaphylactic reactions to murine proteins or to any component of this product. (See WARNINGS.)

WARNINGS (see BOXED WARNINGS)
Infusion-Related Events (see BOXED WARNING): An infusion-related symptom complex consisting of fever and chills/rigors occurred in the majority of patients during the first RITUXAN infusion. Other frequent infusion-related symptoms included nausea, urticaria, fatigue, headache, pruritus, bronchospasm, dyspnea, sensation of tongue or throat swelling (angioedema), rhinitis, vomiting, hypotension, flushing, and pain at disease sites. These reactions generally occurred within 30 minutes to 2 hours of beginning the first infusion, and resolved with slowing or interruption of the RITUXAN infusion and with supportive care (diphenhydramine, acetaminophen, IV saline, and vasopressors). RITUXAN should be interrupted for severe reactions. In most cases, the infusion can be resumed at a 50% reduction in rate (e.g., from 100 mg/hr to 50 mg/hr) when symptoms have completely resolved. In clinical studies, the incidence of infusion-related events decreased from 80% (7% Grade 3/4) during the first infusion to approximately 40% (5% to 10% Grade 3/4) with subsequent infusions. Mild to moderate hypotension requiring interruption of RITUXAN infusion with or without the administration of IV saline occurred in 32 (10%) patients. Angioedema was reported in 41 (13%) patients and was serious in one patient. Bronchospasm occurred in 24 (8%) patients; one-quarter of these patients were treated with bronchodilators.

Tumor Lysis Syndrome (see BOXED WARNING): TLS, characterized by rapid reduction in tumor volume, renal insufficiency, hyperkalemia, hypocalcemia, hyperuricemia, or hyperphosphatasemia, has been reported within 12 to 24 hours after the first RITUXAN infusion at a reported rate of 0.04%–0.05%. The risks of TLS appear to be higher in patients with high numbers of circulating malignant cells. Correction of electrolytes abnormalities, monitoring of renal function and fluid balance, and supportive care, including dialysis, should be instituted as indicated. Following complete resolution of the complications of TLS, RITUXAN has been tolerated when re-administered in conjunction with prophylactic therapy for TLS in a limited number of cases.

General
RITUXAN is associated with hypersensitivity reactions which may respond to adjust-ments in the infusion rate. Hypotension, bronchospasm, and angioedema have occurred in association with RITUXAN infusion as part of an infusion-related symptom complex. RITUXAN infusion should be interrupted for severe reactions and can be resumed at a 50% reduction in rate (e.g., from 100 mg/hr to 50 mg/hr) when symptoms have completely resolved. Treatment of these symptoms with diphenhydramine and acetaminophen is recommended; additional treatment with bronchodilators or IV saline may be indicated. In most cases, patients who have experienced non-life-threatening reactions have been able to complete the full course of therapy. (See DOSAGE and ADMINISTRATION section of full prescribing information.) Medications for the treatment of hypersensitivity reactions, e.g., epinephrine, antihistamines and corticosteroids, should be available for immediate use in the event of a reaction during administration.

Cardiovascular
Infusions should be discontinued in the event of serious or life-threatening cardiac arrhythmias. Patients who develop clinically significant arrhythmias should undergo cardiac monitoring during and after subsequent infusions of RITUXAN. Patients with preexisting cardiac conditions including arrhythmias and angina have had recurrences of these events during RITUXAN therapy and should be monitored throughout the infusion and immediate post-infusion period.

PRECAUTIONS
Laboratory Monitoring: Complete blood counts (CBC) and platelet counts should be obtained at regular intervals during RITUXAN therapy and more frequently in patients who develop cytopenias (see ADVERSE REACTIONS).

Drug/Laboratory Interactions: There have been no formal drug interaction studies performed with RITUXAN.

HAMA/HACA Formation: Human anti-murine antibody (HAMA) was not detected in 67 patients evaluated. Less than 1.0% (3/355) of patients evaluated for human anti-chimeric antibody (HACA) were positive. Patients who develop HAMA/HACA titers may have allergic or hypersensitivity reactions when treated with this or other murine or chimeric monoclonal antibodies.

Immunization: The safety of immunization with any vaccine, particularly live viral vaccines, following RITUXAN therapy has not been studied. The ability to generate a primary or anamnestic humoral response to any vaccine has also not been studied.

Carcinogenesis, Mutagenesis, Impairment of Fertility: No long-term animal studies have been performed to establish the carcinogenic or mutagenic potential of RITUXAN, or to determine its effects on fertility in males or females. Individuals of childbearing potential should use effective contraceptive methods during treatment and for up to 12 months following RITUXAN therapy.

Pregnancy Category C: Animal reproduction studies have not been conducted with RITUXAN. It is not known whether RITUXAN can cause fetal harm when admin-istered to a pregnant woman or whether it can affect reproductive capacity. Human IgG is known to pass the placental barrier, and thus may potentially cause fetal B-cell depletion; therefore, RITUXAN should be given to a pregnant woman only if clearly needed.

Nursing Mothers: It is not known whether RITUXAN is excreted in human milk. Because human IgG is excreted in human milk and the potential for absorption and immunosuppression in the infant is unknown, women should be advised to discontinue nursing until circulating drug levels are no longer detectable. (See CLINICAL PHARMACOLOGY section of full prescribing information.)

Pediatric Use: The safety and effectiveness of RITUXAN in pediatric patients have not been established.

ADVERSE REACTIONS
Safety data, except where indicated, are based on 315 patients treated in five single-agent studies of RITUXAN. These include patients with bulky disease (lesions >10 cm), those who have received more than one course of RITUXAN, and patients receiving 375 mg/m² for eight doses.

Infusion-Related Events: (See BOXED WARNING and WARNINGS.)

Immunologic Events: RITUXAN induced B-cell depletion in 70 to 80% of patients and was associated with decreased serum immunoglobulins in a minority of patients. The incidence of infection did not appear to be increased. During the treat-ment period, 50 out of 166 patients (30%) in the pivotal trial developed 68 infectious events; six (9%) were Grade 3 in severity and none were Grade 4 events. Of the six serious infectious events, none were associated with neutropenia. The infectious events included sepsis due to *Listeria* (n=1), *Staphylococcal* bacteremia (n=1), and polymicrobial sepsis (n=1). In the posttreatment period (30 days to 11 months following the last dose), bacterial infections included sepsis (n=1); significant viral infections included *Herpes simplex* infections (n=2) and *Herpes zoster* (n=3). Additional reports of focal bacterial infections, sepsis, and viral infections have been received in the postmarketing setting. Serious infections, including sepsis, have been reported in patients with and without neutropenia.

Retreatment Events: Twenty-one patients have received more than one course of RITUXAN. The percentage of patients reporting any adverse event upon retreatment was similar to the percentage of patients reporting adverse events upon initial expo-sure. The following adverse events were reported more frequently in retreated subjects: asthenia, throat irritation, flushing, tachycardia, anorexia, leukopenia, thrombocytopenia, anemia, peripheral edema, dizziness, depression, respiratory symptoms, night sweats, and pruritus.

Hematologic Events: Severe cytopenias were reported including thrombocy-topenia (1.3%), neutropenia (1.9%), and anemia (1.0%). A single occurrence of transient aplastic anemia (pure red cell aplasia) and two occurrences of hemolytic anemia following RITUXAN therapy were reported. In addition, there have been rare postmarketing reports of prolonged pancytopenia and marrow hypoplasia.

Cardiac Events (see BOXED WARNING): Four patients developed ventricular or supraventricular arrhythmias and one patient developed angina in association with the RITUXAN infusion. Rare, fatal cardiac failure with symptomatic onset weeks after RITUXAN has also been reported. Patients who develop clinically significant cardiopulmonary events should ha[ve] RITUXAN infusion discontinued.

Pulmonary Events (see BOXED WARNING): Three pulmona[ry] events have been reported in temporal association with RITUX[AN] infusion as a single agent: acute, infusion-related bronchospasm, an acute pneumonitis presenting 1–4 weeks post-RITUXAN infusion, and bronchiolitis obliterans. The bronchiolitis obliterans was associated with progressive pulmonary symptoms and culminated in death several months following the last RITUXAN infusion. The safety of resumption o[f] continued administration of RITUXAN in patients with pneumonitis or bronchiolitis obliterans is unknown.

Table 1
Adverse Events ≥5% of Patients (N=315)

	Incidence All Grades	
	N	%
Any Adverse Event	275	87
Body As A Whole		
Fever	154	49
Chills	102	32
Asthenia	49	16
Headache	43	14
Throat Irritation	19	6
Abdominal Pain	18	6
Cardiovascular System		
Hypotension	32	10
Digestive System		
Nausea	55	18
Vomiting	23	7
Hemic and Lymphatic System		
Leukopenia	33	11
Thrombocytopenia	25	8
Neutropenia	21	7
Metabolic and Nutritional System		
Angioedema	41	13
Musculo-Skeletal System		
Myalgia	21	7
Nervous System		
Dizziness	23	7
Respiratory System		
Rhinitis	25	8
Bronchospasm	24	8
Skin and Appendages		
Pruritus	32	10
Rash	31	10
Urticaria	24	8

Severe and life-threatening (Grade 3 and 4) events were reported in 10% (32/315) of patients. The following Grade 3 and 4 adverse events were reported: neutropenia (1.9%), chills (1.6%), leukopenia and thrombocytopenia (1.3% for each), hypotension, anemia, bronchospasm, and urticaria (1.0% for each), headache, abdominal pain, and arrhythmia (0.6% for each), asthenia, hypertension, nausea, vomiting, coagulation disorder, angioedema, arthralgia, pain, rhinitis, increased cough, dyspnea, bronchiolitis obliterans, hypoxia, asthma, pruritus, and rash (one patient each, 0.3%).

The following adverse events occurred in ≥1.0% but <5.0% of patients, in order of decreasing incidence: flushing, arthralgia, diarrhea, anemia, cough increase, hyper-tension, lacrimation disorder, pain, hyperglycemia, back pain, peripheral edema, paresthesia, dyspepsia, chest pain, anorexia, anxiety, malaise, tachycardia, agitation, insomnia, sinusitis, conjunctivitis, abdominal enlargement, postural hypotension, LDH increase, hypocalcemia, hypesthesia, respiratory disorder, tumor pain, pain at injection site, bradycardia, hypertonia, nervousness, bronchitis, and taste perversion.

Multisystem adverse events—The following serious adverse reactions have been reported at a frequency of less than 0.1% in the postmarketing setting:
Body as a Whole: Lupus-like syndrome and serum sickness
Cardiovascular System: Systemic vasculitis
Musculoskeletal System: Polyarticular arthritis
Respiratory System: Pleuritis
Skin and Appendages: Severe bullous skin reactions (including toxic epidermal necrolysis) and pemphigus; some with fatal outcome
Special Senses: Optic neuritis and uveitis

Several of these events were reported as individual components of multisystem processes (e.g., optic neuritis in a patient with systemic vasculitis, pleuritis in association with lupus-like syndrome, etc.) and often in conjunction with rash and polyarthritis.

The proportion of patients reporting any adverse event was similar in patients with bulky disease and those with lesions < cm in diameter. However, the incidence of dizziness, neutropenia, thrombocytopenia, myalgia, anemia, and chest pain was higher in patients with lesions >10 cm. The incidence of any Grade 3 and 4 event was higher (31% vs. 13%) and the incidence of Grade 3 or 4 neutropenia, anemia, hypotension, and dyspnea was also higher in patients with bulky disease compared with patients with lesions <10 cm.

OVERDOSAGE
There has been no experience with overdosage in human clin[ical] trials. Single doses higher than 500 mg/m² have not been tested.

Jointly Marketed by:

IDEC Pharmaceuticals Corporation
11011 Torreyana Road
San Diego, CA 92121

Genentech, Inc.
1 DNA Way
South San Francisco, CA
94080-4990

7140903

(4809703 Revised July 199[9])

Genentech
BIO●ONCOLOGY

IDE[C]
Pharmaceuticals Corporati[on]

attracted nationwide fame. In 1994, during the pastor's 30th-anniversary celebration, singers Angela Bofill and Bobby McFerrin joined comedian Robin Williams, author Maya Angelou, and talk-show queen Oprah Winfrey to honor him publicly. Williams's nondogmatic, fun Sunday services attract a diverse audience that crosses all socioeconomic boundaries. Go for an uplifting experience.

Grace Cathedral. California St. (between Taylor and Jones sts.). ☎ **415/749-6300.**

Although this Nob Hill cathedral, designed by architect Lewis P. Hobart, appears to be made of stone, it is in fact constructed of reinforced concrete, beaten to achieve a stone-like effect. Construction began on the site of the Crocker mansion in 1928 but was not completed until 1964. Among the more interesting features of the building are its stained-glass windows, particularly those by the French Loire studios, depicting such modern figures as Thurgood Marshall, Robert Frost, and Albert Einstein; the replicas of Ghiberti's bronze *Doors of Paradise* at the east end; the series of religious frescoes completed in the 1940s by Polish artist John de Rosen; and the 44-bell carillon.

✪ **Mission Dolores.** 16th St. (at Dolores St.). ☎ **415/621-8203.** Donations appreciated. May–Oct daily 9am–4:30pm; Nov–Apr daily 9am–4pm; Good Friday 10am–noon. Closed Thanksgiving, Dec 25. Muni Metro: J. Bus: 14, 22, 26, or 53 to the corner of Church and 16th sts.

San Francisco's oldest standing structure, the Mission San Francisco de Assisi (a.k.a. Mission Dolores) has withstood the test of time, as well as two major earthquakes, relatively intact. In 1776, at the behest of Franciscan missionary Junípero Serra, Father Francisco Palou came to the Bay Area to found the sixth in a series of missions that dotted the California coastline. From these humble beginnings grew what was to become the city of San Francisco. The mission's small, simple chapel, built solidly by Native Americans who were converted to Christianity, is a curious mixture of native construction methods and Spanish-colonial style. A statue of Father Serra stands in the mission garden, although the portrait looks somewhat more contemplative, and less energetic, than he must have been in real life. A 45-minute audio tour costs $5 for adults, $4 for children.

7 Architectural Highlights

MUST-SEES FOR ARCHITECTURE BUFFS

ALAMO SQUARE HISTORIC DISTRICT   San Francisco's collection of Victorian houses, known as **"Painted Ladies,"** is one of the city's most famous assets. Most of the 14,000 extant structures date from the second half of the 19th century and are private residences. Spread throughout the city, many have been beautifully restored and ornately painted. The small area bordered by Divisadero Street on the west, Golden Gate Avenue on the north, Webster Street on the east, and Fell Street on the south—about 10 blocks west of the Civic Center—has one of the city's greatest concentrations of Painted Ladies. One of the most famous views of San Francisco—seen on postcards and posters all around the city—depicts sharp-edged Financial District skyscrapers behind a row of Victorians. This fantastic juxtaposition can be seen from Alamo Square, in the center of the historic district, at Fulton and Steiner streets.

CITY HALL & CIVIC CENTER   Built in 1881 to a design by Brown and Bakewell, it is part of this "City Beautiful" complex done in the Beaux-Arts style. The dome rises to a height of 308 feet on the exterior and is ornamented with occuli and topped by a lantern. The interior rotunda soars 112 feet and is finished in oak, marble, and limestone, with a monumental marble staircase leading to the second floor.

OTHER ARCHITECTURAL HIGHLIGHTS

San Francisco is a center of many architecturally striking sights. This section concentrates on a few highlights.

Around Union Square and the Financial District is the former **Circle Gallery,** 140 Maiden Lane. Now a gallery housing Folk Art International, Xanadu Tribal Arts, and Boretti Amber & Design, it's the only building in the city designed by Frank Lloyd Wright (in 1948). The gallery was the prototype for the Guggenheim's seashell-shaped circular gallery space, even though it was meant to serve as a retail space for V. C. Morris, a purveyor of glass and crystal. Note the arresting exterior, a solid wall with a circular entryway to the left. Maiden Lane is just off Union Square between Geary and Post streets.

The **Hallidie Building,** 130–150 Sutter St., designed by Willis Polk in 1917, is an ideal example of a glass-curtain building. The vast glass facade is miraculously suspended between the two cast-iron cornices. The fire escapes that course down each side of the building complete the proscenium-like theatrical effect.

Two prominent pieces of San Francisco's skyline are in the Financial District. The **TransAmerica Pyramid,** 600 Montgomery St., between Clay and Washington streets, is one of the tallest structures in San Francisco. This corporate headquarters was completed in 1972, stands 48 stories tall, and is capped by a 212-foot spire. The former **Bank of America World Headquarters,** 555 California St., was designed by Wurster, Bernardi, and Emmons with Skidmore, Owings, and Merrill. This carnelian-marble–covered building dates from 1969. Its 52 stories are topped by a panoramic restaurant and bar, the Carnelian Room (see chapter 10, "San Francisco After Dark," for complete information). The focal point of the building's formal plaza is an abstract black granite sculpture, known locally as the "Banker's Heart," designed by Japanese architect Masayuki Nagare.

The **Medical Dental Building,** 450 Sutter St., is a steel-frame structure beautifully clad in terra-cotta. It was designed by Miller and Pflueger in 1929. The entrance and the window frames are elaborately ornamented with Mayan relief work; the lobby ceiling is similarly decorated with gilding. Note the ornate elevators, too.

At the foot of Market Street you will find the **Ferry Building.** Built between 1895 and 1903, it served as the city's major transportation hub before the Golden Gate and Bay bridges were built; some 170 ferries docked here daily unloading Bay Area commuters until the 1930s. The tower that soars above the building was inspired by the Campanile of Venice and the Cathedral Tower in Seville. Plans are afoot to restore the building to its former glory, opening up the soaring galleries to the sky again. If you stop by the Ferry Building, you might also want to go to **Rincon Center,** 99 Mission St., to see the WPA murals painted by the Russian artist Refregier in the post office.

Several important buildings are on or near Nob Hill. The **Flood Mansion,** 1000 California St., at Mason Street, was built between 1885 and 1886 for James Clair Flood. Thanks to the Comstock Lode, Flood rose from being a bartender to being one of the city's wealthiest men. He established the Nevada bank that later merged with Wells Fargo. The house cost $1.5 million; the fence alone cost $30,000. It was designed by Augustus Laver and modified by Willis Polk after the earthquake to accommodate the Pacific Union Club.

Built by George Applegarth in 1913 for the sugar magnate Adolph Spreckels, the **Spreckels Mansion,** 2080 Washington St., is currently home to romance novelist Danielle Steele (don't even try to get in to see her!). The extraordinary building has rounded-arch French doors on the first and second floors and curved balconies on the second floor. Inside, the original featured an indoor pool in the basement, Adamesque fireplaces, and a circular Pompeian room with fountain.

Finally, one of San Francisco's most ingenious architectural accomplishments is the **San Francisco–Oakland Bay Bridge.** Although it's visually less appealing than the nearby Golden Gate Bridge, the Bay Bridge is in many ways more spectacular. The silvery giant that links San Francisco with Oakland is one of the world's longest steel bridges ($8^1/4$ miles). It opened in 1936, 6 months before the Golden Gate. Each of its two decks contains five automobile lanes. The Bay Bridge is not a single bridge at all, but a superbly dovetailed series of spans joined in midbay, at Yerba Buena Island, by one of the world's largest (in diameter) tunnels. To the west of Yerba Buena, the bridge is really two separate suspension bridges, joined at a central anchorage. East of the island is a 1,400-foot cantilever span, followed by a succession of truss bridges. And it looks even more complex than it sounds. You can drive across the bridge (the toll is $2, paid westbound), or you can catch a bus at the Transbay Terminal (Mission at First Street) and ride to downtown Oakland.

8 Especially for Kids

The following San Francisco attractions have major appeal to kids of all ages:

- Alcatraz Island (*see p. 158*)
- Cable cars (*see p. 164*)
- Cable Car Barn Museum (*see p. 166*)
- California Academy of Sciences, including Steinhart Aquarium (*see p. 177*)
- The Exploratorium (*see p. 166*)

- Golden Gate Bridge (*see p. 165*)
- Golden Gate Park, including the Children's Playground, Bison Paddock, and Japanese Tea Garden (*see p. 174*)
- National Maritime Museum and the historic ships anchored at Hyde Street Pier (*see p. 168*)
- The Metreon Entertainment Center (*see p. 170*)
- The San Francisco Zoo (*see p. 179*)

In addition to the sights listed above, the following attractions are of particular interest to kids.

CHILDREN'S PLAYGROUNDS

One of the most enormous, fun playgrounds for kids is in **Golden Gate Park** (see above). Apartment buildings surround the **Cow Hollow Playground,** Baker Street between Greenwich and Filbert streets, on three of four sides. The landscaped playground features a bilevel play area fitted with well-conceived, colorful play structures, including a tunnel, slides, swings, and a miniature cable car. **Huntington Park,** Taylor Street between Sacramento and California streets, sits atop Nob Hill. This tiny play area contains several small structures particularly well suited to children under 5. **Julius Kahn Playground,** West Pacific Avenue at Spruce Street, is a popular playground inside San Francisco's great Presidio park. Larger play structures and forested surroundings make this area attractive to children and adults alike.

9 Self-Guided & Organized Tours

THE 49-MILE SCENIC DRIVE

The self-guided, 49-mile drive is one easy way to orient yourself and to grasp the beauty of San Francisco and its extraordinary location. Beginning in the city, it follows a rough circle around the bay and passes virtually all the best-known sights from Chinatown to the Golden Gate Bridge, Ocean Beach, Seal Rocks, Golden Gate Park, and Twin Peaks. Originally designed for the benefit of visitors to San Francisco's 1939 and 1940 Golden Gate International Exposition, the route is marked with blue-and-white seagull signs. Although it makes an excellent half-day tour, this mini-excursion can easily take longer if you decide, for example, to stop to walk across the Golden Gate Bridge or to have tea in Golden Gate Park's Japanese Tea Garden.

The San Francisco **Visitor Information Center,** at Powell and Market streets (see "Visitor Information" in chapter 4), distributes free route maps. A few of the Scenic Drive marker signs are missing, so the map comes in handy. Try to avoid the downtown area during the weekday rush hours from 7 to 9am and 4 to 6pm.

A BART TOUR

One of the world's best commuter systems, **Bay Area Rapid Transit (BART)** runs along 71 miles of rail, linking eight San Francisco stations with Daly City to the south and 25 stations in the East Bay. Under the bay, BART runs through one of the longest underwater transit tubes in the world. This link opened in September 1974, 2 years behind schedule and 6 months after the general manager resigned under fire. The train cars are 70 feet long and designed to represent the last word in public transport luxury. Twenty years later, they no longer seem futuristic, but they're still attractively modern, with carpeted floors, tinted picture windows, air-conditioning, and recessed lighting. The trains can hit a top speed of 80 mph; a computerized control system monitors and adjusts their speed.

The people who run BART think so highly of their trains and stations that they sell a $3.80 **"Excursion Ticket,"** which allows you, in effect, to "sightsee" the BART system. Tour the entire system as much as you like for up to 3 hours; you must exit at the station where you entered (if you get out anywhere along the line, the gate instantly computes the normal fare). For more information, call ☎ **650/992-BART** or 650/992-2278.

BOAT TOURS

One of the best ways to look at San Francisco is from a boat bobbing on the bay. There are several cruises to choose from, many of which start from Fisherman's Wharf.

Blue & Gold Fleet, Pier 39, Fisherman's Wharf (☎ **415/773-1188**) tours the bay year-round in a sleek, 400-passenger sightseeing boat, complete with food and beverage facilities. The fully narrated, 1^1/$_4$-hour cruise passes beneath the Golden Gate and Bay bridges and comes within yards of Alcatraz Island. Frequent daily departures from Pier 39's West Marina begin at 10am during summer and 11am in winter. Tickets cost $17 for adults, $13 for seniors over 62 and juniors 12 to 17, $9 for children 5 to 11, free for children under 5. There's a $2.25 charge for ordering tickets by phone.

The **Red & White Fleet,** Pier 43^1/$_2$ (☎ **415/447-0597;** www.redandwhite. com) offers daily Bay Cruises tours that leave from Pier 43^1/$_2$ and cruise under the Golden Gate Bridge, past the Marin Headlands, Sausalito, Tiburon, Angel Island, and Alcatraz. Prices are $17 for adults, $13 for seniors and teens 12 to 18, $9 for children 5 to 11.

BUS TOURS

Gray Line, with offices in the Transbay Terminal, First and Mission streets, Pier 39, and Union Square (☎ **800/826-0202** or 415/558-9400), is San Francisco's largest bus-tour operator. It offers several itineraries daily. There is a free pickup and return service between centrally located hotels and departure locations. Reservations are required for most tours, which are available in several foreign languages, including French, German, Spanish, Italian, Japanese, and Korean.

WALKING TOURS

Javawalk is a 2-hour walking tour by self-described "coffeehouse lizard" Elaine Sosa. As the name suggests, it's loosely a coffee walking tour through North Beach, but there's a lot more going on than drinking cups of brew. Javawalk also serves up a good share of historical and architectural trivia, offering something for everyone. The best part of the tour, however, may be the camaraderie that develops among the participants. Sosa keeps the excursion interactive and fun, and it's obvious she knows a profusion of tales and trivia about the history of coffee and its North Beach roots. It's a guaranteed good time, particularly if you're addicted to caffeine. Javawalk is offered Tuesday to Saturday at 10am. The price is $20 per person, $19 for kids under 13. For information and reservations, call ☎ **415/673-WALK** or 415/673-9255.

Cruisin' the Castro (☎ **415/550-8110;** www.webcastro.com/castrotour) is an informative historical tour of San Francisco's most famous gay quarter. It gives you new insight into the contribution of the gay community to the city's political maturity, growth, and beauty. Trevor Hailey, who was involved in the development of the Castro in the 1970s, conducts the tours. She knew Harvey Milk, the first openly gay politician elected to office in the United States. You'll learn about Milk's rise from shopkeeper to city supervisor and visit Harvey Milk Plaza, where marches, rallies, and protests begin. In addition, you'll explore the Castro Theatre and side streets lined with beautifully restored Victorians, as well as the plethora of community-oriented

The Names Project AIDS Memorial Quilt

The Names Project began in 1987 as a memorial for people who have died from AIDS. The idea was to direct grief into positive action and help the world understand the devastating impact of the disease. Organizers invited the public to make coffin-sized panels for a giant memorial quilt. More than 40,000 individual panels now commemorate the lives of those who have died of complications related to AIDS. Each unique design was sewn by the victims' friends, lovers, and family members.

The AIDS Memorial Quilt, which would cover 24 football fields if laid out end to end, was first displayed on the Capitol Mall in Washington, D.C., during a 1987 national march for lesbian and gay rights. Although sections of the quilt are often on tour throughout the world, portions of the largest community art project in the world are on display at **The Names Project AIDS Memorial Quilt Visitors Center & Panelmaking Workshop,** 2362-A Market St. (☎ 415/ 863-1966). The center is scheduled to move to a new address by the end of 2000; further information is not yet available. Currently, the center is open Monday to Friday noon to 7pm, Sunday noon to 6pm. To get there, take the Muni Metro K, L, or M line to the Castro Street station, or the F line to Church and Market streets; bus no. 24, 33, or 35 will also get you there. A sewing machine, fabrics, and assistance from trained volunteers are available for those interested in making a quilt panel.

stores in the Castro whose owners Hailey knows personally. Tours run Tuesday to Saturday from 10am to 2pm, and begin at Harvey Milk Plaza, atop the Castro Street Muni station. The cost includes lunch at a Castro area restaurant. Reservations are required. The tour, with lunch, costs $40 for adults, $35 for seniors 62 and over; children's prices are negotiable.

On the **Haight-Ashbury Flower Power Walking Tour** (☎ 415/863-1621), you explore hippie haunts with Pam and Bruce Brennan. You'll revisit in 3 short hours the Grateful Dead's crash pad, Janis Joplin's house, and other reminders of the Summer of Love. Tours begin at 9:30am Tuesday and Saturday. The cost is $15 per person. Reservations are required.

San Francisco's Chinatown is always fascinating, but for many visitors with limited time it's hard to know where to search out the "non-touristy" shops, restaurants, and historical spots in this microcosm of Chinese culture. **Wok Wiz Chinatown Walking Tours & Cooking Center,** 654 Commercial St., between Kearny and Montgomery streets (☎ 415/981-8989; www.wokwiz.com), founded 14 years ago by author, TV personality, cooking instructor, and restaurant critic Shirley Fong-Torres, is the answer. The Wok Wiz tours take you into nooks and crannies not usually seen by tourists. Most guides are Chinese, speak fluent Cantonese or Mandarin, and are intimately acquainted with the neighborhood's alleys and small enterprises, as well as Chinatown's history, folklore, culture, and food.

Tours are conducted daily 10am to 1:30pm and include dim sum (Chinese lunch). There's also a less expensive tour that does not include lunch. It's an easy walk, fun and fascinating, and you're bound to make new friends. Groups are generally held to a maximum of 15, and reservations are essential. Prices (including lunch) are $39 for adults, $35 for seniors 62 and older, $37 for children under 12.

Shirley Fong-Torres also operates an **I Can't Believe I Ate My Way Through Chinatown** tour. It starts with breakfast in a noodle house, moves to a wok shop, and stops for nibbles at a vegetarian restaurant, a rice-noodle factory, and a supermarket before taking a break for a sumptuous luncheon. It's offered on most Saturdays and costs $65 per person. The **Walk & Wok** tour includes shopping for food in Chinatown, then cooking (and eating) it together at Shirley's Cooking Center (most Saturdays; $75 per person).

Jay Gifford, founder of the **Victorian Homes Historical Walking Tour** (☎ 415/252-9485; www.victorianwalk.com) and a San Francisco resident for 2 decades, communicates his enthusiasm and love of San Francisco throughout this highly entertaining walking tour. The 2¹/₂-hour tour, at a very leisurely place, incorporates a wealth of knowledge about San Francisco's Victorian architecture and the city's history—particularly the periods before and after the great earthquake and fire of 1906. You'll stroll through Japantown, the Western Addition (where you can take a break to cruise the trendy shops on Fillmore Street), and onward to Pacific Heights and Cow Hollow. In the process you'll see more than 200 meticulously restored Victorians, including the one where *Mrs. Doubtfire* was filmed. Jay's guests often find they are the only ones on the quiet neighborhood streets, where tour buses are forbidden. The tour ends with a trolley bus ride back to Union Square, passing through North Beach and Chinatown.

Tours, which start at Union Square at 11am, are offered daily year-round and cost $20 per person. Reservations are required.

10 Staying Active

Half the fun in San Francisco takes place outdoors. If you're not in the mood to trek it, there are other things to do that allow you to enjoy the surroundings.

BALLOONING

Although you must drive 1 hour to get there, hot-air ballooning is an ethereal and silent flight over the Wine Country.

Adventures Aloft, P.O. Box 2500, Vintage 1870, Yountville, CA 94599 (☎ 800/944-4408 or 707/944-4408; www.nvaloft.com), is the Napa Valley's oldest hot-air balloon company, staffed with full-time professional pilots. Groups are small, and the flight lasts about an hour. The cost of $185 per person ($150 ages 6 to 16) includes a post-adventure champagne brunch and a framed "first-flight" certificate. Flights are daily 6 to 7am (weather permitting).

BEACHES

For beach information, call ☎ 415/391-2000. Most days it's too chilly to hang out at the beach, but when the fog evaporates and the wind dies down, one of the best ways to spend the day is oceanside in the city. On any truly hot day, thousands flock to worship the sun, build sandcastles, and throw the ball around. Without a wet suit, swimming is a fiercely cold endeavor. Only two beaches are considered safe for swimming: **Aquatic Park,** adjacent to the Hyde Park Pier, and **China Beach,** a small cove on the western edge of the South Bay. But dip at your own risk—there are never lifeguards on duty.

Also on the South Bay, **Baker Beach** is ideal for picnicking, sunning, walking, or fishing against the backdrop of the Golden Gate.

Ocean Beach, at the end of Golden Gate Park, on the westernmost side of the city, is San Francisco's largest beach—4 miles long. Just offshore, at the northern end of the beach in front of Cliff House, are the jagged Seal Rocks inhabited by various shore birds and a large colony of barking sea lions (bring binoculars for a close-up view). To the left, Kelly's Cove is one of the more challenging surf spots in town. Ocean Beach is ideal for strolling or sunning, but don't swim here—tides are tricky, and each year bathers drown in the rough surf.

Stop by Ocean Beach bus terminal at the corner of Cabrillo and La Playa to learn about San Francisco's playful history in local artist Ray Beldner's whimsically historical sculpture garden. Then hike up the hill to explore the Cliff House and the ruins of Sutro Baths. These baths, able to accommodate 24,000 bathers, were lost to fire in 1966.

OTHER MUNICIPAL PARKS

In addition to **Golden Gate Park** and the **Golden Gate National Recreation Area** (discussed above), San Francisco boasts more than 2,000 additional acres of parkland, most of which is perfect for picnicking or throwing around a Frisbee.

Smaller city parks include **Buena Vista Park** (Haight Street between Baker and Central streets), which affords fine views of the Golden Gate and is also a favored lounging ground for gay lovers; **Ina Coolbrith Park** (Taylor Street between Vallejo and Green streets), offering views of the Bay Bridge and Alcatraz; and **Sigmund Stern Grove** (19th Avenue and Sloat Boulevard) in the Sunset District, which is the site of the famous free summer music festival.

One of our personal favorites is **Lincoln Park,** a 270-acre green on the northwestern side of the city at Clement Street and 34th Avenue. The California Palace of the Legion of Honor is here (see "Museums," earlier in this chapter), as is a scenic 18-hole municipal golf course (see "Activities," below). But the best things about this park are the 200-foot cliffs that overlook the Golden Gate Bridge and San Francisco Bay. To get to the park, take bus no. 38 from Union Square to 33rd and Geary streets, and walk a few blocks to the park.

ACTIVITIES

BIKING   The Parks and Recreations department maintains two city-designated bike routes. One winds 7¹/₂ miles through Golden Gate Park to Lake Merced; the other traverses the city, starting in the south, and continues over the Golden Gate Bridge. These routes are not dedicated to bicyclists, who must exercise caution to avoid crashing into pedestrians. Helmets are recommended for adults and required by law for kids under 18. A bike map is available from the San Francisco Visitor Information Center, at Powell and Mason streets (see "Visitor Information" in chapter 4), and from bicycle shops all around town.

Ocean Beach has a public walk- and bikeway that stretches along 5 waterfront blocks of the Great Highway between Noriega and Santiago streets. It's an easy ride from Cliff House or Golden Gate Park.

Park Cyclery, 1749 Waller St. (☎ 415/751-7368), is a shop in the Haight that rents bikes. Located next to Golden Gate Park, the cyclery rents mountain bikes and cross bikes exclusively, along with helmets. The charge is $5 per hour, $25 per day. Open daily 10am to 6pm.

BOATING   At the **Golden Gate Park Boat House** (☎ 415/752-0347) on Stow Lake, the park's largest body of water, you can rent a rowboat or pedal boat by the hour and steer over to Strawberry Hill, a large, round island in the middle of the lake, for lunch. There's usually a line on weekends. The boathouse is open daily, June to September 9am to 5pm, the rest of the year 9am to 4pm.

Cass Marina, 1702 Bridgeway, Sausalito (☎ **800/472-4595** or 415/332-6789; www.cassmarina.com), is a certified sailing school that rents sailboats measuring 22 to 101 feet. Sail to the Golden Gate Bridge on your own or with a licensed skipper. In addition, large sailing yachts leave from San Francisco and Sausalito on a regularly scheduled basis. Call or check the Web site for schedules, prices, and availability of sailboats. The marina is open daily from 9am to sunset.

CITY STAIR CLIMBING   Many health clubs have stair-climbing machines and step classes, but in San Francisco, you need only to go outside. The following city stair climbs will give you not only a good workout, but great sightseeing too.

Filbert Street Steps, between Sansome Street and Telegraph Hill, are a particular challenge. Scaling the sheer eastern face of Telegraph Hill, this 377-step climb wends through verdant flower gardens and charming 19th-century cottages. Napier Lane, a narrow wooden plank walkway, leads to Montgomery Street. Turn right, and follow the path to the end of the cul-de-sac where another stairway continues to Telegraph's panoramic summit.

The **Lyon Street Steps,** between Green Street and Broadway, were built in 1916. This historic stairway street contains four steep sets of stairs totaling 288 steps. Begin at Green Street and climb all the way up, past manicured hedges and flower gardens, to an iron gate that opens into the Presidio. A block east, on Baker Street, another set of 369 steps descends to Green Street.

CROQUET   The **San Francisco Croquet Club** (☎ **415/776-4104**) offers free public lessons (by reservation) from 10am to 1pm on the first Saturday of each month (or anytime by reservation for parties of four or more). The game is taught according to American national six-wicket rules at the croquet lawns in Stern Grove, 19th Avenue and Wawona Street.

FISHING   **New Easy Rider Sport Fishing,** 225 University Ave., Berkeley (☎ **415/ 285-2000**), makes daily trips from Fisherman's Wharf for ling cod, rock fish, and many other types of game fish all year, and salmon runs from June through October. Fishing equipment is available; the cost, including bait, is $55 per person, $60 during winter when it's a crab and fish combo. Reservations are required, as are licenses for adults. One-day licenses can be purchased before departure. Excursions run daily 6am to 4pm. Fish are cleaned, filleted, and bagged on the return trip for a small fee.

GOLF   San Francisco has a few beautiful golf courses. One of the most lavish, the **Presidio Golf Course** (☎ **415/561-4664**), recently opened to the public for the first time. Greens fees are $42 Monday to Thursday, $52 Friday, $72 Saturday and Sunday. There are also two decent municipal courses in town.

The 9-hole **Golden Gate Park Course,** 47th Ave. and Fulton St. (☎ **415/ 751-8987**), charges greens fees of $10 per person weekdays, $13 weekends. The 1,357-yard course is par 27. All holes are par 3, tightly set, and well trapped with small greens. The course is a little weathered in spots, but it's casual, fun, and inexpensive. Open daily at 6am.

The 18-hole **Lincoln Park Golf Course,** 34th Ave. and Clement St. (☎ **415/ 221-9911**), charges greens fees of $23 per person weekdays, $27 weekends. It's San Francisco's prettiest municipal course, with terrific views and fairways lined with Monterey cypress trees. The 5,081-yard layout plays to par 68, and the 17th hole has a glistening ocean view. This is the oldest course in the city and one of the oldest in the West. Open daily at 6:30am.

A good place for a tune-up is the **Mission Bay Golf Center,** Sixth St. at Channel St. (☎ **415/431-7888).** San Francisco's most popular driving range is an impeccably maintained 7-acre facility that consists of a double-decker steel and concrete arc containing 66 covered practice bays. The grass landing area extends 300 yards, has nine target greens, and is lit for evening use. There's a putting green and a chipping and bunker practice area. The center is open Monday 11:30am to 11pm, Tuesday to Sunday 7am to 11pm. A bucket of balls costs $7, and the last bucket is sold at 10pm. To get there from downtown San Francisco, take Fourth Street south to Channel Street and turn right.

HANDBALL   The city's best handball courts are in Golden Gate Park, opposite Seventh Avenue, south of Middle Drive East. Courts are available free, on a first-come, first-served basis.

RUNNING   The **Bay to Breakers Foot Race** (☎ 415/777-7770; www. baytobreakers.com) is an annual 7½-mile run from downtown to Ocean Beach. About 80,000 entrants take part in one of San Francisco's trademark events. Costumed participants and hordes of spectators add to the fun. The event, sponsored by the *San Francisco Examiner,* is held on the third Sunday of May.

The San Francisco Chronicle Marathon takes place annually in the middle of July. For more information, contact **West End Management** (☎ **415/284-9492).**

SKATING (CONVENTIONAL & IN-LINE)   Although people skate in Golden Gate Park all week long, Sunday is best; John F. Kennedy Drive between Kezar Drive and Transverse Road is closed to automobiles. A smooth "skate pad" is on your right, just past the Conservatory. Another hot skating, biking, and walking spot is the newly renovated **Embarcadero promenade,** which stretches from the new Pacific Bell Park (Townsend Street and Embarcadero) to Fisherman's Wharf. **Skates on Haight,** 1818 Haight St. (☎ **415/752-8376),** 1 block from the park, is the best place to rent inline or conventional skates. The cost of $8 per hour, $24 per day, includes protective wrist guards and knee pads. Major credit card and ID deposit are required. The shop is open Monday to Friday 11am to 7pm, Saturday and Sunday 10am to 6pm.

TENNIS   The **San Francisco Parks and Recreations Department** (☎ 415/ 753-7001) maintains more than 100 courts throughout the city. Almost all are available free, on a first-come, first-served basis. The exceptions are the 21 courts in **Golden Gate Park,** which cost $4 to $6. Courts must be reserved for weekend play by calling ☎ 415/753-7101 on Wednesday from 4 to 6pm.

WALKING & HIKING   The **Golden Gate National Recreation Area** offers plenty of opportunities. One pleasant walk (or bike ride) is along the Golden Gate Promenade, from Aquatic Park to the Golden Gate Bridge. The 3½-mile paved trail leads along the northern edge of the Presidio, out to Fort Point. You can also hike along the Coastal Trail all the way from near Fort Point to the Cliff House. The park service maintains several other trails in the city. For more information or to pick up a map of the Golden Gate National Recreation Area, stop by the park service headquarters at Fort Mason at the north end of Laguna Street (☎ **415/556-0560).**

Although most drive to this spectacular vantage point, a more rejuvenating way to experience Twin Peaks is to walk up from the back roads of U.C. Medical Center (off Parnassus) or from either of the two roads that lead to the top (off Woodside or Clarendon avenues). The best time to trek is early morning, when the city is quiet, the air is crisp, and the sightseers haven't crowded the parking lot. Keep an eye out for cars, because there's no real hiking trail, and be sure to walk beyond the lot and up to the highest vantage point.

11 Spectator Sports

The Bay Area's sports scene includes several major professional franchises. Check the local newspapers' sports sections for daily listings of local events.

BASEBALL

The **San Francisco Giants** play at the new and absolutely stunning **Pacific Bell Park,** Third and King streets (☎ **415/972-2000;** www.sfgiants.com), in the China Basin section of SoMa. From April through October, 40,800 fans root for the National League Giants. The unobstructed bay vistas take in bobbing boats beyond the outfield at the recently completed $319 million "Pac Bell Park." Tickets are hard to come by; you can try to track them down through **BASS Ticketmaster** (☎ **510/762-2277**). Special express bus service is available from Market Street on game days; call **Muni** (☎ **415/673-6864**) for pickup points and schedule information.

The American League's **Oakland Athletics** play across the bay at the Oakland Coliseum Complex, at the Hegenberger Road exit from I-880, Oakland (☎ **510/ 430-8020**). The stadium holds close to 50,000 spectators and is accessible through BART's Coliseum station. Tickets are available from the Coliseum Box Office or by phone through **BASS Ticketmaster** (☎ **510/762-2277**).

PRO BASKETBALL

The **Golden State Warriors** of the NBA play at the Oakland Coliseum Complex, at the Hegenberger Road exit from I-880, Oakland (☎ **510/986-2200**). The Warriors play in the 15,025-seat Oakland Coliseum Arena. The season runs from November through April, and most games start at 7:30pm. Tickets are available at the arena and by phone through **BASS Ticketmaster** (☎ **510/762-2277**).

PRO FOOTBALL

The **San Francisco 49ers** play at 3Com/Candlestick Park, Giants Drive and Gilman Avenue (☎ **415/468-2249**), on Sundays from August through December; kickoff is usually at 1pm. Tickets sell out early in the season, but are available at higher prices through ticket agents beforehand and from scalpers at the gate. Ask your hotel concierge or visit **City Box Office,** 153 Kearny St., Suite 302 (☎ **415/392-4400**). Special express bus service is available from Market Street on game days; call **Muni** (☎ **415/673-6864**) for pickup points and schedule information.

The 49ers' archenemies, the **Oakland Raiders,** play at the Oakland Alameda County Coliseum, off the 880 freeway (Nimitz). Call ☎ **800/949-2626** for ticket information.

COLLEGE FOOTBALL

The **University of California Golden Bears** play at Memorial Stadium, 61 Harmon Gym, University of California, Berkeley (☎ **800/GO-BEARS** or 510/642-3277), on the university campus across the bay. Tickets usually are available at game time. Phone for schedules and information.

HORSE RACING

Ten miles northeast of San Francisco is scenic Golden Gate Fields, Gilman Street off I-80, Albany (☎ **510/559-7300**). It schedules thoroughbred racing from November 15 to December 31. The track is on the seashore. Call for admission prices and post times.

Bay Meadows, 2600 S. Delaware St., off U.S. 101, San Mateo (☎ **650/ 574-7223**), is a thoroughbred and quarter-horse track on the peninsula about 20 miles south of downtown San Francisco. It schedules races 4 or 5 days a week from September through January. Call for admission and post times.

City Strolls

Despite a handful of killer hills, San Francisco is best explored on foot. In this chapter, you'll find suggestions for introductory walks in two of the city's many great neighborhoods. For more extensive city walks, check out *Frommer's Memorable Walks in San Francisco.*

Walking Tour 1—Chinatown: History, Culture, Dim Sum & Then Some

Start: Corner of Grant Avenue and Bush Street.
Public Transportation: 2, 3, 4, 9X, 15, 30, 38, 45, or 76 bus.
Finish: Commercial Street, between Montgomery and Kearny streets.
Time: 2 hours, not including museum or shopping stops.
Best Times: Daylight hours, when there's the most action.
Worst Times: Too early or too late, because shops are closed and no one is milling around.
Hills That Could Kill: None.

This tiny section of San Francisco, bounded loosely by Broadway and Stockton, Kearny, and Bush streets, is said to harbor one of the largest Chinese populations outside Asia. Daily proof is the crowds of Chinese residents who flock to the herbal stores, vegetable markets, restaurants, and businesses. Chinatown also marks the spot where the city began its development in the mid-1800s. On this walk, you'll learn why Chinatown remains intriguing to all who wind through its narrow, crowded streets and how its origins are responsible for the town as we know it.

To begin the tour, make your way to the corner of Bush Street and Grant Avenue, where you can't miss the:

1. **Chinatown Gateway Arch.** Traditional Chinese villages have ceremonial gates like this one. This gate is a lot less formal than those in China, built here more for the benefit of the tourist industry than anything else.

Once you cross the threshold, you'll be at the beginning of Chinatown's portion of:

2. **Grant Avenue,** a.k.a. the mecca for tourists who wander in and out of gift shops that offer a variety of unnecessary junk interspersed with quality imports. You'll also find decent restaurants and grocery stores frequented by Chinese residents, ranging from children to the oldest living people you've ever seen.

Walking Tour—Chinatown

Legend
"Take a Break"

0   1/8 mi
0   .125 km

Jackson St.

Columbus Ave.

Ross Alley

Portsmouth Square

Washington St.

Merchant St.
finish here

Walter U. Lum Pl.

Clay St.

Stockton St.

Wavely Pl.

Grant Ave.

Commercial St.

Kearny St.

Sacramento St.

Montgomery St.

California St.

St. Mary's Square

Pine St.

Bush St.

start here

Sutter St.

Stockton St.

1 Chinatown Gateway Arch	**11** Ten Ren Tea Co., Ltd.
2 Grant Avenue	**12** Ross Alley
3 St. Mary's Square	**13** Golden Gate Fortune
4 Old St. Mary's Church	Cookie Company
5 Canton Bazaar	**14** Stockton Street
6 Bank of America	**15** Great China Herb Co.
7 Chinatown Kite Shop	**16** Waverly Place
8 The Wok Shop	**17** Tin How Temple
9 The original street of	**18** Portsmouth Square
"American" California	**19** Chinese Cultural Center
10 Bank of Canton	

Tear yourself away from the shops and go right at the corner of Pine Street. Cross to the left side of Pine, and on your left you'll come to:

3. **St. Mary's Square,** where you'll find a huge metal-and-granite statue of Dr. Sun Yat-sen, the founder of the Republic of China. A native of Guandong (Canton) Province, Sun Yat-sen led the rebellion that ended the reign of the Qing Dynasty.

Note also the second monument in the square, which honors Chinese-American victims of both world wars. (A pay toilet is strategically placed here, too.)

Walk to the other end of the square, toward California Street, cross California, and you'll be standing in front of:

4. **Old St. Mary's Church.** The first Catholic cathedral in San Francisco and the site of the Chinese community's first English-language school, St. Mary's was built primarily by Chinese laborers and dedicated on Christmas Day, 1854.

Step inside to find a written history of the church and turn-of-the-century photos of San Francisco. Stop in on a Tuesday or Thursday at 12:30 pm for a free half-hour classical music performance.

Upon leaving the church, take a right and walk to the corner of Grant Avenue and California Street, then go right on Grant. Here you'll find a shop called the:

5. **Canton Bazaar,** 616 Grant Ave. Of the knickknack and import shops lining Grant Avenue, this is one of the most popular.

Continue in the same direction on Grant Avenue, and cross Sacramento Street and Grant Avenue to arrive at the northwest corner and the doorstep of the:

6. **Bank of America,** which is in the traditional Chinese architectural style. Notice dragons subtly portrayed on many parts of the building.

Heading in the same direction (north) on Grant, a few doors down is the:

7. **Chinatown Kite Shop,** 717 Grant Ave. This store's assortment of flying objects includes attractive fish kites, nylon or cotton windsock kites, hand-painted Chinese paper kites, wood-and-paper biplanes, and pentagonal kites.

Other take-home treasures of a more functional kind can be found across the street at:

8. **The Wok Shop,** 718 Grant Ave., where you can purchase just about any utensil, cookbook, or vessel you might need to do Chinese-style cooking in your own kitchen.

When you come out of the Wok Shop, go right. Walk past Commercial Street and you'll arrive at the corner of Grant Avenue and Clay Street; cross Clay and you'll be standing on the:

9. **Original street of "American" California.** Here an English seaman named William Richardson set up the first tent in 1835.

Continue north on Grant to Washington Street. Go right, and at 743 Washington St. you will be standing in front of the:

10. **Bank of Canton,** which boasts the oldest (1909) Asian-style edifice in Chinatown. This three-tiered temple-style building once housed the China Telephone Exchange, known as "China-5" until 1945.

You're probably getting thirsty by now, so follow Washington Street a few doors down (east); on your right-hand side you will come upon:

☕ **TAKE A BREAK   Washington Bakery & Restaurant,** 733 Washington St. No need to have a full meal here—the service can be abrupt, and the food's mediocre. Do stop in, however, for a little potable adventure: snow red beans with ice cream. The sugary-sweet drink mixed with whole beans and ice cream is not something you're likely to have tried elsewhere, and it happens to be quite tasty. Whatever you do, don't fill up— a few blocks away some wonderfully fresh dim sum awaits you.

Go back to Grant Avenue, cross Washington Street and then Grant, and follow the west side of Grant 1 block to:

11. Ten Ren Tea Co., Ltd., 949 Grant Ave. In this amazing shop you can sample a freshly brewed tea variety and check out the dozens of drawers and canisters labeled with over 40 kinds of tea.

Leave Ten Ren, take a left, and when you reach Jackson Street, make another left. On the left side at 735 Jackson St., through the storefront window you'll notice stacks of steaming wooden baskets manned by a Chinese cook. You've reached your snacking destination.

☕ **TAKE A BREAK**   It's the **House of Dim Sum**—nothing fancy, for sure, but the dumplings are fresh, cheap, and delicious, and the staff is friendly. Order at the counter: pork, chive and shrimp, and shark-fin dumplings; sweet buns; turnip cake; or sweet rice with chicken wrapped in a lotus leaf. Unless they're taken, it's best to sit at one of the two tables to enjoy your feast.

As you leave the House, turn left up the hill and make another left on:

12. Ross Alley. As you walk along the narrow street, it's not difficult to imagine that this block was once rife with gambling dens.

As you follow the alley south, on the left side of the street you'll see:

13. Golden Gate Fortune Cookie Company, 56 Ross Alley. It's just a tiny place where one woman sits at a conveyer belt, folding messages into warm cookies as the manager exhorts tourists to buy a big bag of the fortune-telling treats.

Sometimes staff members push a purchase; other times someone might hand you a free warm cookie.

As you exit the alley, take a right on Washington Street and follow it up to:

14. Stockton Street. From Broadway to Sacramento Street, Stockton is where most of the residents of Chinatown do their daily shopping.

A good stop if you're in the market for jewelry is **Jade Galore,** 1000 Stockton St., at Washington Street.

You might want to wander up Stockton Street to absorb the atmosphere and street life of this less tourist-oriented Chinese community before doubling back to Washington Street.

Once back at Stockton and Washington streets, turn left down Washington and head back toward Grant Avenue. On the right side of the street you will stumble upon the:

15. Great China Herb Co., 857 Washington St. Chinese and holistic Westerners come to shops like this one—full of exotic herbs, roots, and other natural substances—to buy what they believe cures all types of ailments and ensures good health and long life. Thankfully, unlike the proprietors of many similar shops in the area, owners Mr. and Mrs. Ho speak English, so you will not be met with a blank stare as you inquire what exactly is in each box, bag, or jar along the dozens of shelves.

Continue back toward Grant Avenue, and take a right on:

16. Waverly Place, or "The Street of Painted Balconies." This is probably Chinatown's most popular side street or alleyway because of its painted balconies and colorful architectural details—a sort of Chinese-style New Orleans street.

Most buildings aren't open to the public, but one temple you can visit (make sure it's open before you climb the long, narrow stairway) is the:

17. Tin How Temple, 125 Waverly Place. Accessible by way of a narrow stairway four floors up, this incense-laden sanctuary decorated in traditional black, red, and gold lacquered wood is a house of worship. Chinese Buddhists come here to pray, meditate, and send offerings to their ancestors and to Tin How, the Queen of the Heavens and Goddess of the Seven Seas. When you visit, try to be as unobtrusive as possible. It is customary to give a donation or buy a bundle of incense during your visit.

Once you've finished exploring Waverly Place, walk down Clay Street past Grant Avenue. Continue until you come upon the block-wide urban playground that is also the most important site in San Francisco's history:

18. **Portsmouth Square.** This very spot was the center of the region's first township, which was called Yerba Buena before it was renamed San Francisco in 1847.

Around 1846, before any semblance of a city had taken shape, this plaza was at the foot of the eastern shoreline of the bay. There were fewer than 50 nonnative residents and no substantial buildings to speak of. The few boats that pulled into the cove did so less than a block from where you're standing.

In 1846, when California was claimed as American territory, the Marines who landed here named the square after their ship, USS *Portsmouth*. (A bronze plaque marks the spot where they raised the American flag.)

Yerba Buena remained a modest township until the gold rush of 1849. Immediately following the rush, the population grew from under 1,000 to over 19,000 as gold-seekers from around the world made their way here.

When the square became crowded, long wharves were constructed to support new buildings above the bay. Eventually, the entire area became landfill. That was almost 150 years ago, but today the square still serves as an important neighborhood meeting place—a sort of communal outdoor living room. Some practice tai chi here in the early morning; children play, and elderly men gamble over Chinese cards. It is said that Robert Louis Stevenson used to love sitting on a bench here and watching life going on all around him. You'll find a monument to his memory at the northeast corner of the square.

Cross the bridge leading from Portsmouth Square over the traffic and across the street to the Holiday Inn at 750 Kearny St. Cross the street, enter the hotel, and take the elevator to the third floor, where you'll find the:

19. **Chinese Cultural Center,** which serves both the community and tourists. It offers lectures, films, and seminars; there are also interesting display cases housing Chinese art and a gallery with rotating exhibits of Asian art and writing.

Do-It-Yourself Excursions

The Convention & Visitors Bureau distributes a new brochure detailing self-guided walking tours of North Beach, Union Square, Fisherman's Wharf, and Chinatown. Send a self-addressed business-size envelope to the San Francisco Convention & Visitors Bureau, P.O. Box 429097, San Francisco, CA 94142-9097, or visit **www.sfvisitor.org/visitorinfo/html/walkpdfs.html.**

Walking Tour 2—Noshing Through North Beach

Start: Intersection of Montgomery Street, Columbus Avenue, and Washington Street.
Public Transportation: 15, 30X, 41, or 42 bus.
Finish: Washington Square.
Time: 3 hours, including a stop for lunch.
Best Times: Start the tour Monday to Saturday anytime between 11am and 4pm.
Worst Times: Sunday, when shops are closed.
Hills That Could Kill: The Montgomery Street hill from Broadway to Vallejo Street; otherwise, this is an easy walk.

Along with Chinatown, North Beach is one of the city's oldest neighborhoods. Originally the Latin Quarter, it became the city's Italian district when Italian immigrants moved "uphill" in the early 1870s, crossing Broadway from the Jackson Square area and settling in. They quickly established restaurants, cafes, bakeries, and other businesses familiar to them from their homeland. The "Beat Generation" helped put North Beach on the map, with the likes of Jack Kerouac and Allen Ginsberg holding court in the area's cafes during the 1950s. Although most of the original beat poets are gone, their spirit lives on in North Beach, which is still a haven for bohemian artists and writers. The neighborhood, thankfully, retains its Italian village feel, where residents from all walks of life enjoy taking time for conversation over a pastry and a frothy cappuccino.

If there's one landmark you can't miss, it's the familiar building on the corner of Montgomery Street and Columbus Avenue, the:

1. **TransAmerica Pyramid.** Noted for its spire (which rises 212 feet above the top floor) and its "wings" (which begin at the 29th floor and stop at the spire), the pyramid is San Francisco's tallest building and a hallmark of the skyline. You might want to take a peek at one of the rotating art exhibits in the lobby, or go around to the right and into half-acre Redwood Park, which is part of the TransAmerica Center.

The TransAmerica Pyramid occupies part of the 600 block of Montgomery Street, which once held a historic building called:

2. **The Montgomery Block.** Originally four stories high, it was the tallest building in the West when it was built in 1853. San Franciscans called it "Halleck's Folly" because it was built on a raft of redwood logs that had been bolted together and floated at the edge of the ocean (which was right at Montgomery Street at that time). The building was demolished in 1959 but is fondly remembered for its historic importance as the power center of the city. Its tenants included artists and writers of all kinds, among them Jack London, George Sterling, Ambrose Bierce, Bret Harte, and Mark Twain.

From the southeast corner of Montgomery and Washington streets, look across Washington to the corner of Columbus Avenue, and you'll see the:

3. **Original TransAmerica Building** (now Sanwa Bank), 4 Columbus Ave. A Beaux Arts flat-iron building covered in white terra-cotta, it was also the home of the old Fugazi Bank. Built for the Banco Populare Italiano Operaia Fugazi in 1909, it was originally a two-story building and gained a third floor in 1916. In 1928, Fugazi merged his bank with the Bank of America, which was started by A. P. Giannini, who also created the TransAmerica Corporation.

Walking Tour—North Beach

1 TransAmerica Pyramid
2 The Montgomery Block
3 Original TransAmerica Building
4 Golden Era Building
5 400 block of Jackson Square
6 Columbus Tower
7 Purple Onion
8 1010 Montgomery Street
9 hungry i
10 Former site of the Condor Club
11 City Lights Bookstore
12 Vesuvio
13 Spec's Adler Museum Café
14 Caffè Trieste
15 Biordi Art Imports
16 Molinari Delicatessen
17 Club Fugazi
18 Mario's Bohemian
    Cigar Store
19 Washington Square

Cross Washington Street and continue north on Montgomery Street to no. 730, the:

4. **Golden Era Building,** erected in about 1852. The building is named after the literary magazine the *Golden Era,* which was published here. Some of the young writers who worked on the magazine were known as the Bohemians; they included Samuel Clemens (a.k.a. Mark Twain) and Bret Harte (who began as a typesetter here). Backtrack a few dozen feet and stop for a minute to admire the annex, at no. 722 (marked by a faded black-and-white-striped awning). The Belli Annex, as it is currently known, is registered as a historic landmark.

Continue again and take the first right onto Jackson Street. Now you're in the:

5. **400 block of Jackson Street,** where you'll find some of the only commercial buildings to survive the 1906 earthquake and fire. 415 Jackson (ca. 1853) served as the headquarters for the Ghirardelli Chocolate Company from 1855 to 1894. The Hotaling Building (no. 451) was built in 1866. At no. 472 is another of the buildings that survived the disaster of 1906.

Continue toward the intersection of Columbus Avenue and Jackson Street. Turn right on Columbus and look across the street for the small triangular building at the junction of Kearny Street and Columbus Avenue, the:

6. **Columbus Tower** (a.k.a. Sentinel Building). If you walk up a little farther, then turn around and look back down Columbus, you'll be able to get a better look. The flat-iron beauty—a building shaped to a triangular site—went up between 1905 and 1907. Movie director and producer Francis Ford Coppola bought and restored it in the mid-1970s; it is now home to his film production company, American Zoetrope Studios. The cafe showcases all things Niebaum-Coppola (as in Francis Ford Coppola and his winery)—including olive oil, parmesan cheese, and wine. It's a great place to stop for a glass of wine, an espresso, or a thin-crusted pizza snack. This is one of the few pre-1906 earthquake buildings in the city center.

Across the street from the Tower on Columbus Avenue is the:

7. **Purple Onion,** 140 Columbus Ave. Many famous headliners have played here, often before they were famous. Phyllis Diller, who's now so big that she's famous for something as simple as her laugh, was still struggling when she played a 2-week engagement here in the late 1950s.

Turn right on Pacific Avenue. Just after you cross Montgomery Street, you'll find brick-lined **Osgood Place** on the left. A registered historic landmark, it is one of the few quiet—and car-free—little alleyways left in the city. Stroll up Osgood and go left on Broadway to:

8. **1010 Montgomery St. (at Broadway).** This is where Allen Ginsberg lived during the time he wrote his legendary poem "Howl," first performed on October 13, 1955, in a converted auto-repair shop at the corner of Fillmore and Union streets. By the time Ginsberg finished reading, he was crying and the audience was going wild. Jack Kerouac proclaimed, "Ginsberg, this poem will make you famous in San Francisco." Continue along Broadway toward Columbus Avenue. This stretch of Broadway is San Francisco's answer to New York's Times Square, complete with strip clubs and peep shows that are being pushed aside by restaurants, clubs, and an endless crowd of visitors. It's among the most sought-after locations in the city as more and more profitable restaurants and clubs spring up.

Along the way, on the right side of the street, you'll come to **Columbus Books,** 540 Broadway. It sells new and used discount books and is worth a quick trip inside for a good, cheap read.

A few dozen yards farther up Broadway is the current location of the:

9. **hungry i, 546 Broadway.** Now a seedy strip club, the original hungry i (at 599 Jackson St.) was owned and operated by the vociferous "Big Daddy" Nordstrom. If you had been here while Enrico Banducci (also of Enrico's restaurant) was in charge, you would have found only a plain room with an exposed brick wall and director's chairs around small tables. A who's who of nightclub entertainers fortified their careers at the original hungry i, including Lenny Bruce, Billie Holiday (who first sang "Strange Fruit" there), Bill Cosby, Richard Pryor, Woody Allen, and Barbra Streisand.

At the corner of Broadway and Columbus Avenue, you will see the:

10. **Former site of the Condor Club,** 300 Columbus Ave., where Carol Doda scandalously bared her breasts and danced topless for the first time in 1964. Note the bronze plaque claiming the Condor Club as BIRTHPLACE OF THE WORLD'S FIRST TOPLESS & BOTTOMLESS ENTERTAINMENT. Go inside what is now the Condor Bistro and have a look at the framed newspaper clippings that hang around the dining room. From the elevated back room you can see Doda's old dressing room and, on the floor below, an outline of the piano that would descend from the second floor with her atop it.

When you leave the Condor Bistro, cross to the south side of Broadway. Note the mural of jazz musicians painted on the whole side of the building directly across Columbus Avenue. Diagonally across the intersection from the Condor Bistro is:

11. **City Lights Bookstore,** 261 Columbus Ave. Owned by one of the first Beat poets to arrive in San Francisco, Lawrence Ferlinghetti, City Lights is now a city landmark and literary mecca. It's one of the last of the Beat-era hangouts in operation. An active participant in the Beat movement, Ferlinghetti established his shop as a meeting place where writers and bibliophiles could (and still do) attend poetry readings and other events. It's still a vibrant part of the literary scene; the well-stocked bookshop prides itself on its collection of art, poetry, and political paperbacks.

Upon exiting City Lights Bookstore, turn right, cross aptly named Jack Kerouac Street, and stop by the bar named:

12. **Vesuvio,** 255 Columbus Ave. (at Broadway). Because of its proximity to City Lights Bookstore, Vesuvio became a favorite hangout of the Beats. Dylan Thomas used to drink here, as did Jack Kerouac, Ferlinghetti, and Ginsberg. Even today, Vesuvio, which opened in 1949, maintains its original bohemian atmosphere. The building dates from 1913, and is an excellent example of pressed-tin architecture.

Facing Vesuvio across Columbus Avenue are two other favorite spots of the Beat Generation:

13. **Spec's Adler Museum Café,** 12 Saroyan Place, is one of the city's funkiest bars, a small, dimly lit watering hole with ceiling-hung maritime flags and exposed brick walls crammed with memorabilia. Within the bar is a mini-museum that consists of a few glass cases filled with mementos brought back and dropped off by seamen who have frequented the pub.

From here, go up Columbus across Broadway to Grant Avenue. Turn right, walking until you come to Vallejo Street. At 606 Vallejo St. (at Grant Avenue) is:

14. **Caffè Trieste,** yet another favorite spot of the Beats. Founded by Gianni Giotta in 1956, it's still run by family members. The quintessential San Francisco coffeehouse, Trieste features opera on the jukebox and the real thing, performed by

the Giottas, on Saturday afternoons. Any day of the week is a good one to stop in for a cappuccino or espresso—the beans are roasted right next door.

Go left out of Caffè Trieste onto Vallejo Street, turn right on Columbus Avenue, and bump into the loveliest shop in all of North Beach:

15. Biordi Art Imports, 412 Columbus Ave. The shopkeepers have imported hand-painted majolica pottery from the hill towns of central Italy for more than 50 years. Some of the colorful patterns date from the 14th century. Biordi hand-picks its artisans, and its catalog includes biographies of those who are currently represented.

Across Columbus Avenue at the corner of Vallejo Street is:

16. Molinari Delicatessen, 373 Columbus Ave. (☎ **415/421-2337**), which has been selling its pungent, air-dried salamis since 1896. Ravioli and tortellini are made in the back of the shop, but it's the mouthwatering selection of cold salads, cheeses, and marinades up front that captures the attention of most folks. The Italian subs are big enough for two hearty appetites.

Walk north to the lively intersection of Columbus, Green, and Stockton, cross Columbus Avenue, and continue west on Green to:

17. Club Fugazi, 678 Beach Blanket Babylon Blvd. (an extension of Green Street, between Columbus and Powell streets). It doesn't look like much from the outside, but Club Fugazi stages San Francisco's legendary musical revue "Beach Blanket Babylon." The show evolved from Steve Silver's Rent-a-Freak service, which consisted of a group of party-givers who attended parties dressed as any number of characters in outrageous costumes. The fun caught on, and soon came "Beach Blanket Babylon." You'll love this super-charged show, which is definitely worth the price of admission.

On the way back to Columbus Avenue, be sure to stop in at **O'Reilly's Irish Pub** (622 Green St.) to see the mural of Irish authors that peers out from the back wall (how many can you name?). As you come out of O'Reilly's, turn left, cross Columbus Avenue, and proceed 1 block northwest on Columbus to:

18. Mario's Bohemian Cigar Store, 566 Columbus Ave. Across the street from Washington Square is one of North Beach's most popular neighborhood hangouts: Mario's. This historic, tiny, and charmingly threadbare bar has long been a popular meeting place for aged Sicilians and beat poets, although nowadays it attracts all types, including the occasional tourist in search of a cigar. Oddly enough, it doesn't serve regular ol' coffee, but the hot focaccia sandwiches are superb.

Our last stop, directly across Union Street, is:

19. Washington Square, one of the oldest parks in the city. This land was designated a public park in 1847 and has undergone many changes. Its current landscaping dates from 1955. Even though it's called a "square," this little oasis in the middle of such a bustling neighborhood lost its square status when Columbus Avenue was laid out and one of its four corners was lopped off. Why isn't it named Columbus Square? Because the park was named in the 1850s, before Montgomery Avenue became Columbus Avenue.

9 Shopping

Like its population, San Francisco's shopping is both worldly and intimate. Every persuasion, style, era, and fetish is represented, not in big, tacky shopping malls, but in hundreds of quaint, dramatically different boutiques scattered throughout the city. Whether you're looking for Chanel or Chinese herbal medicine, San Francisco's got it. Just pick a neighborhood and break out your credit cards—you're sure to end up with at least a few take-home treasures.

1 The Shopping Scene

MAJOR SHOPPING AREAS

San Francisco has many shopping areas, but the following places are where you'll find most of the action:

UNION SQUARE & ENVIRONS San Francisco's most congested and popular shopping mecca is centered on Union Square and enclosed by Bush, Taylor, Market, and Montgomery streets. Most of the big department stores and many high-end specialty shops are here. Be sure to venture to Grant Avenue, Post and Sutter streets, and Maiden Lane. This area is a hub for public transportation; all Market Street and several other buses run here, as do the Powell-Hyde and Powell-Mason cable-car lines. You can also take Muni Metro to Powell Station.

CHINATOWN When you pass under the gate to Chinatown on Grant Avenue, say good-bye to the world of fashion and hello to a swarm of cheap tourist shops selling everything from linen and jade to plastic toys and $2 slippers. But that's not all Chinatown has to offer. The real gems are tucked on side streets or are small, one-person shops selling Chinese herbs, original art, and jewelry. Grant Avenue is the area's main thoroughfare, and the side streets between Bush Street and Columbus Avenue are full of restaurants, markets, and eclectic shops. Walking is best, since traffic through this area is slow at best and parking is next to impossible. Most stores in Chinatown are open daily from 10am to 10pm. Take bus no. 9X, 15, 30, 41, or 45.

UNION STREET Union Street, from Fillmore Street to Van Ness Avenue, caters to the upper–middle-class crowd. It's a great place to stroll, window-shop the plethora of boutiques, cafes, and restaurants, and watch the beautiful people parade by. Take bus no. 22, 41, 42, or 45.

CHESTNUT STREET   Parallel and a few blocks north, Chestnut is a younger version of Union Street. It holds endless shopping and dining choices, and an ever-tanned, superfit population of postgraduate singles who hang around cafes and scope each other out. Take bus no. 22, 28, 30, 41, 42, 43, or 76.

FILLMORE STREET   Some of the best shopping in town is packed into 5 blocks of Fillmore Street in Pacific Heights. From Jackson to Sutter streets, Fillmore is the perfect place to grab a bite and peruse the high-priced boutiques, craft shops, and incredible housewares stores. Don't miss Zinc Details and Fillamento. Take bus no. 1, 2, 3, 4, 12, 22, or 24.

HAIGHT STREET   Green hair, spiked hair, no hair, or mohair—even the hippies look conservative next to Haight Street's dramatic fashion freaks. The shopping in the 6 blocks of upper Haight Street between Central Avenue and Stanyan Street reflects its clientele. It offers everything from incense and European and American street styles to furniture and antique clothing. Bus lines 7, 66, 71, and 73 run the length of Haight Street. The Muni Metro N line stops at Waller Street and Cole Street.

SOMA   Although this area isn't suitable for strolling, you'll find almost all the discount shopping in warehouse spaces South of Market. You can pick up a discount-shopping guide at most major hotels. Many bus lines pass through this area.

HAYES VALLEY   It's not the prettiest area in town, with some of the shadier housing projects a few blocks away. But while most neighborhoods cater to more conservative or trendy shoppers, lower Hayes Street, between Octavia and Gough, celebrates anything vintage, artistic, or downright funky. Still in its developmental stage, it's definitely the most interesting new shopping area in town, with furniture and glass stores, thrift shops, trendy shoe stores, and men's and women's clothiers. There are lots of great antique shops south on Octavia and on nearby Market Street. Take bus no. 16AX, 16BX, or 21.

FISHERMAN'S WHARF & ENVIRONS   The tourist-oriented malls run along Jefferson Street and include hundreds of shops, restaurants, and attractions. They include Ghirardelli Square, Pier 39, the Cannery, and the Anchorage (see "Shopping Centers & Complexes," below).

2 Shopping A to Z

ANTIQUES

Jackson Square, a historic district just north of the Financial District's Embarcadero Center, is the place to go for the top names in fine furniture and fine art. There are also a lot of Asian-art dealers here. More than a dozen dealers on the 2 blocks between Columbus and Sansome streets specialize in European furnishings from the 17th to the 19th centuries. Most shops here are open Monday to Friday 9am to 5pm and Saturday 11am to 4pm.

Butterfield & Butterfield. 220 San Bruno Ave. (at 16th St.). ☎ **415/861-7500.**

This renowned auction house holds preview weekends for upcoming auctions of furnishings, silver, antiques, art, and jewelry. The office is open Monday to Friday 8:30am to 5pm.

Fumiki Fine Asian Arts. 2001 Union St. (at Buchanan St.) ☎ **415/922-0573.**

Come here for one of the largest collections of antique Japanese Imari and Korean and Japanese *tansus* (clothing chests) in the country. There's an extensive collection of

Hours, Taxes & Shipping

Store hours are generally Monday to Saturday 10am to 6pm and Sunday noon to 5pm. Most department stores stay open later, as do shops around Fisherman's Wharf, the most heavily visited area.

Sales tax in San Francisco is 8.5%, which is added on at the register for all goods and services purchased. If you live out of state and buy an expensive item, you might want to consider having the store ship it home for you. You escape paying the sales tax but have to pay for shipping.

Most of the city's shops can wrap your purchase and ship it anywhere in the world via United Parcel Service (UPS). If they can't, you can send it yourself, either through **UPS** (☎ **800/742-5877**) or through the U.S. mail (see "Fast Facts: San Francisco" in chapter 4, "Getting to Know San Francisco").

Asian art and antiques, including Japanese baskets and Chinese artifacts and embroidery. Open Monday to Saturday 10am to 6pm, Sunday noon to 5pm.

ART

The San Francisco Gallery Guide, a comprehensive, bimonthly publication listing the city's current shows, is available free by mail. Send a self-addressed, stamped envelope to San Francisco Bay Area Gallery Guide, 1369 Fulton St., San Francisco, CA 94117 (☎ **415/921-1600**), or pick one up at the San Francisco Visitor Information Center at 900 Market St. Most of the city's major art galleries are clustered downtown in the Union Square area.

Atelier Dore. 771 Bush St. (between Mason and Powell sts.). ☎ **415/391-2423.**

Atelier Dore features American and European paintings from the 19th and 20th centuries, including some WPA art. Open Tuesday to Saturday 11am to 5pm; Monday by appointment only.

✪ **Catharine Clark Gallery.** 49 Geary St. (between Kearny and Grant sts.), 2nd floor. ☎ **415/399-1439.**

Catharine Clark's is a different kind of gallery experience. While many galleries focus on established artists and out-of-this world prices, Catharine's exhibits up-and-coming contemporary artists (mainly from California) and nurtures beginning collectors by offering a purchasing plan that's almost unheard of in the art business. You can buy a piece on layaway and take up to a year to pay for it—interest free! Prices here make art a realistic purchase for everyone for a change, but serious collectors still frequent the shows because Clark has such a keen eye for talent. Shows change every 4 to 6 weeks. Open Tuesday to Friday 10:30am to 5:30pm, Saturday 11am to 5:30pm; first Thursday of the month 10:30am to 7:30pm.

Eleonore Austerer. 540 Sutter St. (between Powell and Mason sts.). ☎ **415/986-2244.**

Here you'll find limited-edition graphics by modern masters like Braque, Matisse, Miró, Picasso, Calder, Chagall, and Hockney, as well as original works by European and American contemporary artists. The gallery, in a beautiful old building near Union Square, is open Monday to Saturday 10am to 6pm.

Fraenkel Gallery. 49 Geary St., 4th floor (between Grant Ave. and Kearny St.). ☎ **415/981-2661.**

This photography gallery features works by contemporary American and European artists. Excellent shows change frequently. Open Tuesday to Friday 10:30am to 5:30pm, Saturday 11am to 5pm.

Images of the North. 1782 Union St. (at Octavia St.). ☎ **415/673-1273.**

The highlight here is one of the most extensive collections of Canadian and Alaskan Inuit art in the United States. There's also a fine collection of Native American masks and jewelry. Open Monday to Saturday 11am to 5:30pm, Sunday noon to 4pm.

Maxwell Galleries. 559 Sutter St. (between Powell and Mason sts.). ☎ **415/421-5193.**

The specialties at Maxwell Galleries are 19th- and 20th-century European and American sculpture and paintings, including works by Raphael and Butler. Open Monday to Friday 9:30am to 5:15pm, Saturday 11am to 5pm.

Meyerovich Gallery. 251 Post St. (at Stockton St.), 4th floor. ☎ **415/421-7171.** www.meyerovichgallery.com.

Works on paper by modern and contemporary masters here include Chagall, Matisse, Miró, and Picasso. Its new Contemporary Gallery, across the hall, features works by Lichtenstein, Motherwell, Dine, and Hockney. Open Monday to Friday 9:30am to 6pm, Saturday 10am to 5pm, and by appointment.

BOOKS

In addition to the listings below, there's a **Barnes & Noble** superstore at 2550 Taylor St., between Bay and North Point streets, near Fisherman's Wharf (☎ **415/ 292-6762**).

The Booksmith. 1644 Haight St. (between Clayton and Cole sts.). ☎ **800/493-7323** or 415/863-8688. www.booksmith.com. E-mail: read@booksmith.com.

Haight Street's best selection of new books is in this large, well-maintained shop. It carries all the top titles, along with works from smaller presses, and more than 1,000 different magazines. Open Monday to Saturday 10am to 9pm, Sunday 10am to 6pm.

Borders Books & Music. 400 Post St., at Union Square. ☎ **415/399-1633.**

With four stories neatly packed with books, magazines, videos, a cafe, and plenty of reading nooks, it's a good thing this megastore is open late—you could spend hours browsing the selections. Open Monday to Thursday 9am to 11pm, Friday and Saturday 9am to midnight, Sunday 9am to 9pm.

✪ **City Lights Booksellers & Publishers.** 261 Columbus Ave. (at Broadway). ☎ **415/362-8193.** www.citylights.com.

Brooding literary types browse this famous bookstore owned by Lawrence Ferlinghetti, the renowned Beat Generation poet. The three-level bookshop prides itself on a comprehensive collection of art, poetry, and political paperbacks, as well as more mainstream books. Open daily 10am to midnight.

✪ **A Clean, Well-Lighted Place for Books.** 601 Van Ness Ave. (between Turk St. and Golden Gate Ave.). ☎ **415/441-6670.** www.bookstore.com.

Voted best bookstore by the *San Francisco Bay Guardian,* this independent store has good new fiction and nonfiction sections, and specializes in music, art, mystery, and cookbooks. The store is well known for its author readings and events. For a calendar of events, call or check the Web site. Open Monday to Thursday 10am to 11pm, Friday and Saturday 10am to 11pm, Sunday 10am to 9pm.

✪ **Green Apple Books.** 506 Clement St. (at 6th Ave.). ☎ **415/387-2272.**

The local favorite for used books, Green Apple is crammed with titles—more than 60,000 new and 100,000 used books. Its extended sections in psychology, cooking, art, history; collection of modern first editions; and rare graphic comics are superseded only by the staff's superlative service. Open Sunday to Thursday 10am to 10:30pm, Friday and Saturday 10am to 11:30pm.

CHINA, SILVER & GLASS

The Enchanted Crystal. 1895 Union St. (at Laguna St.). ☎ **415/885-1335.**

This shop has an extensive collection of fine crystal, art glass, jewelry, and one-of-a-kind decorative art, including one of the largest crystal balls in the world (from Madagascar). Open Monday to Saturday 10am to 6pm, Sunday noon to 5pm.

✪ **Gump's.** 135 Post St. (between Kearny St. and Grant Ave.). ☎ **415/982-1616.**

Founded over a century ago, Gump's offers gifts and treasures ranging from Asian antiquities to contemporary art glass and exquisite jade and pearl jewelry. Many items are made specifically for the store. Gump's also has one of the city's most revered holiday window displays. Open Monday to Saturday 10am to 6pm.

CRAFTS

The Canton Bazaar. 616 Grant Ave. (between Sacramento and California sts.). ☎ **415/362-5750.**

Amid a wide variety of handicrafts you'll find an excellent selection of rosewood and carved furniture, cloisonné enamelware, rose Canton chinaware, porcelain, carved jade, embroideries, jewelry, and antiques from mainland China. Open daily 10am to 10pm.

The New Unique Company. 838 Grant Ave. (between Clay and Washington sts.). ☎ **415/981-2036.**

Primarily a calligraphy- and watercolor-supplies store, the shop also has a good assortment of books on these topics. In addition, there's a wide selection of carved stones for use as seals on letters and documents. Should you want a special design or group of initials, the store will carve seals to order. Open Monday to Saturday 10:30am to 6pm, Sunday 11am to 6pm.

Silkroute International. 3119 Fillmore St. (at Filbert St.). ☎ **415/563-4936.**

Owned and operated by an Afghan who offers fascinating wares, old and new, from his native country, the shop sells Oriental and tribal rugs, kilims, dhurries, textiles, jewelry, clothing, pillows, art, and antiques. Open Monday to Saturday 11am to 6pm, Sunday noon to 5pm.

DEPARTMENT STORES

Macy's. Stockton and O'Farrell sts., Union Square. ☎ **415/397-3333.**

The seven-story Macy's West features contemporary fashions for women, juniors, and children, plus jewelry, fragrances, cosmetics, and accessories. The sixth floor offers a "hospitality suite" where visitors can leave their coats and packages, grab a cup of coffee, or find out more about the city from the concierge. The top floors contain home furnishings, and the Cellar sells kitchenware and gourmet foods. You'll even find a Boudin Cafe (great sandwiches!) and Wolfgang Puck Cafe on the premises. Across the street, Macy's East has five floors of men's fashion, the largest Men's Polo by Ralph Lauren shop in the country, and the Fresh Choice cafe. Open Monday to Saturday 10am to 8pm, Sunday 11am to 7pm.

Neiman Marcus. 150 Stockton St., Union Square. ☎ **415/362-3900.**

Some call this unit of the Texas-based chain "Needless Mark-up." But if you've got the cash, the men's and women's clothes, precious gems, and conservative formal wear are some of the most glamorous in town. The Rotunda Restaurant, on the top floor, is a beautiful, relaxing place for lunch and afternoon tea. Open Monday to Wednesday and Friday and Saturday 10am to 7pm, Thursday 10am to 8pm, Sunday noon to 6pm.

Nordstrom. In the San Francisco Shopping Centre, 865 Market St. ☎ **415/243-8500.**

Renowned for its personalized service, this is the largest branch of the Seattle-based fashion department-store chain. Nordstrom occupies the top five floors of the San Francisco Shopping Centre (see "Shopping Centers & Complexes," below) and is the mall's primary anchor. Equally devoted to women's and men's fashions, the store has one of the best shoe selections in the city and thousands of suits in stock. The City Centre Grill, on the fourth floor, has a panoramic view and is an ideal place for an inexpensive lunch or light snack. Nordstrom Spa, on the fifth floor, is the perfect place to relax after a hectic day of bargain hunting. Open Monday to Saturday 9:30am to 9pm, Sunday 10am to 7pm.

DISCOUNT SHOPPING

San Francisco's many factory-outlet stores sell overstocked and discontinued fashions at bargain prices. All of the following shops are south of Market Street, in the city's warehouse district (SoMa).

Esprit Outlet Store. 499 Illinois St. (at 16th St.). ☎ **415/957-2550.**

All the Esprit collections are available here at 20% or more off regular prices. In addition to clothes, the store sells accessories, shoes, and assorted other items. Open Monday to Friday 10am to 8pm, Saturday 10am to 7pm, and Sunday 11am to 6pm.

✪ **Jeremy's.** 2 South Park (between Bryant and Brannan sts. at Second St.). ☎ **415/882-4929.**

This boutique offers top designer fashions, from shoes to suits, at rock-bottom prices. There are no cheap knockoffs here, just good men's and women's clothes and accessories. Jeremy's also has its own stylish clothing line. Open Monday to Friday 11am to 7pm, Saturday 11am to 6pm, and Sunday 11am to 5pm.

The North Face. 1325 Howard St. (between 9th and 10th sts.). ☎ **415/626-6444.**

Well known for its sporting, camping, and hiking equipment, this off-price outlet carries a limited but high-quality selection of ski wear, boots, sweaters, and goods such as tents, packs, and sleeping bags. The North Face makes heavy use of Gore-Tex, down, and other durable, lightweight materials. Open Monday to Wednesday 10am to 6pm, Thursday to Saturday 10am to 7pm, Sunday 11am to 5pm.

FABRICS

Britex Fabrics. 146 Geary St. (between Stockton and Grant sts.). ☎ **415/392-2910.**

A San Francisco institution since 1952, Britex offers an absurd amount and variety of fabrics, not to mention over 30,000 button selections. Open Monday to Wednesday and Saturday 9:30am to 6pm, Thursday and Friday 9:30am to 7pm. Closed Sunday.

FASHION

See also "Vintage Clothing," later in this section.

Grand Women's Boutique. 1429 Haight St. (between Ashbury and Masonic aves.). ☎ **415/255-1214.**

Invited to an underground club and forgot your funky rave attire? Grand's North Beach shop features the latest in fashion-forward street wear by local designers. Garb comes both baggy and tight; the style is club, and the price is right. Open daily 11:30am to 7pm.

Gucci America. 200 Stockton St. (between Geary and Post sts.). ☎ **415/392-2808.**

Donning Gucci's golden Gs is not a cheap endeavor. But if you've got the cash, you'll find all the latest lines of shoes, leather goods, scarves, and pricey accessories, such as a $7,000 handmade crocodile bag. Open Monday to Saturday 10am to 6pm, Sunday noon to 5pm.

Niketown. 278 Post St. (at Stockton St.). ☎ **415/392-6453.**

Here it's not "I can," but "I can spend." At least that's what the kings of sportswear were banking on when they opened this megastore in 1997. As you'd expect, inside the doors it's Nike's world, offering everything the merchandising team could create. Open Monday to Friday 10am to 8pm, Saturday 10am to 7pm, Sunday 11am to 6pm.

Three Bags Full. 2181 Union St. (at Fillmore St.). ☎ **415/567-5753.** www. threebagsfull.com.

Snuggling up in a cozy sweater can be a fashionable event if you do your shopping at this pricey boutique, which carries the gamut in handmade and one-of-a-kind playful and extravagant knitwear. Open Monday through Saturday 10:30am to 5pm, Sunday 10am to 5pm. Other city locations are 500 Sutter St. (closed Sunday) and 3314 Sacramento St. (closed Sunday and Monday).

✪ **Wilkes Bashford.** 375 Sutter St. (at Stockton St.). ☎ **415/986-4380.**

Wilkes Bashford is one of the most expensive and best-known clothing stores in the city. In its three-plus decades in business, the boutique has garnered a reputation for stocking only the finest clothes in the world (which can often be seen on Mayor Willie Brown, who does his suit shopping here). Most fashions come from Italy and France; they include women's designer sportswear and couture and men's Kiton and Brioni suits (at $2,500 and up, they're considered the most expensive suits in the world). Open Monday to Wednesday and Friday and Saturday 10am to 6pm, Thursday 10am to 8pm. Closed Sunday.

MEN'S FASHIONS

All American Boy. 463 Castro St. (between Market and 18th sts.). ☎ **415/861-0444.**

Long known for setting the mainstream style for gay men, All American Boy is the quintessential Castro clothing shop. Open Monday to Thursday and Sunday 10am to 7pm, Friday and Saturday 10am to 8pm.

Brooks Brothers. 201 Post St. (at Grant Ave.). ☎ **415/397-4500.**

In San Francisco, this bulwark of tradition is 1 block east of Union Square. Brooks Brothers introduced the button-down collar and single-handedly changed the standard of the well-dressed businessman. The multilevel shop also sells traditional casual wear, including sportswear, sweaters, and shirts. Open Monday to Friday 9:30am to 7pm, Saturday 9:30am to 6pm, Sunday 11am to 6pm.

Cable Car Clothiers. 441 Sutter St. (between Stockton. and Powell sts.). ☎ **415/397-4740.**

Dapper men head to this beautiful landmark building for traditional attire, such as three-button suits with natural shoulders, Aquascutum coats, McGeorge sweaters, and Atkinson ties. Open Monday to Saturday 9:30am to 5:30pm.

Citizen Clothing. 536 Castro St. (between 18th and 19th sts.). ☎ **415/558-9429.**

The Castro has some of America's best men's casual clothing stores, and this is one of them. Stylish (but not faddish) pants, tops, and accessories are in stock. Open Monday to Saturday 10am to 8pm, Sunday 11am to 7pm.

MAC. 5 Claude Lane (off Sutter St. between Grant Ave. and Kearny St.). ☎ **415/837-0615.**

The more-classic-than-corporate man shops here for imported tailored suits in new and intriguing fabrics. Lines include London's Katharine Hamnett, Belgium's SO, Italy's Alberto Biani, and New York's John Bartlett. Open Monday to Saturday 11am to 6pm, Sunday noon to 5pm. Its women's store is at 1543 Grant Ave., between Filbert and Union streets (☎ **415/837-1604**).

WOMEN'S FASHIONS

The Chanel Boutique. 155 Maiden Lane (between Stockton St. and Grant Ave.). ☎ **415/981-1550.**

Ever fashionable and expensive, Chanel is appropriately located on Maiden Lane, the quaint downtown side street where the most exclusive stores and spas cluster. You'll find what you'd expect from Chanel: clothing, accessories, scents, cosmetics, and jewelry. Open Monday to Saturday 10am to 6pm, Sunday noon to 5pm.

✪ **Métier.** 355 Sutter St. (between Grant and Stockton sts.). ☎ **415/989-5395.**

Here you'll find classic, sophisticated, and expensive creations. Offerings include European ready-to-wear lines and designers Peter Cohen, Georgina Von Etzdorf, Alberto Biani, and local Lat Naylor, as well as a distinguished collection of antique-style, high-end jewelry from L.A.'s Kathie Waterman. Open Monday to Saturday 10am to 6pm. Closed Sunday.

Solo Fashion. 1599 Haight St. (at Clayton St.). ☎ **415/621-0342.**

While strolling upper Haight, stop in here for a good selection of upbeat, contemporary, English-style street wear, along with a collection of dresses designed exclusively for this shop. Open daily 11am to 7pm.

CHILDREN'S FASHIONS

Minis. 2042 Union St. (between Webster and Buchanan sts.). ☎ **415/567-9537.**

Christina Profili, a San Francisco native who used to design for Banana Republic, opened this children's clothing store to sell her own creations. Every piece, from shirts to pants and dresses, is made from cotton or organic cotton. Every outfit perfectly coordinates with everything else in the store. Minis also offers educational and creative toys and books with matching dolls, and maternity wear. Open daily 10:30am to 6:30pm.

FOOD

Golden Gate Fortune Cookies Co. 56 Ross Alley (between Washington and Jackson sts.). ☎ **415/781-3956.**

This tiny, touristy factory sells fortune cookies hot off the press. You can purchase them in small bags or in bulk, and if your order is large enough, you might even be able to negotiate your own message. Even if you're not buying, stop in to see how these sugary treats are made (although the staff can get pushy for you to buy). Open daily 10am to 7pm.

✪ **Joseph Schmidt Confections.** 3489 16th St. (at Sanchez St.). ☎ **800/861-8682** or 415/861-8682.

Chocolate takes the shape of exquisite sculptural masterpieces—such as long-stemmed tulips and heart-shaped boxes—that are so beautiful, you'll be hesitant to bite the head off your adorable panda bear. Once you do, you'll know why this is the most popular chocolatier in town. Prices are remarkably reasonable. Open Monday to Saturday 10am to 6:30pm.

✪ **Ten Ren Tea Co.** 949 Grant Ave. (between Washington and Jackson sts.). ☎ **415/362-0656.**

At the Ten Ren Tea Co. you will be offered a steaming cup of tea. In addition to a selection of almost 50 traditional and herbal teas, the company stocks related paraphernalia, such as pots, cups, and infusers. If you can't make up your mind, take home a mail-order form. Open daily 9am to 9pm.

GIFTS

Art of China. 839–843 Grant Ave. (between Clay and Washington sts.). ☎ **415/981-1602.**

Amid a wide variety of collectibles, this shop features exquisite, hand-carved Chinese figurines. You'll also find a lovely assortment of ivory beads, bracelets, necklaces, and earrings. Pink-quartz dogs, jade figurines, porcelain vases, cache pots, and blue-and-white barrels suitable for use as table bases are just some of the many items. Open daily 10am to 6pm.

Babushka. 333 Jefferson St. (at Leavenworth St.). ☎ **415/673-6740.**

Located near Fisherman's Wharf, adjacent to the Anchorage Shopping Center, Babushka sells only Russian products, most of which are wooden nesting dolls. Open Monday to Friday 9am to 10pm, Saturday and Sunday 9am to 10:30pm.

Cost Plus Imports. 2552 Taylor St. (between North Point and Bay sts.). ☎ **415/928-6200.**

At the Fisherman's Wharf cable-car turntable, Cost Plus is a vast warehouse crammed to the rafters with Chinese baskets, Indian camel bells, Malaysian batik scarves, and innumerable other items from Algeria to Zanzibar. More than 20,000 items from 40 nations, imported directly from their country of origin, pack this well-priced warehouse. There's also a decent wine shop. Open daily 9am to 9pm.

✪ **Dandelion.** 55 Potrero Ave. (at Alameda St.). ☎ **415/436-9500.**

Many locals were dismayed when, after almost 20 years in business, Dandelion closed its doors on California Street a few years back. But owners Steve, Del, and Carl weren't finished. Their new location is larger and even more packed with the most wonderful collection of gifts, collectibles, and furnishings. There's something for every taste and budget here, from an excellent collection of teapots, decorative dishes, and gourmet foods, to silver, books, cards, and picture frames. Don't miss the Zen-like second floor, with its variety of peaceful furnishings in Indian, Japanese, and Western styles. Open Tuesday through Saturday 10am to 6pm. Closed Sunday and Monday.

Distractions & Euphoria. 1552 Haight St. (between Ashbury and Clayton sts.). ☎ **415/252-8751.**

This is the best of the Haight Street shops selling underground-rave wear, street fashion, and underground electronica CDs. You'll find pipes, toys, and stickers liberally mixed with lots of cool stuff to look at. Open daily 10:30am to 7:30pm.

Flax. 1699 Market St. (at Valencia and Gough sts.). ☎ **415/552-2355.** www.flaxart.com.

If you're the type of person who goes into an art store for a special pencil and comes out $300 later, don't go near this shop. Flax has everything you can think of in art and design supplies, an amazing collection of local arts and crafts, blank bound books, children's art supplies, frames, calendars—you name it. There's a gift for every type of person here, especially you. If you can't stop by, call for a mail-order catalog. Open Monday to Saturday 9:30am to 6pm.

Good Vibrations. 1210 Valencia St. (at 23rd St.). ☎ **800/BUY-VIBE** or 415/974-8980 (for mail order). www.goodvibes.com.

A laypersons' sex-toy, book, and video emporium, Good Vibrations is specifically (but not exclusively) designed for women. Unlike most sex shops, it's not a back-alley business, but a straightforward shop with healthy, open attitudes about human sexuality. It also has a vibrator museum. Open Sunday to Thursday 11am to 7pm, Friday and Saturday 11am to 8pm. A second location is at 2504 San Pablo Ave., Berkeley (☎ **510/841-8987**).

Quantity Postcards. 1441 Grant St. (at Green St.). ☎ **415/986-8866.**

You'll find the perfect postcard for literally everyone you know here, as well as some depictions of old San Francisco, movie stars, and Day-Glo posters featuring concert-poster artist Frank Kozik. Prices range from 35¢ to $2 per card. Even if you don't need any cards, you'll enjoy browsing the eclectic collection of mailables. Open Sunday to Thursday 11am to 11pm, Friday and Saturday 11am to 12:30am.

✪ **SFMOMA Museum Store.** 151 Third St. (2 blocks south of Market St., across from Yerba Buena Gardens). ☎ **415/357-4035.** www.sfmoma.org.

With an array of artistic cards, books, jewelry, housewares, knickknacks, and creative tokens of San Francisco, it's virtually impossible not to find something you'll consider a must-have. (Check out the Fog Dome!) Aside from being one of the locals' favorite shops, it offers far more tasteful mementos than most Fisherman's Wharf options. Open daily from 10:30am to 6:30pm. You can also request a catalog by e-mail (museumstore@sfmoma.org).

Smile. 500 Sutter St. (between Powell and Mason sts.). ☎ **415/362-3436.**

Need a little humor in your life? Smile specializes in whimsical art, furniture, clothing, jewelry, and American crafts guaranteed to make you grin. Open Monday to Saturday 9:30am to 5:30pm.

HOUSEWARES/FURNISHINGS

✪ **Biordi Art Imports.** 412 Columbus Ave. (at Vallejo St.). ☎ **415/392-8096.**

Whether you want to decorate your dinner table, color your kitchen, or liven up the living room, Biordi's Italian majolica pottery is the most exquisite and unusual way to do it. The owner has been importing these hand-painted collectibles for 54 years, and every piece is a showstopper. Call for a catalog. They'll ship anywhere. Open Monday to Saturday 9:30am to 6pm. Closed Sunday.

✪ **Fillamento.** 2185 Fillmore St. (at Sacramento St.). ☎ **415/931-2224.**

The best housewares store in the city, Fillamento has three floors that are always packed with shoppers searching for classic, artistic, and refined items. Whether you're looking to set a good table or revamp your bedroom, you'll find it all here. Open Monday through Saturday 11am to 7pm, Sunday noon to 5pm.

Victorian Interiors. 575 Hayes St. (at Laguna St.). ☎ **415/431-7191.**

Draped with an array of period floral wallpapers, this little store is the perfect place for any Victoriana fanatic. Along with traditional Victorian wallpapers, moldings, drapery cornices and rods, tiles, fabrics, and carpets, you'll find a great collection of old pipes and knickknacks. Open Tuesday to Saturday 11am to 6pm, Sunday noon to 5pm.

The Wok Shop. 718 Grant Ave. (at Clay St.). ☎ **888/780-7171** for mail order, or 415/989-3797. www.wokshop.com.

This shop has every conceivable implement for Chinese cooking, including woks, brushes, cleavers, circular chopping blocks, dishes, oyster knives, bamboo steamers, and strainers. It also sells a wide range of kitchen utensils, baskets, handmade linens from China, and aprons. Open Sunday to Friday 10am to 6pm, Saturday 10am to 9pm.

✪ **Zinc Details.** 1905 Fillmore St. (between Bush and Pine sts.). ☎ **415/776-2100.**

One of my favorite stores in the city, Zinc Details has received accolades everywhere from *Elle Decor Japan* to *Metropolitan Home* for its amazing collection of locally hand-crafted glass vases, pendant lights, ceramics, and furniture. Each piece (except vintage items) is a true work of art created specifically for the store, and the pieces are in such high demand that the store's wholesale accounts include Barneys New York and the Guggenheim Museum Store. Open Monday to Saturday 11am to 7pm, Sunday noon to 6pm.

JEWELRY

Dianne's Old & New Estates. 2181A Union St. (at Fillmore St.). ☎ **888/346-7525** or 415/346-7525.

Buy yourself a bauble and treat yourself to a trinket at this shop featuring top-of-the-line antique jewelry—pendants, diamond rings, necklaces, bracelets, and natural pearls. For a special gift, check out the collection of platinum wedding and engagement rings and vintage watches. Don't worry if you can't afford it now—the shop offers 1-year interest-free layaway. Open Thursday to Monday 11am to 6pm.

Jerusalem Shoppe. 313 Noe St. (at Market St.). ☎ **415/626-7906.**

Known for its extensive collection of silver and gold gemstone jewelry by more than 300 local and international artists, this shop displays other unique treasures, from clothing and accessories to imported antique Indian quilts. Open Monday to Saturday 11am to 8pm, Sunday 11am to 7pm.

The Magical Trinket. 524 Hayes St. (between Laguna and Octavia sts.). ☎ **415/626-0764.**

Do-it-yourself jewelry makers, beware. This store, brimming with beads, baubles, and bangles, will inspire you to make your own knickknacks and kick yourself for the prices you've been paying for costume jewelry in retail stores. If you're overwhelmed by all the bead options, colors, shapes, and styles, owner Eve Blake calmly explains how to create your wearable masterpiece. She offers more extensive classes for those who are really bead-dazzled. Open Monday noon to 5pm, Tuesday to Saturday 11am to 7pm, Sunday noon to 5pm.

Pearl & Jade Empire. 427 Post St. (between Powell and Mason sts.). ☎ **415/362-0606.**

The Pearl & Jade Empire has been importing jewelry from all over the world since 1957. It specializes in unusual pearls and jade and offers restringing on the premises. Open Monday to Saturday 9:30am to 6pm.

Tiffany & Co. 350 Post St. (at Powell St.). ☎ **415/781-7000.**

Even if you don't have lots of cash to buy an exquisite bauble that comes in Tiffany's famous light-blue box, enjoy this renowned store à la Audrey Hepburn in *Breakfast at Tiffany's*. The designer collection features Paloma Picasso, Jean Schlumberger, and Elsa Peretti in both silver and 18-karat gold, and there's an extensive gift collection in sterling, china, and crystal. Open Monday to Saturday 10am to 6pm.

Union Street Goldsmith. 1909 Union St. (at Laguna St.). ☎ **415/776-8048.**

A showcase for Bay Area goldsmiths, this exquisite shop sells a contemporary collection of fine custom-designed jewelry in all platinum and all karats of gold. Many pieces emphasize colored stones in their settings. Open Monday to Saturday 11am to 5:45pm, Sunday noon to 4:45pm.

MARKETS/PRODUCE

✪ **Farmers Market.** Embarcadero, at Green St. ☎ **510/528-6987.**

Every Saturday from 8am to 1:30pm, northern California fruit, vegetable, bread, and dairy vendors join local restaurateurs in selling fresh, delicious edibles. There's no better way to enjoy a bright San Francisco morning than strolling this gourmet street market and snacking your way through breakfast. You can also pick up locally made vinegars and oils—they make wonderful gifts. There's another market on Tuesday at Justin Herman Plaza (Market Street and Embarcadero) from 10:30am to 2:30pm.

MUSIC

Recycled Records. 1377 Haight St. (between Central and Masonic sts.). ☎ **415/ 626-4075.**

Easily one of the best used-record stores in the city, this loud shop in the Haight has a good selection of promotional CDs and cases of used "classic" rock LPs. Sheet music, tour programs, and old *TV Guides* are for sale, too. Open Monday to Friday 10am to 7pm, Saturday 10am to 9pm, Sunday 11am to 7pm.

Streetlight Records. 3979 24th St. (between Noe and Sanchez sts.). ☎ **415/282-3550.**

Overstuffed with used music in all three formats, this place is best known for its records and excellent CD collection. Rock music is cheap, and the money-back guarantee guards against defects. Its second location is at 2350 Market St., between Castro and Noe streets (☎ **415/282-8000;** call for open hours). Open Monday to Saturday 11am to 9pm, Sunday 11am to 8pm.

Virgin Megastore. 2 Stockton St. (at Market St.). ☎ **415/397-4525.**

With thousands of CDs, including an impressive collection of imports, videos, DVDs, a multimedia department, a cafe, and related books, any music-lover could blow his or her entire vacation fund in this enormous Union Square store. Open Sunday to Thursday 9am to 10pm, Friday and Saturday 9am to midnight.

SHOES

Birkenstock. 42 Stockton St. (between Market and O'Farrell sts.). ☎ **415/989-2475.**

This relaxed store is known for its earthy California-style, form-fitting sandals, clogs, and lace-ups. Open Monday to Saturday 10am to 6pm, Sunday noon to 6pm.

Bulo. 437A Hayes St. (at Gough St.). ☎ **415/864-3244.**

If you have a fetish for foot fashions, you must check out Bulo, which carries nothing but imported Italian men's shoes. The selection is small but styles run the gamut, from casual to dressy, reserved to wildly funky. New shipments come in every three to four weeks, so the selection is ever-changing, eternally hip, and unfortunately, ever-expensive, with many pairs going for close to $200. Open Monday to Saturday 11am to 6:30pm, Sunday noon to 6pm. The women's shoe store is across the street at 418 Hayes St. (☎ **415/255-4939**).

Gimme Shoes. 2358 Fillmore St. (at Washington St.). ☎ **415/441-3040.**

The staff is funky-fashion snobby, the prices are steep, and the European shoes and accessories are utterly chic; everyone's crazy for the Katharine Hamnett watch collection. Open Monday to Saturday from 11am to 7pm and Sunday from 11am to 6pm.

Kenneth Cole. 865 Market St. (in the San Francisco Shopping Centre). ☎ **415/227-4536.**

This trendy shop carries high-fashion footwear for men and women. There is also an innovative collection of handbags and small leather goods and accessories. Other shops are at 2078 Union St., at Webster Street (☎ **415/346-2161**), and 166 Grant St., at Post Street (☎ **415/981-2653**). Open Monday to Saturday 9:30am to 8pm, Sunday 11am to 6pm.

SHOPPING CENTERS & COMPLEXES

The Anchorage. 2800 Leavenworth St. (at Beach and Jefferson sts. on Fisherman's Wharf). ☎ **415/775-6000.**

This touristy waterfront mall has close to 55 stores that offer everything from music boxes to home furnishings; street performers entertain during open hours. Generally open daily from 10am to 9pm.

The Cannery. 2801 Leavenworth St. (at Jefferson St.). ☎ **415/771-3112.**

Once a Del Monte fruit-canning plant, this complex now contains a score or two of shops, restaurants, and nightspots, and thankfully only a few chain stores. Shops include **Gourmet Market** (☎ **415/673-0400**), which sells international foods, coffees, and teas; **The Print Store** (☎ **415/771-3576**), with a well-chosen selection of fine-art prints and local original art; and the **Basic Brown Bear Factory** (☎ **415/931-6670**), where you can stuff your own teddy bear. Vendors' stalls and sidewalk cafes occupy the courtyard, amid a grove of olive trees. On summer weekends street performers entertain. The **Museum of the City of San Francisco** (☎ **415/928-0289**) is on the third floor.

Cobb's Comedy Club (see chapter 10, "San Francisco After Dark") is also here, as are several restaurants. The Cannery is open Monday to Saturday 10am to 6pm, Sunday 11am to 6pm; there are extended hours during the summer and on holidays.

Crocker Galleria. 50 Post St. (at Kearny St.). ☎ **415/393-1505.**

Modeled after Milan's Galleria Vittorio Emanuele, this glass-domed, three-level pavilion, about 3 blocks east of Union Square, features around 40 high-end shops. Fashions include Nicole Miller, Gianni Versace, and Polo/Ralph Lauren. Open Monday to Saturday 10am to 6pm.

Ghirardelli Square. 900 North Point (between North Point and Beach sts.). ☎ **415/775-5500.**

This former chocolate factory is one of the city's largest malls and most popular landmarks. It dates from 1864 when it served as a factory making Civil War uniforms, but it's best known as the former chocolate and spice factory of Domingo Ghirardelli (say "Gear-a-deli"). A clock tower, an exact replica of the one at France's Château de Blois, crowns the complex. Inside the tower, on the mall's plaza level, is the Ghirardelli soda fountain. It still makes and sells small amounts of chocolate, but the big draw is the old-fashioned ice-cream parlor. (Got a late-night craving? The place stays open until midnight on Friday and Saturday.) A free map and guide to the mall is available from the information booth in the center courtyard.

Many chain stores are located here, including the women's clothier **Ann Taylor** (☎ 415/775-2872) and **The Sharper Image** (☎ 415/776-1443), for unique, upscale electronics and designs.

The complex is open Sunday to Thursday 10am to 6pm, Friday and Saturday 10am to 9pm. Main plaza shops' and restaurants' hours vary, with extended hours during the summer. (Incidentally, the Ghirardelli Chocolate Company still makes chocolate in the East Bay.)

Pier 39. Embarcadero and Beach St. (on the waterfront). ☎ **415/981-PIER.**

The automated information line boasts that Pier 39 is the "third most visited attraction in the country" and in almost the same breath reminds callers not to forget to bring their Visa cards. To residents, that pretty much wraps up Pier 39—an expensive tourist trap where out-of-towners go to waste money on worthless souvenirs and greasy fast food. For vacationers, though, Pier 39 does have some redeeming qualities—fresh crab (in season), playful sea lions, phenomenal views, and plenty of fun for the kids. If you want to get to know the real San Francisco, skip the cheesy T-shirt shops and limit your time here to one afternoon.

Some of the most interesting stores include **Puppets on the Pier** (☎ 415/781-4435), a store that sells—you guessed it—puppets, and **Kite Flight** (☎ 415/956-3181), where you can buy a fanciful creation to fly in the breezes off the bay.

Open weekdays 10:30am to 8:30pm, weekends 10am to 8:30pm, with extended hours during the summer. Store and restaurant hours vary.

San Francisco Shopping Centre. 865 Market St. (at Fifth St.). ☎ **415/495-5656.**

Opened in 1988, this $140 million complex is one of the few vertical malls in the United States. Its most stunning features are the four-story spiral escalators that circle up to Nordstrom (see "Department Stores," above) and the nine-story atrium covered by a retractable skylight. More than 70 specialty shops include Abercrombie & Fitch, Ann Taylor, bebe, Benetton, Footlocker, J. Crew, and Victoria's Secret. Open Monday to Saturday 9:30am to 8pm, Sunday 11am to 6pm; holiday hours may vary.

TOYS

The Chinatown Kite Shop. 717 Grant Ave. (between Clay and Sacramento sts.). ☎ **415/391-8217.**

This shop's playful assortment of flying objects includes attractive fish kites, windsocks, hand-painted Chinese paper kites, wood-and-paper biplanes, pentagonal kites, and do-it-yourself kite kits, all of which make great souvenirs or decorations. Computer-designed stunt kites have two or four control lines to manipulate loops and dives. Open daily 10:30am to 8:30pm.

The Disney Store. 400 Post St. (at Powell St.). ☎ **415/391-6866.**

Capitalizing on the world's love for The Mouse and his friends, this store offers everything Disney-oriented you could possibly want—from clothes and toys to high-end commissioned art from the Disney gallery. Those looking for a simple token can fork over $3 for a plastic character, while more serious collectors can throw down $9,000 for a Yamagata Disney lithograph. Open in winter Monday to Friday 10am to 7pm, Saturday 10am to 7pm, Sunday 11am to 5pm. Hours are extended during the summer and holiday season; call for details. Another location is at Pier 39 (☎ 415/391-4119).

F.A.O. Schwarz. 48 Stockton St. (at O'Farrell St.). ☎ **415/394-8700.**

The world's greatest—and most overpriced—toy store for both children and adults is filled with every imaginable plaything, from hand-carved, custom-painted carousel rocking horses, Barbie dolls, and stuffed animals, to gas-powered cars, train sets, and hobby supplies. At the entrance is a singing 22-foot clock tower with 1,000 moving parts. Call for store hours.

TRAVEL GOODS

On the Road Again. Embarcadero and Beach St. (in Pier 39). ☎ **415/434-1482.**

In addition to lightweight luggage, this smart shop sells toiletry kits, travel bottles, travel-sized items, and a good selection of other related goods. Open daily 10am to 8:30pm.

Thomas Bros. Maps & Books. 550 Jackson St. (at Columbus Ave.). ☎ **800/969-3072** for mail order, or 415/981-7520.

The best map shop in the city, Thomas Bros. sells street, topographic, and hiking maps depicting San Francisco, California, and the world, as well as an extensive selection of travel guides and atlases. Open Monday to Friday 9:30am to 5:30pm, Saturday 10am to 5:30pm.

VINTAGE CLOTHING

Aardvark's. 1501 Haight St. (at Ashbury St.). ☎ **415/621-3141.**

One of San Francisco's largest secondhand clothing dealers, Aardvark's has seemingly endless racks of shirts, pants, dresses, skirts, and hats from the past 30 years. Open daily 11am to 7pm.

Buffalo Exchange. 1555 Haight St. (between Clayton and Ashbury sts.). ☎ **415/431-7733.**

This large storefront on upper Haight Street is crammed with racks of antique and new fashions from the 1960s, 1970s, and 1980s. It stocks everything from suits and dresses to neckties, hats, handbags, and jewelry. Buffalo Exchange anticipates some of the hottest new street fashions. Open Monday to Saturday 11am to 7pm, Sunday noon to 6pm. A second shop is at 1800 Polk St., at Washington Street (☎ **415/346-5726**).

✪ **Good Byes.** 3464 Sacramento St. and 3483 Sacramento St. (between Laurel and Walnut sts.). ☎ **415/346-6388.**

One the best new- and used-clothes stores in San Francisco, Good Byes carries only high-quality clothing and accessories, including an exceptional selection of men's fashions at unbelievably low prices (for example, $350 pre-owned shoes for $35). Women's wear is in a separate boutique across the street. Open Monday to Wednesday and Friday and Saturday 10am to 6pm, Thursday 10am to 8pm, Sunday 11am to 5pm.

La Rosa. 1711 Haight St. (at Cole St.). ☎ **415/668-3744.**

On a street packed with vintage-clothing shops, this is one of the more upscale options. It features a selection of high-quality, dry-cleaned secondhand goods. Formal suits and dresses are its specialty, but you'll also find sport coats, slacks, and shoes. You might also want to visit its more moderately priced sister store, **Held Over,** 1543 Haight St., near Ashbury. Open Wednesday to Friday noon to 6pm, Saturday 11am to 7pm, Sunday and Monday noon to 6pm.

WINE

✪ **Wine Club San Francisco.** 953 Harrison St. (between Fifth and Sixth sts.). ☎ **415/512-9086.**

The Wine Club is a discount warehouse that offers bargain prices on more than 1,200 domestic and foreign wines. Bottles cost between $4 and $1,100. Open Monday to Saturday 9am to 7pm, Sunday 11am to 6pm.

San Francisco After Dark

For a city with fewer than a million inhabitants, San Francisco boasts an arts scene that's nothing short of phenomenal. The city's opera is justifiably world renowned, the ballet is well respected, and the theaters are high in both quantity and quality. Dozens of piano bars and top-notch lounges augment one of the best dance-club cultures this side of New York, and skyscraper lounges offer some of the most dazzling city views in the world. In short, there's always something going on, so get off your fanny and get out there.

For up-to-date nightlife information, turn to the *San Francisco Weekly* and the *San Francisco Bay Guardian,* both of which run comprehensive listings. They are available free at bars and restaurants and from street-corner boxes all around the city. *Where,* a free tourist-oriented monthly, also has information on programs and performance times; it's available in most of the city's finer hotels. The Sunday edition of the *San Francisco Examiner* and *Chronicle* features a "Date-book" section, printed on pink paper, with information and listings on the week's events.

TICKETS

Tix Bay Area (☎ 415/433-7827) sells half-price tickets to theater, dance, and music performances on the day of the show only; tickets for Sunday and Monday events, if available, are sold on Saturday. It also sells advance, full-price tickets for most performance halls, sporting events, concerts, and clubs. A service charge, ranging from $1 to $3, is levied on each ticket. Only cash and traveler's checks are accepted for half-price tickets; Visa and MasterCard are accepted for full-price tickets. Tix is on Stockton Street, between Post and Geary streets on the east side of Union Square (opposite Maiden Lane). It's open Tuesday to Thursday 11am to 6pm, Friday and Saturday 11am to 7pm.

You can also get tickets to most theater and dance events through **City Box Office,** 153 Kearny St., Suite 402 (☎ 415/392-4400). American Express, MasterCard, and Visa are accepted.

BASS Ticketmaster (☎ 510/762-2277) sells computer-generated tickets to concerts, sporting events, plays, and special events, and imposes a hefty service charge. Downtown BASS Ticketmaster offices include Tix Bay Area (above) and Warehouse stores throughout the city. The most convenient location is at 30 Powell St.

1 The Performing Arts

Special concerts and performances take place in San Francisco year-round. **San Francisco Performances,** 500 Sutter St., Suite 710 (☎ **415/398-6449**), has brought acclaimed artists to the Bay Area for more than 15 years. Shows run the gamut from chamber music to dance and jazz. Performances are in several venues, including the Performing Arts Center, Herbst Theater, and the Center for the Performing Arts at Yerba Buena Center. The season runs from late September through May. Tickets cost $12 to $55 and are available through **City Box Office** (☎ 415/392-4400).

The **EC Cabaret,** 3 Embarcadero Center (☎ **415/398-6449** for information), mounts a 6pm Thursday after-work concert series in fall and winter; admission is $6 at the door.

CLASSICAL MUSIC

In addition to the world-class groups described below, visitors might be interested in the **San Francisco Contemporary Music Players** (☎ 415/252-6235). They perform modern chamber works by international artists at the Center for the Arts at Yerba Buena Gardens. Tickets, available by phone (☎ 415/978-ARTS), cost $14 for adults, $10 for seniors, $6 for students. Another commendable group is the **Women's Philharmonic** (☎ 415/437-0123). For more than 15 years, the critically acclaimed orchestra has played works by historical and contemporary female composers. Most performances, at least for the next season, are at Herbst Theater. Phone for dates, programs, and ticket prices.

Philharmonia Baroque Orchestra. Performing in Herbst Theater, 401 Van Ness Ave. ☎ **415/392-4400** (box office) or 415/252-1288 (administrative offices). www. philparmonia.org. Tickets $30–$42.

Acclaimed by the *New York Times* as "the country's leading early music orchestra," Philharmonia Baroque performs in San Francisco and all around the Bay Area. The season lasts from September through April.

San Francisco Symphony. Performing at Davies Symphony Hall, 201 Van Ness Ave. (at Grove St.). ☎ **415/864-6000** (box office). Tickets $12–$73.

Founded in 1911, the internationally respected San Francisco Symphony has long been an important part of the city's cultural life under such legendary conductors as Pierre Monteux and Seiji Ozawa. In 1995, Michael Tilson Thomas took over from Herbert Blomstedt; he has led the orchestra to new heights and crafted an exciting repertoire of classical and modern music. The season runs from September through June. Summer symphony activities include a Composer Festival and a Summer Pops series.

OPERA

In addition to San Francisco's major opera company, you might check out the amusing **Pocket Opera,** 44 Page St., Suite 200 (☎ 415/575-1100). From mid-February to mid-June, the comic company stages farcical performances of well-known operas in English. The staging is intimate and informal, without lavish costumes and sets. The cast ranges from 3 to 16 players, supported by a chamber orchestra. The rich repertoire includes such works as *Don Giovanni* and *The Barber of Seville.* Performances are on Friday, Saturday, or Sunday. Call the box office (☎ 415/575-1102) for complete information and show times. Tickets cost $13 (students) to $27.

San Francisco Opera. Performing at War Memorial Opera House, 301 Van Ness Ave. (at Grove St.). ☎ **415/864-3330** (box office). Tickets $10–$140.

The San Francisco Opera was the first municipal opera in the United States and is one of the city's cultural icons. Brilliantly balanced casts may feature celebrated stars like Frederica Von Stade and Placido Domingo, along with promising newcomers and regular members, in productions that range from traditional to avant-garde. All productions have English supertitles. The season starts in September and lasts just 14 weeks. Performances are held most evenings, except Monday, with matinees on Sundays. Tickets go on sale as early as June, and the best seats sell out quickly. Unless Pavarotti or Domingo is in town, some less coveted seats are usually available until curtain time.

THEATER

After 13 successful years, **Climate,** 252 Ninth St., at Folsom Street (☎ **415/978-2345**), is still showcasing avant-garde and experimental works in a casual, intimate atmosphere. **Eureka Theatre Company,** 330 Townsend St., Suite 210, at Fourth Street (☎ **415/243-9899**), produces contemporary plays. The season runs from September through June, and performances are usually Wednesday to Sunday. Tickets cost $16 to $22, with discounts for students and seniors. Call for specific theater location. **Theatre Rhinoceros,** 2926 16th St. (☎ **415/861-5079**), founded in 1977, was America's first (and remains its foremost) theater ensemble devoted solely to works addressing gay and lesbian issues. The company presents five main-stage shows and a dozen studio productions of new and classic works each year. The theater is 1 block east of the 16th Street/Mission BART station.

○ **American Conservatory Theater (A.C.T.).** Performing at the Geary Theater, 415 Geary St. (at Mason St.). ☎ **415/749-2228.** Tickets $14–$55.

The American Conservatory Theater made its debut in 1967 and quickly established itself as the city's premier resident theater group and one of the nation's best. The A.C.T. season runs from September through July and features both classic and experimental works.

A.C.T. recently returned to its home, the fabulous **Geary Theater** (1910), a national historic landmark, after the theater sustained severe damage in the 1989 earthquake and closed for renovations. Now it's fully refurbished and modernized to such an extent that it's regarded as one of America's finest performance spaces.

Lorraine Hansberry Theatre. Performing at 620 Sutter St. ☎ **415/474-8800.** Tickets $15–$26.

San Francisco's top African-American theater group performs in a 300-seat theater off the lobby of the Sheehan Hotel, near Mason Street. It mounts special adaptations from literature along with contemporary dramas, classics, and world premieres. Tickets range from $15 to $26. Phone for dates and programs.

The Magic Theatre. Performing at Building D, Fort Mason Center, Marina Blvd. (at Buchanan St.). ☎ **415/441-8822.** Tickets $18–$32. Discounts for students and seniors.

The highly acclaimed Magic Theatre is a major West Coast company dedicated to presenting the works of new playwrights; over the years it has nurtured the talents of such luminaries as Sam Shepard and Jon Robin Baitz. Shepard's Pulitzer Prize–winning play *Buried Child* had its premiere here. More recent productions have included works by Athol Fugard, Claire Chafee, and Nilo Cruz. The season usually runs from September through July; performances are Wednesday to Sunday.

DANCE

In addition to the local companies, top traveling troupes like the Joffrey Ballet and the American Ballet Theatre make regular appearances. Primary modern dance spaces include the **Theatre Artaud,** 450 Florida St., at 17th Street (☎ **415/621-7797**); the **Cowell Theater,** at Fort Mason Center, Marina Boulevard, at Buchanan Street (☎ **415/441-3400**); **Dancer's Group/Footwork,** 3221 22nd St., at Mission Street (☎ **415/824-5044;** www.dancersgroup.org); and the **ODC Theatre,** 3153 17th St., at Shotwell in the Mission District (☎ **415/863-9834**). Check the local papers for schedules or contact the theater box offices.

San Francisco Ballet. Performing at War Memorial Opera House, 301 Van Ness Ave. (at Grove St.). ☎ **415/865-2000** for tickets and information. Tickets $7–$100.

Founded in 1933, the San Francisco Ballet is the oldest professional ballet company in the United States and is regarded as one of the country's finest. It performs an eclectic repertoire of full-length, neoclassical, and contemporary ballets. Even the *New York Times* proclaimed, "The San Francisco Ballet under Helgi Tomasson's leadership is one of the spectacular success stories of the arts in America." The 2001 Repertory Season runs from February through April; the company performs *The Nutcracker* each December. The San Francisco Ballet Orchestra accompanies all performances.

2 Comedy & Cabaret

Bay Area Theatresports (BATS). Performing at Center for Improvisational Theatre at the Fort Mason Center, Building B, 3rd floor. ☎ **415/474-8935.** Tickets $5–$15.

Combining improvisation with competition, Bay Area Theatresports (BATS) operates an improvisational tournament, in which four-actor teams compete against each other, taking on hilarious challenges from the audience. Judges flash scorecards good-naturedly or honk a horn for scenes that just aren't working. Shows are on Monday only. Phone for reservations.

✪ **Beach Blanket Babylon.** At Club Fugazi, Beach Blanket Babylon Blvd., 678 Green St. (between Powell St. and Columbus Ave.). ☎ **415/421-4222.** Tickets $20–$55.

A San Francisco tradition, Beach Blanket Babylon evolved from Steve Silver's Rent-a-Freak service—a group of party-givers extraordinaire who hired themselves out as a "cast of characters" to entertain, complete with fabulous costumes and sets, props, and gags. After their act caught on, it moved into the Savoy-Tivoli, a North Beach bar. By 1974, the audience had grown too large for the facility, and Beach Blanket has been at the 400-seat Club Fugazi ever since.

The show is a comedic musical send-up that is best known for outrageous costumes and oversized headdresses. It's been playing for almost 27 years, and almost every performance sells out. The show is updated often enough that locals still attend. Those under 21 are welcome at Sunday matinees at 3pm, when no alcohol is served; photo ID is required for evening performances. Write for weekend tickets at least 3 weeks in advance, or get them through Tix (see "Tickets," above). *Note:* Tickets are within a specific section depending on price; seating is first-come, first-seated within that section. Performances are Thursday through Saturday at 8pm, Sunday at 3 and 7pm.

Cobb's Comedy Club. The Cannery, 2801 Leavenworth St. (at Beach St.). ☎ **415/ 928-4320.** Cover $7 Mon–Wed, $10 Thurs and Sun, $13 Fri–Sat. 2-beverage minimum nightly. Validated parking.

Located in the Cannery at Fisherman's Wharf, Cobb's features such national headliners as Pam Stone, Brian Regan, and Jake Johannsen. There is comedy every night,

Smoke Signals

California forbids smoking in bars, restaurants, hotel lobbies, and public areas of any kind. Some bars break the rules. Others ask their guests to step outside. Either way, don't count on lighting up inside any public place. Establishment owners are quick to enforce the rule, because they can be fined if patrons disobey.

including a 15-comedian All-Pro Monday showcase (a 3-hour marathon). Cobb's is open to those 18 and over, and occasionally to kids 16 and 17 if they are accompanied by a parent or legal guardian (call ahead). Food is served from adjoining Belle Roux Louisiana Kitchen. Shows are Monday through Wednesday at 8pm, Thursday and Sunday at 9pm, Friday and Saturday at 8 and 10pm.

Punch Line. 444 Battery St. (between Washington and Clay sts.), plaza level. ☎ **415/ 397-4337,** or 415/397-7573 for recorded information. Cover $5 Sun, $8–$15 Tues–Sat. 2-drink minimum nightly.

Adjacent to the Embarcadero One office building, this is the largest comedy nightclub in the city. Three-person shows with top national and local talent are featured Tuesday to Saturday. Showcase night is Sunday, when 15 to 20 rising stars take the mike. There's an all-star showcase or a special event on Monday. If you don't want to wait in line, buy tickets in advance from **Ticketmaster** outlets (☎ **415/421-TIXS**). Shows are Tuesday to Thursday and Sunday at 9pm, Friday and Saturday at 9 and 11pm.

3 The Club & Music Scene

The greatest legacy from the 1960s is the city's continued tradition of live entertainment and music, which explains the great variety of clubs and music. The hippest dance places are South of Market Street (SoMa), in former warehouses; the artsy bohemian scene centers on the Mission; and most popular cafe culture is still in North Beach.

Note: The club and music scene is always changing, often outdating recommendations before the ink can dry on a page. Most of the venues below are promoted as different clubs on various nights of the week, each with its own look, sound, and style. Discount passes and club announcements are often available at clothing stores and other shops along upper Haight Street.

If you prefer to let someone else take the lead (and the driver's seat) for a night out, call **3 Babes and a Bus** (☎ **415/552-2582**). The nightclub tour company (the head babe is a stockbroker by day) will take you and a gaggle of 20- to 40-something partyers (mostly single women) out on the town, skipping lines and cover charges, for $35 per person.

Drink prices at most bars, clubs, and cafes range from about $3.50 to $6, unless otherwise noted.

ROCK & BLUES CLUBS

In addition to the following listings, see "Dance Clubs," below, for (usually) live, danceable rock.

Biscuits and Blues. 401 Mason (at Geary St.). ☎ **415/292-2583.** Cover (during performances) $5–$25.

With a crisp, blow-your-eardrums-out sound system, New Orleans–speakeasy (albeit commercial) appeal, and a nightly line-up of live entertainment, there's no better place to muse the blues than at this basement-cum-nightclub. During performances, prices can be hefty (up to $25), but entrance is free during happy hour (Monday to Friday 5 to 7pm). There's usually recorded music, drink specials, and inexpensive snacks—not to mention the only opportunity to socialize. Once the bands get going, it's so loud you can't even hear yourself holler. *Note:* There's a full dinner menu, but the only notable treat is the moist, flaky biscuits.

The Fillmore. 1805 Geary Blvd. (at Fillmore St.). ☎ **415/346-6000.** www.thefillmore.com. Tickets $9–$25.

Reopened after years of neglect, the Fillmore, made famous by promoter Bill Graham in the 1960s, is attracting big names again. Check listings in magazines, or call the theater for information on upcoming events.

Grant & Green. 1371 Grant Ave. (at Green St.). ☎ **415/693-9565.** No cover.

The atmosphere at this North Beach dive rockery is not that special, but the local bands are pretty good. Look for daytime shows on weekends.

Lou's Pier 47 Club. 300 Jefferson St. (at Jones St.). ☎ **415/771-5687.** Cover $5–$10.

There are few locals in the place, but Lou's happens to be good, old-fashioned fun. It's a casual spot where you can let your hair down with Cajun seafood (downstairs) and live blues bands (upstairs). Major happy hour specials (Monday through Friday 4 to 7pm) and a vacation attitude make the place one of the more, um, jovial spots near the Wharf. There's no cover for the first band, which plays nightly from 4 to 8pm, but the second, which comes on at 9pm, will cost you.

The Saloon. 1232 Grant Ave. (at Vallejo St.). ☎ **415/989-7666.** Cover $4–$5 Fri–Sat.

An authentic Gold Rush survivor, this North Beach dive is the oldest bar in the city. Popular with both bikers and daytime pinstripers, it schedules live blues nightly.

Slim's. 333 11th St. (at Folsom St.). ☎ **415/522-0333.** Cover free to $20. 2-drink minimum when seated at a table.

Co-owned by musician Boz Scaggs, who sometimes takes the stage under the name "Presidio Slim," this glitzy restaurant and bar seats 300, serves California cuisine, and specializes in excellent American music—homegrown rock, jazz, blues, and alternative music—almost nightly. Menu items range from $3 to $8.50.

JAZZ & LATIN CLUBS

✪ **Cafe du Nord.** 2170 Market St. (at Sanchez St.). ☎ **415/861-5016.** Cover $3–$10.

Although it's been around since 1907, this basement supper club has finally been recognized as a respectable jazz, swing, and salsa music venue. With a younger generation now appreciating the music, the place is often packed from the 40-foot mahogany bar to the back room (which has a pool table). *Note:* If Lavay Smith and the Red Hot Skillet Lickers are in the house, definitely stop by. Du Nord puts out its own compilation CDs, which are definitely worth purchasing.

Jazz at Pearl's. 256 Columbus Ave. (at Broadway). ☎ **415/291-8255.** No cover. 2-drink minimum.

This is one of the best jazz venues in the city. The live jams last until 2am nightly. Ribs and chicken are served, too; prices run $4 to $8.95.

Rasselas. 2801 California St. (at Divisadero St.). ☎ **415/567-5010.** No cover. 2-drink minimum.

Large, casual, and comfortable, with couches and small tables, this is a favorite spot for local jazz and R&B combos. The adjacent restaurant serves Ethiopian cuisine under an elegant Bedouin tent. Menu items range from $3 to $10.75.

Up & Down Club. 1151 Folsom St. (between 7th and 8th sts.). ☎ **415/626-2388.** Cover $5–$10.

One of the original homes for SoMa's now-familiar new-jazz scene, the Up & Down supper club attracts a trendy crowd to its restaurant and dance floor. Dinner's at 8pm (reservations required), music starts at 9:30, and dancing begins at 10.

DANCE CLUBS

Although a lot of clubs allow dancing, the following are the places to go if all you want to do is shake your groove thang.

Club Ten 15. 1015 Folsom St. (at Sixth St.). ☎ **415/431-1200.** Cover $5–$15.

Get decked out and plan for a late night if you're headed to this enormous party warehouse. Three levels, a full-color laser system, and 4,000 feet of dance floor make for an extensive variety of dancing venues, complete with a 20- and 30-something gyrating mass who live for the DJs' pounding house, disco, and acid-jazz music. Each night is a different club that attracts its own crowd ranging from yuppie to hip-hop. A recent $1.5 million renovation added 6,000 square feet of dance floor and a VIP area. This place just keeps getting wilder. Call ahead for a complete schedule of events.

The EndUp. 401 Sixth St. (at Harrison St.). ☎ **415/357-0827.** www.theendup.com. Cover varies from free to $10.

For over a decade, this place has thrown some of the most kickin' parties in town. There's a different theme every night: Wednesday is Reggae with Club Dread; Thursday sets swinging singles loose at the Kit Kat Club; Fag Friday is just what it sounds like, plus lots of throw-down dancing; Saturday is the festive lesbian club the G Spot; and Sunday is ever-popular with the sleepless dance-all-day crowd that comes here after the other clubs close (it opens at 5:30am). Call to confirm nights—offerings change from time to time.

HiFi. 2125 Lombard St. (at Fillmore St.). ☎ **415/345-8663.** Cover $3–$6.

Previously a small, dark blues bar, its latest incarnation is a '50s and '60s "jet set lounge" perfectly poised to attracted the partying yuppie set. Most nights a DJ spins house, Latin, soul, and disco; live bands rock the place on Sundays.

Nickie's Bar-be-cue. 460 Haight St. (between Fillmore and Webster sts.). ☎ **415/621-6508.** www.nickies.com. Cover $3–$5.

Don't show up here for dinner—the only hot thing you'll find is the small, crowded dance floor. But don't let that stop you from checking it out—Nickie's is a sure thing.

Dial-A-Scene

The local newspapers won't direct you to the city's underground club scene, nor will they advise you which of the dozens of clubs are truly hot. To get dialed in, do what the locals do—turn to the **Be-At Line** (☎ **415/626-4087**) for its daily recorded update on the town's most hoppin' hip-hop, acid-jazz, and house clubs. The scene is reported by one of its coolest residents, Mayor Brown's street-suave son, Michael. For the grooviest message and inside scoop on the feel-good, underground party scene, consult the **Bug Out Line** (☎ **415/437-6905**). **Housewares Rave** (☎ **415/281-0125**) highlights the heavy techno scene. The far more commercial **Club Line** (☎ **415/979-8686**) offers up-to-date schedules for the city's larger dance venues.

Every time we come here, the old-school disco hits are in full force, casually dressed dancers lose all their inhibitions, and the crowd consists of all types of friendly San Franciscans. This place is perpetually hot, so dress accordingly; you can always cool down with a pint from the wine-and-beer bar. Keep in mind that lower Haight is on the periphery of a shady neighborhood, so don't make your rental car look tempting, and stay alert as you walk through the area.

Paradise Lounge. 1501 Folsom St. (at 11th St.). ☎ **415/861-6906.** Cover $3–$15.

Labyrinthine Paradise features three dance floors simultaneously vibrating to different beats. Smaller, auxiliary spaces include a pool room with a half-dozen tables. Poetry readings are fairly common here.

Sound Factory. 525 Harrison St. (at First St.). ☎ **415/243-9646.** Cover $10 Fri, $15 Sat.

Herb Caen dubbed this disco theme park the "mother of all discos." The maze of rooms and nonstop barrage of house, funk, lounge vibes, and club classics attracts swarms of young urbanites looking to rave it up, sometimes until as late as 6am. Management tries to eliminate the riffraff by enforcing a dress code (no sneakers, hooded sweatshirts, or sports caps).

SUPPER CLUBS

If you can eat dinner, listen to live music, and dance (or at least wiggle in your chair) in the same room, it's a supper club—that's our criteria.

330 Ritch. 330 Ritch (between Third and Fourth sts. off Townsend St.). ☎ **415/541-9574** or 415/522-9558 (for recorded band information). Cover $3–$10.

If you can find the place, you must be cool. It's on a 2-block alley in SoMa, and even locals have a hard time remembering how to get there. You'll find happy-hour cocktails (specials on a few select mixed drinks and draft brews), pool tables, and a hip, young crowd at play. The place really livens up when bands take center stage on Fridays. Free swing-dancing lessons (with $5 cover charge) are offered every Wednesday to the Bay Area's best swing bands. A "hearty American" dinner is served Wednesday to Saturday from 6 to 10pm. Closed Monday and Tuesday.

✪ **Blue Bar.** Below the Black Cat Cafe, 501 Broadway (at Kearny St.). ☎ **415/981-2233.** Cover $5 Wed–Sun.

Whether you're passing by North Beach or finishing a night at Reed Hearon's Black Cat Cafe (see the review in chapter 6, "Where to Dine," for complete details), drop into this chic-cozy live jazz and blues venue with cushy couches and a laid-back atmosphere. The restaurant's full menu is available here—a plus for late-night eaters and a bummer for those who come exclusively for the music.

✪ **Harry Denton's Starlight Room.** Atop the Sir Francis Drake Hotel, 450 Powell St., 21st floor. ☎ **415/395-8595.** Cover $5 Wed–Thurs after 8pm, $10 Fri–Sat after 8pm.

Come dressed to the nines or in casual attire to this celestial high-rise cocktail lounge and nightclub, where tourists and locals watch the sunset at dusk and boogie down to live swing and big-band tunes after dark. The room is classic 1930s San Francisco, with red-velvet banquettes, chandeliers, and fabulous views. But what really attracts flocks of all ages is a night of Harry Denton–style fun, which usually includes plenty of drinking and unrestrained dancing. The full bar stocks a decent collection of single-malt scotches and champagnes, and you can snack from the pricey Starlight appetizer menu. Like Harry's SoMa dance club, early evening is more relaxed, but come the weekend, this place gets loose.

Julie's Supper Club. 1123 Folsom St. (at Seventh St.). ☎ **415/861-0707.** No cover.

Julie's is a longtime standby for cocktails and late dining. The vibe in both rooms is very 1950s cartoon, with a space-age Jetsons appeal. Good-looking singles prowl, cocktails in hand, as live music plays by the front door. The food is hit-and-miss, but the atmosphere is definitely a winner—casual and playful. A little interesting history: This building is one location where the Symbionese Liberation Army held Patty Hearst hostage in the 1970s. Menu items range from $7.50 to $16.

RETRO CLUBS

Club Deluxe. 1511 Haight St. (at Ashbury St.). ☎ **415/552-6949.** Cover $2–$10.

Before the recent 1940s trend hit the city, Deluxe and its fedora-wearing clientele had been celebrating the bygone era for years. Fortunately, even with all the retro hype, the vibe here hasn't changed. Expect an eclectic mix of throwbacks and generic San Franciscans in the intimate, smoky bar and adjoining lounge, and live jazz or blues most nights. Although many regulars dress the part, there's no attitude here, so come as you like.

✪ **HiBall Lounge.** 473 Broadway (between Kearny and Montgomery sts.). ☎ **415/397-9464.** Cover $2–$8.

Retro jazz is in full swing in the city, and one of the most popular places to hear it—and dance to it—is this North Beach joint. Harking back to Broadway at its best, the vibe is full-on 1940s and '50s, from the red banquettes and stage curtains to the small, dark room. Live bands perform nightly to a young, swingin' crowd. There's also a swing-dance class Wednesday through Sunday. The kitschy-fun adjoining Bamboo Hut lounge celebrates classic tiki cocktails. The dress code: no baseball caps, tennis shoes, T-shirts, or ripped jeans.

4 The Bar Scene

Finding your idea of a comfortable bar has a lot to do with picking a neighborhood filled with your kind of people and investigating that area. There are hundreds of bars throughout San Francisco, and although many are obscurely located and can't be classified by their neighborhood, the following is a general description of what you'll find and where:

- **Chestnut and Union Street** bars attract a postcollegiate crowd.
- Young alternatives frequent **Mission District** haunts.
- **Upper Haight** caters to eclectic neighborhood cocktailers.
- **Lower Haight** is skate- and snowboarder grungy.
- Tourists mix with theatergoers and thirsty businesspeople in **downtown** pubs.
- **North Beach** serves all types.
- **Castro** caters to gay locals and tourists.
- **South of Market (SoMa)** offers an eclectic mix.

The following is a list of a few of San Francisco's more interesting bars.

Albion. 3139 16th St. (between Valencia and Guerrero sts.). ☎ **415/552-8558.**

This Mission District club is a grit-and-leather in-crowd place packed with artistic types and various SoMa hipsters. Live music (Sunday 4 to 7pm) ranges from ragtime and blues to jazz and swing.

Backflip. 601 Eddy St. (at Larkin St.). ☎ **415/771-FLIP.**

Adjoining the funky Phoenix Hotel, this shimmering aqua-blue cocktail lounge—designed to induce the illusion that you're carousing in the deep end—serves tapas and

Caribbean-style appetizers to a mostly young, fashionable crowd (so please don't order a Cosmopolitan). While the scene continues to change, Thursday the crowd seems to be young and gay/alternative; weekends, wanna-be-cool yuppies tend to pack the place. Regardless, if you're headed here, you can expect the unexpected, kick back with a martini, and enjoy the city's varied eye candy.

✪ **Bottom of the Hill.** 1233 17th St. (at Missouri St.). ☎ **415/621-4455.** Cover $4–$10.

Voted one of the best places to hear live rock in the city by the *San Francisco Bay Guardian,* this popular neighborhood club attracts an eclectic crowd ranging from rockers to real-estate salespeople. The main attraction is live music every night, but it also offers pretty good burgers and kebabs, outdoor seating on the back patio, and an awesome $4 all-you-can-eat barbecue on Sunday from 4 to 7pm. Happy hour runs Monday to Friday from 4 to 7pm.

Caribbean Zone. 55 Natoma St. (between First and Second sts.). ☎ **415/541-9465.** No cover.

Not just another restaurant bar, this is a visual Disneyland, jam-packed with a cluttered, tropical decorations that include a full-size airplane fuselage. It's been around a little too long, but tourists seem to love it. Dinner ranges from $14 to $19.

Chalkers Billiard Club. One Rincon Center, 101 Spear St. (at Mission St.). ☎ **415/ 512-0450.** www.chalkers.com.

Pool hall meets men's smoking club at this enormous, classy billiards joint. Food and drinks are delivered to the 30 cherrywood tables, which you can rent by the hour. Pool sharks especially appreciate the custom cue shop, where savvy sticks can go for up to $25,000. Happy hour (weekdays 5 to 7pm) offers more beer for your buck.

Edinburgh Castle. 950 Geary St. (between Polk and Larkin sts.). ☎ **415/885-4074.**

Since 1958, this legendary Scottish pub has been known for unusual British ales on tap and the best selection of single-malt scotches in the city. The huge pub is decorated with Royal Air Force mementos, horse brasses, steel helmets, and an authentic Ballantine caber (a long wooden pole) used in the annual Scottish games. Fish-and-chips and other traditional foods are available until 11pm.

The Great Entertainer. 975 Bryant (at Eighth St.). ☎ **415/861-8833.**

This is a glorified pool hall, with 50 tables, five private billiard suites, snooker, shuffleboard, darts, table tennis, and a video arcade. Drinks, pizza, and other dishes accompany the games. Menu items run $2 to $20.

Li Po Cocktail Lounge. 916 Grant Ave. (between Washington and Jackson sts.). ☎ **415/ 982-0072.**

A divey Chinese bar, Li Po stands out for its clutter of dusty Asian furnishings and mementos. They include an unbelievably huge rice-paper lantern hanging from the ceiling and a glittery golden shrine to Buddha behind the bar.

Perry's. 1944 Union St. (at Laguna St.). ☎ **415/922-9022.**

If you read *Tales of the City,* you already know that this bar and restaurant has a colorful history as a pickup place for Pacific Heights and Marina singles. Although the times are not as wild, locals still come to casually check out the happenings at the dark mahogany bar. A separate dining room offers breakfast, lunch, dinner, and weekend brunch at candlelit tables. It's a good place for hamburgers, simple fish dishes, and pasta. Menu items range from $7 to $20.

Persian Aub Zam Zam. 1633 Haight St. (at Clayton St.). ☎ **415/861-2545.**

If you make it through the forbidding metal doors, you'll feel as though you're in Casablanca, but unfortunately, most people don't get that far. The owner and bartender, Bruno, who has poured here for over 40 years, opens the place when he wants some company and arbitrarily chooses who's allowed to join him at the bar. If you meet his random requirements, play it safe and order a martini—a drink Bruno likes to serve (we've been ousted for ordering a Coors Light). Along with the challenge of getting in, locals love Bruno's ne'er-changing rituals: yesteryear's prices, a classic martini, and 50-cent pieces as change. Strategic tips to better your chances of entering and being allowed to stay: Don't come with a large party (he never lets anyone sit at the tables, and seating at the bar is limited); don't wear unusual attire (backward baseball caps are definitely out of the question!); drink beer from a glass, not the bottle; and don't order fancy cocktails. Then just sit back and enjoy watching everyone else get kicked out.

Pied Piper Bar. In the Sheraton Palace Hotel, 2 New Montgomery (at Market St.). ☎ **415/ 512-1111.**

The huge Pied Piper mural by Edwardian illustrator Maxfield Parrish steals the show at this historic mahogany bar, where high stakes were once won and lost on the roll of the dice.

The Red Room. In the Commodore Hotel, 827 Sutter St. (at Jones St.). ☎ **415/346-7666.**

Ultramodern and deliciously dim, this lounge reflects no other color but ruby red. It's a sexy place to sip the latest cocktail.

The Savoy-Tivoli. 1434 Grant Ave. (at Green and Union sts.). ☎ **415/362-7023.**

Euro-trash and wanna-bes crowd the few pool tables and indoor and patio seating, smoking cigarettes and looking cool, at this popular, trendy bar. Tourists and newcomers dominate, because posing gets tiring after a while, and there are far cooler bars in town. But a sidewalk-facing table in the heart of North Beach allows for great people-watching, and the high-profile clientele does create an entertaining atmosphere. The waitresses have been known to overcharge for drinks, which are supposed to range from $3.50 to $6.

✪ **Spec's.** 12 Saroyan Place (off Columbus Ave.). ☎ **415/421-4112.**

Spec's location on Saroyan Place, a tiny alley at 250 Columbus Ave., makes it less of a walk-in bar and more of a lively local hangout. Its funky decor—maritime flags hang from the ceiling; posters, photos, and various oddities line the exposed-brick walls—gives it character that intrigues every visitor. A "museum," displayed under glass, contains memorabilia and items brought back by seamen who drop in between voyages, and the clientele is funky enough to keep you preoccupied while you drink a beer.

Toronado. 547 Haight St. (at Fillmore St.). ☎ **415/863-2276.**

Lower Haight isn't exactly a charming street, but there's plenty of nightlife here catering to an artistic/grungy/skateboarding 20-something crowd. While Toronado definitely draws in the young'uns, its 40-plus microbrews on tap and 60 bottled beers also entice a more eclectic clientele in search of beer heaven. The brooding atmosphere matches the surroundings: an aluminum bar, a few tall tables, dark lighting, and a back room packed with tables and chairs. A DJ picks up the pace on Friday and Saturday nights.

✪ **Tosca.** 242 Columbus Ave. (between Broadway and Pacific Ave.). ☎ **415/986-9651.**

Open daily from 5pm to 2am, Tosca is a popular watering hole for local politicos, writers, media types, and similar cognoscenti of unassuming classics. Visiting celebrities have been known to drop in as impromptu bartenders, serving martinis in chilled long-stemmed glasses. Equipped with dim lights, red leather booths, and the requisite vintage jukebox spilling out Italian arias, it's everything you'd expect an old North Beach legend to be.

✪ **Vesuvio.** 255 Columbus Ave. (at Broadway). ☎ **415/362-3370.** www.vesuvio.com.

Situated along Jack Kerouac Alley across from the famed City Lights Bookstore, this renowned literary beatnik hangout is not just riding its historic coattails. The atmosphere is way cool, as are the customers. Bring a chessboard, borrow a game here, or write in a notebook, but whatever you do, make sure you look brooding and intense. Popular with neighborhood writers, artists, songsters, and wanna-bes, Vesuvio is crowded with self-proclaimed philosophers, and everyone else ranging from longshoremen and cab drivers to businesspeople. The convivial space is two stories of cocktail tables, complemented by a changing exhibition of local art and an ongoing slide show. In addition to drinks, Vesuvio features an espresso machine. No credit cards.

BREW PUBS

20 Tank Brewery. 316 11th St. (at Folsom St.). ☎ **415/255-9455.**

Right in the heart of SoMa's popular strip, this huge, come-as-you-are bar is known for serving good beer at fair prices. Pizzas, sandwiches, chilis, and assorted appetizers are also available. Menu items range from $4.95 to $14. Pub games include darts, shuffleboard, and dice.

Gordon Biersch Brewery Restaurant. 2 Harrison St. (on the Embarcadero). ☎ **415/243-8246.**

Gordon Biersch Brewery is San Francisco's largest brew restaurant, serving decent food and tasty beer to an attractive crowd of mingling professionals. There are always several beers to choose from, ranging from light to dark. Menu items run $4.50 to $19.95. (See chapter 6 for more information.)

San Francisco Brewing Company. 155 Columbus Ave. (at Pacific St.). ☎ **415/434-3344.** www.sfbrewing.com.

Surprisingly low-key for an alehouse, this cozy brew pub serves its creations along with burgers, fries, and the like. The bar is one of the city's few remaining old saloons, aglow with stained-glass windows, tile floors, skylit ceiling, beveled glass, and mahogany bar. A massive overhead fan runs the full length of the bar—a bizarre contraption crafted from brass and palm fronds. The handmade copper brew kettle is visible from the street. There's music most evenings. Darts, chess, backgammon, cards, and dice are all available. Menu items range from $3.25 to $16. The happy-hour special, a dollar per 10-ounce microbrew beer (or $1.75 a pint), runs daily from 4 to 6pm and midnight to 1am.

Thirsty Bear Brewing Company. 661 Howard St. (1 block east of the Moscone Center). ☎ **415/974-0905.**

Seven superb, handcrafted varieties of brew, ranging from fruit-flavored Strawberry Ale to a steak-in-a-cup stout, are always on tap at this stylish high-ceilinged brick edifice. Excellent Spanish food, too (see chapter 6). Pool tables and dartboards are upstairs, and live music (jazz, flamenco, blues, alternative, and classical) can be heard most nights.

COCKTAILS WITH A VIEW

See "Supper Clubs," above, for a full review of ✪ **Harry Denton's Starlight Room.**

The Carnelian Room. 555 California St., in the Bank of America Building (between Kearny and Montgomery sts.). ☎ **415/433-7500.**

On the 52nd floor of the Bank of America Building, the Carnelian Room offers uninterrupted views of the city. From a window-front table you feel as though you can reach out, pluck up the TransAmerica Pyramid, and stir your martini with it. In addition to cocktails, it serves "Discovery Dinners" ($39 per person). Jackets and ties are optional, but encouraged, for men. *Note:* The restaurant has the most extensive wine list in the city—1,275 selections, to be exact.

Cityscape. Hilton Tower I, 333 O'Farrell St. (at Mason St.), 46th floor. ☎ **415/923-5002.**

When you sit under the glass roof and sip a drink here, it's as though you're sitting out under the stars and enjoying views of the bay. Dinner is available, and there's dancing to a DJ's picks nightly from 10pm. The mirrored columns and floor-to-ceiling draperies help create an elegant and romantic ambience.

Crown Room. In the Fairmont Hotel, 950 Mason St., 24th floor. ☎ **415/772-5131.**

Of all the bars listed here, the Crown Room is definitely the plushest. Reached by an external glass elevator, it has a panoramic view that will encourage you to linger. It serves drinks (steep at $7 to $9) and dinner buffets ($36.50).

Equinox. In the Hyatt Regency Hotel, 5 Embarcadero Center. ☎ **415/788-1234.**

The hook of the 17-story Hyatt's rooftop Equinox is a revolving floor that gives each table a 360-degree panoramic view of the city every 45 minutes. In addition to cocktails, it serves dinner daily.

✪ **Top of the Mark.** In the Mark Hopkins Intercontinental, 1 Nob Hill (California and Mason sts.). ☎ **415/616-6916.**

This is one of the most famous cocktail lounges in the world, and for good reason—the spectacular glass-walled room features an unparalleled 19th-floor view. During World War II, Pacific-bound servicemen toasted their good-bye to the States here. Live entertainment starts at 8:30 nightly, with a cover charge of $6 to $10. There are free dance lessons on Tuesday nights. Afternoon tea runs from 3 to 5pm Monday to Friday. Sunday brunch, served from 10am to 2pm, costs $39 without champagne ($27 for children 5 to 14), $55 with. Drinks are also pricey, ranging from $6 to $8.

PIANO BARS

San Francisco is lucky to have several lively piano bars. As in other cities, these specialized lounges perfectly suit the grand hotels in which they are usually located.

Nob Hill Terrace. In the Mark Hopkins Intercontinental, 1 Nob Hill (California and Mason sts.). ☎ **415/392-3434.**

Drinks ($5 to $10) are served nightly in a delightfully intimate, skylit room with hand-painted murals. It's just off the lobby.

✪ **The Redwood Room.** In the Clift Hotel, 495 Geary St. ☎ **415/775-4700.**

A true Art Deco beauty, this ground-floor lounge is one of San Francisco's most comfortable and nostalgic piano bars. Its gorgeous redwood interior came from a single 2,000-year-old tree. It's further enhanced by the large, brilliantly colored Gustav Klimt murals. Drinks go for $6 to $9.

Midnight (or Midday) Mochas

If you happen to be wandering around North Beach past your bedtime and need your caffeine fix, seek out these two cafes. They offer not only excellent espresso, but also a glimpse into what it must have been like back in the days of the beatniks, when nothing was as crucial as a strong cup of coffee, a good smoke, and a stimulating environment.

Doing the North Beach thing is little more than hanging out in a sophisticated but relaxed atmosphere over a well-made cappuccino. You can do it at **Caffè Greco,** 423 Columbus Ave., between Green and Vallejo streets (☎ **415/ 397-6261**), and grab a bite, too. The affordable cafe fare includes beer, wine, a good selection of coffees, focaccia sandwiches, and desserts (try the gelato or homemade tiramisu).

Caffè Trieste, 601 Vallejo St., at Grant Avenue (☎ **415/392-6739**), is one of San Francisco's most beloved cafes—very down-home Italian, with only espresso drinks, pastries, and indoor and outdoor seating. Opera is always on the jukebox, unless it's Saturday afternoon, when the family and their friends break out in arias from 2 to 5pm.

SPORTS BARS

Bayside Sports Bar and Grill. 1787 Union St. (at Octavia St.). ☎ **415/673-1565.**

This is easily one of the largest sports bars in the city, equipped with a state-of-the-art super-large-screen television, 30 smaller ones, 19 beers on tap, and two pool tables. The crowd is mainly Marina yuppies (lots of baseball caps, sweatshirts, and Lycra shorts), which is made bearable by the fast, friendly food service (mostly burgers, sandwiches, and such) and the myriad of sports channels. Happy hour is Monday to Friday from 4 to 6pm.

Greens Sports Bar. 2239 Polk St. (at Green St.). ☎ **415/775-4287.** www.citysearch.com/ sfo/greenssportsbar.

If you think San Francisco sports fans aren't as enthusiastic as those on the East Coast, we dare you to try to get a seat at Green's (or even get in) during a 49ers game. It's a classic old sports bar, with lots of polished dark wood and windows that open onto Polk Street, but it's loaded with modern appliances, including a large-screen television and 10 smaller ones. There are 18 beers on tap and a pool table. They don't serve food here, but you can bring in grub for the game. A late-night happy hour runs Sunday to Wednesday from 10pm to 2am.

WINE & CHAMPAGNE BARS

The Bubble Lounge. 714 Montgomery St. (at Columbus Ave.). ☎ **415/434-4204.**

San Francisco nightlife is in full swing, and toasting the town is a nightly event at this two-level champagne bar. With 300 champagnes, around 30 by the glass, brick walls, couches, velvet curtains, and a pool table, there's plenty of pop in this fizzy lounge.

Eos. 101 Carl St. (at Cole St.). ☎ **415/566-3063.**

If you're downtown, head for the London Wine Bar. If you're around the Civic Center, make it Hayes and Vine. For anything west of these two, your top choice is Eos, a fairly new, highly successful restaurant and wine bar in Cole Valley (near the Haight). Around the corner from the restaurant is this chic, lively wine bar filled mostly with young patrons who dabble among the 400 vintages from around the world.

Hayes and Vine. 377 Hayes St. (at Gough St.). ☎ **415/626-5301.**

You'll find 750 wines (with over 50 by the glass!) from around the world at this unpretentious wine bar staffed by true cognoscenti of fine wine. (It's a good thing, too, because you have probably never heard of 90% of these wines.) Be sure to ask about taking a "flight," which allows you to try several different wines for a fixed price. Cheese, breads, antipasti, charcuterie, and desserts are also served.

London Wine Bar. 415 Sansome St. (between Sacramento and Clay sts.). ☎ **415/788-4811.**

This British-style wine bar and store is a popular after-work hangout for Financial District suits. It's more of a place to drink and chat than to admire fine wines. Usually two to three dozen wines are open at any given time, mostly from California. It's a great venue for sampling local Napa Valley wines before you buy.

5 Gay & Lesbian Bars & Clubs

Just like straight establishments, gay and lesbian bars and clubs target varied clienteles. Whether you're into leather or Lycra, business or bondage, there's gay nightlife just for you.

Check the free weeklies, the *San Francisco Bay Guardian* and *San Francisco Weekly,* for listings of events and happenings. The *Bay Area Reporter* is a gay paper with comprehensive listings, including a weekly community calendar. All the above papers are free and distributed weekly on Wednesday or Thursday. They can be found stacked at the corner of 18th and Castro streets and Ninth and Harrison streets, as well as in bars, bookshops, and stores around town. To find out what's up with lesbian events in San Francisco, ranging from women's golf to nightlife, call **Girl Spot** (☎ 415/337-4962). There are also a number of gay and lesbian guides to San Francisco. See "For Gays & Lesbians," in chapter 2, "Planning Your Trip: The Basics," for further details.

Listed below are some of the city's more established, mainstream gay hangouts.

Alta Plaza. 2301 Fillmore St. (at Clay St.). ☎ **415/922-1444.** www.altaplaza.com. No cover.

Pacific Heights's wealthy gays flock to this classy Fillmore bar and restaurant. Cocktail hour, from 4 to 7pm nightly, offers $3 well and call drinks and is especially festive on Friday and Saturday. Later in the evening, the restaurant fills with yuppie diners who come for the northern California cuisine with Pacific Rim and Italian influences—or to hang in the bar area and check out the hotties. There's live jazz Sunday to Thursday and a DJ on weekend nights.

✪ **The Café.** 2367 Market St. (at Castro St.). ☎ **415/861-3846.**

When this place first got jumping, it was the only predominantly lesbian dance club on Saturday nights in the city. Once the guys found out how much fun the girls were having, they joined the party. Today, it's a happening mixed gay and lesbian scene with two bars, a steamy, free-spirited dance floor, and a small patio.

Castro Station. 456B Castro St. (between 17th and 18th sts.). ☎ **415/626-7220.** No cover.

A well-known gay hangout in the Castro District, this bar is popular with the leather and Levi's crowd, as well as trendy boys from around the country who come here looking for action. Drinks cost $2.25 to $6.

The Cinch Saloon. 1723 Polk St. (near Washington St.). ☎ **415/776-4162.** No cover.

Among the popular attributes of this cruisey neighborhood bar are the outdoor patio, Sunday barbecue or buffet, and progressive music and videos. 49er fans also gather here for televised games. Decorated in a Southwestern theme ("down home in

Arizona"), the bar attracts a mixed crowd of gays, lesbians (now that there are almost no exclusively lesbian bars left in San Francisco), and gay-friendly straights. There are "beer busts" or theme drink nights weekly. The nominal charge for barbecues and buffets is donated entirely to various AIDS organizations.

Detour. 2348 Market St. (near Castro St.). ☎ **415/861-6053.** No cover.

Right in the heart of gay San Francisco, this bar attracts a young, often hot crowd of boys, with its low lighting and throbbing house music. Chain-link fences seem to hold in the action while a live DJ spins a web of popular hits. Special events, including Saturday go-go dancers, keep this place jumping.

The Eagle. 398 12th St. (at Harrison St.). ☎ **415/626-0880.** www.sfeagle.com.

One of the city's most traditional Levi's-leather bars, the Eagle boasts a heated outdoor patio, a happy hour (Monday to Friday 4 to 8pm), and a popular Sunday-afternoon beer fest from 3 to 6pm.

The EndUp. 401 Sixth St. (at Harrison St.). ☎ **415/357-0827.** Cover varies.

It's a different nightclub every night of the week, but regardless of who's throwing the party, the place is always jumping with the DJ's blasting tunes. There are two pool tables, a flaming fireplace, outdoor patio, and a mob of gyrating souls on the dance floor. Some nights are straight, so call ahead.

Giraffe Lounge. 1131 Polk St. (near Sutter St.). ☎ **415/474-1702.** No cover.

Favored by a younger, action-seeking crowd, this video bar, with its 15 ceiling-mounted monitors, is a good place for cruising or shooting pool. It's a friendly neighborhood hangout during the week and livens up on weekends.

Kimo's. 1351 Polk St. (at Pine St.). ☎ **415/885-4535.** Free to nominal cover.

This neighborhood bar in the seedier gay section of town is a friendly oasis, decorated with plants, pictures, and "gay banners." The bar provides a relaxing venue for chatting, drinking, and quiet cruising, and things occasionally liven up during drag shows.

Lone Star Saloon. 1354 Harrison St. (between Ninth and Tenth sts.). ☎ **415/863-9999.** No cover.

Expect dykes and a heavier, furrier motorcycle crowd (both men and women) most every night. The Sunday-afternoon beer bust on the patio is especially popular.

Metro. 3600 16th St. (at Market St.). ☎ **415/703-9750.** No cover.

With modern art on the walls and much use of terra-cotta, the Metro provides the gay community with high-energy dance music and the best view of the Castro District from its large balcony. The bar seems to attract people of all ages who enjoy the friendly bartenders and the highly charged, cruising atmosphere. There's a Chinese restaurant on the premises if you get hungry.

The Mint. 1942 Market St. (at Laguna St.). ☎ **415/626-4726.** No cover.

Come out of the shower and into the Mint, a gay and lesbian karaoke bar where you can sing show tunes every night. Along with song, you'll encounter a mixed 20- to 40-something crowd that combines cocktails with do-it-yourself cabaret.

Rawhide II. 280 Seventh St. (at Folsom St.). ☎ **415/621-1197.** Weekend cover charge $5; includes 1 drink.

Gay or straight, this was one of the city's top country-western dance bars until it recently changed to feature alternative music. It's still patronized by both men and women. Dance lessons ($5) are offered Tuesday to Friday from 7:30 to 9:30pm.

The Stud. 399 Ninth St. (at Harrison St.). ☎ **415/863-6623.** Cover $2–$6 weekends.

The Stud has been around for 30 years, is one of the most successful gay establishments in town, and is mellow enough for straights as well. The interior has an antique-shop look and a miniature train circling over the bar and dance floor. Music is a balanced mix of old and new, and nights vary from cabaret and oldies to disco. Call in advance for the evening's offerings. Drink prices range from $2 to $6. Happy hour runs daily from 5 to 9pm.

The Swallow. 1750 Polk St. (between Clay and Washington sts.). ☎ **415/775-4152.** No cover.

Some consider this classy piano bar for the middle-aged-and-up crowd the best gay bar on Polk Street. There's live cabaret here nightly.

Twin Peaks Tavern. 401 Castro St. (at 17th and Market sts.). ☎ **415/864-9470.** No cover.

Right at the intersection of Castro, 17th, and Market streets is one of the Castro's most famous gay hangouts, which caters to an older crowd and claims to be the first gay bar in America. Because of its relatively small size and desirable location, the place becomes fairly crowded and convivial by 8pm, earlier than many neighboring bars.

6 Film

The **San Francisco International Film Festival** (☎ 415/931-FILM; www.sfiff.org), held in March, is one of America's oldest film festivals. Tickets are relatively inexpensive. Entries include new films by beginning and established directors. Call or surf ahead for a schedule or information. You can charge tickets by phone through **BASS TicketMaster** (☎ 510/762-2277).

Even if you're not here in time for the festival, don't despair. The classic, independent, and mainstream cinemas in San Francisco are every bit as good as the city's other cultural offerings.

REPERTORY CINEMAS

Castro Theatre. 429 Castro St. (near Market St.). ☎ **415/621-6120.**

Built in 1922, the beautiful Castro Theatre is known for its screenings of classics and for its Wurlitzer organ, which is played before each show. There's a different feature almost nightly, and more often than not it's a double feature. Bargain matinees are usually offered on Wednesday, Saturday, Sunday, and holidays. Phone for schedules, prices, and show times.

Red Vic. 1727 Haight St. (between Cole and Shrader sts.). ☎ **415/668-3994.**

The worker-owned Red Vic movie collective recently moved from the Victorian building that gave it its name. The theater specializes in independent releases and contemporary cultish hits. Prices are $6.50 for adults ($4.50 for matinees), $3 for seniors and kids 12 and under. Tickets go on sale 20 minutes before each show. Phone for schedules and show times.

Roxie. 3117 16th St. (at Valencia St.). ☎ **415/863-1087.**

The Roxie consistently screens the best new alternative films anywhere. The low-budget contemporary features are largely devoid of Hollywood candy coating; many are West Coast premieres. Films change weekly, and sometimes more often. Phone for schedules, prices, and show times.

Side Trips from San Francisco

The Bay City is, without question, captivating, but don't let it ensnare you to the point of ignoring its environs. The area contains a multitude of natural spectacles like Mount Tamalpais and Muir Woods; scenic communities like Tiburon and Sausalito; and cities like gritty Oakland and its youth-oriented next-door neighbor, Berkeley. To the southwest lies Half Moon Bay, an adorable little coastal town perched on a wide expanse of golden beach.

From San Francisco you can reach any of these points in an hour or less by car. Another option is to hitch a ride with **Tower Tours** (☎ **415/434-8687**), which runs regularly scheduled microbus tours to neighboring towns and the countryside. Half- and full-day trips to Muir Woods, Sausalito, Napa, and Sonoma are available, as are excursions to Yosemite and the Monterey Peninsula. Phone for prices and schedules.

1 Berkeley

10 miles NE of San Francisco

Berkeley is famous as the home of the University of California at Berkeley, which is world-renowned for its academic standards, 16 Nobel Prize winners, and protests that led to the most famous student riots in U.S. history. Today, there's still hippie idealism in the air, but the radicals have aged; the '60s are present only in tie-dye and paraphernalia shops, and the students have less angst. The biggest change the town is facing is yuppification; as San Francisco's rent and property prices soar, everyone with less than a small fortune is seeking shelter elsewhere, and Berkeley is one of the top picks. It's a charming town teeming with all types of people, a beautiful campus, vast parks, great shopping, and some incredible restaurants.

ESSENTIALS

The Berkeley **Bay Area Rapid Transit** (BART) station is 2 blocks from the university. The fare from San Francisco is less than $3.

If you are coming **by car** from San Francisco, take the Bay Bridge (go during the evening commute, and you'll think Los Angeles traffic is a breeze). Follow I-80 east to the University Avenue exit, and follow University until you hit the campus. Parking is tight, so either leave your car at the Sather Gate parking lot on Telegraph and Durant, or expect to fight for a spot.

The Bay Area

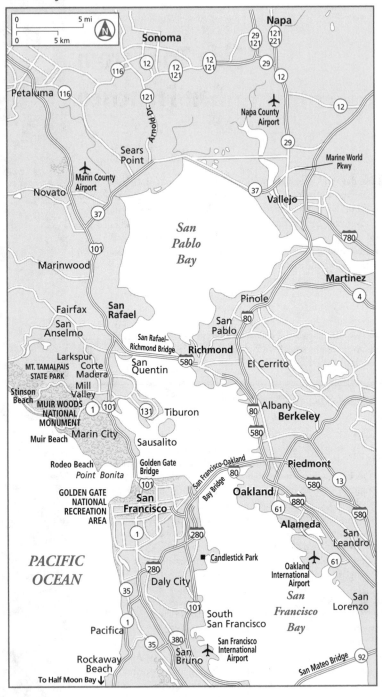

Phone the **Visitor Hot Line** (☎ 510/549-8710) for automated information on events and happenings in Berkeley.

WHAT TO SEE & DO

Hanging out is the preferred Berkeley pastime, and the best place to do it is on Telegraph Avenue; the street that leads to the campus's southern entrance. Most of the action lies between Bancroft Way and Ashby Avenue, where coffeehouses, restaurants, shops, great book and record stores, and craft booths swarm with life. Pretend you're local: Plant yourself at a cafe, sip a latte, and ponder something intellectual or survey the town's unique residents.

Bibliophiles must stop at **Cody's Books,** 2454 Telegraph Ave. (☎ 510/845-7852), to peruse its gargantuan selection of titles, independent-press books, and magazines. Vendors selling everything from T-shirts and jewelry to I Ching and tarot-card readings pack the avenue.

UC BERKELEY CAMPUS

The University of California at Berkeley is worth a stroll. It's a beautiful old campus with plenty of woodsy paths, architecturally noteworthy buildings, and, of course, 31,000 students, many of them scurrying to and from classes. Among the architectural highlights of the campus are a number of buildings by Bernard Maybeck, Bakewell and Brown, and John Galen Howard.

Contact the **Visitor Information Center,** 101 University Hall, 2200 University Ave., at Oxford Street (☎ 510/642-5215), to join a free, regularly scheduled campus tour. They start Monday through Saturday at 10am, Sunday at 1pm; no tours from mid-December to mid-January. Or stop by the office and pick up a self-guided walking-tour brochure.

The university's southern entrance is at the northern end of Telegraph Avenue, at Bancroft Way. Walk through the main entrance into Sproul Plaza, and when school is in session, you'll encounter the gamut of Berkeley's inhabitants: colorful street people, rambling political zealots, chanting Hare Krishnas, and ambitious students. You'll also find the Student Union, complete with a bookstore, cafes, and an information desk on the second floor where you can pick up a free map of Berkeley and the student newspaper (also found in dispensers throughout campus).

You might be lucky enough to stumble upon some impromptu musicians or a heated, and sometimes absurd, debate. There's always something going on, so stretch out on the grass for a few minutes and take in the Berkeley vibe.

For viewing more traditional art forms, there are some noteworthy museums, too. The **Lawrence Hall of Science** (☎ 510/642-5132), offering hands-on science exploration, is open 10am to 5pm daily and is a wonderful place to watch the sunset. Admission is $6 for adults; $4 for seniors, students, and children 7 to 18; $2 for children 3 to 6; free for kids under 3. The **University Art Museum** (☎ 510/642-0808) is open 11am to 5pm on Wednesday and Friday through Sunday, and Thursday 11am to 9pm. Admission is $6 for adults; $4 for seniors, students, and children 12 to 17; free for kids under 12 and U.C. students. This museum contains a substantial collection of Hans Hofmann paintings, a sculpture garden, and the Pacific Film Archive.

If you're interested in notable off-campus buildings, contact the **Berkeley Convention and Visitors Bureau** (☎ 510/549-7040) for an architectural walking-tour brochure.

Berkeley

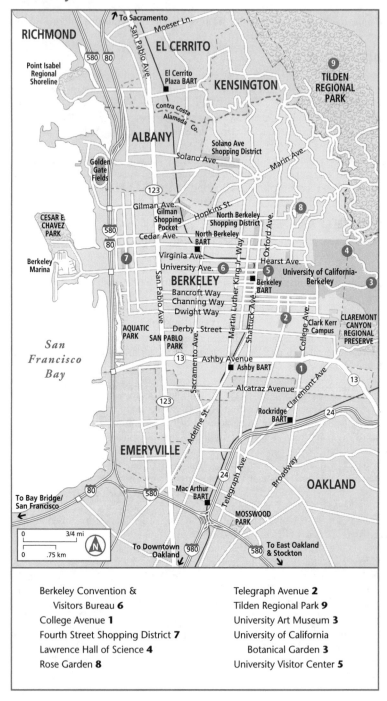

Berkeley Convention & Visitors Bureau **6**	Telegraph Avenue **2**
	Tilden Regional Park **9**
College Avenue **1**	University Art Museum **3**
Fourth Street Shopping District **7**	University of California
Lawrence Hall of Science **4**	Botanical Garden **3**
Rose Garden **8**	University Visitor Center **5**

PARKS

Unbeknownst to many travelers, Berkeley has some of the most extensive and beautiful parks around. If you want to wear out the kids or enjoy hiking, swimming, or just getting a breath of California air and sniffing a few roses, jump in your car and make your way to **Tilden Park.** On the way, stop at the colorful terraced Rose Garden, in north Berkeley on Euclid Avenue between Bay View and Eunice Street. Then head high into the Berkeley hills to Tilden, where you'll find plenty of flora and fauna, hiking trails, an old steam train and merry-go-round, a farm and nature area for kids, and a chilly tree-encircled lake. By public transit, line no. 67 goes to the north end of the park, and no. 8 skirts the edge of the park. Call ☎ **510/843-2137** for further information.

Another worthy nature excursion is the **University of California Botanical Garden** (☎ **510/642-3343**), which features a vast collection of herbage ranging from cacti to redwoods. It's on campus in Strawberry Canyon on Centennial Drive; line no. 8 from the Berkeley BART station runs there.

SHOPPING

If you're itching to exercise your credit cards, head to one of two places. College Avenue from Dwight to the Oakland border overflows with eclectic boutiques, antique shops, and restaurants. The other option is Fourth Street, in west Berkeley 2 blocks north of the University Avenue exit. This 2-block expanse is the perfect place to go on a sunny morning. Grab a cup of java, read the paper at a patio table, then hit the **Crate and Barrel Outlet,** 1785 Fourth St., between Hearst and Virginia (☎ **510/528-5500**). Prices are 30% to 70% off retail. It's open Monday to Saturday 10am to 6pm, Sunday 11am to 6pm. This area also boasts small, wonderful stores crammed with imported and locally made housewares. Nearby is **REI,** the Bay Area's favorite outdoor outfitter, 1338 San Pablo Ave., near Gilman Street (☎ **510/527-4140**).

WHERE TO STAY

Bed and Breakfast California, 12711 McCartysville Place, Saratoga, CA 95070 (☎ **800/872-4500** or 408/867-9662; fax 408/867-0907; www.bbintl.com; e-mail: info@bbintl.com), accommodates visitors in more than 150 private homes and apartments in the San Francisco–Berkeley area. The cost ranges from $65 to $300 per night, and there's a 2-night minimum. The **Berkeley Convention and Visitors Bureau,** 2015 Center St., Berkeley, CA 94704 (☎ **800/847-4823,** 510/549-7040, or 510/549-8710 for the Visitor Hot Line), can find accommodations and supply free visitor guides, maps, and area literature. It's staffed Monday to Friday 9am to 5pm.

WHERE TO DINE

East Bay dining is a relaxed alternative to the city's gourmet scene. There are plenty of ambitious Berkeley restaurants and, unlike San Francisco, plenty of parking.

If you want to dine student style, eat on campus Monday to Friday. Buy something at a sidewalk stand or in the building directly behind the Student Union. The least expensive food is available downstairs in the **Cafeteria,** on Lower Sproul Plaza. There's also the **Bear's Lair Pub and Coffee House,** the **Terrace,** and the **Golden Bear Restaurant.** All the university eateries have both indoor and outdoor seating.

Telegraph Avenue has an array of small, ethnic restaurants, cafes, and sandwich shops. Follow the students: If the place is crowded, it's good, super cheap, or both.

People's Park/People's Power

In late 1967, the university demolished an entire block of buildings north of Telegraph Avenue. The destruction, which forced hippies and other "undesirables" from the slum housing that stood there, was done under the guise of university expansion and urban renewal—good liberal causes. But after the lot lay vacant for almost 2 years, a group of Berkeley radicals, whose names read like a who's who of 1960s leftists, including Jerry Rubin, Bobby Seale, and Tom Hayden, decided to take the land for "the people."

On April 29, 1969, hundreds of activists invaded the vacant lot with gardening tools and tamed the muddy ground into a park. One month later, Berkeley's Republican mayor sent 250 police officers into the park, and 4,000 demonstrators materialized to challenge them. A riot ensued, and the police fired buckshot at the crowd. One rioter was killed and another blinded. Gov. Ronald Reagan sent in the National Guard, and for the next 17 days, the guardsmen repeatedly gassed innocent students, faculty, and passersby. Berkeley was a war zone, and People's Park became the decade's most important symbol of "people power."

People's Park again sparked controversy in 1992, when university officials decided to build volleyball courts there. In August, a park activist broke into the campus home of the university's chancellor. When a police officer arrived, the activist lunged at him with a machete and was shot dead. On the victim's body was a note with the message: "We are willing to die for this land. Are you?" On news of the contemporary radical's death, more than 150 of her supporters rioted. Postscript: The nets didn't get much use, and now basketball courts have taken their place.

EXPENSIVE

✪ **Chez Panisse.** 1517 Shattuck Ave. (between Cedar and Vine). ☎ **510/548-5525;** cafe reservations 415/548-5049. Fax 510/548-0140. Reservations essential. Restaurant fixed-price menu $38–$68; cafe main courses $13–$18. AE, CB, DC, DISC, MC, V. Restaurant seatings Mon–Sat 6–6:30pm and 8:30–9:15pm. Cafe Mon–Thurs 11:30am–3pm and 5–10:30pm; Fri–Sat 11:30am–4pm and 5–11:30pm. From I-80 north, take the University Ave. exit and turn left onto Shattuck Ave. BART: Berkeley. CALIFORNIA.

California cuisine is so much a product of Alice Waters's genius that all other restaurants following in her wake should be dated "AAW" (After Alice Waters). Read the menus posted outside and you'll understand why. Most of the produce and meat comes from local farms and is organically produced, and after all these years, Alice still attends to her restaurant with great integrity and innovation.

Chez Panisse is a delightful redwood and stucco cottage with a brick terrace filled with flowering potted plants. The two dining areas, the cafe and the restaurant, both serve Mediterranean-inspired cuisine.

In the upstairs cafe are displays of pastries and fruit, and large bouquets of fresh flowers adorn an oak bar. At lunch or dinner, the menu might feature delicately smoked gravlax or roasted eggplant soup with pesto, followed by lamb ragout garnished with apricots, onions, and spices served with couscous.

The cozy downstairs restaurant, strewn with blossoming floral bouquets, is an appropriately warm environment to indulge in the fixed-price four-course gourmet dinner, which is served Tuesday to Thursday. Friday and Saturday, it's four courses plus an aperitif, and Monday is bargain night with a three-course dinner for $39.

The restaurant posts the menu, which changes daily, each Saturday for the following week. There's an excellent wine list ($20 to $200).

MODERATE

✪ **Cafe Rouge.** 1782 Fourth St. (between Delaware and Hearst). ☎ **510/525-1440.** Reservations recommended. Main courses $9.50–$24. AE, MC, V. Mon–Sat 11:30am–3pm; Tues–Sat 3–5pm (interim menu); Tues–Thurs 5:30–9:30pm; Fri–Sat 5:30–10:30pm; Sun 5–9pm. BISTRO.

After cooking at San Francisco's renowned Zuni Cafe for 10 years, chef-owner Marsha McBride launched her own restaurant, a sort of Zuni East. She brought former staff members and some of the restaurant's flavor with her, and now her sparse, loft-like dining room serves salads, rotisserie chicken with oil and thyme, grilled lamb chops, steaks, and homemade sausages. East Bay carnivores are especially happy with the burger; like Zuni's, it's top-notch.

O Chamé. 1830 Fourth St. (near Hearst). ☎ **510/841-8783.** Reservations recommended Fri–Sat. Main courses $8.50–$18.50. AE, DC, MC, V. Mon–Sat 11:30am–3pm; Mon–Thurs 5:30–9pm; Fri–Sat 5:30–9:30pm. JAPANESE.

Spare and plain in its decor, with ochre-colored walls marked with etched patterns, this spot has a meditative air to complement the traditional and experimental Japanese-inspired cuisine. The menu, which changes daily, offers meal-in-a-bowl dishes ($8.50 to $12.50) that allow a choice of soba or udon noodles in a clear soup with a variety of toppings—from shrimp and wakame seaweed to beef with burdock root and carrot. Appetizers include a flavorful melding of grilled shiitake mushrooms and sweet peppers, and portabello mushrooms, watercress, and green-onion pancakes. There's a sashimi of the day, and specials ($10 to $17.50) always include delicious roasted salmon.

✪ **Rivoli.** 1539 Solano Ave. ☎ **510/526-2542.** Reservations recommended. Main courses $14–$17. AE, DISC, MC, V. Mon–Thurs 5:30–9:30pm; Fri 5:30–10pm; Sat 5–10pm; Sun 5–9pm. CALIFORNIA.

One of the favored dinner destinations in the East Bay, Rivoli offers top-notch food at amazingly reasonable prices. In an otherwise uninteresting space, the owners have created a warm, intimate dining room, which overlooks a sweet little garden with visiting raccoons and possums. There's a wine bar near the entrance. Aside from a few house favorites, the menu changes entirely every 3 weeks to feature whatever's freshest and in season; the wine list follows suit with around a dozen by-the-glass options hand-picked to match the food. While many love it, I wasn't thrilled with the portabello-mushroom fritter, which in my mind was a glorified variation of the fried zucchini stick. However, plenty of dishes shine, including spring cassoulet with Liberty duck confit, Wilis Ranch pork, and house-made chicken sausage, white beans, fava beans, thyme, tomato, and bread crumbs. Finish the evening with a hot fudge sundae with whipped cream and toasted nuts.

INEXPENSIVE

Cambodiana's. 2156 University Ave. (between Shattuck and Oxford). ☎ **510/843-4630.** Reservations recommended. Main courses $6.25–$14; fixed-price dinner $11.50. AE, CB, DC, JCB, MC, V. Mon–Fri 11:30am–3pm; Sun–Thurs 5–9:30pm; Fri–Sat 5–10:30pm. CAMBODIAN.

For those who relish the spicy cuisine of Cambodia, this is quite a find. The decor is as colorful as the fare—brilliant blue, yellow, and green walls with Breuer-style chairs. Especially tasty choices include curry (chicken, beef, and so on), and Naga dishes with a sauce of tamarind, turmeric, lemongrass, shrimp paste, coconut-milk galinga, shallot, lemon leaf, sugar, and green chili. This sauce may smother salmon, prawns, chicken, or steak. Another tempting dish is chicken *chaktomuk,* prepared with pineapple, red peppers, and zucchini in soy and oyster sauce. There are plenty of vegetarian and low-cal options, and the three-course fixed-price dinner is an excellent value.

2 Oakland

10 miles E of San Francisco

Although it's less than a dozen miles from San Francisco, Oakland is worlds apart from its sister city across the bay. Originally little more than a cluster of ranches and farms, Oakland exploded in size and stature practically overnight when the last mile of transcontinental railroad track was laid down. Major shipping ports soon followed, and to this day, Oakland remains one of the busiest industrial ports on the West Coast.

The price for economic success, however, is Oakland's lowbrow reputation for being a predominantly working-class city, forever in the shadow of chic San Francisco. But with all its shortcomings and bad press, Oakland still manages to offer a few pleasant surprises for the handful of tourists who venture this way. Rent a sailboat on Lake Merritt, stroll along the waterfront, explore the fantastic Oakland Museum: They're all great reasons to hop the bay and spend a fog-free day exploring one of California's largest and most ethnically diversified cities.

ESSENTIALS
Bay Area Rapid Transit (BART) connects San Francisco and Oakland through one of the longest underwater transit tunnels in the world. Fares range from $1 to $4, depending on your station of origin; children under 5 ride free. BART trains operate Monday to Friday from 4am to midnight, Saturday 6am to midnight, Sunday 8am to midnight. Exit at the 12th Street station for downtown Oakland.

By car from San Francisco, take I-80 across the San Francisco–Oakland Bay Bridge and follow signs to downtown Oakland. Exit at Grand Avenue South for the Lake Merritt area.

Downtown Oakland lies between Grand Avenue on the north, I-980 on the west, Inner Harbor on the south, and Lake Merritt on the east. Between these landmarks are three BART stations (12th Street, 19th Street, and Lake Merritt), City Hall, the Oakland Museum, Jack London Square, and several other sights.

WHAT TO SEE & DO
Lake Merritt is Oakland's primary tourist attraction, along with Jack London Square (see below). Three and a half miles in circumference, the tidal lagoon was bridged and dammed in the 1860s and is now a wildlife refuge that is home to flocks of migrating ducks, herons, and geese. The 122-acre **Lakeside Park,** a popular place to picnic, feed the ducks, and escape the fog, surrounds the lake on three sides. At the **Sailboat House** (☎ 510/444-3807), in Lakeside Park along the north shore, you can rent sailboats, rowboats, pedal boats, or canoes for $6 to $12 per hour.

Another site worth visiting is Oakland's **Paramount Theatre,** 2025 Broadway (☎ 510/893-2300), an outstanding example of art deco architecture and decor. Built in 1931 and authentically restored in 1973, it's the city's main performing-arts center. Guided tours of the 3,000-seat theater are given the first and third Saturday of each month, excluding holidays. No reservations are necessary; just show up at 10am at the box office entrance on 21st Street at Broadway. Cameras are allowed, and admission is $1.

If you take pleasure in strolling sailboat-filled wharves or are a die-hard fan of Jack London, you might enjoy a visit to **Jack London Square.** Oakland's only patently tourist area, this low-key version of San Francisco's Fisherman's Wharf shamelessly plays up the fact that Jack London spent most of his youth along the waterfront. The square fronts the harbor, housing a tourist-tacky complex of boutiques and eateries that are about as far from the "call of the wild" as you can get. Most are open Monday to Saturday 10am to 7pm (some restaurants stay open later). One of the best options is live jazz at Yoshi's restaurant and club, 510 Embarcadero West (☎ **510/238-9200**). In the center of the square is a small reconstructed Yukon cabin in which Jack London lived while prospecting in the Klondike during the gold rush of 1897.

In the middle of Jack London Square you'll find a more authentic memorial, **Heinold's First and Last Chance Saloon**—a funky, friendly little bar and historic landmark that's worth a visit. This is where London did some of his writing and most of his drinking; the corner table he used has remained exactly as it was nearly a century ago. Also in the square are the mast and nameplate from USS *Oakland,* a ship that saw extensive action in the Pacific during World War II, and a wonderful museum filled with interesting London memorabilia.

The square is at Broadway and Embarcadero. Take I-880 to Broadway, turn south, and go to the end. Ride BART to 12th Street station, then walk south along Broadway (about half a mile); a free shuttle runs Monday through Friday 11am to 2pm. Or take bus no. 51A to the foot of Broadway.

Oakland Museum of California. 1000 Oak St. (at 10th St.) ☎ **888/625-6873**, or 510/238-2200 for recorded information. Admission $6 adults, $4 students and seniors, free for children under 6. Wed–Sat 10am–5pm; Sun noon–5pm. Closed Jan 1, July 4, Thanksgiving, Dec 25. From I-880 north, take the Oak St. exit; the museum is 5 blocks east. Or take I-580 to I-980 and exit at the Jackson St. ramp. BART: Lake Merritt station; walk 1 block north.

Two blocks south of the lake, the Oakland Museum of California incorporates just about everything you'd want to know about the state and its people, history, culture, geology, art, environment, and ecology. Inside a low, modern building set among sweeping gardens and terraces, it's actually three museums in one: exhibitions of works by California artists from Bierstadt to Diebenkorn; collections of historic artifacts, from Pomo Indian basketry to Country Joe McDonald's guitar; and re-creations of California habitats from the coast to the White Mountains. The museum holds major shows of California artists and exhibitions dedicated to major California movements, such as an "Awakening from the California Dream: An Environmental History." The museum also frequently shows photography from its huge collections.

Forty-five-minute guided tours leave from the gallery information desks on request or by appointment. There is a fine cafe, a **gallery** (☎ **510/834-2296**) that sells works by California artists, and a book and gift shop. The cafe is open Wednesday to Saturday 10am to 4pm, Sunday noon to 4pm.

WHERE TO DINE
EXPENSIVE

Citron. 5484 College Ave. (off the northeast end of Broadway between Taft and Lawton sts.). ☎ **510/653-5484.** Reservations recommended. Main courses $18–$28; 3-course fixed-price menu (Sun–Wed only) $26–$32. AE, DC, DISC, MC, V. Mon–Thurs 5:30–9:30pm; Fri 5:30–10pm; Sat 5–10pm; Sun 5–9pm. FRENCH/MEDITERRANEAN.

This petite, adorable French bistro was an instant smash when it opened in 1992, and it continues to earn raves for its small yet enticingly eclectic menu. Chef Chris Rossi draws the flavors of France, Italy, and Spain together with fresh California produce for Chez Panisse–like results. The menu changes every few weeks; dishes range from grilled Colorado lamb sirloin with wild-mushroom spoon bread and rosemary *jus,* to osso buco of lamb on a bed of flageolet bean and sun-dried tomato ragout, sprinkled with a pistachio gremolata garnish. The fresh salads and Citron "40 clove" chicken are also superb.

♥ Oliveto Cafe & Restaurant. Rockridge Market Hall, 5655 College Ave. (off the northeast end of Broadway at Shafter/Keith St., across from the Rockridge BART station). ☎ **510/547-5356.** Reservations recommended for restaurant. Main courses $16–$22. AE, DC, MC, V. Mon–Fri 11:30am–2pm; Mon–Sat 5:30–10pm; Sun 5–9pm. ITALIAN.

Paul Bertolli, former chef at the world-renowned Chez Panisse restaurant, jumped ship to open one of the top Italian restaurants in the Bay Area (and certainly the best in Oakland). During the week it's a madhouse at lunchtime, when local workers pile in for the wood-fired pizzas and tapas served in the lower-level cafe. The upstairs restaurant—with suave neo-Florentine decor and a partial open kitchen—is slightly more civil, packed nightly with fans of Bertolli's house-made pastas, sausages, and prosciutto. Oliveto has a wood-burning oven, flame-broiled rotisserie, and high-end liquor cabinet (that is, hard alcohol, but no mixed drinks). An assortment of pricey grills, braises, and roasts anchor the daily changing menu, but it's the reasonably priced pastas, pizzetas, and awesome salads that offer the most tang for your buck. *Tip:* There's free parking in the lot at the rear of the Market Hall building.

MODERATE

Bay Wolf. 3853 Piedmont Ave. (off Broadway between 40th St. and MacArthur Blvd.). ☎ **510/655-6004.** Reservations recommended. Main courses $15.50–$19.50. AE, MC, V. Mon–Fri 11:30am–2pm and 6–9pm; Sat–Sun 5:30–9:30pm. CALIFORNIA.

The life span of most Bay Area restaurants is about a year; Bay Wolf, one of Oakland's most revered restaurants, has been going strong for more than 2 decades. The converted brown Victorian is a comfortably familiar sight for most East Bay diners, who have come here for years to let chef-owner Michael Wilds do the cooking. Bay Wolf enjoys a reputation for simple yet sagacious preparations using only fresh ingredients. Main courses include highly regarded Liberty Ranch duck with sweet potato flan and chard; flavorful seafood stew seasoned with saffron and brimful of cracked Dungeness crab, prawns, rockfish, and mussels; and tender braised lamb shank with white beans, artichokes, and rosemary. Informal service means you can leave the tie at home. The front deck has heat lamps, allowing for open-air evening dining—a treat San Franciscans rarely experience.

3 Angel Island & Tiburon

8 miles N of San Francisco

A federal and state wildlife refuge, Angel Island is the largest of the San Francisco Bay's three islets (the others being Alcatraz and Yerba Buena). The island has been, at various times, a prison, a quarantine station for immigrants, a missile base, and even a favorite site for duels. Nowadays, most visitors are content with picnicking on the large green lawn that fronts the docking area; loaded with the appropriate recreational supplies, they claim a barbecue, plop their fannies down on the lush green grass, and while away an afternoon free of phones, televisions, and traffic. Hiking, mountain biking, and guided tram tours are other popular activities.

Tiburon, situated on a peninsula of the same name, looks like a cross between a fishing village and a Hollywood western set—imagine San Francisco reduced to toy dimensions. The seacoast town rambles over a series of green hills and ends up at a spindly, multicolored pier on the waterfront, like a Fisherman's Wharf in miniature. But in reality it's an extremely plush patch of yacht-club suburbia, as you'll see by the

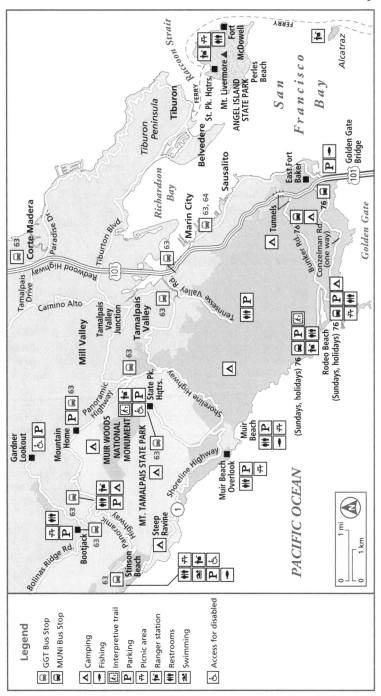

Legend

☐🚌	GGT Bus Stop
☐🚌	MUNI Bus Stop
⬛	Camping
☗	Fishing
🚶	Interpretive trail
P	Parking
⛱	Picnic area
👫	Ranger station
🚻	Restrooms
🏊	Swimming
♿	Access for disabled

marine craft and the homes of their owners. Ramshackle, color-splashed old frame houses line Main Street, sheltering chic boutiques, souvenir stores, antique shops, and art galleries. Other roads are narrow, winding, and hilly, and lead up to dramatically situated homes. The view of San Francisco's skyline and the islands in the bay is a good enough reason to pay the precious price to live here.

ESSENTIALS

Ferries of the **Blue & Gold Fleet** (☎ 415/705-5555) from Pier 41 (Fisherman's Wharf) travel to both Angel Island and Tiburon. Boats run on a seasonal schedule; phone for departure information. The round-trip fare is $12 to Angel Island or Tiburon, half-price for kids 5 to 11, and free for kids under 5.

By car from San Francisco, take U.S. 101 to the Tiburon/Highway 131 exit, then follow Tiburon Boulevard all the way into downtown, a 40-minute drive from San Francisco. Catch the **Tiburon–Angel Island Ferry** (☎ 415/435-2131) to Angel Island from the dock at Tiburon Boulevard and Main Street. The 15-minute round-trip, which runs only on weekends, costs $7 for adults, $5 for children 5 to 11, $1 for bikes. One child under 5 is free with each paying adult.

WHAT TO SEE & DO ON ANGEL ISLAND

Passengers disembark from the ferry at **Ayala Cove,** a small marina abutting a huge lawn area equipped with tables, benches, barbecue pits, and rest rooms. Also at Ayala Cove are a small store, gift shop, cafe (with surprisingly good grub), and overpriced mountain-bike rental shop.

Angel Island's 12 miles of hiking and mountain-bike trails include the **Perimeter Road,** a partly paved path that circles the island. It winds past disused troop barracks, former gun emplacements, and other military buildings; several turnoffs lead to the top of Mount Livermore, 776 feet above the bay. Sometimes referred to as the "Ellis Island of the West," Angel Island was used as a holding area for Chinese immigrants awaiting their citizenship papers from 1910 to 1940. You can still see some faded Chinese characters on the walls of the barracks where the immigrants were held. During the warmer months you can camp at a limited number of sites; reservations are required.

Guided sea-kayak tours are also available. The all-day trips, which include a catered lunch, combine the thrill of paddling stable two- or three-person kayaks with an informative, naturalist-led tour that encircles the island (conditions permitting). All equipment is provided, kids are welcome, and no experience is necessary. Rates run about $95 per person. For more information, call **Sea Trek** (☎ 415/332-8494).

The 1-hour **Angel Island Tram Tour** (☎ 925/426-3058) costs $10 for adults, $9 for seniors, $7 for children 6 to 12; children under 6 are free.

For recorded information about **Angel Island State Park,** call ☎ 415/435-1915.

WHAT TO SEE & DO IN TIBURON

The main thing to do in Tiburon is stroll along the waterfront, pop into the stores, and spend an easy $50 on drinks and appetizers before heading back to the city. For a taste of the wine country, stop in at **Windsor Vineyards,** 72 Main St. (☎ 800/214-9463 or 415/435-3113)—its Victorian tasting room dates from 1888. Thirty-five choices are available for a free tasting with a wine purchase. Wine accessories and gifts—glasses, cork pullers, carry packs (which hold six bottles), gourmet sauces, posters, and maps—are also available. Ask about personalized labels for your selections. The shop is open Sunday to Thursday 10am to 6pm, Friday and Saturday 10am to 7pm.

WHERE TO DINE IN TIBURON

Guaymas. 5 Main St. ☎ **415/435-6300.** Reservations recommended. Main courses $12–$20. AE, CB, DC, DISC, MC, V. Mon–Thurs 11:30am–10pm; Fri–Sat 11:30am–11pm; Sun 10:30am–10pm. Ferry: Walk about 10 paces from the landing. From U.S. 101, exit at Tiburon/Hwy. 131; follow Tiburon Blvd. 5 miles and turn right onto Main St. Restaurant is behind the bakery. MEXICAN.

Guaymas offers authentic Mexican regional cuisine and a spectacular panoramic view of San Francisco and the bay. In good weather, the two outdoor patios are almost always packed with diners soaking in the sun and scene. Inside, colorful Mexican artwork brightens the beige walls. Should you feel chilled, to the rear of the dining room is a beehive-shaped adobe fireplace.

Guaymas is named after a fishing village on Mexico's Sea of Cortez, and both the town and the restaurant are famous for their *camarones* (giant shrimp). The restaurant also features ceviche, handmade tamales, and charcoal-grilled beef, seafood, and fowl. Save room for dessert, especially the outrageously scrumptious fritter with "drunken" bananas and ice cream. In addition to a good selection of California wines, the restaurant offers an exceptional variety of tequilas, Mexican beers, and mineral waters flavored with flowers, grains, and fruits.

✪ **Sam's Anchor Café.** 27 Main St. ☎ **415/435-4527.** Main courses $8–$18.95. AE, DC, DISC, MC, V. Mon–Thurs 11am–10pm; Fri 11am–10:30pm; Sat 10am–10:30pm; Sun 9:30am–10pm. Ferry: Walk from the landing. From U.S. 101, exit at Tiburon/Hwy. 131, follow Tiburon Blvd. 4 miles, and turn right onto Main St. SEAFOOD.

Summer Sundays are liveliest in Tiburon, when weekend boaters tie up at the docks of waterside restaurants like this one. Sam's is the kind of place where you and your cronies can take off your shoes and have a fun, relaxed time eating burgers and drinking margaritas outside on the pier. The fare is typical—sandwiches, salads, and seafood such as deep-fried oysters—but the quality and selection is inconsequential: beers, burgers, and a designated driver are all you really need.

4 Sausalito

5 miles N of San Francisco

Just off the northern end of the Golden Gate Bridge is the eclectic little town of Sausalito, a slightly bohemian, nonchalant, studiedly quaint adjunct to San Francisco. With approximately 7,500 residents, Sausalito feels rather like St. Tropez on the French Riviera—minus the starlets and the social rat race. It has its quota of paper millionaires, but they rub their permanently suntanned shoulders with a good number of hard-up artists, struggling authors, shipyard workers, and fishers. Next to the swank restaurants, plush bars, and antique shops and galleries, you'll see hamburger joints, beer parlors, and secondhand bookstores. Sausalito's main strip is Bridgeway, which runs along the water. Those in the know make a quick detour to Caledonia Street, 1 block inland; not only is it less congested, but there's a far better selection of cafes and shops.

ESSENTIALS

The **Golden Gate Ferry Service** fleet, Ferry Building (☎ **415/923-2000**), operates between the San Francisco Ferry Building, at the foot of Market Street, and downtown Sausalito. Service is frequent, departing at reasonable intervals every day of the year except January 1, Thanksgiving, and December 25. Phone for an exact schedule. The ride takes a half hour, and one-way fares are $4.80 for adults and $3.55 for kids 6 to 12. Seniors and passengers with disabilities ride for $2.35; children 5 and under ride free. Family rates are available on weekends.

Ferries of the **Blue & Gold Fleet** (☎ 415/705-5555) leave from Pier 41 (Fisherman's Wharf) and cost $12 round-trip; half-price for kids 5 to 11. Boats run on a seasonal schedule; phone for departure information.

By car from San Francisco, take U.S. 101 north, then the first right after the Golden Gate Bridge (Alexander exit). Alexander becomes Bridgeway in Sausalito.

WHAT TO SEE & DO

Above all, Sausalito has scenery and sunshine, for once you cross the Golden Gate Bridge you're out of the San Francisco fog patch and under blue California sky (we hope). Houses cover the town's steep hills, overlooking a forest of masts on the waters below. Most of the tourist action, which is almost singularly limited to window shopping and eating, takes place at sea level on Bridgeway.

Sausalito is a mecca for shoppers seeking handmade, original, and offbeat clothes and footwear, as well as arts and crafts. The town's best shops are in the alleys, malls, and second-floor boutiques reached by steep, narrow staircases on and off Bridgeway. Caledonia Street, which runs parallel to Bridgeway 1 block inland, is home to more shops.

Bay Model Visitors Center. 2100 Bridgeway. ☎ **415/332-3871.** Free admission. Labor Day–Memorial Day Tues–Sat 9am–4pm; Memorial Day–Labor Day Tues–Fri 9am–4pm, Sat–Sun and holidays 10am–5pm.

The U.S. Army Corps of Engineers uses this high-tech, $1^1/_2$-acre model of San Francisco's bay and delta to resolve problems and observe the impact changes in water flow will have. The model reproduces (in scale) the rise and fall of tides, the flows and currents of water, and the mixing of fresh water and saltwater, and indicates trends in sediment movement. There's a 10-minute film and a tour, but the most interesting time to visit is when it's in use, so call ahead.

WHERE TO STAY
VERY EXPENSIVE

✪ **The Inn Above Tide.** 30 El Portal (next to the Sausalito Ferry Landing), Sausalito, CA 94965. ☎ **800/893-8433** or 415/332-9535. Fax 415/332-6714. www.innabovetide.com. 30 units. A/C TV TEL. $215–$540 double. Rates include continental breakfast and evening wine and cheese. 2-night minimum stay on weekends. AE, DC, MC, V. Valet parking $8.

Perched directly over the bay atop well-grounded pilings, this former luxury apartment complex underwent a $4 million transformation into one of Sausalito's—if not the Bay Area's—finest accommodations. The view clinches it: Every room affords an unparalleled panorama of the San Francisco Bay, including a postcard-quality vista of the city glimmering in the distance. Should you manage to tear yourself away from your private deck, you'll find that 22 of the sumptuously appointed rooms sport a romantic little fireplace. Some have a vast sunken tub with Jacuzzi jets, remote-control air-conditioning, and wondrously comfortable queen- or king-size beds. Soothing shades of pale green and blue highlight the decor, which blends in well with the bayscape outside. Be sure to request that your breakfast and newspaper be delivered to your deck, then cancel your early appointments: On sunny mornings, nobody checks out early.

EXPENSIVE

Casa Madrona. 801 Bridgeway, Sausalito, CA 94965. ☎ **800/567-9524** or 415/332-0502. Fax 415/332-2537. 35 units. MINIBAR TEL. $188–$280 double; $300 Madrona Villa suite. Rates include breakfast (served 7:30–9:30am). 2-night minimum stay on weekends. AE, MC, V. Parking $7. Ferry: Walk across the street from the landing. From U.S. 101 north, take the first right after the Golden Gate Bridge (Alexander exit); Alexander becomes Bridgeway.

Sooner or later most visitors to Sausalito look up and wonder at the ornate mansion on the hill. It's part of Casa Madrona, a hideaway by the bay built in 1885 by a wealthy lumber baron. The epitome of luxury in its day, the mansion had slipped into decay when Henri Deschamps converted it into a hotel and restaurant. Successive renovations and extensions have added a rambling, New England–style building to the hillside below the main house. Now a certified historic landmark, the hotel offers rooms, suites, and cottages. The 16 newest units are uniquely decorated by local designers. The "1,000 Cranes" is Asian in theme, with lots of ash wood and lacquer. "Artist's Loft" is reminiscent of a rustic Parisian artist's studio. "Summer House" is decked out in white wicker. Other rooms in the mansion are decorated in a variety of styles; some have Jacuzzis, and others have fireplaces. The newest rooms overlook the water, with panoramic views of the San Francisco skyline and bay.

Dining/Diversions: Mikayla Restaurant (☎ **415/331-5888**) serves superb West Coast cuisine in an unbelievably beautiful setting overlooking the bay and San Francisco skyline. Renowned local artist and designer Laurel Burch orchestrated the decor. It's open for dinner nightly 6 to 10pm and for Sunday brunch 10:30am to 2:30pm.

WHERE TO DINE
EXPENSIVE

Ondine. 558 Bridgeway. ☎ **415/331-1133.** www.ondinerestaurant.com. Reservations recommended. Main courses $24–$35. AE, DC, JCB, MC, V. Daily 5–10pm; Sun 10am–2pm. ASIAN/FRENCH.

Sausalito's best restaurant entered the scene in 1999, delighting Marin diners—and legions of fans crossing the bridge. It offers the ultimate in bayfront views, elegance, service, and the East-meets-West delights of Japanese-trained chef Seiji Wakabayashi, who hails from Wolfgang Puck's Spago. Along with a panoramic vista of the Alcatraz, Angel Island, Bay Bridge, and Tiburon and the wildly colorful room itself, the view on the plate is worth extra attention. Chef "Waka" takes kung-pao cooking to new heights: His luxurious version includes lobster, shrimp, and squid sausage with peanuts, Thai basil, and chiles. Grilled tuna and rock shrimp risotto goes exotic, with coconut-banana curry sauce. Salmon? Perhaps sesame-crusted and served with ginger-sake beurre blanc. Desserts, also whipped up by Waka, are almost as sweet and decadent as the view.

MODERATE

Guernica. 2009 Bridgeway. ☎ **415/332-1512.** Reservations recommended. Main courses $11.75–$17. AE, MC, V. Daily 5–10pm. From U.S. 101 north, take the first right after the Golden Gate Bridge (Alexander exit); Alexander becomes Bridgeway in Sausalito. FRENCH/BASQUE.

Established in 1976, Guernica is one of those funky old restaurants that you'd probably pass up for something more chic and modern down the street if you didn't know better. What? You don't know about Guernica's legendary Paella Valenciana? Well, now you do. Be sure to call ahead and order it in advance, and bring a partner, 'cause it's served for two but will feed three. Begin with an appetizer of artichoke hearts or escargots. Other main courses range from pork loin "New Orleans style" to hearty rack of lamb Guernica. Rich desserts include such in-season specialties as strawberry tart, peach Melba, and Basque-style rice pudding.

PICNIC, ANYONE?

Even Sausalito's naysayers have to admit that it's hard not to enjoy eating your way down Bridgeway on a warm, sunny day. If the crowds are too much or the prices too steep at the bayside restaurants, grab a bite to go for an impromptu picnic in the park fronting the marina.

Caledonia Kitchen. 400 Caledonia St. ☎ **415/331-0220.** No credit cards. Daily 8am–7pm. DELI.

Caledonia Kitchen is the sort of place you wish were just around the corner from your house. The beautiful little cafe serves a huge assortment of fresh salads, soups, chili, gourmet sandwiches, and inexpensive entrees like herbed roast chicken or vegetarian lasagna for only $4.95. Continental-style breakfast items and good coffee and espresso drinks are also on the menu.

Hamburgers. 737 Bridgeway. ☎ **415/332-9471.** No credit cards. Daily 11am–5pm. BURGERS.

Like the name says, the specialty at this tiny, narrow cafe is juicy flame-broiled hamburgers, arguably Marin County's best. Look for the rotating grill in the window off Bridgeway, then stand in line and salivate with the rest. Chicken burgers are a slightly healthier option. Order a side of fries, grab a bunch of napkins, and head to the park across the street.

5 Muir Woods & Mount Tamalpais

12 miles N of the Golden Gate Bridge

While the rest of Marin County's redwood forests were being devoured to feed San Francisco's turn-of-the-century building spree, Muir Woods, in a remote ravine on the flanks of Mount Tamalpais, escaped destruction in favor of easier pickings.

MUIR WOODS

Although the magnificent California redwoods have been successfully transplanted to five continents, their homeland is a 500-mile strip along the mountainous coast of southwestern Oregon and northern California. The coast redwood, or *Sequoia sempervirens,* is the tallest tree in the immediate region; the largest known specimen, in the Redwood National Forest, towers 367.8 feet. It has an even larger relative, the *Sequoiadendron giganteum* of the California Sierra Nevada, but the coastal variety is stunning enough. Soaring toward the sky like a wooden cathedral, Muir Woods is unlike any other forest in the world and an experience you won't soon forget.

Granted, Muir Woods is tiny compared to the Redwood National Forest farther north, but you can still get a pretty good idea of what it must have been like when these giants dominated the entire coastal region. What is truly amazing is that they exist a mere 6 miles (as the crow flies) from San Francisco—close enough, unfortunately, that tour buses arrive in droves on the weekends. You can avoid the masses by hiking up the Ocean View Trail and returning on the Fern Creek Trail. The moderately challenging hike shows off the woods' best sides and leaves the lazy-butts behind.

To reach Muir Woods from San Francisco, cross the Golden Gate Bridge heading north on Highway 101, take the Stinson Beach/Highway 1 exit heading west, and follow the signs (and the traffic). The park is open daily 8am to sunset, and there's an admission fee of $2 per person over 16. There's also a small gift shop, educational displays, and docent-led tours that you're welcome to stand in on. For more information, call the **Muir Woods information line** (☎ **415/388-2595**).

If you don't have a car, you can book a bus trip with the **Red & White Fleet** (☎ **877/855-5506** or 415/447-0597), which takes you straight to Muir Woods and makes a short stop in Sausalito on the way back. The 3¹/₂-hour tours run several times daily and cost $28 for adults, $13 for children. Call for information and departure times.

MOUNT TAMALPAIS

The birthplace of mountain biking, Mount Tam—as the locals call it—is the Bay Area's favorite outdoor playground and the most dominant mountain in the region. Most every local has his or her secret trail and scenic overlook, as well as an opinion on the raging debate between mountain bikers and hikers (a touchy subject). The main trails—mostly fire roads—see a lot of foot and bicycle traffic on weekends, particularly on clear, sunny days when you can see a hundred miles in all directions, from the foothills of the Sierra to the western horizon. It's a great place to escape from the city for a leisurely hike and to soak in breathtaking views of the bay.

To get to Mount Tamalpais **by car,** cross the Golden Gate Bridge heading north on Highway 101, and take the Stinson Beach/Highway 1 exit. Follow the shoreline highway about 2$^{1}/_{2}$ miles, turn into Pantoll Road, and continue for about a mile to Ridgecrest Boulevard. Ridgecrest winds to a parking lot below East Peak. From there, it's a 15-minute hike up to the top.

6 Point Reyes National Seashore

35 miles N of San Francisco

The National Seashore system was created to protect rural and undeveloped stretches of the coast from the pressures brought on by soaring real-estate values and increasing population. Nowhere is the success of the system more evident than at Point Reyes. Residents of the surrounding towns—Inverness, Point Reyes Station, and Olema—have steadfastly resisted runaway development. You won't find any strip malls or fast-food joints here, just a laid-back coastal town with cafes and country inns, where gentle living prevails.

Although the peninsula's people and wildlife live in harmony above the ground, the situation beneath the soil is much more volatile. The infamous San Andreas Fault separates Point Reyes—the northernmost land mass on the Pacific Plate—from the rest of California, which rests on the North American Plate. Point Reyes is making its way toward Alaska at a rate of about 2 inches per year, but at times, it has moved much faster. In 1906, Point Reyes jumped north almost 20 feet in an instant, leveling San Francisco and jolting the rest of the state. The half-mile Earthquake Trail, near the Bear Valley Visitor Center, illustrates this geological drama with a loop through an area torn by the slipping fault. Shattered fences, rifts in the ground, and a barn knocked off its foundation by the quake illustrate how alive the earth is. If that doesn't convince you, a seismograph in the visitor center will.

ESSENTIALS

Point Reyes is only 30 miles northwest of San Francisco, but it takes at least 90 minutes to reach by car (it's all the small towns, not the topography, that slow you down). The easiest route is Sir Francis Drake Boulevard from Highway 101 south of San Rafael; it takes its bloody time getting to Point Reyes, but does so without any detours. For a much longer but more scenic route, take the Stinson Beach/Highway 1 exit off Highway 101 just south of Sausalito and follow Highway 1 north.

As soon as you arrive at Point Reyes, stop at the **Bear Valley Visitor Center** (☎ **415/663-1092**) on Bear Valley Road (look for the small sign just north of Olema on Highway 1) and pick up a free Point Reyes trail map. The rangers are extremely friendly and helpful and can answer any questions about the National Seashore. Be sure to check out the great natural-history and cultural displays. The center is open weekdays from 9am to 5pm, weekends from 8am to 5pm.

Entrance to the park is free. **Camping** is $10 per site per night, and permits are required. Reservations can be made up to 3 months in advance by calling ☎ **415/663-8054** Monday to Friday 9am to 2pm.

WHAT TO SEE & DO

When headed to any part of the Point Reyes coast, expect to spend the day surrounded by nature at its finest; however, bear in mind that as beautiful as the wilderness can be, it's also untamable. The bone-chilling waters in these areas are not only home to a vast array of sea life, including sharks, but are also unpredictable and dangerous. There are no lifeguards on duty, and swimming is strongly discouraged because of the waves and rip tides. Pets are not permitted on any of the area's trails.

By far the most popular—and crowded—attraction at Point Reyes National Seashore is the venerable **Point Reyes Lighthouse** (☎ **415/669-1534**) at the westernmost tip of Point Reyes. Even if you plan to forgo the 308 steps to the lighthouse, it's still worth a visit. The dramatic scenery includes thousands of common murres and prides of sea lions that bask on the rock far below (binoculars come in handy).

The lighthouse is also the top spot on the California coast to observe **gray whales** as they make their southward and northward migration along the coast from January through April. The annual round trip is 10,000 miles—one of the longest mammal migrations known. The whales head south in December and January and return north in March. *Note:* If you plan to drive to the lighthouse to whale watch, arrive early, because parking is limited. If possible, come on a weekday. On a weekend or holiday from December through April, it's wise to park at the Drake's Beach Visitor Center and take the shuttle bus (weather permitting) to the lighthouse and on to Chimney Rock to watch elephant seals. The shuttle bus fare is $3.50 for adults, free for children under 13. Dress warmly—it's often quite cold and windy—and bring binoculars.

Whale watching is far from the only activity at the Point Reyes National Seashore. On weekends rangers conduct many different tours: You can walk along the Bear Valley Trail, spotting the wildlife at the ocean's edge; see the waterfowl at Fivebrooks Pond; explore tide pools; view some of North America's most beautiful ducks in the wetlands of Limantour; hike to the promontory overlooking Chimney Rock to see the sea lions, harbor seals, elephant seals, and seabirds; or take a guided walk along the San Andreas Fault to observe the site of the epicenter of the 1906 earthquake and learn about the regional geology. And this is just a sampling. Tours vary seasonally; call the **Bear Valley Visitors Center** (☎ **415/663-1092**) or request a copy of *Park Paper,* which includes a schedule of activities and other useful information. Many tours are suitable for travelers with disabilities.

Some of the park's best—and least crowded—highlights can be approached only on foot. They include **Alamere Falls,** a freshwater stream that cascades down a 40-foot bluff onto Wildcat Beach, and **Tomales Point Trail,** which passes through the Tule Elk Reserve, a protected haven for roaming herds of tule elk that once numbered in the thousands. Hiking most of the trails usually ends up being an all-day outing, however, so it's best to split a 2-day trip into a "by car" day and a "by foot" day.

If you're into bird watching, you'll definitely want to visit the **Point Reyes Bird Observatory** (☎ **415/868-1221**), one of the few full-time ornithological research stations in the United States. It's at the southeast end of the park on Mesa Road. This is where ornithologists keep an eye on more than 400 feathered species. Admission to the visitor center and nature trail is free, and visitors are welcome to observe the tricky process of catching and banding the birds. The observatory is open daily from 15 minutes after sunrise to sunset. Banding hours vary; call (☎ **415/868-0655**) for exact times.

Johnson's Oyster Farm

If you want to escape the crowds and enjoy some stinky man-made entertainment, head to Johnson's Oyster Farm. Located on the edge of Drakes Estero (a large saltwater lagoon on the Point Reyes peninsula that produces nearly 20% of California's commercial oyster yield), Johnson's might look and smell like a dump, but those tasty bivalves don't come any fresher or cheaper. Granted, it doesn't look like much—a cluster of trailer homes, shacks, and oyster tanks surrounded by huge piles of oyster shells—but that certainly doesn't detract from the taste of fresh-out-of-the-water oysters dipped in Johnson's special sauce. The popular modus operandi is 1) buy a couple of dozen, 2) head for an empty campsite along the bay, 3) fire up the barbecue pit (don't forget the charcoal), 4) split and 'cue the little guys, 5) slather them in Johnson's special sauce, and 6) slurp 'em down. Johnson's (☎ 415/669-1149) is off Sir Francis Drake Boulevard, about 6 miles west(ish) of Inverness. Open Tuesday to Saturday 8am to 4:30pm, Sunday 9am to 4:30pm.

One of my favorite things to do in Point Reyes is paddling through placid Tomales Bay, a haven for migrating birds and marine mammals. **Tamal Saka Tomales Bay Kayaking** (☎ 415/663-1743; www.tamalsaka.com) organizes kayak trips, including 3-hour sunset outings, $3^{1}/_{2}$-hour full-moon paddles, yoga tours, day trips, and longer excursions. Instruction, clinics, and boat delivery are available, and all ages and levels are welcome. Prices for tours start at $45. Rentals begin at $25 for one person, $35 for two. Don't worry—the kayaks are very stable, and there are no waves to contend with. The launching point is on Highway 1 at the Marshall Boatworks in Marshall, 8 miles north of Point Reyes Station. Open daily 9am to 6pm and by appointment.

WHERE TO STAY

Inns of Marin, P.O. Box 547, Point Reyes Station, CA 94956 (☎ 800/887-2880 or 415/663-2000), is a free service that can help you find accommodations ranging from one-room cottages to inns to complete vacation homes. Many places have a 2-night minimum, but at slow times they might make an exception. They can also refer you to restaurants, hiking, and area attractions.

EXPENSIVE

✪ **Manka's Inverness Lodge & Restaurant.** 30 Callendar St. (at Argyle St. off Sir Francis Drake Blvd., 3 blocks north of downtown Inverness), P.O. Box 1110, Inverness, CA 94937. ☎ **800/58-LODGE** or 415/669-1034. Fax 415/669-1598. www.mankas.com. 14 units, 2 cabins. $185–$415 double; $265–$450 cabin. MC, V.

If there was ever a reason to pack your bags and leave San Francisco for a day or two, this is it. A former hunting and fishing lodge, Manka's looks like something out of a Hans Christian Andersen fairy tale, right down to the tree-limb bed stands and the cook's roasted venison sausage in front of the hearth. It's all terribly romantic in a Jack London–ish sort of way, and tastefully done. The lodge consists of a superb restaurant on the first floor, four rooms upstairs (*Tip:* Rooms 1 and 2 have large private decks), and four rooms in the Redwood Annex. Two spacious one-bedroom cabins, behind the lodge and on the water, have living rooms and kitchenettes. For the ultimate romantic splurge, inquire about the three secluded guesthouses: Grizzly Lodge, Boat House, and Chicken Ranch.

Dining/Diversions: The lodge's reputation is built on its rustic and romantic restaurant, which dominates the bottom floor. The specialty of the house is game and fish, including oysters from Tomales Bay. The fixed-price offerings go for $48 to $68. The limited menu might feature pheasant with Madeira *jus,* mashed potatoes, and wild-huckleberry jam; black-buck antelope chops with sweet-corn salsa; or, everybody's favorite, pan-seared elk tenderloin. It's open for dinner Thursday to Monday, spring through fall, and weekends only during the winter.

MODERATE

Bear Valley Inn. 88 Bear Valley Rd., Olema, CA 94950. ☎ **415/663-1777.** 3 units, none with bathroom. $120 double. Rates include breakfast. MC, V.

This venerable two-story 1899 house has survived everything from a major earthquake to a recent forest fire, which is lucky for you because you'll be hard pressed to find a better B&B for the price in Point Reyes. Granted, the Bear Valley Inn isn't perfect—the rooms lack private bathrooms and the main highway is a tad too close—but it's loaded with turn-of-the-19th-century English country farmhouse charm, right down to the profusion of flowers and vines outside and comfy chairs fronting a toasty-warm woodstove inside. It's in a great location, too, with three good restaurants only a block away, and the entire National Seashore at your doorstep.

INEXPENSIVE

Motel Inverness. 12718 Sir Francis Drake Blvd., Inverness, CA 94937. ☎ **415/669-1081.** 7 units. TV. From $89 double. AE, DISC, MC, V.

Finding an inexpensive place to stay in Point Reyes is next to impossible, because hoity-toity B&Bs reign supreme. There is, however, one exception—Motel Inverness, a homey, well-maintained lodging fronting Tomales Bay. For the outdoor adventurer who plans on spending as little time indoors as possible, it's the perfect place to hole up. (Those seeking a little romance should dig a little deeper and opt for Manka's; see above.) Each guest room—all of which were completely renovated and refurnished in May 1998—comes with a queen-size bed, skylight, new mattresses, and cable TV. Attached to the hotel is a giant "great" room, complete with pool table to distract the kids; parents can relax on the back lawn overlooking the bay, bird sanctuary, and rolling green hills beyond. No smoking.

WHERE TO DINE

See "Where to Stay," above, for details on the highly recommended **Manka's Inverness Lodge and Restaurant.**

MODERATE

Station House Café. Main St., Point Reyes Station. ☎ **415/663-1515.** Reservations recommended. Breakfast $4.45–$7.50; main courses $9–$20. DISC, MC, V. Sun–Thurs 8am–9pm; Fri–Sat 8am–10pm. AMERICAN.

For more than 2 decades the Station House Café has been a favorite pit stop for Bay Areans headed to and from Point Reyes. It's a friendly, low-key place with an open kitchen, an outdoor garden dining area (key on sunny days), and live music on weekends. Breakfast dishes include a Hangtown fry with local oysters and bacon, and eggs with creamed spinach and mashed-potato pancakes. Lunch and dinner specials might include fettuccine with fresh local mussels steamed in white wine and butter sauce, two-cheese polenta served with fresh spinach sauté and grilled garlic-buttered tomato, or a daily fresh salmon special—all made from local produce, seafood, and organically raised Niman-Schell Farms beef. The cafe has an extensive list of fine California wines and local imported beers.

INEXPENSIVE

The Gray Whale. 12781 Sir Francis Drake Blvd., Inverness. ☎ **415/669-1244.** Main courses $6–$10. MC, V. Sun–Thurs 11am–8pm; Fri–Sat 11am–9pm. ITALIAN.

For more than a decade, the Gray Whale cafe has been another popular stop for visitors to the lighthouse at Point Reyes. Why so popular? First, it's cheap: Sandwiches—such as roasted eggplant with pesto and mozzarella—are only $5, as are most salads and pastas. Second, it's pretty good. Personal favorites are the specialty pizzas, such as the Californian (artichoke hearts, fresh basil, and tomatoes) and the Vegetarian (baked eggplant, roasted onions and romas, broccoli, and piles of freshly grated Parmesan cheese). Veteran hikers and mountain bikers stop by for an espresso booster, sipped on the small patio overlooking the block-long town of Inverness.

Taqueria La Quinta. 11285 Hwy. 1 (at Third and Main sts.), Point Reyes Station. ☎ **415/663-8868.** Main courses $4–$9. No credit cards. Wed–Mon 11:30am–7pm. MEXICAN.

Fresh, good, fast, and cheap: What more could you ask for in a restaurant? Taqueria La Quinta has been one of my favorite lunch stops in downtown Point Reyes for years and years. A huge selection of Mexican-American standards is posted above the counter, but those in the know inquire about the seafood specials. It's all self-serve. Watch out for the salsa—that sucker's hot.

7 Half Moon Bay

28 miles SW of San Francisco

A mere 45-minute drive from the teeming streets of San Francisco, lies a heavenly little seaside hamlet called Half Moon Bay, one of the finest—and friendliest—small towns on the California coast. Other coastal communities, like Bolinas, make tourists unwelcome, but Half Moon Bay residents are disarmingly amicable, bestowing greetings on anyone and everyone who stops for a visit.

Only in the past decade has Half Moon Bay begun to capitalize on its golden beaches, mild climate, and proximity to San Francisco, so you won't find the ultra-touristy machinations that result in gaudy theme parks and time-share condos. What you will find is a peaceful, unfettered slice of textbook California: pristine beaches, redwood forests, nature preserves, rustic fishing harbors, horse ranches, organic farms, and a host of superb inns and restaurants—everything you need for the perfect weekend getaway.

ESSENTIALS

GETTING THERE   There is no public transportation from San Francisco to Half Moon Bay. There are two ways to get here: the fast way and the scenic way. To save time, take Highway 92 west from Highway 280 or Highway 101 out of San Francisco, which takes you over a small mountain range and drops you directly into Half Moon Bay. A better—and far prettier—route is Highway 1, which technically starts at the south end of the Golden Gate Bridge and veers southwest to the shoreline a few miles south of Daly City. Both routes to Half Moon Bay are clearly marked with numerous signs.

Downtown Half Moon Bay is easy to miss, because it is not on Highway 1. It's a few hundred yards inland; head 2 blocks up Highway 92 from the Highway 1 intersection, then turn south at the Shell gas station onto Main Street until you cross a small bridge.

Travel Tip

Temperatures rarely venture into the 70s in Half Moon Bay, so be sure to pack for cool (and often wet) weather.

VISITOR INFORMATION For more information, contact the **Half Moon Bay Coastside Chamber of Commerce,** 520 Kelly Ave., Half Moon Bay, CA 94019 (☎ **650/726-8380;** www.halfmoonbaychamber.org).

WHAT TO SEE & DO

The best things to do in Half Moon Bay are the same things the locals do. For example, there's a wonderful paved beach trail that winds 3 miles from Half Moon Bay to Pillar Point Harbor. Walking, biking, jogging, and skating are all kosher, and be sure to keep a lookout for dolphins and whales. Bicycles can be rented from the **Bicyclery,** 101A & B Main St. (☎ **650/726-6000**), in downtown Half Moon Bay. Prices range from $8 to $12 an hour to $25 to $30 per day.

Half Moon Bay is also known for its organically grown produce. The best place to stock up on fruits and vegetables is the **Andreotti Family Farm,** 329 Kelly Ave., off Highway 1 (☎ **650/726-9461** or 650/726-9151). Every Friday, Saturday, and Sunday a member of the family slides open the door to the weathered old barn at 10am sharp to reveal a cornucopia of strawberries, artichokes, cucumbers, and the like. It's a terribly charming old-fashioned outfit that's been in business since 1926. To get there, head toward the beach and you'll see it on your right-hand side. Open until 6pm year-round.

A few miles up Highway 92 is the **Obester Winery,** 12341 San Mateo Rd. (☎ **650/726-9463**), a small wooden shack filled with award-winning wines that are free for the tasting. It's open daily from 10am to 5pm. Exactly 3 miles up Highway 92 from the winery is **Half Moon Bay Nursery,** 11691 San Mateo Rd. (☎ **650/ 726-5392**), a wonderful family-owned nursery where the county's serious green thumbs go for prized perennials. It's open daily from 9am to 5pm.

If you're the adventurous type, you might want to consider a day of deep-sea fishing with **Captain John's Fishing Trips** (☎ **800/391-8787** or 650/726-2913) or **Huck Finn Sportfishing** (☎ **800/572-2934** or 650/726-7133). Either outfit will take you out for a full day for about $50. You don't need experience, tackle, or even a fishing license; they provide everything, and will clean, fillet, and bag your catch. January through March they also offer whale-watching trips for $30 per adult, $20 per child (reservations recommended). Both charters depart from picturesque Pillar Point Harbor, a full-service harbor that houses over 350 commercial fishing vessels and recreational boats. Whether you plan to go fishing or not, it's worth a gander to watch the trawlers unload their daily catch.

One of the most popular activities in Half Moon Bay is horseback riding along the beach. **Sea Horse Ranch,** a.k.a. Friendly Acres Horse Ranch, Highway 1, 1 mile north of Half Moon Bay (☎ **650/726-2362** or 650/726-8550), offers guided or unguided (assuming you know how to ride) excursions along the beach or on well-worn trails for about $40. Early-bird special rates apply before 10am. Open daily from 8am to 6pm.

And, of course, there's the requisite golf course, **Half Moon Bay Golf Links,** 2000 Fairway Dr., at the south end of Half Moon Bay adjacent to the Half Moon Bay Lodge (☎ **650/726-6384**). Designed by Arnold Palmer, the oceanside 18-hole layout has been rated among the top 100 courses in the country, as well as no. 1 in the Bay Area. It ain't cheap, though, with greens fees ranging from $95 to $135. Make reservations as far in advance as possible.

BEACHES & PRESERVES

The 4-mile arc of golden-colored sand that rings Half Moon Bay consists of three state-run beaches (Dunes, Venice, and Francis), all part of **Half Moon Bay State**

Beach. There's a $5 per vehicle entrance fee for all three beaches, but unless you plan on camping or using the rest room often, you're better off saving your lunch money and entering the beach farther north at Mirada Road. Although surfing is allowed, swimming isn't a good idea unless you happen to be cold-blooded.

When the surf is really up, be sure to check out the banzai surfers at **Maverick Beach,** just south of the radar-tracking station past Pillar Point Harbor. To get there, take Westpoint Road to the West Shoreline Access parking lot and follow the trail to the beach. While you're there, keep a lookout for sea lions basking on the offshore rocks. Also adjacent to the parking lot is tiny **Pillar Point Marsh,** a unique fresh- and saltwater marsh that's home and way station to nearly 20% of all North American bird species—from great blue herons to snowy egrets to red-winged black birds.

A few miles farther north on Highway 1 is the **Fitzgerald Marine Reserve** (☎ 650/728-3584), a 35-acre tidal reef housing more than 200 species of marine animals, including starfish, snails, urchins, sponges, sea anemones, and hermit and rock crabs. In fact, it's one of the most diverse tidal basins on the West Coast, as well as one of the safest, thanks to a wave-buffering rock terrace 50 yards from the beach. Call before coming to find out when it's low tide (everything's hidden at high tide) and about the docent-led tour schedules (usually offered on Sunday). No dogs are allowed, and rubber-soled shoes are recommended. It's at the west end of California Avenue off Highway 1 in Moss Beach.

Sixteen miles south of Half Moon Bay on Highway 1 (at the turnoff to Pescadero) is the **Pescadero Marsh Natural Preserve,** one of the few remaining natural marshes on the central California coast. Part of the Pacific flyway, it's a resting stop for nearly 200 bird species, including great blue herons that nest in the northern row of eucalyptus trees. Passing through the marsh is the mile-long **Sequoia Audubon Trail,** accessible from the parking lot at Pescadero State Beach on Highway 1 (the trail starts below the Pescadero Creek Bridge).

Starting in December and continuing through March, the **Año Nuevo State Reserve** is home to one of California's most amazing animal attractions—the hallowed breeding grounds of the **northern elephant seal.** Every winter people reserve tickets months in advance for a chance to witness a fearsome clash between the 2^1/$_2$-ton bulls over mating privileges among the harems of females. Reservations are required for 2^1/$_2$-hour naturalist-led tours (held rain or shine December 15 to March 31). For tickets and tour information, call ☎ 800/444-4445. Even if it's not mating season, you can still see the elephant seals lolling around the shore almost year-round, particularly between April and August when they come ashore to molt.

WHERE TO SHOP

Half Moon Bay's Main Street is a shopper's paradise. Dozens of small stores and boutiques—ranging from chic to shit-kickin'—line the half-mile strip; you'll find everything from feed and tack stores (should you be on the lookout for a used saddle) to custom furniture and camping gear. Must-see stores (from north to south) include the **Buffalo Shirt Company,** 315 Main St. (☎ 650/726-3194), which carries a fine selection of casual wear, Indian rugs, and outdoor gear; **Cartwheels,** 330 Main St. (☎ 650/726-6060), a nifty store specializing in rustic wood furniture, rugs, and toys; and **Half Moon Bay Feed & Fuel,** 331 Main St. (☎ 650/726-4814), a great place to pick up a treat for your pet.

No country boy can survive without **Cunha's Country Store,** 448 Main St. (☎ 650/726-4071), the town's beloved grocery and general store that's a mandatory stop for regular visitors from the Bay Area. And, of course, what would Half Moon

Bay be without a good bookstore? **Coastside Books,** 432 Main St. (☎ **650/ 726-5889**), also carries a fair selection of children's books and postcards.

End your shopping spree with a stop at **Cottage Industries,** 621 Main St. (☎ **650/ 712-8078**), to marvel at the high-quality handcrafted furniture.

WHERE TO STAY

Beach House Inn. 4100 N. Cabrillo Hwy. (Hwy. 1), Half Moon Bay, CA 94019. ☎ **800/ 315-9366** or 650/712-0220. Fax 650/712-0693. 54 units. MINIBAR TV TEL. $185–$350 double. Rates include continental breakfast. AE, DC, DISC, MC, V. From Half Moon Bay, go 3 miles north on Hwy. 1.

It was only a matter of time before big-time developers clued in to the potential of Half Moon Bay, so no one was surprised when ground was broken for the three-story Beach House Inn & Conference Center. (Everyone *was* shocked when someone burned the first version down in retaliation for blocking the neighbors' ocean view.) Although the facade has a rather unimaginative Cape Cod look, the rooms are surprisingly well designed; they have modern prints, stylish furnishings, and spectacular views of the bay and harbor. Every room comes fully loaded with a wood-burning fireplace, king-size bed and sleeper sofa, large bathroom, stereo with CD player, private patio or deck access, two color TVs, four telephones with data ports and voicemail, microwave, and refrigerator. *Tip:* Opt for one of the corner rooms, which offer a more expansive view for the same price. Rates include evening wine tasting on Friday and Saturday only.

Amenities: Heated pool, ocean-view whirlpool, fitness room, conference room, free daily newspaper.

✪ **Cypress Inn on Miramar Beach.** 407 Mirada Rd., Half Moon Bay, CA 94019. ☎ **800/ 83-BEACH** or 650/726-6002. Fax 650/712-0380. 12 units. TV. $185–$295 double. Rates include breakfast; afternoon tea, wine, and hors d'oeuvres; after-dinner treats. AE, DISC, MC, V. From the junction of Hwys. 92 and 1, go 3 miles north, then turn west and follow Medio to the end; hotel is at Medio and Mirada.

A favorite place to stay in Half Moon Bay, the Cypress Inn is blissfully free of Victorian charm (nary a lace curtain in this joint). It's a modern, artistically designed and decorated building with colorful native folk art and rustic furniture made of pine and heavy wicker. Each room has a billowy feather bed, private balcony, gas fireplace, and unobstructed ocean view. Adjacent to the inn are four Beach House rooms equipped with built-in stereo systems and hidden TVs, but they lack the Santa Fe–meets–California effect that I adore in the main house. The ace in the hole is that it's the only B&B perched right on the beach.

Mill Rose Inn. 615 Mill St. (1 block west of Main St.), Half Moon Bay, CA 94019. ☎ **650/ 726-9794.** Fax 650/726-3031. 6 units. TV TEL. $165–$285 double. Rates include breakfast and afternoon tea, wine, and hors d'oeuvres. AE, DC, DISC, MC, V.

Fashioned after an English country house, the Mill Rose Inn looks as if it was pulled from the cover of a Harlequin romance. The elaborate gardens abound with flowers (literally thousands of them), and the rooms are equally gussied up, with a profusion of brass, porcelain, antiques, and lace—a textbook antithesis to the Cypress Inn. The spacious rooms are loaded with comforts, such as private entrances, king- or queen-size feather beds, fireplaces (with the exception of the Baroque Rose room), well-stocked refrigerators, cable TV, VCRs, and access to a Jacuzzi that's tucked inside a frosted-glass gazebo. It's in a good spot, too, just off Main Street in a quiet neighborhood.

Dinner at Duarte's

Always a worthy side trip from Half Moon Bay, is a jaunt down the coast to Pescadero. Nightlife in the tiny coastal community revolves around **Duarte's Tavern,** 202 Stage Rd. (☎ 650/879-0464), which is owned and operated by the family that built it in 1894. The town's population literally triples on weekends as folks pile into the unassuming wood-paneled restaurant for a bowl of its legendary artichoke soup. You'll also find steak, prime rib, and plenty of fresh seafood on the menu, as well as fruits and vegetables straight from the Duartes' gardens behind the restaurant. It's open for breakfast, lunch, and dinner every day, and reservations are recommended for dinner.

Before dinner, you might want to stop at **Phipps Ranch,** 2700 Pescadero Rd. (☎ 650/879-0787), a sort of Knott's Berry Farm in miniature, located a few miles east of Duarte's Tavern on Pescadero Road. You'll find a huge assortment of fresh, organically grown fruits and vegetables, as well as an amazing selection of dried beans. Green thumbs will enjoy browsing the nursery and gardens. A popular early-summer pastime is picking your own olallieberries, strawberries, raspberries, and boysenberries in the adjacent fields. It's open daily from 10am to 7pm (until 6pm in the winter).

✪ **Seal Cove Inn.** 221 Cypress Ave., Half Moon Bay, CA 94038. ☎ **650/728-4114.** Fax 650/728-4116. 10 units. MINIBAR TV TEL. $190–$270 double. Rates include breakfast, wine, and sherry. DISC, MC, V. The inn is 6 miles north of Half Moon Bay off Hwy. 1; follow signs to Moss Beach Distillery.

Before Karen Herbert and her husband, Rick, opened this top-notch B&B, she was the writer and publisher of Karen Brown's Country Inns Series, so you can bet she knows what it takes to create and run a superior bed-and-breakfast. The result is a stately, sophisticated B&B that harmoniously blends California, New England, and European influences in a spectacular setting. All rooms have wood-burning fireplaces, country antiques, original watercolors, grandfather clocks, hidden televisions with VCRs, and refrigerators stocked with free beverages. They overlook distant cypress trees and a colorful half-acre wildflower garden dotted with birdhouses. You'll find coffee and a newspaper outside your door in the morning, brandy and sherry by the living-room fireplace in the evening, and chocolates beside your turned-down bed at night. The ocean is just a short walk away.

WHERE TO DINE

Moss Beach Distillery. Beach St. (at Ocean St.), Moss Beach (6 miles north of Half Moon Bay off Hwy. 1). ☎ **650/728-5595.** Reservations recommended. Main courses $14–$26. AE, CB, DC, DISC, MC, V. Mon–Sat noon–10pm (closing hours vary); Sun brunch 10am–3pm (closing hours vary). CALIFORNIA/CONTINENTAL.

Ever since its bootlegging days during Prohibition almost a century ago, this old stucco distillery on a cliff above Moss Beach has been a wildly popular hangout for both locals and city folk. In the 1920s, silent-film stars and San Francisco politicos frequented the distillery for drinks and the bordello next door for . . . other pastimes. Time and weather have aged it considerably, but a recent renovation spiffed things up. The food—pasta primavera, grilled pork chops, Dungeness crab cakes, chicken Marsala—has never been the main draw; rather, it's the phenomenal view of the rugged coast from almost every window. Your best bet is to come at sunset, order off the appetizer menu (the oysters are always fresh), and snuggle with your partner in the cocktail lounge.

✪ **Pasta Moon.** 315 Main St., Half Moon Bay. ☎ **650/726-5125.** Reservations recommended. Main courses $8–$23. AE, DISC, MC, V. Mon–Fri 11:30am–2:30pm, Sat noon–3pm, Sun brunch 11am–2:30pm; Sun–Thurs 5:30–9:30pm; Fri–Sat 5:30–10pm. ITALIAN.

When visitors ask, "Where is the best place to eat around here?" the inevitable answer is Pasta Moon, a handsome nouveau Italian restaurant in downtown Half Moon Bay. It specializes in making everything from scratch and using only the freshest ingredients. Pasta dishes, which are always freshly made and perfectly cooked, earn the highest recommendations. They include house-made black-pepper fettuccine with spicy calabrese sausage and braised winter greens, and hand-cut pappardelle with sweet fennel sausage, tomatoes, and cream. Another favorite is fresh oak-smoked pork tenderloin braised with savoy cabbage. For dessert, try the wonderful tiramisu, with its layers of Marsala-and-espresso–soaked ladyfingers and creamy mascarpone.

✪ **Sushi Main Street.** 696 Mill St., Half Moon Bay. ☎ **650/726-6336.** Main courses $5–$10. MC, V. Mon–Sat 11:30am–2:30pm and 5–9pm; Sun 5–9pm. JAPANESE.

Who woulda thunk that one of the most exquisite Japanese restaurants in California would be in tiny Half Moon Bay? Chef-owner Hirohito Shigeta started out a decade ago in a tiny space on Main Street and kept the old name when he moved into larger digs down the street. His wife, Karolynne—an interior designer with impeccable taste—decorated the new space with her vast collection of museum-quality Balinese artifacts, and the result is astoundingly beautiful. But even if it looked like the inside of a trailer home, it would still be worth a visit for the exceptional sushi, tempura, and soba. Adventurous sushi warriors will want to try the New Zealand roll (mussels, radish, sprouts, avocado, and teriyaki), unagi papaya, and marinated salmon roll with cream cheese and spinach. For a traditional shoeless Japanese meal, request the knee-high table in the corner.

The Wine Country **12**

Even if you're having the time of your life in downtown San Francisco, I highly recommend you consider at least a quick jaunt to the Wine Country, an hour or so north by car. Amid the mountains dipping into a grapevine-trellised valley, you'll experience an entirely different northern California: fresh country air, hot weather, some of the world's finest wineries, incredible restaurants, green pastures, and virtually nothing to do but overindulge. With eating, drinking, and lounging the encouraged attractions, there's virtually no better definition of a vacation than a few days here.

To decide which of the Wine Country's two distinct valleys (Napa and Sonoma) you prefer to visit, you need to consider their differences. The most obvious is size—Napa Valley dwarfs Sonoma Valley in population, number of wineries, and sheer volume of tourism (and traffic). Napa is definitely the more commercial of the two, with many more wineries to visit, spas (at far cheaper rates) to choose from, and a superior selection of fine restaurants, hotels, and quintessential Wine Country activities, like hot-air ballooning. Further, if your goal is to really learn about the wonderful world of winemaking, Napa Valley is your choice. World-class wineries such as Sterling and Robert Mondavi offer the most interesting and edifying wine tours in North America, if not the world (although Sonoma's Benziger Winery gives them a run for their money).

If you're planning a more extensive trip to the area, consult *Frommer's Portable California Wine Country.*

1 Napa Valley

55 miles N of San Francisco

The city of Napa and its neighboring towns have an overall tourist and big-business feel. You'll see plenty of rolling hills, flora and fauna, and vast stretches of vineyards, but they come hand-in-hand with upscale restaurants, designer discount outlets, rows of hotels, and, in summer, plenty of traffic. Even with hordes of visitors year-round, Napa is still pretty sleepy, focusing on daytime attractions (wine, outdoor activities, and spas) and, of course, food. Nightlife is very limited, but after indulging all day, most visitors are ready to turn in early anyway.

Although "Napa Valley" seems ominous on a map, it's actually relatively condensed and only 25 miles long. You can venture from the town of Napa all the way to Calistoga in less than half an hour (traffic permitting).

The Wine Country

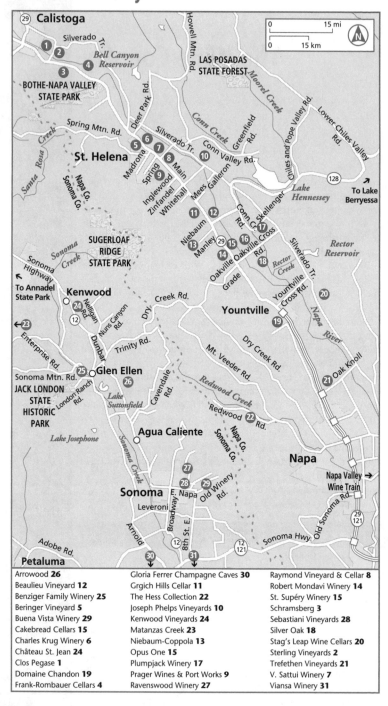

Calistoga

Silverado Tr.
Bell Canyon Reservoir
Howell Mtn. Rd.
LAS POSADAS STATE FOREST
Moorel Creek

BOTHE-NAPA VALLEY STATE PARK

Deer Park Rd.
Conn Creek
Greenfield Rd.
Chiles and Pope Valley Rd.
Lower Chiles Valley Rd.

Spring Mtn. Rd.
Silverado Tr.
Conn Valley Rd.

St. Helena

Madrona
Spring
Main
Inglewood
Zinfandel
Whitehall
Mees
Galleron
Conn Cr.
Skellenger Ln.

Napa Co.
Sonoma Co.

Santa Rosa Creek

Lake Hennessey
To Lake Berryessa

Niebaum
Manley
Oakville Cross Rd.
Oakville Grade
Rector Creek
Silverado Tr.
Rector Reservoir

SUGERLOAF RIDGE STATE PARK

Sonoma Creek
Sonoma Highway

To Annadel State Park

Kenwood
Nelligan Rd.
Nuns Canyon Rd.
Dry Creek Rd.

Yountville

Yountville Cross Rd.
Napa River

To Annadel State Park

Enterprise Rd.
Dunbar
Trinity Rd.
Mt. Veeder Rd.
Dry Creek Rd.
Oak Knoll

Glen Ellen
Sonoma Mtn. Rd.
London Ranch Rd.
Lake Suttonfield
Cavendale Rd.
Redwood Creek
Redwood Rd.

JACK LONDON STATE HISTORIC PARK

Lake Josephone

Agua Caliente

Napa Co.
Sonoma Co.

Napa

Sonoma
E. Napa
Old Winery Rd.
Leveroni
Broadway
8th St. E.
Napa Valley Wine Train

Arnold
Adobe Rd.
Petaluma
Sonoma Hwy.
Old Sonoma Rd.

Arrowood **26**	Gloria Ferrer Champagne Caves **30**	Raymond Vineyard & Cellar **8**
Beaulieu Vineyard **12**	Grgich Hills Cellar **11**	Robert Mondavi Winery **14**
Benziger Family Winery **25**	The Hess Collection **22**	St. Supéry Winery **15**
Beringer Vineyard **5**	Joseph Phelps Vineyards **10**	Schramsberg **3**
Buena Vista Winery **29**	Kenwood Vineyards **24**	Sebastiani Vineyards **28**
Cakebread Cellars **15**	Matanzas Creek **23**	Silver Oak **18**
Charles Krug Winery **6**	Niebaum-Coppola **13**	Stag's Leap Wine Cellars **20**
Château St. Jean **24**	Opus One **15**	Sterling Vineyards **2**
Clos Pegase **1**	Plumpjack Winery **17**	Trefethen Vineyards **21**
Domaine Chandon **19**	Prager Wines & Port Works **9**	V. Sattui Winery **7**
Frank-Rombauer Cellars **4**	Ravenswood Winery **27**	Viansa Winery **31**

ESSENTIALS

GETTING THERE   From San Francisco, cross the Golden Gate Bridge and continue north on U.S. 101. Turn east on California Highway 37, then north on Highway 29, the main road through the Wine Country.

Highway 29 (the St. Helena Highway) runs the length of Napa Valley. You really can't get lost—there's just one north-south road, on which most of the wineries, hotels, shops, and restaurants are located.

VISITOR INFORMATION   The **Wine Institute,** 425 Market St., Suite 1000, San Francisco, CA 94105 (☎ **415/512-0151**), distributes maps and brochures. Once in Napa Valley, stop first at the **Napa Valley Conference and Visitors Bureau,** 1310 Town Center Mall, Napa, CA 94559 (☎ **707/226-7459;** www.napavalley.com/nvcvb.html). It offers a $10 package that includes *The Napa Valley Guide,* a bunch of brochures, a map, a *Four Perfect Days in The Wine Country Itinerary,* and hot-air balloon discount coupons. If you want less to recycle, call **Vintage Publications,** 2929 Conifer Court, Napa, CA 94558 (☎ **800/651-8953**), to mail-order just the guide ($6, plus $3 for shipping within the U.S.). The Web site dispenses lots of the same information free.

TOURING THE VALLEY & WINERIES

Napa Valley claims 34,000 acres of vineyards, making it the most densely planted wine-growing region in the United States. It's an easy venture from one end to the other; you can drive it in less than half an hour (but expect it to be closer to 50 minutes during high season).

Conveniently, most of the large wineries—as well as most of the hotels, shops, and restaurants—are along a single road, Highway 29. It starts at the mouth of the Napa River, near the north end of San Francisco Bay, and continues north to Calistoga and the top of the growing region. When planning your tour, keep in mind that most wineries are closed on major holidays.

All the Napa Valley establishments in this chapter—every town, winery, hotel, and restaurant—is organized below from south to north, beginning in the village of Napa, and can be reached from this main thoroughfare.

NAPA

55 miles from San Francisco

The city of Napa serves as the commercial center of the Wine Country and the gateway to Napa Valley—hence the high-speed freeway that whips you right past it and on to the "tourist" towns of St. Helena and Calistoga. However, if you veer off the highway, you'll be surprised to discover a small but burgeoning community of 63,000 residents with the most cosmopolitan (if you can call it that) atmosphere in the county—and some of the most affordable accommodations in the valley. Unfortunately, any charm Napa may exude is all but squelched by the used-car lots and warehouse superstores surrounding the quaint neighborhoods. Head even a few minutes north of Napa and the real Wine Country atmosphere begins instantly, with wineries, vineyards, and wide-open country views.

✪ **The Hess Collection.** 4411 Redwood Rd., Napa. ☎ **707/255-1144.** www.hesscollection.com. Daily 10am–4pm. From Hwy. 29 north, exit at Redwood Rd. west, and follow Redwood Rd. for 6^1/$_2$ miles.

No place in the valley brings together art and wine better than this winery and art gallery on the side of Mount Veeder. While others strive to pair wine with food, Swiss art collector Donald has gone went a different route: After acquiring the old Christian

Napa Valley Traffic Tip

Travel the Silverado Trail as often as possible to avoid California Highway 29's traffic. The Silverado Trail runs parallel to and about 2 miles east of Highway 29. You get there from the city of Napa or by taking any of the "cross roads" from Highway 29. Cross roads are not well signposted, but clearly defined on most maps. Avoid passing through Main Street in St. Helena during high season. While a wintertime cruise from Napa to Calistoga can take 20 minutes, in summer you can expect the trek to take closer to 50 minutes.

Brothers winery in 1978, he continued to produce wine while funding a huge restoration and expansion project that would honor both wine and the fine arts. The result is a working winery interspersed with gloriously lit rooms that exhibit his stunning art collection; the free self-guided tour takes you through the galleries as it introduces you to the winemaking process.

For a $3 fee, you can sample the winery's current cabernet and chardonnay and one other featured wine. If you want to take some with you, prices start at $9.95 for a bottle of the second-label Hess select brand; most other selections range from $15 to $35.

Trefethen Vineyards. 1160 Oak Knoll Ave. (east of Hwy. 29), Napa. ☎ **707/255-7700.** www.trefethen.com. Daily 10am–4:30pm. Tours by appointment only.

Listed on the National Register of Historic Places, the vineyard's main building was built in 1886 and is Napa's only wooden, gravity-flow winery. Although Trefethen is one of the valley's oldest wineries, it didn't produce its first chardonnay until 1973—but thank goodness it did. The award-winning whites and reds are a pleasure to the palate. Tastings are free, but if you want to sample a reserve wine, it'll cost you $5.

Stag's Leap Wine Cellars. 5766 Silverado Trail, Napa. ☎ **707/944-2020.** www.cask23.com. Daily 10am–4pm. Tours by appointment only. From Hwy. 29, go east on Trancas St. or Oak Knoll Ave., then north to the cellars.

Founded in 1972, Stag's Leap shocked the oenological world in 1976 when its 1973 cabernet won first place over French wines in a Parisian blind tasting. For $5 per person, you can be the judge of the winery's current releases, or you can fork over another fiver for one of Stag's Leap's best-known wines, Cabernet Sauvignon Cask 23. The 1-hour tour runs through everything from the vineyard to production facilities and ends with a tasting; by August 2000, it could also include their new caves, which are currently under construction.

YOUNTVILLE

70 miles from San Francisco

Yountville (pop. 3,700) was founded by the first white American to settle in the valley, George Calvert Yount. While it lacks the small-town charm of neighboring St. Helena and Calistoga—primarily because it has no rambunctious main street—it does serve as a good base for exploring the valley. It's home to a handful of excellent wineries, inns, and a small stretch of fab restaurants, including the world-renowned French Laundry.

✪ **Domaine Chandon.** 1 California Dr. (at Hwy. 29), Yountville. ☎ **707/944-2280.** www.dcchandon.com. Jan–Mar Wed–Sun 10am–6pm; Apr–Dec daily 10am–8pm. Free tours every hour on the hour from 11am to 5pm; no reservations necessary.

French champagne house Moët et Chandon founded the valley's most renowned sparkling winery in 1973. The grounds suit Domaine Chandon's reputation perfectly—

this is the kind of place where the world's wealthy might stroll the beautifully manicured gardens under the shade of a delicate parasol, stop at the outdoor patio for sips of the famous sparkling wine, then glide into the dining room for a luncheon.

If you can pull yourself away from the bubbly (sold in tastings for $8 to $12 and served with complimentary bread and spread), the comprehensive tour of the facilities is worth the time. There's a shop, and a small gallery housing artifacts from Moët et Chandon that depict the history of champagnes.

OAKVILLE
68 miles from San Francisco

Driving farther north on Highway 29 brings you to Oakville, most easily recognized by Oakville Cross Road.

✪ **Robert Mondavi Winery.** 7801 St. Helena Hwy. (Hwy. 29), Oakville. ☎ **800/MONDAVI** or 707/226-1395. www.robertmondaviwinery.com. May–Oct daily 9:30am–5:30pm; Nov–Apr daily 9:30am–4:30pm. Reservations recommended for guided tour; book 1 week ahead, especially for weekend tours.

If you continue on Highway 29 to Oakville, you'll arrive at the ultimate high-tech Napa Valley winery, housed in a magnificent Mission-style facility. At Mondavi, computers control almost every variable in the winemaking process—it's fascinating to watch. After the tour, you can taste the results of all this attention to detail in selected current wines (free). You can also taste without taking the tour, but it will cost you: The Rose Garden (an outdoor tasting area open in summer) offers an etched Reidel glass and three wines for $10; tastings in the ToKalon Room go from $3 for a 3-ounce taste to $25 for a rare library wine.

Fridays feature an "Art of Wine and Food" program. It includes a slide presentation on the history of wine, a tour of the winery, and a three-course luncheon with wine pairing; the cost is around $60, and you must reserve in advance. Although there's no picnicking on the grounds, Mondavi does offer gourmet picnic lunches from time to time. The Vineyard Room usually features an art show, and you'll find some exceptional antiques in the reception hall. In summer, the winery also schedules some great outdoor jazz concerts. Call to learn about upcoming events.

Opus One. 7900 St. Helena Hwy. (Hwy. 29), Oakville. ☎ **707/944-9442.** www. opusonewinery.com. Daily 10:30am–3:30pm. Tours by appointment only; in high season, book a month in advance.

Unlike most other vineyard experiences, a visit to Opus One is a serious and stately affair that takes after its wine and its owners: Robert Mondavi and Baroness Phillipe de Rothschild, who, after years of discussion, embarked on this state-of-the-art collaboration. Architecture buffs in particular will appreciate the tour, which takes in both the impressive Greco-Roman-meets-20th-century building and the no-holds-barred ultra-high-tech production and aging facilities. *Take note:* Newcomers to wine tasting might not appreciate the haute attitude here.

The entire facility caters to one ultra-premium wine, which is offered here for a whopping $25 per 4-ounce taste (and a painful $125 per bottle). But wine lovers should happily fork over the cash: It's likely to be one of the most memorable reds you'll ever sample. Grab your glass and head to the redwood rooftop deck to enjoy the view.

RUTHERFORD
3 miles from Oakville

If you so much as blink after Oakville, you're likely to overlook Rutherford, the next small town that borders on St. Helena. Each town has its share of spectacular wineries, but you won't see most of them while driving along Highway 29.

Silver Oak Wine Cellars. 915 Oakville Cross Rd. (at Money Rd.), Oakville. ☎ **707/ 944-8808.** www.silveroak.com. Tasting room Mon–Sat 9am–4pm. Tours Mon–Fri at 1:30pm, by appointment only.

Twenty-five years ago, an oil man from Colorado, Ray Duncan, and a former Christian Brothers monk, Justin Meyer, formed a partnership and launched a mission to create the finest cabernet sauvignon in the world. "We still haven't produced the best bottle of cabernet sauvignon of which Silver Oak is capable," admits Meyer, but this small winery is the Wine Country's undisputed king of cabernet.

A narrow tree-lined road leads to the handsome Mediterranean-style winery, which produces roughly 40,000 cases of 100% varietal cab annually. (The partners' Alexander Valley winery in Geyserville produces an additional 10,000 cases annually.) The elegant tasting room is refreshingly quiet and soothing, adorned with redwood panels stripped from old wine tanks and warmed by a wood fire. Tastings and tours are $10, which includes a beautiful German-made burgundy glass. At press time, only two wines were released: a 1995 Alexander Valley and a 1995 Napa Valley. If the $50 and $75 per-bottle price tags are a bit much, for half the price you can take home one of the winery's noncab releases—a velvety Meyer Family Port. No picnic facilities are available.

✪ PlumpJack Winery. 620 Oakville Cross Rd. (just west of the Silverado Trail), Oakville. ☎ **707/945-1220.** www.plumpjack.com. Daily 10am–4:30pm.

If most wineries are like a Brooks Brothers suit, PlumpJack stands out as the Todd Oldham of wine tasting: chic, colorful, a little wild, and popular with a young, hip crowd. Like the franchise's PlumpJack restaurant and wine shop in San Francisco and its resort in Tahoe, this playfully medieval winery is a welcome diversion from the same old same old. With Getty bucks behind what was once Villa Mt. Eden winery, the budget covers far more than just atmosphere: There's some serious winemaking going on here, too. For $5 you can sample the cabernet, petite sirah, Riesling, and chardonnay—each an impressive product from a winery that's only been open to the public since mid-1997. The few vintages for sale currently cost $25 to $45. There are no tours or picnic spots, but this refreshingly stylized, friendly facility will make you want to hang out for a while nonetheless.

Cakebread Cellars. 8300 St. Helena Hwy. (Hwy. 29), Rutherford. ☎ **800/588-0298** or 707/963-5221. www.cakebread.com. Daily 10am–4pm. Tours by appointment only.

This winery's moniker is actually the owners' surname, but it suits the wines produced here—the focus is on making wine that pairs well with food. The owners have done such a good job that 85% of their 85,000 annual cases go directly to restaurants, which means only a select few get to take home a bottle. Even if you've found the label in your local wine store, your choice has been limited: Just three varieties are distributed nationally. Here you can sample the sauvignon blanc, chardonnay, cabernet, merlot, zinfandel, pinot noir, Rubaiyat-blend wine, and dry rose Vin de Porche, which are all made from Napa Valley grapes. Prices range from an affordable $15 for a bottle of 1998 sauvignon blanc to a pricey $80 for the 1996 reserve cab, but the average bottle sells for just a little more than $20. In the tasting room, a large barnlike space, the hospitable hosts pour a $5 or $10 sampling; both include a keepsake wineglass.

✪ St. Supéry Winery. 8440 St. Helena Hwy. (Hwy. 29), Rutherford. ☎ **800/942-0809** or 707/963-4507. www.stsupery.com. Daily 9:30am–5pm (until 6pm during summer). Tours every hour on the hour.

The outside may look like a modern corporate office building, but inside you'll find a functional, welcoming winery that encourages first-time tasters to learn more about oenology. On the self-guided tour, you can wander through the demonstration vine-yard, where you'll learn about growing techniques. Inside, kids gravitate toward "SmellaVision," an interactive display that teaches you how to identify different wine ingredients. Adjoining is the Atkinson House, which chronicles more than 100 years of winemaking history. For $3 you'll get lifetime tasting privileges, and although the ever-popular Moscato dessert wine probably won't be available, the sauvignon blanc and chardonnay flow freely. Even the prices make visitors feel at home: Many bottles go for around $8, although the 1995 Meritage cabernet will set you back $40.

Niebaum-Coppola. 1991 St. Helena Hwy. (Hwy. 29), Rutherford. ☎ **707/968-1100.** www.niebaumcoppola.com. Daily 10am–5pm (until 6pm Memorial Day–Labor Day). Tours daily at 11am and 2pm.

In March 1995, Hollywood met Napa Valley when Francis Ford Coppola bought his-toric Inglenook Vineyards. Although the renowned film director has long dabbled in wine production—he's had a home in the valley for over 25 years—Niebaum-Coppola (pronounced *Nee*-bomb *Coh*-pa-la) is his biggest endeavor yet. He plunked down mil-lions to renovate the beautiful 1880s ivy-draped stone winery and restore the surround-ing property to its historic dimensions, gilding it with the glitz and glamour you'd expect from Tinseltown. On display are Academy awards and memorabilia from such Coppola films as *The Godfather* and *Bram Stoker's Dracula;* the Centennial Museum chronicles the history of the estate and its winemaking as well as Coppola's filmmaking.

In all the Hollywood hullabaloo, wine is not forgotten. Available for tasting are a Rubicon (a blend of estate-grown cabernet, cabernet franc, and merlot, aged for more than 5 years), cabernet franc, merlot, chardonnay, zinfandel, and others. All are made from organically grown grapes and cost around $10 to more than $80. There's also a variety of expensive and affordable gift items. Speaking of expensive, the steep $7.50-per-person tasting fee might make you wonder whether a movie is included in the price—it's not, but at least you'll get to keep the souvenir glass. And at $20 a pop for the château and garden tour, you've gotta wonder whether you're *funding* his next film. But the grounds are indeed spectacular, and the 1½-hour journey includes a private tasting and a glass. Don't let the prices deter you; if nothing else, at least visit the stun-ning grounds—it costs nothing to stroll. You're welcome to picnic at any of the des-ignated garden sites.

Beaulieu Vineyard. 1960 St. Helena Hwy. (Hwy. 29), Rutherford. ☎ **707/967-5230.** www.bvwine.com. Daily 10am–5pm. Tours daily 11am–4pm.

Bordeaux native Georges de Latour founded the third-oldest continuously operating winery in Napa Valley in 1900. With the help of legendary oenologist André Tche-listcheff, he produced world-class, award-winning wines that have been served by every president of the United States since Franklin D. Roosevelt. The brick-and-redwood tasting room isn't much to look at, but with Beaulieu's (pronounced

Wine Tasting on the Web

Soon there may be no need to lug your vacation wine bounty on the plane or navigate the confusing shipping laws surrounding wine. WineShopper.com, a San Francisco-based company that launched in 2000, plans to offer thousands of wines—including those you taste in Napa and Sonoma—online. Once the firm gets through the gnarled path of regulations surrounding distribution and shippig, these bottles can lawfully be sent nationwide. Currently, the company is rolling out the service state by state.

*Bowl-*you) stellar reputation, it has no need to visually impress. Tastings cost $5, and a variety of bottles sell for under $20. The Private Reserve Tasting Room offers a "flight" of reserve wines to taste for $18, but if you want to take a bottle to go, it may cost as much as $75. A free tour explains the winemaking process and the vineyard's history. No reservation is necessary.

Grgich Hills Cellar. 1829 St. Helena Hwy. (Hwy. 29), north of Rutherford Cross Rd., Rutherford. ☎ **707/963-2784.** Daily 9:30am–4:30pm. Free tours by appointment only, Mon–Fri 11am and 2pm, Sat–Sun 11am and 1:30pm.

Yugoslavian émigré Miljenko (Mike) Grgich made his presence known to the world when his Château Montelena chardonnay bested the top French white burgundies at the famous 1976 Paris tasting. Since then, the master vintner has teamed up with Austin Hills (of the Hills Brothers coffee fortune) and started this extremely successful and respected winery.

The ivy-covered stucco building isn't much to behold, and the tasting room is even less appealing, but people don't come here for the scenery: As you might expect, Grgich's (pronounced *Grr-*gitch) chardonnays are legendary—and priced accordingly. The smart buys are the outstanding zinfandel and cabernet sauvignon, which cost around $20 and $45, respectively. The winery also produces a fantastic fumé blanc for as little as $18 a bottle. Before you leave, be sure to poke your head into the barrel-aging room and inhale the divine aroma. Tastings cost $3 (which includes the glass) on weekends, and are free on weekdays. No picnic facilities are available.

St. Helena

73 miles from San Francisco

Located 17 miles north of Napa on Highway 29, this former Seventh-Day Adventist village maintains a pseudo Old West feel while simultaneously catering to upscale shoppers with deep pockets—hence Vanderbilt and Company, purveyor of fine housewares, at 1429 Main St. It's a quiet, attractive little town where you'll find a slew of beautiful old homes and first-rate restaurants and accommodations.

Raymond Vineyard & Cellar. 849 Zinfandel Lane (off Hwy. 29 or the Silverado Trail), St. Helena. ☎ **800/525-2659** or 707/963-3141. www.raymondwine.com. Daily 10am–4pm. Tours by appointment only.

As fourth-generation vintners from Napa Valley and relations of the Beringers, brothers Walter and Roy Raymond have had plenty of time to develop terrific wines—and an excellent wine-tasting experience. The short drive through vineyards to reach the friendly, unintimidating cellar is case in point: Passing the heavy-hanging grapes makes you feel you're really in the thick of things before you even get in the door. The spacious, warm room, complete with dining table and chairs, is a perfect setting for sampling the four tiers of wines. Most are free for the tasting and well priced to appeal to all levels of wine drinkers: The Amber Hill label starts at $6 a bottle for chardonnay and $11 for cab; the reserves are priced in the low twenties, while the "Generations" cab costs $50.

Along with the overall experience, there's a great gift selection, which includes barbecue sauces, mustard, a chocolate wine syrup, and a gooey hazelnut merlot fudge sauce. Private reserve tastings cost $2.50. There are no picnic facilities.

✪ V. Sattui Winery. 1111 White Lane (at Hwy. 29), St. Helena. ☎ **707/963-7774.** www.vsattui.com. Winter daily 9am–5pm; summer daily 9am–6pm.

This winery, enormous gourmet deli, and picnic area is a favorite for beginner wine tasters and families. Why? You can fill up on wine, pâté, and cheese samples without ever reaching for your pocketbook, and you can let the kids romp over the grounds while you enjoy your just-bought booty under the shade of a tree. The gourmet store stocks more than 200 cheeses, sandwich meats, pâtés, breads, exotic salads, and delicious desserts such as white-chocolate cheesecake. (It would be an easy place to graze were it not for the continuous mob scene at the counter.)

The long wine bar in the back offers everything from chardonnay, sauvignon blanc, Riesling, cabernet, and zinfandel to a tasty Madeira and a muscat dessert wine. The wines aren't distributed, so if you taste something you simply must have, buy it. (If you buy a case, ask to talk with a manager, who'll give you access to the less crowded, more exclusive private tasting room.) Wine prices start at around $9, with many in the $13 neighborhood; reserves top out at around $75.

This is one of the most popular stops along Highway 29, so prepare for an enormous picnic party and you won't be disappointed. *Note:* To use the picnic area, you must buy food and wine here.

✪ **Joseph Phelps Vineyards.** Taplin Rd. (off the Silverado Trail), P.O. Box 1031, St. Helena. ☎ **800/707-5789.** www.jpvwines.com. Mon–Sat 9am–5pm; Sun 9am–4pm. Tours and tastings by appointment only.

Visitors interested in intimate, comprehensive tours and a knockout tasting should schedule a tour at this stellar winery. A quick turn off the Silverado Trail in Spring Valley (there's no sign—watch for Taplin Road or you'll blast right by), Joseph Phelps was founded in 1973 and is a major player in both the region and the worldwide wine market. Phelps himself accomplished a long list of valley firsts, including launching the syrah varietal in the valley and extending the 1970s Berkeley food revolution (led by Alice Waters) to the Wine Country at his store, the Oakville Grocery (see p. 287).

Joseph Phelps is a favorite stop for serious wine lovers. The modern, state-of-the-art winery and big-city vibe are proof that Phelps's annual 100,000 cases prove fruitful in more ways than one. When you pass through the wisteria-covered trellis to the entrance of the redwood building, you'll encounter an air of seriousness that hangs heavier than harvest grapes. Fortunately, the mood lightens as the well-educated tour guide explains the details of what you're tasting while pouring samples of five to six wines, which may include Riesling, sauvignon blanc, gewürztraminer, syrah, merlot, zin, and cab. (Unfortunately, some wines are so popular that they sell out quickly; come late in the season and you may not be able to taste or buy them.) The three excellently located picnic tables, on the terrace overlooking the valley, are available by reservation.

✪ **Prager Winery & Port Works.** 1281 Lewelling Lane (just west of Hwy. 29, behind Sutter Home), St. Helena. ☎ **800/969-PORT** or 707/963-7678. www.pragerport.com. Daily 10:30am–4:30pm.

If you want a real down-home, off-the-beaten-track experience, Prager's can't be beat. Turn the corner from Sutter Home and roll into the small gravel parking lot; you're on the right track, but when you pull open the creaky old wooden door to this shack of a wine-tasting room, you'll begin to wonder. Don't turn back! Pass the oak barrels and you'll quickly come upon the clapboard tasting room, made homey with a big Oriental rug, a cat, and, during winter, a small space heater. Most days, your host will be Jim Prager himself, a sort of modern Santa Claus in both looks and demeanor. But you won't have to sit on his lap for your wish to come true: Just fork over $5 (refundable with purchase) and he'll pour you samples of his delicious $45 Sweet Claire dessert wine, a late-harvest Johannesburg Riesling, and the recently released 10-year-old port (which costs $45 per bottle and has won various awards). Other yummy selections include chardonnay and cab, which retail in the mid-30s. Also available is "Prager Chocolate Drizzle," a chocolate liqueur that tops ice creams and other desserts.

The Ins & Outs of Shipping Wine Home

Perhaps the only thing more complex than that $400 case of cabernet you just purchased, are the rules and regulations about shipping it home. Because of absurd and forever fluctuating "reciprocity laws"—which supposedly protect the business of the country's wine distributors—wine shipping is limited by regulations that vary in each of the 50 states. Shipping rules also vary from winery to winery. To make matters more confusing, according to at least one shipping company, the list of reciprocal states (those having agreements with California that make it no problem to ship wine there) changes almost daily! Depending on which state you live in, sending even a single bottle of wine can be a truly Kafkaesque experience.

If you happen to live in a reciprocal state and the winery you're buying from offers shipping, you're in luck. You buy and pay the postage, and the winery sends your purchase for you. It's as simple as that. If that winery doesn't ship, it can most likely give you an easy solution.

If you live in a nonreciprocal state, the winery might still have shipping advice for you, so definitely ask! Some refuse to ship at all; others are more than accommodating. Be cautious of wineries that tell you they can ship to nonreciprocal states, and make sure you get a firm commitment: When one of my New York–based editors visited Napa, a winery promised to ship her purchase; when she got home, the winery reneged, leaving her with no way to get the wine and no potable memories of the trip.

You may face the challenge of finding a shipping company yourself. If that's the case, keep in mind that it's technically illegal to box your own wine and send it to a nonreciprocal state; the shipper could lose its license, and you could lose your wine. If you do get stuck shipping illegally (not that we're recommending you do that), you might want to head to a post office, UPS, or other shipping

---

I recommend tasting here, even if you can't afford to purchase; if you do want to buy, this is the only place to do it because Prager doesn't distribute. If you're looking for a special gift, Jim's daughter custom-etches bottles for around $100 in the design of your choice, plus the cost of the wine.

Beringer Vineyards. 2000 Main St. (Hwy. 29), St. Helena. ☎ **707/963-7115.** www.beringer.com. Off-season daily 9:30am–5pm (last tour 4pm, last tasting 4:30pm); summer 9:30am–6pm (last tour 5pm, last tasting 5:30pm). Free 45-min. tours every 30 min.; no reservations necessary.

Follow the line of cars just north of St. Helena's business district to Beringer Vineyards, where everyone stops at the remarkable Rhine House to taste wine and view the hand-dug tunnels carved out of the mountainside. Founded in 1876 by brothers Jacob and Frederick, this is the oldest continuously operating winery in Napa Valley—it was open even during Prohibition, when Beringer stayed afloat by making "sacramental" wines. While white zinfandel is the winery's most popular nationwide seller, the 1994 chardonnay is the choice for more discerning palates: It won *Wine Spectator*'s 1996 Wine of the Year award. Beringer won *Food and Wine*'s winery of the year for 1999. Tastings of current vintages ($3) are conducted in the upstairs gift shop, where there's also a large selection of bottles for less than $20. Reserve wines are available in the Rhine House for a fee of $2 to $7 per taste.

company outside the Wine Country area. It's less obvious that you're shipping wine from Vallejo or San Francisco than from Napa Valley.

Napa Valley Shipping Companies

Aero Packing, 163 Camino Dorado, at Highway 29, Napa (☎ **707/255-8025**), will pack and ship to reciprocal states and insures the first $100 (it's 50¢ extra per $100 beyond the first). Ground shipping of one case to Los Angeles is $20; to Florida, $45. Currently does not ship to a handful of states, including New York and Massachusetts.

The **St. Helena Mailing Center,** 1241 Adams St., at Highway 29, St. Helena (☎ 707/963-2686), tells me that they will pack and ship anywhere in the United States. Rates are around $21 per case for ground delivery to Los Angeles, $66 to New York. While those who live in reciprocal states insure their package for up to $100 (it costs extra beyond the first $100), the Mailing Center does not insure packages shipped to nonreciprocal states. However, it's no big deal; each bottle is packed in styrofoam and should make it home without a problem.

Sonoma Valley Shipping Companies

Mail Boxes, Etc., 19229 Sonoma Hwy., at Verano Street, Sonoma (☎ **707/ 935-3438**), has a lot of experience with shipping wine. It claims it will ship your wine to any state, via UPS (which currently ships to only a dozen states) or Federal Express. Prices vary from $20 to L.A. (UPS) to as much as $85 to the East Coast (FedEx).

The **Wine Exchange of Sonoma,** 452 First St. E., between East Napa and East Spain streets, Sonoma (☎ **707/938-1794**), will ship your wine, but there's a catch: You must buy an equal amount of the same wine at the store (which they assured me would be in stock, and probably at a better rate). Shipping rates range from $20 to L.A. to $45 to the East Coast.

Charles Krug Winery. 2800 St. Helena Hwy. (just north of the tunnel of trees at the northern end of St. Helena), St. Helena. ☎ **707/963-5057**. www.charleskrugwinery.com. Daily 10:30am–5:30pm. Tours daily at 11:30am, 1:30, and 3:30pm.

Founded in 1861, Krug was the first winery built in the valley. The family of Peter Mondavi (yes, Robert is his brother) owns it today. It's worth paying your respects here with a $3 tour, which takes just under an hour and encompasses a walk through the redwood Italianate wine cellar, built in 1874, as well as the vineyards, where you'll learn more about grapes and varietals. The tour ends with a tasting in the retail center. But you don't have to tour to taste: Just stop by and fork over $3 to sip current releases, $5 to sample reserves; you'll also get a souvenir glass. On the grounds are picnic facilities with umbrella-shaded tables overlooking vineyards or the wine cellar.

CALISTOGA

81 miles from San Francisco

Calistoga, the last tourist town in Napa Valley, was named by Sam Brannan, entrepreneur extraordinaire and California's first millionaire. After making a bundle supplying miners during the gold rush, he went on to take advantage of the natural geothermal springs at the north end of the valley by building a hotel and spa in 1859. Flubbing up a speech, in which he compared this natural California wonder to New

York State's Saratoga Springs resort, he serendipitously coined the name "Calistoga," and it stuck. Today, this small, simple resort town with 4,713 residents and an old-time main street (no building along the 6-block stretch is more than two stories high) is popular with city folk who come here to unwind. Calistoga is a great place to relax and indulge in mineral waters, mud baths, Jacuzzis, massages, and, of course, wine. The vibe is more casual—and a little groovier—than you find in neighboring towns to the south.

✪ Frank-Rombauer Cellars. 1091 Larkmead Lane (just off the Silverado Trail), Calistoga. ☎ **707/942-0859.** Daily 10am–5pm.

You've gotta love this place. "Wine dudes" Bob, Holly, and Rich will do practically anything to maintain their self-proclaimed reputation as the "friendliest winery in the valley." They'll serve you all the bubbly you want (four to six varieties: Brut, blanc de blanc, blanc de noir, and extra-dry reserve, ranging from $20 to $70 a bottle) and guarantee that you'll never wait more than 10 minutes to take the 20-minute tour of the oldest champagne cellar in the region.

Former Disney president Richard Frank owns the winery, which used to be Kornell Champagne Cellars. As one employee pointed out, it's not surprising that the unpretentious place is a "celebrity stopover." While the tasting room is so casual you may find yourself kicking back on a case of wine, the stone cellar (listed on the National Register of Historic Places) captures the essence of Wine Country history. Be sure to meander into the Back Room, where chardonnay, zinfandel, and cabernet are poured. The winery makes fewer than 500 cases of still wines a year (versus 10,000 cases of champagne), which means that if you don't try and buy the wine here, you may never get another chance. The same goes for the T-shirt with the slogan "Kiss French, Drink California." Behind the tasting room is a choice picnic area, situated under the oaks and overlooking the vineyards.

✪ Schramsberg. 1400 Schramsberg Rd. (off Hwy. 29), Calistoga. ☎ **707/942-2414.** www.schramsberg.com. Daily 10am–4pm. Tours and tastings by appointment only.

This 200-acre champagne estate, a landmark once frequented by Robert Louis Stevenson, has a wonderful Old World feel. It's one of my all-time favorite places to explore. Schramsberg is the label that presidents serve when toasting dignitaries from around the globe, and there's plenty of historic memorabilia in the front room to prove it. But the real mystique begins when you enter the champagne caves, which wind 2^1/$_2$ miles (reputedly the longest in North America) and were partly hand-carved by Chinese laborers in the 1800s. The caves have an authentic Tom Sawyer ambience, complete with dangling cobwebs and seemingly endless passageways; you can't help but feel you're on an adventure. The comprehensive, unintimidating tour ends in a charming tasting room, where you'll sit around a big table and sample several surprisingly varied selections of bubbly. Tastings are a bit dear ($7.50 per person), but it's money well spent. Note, however, that tastings are offered only to those who take the free tour, and you must reserve in advance.

✪ Clos Pegase. 1060 Dunaweal Lane (off Hwy. 29 or the Silverado Trail), Calistoga. ☎ **707/942-4981.** www.clospegase.com. Daily 10:30am–5pm. Tours daily at 11am and 2pm.

What happens when a man falls in love with art and winemaking, purchases more than 450 acres of prime growing property, and sponsors a competition commissioned by the San Francisco Museum of Modern Art to create a "temple to wine"? You'll find out when you visit this magnificent winery. Renowned architect Michael Graves designed this incredible oasis, which integrates art, 20,000 square feet of aging caves, and a luxurious hilltop private home. Viewing the art is as much the point as tasting the wines—which, by the way, don't come cheap: Prices range from $13 for the 1998 Vin Gris Merlot to as much as $60 for the 1996 Hommage Artist Series Reserve, an extremely limited blend of the winery's finest lots of cabernet sauvignon and merlot. Tasting current releases costs $2.50 to $5 for samples of three premium wines. The grounds at Clos Pegase (pronounced Clo Pay-*goss*) feature an impressive sculpture garden as well as scenic picnic spots.

✪ **Sterling Vineyards.** 1111 Dunaweal Lane (off Hwy. 29, just south of Calistoga), Calistoga. ☎ **707/942-3300.** www.sterlingvineyards.com. Daily 10:30am–4:30pm.

No, you don't need climbing shoes to reach this dazzling white Mediterranean-style winery, perched 300 feet up on a rocky knoll. Just fork over $6 and take the aerial tram, which offers dazzling bucolic views along the way. Once on land, follow the self-guided tour (the most comprehensive in the Wine Country) of the winemaking process. Currently owned by the Seagram company, the winery produces more than 200,000 cases per year. Samples at the panoramic tasting room are included in the tram fare. Expect to pay anywhere from $10 to $60 for a souvenir bottle ($20 is the average). If you can find a bottle of 1996 Napa Valley Reserve Cabernet Sauvignon, which currently goes for about $60, buy it—the *Wine Spectator* gave it a 94.

BEYOND THE WINERIES: WHAT TO SEE & DO IN NAPA VALLEY
NAPA/ST. HELENA

If you have plenty of time and a penchant for Victorian architecture, the **Napa Valley Conference and Visitors Bureau,** 1310 Napa Town Center Mall, off First Street (☎ **707/226-7459;** www.napavalley.com), offers self-guided walking tours of the town's historic buildings.

Anyone with an appreciation for art absolutely must visit the ✪ **di Rosa Preserve,** which until recently was closed to the public. Rene and Veronica di Rosa, who have collected contemporary American art for more than 40 years, converted their 88 acres of prime property into a monument to northern California's regional art and nature. Their world-renowned collection features 1,500 works in all media by more than 600 greater Bay Area artists. Their treasures are on display practically everywhere—along the shores of their 30-acre lake and in each nook and cranny of their 110-year-old winery-turned-residence, adjoining building, two new galleries, and gardens. With hundreds of surrounding acres of rolling hills (protected under the Napa County Land Trust), this place is a must-see for both art and nature lovers. It's at 5200 Sonoma Hwy. (Highway 121/12); look for the blue gate. Visits are by appointment only. Each tour lasts 2 to 2¹/₂ hours, has a maximum of 25 guests, and costs $10 per person. Call ☎ **707/226-5991** to make reservations.

SHOPPING   Plan to spend at least an hour if you visit **Red Hen's** co-op collection of antiques. You'll find everything from baseball cards to living-room sets, and prices are remarkably affordable. You can't miss the enormous red barn-style building at 5091 St. Helena Hwy., on Highway 29 at Oak Knoll Avenue West (☎ **707/ 257-0822**). Its sister property in central Napa is the **Riverfront Antique Center,** 705 Soscol Ave., at Third Street (☎ **707/253-1966**). Here, 70 antique-art dealers exhibit their collections in stalls throughout a mazelike warehouse. During winter, bring a scarf and mittens—there's no indoor heating. Both locations are open daily from 10am to 5:30pm.

St. Helena's Main Street is the best place to go if you're suffering serious retail withdrawal. Take, for example, ✪ **Vanderbilt and Company,** 1429 Main St., between Adams and Pine streets (☎ **707/963-1010**). It offers the crème de la crème of cookware, hand-painted Italian dishes, and everything else you could possibly convince yourself you need for your gourmet kitchen and dining room. Open daily from 9:30am to 5:30pm.

Shopaholics won't be able to avoid at least one sharp turn off Highway 29 for a stop at the **St. Helena Premium Outlets,** 2 miles north of downtown St. Helena (☎ 707/963-7282). Featured designers include Donna Karan, Coach, Movado, London Fog, and more. The stores are open daily from 10am to 6pm.

One last favorite stop: **Napa Valley Olive Oil Manufacturing Company,** 835 Charter Oak Rd., at the end of the road behind Tra Vigne restaurant (☎ 707/963-4173). The tiny market presses and bottles its own oils and sells them at a fraction of the price you'll pay elsewhere. In addition, it has an extensive selection of Italian cooking ingredients, imported snacks, and the best deals on exotic mushrooms. You'll also love the age-old method for totaling the bill, which you simply must find out for yourself.

SPA-ING IT   If the Wine Country's slow pace and tranquil vistas aren't soothing enough for you, the region's diverse selection of spas can massage, bathe, wrap, and steam you into an overly pampered pulp. Should you choose to indulge, do so toward the end of your stay—when you've wined and dined to the point where you have only enough energy left to make it to and from the spa.

Compared to the cosmopolitan-chic day spas of Sonoma Mission Inn (Sonoma) and Health Spa Napa Valley (St. Helena), ✪ **White Sulphur Springs Retreat & Spa,** 3100 White Sulphur Springs Rd. (☎ 707/963-4361), offers a more spiritual day of cleansing and pampering. Yes, you will encounter massages, aromatherapy treatments, seaweed or mineral mud wraps, and a pool and Jacuzzi for guests' use. But the most blissful benefits are not the product of some well-known architect or fancy new massage oil. Mother Nature takes the credit for the magic here: acres of redwoods, streams, grassy fields, wooded groves, and hiking trails galore. The spa treatments only make the experience that much more relaxing. The resident spotted owls, woodpeckers, raccoon, deer, and fox don't take advantage of the natural outdoor hot sulfur spring, pool, Jacuzzi, or sauna (free for spa-goers), but you might catch a glimpse of them as you bathe. Massages ($80 to $95 per hour) are given in the homey spa building or outside amid the redwoods. A day of peaceful pampering doesn't come any cheaper, but take note: This is a casual place.

BIKING   The quieter northern end of the valley is an ideal place to rent a bicycle and ride the Silverado Trail. **St. Helena Cyclery,** 1156 Main St. (☎ 707/963-7736), rents bikes for $7 per hour or $25 a day, including rear rack, helmet, lock, and picnic bag.

CALISTOGA

BICYCLING   Cycling enthusiasts can rent bikes from **Getaway Adventures BHK,** 1117 Lincoln Ave. (☎ 800/499-BIKE or 707/942-0332; www.getawayadventures. com). Full-day tours cost $95 and include lunch and a visit to four or five wineries; downhill cruises are available for people who hate to pedal. Bike rental without a tour costs $9 an hour, $20 per half-day, or $28 per day.

HORSEBACK RIDES   If you like horses and venturing through cool, misty forests, then $50 will seem like a bargain for a 1¹/₂-hour ride with a friendly tour guide from **Napa Valley Trail Rides,** P.O. Box 877, Glen Ellen, CA 95442 (☎ 707/996-8566; www.thegrid.net/trailrides/). After a lesson in the basics of horse handling at the stable, you'll be led on a leisurely stroll, with the occasional trot thrown in for excitement. The ride goes through beautiful Bothe-Napa Valley State Park, off Highway 29 near Calistoga.

✪ **MUD BATHS**   The one thing you should do while you're in Calistoga is what people have been doing here for the past 150 years: Take a mud bath. The natural baths contain local volcanic ash, imported peat, and naturally boiling mineral hot-springs water, mulled together to produce a thick mud that simmers at a temperature of about 104°F.

Indulge yourself at any of these Calistoga spas: **Dr. Wilkinson's Hot Springs,** 1507 Lincoln Ave. (☎ 707/942-4102); **Lincoln Avenue Spa,** 1339 Lincoln Ave. (☎ 707/942-5296); **Golden Haven Hot Springs Spa,** 1713 Lake St. (☎ 707/942-6793); **Calistoga Spa Hot Springs,** 1006 Washington St. (☎ 707/942-6269), **Calistoga Village Inn & Spa,** 1880 Lincoln Ave. (☎ 707/942-0991); **Eurospa & Inn,** 1202 Pine St. (☎ 707/942-6829); **Indian Springs Resort,** 1712 Lincoln Ave. (☎ 707/942-4913); **Lavender Hill Spa,** 1015 Foothill Blvd. (☎ 800/528-4772 or 707/942-4495); **Mount View Spa,** 1457 Lincoln Ave. (☎ 707/942-5789); **Nance's Hot Springs,** 1614 Lincoln Ave. (☎ 707/942-6211); or **Roman Spa Motel,** 1300 Washington St. (☎ 707/942-4441).

NATURAL WONDERS   **Old Faithful Geyser of California,** 1299 Tubbs Lane (☎ **707/942-6463**), is one of only three "old faithful" geysers in the world. It's been blowing off steam at regular intervals for as long as anyone can remember. The 350°F water spews at a height of about 60 feet every 40 minutes, day and night. The performance lasts about a minute, and you can bring a picnic lunch to munch on between spews. An exhibit hall, gift shop, and snack bar are open every day. Admission is $6 for adults, $5 for seniors, $2 for children 6 to 12, free for children under 6. Open daily from 9am to 6pm (to 5pm in winter). To get there, follow the signs from downtown Calistoga; it's between Highway 29 and Calif. 128.

You won't see thousands of trees turned into stone, but you'll still find many interesting petrified specimens at the **Petrified Forest,** 4100 Petrified Forest Rd. (☎ **707/942-6667**). Volcanic ash blanketed this area after the eruption of Mount St. Helena 3 million years ago. You'll find redwoods that have turned to rock through the slow infiltration of silicas and other minerals, as well as petrified seashells, clams, and marine life indicating that water covered this area before the redwood forest appeared. Admission is $4 for adults, $3 for seniors and youths 12 to 17, $1 for children 4 to 11, free for children under 4. Open daily 10am to 5:30pm (to 4:30pm in winter). Heading north from Calistoga on Calif. 128, turn left onto Petrified Forest Road, just past Lincoln Street.

WHERE TO STAY IN NAPA VALLEY

Accommodations here run the gamut—from motels and B&Bs to world-class luxury retreats—and all are easily accessible from the main highway. While I recommend shacking up in the more romantically pastoral areas such as St. Helena, there's no question you're going to find better deals in the towns of Napa or laid-back Calistoga.

The listings below are arranged first by area, then by price, using the following categories: **Very Expensive,** more than $250 per night; **Expensive,** $200 to $250 per night; **Moderate,** $150 to $200 per night; and **Inexpensive,** less than $150 per night. The reality is that anything less than $150 a night qualifies as inexpensive in these parts.

When planning your trip, keep in mind that during the high season—June to November—most hotels charge peak rates and sell out completely on weekends; many have a 2-night minimum. If you need help organizing your Wine Country vacation, contact an agency. **Accommodation Referral Bed & Breakfast Exchange** (☎ **800/240-8466,** 800/499-8466 in Calif., or 707/963-8466), which also represents hotels and inns, will ask for dates, price range, and what kind of accommodation you're look-ing for before coming up with recommendations. **Bed & Breakfast Inns of Napa Val-ley** (☎ 707/944-4444), an association of 26 B&Bs, provides descriptions and makes reservations. **Napa Valley Reservations Unlimited** (☎ 800/251-NAPA or 707/252-1985) is also a source for everything from hot-air balloon and glider rides to wine-tasting tours by limousine.

NAPA

Wherever tourist dollars are to be had, you're sure to find big hotels with familiar names catering to independent vacationers, business travelers, and groups. **Embassy Suites,** 1075 California Blvd., Napa, CA 94559 (☎ 800/362-2779 or 707/253-9540), offers 205 of its usual two-room suites. Each has a kitchenette, cof-feemaker, modem capability, and two TVs; there are indoor and outdoor pools and a restaurant. Rates range from $190 to $280 and include cooked-to-order breakfast. The 191-room **Napa Valley Marriott,** 3425 Solano Ave., Napa, CA 94558 (☎ 800/228-9290 or 707/253-7433), has lighted tennis courts, an exercise room, a heated outdoor pool and spa, and two restaurants; rates range from $189 to $249.

Moderate

✪ **Cedar Gables Inn.** 486 Coombs St., Napa, CA 94559. ☎ **800/309-7969** or 707/224-7969. Fax 707/224-4838. www.CedarGablesInn.com. 9 units. $139–$259 double; win-ter $129–$249 double. Rates include full breakfast and port. AE, DISC, MC, V. From Hwy. 29 north, exit onto First St. and follow signs to downtown; turn right onto Coombs St.; the house is at the corner of Oak St.

Innkeepers Margaret and Craig Snasdell have developed quite a following with their grand, romantic B&B in Old Town Napa. The Victorian was built in 1892, and rooms reflect the era, with rich tapestries and stunning gilded antiques. Five rooms have fireplaces, five have whirlpool tubs, and all feature queen-size brass, wood, or iron beds. Guests meet each evening in front of the roaring fireplace in the family room for wine and cheese. At other times, it's a perfect place to cuddle up and watch the large-screen TV.

Inexpensive

Chablis Inn. 3360 Solano Ave., Napa, CA 94558. ☎ **707/257-1944.** Fax 707/226-6862. www.chablisinn.com. 34 units. A/C TV TEL. Apr to mid-Nov $80–$130 double; mid-Nov to Mar $70–$100 double. Rates include continental breakfast. AE, DC, DISC, MC, V.

There's no way around it. If you want to sleep cheaply in a town where the *average* room rate tops $200 per night in high season, you're destined for a motel. But look on the bright side: Because your room is likely to be little more than a crash pad after a day of eating and drinking, a clean bed and a remote control are all you'll really need anyway. Chablis offers much more than that. Each of the superclean motel-style rooms has a new mattress, refrigerator, and coffeemaker; some even boast kitchenettes, whirlpool tubs, or both. Guests have access to an outdoor heated pool and hot tub, plus a basic continental breakfast. Friendly owner Ken Patel is on hand most of the time and is constantly upgrading his tidy highway-side hostelry; his most recent pro-ject: replacing all furniture in July 1999.

Wine Valley Lodge. 200 S. Coombs St. (between First and Imola sts.), Napa, CA 94558. ☎ **707/224-7911.** 53 units. A/C TV TEL. $69–$119 double; $120–$165 deluxe. AE, CB, DC, DISC, MC, V.

Dollar for dollar, the Wine Valley Lodge offers the most for the least in all of Wine Country. At the south end of town in a quiet residential neighborhood, the Mission-style motel is extremely well kept and accessible, just a short drive from Highway 29 and the wineries to the north. The reasonably priced deluxe rooms hold two bedrooms connected by a bathroom. A $500,000 room renovation, begun in February 2000, promises continued improvements by year's end.

YOUNTVILLE

Expensive

✪ **Napa Valley Lodge.** 2230 Madison St., Yountville, CA 94599. ☎ **800/368-2468** or 707/944-2468. Fax 707/944-9362. www.woodsidehotels.com. 55 units. A/C MINIBAR TV TEL. $212–$525 double. Rates include champagne breakfast buffet. AE, CB, DC, DISC, MC, V.

Many frequent visitors compare this contemporary hotel to the nearby, upscale Vintage Inn, noting that it's even more personable and accommodating. The lodge is just off Highway 29, beyond a wall that does a good job of disguising the road. Guest rooms, which were upgraded in 1999, are large, ultraclean, and better appointed than many in the area. Many have vaulted ceilings, and 33 have fireplaces. All come with a king- or queen-size bed, wicker furnishings, coffeemaker, robes, and a private balcony or a patio. In 1997 all the bathrooms were upgraded to include a vanity area and nice tile work. The cheapest units, at ground level, are smaller and get less sunlight than those on the second floor. Facilities include a pool, redwood sauna, and small exercise room. Extras include concierge, on-demand video, afternoon tea and cookies in the lobby, Friday-evening wine tasting in the library, and a full champagne breakfast—with all this, it's no wonder AAA gave the Napa Valley Lodge the four-diamond award for excellence. Ask about winter discounts, which can be as high as 30%.

Moderate

✪ **Maison Fleurie.** 6529 Yount St. (between Washington St and Yountville Cross Rd.), Yountville, CA 94599. ☎ **800/788-0369** or 707/944-2056. Fax 707/944-2056. www.foursisters.com. 13 units. A/C TV TEL. $110–$260 double. Rates include full breakfast and afternoon hors d'oeuvres. AE, DC, MC, V.

Maison Fleurie is one of the prettiest hotels in the Wine Country, a trio of beautiful 1873 brick-and-fieldstone buildings overlaid with ivy. The main house—a charming Provençal replica with thick brick walls, terra-cotta tile, and paned windows—holds seven rooms; the rest are in the old bakery building and the carriage house. Some feature private balconies, patios, sitting areas, Jacuzzi tubs, and fireplaces. Breakfast is served in the quaint little dining room; afterward, you're welcome to wander the landscaped grounds, use the pool or outdoor spa, or borrow a mountain bike (free of charge) to ride around town, returning in time for afternoon hors d'oeuvres. It's impossible not to enjoy your stay at Maison Fleurie.

Inexpensive

Napa Valley Railway Inn. 6503 Washington St. (adjacent to the Vintage 1870 shopping complex), Yountville, CA 94599. ☎ **707/944-2000.** 9 units. A/C TV. $75–$140 double. AE, MC, V.

This is a favorite place to stay in the Wine Country. Why? Because it's inexpensive and it's cute as all get-out. Looking hokey as heck from the outside, the Railway Inn consists of two rows of sun-bleached cabooses and rail cars sitting on a stretch of Yountville's original track and connected by a covered wooden walkway. Things get considerably better when you enter your private caboose or car. They're sumptuously appointed, with comfy love seats, queen-size brass beds, and tiled baths. The coups de grâce are the bay windows and skylights, which let in plenty of California sunshine. The cars are all suites, so if you're looking to save your pennies, opt for a caboose. Adjacent to the inn is Yountville's main shopping complex, which offers wine tastings and contains some good low-priced restaurants.

OAKVILLE & RUTHERFORD
Very Expensive

✪ **Auberge du Soleil.** 180 Rutherford Hill Rd., Rutherford, CA 94573. ☎ **707/963-1211.** Fax 707/963-8764. www.aubergedusoleil.com. 50 units. A/C MINIBAR TV TEL. $350–$535 double; $750–$950 suite; $2,000 cottage suite. Discounts available Dec–Mar. AE, CB, DC, DISC, JCB, MC, V. From Rutherford, turn right on Calif. 128 and go 3 miles to the Silverado Trail; turn left, head north about 200 yds. to Rutherford Hill Rd., turn right.

This spectacular Relais & Châteaux member is the kind of place you'd imagine movie stars frequenting for clandestine affairs or weekend retreats. Set high above Napa Valley in a 33-acre olive grove, it's quiet, indulgent, and luxuriously romantic. The Mediterranean-style rooms are large enough to get lost in, and you might want to once you discover all the amenities. The bathtub alone—an enormous hot tub with a skylight overhead—will entice you to grab a glass of California red and settle in for a while. Oversized, cushy furniture surrounds a wood-burning fireplace—the ideal place to relax and listen to CDs (the stereo comes with a few selections, and there's also a VCR). Fresh flowers, original art, terra-cotta floors, and wood and leather furnishings whisk you out of the Wine Country and into the Southwest. Each sun-washed private deck has views of the valley that are nothing less than spectacular. Those with money to burn should opt for the $2,000-per-night cottage suite; the 1,800-square-foot hideaway has two fireplaces, two full baths, a den, and a patio Jacuzzi. Now that's living. All guests have access to a celestial swimming pool and a tiny exercise room. Overall, this is one of my favorite Wine Country places.

Dining/Diversions: Another ethereal experience. See "Where to Dine in Napa Valley," below.

Amenities: Concierge, newspaper delivery, valet parking, 24-hour room service, twice-daily maid service, laundry and valet, complimentary shoeshine. Outdoor pool with sundeck, massage rooms, three tennis courts, exercise room, beauty salon. Sculpture and nature trail with picnic areas that criss-crosses the property.

Moderate

Rancho Caymus Inn. 1140 Rutherford Rd. (P.O. Box 78), Rutherford, CA 94573. ☎ **800/845-1777** or 707/963-1777. Fax 707/963-5387. 26 suites. A/C MINIBAR TV TEL. $155–$205 double; from $285 Master Suite; $385 2-bedroom suite. Rates include continental breakfast. AE, CB, DC, MC, V. From Hwy. 29 north, turn right onto Rutherford Rd./Calif. 128 E.; the hotel is on your left.

This Spanish-style hacienda, with two floors opening onto wisteria-covered balconies, was the creation of sculptor Mary Tilden Morton (of Morton Salt). Morton wanted each room in the hacienda to be a work of art, and hired the most skilled craftspeople she could find. She designed the adobe fireplaces herself, and wandered through Mexico and South America purchasing artifacts for the property, which was completed in 1985.

Guest rooms surround a whimsical garden courtyard with an enormous outdoor fireplace. The mix-and-match decor is on the funky side, with overly varnished darkwood furnishings and braided rugs. The inn is cozy, however, and rooms are decent-sized, split-level suites with queen beds, wet bars, sofa beds in the sitting areas, and small private patios. Most of the suites have fireplaces, and five have kitchenettes and whirlpool tubs. Breakfast, which includes fresh fruit, granola, orange juice, and breads, is served in the inn's dining room. Since chef Ken Frank's La Toque opened here, this funky inn has also become a dining destination (see "Where to Dine in Napa Valley," for complete details).

ST. HELENA
Very Expensive
The Inn at Southbridge. 1020 Main St., St. Helena, CA 94574. ☎ **800/520-6800** or 707/967-9400. Fax 707/967-9486. www.placestostay.com/napavalley. MINIBAR TV TEL. Mid-Nov to early Mar $235–$445 double; Mar–Apr $255–$495; May to mid-Nov $275–$515 double. AE, CB, DC, , MC, V.

Eschewing the lace-and-latticework theme that plagues most Wine Country inns, the Inn at Southbridge takes an unswervingly modern, pragmatic approach. Instead of stuffed teddy bears, you'll find terry robes, fireplaces, bathroom skylights, down comforters, private balconies, and a host of other little luxuries. The decor is upscale Pottery Barn trendy, and for some a welcome departure from quaintly traditional hotel-style stuff. Functional touches include voicemail and fax modems. One notable bummer: The inn is along the highway, so it lacks that reclusive feel many other upscale hotels offer.

Dining/Diversions: On the premises is Tomatina, owned and run by the owners of Tra Vigne, an Italian restaurant conveniently located next door (see "Where to Dine in Napa Valley," below).

Amenities: Concierge, limited room service, dry cleaning, laundry, newspaper delivery, in-room massage, twice-daily maid service, baby-sitting, secretarial services, complimentary refreshments in lobby. The spa offers access to an excellent gym (including classes), steam room, sauna, outdoor heated pool, Jacuzzi, and spa treatments.

✪ **Meadowood Napa Valley.** 900 Meadowood Lane, St. Helena, CA 94574. ☎ **800/458-8080** or 707/963-3646. Fax 707/963-3532. www.meadowood.com. 85 units. A/C MINIBAR TV TEL. $320–$465 double; 1-bedroom lodge from $540; 2-bedroom from $850; 3-bedroom from $1,180; 4-bedroom from $1,575. Ask about promotional offers and off-season rates. 2-night minimum stay on weekends. AE, DISC, DC, MC, V.

This ultra-luxurious resort, tucked away on 256 acres of pristine mountainside in a forest of madrone and oak trees, is quiet and secluded enough to make you forget that the busy wineries are just 10 minutes away. Originally a private country club for Napa's well-to-do families, Meadowood is one of California's top-ranked resorts, a favorite retreat for celebrities and CEOs. Rooms are furnished with American country classics and have beamed ceilings, private patios, stone fireplaces, and views of the forest. Many are individual suite-lodges so far removed from the common areas that you must drive to get to them. Lazier folks can opt for more centrally located accommodations.

The resort offers a wealth of activities: golf on a challenging 9-hole course, tennis on seven championship courts, and croquet (yes, croquet) on two international regulation lawns. There are private hiking trails, a health spa, heated pools, and a whirlpool. Those who might actually want to leave and do some wine tasting can check in with John Thoreen, the hotel's wine tutor, whose sole purpose is to help guests better understand and enjoy Napa Valley wines.

Dining/Diversions: See "Where to Dine in Napa Valley," below.

Amenities: Concierge, room service, dry cleaning and laundry, full-service spa, newspaper delivery, secretarial service, baby-sitting. Nine-hole golf course, croquet lawns, two outdoor pools with sundeck, massage rooms, seven tennis courts, exercise room, hiking trails, executive conference center.

Moderate
✪ **Deer Run Bed & Breakfast.** 3995 Spring Mountain Rd., P.O. Box 311, St. Helena, CA 94574. ☎ **800/843-3408** or 707/963-3794. Fax 707/963-9026. 4 units (all with shower only). A/C TV. $150–$195 double. Rates include full breakfast. AE, MC, V.

Regardless of your budget, if romantic solitude is a big part of your vacation plan, Deer Run had better be on your itinerary. On a winding mountain road 4¹/₂ miles

(10 minutes by car) from downtown St. Helena, this B&B is the ultimate heavenly hideaway. The wood-paneled rooms look onto owners Tom and Carol Wilson's 4 acres of forest. Each has gorgeous antiques, feather beds, a private entrance, a deck, a decanter of brandy, a fridge, coffee and tea, robes, and a hair dryer. Deer often meander by the Honeymoon Suite (the most secluded), a sweet split-level cottage with a separate bedroom and gas fireplace; its price includes breakfast delivered to your doorstep. The full breakfast served in the main house may include a frittata or apple crêpes with chicken-apple sausage. Outside you'll find Cody, the resident chocolate Lab, hanging out by the very small pool. Guests also have access to hiking trails.

✪ White Sulphur Springs Retreat & Spa. 3100 White Sulphur Springs Rd., St. Helena, CA 94574. ☎ **800/593-8873** in CA or 707/963-8588. Fax 707/963-2890. www.whitesulphursprings.com. 28 units, 14 with bathroom; 9 cottages. Carriage House (shared bathroom) $85–$105 double; Inn $105–$125 double; Creekside Cottages $135–$195. Extra person $15. Off-season and midweek discounts available. 2-night minimum stay on weekends Apr–Oct and all holidays. MC, V.

If your idea of the ultimate vacation is a cozy cabin on 330 acres, paradise is a short, winding drive away from downtown St. Helena. Established in 1852, Sulphur Springs claims to be the oldest resort in California. The property holds creeks, waterfalls, hot springs, hiking trails, and redwood, madrone, and fir trees. Guests stay in small and large creekside cabins, which were renovated in 1998 and '99, or at the inn. The cabins are decorated with simple but homey furnishings; some have a fireplace or woodburning stove, some have a kitchenette, and some have both. From here you can venture off on a hike; take a dip in the natural hot sulphur spring; lounge by the pool; sit under a tree and watch for deer, fox, raccoon, spotted owl, or woodpecker; or schedule a day of massage, aromatherapy, and other spa treatments. *Note:* No RVs are allowed without advance notice.

✪ Wine Country Inn. 1152 Lodi Lane, St. Helena, CA 94574. ☎ **707/963-7077.** Fax 707/963-9018. www.wine-country-inn.com. 24 units (12 with shower only). A/C TEL. $130–$345 double. Rates include breakfast and appetizers. MC, V.

Just off the highway behind Freemark Abbey vineyard, this attractive wood-and-stone inn, complete with a French-style mansard roof and turret, overlooks a pastoral landscape of vineyards. The individually decorated rooms contain iron or brass beds, antique furnishings, and handmade quilts; most have fireplaces and private terraces overlooking the valley, while others have private hot tubs. One of the inn's best features (besides the absence of TVs) is the heated outdoor pool, which is attractively landscaped into the hillside. Another favorite is the selection of suites, which come with stereos, plenty of space, and lots of privacy. The family that runs this place puts personal touches everywhere and makes every guest feel welcome. They serve wine and plenty of appetizers nightly, along with a big dash of hotel-staff hospitality in the inviting living room. A full buffet breakfast is served there, too. Five new cottages are slated to open in late 2000.

Inexpensive

✪ El Bonita Motel. 195 Main St. (at El Bonita Ave.), St. Helena, CA 94574. ☎ **800/541-3284** or 707/963-3216. Fax 707/963-8838. www.elbonita.com. 41 units. A/C MINIBAR TV TEL. May–Oct $109–$239 double; Mar and Nov $99–$199 double; Dec–Feb $85–$159 double. Rates include continental breakfast. AE, CB, DC, DISC, MC, V.

This 1930s Art Deco motel is a bit too close to Highway 29 for comfort, but the 2½ acres of beautifully landscaped gardens behind the building (away from the road) help even the score. The rooms, while small, are spotlessly clean and decorated with new furnishings; all have microwaves and coffeemakers, and some have kitchens or whirlpool baths. Many families, attracted to the larger bungalows with kitchenettes, consider El Bonita one of the best values in Napa Valley—especially considering the heated outdoor pool, Jacuzzi, sauna, and new massage facility.

CALISTOGA

Expensive

✪ **Cottage Grove Inn.** 1711 Lincoln Ave., Calistoga, CA 94515. ☎ **800/799-2284** or 707/942-8400. Fax 707/942-2653. www.cottagegrove.com. 16 cottages. A/C TV TEL. $215–$275 double. Rates include continental breakfast and evening wine and cheese. AE, CB, DC, DISC, MC, V.

Standing in two parallel rows at the end of the main strip in Calistoga is the perfect retreat—new cottages that, though on a residential street, seem removed from the action once you've stepped across the threshold. Each compact guesthouse comes with a wood-burning fireplace, homey furnishings, cozy quilts, and an enormous bathroom with a skylight and a deep, two-person Jacuzzi tub. Guests enjoy such niceties as gourmet coffee, a stereo with CD player, VCR (the inn has a video library), wet bar, and fridge. Several major spas are within walking distance. This is a top pick if you want to do the Calistoga spa scene in comfort and style. Smoking on the small front porch only.

Moderate

Eurospa and Inn. 1202 Pine St. (between Myrtle and Cedar sts.), Calistoga, CA 94515. ☎ **707/942-6829.** Fax 707/942-1138. www.eurospa.com. 12 units. A/C TV. $99–$199 double. Rates include continental breakfast. Weekend packages $369; off-season and midweek package discounts available. AE, CB, DC, DISC, MC, V.

In a quiet residential section of Calistoga, this small European-style inn and spa provides a level of solitude and privacy that few other spas can match. The horseshoe-shaped inn consists of a dozen stucco bungalows, a spa center, and an outdoor patio where a light breakfast and snacks are served. The rooms, although small, are pleasantly decorated with pine furnishings and soft pastels; a few have kitchenettes. Spa treatments range from Fango Naturium mud baths to honey-almond body scrubs, seaweed body wraps, and de-stress massage. If you're worried about going over your budget, opt for the "Wellness Packages," which include lodging, mineral bath, an hour of spa treatments, continental breakfast, and dinner voucher for $229 per person ($319 per couple) per night. Weekend packages include lodging plus 90 minutes of spa treatments each for two people.

Inexpensive

Calistoga Spa Hot Springs. 1006 Washington St. (at Gerrard St.), Calistoga, CA 94515. ☎ **707/942-6269.** www.calistogaspa.com. 57 units, 1 family unit. A/C TV TEL. Winter $70 double, $95 family unit; summer $85 double, $110 family unit. MC, V.

Very few hotels in the Wine Country cater specifically to families with children, which is why I strongly recommend the Calistoga Spa Hot Springs if you're bringing the little ones. In any case, it's a great bargain, offering unpretentious yet comfortable rooms with kitchenettes, as well as a plethora of spa facilities. All of Calistoga's best shops and restaurants are within easy walking distance, and you can even whip up your own grub at the barbecues near the large pool and patio area.

WHERE TO DINE IN NAPA VALLEY

Recently, Napa's restaurants have drawn as much attention to the valley as its award-winning wineries. Nowhere else in the state are kitchens as deft at mixing fresh seasonal, local, organic produce into edible magic, which means that menus change constantly to reflect the best available ingredients. Add that to a great bottle of wine and stunning views, and you have one heck of an eating experience.

To best enjoy Napa's restaurant scene, keep one thing in mind: Reserve—especially for a seat in a famous room.

NAPA
Moderate
Bistro Don Giovanni. 4110 St. Helena Hwy. (Hwy. 29, just north of Salvador Ave.), Napa. ☎ 707/224-3300. Reservations recommended. Main courses $11–$17. AE, DC, DIS, MC, V. Mon–Thurs 11:30am–10pm; Fri–Sat 11:30am–11pm. REGIONAL ITALIAN.

Donna and Giovanni Scala—who also run the fantastic Scala's Bistro in San Francisco—serve refined Italian fare prepared with quality ingredients and California flair at this large, lively, Mediterranean-style restaurant. The menu features pastas, risottos, pizzas (baked in a wood-burning oven), and half a dozen other main courses such as braised lamb shank and Niman-Schell bistro burgers. Less traditional appetizers include a grilled pear with frisée-and-arugula salad with blue cheese, caramelized walnuts, and bacon. Pasta lovers go for farfalle with asparagus, porcini, wild mushrooms, pecorino cheese, and truffle oil; seared salmon with tomato, white wine, and chive sauce is another winner. Alfresco dining in the vineyards is available—and highly recommended on a warm, sunny day.

Inexpensive
Alexis Baking Company. 1517 Third St. (between Main and Jefferson Sts.), Napa. ☎ 707/258-1827. Main courses $3.25–$7.95 at breakfast, $6.95–$9.95 at lunch, $6.75–$13 at dinner. Mon–Wed 6:30am–6pm; Thurs–Fri 6:30pm–8pm; Sat 7:30am–3pm; Sun 8am–2pm. BAKERY/CAFE.

Alexis (a.k.a. ABC) is a quaint, casual stop for residents and in-the-know tourists. On weekend mornings, the line stretches out the door. But once you order from the counter and find a seat in the sunny room, you can relax, enjoy the coffeehouse atmosphere, and start your day with spectacular pastries, coffee drinks, and breakfast goodies like pumpkin pancakes with sautéed pears. Lunch also bustles with locals who come for daily specials like fusilli pasta with roasted pumpkin, white beans, ham, and Parmesan in cream sauce; grilled-chicken Caesar salad; roast-lamb sandwich with minted mayo and roasted shallots on rosemary bread; and lentil bulgar orzo salad. Desserts run the gamut; during the holidays, they include a moist and magical steamed persimmon pudding.

OAKVILLE & RUTHERFORD
Expensive
Auberge du Soleil. 180 Rutherford Hill Rd., Rutherford. ☎ 707/963-1211. Reservations recommended. Main courses $25–$30. AE, DISC, MC, V. Daily 7–11am, 11:30am–2:30pm, and 6–9:30pm. WINE COUNTRY CUISINE.

Auberge du Soleil may be better known for its inn, but it was the restaurant that started all the fuss over this world-class resort. Alfresco dining rises to an entirely new level here, particularly on warm summer nights when diners have a gorgeous sunset view of the mountains. Inside, a magnificent fireplace, huge wood pillars, and fresh flowers create a warm, rustic ambience. Chef Andrew Sutton characterizes his cooking as "Wine Country cuisine," a reflection of the region's produce and international influences (Pacific Rim, Southwestern, and Mediterranean styles predominate). Signature dishes include a tasting platter of truffled deviled quail egg, smoked sturgeon, Thai lobster salad, caviar, and more; and grapevine smoked salmon with walnut-wheat croutons and roasted shallot-caper relish. Regardless of what you order, be sure to reserve terrace seating (or arrive before sunset and beg for it).

✪ **La Toque.** 1140 Rutherford Cross Rd., Rutherford. ☎ **707/963-9770.** Reservations recommended. Fixed-price menu $65. Wed–Sat 5:30–10pm; Sunday 1:30pm–10pm. FRENCH-INSPIRED.

Don't come here without an appetite. Renowned chef Ken Frank left Los Angeles's fenix at the Argyle Hotel to open one of the Wine Country's most formal dining rooms—and once you sit down to the five-course extravaganza you can't refrain from gobbling up all the delicious—and generous—creations that come your way. Each table at the elegant restaurant adjoining Rancho Caymus Inn is well spaced, making plenty of room to showcase the chef-owner's memorable and innovative French-inspired cuisine. The menu might feature an incredible Indian spice–rubbed foie gras with Madras carrot purée (one of the best I've had); melt-in-your-mouth yellowfin tuna with braised daikon, red wine, and sautéed pea sprouts; knock-out Maine lobster with creamy orzo and lobster cabernet sauce; and, should you find room and the extra few bucks for the cheese course, delicious selections served with walnut bread. For an additional $32 per person, my party drank splendid, well-paired wines with each course. Alas, we did not have room for desserts of chocolate panna cotta with vanilla Anglaise and toasted pineapple fritter with vanilla bean ice cream—but we ate it anyway.

YOUNTVILLE
Expensive

✪ **The French Laundry.** 6640 Washington St. (at Creek St.), Yountville. ☎ **707/944-2380.** Reservations required. Vegetarian menu $80; 5-course menu $90; chef's 9-course tasting menu $105. AE, MC, V. Fri–Sun 11am–1pm; daily 5:30–9:30pm. CLASSIC AMERICAN/FRENCH.

It's almost futile to include this restaurant, because you're about as likely to secure a reservation—or get through on the reservation line, for that matter—as you are to drive Highway 29 without passing a winery. Several years after renowned chef-owner Thomas Keller bought the place and caught the attention of epicureans worldwide (including the judges of the James Beard Awards, who named him "Chef of the Nation" in 1997), the discreet restaurant is the hottest dinner ticket *in the world.* At least you can read about it.

The atmosphere is as somber and serious as the oh-so-privileged diners who quietly swoon over the ongoing parade of bite-size delights delivered to the table. Technically, the prix-fixe menu offers a choice of five or nine courses (including a vegetarian menu), but after a slew of cameo appearances from the kitchen, everyone starts to lose count. Signature dishes include Keller's "tongue in cheek" (a marinated and braised round of sliced lamb tongue and tender beef cheeks) and "macaroni and cheese" (sweet butter-poached Maine lobster with creamy lobster broth and orzo with mascarpone cheese). Portions are small, but only because Keller wants his guests to taste as many things as possible. Nobody leaves hungry. The excellent staff is well acquainted with the wide selection of regional wines; there's a $30 corkage fee if you bring your own bottle. On warm summer nights, request a table in the flower-filled garden. *Hint:* If you can't get a reservation, try walking in—on occasion folks don't make their reservation and tables open up, especially during lunch on rainy days.

Moderate

✪ **Bistro Jeanty.** 6510 Washington St. (near Mulberry), Yountville. ☎ **707/944-0103.** http://bistrojeanty.com. Reservations recommended. Appetizers $4.50–$7.50, most main courses $13.75–$18.50. MC, V. Daily 11:30am–10:30pm. Closed Thanksgiving, Dec 25.

This casual, warm bistro, with muted buttercup walls and two dining rooms divided by the bar, is the brainchild of chef Phillipe Jeanty. A few years back, the highly regarded chef left his 18-year post at Domaine Chandon to open one of the hottest (and most moderately priced) new restaurants in town. Jeanty was previously known for formal French cooking, but his cheery bistro is far more laid-back—and equally outstanding. The all-day menu includes legendary tomato soup in puff pastry; foie gras pâté; steak tartare; and house-smoked trout with potato slices. Daube de boeuf is simmered in red wine and served with mashed potatoes, fresh peas, and baby carrots; cassoulet includes white beans, fennel sausage, pork, and duck leg. We'll return frequently for the decadent fall-off-the-bone coq au vin with earthy, smoky red wine sauce, and the delicate deep-fried smelt special, which came in a wax-paper cone accompanied by a seasoned mayo dipping sauce. Like most San Franciscans, we consider this place a must-stop on the Wine Country itinerary.

Bouchon. 6534 Washington St. (at Humbolt), Yountville. ☎ **707/944-8037.** Reservations recommended. Main courses $11.95–$16.95. AE, DC, MC, V. Daily 11:30am–2pm and 5:30–10:30pm. Late-night menu 10:45pm–1:30am. FRENCH BISTRO.

Perhaps to appease the crowds who never get a reservation at French Laundry, Thomas Keller teamed up with his brother Joseph to open this far more casual, but still delicious, French brasserie. Adam Tihany, who also conceptualized New York's Le Cirque 2000, designed the dining room. Along with a raw bar, expect superb renditions of steak frites, mussels marinières, grilled-cheese sandwiches, and other heavenly French classics. Prices and atmosphere are far more down-to-earth than at French Laundry. I do like this place, but far prefer Bistro Jeanty. A bonus, especially for restless residents, is the late hours.

Mustards Grill. 7399 St. Helena Hwy. (Hwy. 29), Yountville. ☎ **707/944-2424.** Reservations recommended. Main courses $11–$27. CB, DC, DISC, MC, V. Apr–Oct daily 11:30am–10pm; Nov–Mar daily 11:30am–9pm. CALIFORNIA.

It's always a pleasant surprise to find a serious restaurant with a strong sense of humor; Mustards is one of those places. Housed in a convivial, barn-style space, it offers an 11-page wine list and an ambitious chalkboard list of specials. My party started out with wonderfully light seared ahi tuna that melted in the mouth the way ahi should. Although the tea-smoked Peking duck with almond onion sauce and grilled rabbit with potatoes, fennel, and saffron broth were tempting, we opted for a moist, perfectly flavored grilled chicken breast with mashed potatoes and fresh herbs. The menu includes something for everyone, from vegetarians to good old burger lovers.

Piatti. 6480 Washington St. (between Washington and Oak sts.), Yountville. ☎ **707/944-2070.** Reservations recommended. Main courses $7–$16. AE, DC, MC, V. Sun–Thurs 11:30am–10pm; Fri–Sat 11:30am–11pm. ITALIAN.

This local favorite—the first (and best) of a swiftly growing northern California chain—is known for serving excellent, reasonably priced food in a rustic Italian-style setting. Chef Peter Hall, a seasoned Napa Valley cook who honed his culinary art at Tra Vigne and Mustards before taking the helm here, performs to a mostly sold-out crowd nightly. For the perfect meal, start with a salad of morning-cut field greens mixed with white corn and Napa Valley strawberry crostini, accompanied by a bowl of spaghetti squash and sweet-potato soup. Although Hall offers a wide array of superb pastas and pizzas, it's the wood-oven-roasted duck—basted with sweet cherry sauce and served over a bed of citrus risotto—that brings back the regulars. There are far fancier and more intimate restaurants in the valley, but none where you can fill up on such outstanding fare at these prices. Piatti also offers patio dining year-round, weather permitting.

Where to Stock Up for a Gourmet Picnic

You could easily plan your whole trip around restaurant reservations, but put together one of the world's best gourmet picnics, and the valley's your oyster.

One of the finest gourmet-food stores in the Wine Country, if not all of California, is the **Oakville Grocery Co.,** 7856 St. Helena Hwy., at Oakville Cross Road, Oakville (☎ **707/944-8802**). You can put together the provisions for a memorable picnic, or, with at least 24 hours' notice, the staff can prepare a picnic basket for you. The store, with its small-town vibe and claustrophobia-inducing crowds, can be quite an experience. You'll find shelves crammed with the best breads and choicest cheeses in the northern Bay Area, as well as pâtés, cold cuts, crackers, top-quality olive oils, fresh foie gras (domestic and French, seasonally), smoked Norwegian salmon, fresh caviar (Beluga, Sevruga, Osetra), and, of course, an exceptional selection of California wines. Open daily 9am to 6pm. The espresso bar tucked in the corner (open daily from 7am to 3pm), offers breakfast and lunch items, house-baked pastries, and 15 wines by the glass or for tasting.

Another of my favorite places to fill a picnic basket is New York City's version of a swank European marketplace, **Dean & DeLuca,** 607 S. Main St. (Highway 29), north of Zinfandel Lane and south of Sulphur Springs Road, St. Helena (☎ **707/967-9980**). The ultimate gourmet grocery store is more like a world's fair of foods, where everything is beautifully displayed and often painfully pricey. As you pace the barn-wood plank floors, you'll stumble upon more high-end edibles than you've ever seen under one roof. They include local organic produce (delivered daily); 200 domestic and imported cheeses (with an on-site aging room to ensure proper ripeness); shelves and shelves of tapenades, pastas, oils, hand-packed dried herbs and spices, chocolates, sauces, and cookware; an espresso bar; one hell of a bakery section; and more. Along the back wall, you can watch the professional chefs prepare gourmet takeout. Try fresh seared salmon with chanterelle mushrooms ($7.50 for a 6-ounce serving), rotisserie meats, salads, and sautéed vegetables. Or order the to-go fireside dinner, a four-course meal that costs $7.50 to $9.50 per person and may include a Caesar salad, rotisserie pork loin with mustard and apricot glaze, French green lentils, sun-dried tomatoes, and root veggies (two-person minimum). Wine master John Hardesty presides over the 1,200-label collection. Adjoining the wine room is a walk-in cedar humidor with that holds over 200 cigars. Open Monday to Saturday 10am to 7pm (the espresso bar opens at 8am), Sunday 10am to 6pm.

ST. HELENA

Expensive

✪ **Pinot Blanc.** 641 Main St., St. Helena. ☎ **707/963-6191.** Main courses $9–$20 at lunch, $16–$24 at dinner. AE, DC, DISC, JCB, MC, V. Daily 11:30am–3pm; limited bar menu daily 3–5:30pm; Sun–Thurs 5:30–9:30pm; Fri–Sat 5:30–10pm. Extended summer hours. FRENCH BISTRO.

Reviews were mixed as L.A. celebrity chef Joachim Splichal's formal new restaurant settled in over the past 3 years, but Pinot Blanc has long surpassed its shaky start. The beautiful dining room, recently renovated to present a more country French atmosphere, is the perfect spot to sample executive chef Sean Knight's gastronomic glories.

Lunch offerings might include potato lasagna with forest shrooms and chanterelle *jus,* or curry chicken salad with sun-dried Napa grapes and apples. The unique menu features such entrees as coq au vin, cannelloni with roasted vegetables, a pot of mussels with Pernod broth and rouille, and planked Atlantic salmon with shallot and apple smoked-bacon crust. Attention is paid to every detail at this restaurant, including the wine list, which features over 200 selections. There is patio seating during the summer.

✪   **Terra.** 1345 Railroad Ave. (between Adams and Hunt sts.), St. Helena. ☎ **707/ 963-8931.** Reservations recommended. Main courses $18.50–$26. CB, DC, MC, V. Sun–Mon and Wed–Thurs 6–9pm; Fri–Sat 6–10pm. CONTEMPORARY AMERICAN.

St. Helena's restaurant of choice is the creation of Lissa Doumani and her husband, Hiro Sone, a master chef who hails from Japan and once worked with Wolfgang Puck at L.A.'s Spago. Sone makes full use of the region's bounty; he seems to know how to coax every nuance of flavor from his fine local ingredients. The recently redecorated dining room is a perfect foil for the extraordinary food. Among the appetizers, the stars of the show are terrine of foie gras with fig and endive salad, and home-smoked salmon with potato latkes, sour cream, and caviar. The main dishes fuse different cooking styles; try grilled salmon with Thai red-curry sauce, or sake-marinated sea bass with shrimp dumplings in shiso broth. A recommended finale? Chocolate truffle cake with espresso ice cream.

Moderate

✪   **Tra Vigne Restaurant.** 1050 Charter Oak Ave., St. Helena. ☎ **707/963-4444.** Reservations recommended. Main courses $12.50–$22. CB, DC, DISC, MC, V. Daily 11:30am–10pm. ITALIAN.

Tra Vigne's combination of good food, high-energy atmosphere, and "reasonable" prices makes this restaurant a long-standing favorite among visitors. The enormous dining room packs 'em in every night. Whether they're on the veranda (heated on cold nights) or in the center of the bustling scene, diners are usually thrilled just to have a seat. Even though the wonderful bread (served with house-made flavored olive oils) is tempting, save room for the robust California dishes, cooked Italian-style. The menu features about five pizzas, including a succulent caramelized onion, thyme, and Gorgonzola version. The dishes of the day might include grilled Sonoma rabbit with teleme-layered potatoes, oven-dried tomatoes, and mustard pan sauce, and a dozen or so antipasti. Equally tempting are the pastas—which include ceppo with sausage, spinach, potatoes, sun-dried tomatoes, and pecorino—and delicious desserts. When ordering, plan wisely: Most dishes are very rich.

The adjoining **Cantinetta** (see below) offers a small selection of sandwiches, pizzas, and lighter meals.

Wine Spectator Greystone Restaurant. At the Culinary Institute of America at Greystone, 2555 Main St., St. Helena. ☎ **707/967-1010.** Reservations recommended. Tastings $4.50–$7; main courses $14–$24. AE, CB, DC, MC, V. Daily 11:30am–10pm. WINE COUNTRY CUISINE.

This place offers a visual and culinary feast that's unparalleled in the area, if not the state. The room is an enormous stone-walled former winery, but the festive decor and heavenly aromas warm the space up. Cooking islands—complete with scurrying chefs, steaming pots, and rotating chicken—provide edible entertainment. New head chef Todd Humphries (formerly of Campton Place in San Francisco) has put his own mark on the cuisine. The "tastings" (appetizer) menu features dishes inspired by fresh ingredients. They include perfect calamari sautéed with paprika, garlic, and rosemary (wonderful every time I come, regardless of the preparation!), a fine seafood and white bean salad, and an unimpressive mushroom piroshki with caramelized onions. Portions are small but affordable; pastas and salads are a bit heftier. Main courses, such as crispy fried lamb shank with cranberry beans, cherry tomatoes and spinach, are well portioned and darn good, but I recommend you opt for a barrage of appetizers for your table to share. You should also order the "Flights of Fancy"—for $14 to $20, you can sample three 3-ounce pours of local wines such as white rhone, pinot, or zinfandel. (Wines by the glass are from the same selection, which, annoyingly, does not list by-the-glass prices.) While the food is serious, the atmosphere is playful—casual enough that you'll feel comfortable in jeans or shorts. If you want to ensure a meal here, reserve far in advance. I prefer to stop by, have a snack at the bar, and eat big meals elsewhere.

Inexpensive

✪ **The Cantinetta.** At Tra Vigne Restaurant, 1050 Charter Oak Ave., St. Helena. ☎ **707/963-8888.** Main courses $4–$8. CB, DC, DISC, MC, V. Daily 11:30am–6pm. ITALIAN.

Regardless of where else I dine while in the valley, I always make a point of stopping at the Cantinetta for an espresso and a snack. Part cafe, part shop, it's a casual place with a few tables and a counter. The focaccias, pasta salads, and pastries are outstanding. There's a selection of cookies and other wonderful treats, flavored oils (free tastings), wines, and an array of gourmet items, many of which were created here. You can also get great picnic grub to go.

Tomatina. At The Inn at Southbridge, 1016 Main St., St. Helena. ☎ **707/967-9999.** Pastas $6–$8; pizzas $8–$19. DC, DISC, MC, V. Daily 11:30am–10pm. ITALIAN.

After spending a week in Wine Country, I usually can't stand the thought of another decadent wine and foie-gras meal. That's when I race to Tomatina for a $3.50 chopped salad, a welcome respite from gluttonous excess. Families and locals come here for another reason: Although the menu is limited, it's a total winner for anyone in search of freshly prepared, wholesome food at atypically cheap Wine Country prices. A Caesar salad, for example, costs a mere $4.50. "Apizzas"—pizzas folded like a soft taco—are the house specialty, and come filled with such delights as fresh Maine clams and oregano. Pizzas are of the build-your-own variety, with gourmet toppings like sautéed mushrooms, fennel sausage, baby spinach, sun-dried tomatoes, and homemade pepperoni. The 26 respectable local wines come by the glass at a toast-worthy $3.75, or $18 per bottle. Dessert, at less than $4 a pop for gelato, biscotti, or pound cake, is an overall sweet deal. Everything is ordered at the counter and brought to the small or family-style tables in the very casual dining area or the outdoor patio. Kids especially like the pool table and big-screen TV.

CALISTOGA

Moderate

All Seasons Café. 1400 Lincoln Ave. (at Washington St.), Calistoga. ☎ **707/942-9111.** Reservations recommended on weekends. Main courses $7.50–$13 at lunch, $10.25–$19 at dinner. MC, V. Mon–Tues and Thurs–Fri 11am–3pm; daily 5:30–10pm. Wine shop Thurs–Tues 11am–7pm. CALIFORNIA.

Wine Country devotees wend their way to the All Seasons Café in downtown Calistoga because of its extensive wine list and knowledgeable staff. The trick is to buy a bottle of wine from the cafe's wine shop, then bring it to your table; the cafe adds a corkage fee of around $7.50 instead of tripling the price of the bottle (as most restaurants do). The diverse menu ranges from pizzas and pastas to such main courses as braised lamb shank osso bucco in an orange, Madeira, and tomato sauce. Anything with house-smoked salmon or spiced sausages is also a safe bet. Chef John Coss saves his guests from any major *faux pas* by matching wines to dishes on the menu, so you know just what's right for smoked salmon and Crescenza cheese pizza.

✪ **Catahoula.** 1457 Lincoln Ave. (between Washington and Fairway sts.), Calistoga. ☎ **707/942-2275.** Reservations recommended. Main courses $11–$20. MC, V. Summer Fri–Sun 8:30–10am; Sat–Sun noon–3:30pm; daily 5:30–10:30pm. Winter Sat–Sun 8:30–10am. AMERICAN/SOUTHERN.

The domain of chef Jan Birnbaum, formerly of New York's Quilted Giraffe and San Francisco's Campton Place, this restaurant is the town's current favorite. And for good reason: It's the only place in Napa where you can get decent rooster gumbo. And you'd have to travel all over Louisiana to find a pan-fried jalapeño-pecan catfish like this one. Catahoula's funky and fun, and the food that comes out of the wood-burning oven—like roast duck with chili cilantro potatoes, or whole roasted fish with lemon broth, orzo, and escarole—is exciting and usually spicy.

Inexpensive

Smokehouse Café. 1458 Lincoln Ave., Calistoga. ☎ **707/942-6060.** Main courses $8–$21. MC, V. Daily 7:30am–10pm (closed for dinner Tues–Wed Jan–Feb). REGIONAL AMERICAN BBQ.

Who would have guessed that some of the best spareribs and house-smoked meats in northern California would come from this little kitchen in Calistoga? Here's the winning game plan: Start with Sacramento delta crawfish cakes and husk-roasted Cheyenne corn. Move on to the slow pig sandwich, a half slab of ribs, or homemade sausages—all of which take up to a week to prepare (not while you wait, luckily). The clincher is the fluffy all-you-can-eat cornbread dipped in pure cane syrup, which comes with every full-plate dinner. Kids are especially welcome—a rarity in these parts—and patio dining is available in summer.

Wappo Bar & Bistro. 1226B Washington St. (off Lincoln Ave.), Calistoga. ☎ **707/942-4712.** Main courses $8.50–$14.50. AE, MC, V. Wed–Mon 11:30am–2:30pm and 6–9:30pm. GLOBAL.

One of the best alfresco dining experiences in the Wine Country is under Wappo's honeysuckle-and-vine-covered arbor, but you'll also be comfortable at one of the well-spaced, well-polished tables inside the small bistro. The menu offers a wide range of choices, from Chilean sea bass with mint chutney to roast rabbit with oven tomato tagliarini. Desserts of choice are black-bottom coconut cream pie and strawberry rhubarb pie.

2 Sonoma County

A pastoral contrast to Napa, Sonoma manages to maintain a backcountry ambience, thanks to its far lower density of wineries, restaurants, and hotels. Small, family-owned wineries are Sonoma's mainstay; tastings are low-key, and they come with plenty of friendly banter with the winemakers (who often do the pouring). Basically, this is the valley to target if your ideal vacation includes visiting a handful of wineries along quiet, woodsy roads, avoiding shopping outlets and Napa's high-end glitz, and simply enjoying the laid-back country atmosphere.

The valley is some 17 miles long and 7 miles wide, and bordered by two mountain ranges: the Mayacamas to the east and Sonoma Mountains to the west. Unlike Napa Valley, you won't find palatial wineries with million-dollar art collections, aerial trams, and Hollywood ego trips (read: Niebaum-Coppola). Rather, the Sonoma Valley offers a refreshing dose of reality, where modestly sized wineries are integrated into the community. If Napa Valley feels like a fantasyland, where everything exists to service the almighty grape and the visitors it attracts, then the Sonoma Valley is its antithesis, an unpretentious gaggle of ordinary towns, ranches, and wineries that welcome tourists but don't necessarily rely on them. The result is a chance to experience what Napa Valley must have been like long before the Seagrams and Moët et Chandons of the world turned the Wine Country into a major tourist destination.

As in Napa, you can also pick up *Wine Country Review* throughout Sonoma. It gives you the most up-to-date information on wineries and related area events.

ESSENTIALS

GETTING THERE   From San Francisco, cross the Golden Gate Bridge and stay on U.S. 101 north. Exit at Highway 37; after 10 miles, turn north onto Highway 121. After another 10 miles, turn north onto Highway 12 (Broadway), which takes you directly into the town of Sonoma.

VISITOR INFORMATION   While you're in Sonoma, stop by the **Sonoma Valley Visitors Bureau,** 453 First St. E. (☎ **707/996-1090;** www.sonomavalley.com). It's open daily from 9am to 7pm in summer and from 9am to 5pm in winter. An additional **Visitors Bureau** is a few miles south of the square at 25200 Arnold Dr. (Highway 121), at the entrance to Viansa Winery (☎ **707/996-5793**); it keeps the same hours.

If you prefer some advance information, the $2 *Sonoma Valley Visitors Guide* lists most every lodging, winery, and restaurant in the valley. Contact the Sonoma Valley Visitors Bureau to order one, or check out the Web site.

TOURING THE VALLEY & WINERIES

Sonoma Valley is currently home to about 35 wineries (including California's first winery, Buena Vista, founded in 1857) and 13,000 acres of vineyards. It produces roughly 25 types of wines totaling more than 5 million cases a year. Cabernet is the varietal for which Sonoma is most noted. Unlike the rigidly structured tours at many of Napa Valley's corporate-owned wineries, tastings and tours on the Sonoma side of the Mayacamas Mountains are usually free and low-key.

The towns and wineries covered below are organized geographically from south to north, starting at the intersection of Highway 37 and Highway 121 in the Carneros District and ending in Kenwood. The wineries tend to be a little more spread out than they are in Napa, but they're easy to find. Still, it's best to decide which wineries you're most interested in and devise a touring strategy before you set out, so you don't do too much backtracking.

I've reviewed some favorite Sonoma Valley wineries here—more than enough to keep you busy tasting wine for a long weekend. If you'd like a complete list of local wineries, be sure to pick up one of the free guides to the valley available at the Sonoma Valley Visitors Bureau (see "Visitor Information," above).

THE CARNEROS DISTRICT

As you approach the Wine Country from the south, you must first pass through the Carneros District, a cool, windswept region that borders the San Pablo Bay and marks the entrance to both Napa and Sonoma valleys. Until the latter part of the 20th century, this mixture of marsh, sloughs, and rolling hills was mainly used as sheep pasture (*carneros* means "sheep" in Spanish). After experimental plantings yielded slow-growing, high-quality grapes—particularly chardonnay and pinot noir—several Napa and Sonoma wineries expanded their plantings here. They eventually established the Carneros District as an American Viticultural Appellation. Although about a dozen wineries are spread throughout the region, there are no major towns or attractions—just plenty of gorgeous scenery as you cruise along Highway 121, the major junction between Napa and Sonoma.

⊙ **Viansa Winery and Italian Marketplace.** 25200 Arnold Dr. (Calif. 121), Sonoma. ☎ **800/995-4740** or 707/935-4700. www.viansa.com. Daily 10am–5pm. Daily self-guided tours.

The first major winery you'll encounter as you enter Sonoma Valley from the south, this sprawling Tuscan-style villa perches atop a knoll overlooking the entire lower valley. Viansa is the brainchild of Sam and Vicki Sebastiani, who left the family dynasty to create their own temple to food and wine. (*Viansa* is a contraction of "Vicki and Sam.") While Sam, a third-generation winemaker, runs the winery, Vicky manages the marketplace, a large room crammed with a cornucopia of high-quality preserves, mustards, olive oils, pastas, salads, breads, desserts, Italian tableware, cookbooks, and wine-related gifts.

The winery, which does an extensive mail-order business through its Tuscany Club (worth joining if you love getting mail and good wine), has quickly established a favorable reputation for its cabernet, sauvignon blanc, and chardonnay. Blended from premium Napa and Sonoma grapes, they're sold in the sexiest-shaped bottles in Sonoma. Sam is also experimenting with Italian grape varieties such as muscat canelli, sangiovese, and nebbiolo, most of which are sold exclusively at the winery. Free tastings are poured at the east end of the marketplace, and the self-guided tour includes a trip through the underground barrel-aging cellar adorned with colorful hand-painted murals.

Viansa is also one of the few wineries in Sonoma Valley that sells deli items—the focaccia sandwiches are delicious. You can dine alfresco under the grape trellis while you admire the bucolic view.

⊙ **Gloria Ferrer Champagne Caves.** 23555 Carneros Hwy. (Calif. 121), Sonoma. ☎ **707/996-7256.** www.gloriaferrer.com. Daily 10am–5:30pm. Tours daily 11am–4pm.

When you have had it up to here with chardonnays and pinots, it's time to pay a visit to Gloria Ferrer, the grande dame of the Wine Country's sparkling-wine producers. Who's Gloria? She's the wife of José Ferrer, whose family has made sparkling wine for 5 centuries. The family business, Freixenet, is the largest producer of sparkling wine in the world; Cordon Negro there is its most popular brand. That equals big bucks, and certainly a good chunk went into building this palatial estate. Glimmering like Oz high atop a gently sloping hill, it overlooks the verdant Carneros District; on a sunny day, enjoying a glass of dry brut while soaking in the magnificent views is a must.

If you're unfamiliar with the term *méthode champenoise,* be sure to take the free 30-minute tour of the fermenting tanks, bottling line, and caves brimming with racks of yeast-laden bottles. Afterward, retire to the elegant tasting room for a flute of brut or cuvée ($3 to $5.50 a glass, $16 and up per bottle), find an empty chair on the veranda, and say, "Ahhh. *This* is the life." There are picnic tables, but it's usually too windy for comfort, and you must buy a bottle of sparkling wine to reserve a table.

SONOMA

At the northern boundary of the Carneros District along Highway 12, is the centerpiece of Sonoma Valley. The midsized town of Sonoma owes much of its appeal to Mexican General Mariano Guadalupe Vallejo, who fashioned this pleasant, slow-paced community after a typical Mexican village—right down to its central plaza, Sonoma's geographical and commercial center. The plaza sits at the top of a T formed by Broadway (Highway 12) and Napa Street. Most of the surrounding streets form a grid pattern around this axis, making Sonoma easy to negotiate. The plaza's Bear Flag Monument marks the spot where the crude Bear Flag was raised in 1846, signaling the end of Mexican rule; the symbol was later adopted by the state of California and placed on its flag. The 8-acre park at the center of the plaza, complete with two ponds populated by ducks and geese, is perfect for an afternoon siesta in the cool shade. A favorite attraction, however, is the gaggle of brilliantly feathered chickens that roam unfettered through the streets of Sonoma—a sight you'll definitely never see in Napa.

Sebastiani Vineyards Winery. 389 Fourth St. E., Sonoma. ☎ **800/888-5532** or 707/938-5532. www.sebastiani.com. Daily 10am–5pm. Tours 10:30am–4pm, every 30 min. in summer, every 45–60 min. in winter; no reservations necessary.

The name Sebastiani is practically synonymous with Sonoma. What started in 1904, when Samuele Sebastiani began producing his first wines, has in three generations grown into a small empire and Sonoma County's largest winery, producing some 6 million cases a year. The winery's setting and structure aren't the most scenic in Sonoma Valley, yet its place in the history and development of the region is unparalleled.

The 25-minute tour is interesting, informative, and well worth the time. You can see the winery's original turn-of-the-century crusher and press, as well as the world's largest collection of oak-barrel carvings, crafted by local artist Earle Brown. If you don't want to take the tour, head straight for the charmingly rustic tasting room, where you can sample an extensive selection of wines free. Bottle prices are reasonable, ranging from $8 for a 1998 white zin to $50 for a 1997 cabernet sauvignon. A picnic area adjoins the cellars, but a far more scenic spot is across the parking lot in Sebastiani's Cherryblock Vineyards.

Buena Vista. 18000 Old Winery Rd. (off E. Napa St., slightly northeast of downtown), Sonoma. ☎ **800/926-1266** or 707/938-1266. www.buenavistawinery.com. Daily 10:30am–5pm. Self-guided tours only.

Count Agoston Haraszthy, the Hungarian émigré who is universally regarded as the father of California's wine industry, founded this historic winery in 1857. A close friend of General Vallejo, Haraszthy returned from Europe in 1861 with 100,000 of the finest vine cuttings, which he made available to all growers. Although Buena Vista's winemaking now takes place at an ultramodern facility in the Carneros District, the winery maintains a tasting room inside the restored 1862 Press House. The beautiful stone-crafted room brims with wines, wine-related gifts, and accessories (as well as a small art gallery along the inner balcony).

Tastings are free for most wines, $3 for the really good stuff; bottle prices range from as low as $8.95 for a buttery 1998 sauvignon blanc to $37 for the Carneros Grand Reserve cabernet sauvignon. You can take the self-guided tour any time during operating hours; a "Historical Presentation," offered daily at 2pm, details the life and times of the Count. After tasting, grab your favorite bottle, a selection of cheeses from the Sonoma Cheese Factory, salami, bread, and pâté (all available in the tasting room), and plant yourself at one of the many picnic tables in the lush, verdant setting.

Ravenswood Winery. 18701 Gehricke Rd. (off Lovall Valley Rd.), Sonoma. ☎ **800/ NO-WIMPY** or 707/938-1960. www.ravenswood-wine.com. Daily 10am–4:30pm. Tours by reservation only.

Compared to old heavies like Sebastiani and Buena Vista, Ravenswood is a relative newcomer to the Sonoma wine scene. It has quickly established itself as the sine qua non of zinfandel, the versatile grape that's quickly gaining ground on the rapacious cabernet sauvignon. In fact, Ravenswood is the first winery in the United States to focus primarily on zins, which make up about three-quarters of its 150,000-case production; it also produces a merlot, cabernet sauvignon, and a small amount of chardonnay.

The winery is smartly designed—recessed into the hillside to protect its treasures from the simmering summers. Tours follow the winemaking process from grape to

---

Touring the Sonoma Valley by Bike

Sonoma and its neighboring towns are so small, close together, and relatively flat that it's not difficult to get around on two wheels. In fact, if you're in no great hurry, there's no better way to tour the Sonoma Valley than by bicycle. You can rent a bike at the ✪ **Goodtime Bicycle Company,** 18503 Sonoma Hwy. (Calif. 12), Sonoma (☎ **888/525-0453** or 707/938-0453). The staff will happily point you to easy bike trails, or you can take an organized excursion to Kenwood-area wineries or south Sonoma wineries. Goodtime provides a gourmet lunch featuring local Sonoma products, and will carry any wine you purchase for you and help with shipping arrangements. Lunch rides start at 10:30am and end around 3pm. The cost, including food and equipment, is $65 per person (that's a darn good deal). Rentals cost $25 a day or $5 per hour, and include helmets, locks, and everything else you'll need. Bikes are also available for rent from **Sonoma Valley Cyclery,** 20093 Broadway, Sonoma (☎ **707/935-3377**), for $20 a day or $6 per hour.

---

glass, and include a visit into the aromatic oak-barrel aging rooms. A gourmet "Barbecue Overlooking the Vineyards" runs from 11am to 4:40pm on weekends from Memorial Day through September; call for details and reservations). You're also welcome to bring your own picnic basket to any of the tables. Tastings are free and generous, although you may not find some of the pourers as witty as they think they are (ours was a jerk; however, I know people who have had great experiences here). Bottle prices range from $8.50 for a light, crisp 1998 French Colombard to $32 for a 1997 meritage style red, but it's the kick-butt zins—priced well, in the low to mid-teens—that you'll want to stock up on.

GLEN ELLEN

About 7 miles north of Sonoma on Highway 12 is the town of Glen Ellen. Although just a fraction of the size of Sonoma, Glen Ellen is home to several of the valley's finest wineries, restaurants, and inns. Aside from the addition of a few new restaurants, this charming town hasn't changed much since the days when Jack London settled on his Beauty Ranch, about a mile west. Other than the wineries, you'll find few real signs of commercialism; the shops and restaurants, along one main winding lane, cater to a small, local clientele—that is, until the summer tourist season, when traffic nearly triples on the weekends. If you're haven't decided where you want to set up camp during your visit to the Wine Country, I highly recommend this lovable little town.

Arrowood. 14347 Sonoma Hwy. (Calif. 12), Glen Ellen. ☎ **707/938-5170.** www. arrowoodvineyards.com. Daily 10am–4:30pm. Tours by appointment only, daily at 10:30am and 2:30pm.

Richard Arrowood had already established a reputation as a master winemaker at Château St. Jean when he and his wife, Alis Demers Arrowood, set out on their own in 1986. Their picturesque winery stands on a gently rising hillside lined with perfectly manicured vineyards. Tastings take place in the Hospitality House, the newer of Arrowood's two stately gray-and-white buildings. They're fashioned after New England farmhouses, complete with wraparound porches. Richard's focus is on making world-class wine with minimal intervention, and his results are impressive: More than one of his current releases has scored over 90 points. Mind you, excellence doesn't come cheap. Prices start at $26 for a 1997 chardonnay and quickly climb to the mid- to high 30s. Arrowood is one of the few wineries in Sonoma that charge for tastings ($3), but if you're curious about what near-perfection tastes like, it's well worth it. No picnic facilities are available.

✪ **The Benziger Family Winery.** 1883 London Ranch Rd. (off Arnold Dr., on the way to Jack London State Historic Park), Glen Ellen. ☎ **800/989-8890** or 707/935-3000. www. benziger.com. Tasting room daily 10am–5pm. Tram tours daily (weather permitting) at 11:30am, 12:30, 2, and 3:30pm.

When Bruno Benziger moved from New York, purchased the plot next to Jack London State Park, and started the Glen Ellen label (see above), he had no idea that he would become the valley's second-largest wine producer. After the Benziger family's fast track to the top, they sold the rights to that label to create lower-volume, higher-quality wines under this one.

A visit here confirms that you are indeed visiting a family winery. At any given time, three generations of Benzigers (pronounced *Ben*-zigger) may be running around tending to chores, and they instantly make you feel as if you're part of the clan. The pastoral, user-friendly property features an exceptional self-guided tour ("The most comprehensive tour in the wine industry," according to *Wine Spectator*), gardens, a spacious tasting room manned by an amiable staff, and an art gallery. The free 40-minute tram tour, pulled by a beefy tractor, is both informative and fun. It winds through the estate vineyards before making a champagne-tasting pit stop on a scenic bluff. *Tip:* Tram tickets—a hot item in the summer—are available on a first-come, first-served basis, so either arrive early or stop by in the morning to pick up afternoon tickets.

Tastings of the standard-release wines are free; bottle prices range from $12 for a 1998 fumé blanc to $21 for a 1996 pinot noir. The best buy is the award-winning 1997 zinfandel (Sonoma County), priced to move at $21 a bottle. You can also purchase a full glass of wine for $5 and tour the estate in style. The winery offers several scenic picnic spots.

KENWOOD

A few miles north of Glen Ellen along Highway 12 is the tiny town of Kenwood, the valley's northernmost outpost. Although Kenwood Vineyards' wines are well known throughout the United States, the town itself consists of little more than a few restaurants, wineries, and modest homes on the wooded hillsides. The nearest lodging, the luxurious Kenwood Inn & Spa, is about a mile south. Kenwood makes for a pleasant day trip—a tour of Château St. Jean, dinner at Kenwood Restaurant—from Glen Ellen or Sonoma.

Kenwood Vineyards. 9592 Sonoma Hwy. (Calif. 12), Kenwood. ☎ **707/833-5891.** www.kenwoodvineyards.com. Daily 10am–4:30pm. Tours at 11:30am and 2:30pm daily.

Kenwood's history dates to 1906, when the Pagani brothers made their living selling wine straight from the barrel and into the jug. In 1970, the Lee family bought the property and dumped a ton of money into converting the aging winery into a modern, high-production facility (most of it cleverly concealed in the original barnlike buildings). Since then, Kenwood has earned a solid reputation for consistent quality with each of its varietals: cabernet sauvignon, chardonnay, zinfandel, pinot noir, merlot, and, most popular, sauvignon blanc—a crisp, light wine with hints of melon.

Although the winery looks rather modest in size, its output is staggering: Over 400,000 cases of ultra-premium wines fermented in steel tanks and French and American oak barrels. Popular with collectors is winemaker Michael Lee's Artist Series cabernet sauvignon, a limited production from the winery's best vineyards, featuring labels with original artwork by renowned artists. The tasting room, housed in one of the old barns, offers free tastings of most varieties and sells gift items. Wine prices are moderate, ranging from $8 for a bottle of 1995 Vintage Red table wine to $22 for a 1997 Sonoma County merlot; the Artist Series runs $50 to $250.

Château St. Jean. 8555 Sonoma Hwy. (Calif. 12), Kenwood. ☎ **800/543-7572** or 707/833-4134. www.chateaustjean.com. Tasting room Mon–Thurs 10am–4:30pm; Fri–Sun 10am–5pm. At the foot of Sugarloaf Ridge, just north of Kenwood and east of Hwy. 12.

Château St. Jean is notable for its exceptionally beautiful buildings, landscaped grounds, and elegant tasting room. Among California wineries, it's a pioneer in vineyard designation—the procedure of making wine from, and naming it for, a single vineyard. A private drive takes you to what was once a 250-acre country retreat built in 1920; a well-manicured lawn overlooking the meticulously maintained vineyards is now a picnic area, complete with a fountain and picnic tables. There's a self-guided tour with detailed and photographic descriptions of the winemaking process. When you're done, be sure to walk to the top of the faux medieval tower for a magnificent view of the valley.

Back in the elegant tasting room—split into three areas to better handle the traffic—you can sample Château St. Jean's wide array of wines. They range from chardonnays and cabernet sauvignon to fumé blanc, merlot, Johannesburg Riesling, and Gewürztraminer. (Don't miss a rare tasting of late-harvest wines—you'll be amazed what a little more time on the vine can do.) Tastings are free, and prices range from $9 for a Sonoma County fumé blanc to $30 for a Durell Vineyards pinot noir; most wines are priced around $20. If you can find a bottle of the 1991 Sonoma County Reserve cabernet, buy it—it's won more awards than Pete Sampras.

JUST UP FROM THE VALLEY: SANTA ROSA

✪ **Matanzas Creek.** 6097 Bennett Valley Rd. (off Warm Springs Rd.), Santa Rosa. ☎ **707/ 528-6464** or 800/590-6464. www.matanzascreek.com. Daily 10am–4:30pm. Tours daily by appointment only at 10:30am, 1, and 3pm. From Hwy. 12 in Kenwood or Glen Ellen, take Warm Springs Rd. turnoff to Bennett Valley Rd.; the drive takes 15–20 min.

It's not technically in Sonoma Valley, but if there's one winery that's worth a detour, it's Matanzas (pronounced Mah-*tan*-zas) Creek. After a scenic 20-minute drive, you'll arrive at one of the prettiest wineries in California, blanketed by fields of lavender (usually in bloom near the end of June), and surrounded by rolling hills of well-tended vineyards.

The winery has a rather unorthodox history. In 1978, Sandra and Bill MacIver, neither of whom had any previous experience in winemaking or business, set out with one goal in mind: to create the finest wines in the country. Actually, they overshot the mark. With the release of their Journey 1990 chardonnay, they were hailed by wine critics as the proud parents of the finest chardonnay ever produced in the United States, comparable to the finest white wines in the world.

This state-of-the-art, environmentally conscious winery produces only three varietals—chardonnay, sauvignon blanc, and merlot—all of which are available for tasting free. Prices for current releases are, as you would imagine, at the higher end. They range from $22 for a 1998 sauvignon blanc to a whopping $95 for the 1995 Estate merlot—but it's easily the finest merlot you'll sample in the Wine Country. Also available for purchase is culinary lavender from Matanzas Creek's own lavender field, the largest outside Provence. Purchase a full glass of wine and bring it outside to savor as you wander through these wonderfully aromatic gardens. Picnic tables hidden under groves of oak have pleasant views of the surrounding vineyards. On the return trip, be sure to take the Sonoma Mountain Road detour for a real backcountry experience.

WHERE TO STAY IN SONOMA COUNTY

Hotel listings are arranged below first by area, then by price, using the following categories: **Very Expensive,** more than $250 per night; **Expensive,** $200 to $250 per night; **Moderate,** $150 to $200 per night; and **Inexpensive,** less than $150 per night. Keep in mind that during the peak season and on weekends, most B&Bs and hotels require a minimum 2-night stay. Of course, that's assuming you can find a vacancy; make reservations as far in advance as possible.

If you are having trouble finding a room, try calling the **Sonoma Valley Visitors Bureau** (☎ **707/996-1090**). The staff will try to refer you to a lodging that has a room to spare, but won't make reservations for you. Another option is the **Bed and Breakfast Association of Sonoma Valley** (☎ **800/969-4667**), which can refer you to a B&B that belongs to the association and make reservations for you, too.

SONOMA
Very Expensive

✪ **Sonoma Mission Inn, Spa & Country Club.** 18140 Sonoma Hwy. (Calif. 12), P.O. Box 1447, Sonoma, CA 94576. ☎ **800/862-4945** or 707/938-9000. Fax 707/935-1205. www.sonomamissioninn.com. 230 units. A/C MINIBAR TV TEL. $120–$380 double. AE, CB, DC, MC, V. From central Sonoma, drive 3 miles north on Highway 12 and turn left on Boyes Blvd.

As you drive through Boyes Hot Springs, you may wonder why someone decided to build a multimillion-dollar spa resort in this ordinary little town. There's no view to speak of, and it certainly isn't within walking distance of any wineries or fancy restaurants. So what's the deal? It's the naturally heated artesian mineral water, piped from directly underneath the spa into the temperature-controlled pools and whirlpools. Set on 12 meticulously groomed acres, the Sonoma Mission Inn consists of a massive three-story replica of a Spanish mission (well, aside from the pink paint job) built in 1927, an array of satellite wings housing numerous super-luxury suites, and, of course, world-class spa facilities. It's a popular retreat for the wealthy and well-known, so don't be surprised if you see Barbra Streisand or Harrison Ford strolling around in skivvies. Big changes have occurred since the resort changed ownership a few years ago. It has gained 70 guest rooms and suites, a $20 million spa facility (you won't even recognize the old one), and the Sonoma Golf Club.

The modern rooms have plantation-style shutters, ceiling fans, down comforters, bathroom scales, hair dryers, and oversize bath towels. The Wine Country rooms feature king-size beds, desks, refrigerators, and huge limestone and marble bathrooms; some offer wood-burning fireplaces, and many have balconies. The older, slightly smaller Historic Inn rooms are sweetly appointed with homey furnishings; most have queen-size beds. For the ultimate in luxury, the opulently appointed (and brand-new) Mission Suites are the way to go.

Dining/Diversions: Mission Grill, run by chef Toni Robertson, is known for its low-calorie, low-sodium, and low-cholesterol California cuisine as well as its 200 varieties of Napa and Sonoma wines (see "Where to Dine in the Sonoma Valley," below). The casual Big 3 Diner serves American cuisine for breakfast, lunch, and dinner.

Amenities: Room service, concierge, laundry, dry cleaning, newspaper delivery, babysitting, secretarial services, valet parking, complimentary refreshments, tennis courts, full spa facilities (see box, "The Super Spa," on p. 298 for the complete rundown).

Moderate

✪ **El Dorado Hotel.** 405 First St. W., Sonoma, CA 95476. ☎ **800/289-3031** or 707/996-3030. Fax 707/996-3148. www.hoteleldorado.com. 26 units. A/C TV TEL. Summer $150–$210 double; winter $120–$160 double. Rates include continental breakfast and split of wine. AE, MC, V.

The Super Spa

The ✪ **Sonoma Mission Inn, Spa & Country Club,** 18140 Sonoma Hwy. (☎ **800/862-4945** or 707/938-9000; www.sonomamissioninn.com), has always been the most complete—and the most luxurious—spa in the whole Wine Country. With its new $20 million, 27,000-square-foot facility, this super spa is now one of the best in the country. The Spanish Mission–style retreat offers more than 50 spa treatments, ever-popular natural mineral baths, and virtually every facility and activity imaginable. You can pamper yourself silly: soak in mineral baths, have a facial set to music, indulge in a grape-seed body wrap, relax with a massage, take a sauna or herbal steam, go for a dip in the pool—the list goes on and on (and, alas, so will the bill). You can also work off those wicked Wine Country meals with aerobics, weights, and cardio machines; get loose in a yoga class; play tennis; or just lounge and lunch by the pool. Or you can opt for a personal favorite—the $199 Rejuvenator, a 1-hour, 45-minute mega-treatment that includes an "oil drip" onto your hair and scalp, a scalp massage, a hair mask that smells so much like cookie dough you'll be tempted to nibble on it, a face mask, and a glorious massage. After the treatment, work out in the exercise room, take a sauna, steam, and mineral plunge, then relax poolside with a good book. Now that's living.

Of course, they have to pay for this fancy upgrade somehow, and here's how:

- Weekend day-use fee for guests: $85
- Weekday day-use fee for guests: $65
- Weekend day-use fee for non-guests: $150
- Weekday day-use fee for non-guests: $85

Steep, yes, but access to the spa facilities is free if you opt for one of the treatments, so you might as well splurge. Either way, a day at the Sonoma Mission Inn Spa is one of my favorite ways to unwind in the Wine Country.

This place may look like a 19th-century Wild West relic from the outside, but inside it's all 20th-century deluxe. Each modern, handsomely appointed guest room—designed by the same folks who put together the ultra-exclusive Auberge du Soleil resort in Rutherford (see "Where to Stay in Napa Valley," above)—has French windows and tiny terraces. Some offer lovely views of the plaza; others overlook the private courtyard and heated lap pool. All rooms (except those for guests with disabilities) are on the second floor, and contain plush towels and hair dryers. The two rooms on the ground floor are off the private courtyard, and each has a partially enclosed patio. The hotel has a concierge, laundry, in-room massage, bicycle rental, and access to a nearby health club. Breakfast, served inside or out in the courtyard, includes coffee, fruits, and freshly baked breads and pastries. Within the hotel is Piatti, a popular restaurant serving regional Italian cuisine (see "Where to Dine in the Sonoma Valley," below).

Inexpensive

Best Western Sonoma Valley Inn. 550 Second St. W. (1 block from the plaza), Sonoma, CA 95476. ☎ **800/334-5784** or 707/938-9200. Fax 707/938-0935. www.sonomavalleyinn. com. 82 units. $89–$379 double. Rates include continental breakfast. AE, CB, DC, MC, V.

There are just two reasons to stay at the Sonoma Valley Inn: 1) it's the only place left with a vacancy, or 2) you're bringing the kids. Otherwise, unless you don't mind staying in a rather drab room with thin walls and a small bathroom, you're probably going to be a little disappointed. Kids, on the other hand, love the place: there's plenty of room to run around, plus a large pool and gazebo-covered spa to play in. The rooms *do* come with a lot of perks, such as continental breakfast delivered to your room, a gift bottle of white table wine from Kenwood Vineyards (chilling in the fridge), cable TV with HBO, and a balcony or deck overlooking the inner courtyard. It's also in a good location, just a block from Sonoma's plaza.

Sonoma Hotel. 110 W. Spain St., Sonoma, CA 95476. ☎ **800/468-6016** or 707/996-2996. Fax 707/996-7014. www.sonomahotel.com. 16 units. A/C TV TEL. Summer $95–$155 double. Winter Sun–Thurs $85–$130 double; Fri–Sat $115–$130 double. Rates include continental breakfast and evening wine and cheese. AE, DC, MC, V.

This cute little historic hotel on Sonoma's tree-lined town plaza emphasizes 19th-century elegance and comfort. Built in 1880 by German immigrant Henry Weyl, it has attractive guest rooms decorated in early California style, with French country furnishings, antique beds, and period decorations. In a bow to modern luxuries, recent additions include private bathrooms, cable TV, phones with data ports, and (and this is crucial) air-conditioning. Perks include fresh coffee and pastries in the morning and wine and cheese in the evening. The popular new restaurant, Heirloom, serves California-French cuisine.

Victorian Garden Inn. 316 E. Napa St., Sonoma, CA 95476. ☎ **800/543-5339** or 707/996-5339. Fax 707/996-1689. www.victoriangardeninn.com. 4 units. $99–$185 double. Rates include breakfast. AE, DC, MC, V.

Proprietor Donna Lewis runs easily the cutest B&B in Sonoma Valley. A small picket fence and a wall of trees enclose an adorable Victorian garden brimming with violets, roses, camellias, and peonies, all shaded under flowering fruit trees. It's truly a marvelous sight in the springtime. The guest rooms—three in the century-old water tower and one in the main building, an 1870s Greek Revival farmhouse—keep up the Victorian theme, with white wicker furniture, floral prints, padded armchairs, and clawfoot tubs. The most popular rooms are the Top o' the Tower and the Woodcutter's Cottage. Each has its own entrance and a garden view; the cottage boasts a sofa and armchairs set in front of the fireplace. After a hard day's wine tasting, spend the afternoon cooling off in the pool or on the shaded wraparound porch, enjoying a mellow merlot while soaking in the sweet garden smells.

GLEN ELLEN

Expensive

✪ **Gaige House Inn.** 13540 Arnold Dr., Glen Ellen, CA 95442. ☎ **800/935-0237** or 707/935-0237. Fax 707/935-6411. www.gaige.com. 15 units. A/C TEL. Summer $230–$395 double; winter $150–$295 double. Rates include full breakfast and evening wines. AE, DC, DISC, MC, V.

When you review hotels and B&Bs for a living—and I've reviewed hundreds of them—it's hard to be impressed. When I visited the Gaige House Inn, not only was I impressed, but I didn't want to leave. Owners Ken Burnet, Jr., and Greg Nemrow have managed to turn what was already a fine B&B into *the* finest in the Wine Country. They've done it by offering a level of service, amenities, and decor normally associated with outrageously expensive resorts—but without the snobbery. Breakfast, for example, is made with herbs from the inn's garden and prepared by a chef who commutes daily from San Francisco. Firm mattresses, wondrously silk-soft linens, and premium down comforters grace the beds, and even the furniture and artwork are of museum quality.

But wait, it gets better. Behind the inn is a 1.5-acre oasis with perfectly manicured lawns, a 40-foot-long pool, and an achingly inviting creek-side hammock shaded by a majestic Heritage oak. All 15 rooms, each artistically decorated in a plantation theme with Asian and Indonesian influences (trust me, they're beautiful), have king- or queen-size beds; two rooms have Jacuzzi tubs, and several have fireplaces. The Gaige Suite is the finest room, bright and airy with large windows, a private balcony overlooking the lawn, a fireplace, and a Jacuzzi tub so large you could swim in it. Personally, I prefer Garden Room no. 10, exquisitely decorated with mahogany trim and flooring, a corner fireplace, a private deck, a huge glass-walled shower with dual heads, and a Jacuzzi tub for two. On sunny days, breakfast is served at individual tables on the large terrace. Evenings are best spent in the reading parlor sipping premium wines.

Inexpensive

Beltane Ranch. 11775 Sonoma Hwy. (Hwy. 12), Glen Ellen, CA 95442. ☎ **707/996-6501.** www.beltaneranch.com. 5 units, 1 cottage. TEL. $130–$180 double. Rates include full breakfast. No credit cards; checks accepted.

The word "Ranch" conjures up a big ol' two-story house in the middle of hundreds of rolling acres, the kind of place where you laze away the day in a hammock watching the grass grow or pitching horseshoes in the garden. Well, friend, you can have all that and more at the Beltane Ranch, a century-old buttercup-yellow manor that's been everything from a bunkhouse to a brothel to a turkey farm. You simply can't help but feel your tensions ease away as you prop your feet up on the shady wraparound porch overlooking the vineyards, sipping a cool, fruity chardonnay while reading *Lonesome Dove* for the third time. Each room is uniquely decorated with American and European antiques; all have sitting areas and separate entrances. Innkeeper Deborah Mahoney serves a big country breakfast in the garden or on the porch overlooking the vineyards. For exercise, you can play tennis on the private court or hike the trails meandering through the 1,600-acre estate. *Tip:* Request one of the upstairs rooms, which have the best views.

✪ **Glenelly Inn.** 5131 Warm Springs Rd. (off Arnold Dr.), Glen Ellen, CA 95442. ☎ **707/ 996-6720.** Fax 707/996-5227. www.glenelly.com. 8 units. $135–$160 double. Rates include full breakfast. MC, V.

The Glenelly Inn is one of my favorite places to stay in the Wine Country. First off, the rates are reasonable, particularly when you factor in breakfast and afternoon snacks. More important, this former railroad inn, built in 1916, is positively drenched in serenity. Located well off the main highway on an oak-studded hillside, the peach-and-cream inn comes with everything you would expect from a country retreat. Long verandas offer comfy wicker chairs and views of the verdant Sonoma hillsides; a hearty country breakfast is served beside a large cobblestone fireplace; and bright, immaculate rooms contain old-fashioned claw-foot tubs, Scandinavian down comforters, and ceiling fans. Innkeeper Kristi Hallamore, a native San Franciscan of Norwegian descent (and a darn good cook), understands that it's the little things that make the difference. Hence the firm mattresses, good reading lights, and a simmering hot tub in a grapevine- and rose-covered arbor. All rooms, decorated with antiques and country furnishings, have queen beds, terry robes, and private entrances. Top picks are the Vallejo and Jack London cottages, both with large private patios, although I also like the rooms on the upper veranda—particularly in the spring, when the terraced gardens below are in full bloom.

KENWOOD

Very Expensive

✪ **Kenwood Inn & Spa.** 10400 Sonoma Hwy., Kenwood, CA 95452. ☎ **800/353-6966** or 707/833-1293. Fax 707/833-1247. www.kenwoodinn.com. 12 units. Apr–Oct $255–$415 double; Nov–Mar $225–$395 double. Rates include gourmet breakfast and bottle of wine. Two-night minimum on weekends Apr–Oct. AE, MC, V.

Inspired by the villas of Tuscany, the Kenwood Inn's honey-colored Italian-style build-ings, flower-filled flagstone courtyard, and pastoral views of vineyard-covered hills are enough to make any northern Italian homesick. I was immediately impressed with the friendly staff who made me feel right at home. Every spacious room is lavishly and exquisitely decorated with imported tapestries, velvets, and antiques. Each has a fireplace, balcony (except on the ground floor), feather bed, CD player, and down comforter—but no phone or TV, so you can relax. A minor caveat is road noise, which you're unlikely to hear from your room, but can be slightly audible over the tranquil pumped-in music around the courtyard and pool.

An impressive two-course gourmet breakfast is served poolside or in the Mediterranean-style dining room. Ours consisted of a poached egg accompanied by light, flavorful potatoes, red bell peppers, and other roasted vegetables, all artfully arranged, followed by a delicious homemade scone with fresh berries, and a small lemon tart.

Amenities: The inn's full-service spa offers aromatherapy, massage (one of the best I've had in a long time), and various skin and body treatments, such as a Mediter-ranean salt scrub with lemon rind and rosemary.

WHERE TO DINE IN THE SONOMA VALLEY

SONOMA

Expensive

Depot Hotel—Cucina Rustica Restaurant. 241 First St. W. (off Spain St.), Sonoma. ☎ 707/938-2980. www.depothotel.com. Reservations recommended. Main courses $17–$20. AE, CB, DC, DISC, MC, V. Wed–Fri 11:30am–5pm; Wed–Sun 5–close. NORTHERN ITALIAN.

Michael Ghilarducci has been the chef and owner here for 13 years, which means he's either independently wealthy or a darn good cook. Fortunately, it's the latter. A block north of the plaza in a handsome 1870 stone building, the Depot Hotel offers pleas-ant outdoor dining in an Italian garden complete with a reflecting pool and cascading Roman fountain. The menu is unwaveringly Italian, featuring classic dishes such as spaghetti bolognese and veal alla parmigiana. Start with the bounteous antipasto misto, and end the feast with a dish of Michael's handmade Italian ice cream and fresh-fruit sorbets.

Mission Grill. At Sonoma Mission Inn, 18140 Sonoma Hwy., Sonoma. ☎ 707/938-9000. Reservations recommended. Main courses $22.50–$27. AE, CB, DC, MC, V. Sun brunch 10am–2pm; daily 6–9:30pm. CALIFORNIA/SPA.

The Mission Grill, one of the best-known restaurants in the Wine Country, has long suffered from a solid reputation for serving high-caliber spa cuisine. The problem, of course, is the word "spa," which conjures up visions of blue-haired ladies eating boiled vegetables and soybean salads. Fortunately, the restaurant has found a solution: award-winning chef Toni Robertson. The former executive chef at the five-star Pan Pacific Hotel in Singapore has also done stints in South Africa, Maui, Beverly Hills, and Chicago. Her emphasis is on healthy, uncomplicated cuisine that relies on fresh ingre-dients and natural flavors. Typical selections from the seasonally changing menu range from lean médaillons of ostrich served with a ragout of fingerling potatoes, artichokes, and dried tomatoes, to roasted sea bass with saffron fettuccine, to grilled Liberty duck breast in roasted plum sauce. Service is professional yet friendly, and the wine list is extensive and expensive.

Moderate

✪ **Café La Haye.** 140 E. Napa St., Sonoma. ☎ 707/935-5994. Reservations recom-mended. Main courses $12–$16. AE, MC, V. Tues–Sat 5:30–9pm; Sat–Sun brunch 9:30am–2pm. ECLECTIC.

"Upscale comfort food" is perhaps the best way to describe what the chefs bring forth from the tiny open kitchen of this popular cafe. Located just off the plaza, the small split-level dining room is pleasantly decorated with hardwood floors, an exposed-beam ceiling, and contemporary artwork. The menu includes a modest selection of simple yet appealing dishes. They range from grilled pork chop with hot sweet mustard and mashed sweet potatoes to flat-iron pot roast served with fresh root vegetables over horseradish mashed potatoes. Enjoyable appetizers are the house smoked salmon with potato pancake and apple-horseradish compote, and organic mixed greens topped with spiced walnuts and roasted chioggia beets (I'm hungry just writing this). Well-prepared, wholesome food, an experienced waitstaff, friendly owners, soothing atmosphere, and reasonable prices—including a modestly priced wine list and an unheard of $7 corkage fee—make La Haye a favorite.

✪ **Maya.** 101 E. Napa St., Sonoma. ☎ **707/935-3500.** Reservations recommended. Main courses $10.50–$19.50. MC, V. Mon–Sat 11:45am–9:30pm; Sun 4–9:30pm. YUCATÁN.

Gourmet Mexican might be the best way to describe the food at this lively new restaurant on the southeast corner of Sonoma's plaza. We're not talking about top-shelf enchiladas here—rather, it's a winning combination of traditional Yucatán dishes prepared with ultra-fresh ingredients. Take salmon à la parilla, for instance: a thick cut of fresh salmon, perfectly cooked within a banana leaf, basted with guava-chili sauce, and served with a medley of grilled onions, sweet peppers, avocado, and cilantro. Wondrous. The commendable Maya pollo rostizado—a spit-roasted half chicken with a Yucatán spice rub—could easily feed two. Other menu items I considered seriously included pan-seared monkfish in papaya vinaigrette, chipotle-braised lamb shank, and grilled center-cut pork chop with maple-balsamic demiglaze. Yes, you're probably going to pay a bit more than you planned for Mexican food, but it's worth the extra few dollars. You'll probably enjoy the faux Mayan village ambience as well: desert earth tones with bright splashes of colorful art and thick, hand-carved wood furnishings. The only caveat is the *muy fuerte* noise level, but a couple of fantastic margaritas on the rocks, and you'll soon be in fiesta mode yourself.

✪ **Meritage.** 522 Broadway, Sonoma. ☎ **707/938-9430.** Reservations recommended. Main courses $13–$19. AE, MC, V. Wed–Mon 11:30am–9pm. SOUTHERN FRENCH/ NORTHERN ITALIAN.

Learning from the previous occupants' mistakes—that Sonoma ain't New York City and shouldn't treat its customers that way—chef-owner Carlo Cavallo has eliminated the big-city attitude and prices at his new restaurant without diminishing style, service, and quality. The former executive chef for Giorgio Armani, Cavallo combines the best of southern French and northern Italian cuisines (hence "Meritage," after a blend made with traditional Bordeaux varieties), giving Sonomans yet another reason to eat out. The menu, which changes twice daily, is a good read: handmade roasted pumpkin tortellini in parmesan cheese sauce; napoleon of escargot in Champagne and wild thyme sauce; organic greens, strawberries, corn, and French feta salad; wild boar chops in white truffle sauce with mashed potatoes. Such edible enticement—combined with reasonable prices, excellent service, a stellar wine list, cozy booth seating, a handsome dining room, and Carlo's practiced charm—make Meritage one of the most exciting new restaurants in the Wine Country.

Piatti. 405 First St. W., Sonoma. ☎ **707/996-2351.** Reservations recommended. Main courses $9.95–$18.95. AE, DC, MC, V. Sun–Thurs 11:30am–10pm; Fri–Sat 11:30am–11pm. ITALIAN.

Part of a northern California chain that originated in Napa, Piatti has built a steadfast clientele by consistently serving large portions of good Italian food at fair prices in a festive setting. The restaurant occupies the ground floor of the El Dorado Hotel at the northwest corner of Sonoma Plaza (just follow your nose). Good pizzas and braised meats—such as superb lamb shank flavored with rich port-wine sauce and fresh mint—emerge from a wood-burning oven. A favorite in the array of satisfying pastas is cannelloni stuffed with roasted veal, spinach, porcini mushrooms, and ricotta. Other recommended dishes include a wonderful roast-vegetable appetizer, a pile of fresh mussels in tomato-and-herb broth, rotisserie chicken with garlic mashed potatoes, and veal scaloppini. Granted, there are fancier and more intimate restaurants in the valley, but none that combine quality and value this deftly. If the sun is out, ask for a courtyard table.

Inexpensive

✪ **Cucina Viansa.** 400 First St. E., Sonoma. ☎ **707/935-5656.** Deli items $5–$9. AE, CB, DISC, MC, V. Sun–Thurs 10am–7pm; Fri–Sat 10am–11pm. ITALIAN DELI.

Cucina Viansa is the sexiest thing going in Sonoma. Sam and Vicki Sebastiani, who also run Viansa Winery, own the suave deli and wine bar. It's a visual masterpiece, with shiny black-and-white-checked flooring, long counters of Italian marble, and track lighting. Start by sampling the preserves and jams near the entrance, then choose from the cured meats, cheese, fruit, pastas, salads, and breads lining the deli. Popular choices are hefty sandwiches on herbed focaccia bread and herb-marinated rotisserie chickens served by the half with your choice of pasta or salad. Roasted turkey, duck, pork, lamb, and rabbit also are available. Opposite the deli is the wine bar, featuring all of Viansa's current releases for both tasting and purchase, as well as a small selection of microbrewed beers on tap. On your way out, stop at the gelateria and treat yourself to some intense Italian ice cream. *Note:* Cucina Viansa schedules live jazz bands every Friday and Saturday from 6 to 11pm.

✪ **Della Santina's.** 133 E. Napa St. (just east of the square), Sonoma. ☎ **707/935-0576.** Reservations recommended. Main courses $8.95–$14.75. AE, DISC, MC, V. Daily 11:30am–3pm and 5pm–9:30pm. ITALIAN.

Those of you who just can't swallow another expensive, chi-chi California meal should follow the locals to this friendly, traditional Italian restaurant. How traditional? Just ask father-and-son team Dan and Robert: When I last dined here they pointed out Signora Santina's hand-embroidered linen doilies as they proudly told me about her Tuscan recipes. (Heck, even the dining room looks like an old-fashioned, elegant Italian living room.) And their pride is merited: Every dish my party tried was refreshingly authentic and well flavored, without overbearing sauces or one *hint* of California pretentiousness. Be sure to start with traditional antipasti, especially sliced mozzarella and tomatoes, or delicious white beans. The nine pasta dishes are, again, wonderfully authentic (gnocchi lovers, rejoice!). The spit-roasted meat dishes are a local favorite (although I found them a bit overcooked); for those who can't choose between chicken, pork, turkey, rabbit, or duck, there's a selection that offers a choice of three. Don't worry about breaking your bank on a bottle of wine, because most of the choices go for under $25. Portions are huge, but save room for a wonderful dessert.

GLEN ELLEN

✪ **The Girl & The Fig.** 13690 Arnold Dr., Glen Ellen. ☎ **707/938-3634.** Reservations recommended. Main courses $12–$19. AE, MC, V. Daily 5:30–9pm. COUNTRY FRENCH.

This modern, attractive cafe with mustard-yellow walls, tile floors, and an open kitchen is the creation of Sondra Bernstein (The Girl). After spending 4 years working at Viansa Winery and Italian Marketplace, she left to open her own restaurant in August 1997. The coup de grâce was convincing San Francisco chefs Gina Marie Armanini and John Gillis to come work for her. They have moved on to open their own place, and their protégé, John Toulze, has taken over the kitchen to rave reviews—including one recently in the *New York Times*. The cuisine is nouveau country with French nuances, and yes, figs are sure to be on the menu in one form or another. The wonderful winter fig salad contains arugula, pecans, dried figs, Laura Chenel goat cheese, and fig-and-port vinaigrette. Toulze uses garden-fresh produce and local meats, poultry, and fish whenever possible, in dishes such as pork tenderloin with a potato-leek pancake and roasted beets, and sea scallops with lobster-scented risotto. For dessert, try the warm pear galette topped with gingered crème fraîche, a glass of Quady Essensia Orange Muscat, and a sliver of raclette from the cheese cart. Sondra knows her wines, and will be happy to choose the best accompaniment to your meal. *Note:* Monday in Glen Ellen has been much more fun since Sondra introduced Fondue Night.

Glen Ellen Inn Restaurant. 13670 Arnold Dr., Glen Ellen. ☎ **707/996-6409.** www.glenelleninn.com. Reservations recommended. Main courses $12–$22. AE, MC, V. Summer daily from 5:30pm; off-season Thurs–Tues from 5:30pm. CALIFORNIA.

Christian and Karen Bertrand run this popular restaurant. The dining room is so quaint and cozy that you feel as if you're dining in their home, and that's exactly the place's charm. Garden seating is the favored choice on sunny days, but the covered, heated patio is always welcoming. First courses from Christian's open kitchen might include a wild-mushroom-and-sausage "purse" served in brandy cream sauce, or warm goat-cheese croquettes. Main courses, which change with the seasons, range from linguine with artichoke hearts and feta to stellar late-harvest ravioli stuffed with pumpkin, walnuts, and sun-dried cranberries on a bed of butternut squash. Other favorites include marinated pork tenderloin on smoked mozzarella polenta, topped with roasted pepper–onion compote, and utterly tender Nebraska corn-fed filet mignon in a foie gras–brandy reduction sauce. On my last visit, the Sonoma Valley mixed green salad, seared ahi tuna, and homemade French vanilla ice cream floating in bittersweet caramel sauce made a perfect meal. The wine list offers numerous Sonoma selections, as well as more than a dozen wines by the glass. *Tip:* There's a small parking lot behind the restaurant.

KENWOOD

Kenwood Restaurant & Bar. 9900 Sonoma Hwy., Kenwood. ☎ **707/833-6326.** Reservations recommended. Main courses $12.50–$24.50. MC, V. Tues–Sun 11:30am–9pm. CALIFORNIA/CONTINENTAL.

This is what Wine Country dining should be—but often, disappointingly, is not. From the terrace of the Kenwood Restaurant, diners enjoy a view of the vineyards set against Sugarloaf Ridge as they imbibe Sonoma's finest at umbrella-covered tables. On nippy days you can retreat inside to the Sonoma-style roadhouse, with shiny wood floors, pine ceiling, vibrant artwork, and cushioned rattan chairs at white-cloth–covered tables. Chef Max Schacher serves first-rate cuisine, perfectly balanced between tradition and innovation, and complemented by a reasonably priced wine list. Great starters are Dungeness crab cake with herb mayonnaise; superfresh sashimi with ginger, soy, and wasabi; and wonderful Caesar salad. Main-dish choices might include poached salmon in creamy caper sauce, prawns with saffron Pernod sauce, or braised Sonoma rabbit with grilled polenta. But the Kenwood doesn't take itself too seriously: Sandwiches and burgers are available.

Appendix A:
History 101

Born as an out-of-the-way backwater of colonial Spain and blessed with a harbor that would have been the envy of any of the great cities of Europe, San Francisco boasts a story as varied as the millions of people who have passed through its Golden Gate.

THE AGE OF DISCOVERY

After Columbus "discovered" the New World in 1492, legends of the fertile land of California were discussed in the universities and taverns of Europe, even though no one really understood where the mythical land was. (Some evidence of arrivals in California by Chinese merchants hundreds of years before Columbus's landing has been unearthed, although few scholars are willing to draw definite conclusions.) The first documented visit by a European to northern California was by the Portuguese explorer Juan Rodriguez Cabrillo, who circumnavigated the southern tip of South America as far north as the Russian River in 1542. Nearly 40 years later, in 1579, Sir Francis Drake landed on the northern California coast, stopping for a time to repair his ships and to claim the territory for Queen Elizabeth of England. Another Portuguese, Sebastian Cermeño, "discovered" Punta de los Reyes (King's Point) in the mid-1590s. All three adventurers completely missed the narrow entrance to San Francisco Bay, either because it was enshrouded in fog or, more likely, because they simply weren't looking for it. Believe it or not, the bay's entrance is nearly impossible to see from the open ocean.

Two more centuries passed before a European actually saw the bay that would later extend Spain's influence over much of the American West. Gaspar de Portolá, a soldier sent from Spain to meddle in a rather ugly conflict between the Jesuits and the Franciscans, accidentally stumbled upon the bay in 1769, en route to somewhere else. He stoically plodded on to his original destination, Monterey Bay, more than 100 miles to the south. Six years later, Juan Ayala actually sailed into San Francisco Bay while on a mapping expedition for the Spanish and immediately realized the enormous strategic importance of his find.

Colonization quickly followed. Juan Bautista de Anza and around 30 Spanish-speaking families marched through the deserts from Sonora, Mexico, arriving after many hardships at the northern tip of modern-day San Francisco in June 1776. They immediately claimed the peninsula for Spain. (Their claim of allegiance to Spain occurred only about

Dateline

- **1542** Juan Rodriguez Cabrillo sails up the California coast.
- **1579** Sir Francis Drake lands near San Francisco, missing the entrance to the bay.
- **1769** Members of the Spanish expedition led by Gaspar de Portolá become the first Europeans to see San Francisco Bay.
- **1775** The *San Carlos* is the first European ship to sail into San Francisco Bay.
- **1776** Captain Juan Bautista de Anza establishes a presidio (military fort); San Francisco de Asis Mission opens.
- **1821** Mexico wins independence from Spain and annexes California.
- **1835** The town of Yerba Buena develops around the port; the United States tries unsuccessfully to purchase San Francisco Bay from Mexico.
- **1846–1848** War between the United States and Mexico.
- **1847** Americans annex Yerba Buena and rename it San Francisco.
- **1848** Gold is discovered in Coloma, near Sacramento.
- **1849** In the year of the gold rush, San Francisco's population swells from about 900 to 26,000.
- **1851** Lawlessness becomes acute before attempts to curb it.
- **1869** The transcontinental railroad reaches San Francisco.
- **1873** Andrew S. Hallidie invents the cable car.
- **1906** The Great Earthquake strikes, and the resulting fire levels the city.
- **1915** The Panama-Pacific International Exposition celebrates San Francisco's restoration and the completion of the Panama Canal.

continues

a week before the 13 English-speaking colonies of North America's Eastern seaboard, a continent away, declared their independence from Britain.) Their headquarters was an adobe fortress, the Presidio, built on the site of today's park with the same name. The settlers' church, a mile to the south, was the first of five Spanish missions later developed around the edges of San Francisco Bay. Although the name of the church was officially *Nuestra Señora de Dolores,* it was dedicated to St. Francis of Assisi and nicknamed San Francisco by the Franciscan priests. Later, the name applied to the entire bay.

In 1821, Mexico broke away from Spain, secularized the Spanish missions, and abandoned all interest in the natives. Freed of Spanish restrictions, California's ports suddenly opened to trade. The region around San Francisco Bay supplied large amounts of hides and tallow for transport around Cape Horn to the tanneries and factories of New England and New York. The prospects for prosperity persuaded an English-born sailor, William Richardson, to jump ship in 1822 and settle on the site of what is now San Francisco. To impress the commandant of the Presidio, whose daughter he loved, Richardson converted to Catholicism and established the beginnings of what would soon became a thriving trading post and colony. Richard named his trading post Yerba Buena (or "good herb") because of a species of wild mint that grew there, near the site of today's Montgomery Street. (The city's original name was recalled with endless mirth 120 years later during San Francisco's hippie era.) He conducted a profitable hide-trading business and eventually became harbormaster and the city's first merchant prince. By 1839, the place was a veritable town, with a mostly English-speaking populace and a saloon of dubious virtue.

Throughout the 19th century, armed hostilities between English-speaking settlers from the Eastern seaboard and the Spanish-speaking colonies of Spain and Mexico erupted in places as widely scattered as Texas, Puerto Rico, and along the frequently shifting U.S.–Mexico border. In 1846, a group of U.S. Marines from the warship *Portsmouth* seized the sleepy main plaza of Yerba Buena, ran the U.S. flag up a pole, and declared California an American territory. The Presidio (occupied by about a dozen unmotivated Mexican soldiers) surrendered without a fuss. The first move the new, mostly Yankee citizenry made was to officially adopt the name of the bay as the name of their town.

THE GOLD RUSH

The year 1848 was one of the most pivotal in European history, with unrest sweeping through Europe, horrendous poverty in Ireland, and widespread disillusionment about hopes for prosperity throughout Europe and the East Coast of the United States. Stories about the golden port of San Francisco and the agrarian wealth of the American West filtered slowly east, attracting slow-moving groups of settlers. Ex-sailor Richard Henry Dana extolled the virtues of California in his best-selling novel, *Two Years Before the Mast,* and helped fire the public's imagination about the territory's bounty, particularly that of the Bay Area.

The first overland party crossed the Sierra and arrived in California in 1841. San Francisco grew steadily, reaching a population of approximately 900 by April 1848, but nothing hinted at the population explosion that was to follow. Historian Barry Parr has referred to the California gold rush as the most extraordinary event to ever befall an American city in peacetime. Even without the lure of gold, San Francisco's winning combination of raw materials, healthful climate, and freedom would eventually have attracted thousands of settlers. But the gleam of the soft metal is said to have compressed 50 years of normal growth into less than six months. In 1848, the year gold was discovered, the population of San Francisco jumped from under 1,000 to 26,000. As many as 100,000 more passed through San Francisco in the space of less than a year on their way to the rocky hinterlands where the gold was rumored to be.

If not for the discovery of some small particles of gold at a sawmill that he owned, Swiss-born John Augustus Sutter would have left a far less flamboyant legacy. Despite Sutter's wish to keep the discovery quiet, his employee, John Marshall, leaked word of the discovery to friends. It eventually appeared in local papers, and smart investors on the East Coast took immediate heed. The rush did not start, however, until Sam Brannan, a Mormon preacher and famous charlatan, ran through the streets of San Francisco shouting, "Gold! Gold in the American River!" (Brannan, incidentally,

- **1936** The Bay Bridge is built.
- **1937** The Golden Gate Bridge is completed.
- **1945** The United Nations Charter is drafted in San Francisco and adopted by the representatives of 50 countries.
- **1950** The Beat Generation moves into the bars and cafes of North Beach.
- **1967** A free concert in Golden Gate Park attracts 20,000 people, ushering in the Summer of Love and the hippie era.
- **1974** BART's high-speed transit system opens the tunnel linking San Francisco with the East Bay.
- **1978** Harvey Milk, a city supervisor and America's first openly gay politician, is assassinated, along with Mayor George Moscone, by political rival Dan White.
- **1989** An earthquake registering 7.1 on the Richter scale hits San Francisco just before a World Series baseball game, as 100 million watch on TV; the city quickly rebuilds.
- **1991** Fire rages through the Berkeley and Oakland hills, destroying 2,800 homes.
- **1993** Yerba Buena Center for the Arts opens.
- **1995** New San Francisco Museum of Modern Art opens.
- **1996** Former Assembly Speaker Willie Brown elected mayor of San Francisco.
- **1998** El Niño deluges San Francisco with its second-highest rainfall in history.
- **2000** Pacific Bell Park opens as the new home of the San Francisco Giants baseball team with an exhibition against the Milwauke Brewers.

bought up all the harborfront real estate he could and cornered the market on shovels, pickaxes, and canned food just before making the announcement that was heard around the world.)

A world on the brink of change responded almost frantically. The gold rush was on. Shop owners hung GONE TO THE DIGGINGS signs in their windows. Flotillas of ships set sail from ports throughout Europe, South America, Australia, and the East Coast, sometimes nearly sinking with the weight of mining equipment. Townspeople from the Midwest headed overland, and the sociology of a nation was transformed almost overnight. Not since the Crusades of the Middle Ages had so many people mobilized in so short a time. Daily business stopped; ships arrived in San Francisco and their crews almost immediately deserted. News of the gold strike spread like a plague through every discontented hamlet in the known world.

Although other settlements were closer to the gold strike, San Francisco was the famous name and, therefore, where the gold-diggers disembarked. Tent cities sprang up, and demand for virtually everything skyrocketed. Although some miners actually found gold, smart merchants quickly discovered more enduring business in servicing the needs of the thousands of miners who arrived ill-equipped and ignorant of the lay of the land. Prices soared. Miners, faced with staggeringly inflated prices for goods and services, barely turned a profit after expenses. Most prospectors failed, many died of hardship, and others committed suicide at the alarming rate of 1,000 a year. Yet despite the tragedies, graft, and vice associated with the gold rush, within mere months, San Francisco was forever transformed from a tranquil Spanish settlement into a roaring, boisterous boomtown.

BOOMTOWN FEVER

By 1855, most of California's surface gold had already been panned out, leaving only the richer but deeper veins of ore, which individual miners couldn't retrieve without massive capital investments. Despite that, San Francisco had evolved into a vast commercial magnet, sucking into its warehouses and banks the staggering riches that overworked newcomers had dragged, ripped, and distilled from the rocks, fields, and forests of western North America.

Investment funds poured into more than mining, however. Speculation on the newly established San Francisco stock exchange could make or destroy an investor in a single day, and several noteworthy writers (including Mark Twain) were among the young men forever influenced by the boomtown spirit. The American Civil War left California firmly in the Union camp, ready, willing, and able to receive hordes of disillusioned soldiers fed up with the internecine warmongering of the Eastern seaboard. In 1869, the transcontinental railway linked the Eastern and Western seaboards of the United States, ensuring the fortunes of the barons who controlled it. The railways shifted economic power bases, however, as cheap manufactured goods from the East undercut the costly articles that sailed or steamed around the tip of South America. The "Big Four"—iron-willed capitalists Leland Stanford, Mark Hopkins, Collis P. Huntington, and Charles Crocker—almost completely controlled ownership of the newly formed Central Pacific and Southern Pacific railroads, and their ruthlessness was legendary. (Much of the bone-crushing railway labor was done by low-paid Chinese newcomers, most of whom arrived in overcrowded ships at San Francisco ports.) As the 19th century came to a close, civil unrest became more frequent as the monopolistic grip of the railways and robber barons became more obvious. Adding to the discontent were the uncounted thousands of Chinese immigrants who fled starvation and unrest in Asia at rates rivaling those of the Italians, Poles, Irish, and British.

During the 1870s, the flood of profits from the Comstock Lode in western Nevada diminished to a trickle, a cycle of droughts wiped out part of California's agricultural bounty, and local industry struggled to survive against the flood of manufactured goods coming by rail from well-established East Coast and Midwest factories. Often, discontented workers blamed their woes on the now-unwanted hordes of Chinese workers, who by preference and for mutual protection had congregated in teeming all-Asian communities.

Despite these downward cycles, the city enjoyed other bouts of prosperity around the turn of the century, thanks to the Klondike gold rush in Alaska and the Spanish-American War. Long accustomed to making a buck off gold fever, San Francisco managed to position itself as a point of embarkation for supplies bound for Alaska. Also during this time, the Bank of America emerged; it eventually grew into the largest bank in the world. Founded in North Beach in 1904, the bank was the brainchild of Italian-born A. P. Giannini, who later funded part of the construction for a bridge that many critics said was preposterous: the Golden Gate.

THE BIG ONE: PART ONE

On the morning of April 18, 1906, San Francisco changed for all time. The city has never experienced an earthquake as destructive as the one that hit at 5:13am (scientists estimate its strength at 8.1 on the Richter scale). All but a handful of the city's 400,000 inhabitants lay fast asleep when the ground went into a series of convulsions. As one eyewitness put it, "The earth was shaking . . . it was undulating, rolling like an ocean breaker." The quake ruptured every water main in the city and simultaneously started a chain of fires that rapidly fused into one gigantic conflagration. The fire brigades were helpless, and for 3 days San Francisco burned.

Militia troops finally stopped the flames from advancing by dynamiting entire city blocks, but not before more than 28,000 buildings lay in ruins. Minor tremors lasted another 3 days. The final damage stretched across a path of destruction 450 miles long and 50 miles wide. In all, 497 city blocks, or about one-third of the city, were razed. As Jack London wrote in a heartrending newspaper dispatch, "The city of San Francisco is no more." The earthquake and subsequent fire so decisively changed the city that post-1906 San Francisco bears little resemblance to the town before the quake. Out of the ashes rose a bigger, healthier, and more beautiful town, although latter-day urbanologists regret that the rebuilding that followed the San Francisco earthquake did not follow a more enlightened plan. So eager was the city to rebuild, that the old, somewhat unimaginative gridiron plan was reinstated, despite the opportunities for more daring visions that the quake's aftermath afforded.

In 1915, in celebration of the opening of the Panama Canal and to prove to the world that San Francisco was restored to its full glory, the city was host to the Panama-Pacific International Exhibition, a world's fair that exposed hundreds of thousands of visitors to the city's unique charms. The frenzy of boosterism, however, reached its peak during the years just before World War I, when investments and civic pride might have reached an all-time high. Despite Prohibition, speakeasies in and around the city did a thriving business, and building sprees were as high-blown and lavish as the profits on the San Francisco stock exchange.

WORLD WAR II

The Japanese attack on Pearl Harbor on December 7, 1941, mobilized the United States into a massive war machine, with many shipyards strategically positioned along the Pacific Coast, including San Francisco. Within less than a year, several shipyards were producing up to one new warship per day, employing hundreds of thousands of people working around the clock. (The largest, Kaiser Shipyards in Richmond, employed more than 100,000 workers.) In search of work and the excitement of life away from their villages and cornfields, workers flooded into the city from virtually everywhere, forcing an enormous boom in housing. Hundreds found themselves separated from their small towns for the first time in their lives and reveled in their newfound freedom.

After the hostilities ended, many soldiers remembered San Francisco as the site of their finest hours and returned to live there permanently. The economic prosperity of the postwar years enabled massive enlargements of the city, including freeways, housing developments, a booming financial district, and pockets of counterculture enthusiasts, such as the beatniks, gays, and hippies.

THE 1950S: THE BEATS

San Francisco's reputation as a rollicking place where anything goes dates from the Barbary Coast days when gang warfare, prostitution, gambling, and drinking were major pursuits, and citizens took law and order into their own hands. Its more modern role as a catalyst for social change and the avant-garde began in the 1950s. A group of young writers, philosophers, and poets challenged the materialism and conformity of American society by embracing anarchy and Eastern philosophy, expressing their notions in poetry. They adopted a uniform of jeans, sweater, sandals, and beret, called themselves "Beats," and hung out in North Beach, where rents were low and cheap wine was plentiful. *San Francisco Chronicle* columnist Herb Caen, to whom they were totally alien, dubbed them "beatniks" in his column.

Allen Ginsberg, Gregory Corso, and Jack Kerouac had begun writing at Columbia University in New York, but it wasn't until they came west and hooked up with Lawrence Ferlinghetti, Kenneth Rexroth, Gary Snyder, and others that the movement gained national attention. The bible of the Beats was Ginsberg's "Howl," which he first read at the Six Gallery on October 13, 1955. By the time he finished reading, Ginsberg was crying, the audience was chanting, and his fellow poets were announcing the arrival of an epic bard. Ferlinghetti published "Howl," which was deemed obscene, in 1956. A trial followed, but the court found that the book had redeeming social value, reaffirming the right of free expression. The other major work, Jack Kerouac's *On the Road*, was published in 1957 and instantly became a best-seller. (He had written it as one long paragraph in 20 days in 1951.) The freedom and sense of possibility the book conveyed became the bellwether for a generation.

While the Beats gave poetry readings and generated controversy, two clubs in North Beach were making waves, notably the "hungry i" and the Purple Onion, where everyone who was anyone or became anyone on the entertainment scene appeared. Mort Sahl, Dick Gregory, Lenny Bruce, Barbra Streisand, and Woody Allen all worked there. Maya Angelou appeared as a singer and dancer at the Purple Onion. The cafes of North Beach—the Black Cat, Vesuvio's, Caffè Trieste, Caffè Tosca, and Enrico's Sidewalk Cafe—were the center of bohemian life in the fifties. When the tour buses started rolling in, rents went up, and Broadway became a sex-club strip in the early 1960s.

Thus ended an era, and the Beats moved on. The alternative scene shifted to Berkeley and the Haight.

THE 1960S: THE HAIGHT

The torch of freedom passed from the Beats and North Beach to the hippies and Haight-Ashbury, but it was a radically different torch. The hippies replaced the Beats' angst, anarchy, negativism, nihilism, alcohol, and poetry with love, communalism, openness, drugs, rock music, and a back-to-nature philosophy. Although the scent of marijuana wafted everywhere—on the streets, in the cafes, in Golden Gate Park—the real drugs of choice were LSD (a tab of good acid cost $5) and other hallucinogenics. Timothy Leary experimented with its effects and exhorted youth to "turn on, tune in, and drop out." Instead of hanging out in coffeehouses, the hippies went to concerts at the Fillmore or the Avalon Ballroom to dance. The first Family Dog Rock 'n' Roll Dance and Concert, "A Tribute to Dr. Strange," was at the Longshoreman's Hall in 1965. It featured Jefferson Airplane, the Marbles, the Great Society, and the Charlatans. At the event, the first major happening of the 1960s, Ginsberg led a snake dance through the crowd. In January 1966, Longshoreman's Hall was the site of the 3-day Trips Festival, organized by rock promoter Bill Graham. The climax came with Ken Kesey and the Merry Pranksters Acid Test show, which used five movie screens, psychedelic visions, and the sounds of the Grateful Dead and Big Brother and the Holding Company. The "be-in" followed in the summer of 1966 at the polo grounds in Golden Gate Park, when an estimated 20,000 heard Jefferson Airplane perform and Ginsberg chant, while the Hell's Angels acted as unofficial police. During the Summer of Love, in 1967, thousands of young people streamed into the city in search of drugs and sex.

The '60s Haight scene was very different from the '50s Beat scene. The hippies were much younger than the Beats had been, constituting the first youth movement to take over the nation. (They also became the first generation of young, independent, and moneyed consumers to be courted by corporations.) Ultimately, the Haight and the hippie movement deteriorated from love and flowers into drugs and crime, drawing a fringe of crazies like Charles Manson and leaving only a legacy of sex, drugs, violence, and consumerism. As early as October 1967, the "Diggers," who had opened a free shop and soup kitchen in the Haight, symbolically buried the dream in a clay casket in Buena Vista Park.

The end of the Vietnam War and the resignation of President Nixon took the edge off politics. The last fling of the mentality that had driven the 1960s occurred in 1974, when the Symbionese Liberation Army kidnapped newspaper heiress Patty Hearst from her Berkeley apartment and took her on a bank-robbing spree before surrendering in San Francisco.

THE 1970S: GAY RIGHTS

The homosexual community in San Francisco developed at the end of World War II, when thousands of military personnel returned to the United States via San Francisco. A substantial number of those men were homosexual and decided to stay in the city. A gay community grew up along Polk Street between Sutter and California. Later, the larger community moved into the Castro, where it remains today.

The gay political-protest movement is usually dated from the 1969 Stonewall raid in Greenwich Village. Although the political movement started in New York, California had already given birth to two major organizations for gay rights: the Mattachine Society, founded in 1951 by Henry Hay in Los Angeles, and the Daughters of Bilitis, a lesbian organization founded in 1955 in San Francisco.

After Stonewall, the Committee for Homosexual Freedom was created in the spring of 1969 in San Francisco; a Gay Liberation Front chapter was organized at Berkeley. In the fall of 1969, Robert Patterson, a columnist for the *San Francisco Examiner,* referred to homosexuals as "semi males," "drag darlings," and "women who aren't exactly women." On October 31 at noon, a group began a peaceful picket of the *Examiner.* Peace reigned until someone threw a bag of printer's ink from an *Examiner* window. Someone wrote "Fuck the Examiner" on the wall, and the police moved in to clear the crowd, clubbing as they went. The remaining picketers retreated to Glide Methodist Church, then marched on city hall. Unfortunately, the mayor was away. Unable to air their grievances, they started a sit-in that lasted until 5pm, when they were ordered to leave. Most did, but three remained and were arrested.

Later that year at an anti-Thanksgiving rally, gays protested against several national and local businesses: Western and Delta airlines (the former for firing lesbian stewardesses, the latter for refusing to sell a ticket to a young man wearing a Gay Power button); KFOG, for its anti-homosexual broadcasting; and some local gay bars for exploitation. On May 14, 1970, a group of gay and women's liberationists invaded the convention of the American Psychiatric Association in San Francisco to protest the reading of a paper on aversion therapy for homosexuals, forcing the meeting to adjourn.

The rage against intolerance was appearing on all fronts. At the National Gay Liberation conference in August 1970 in the city, Charles Thorp, chairman of the San Francisco State Liberation Front, called for militancy and issued a challenge to come out with a rallying cry of "Blatant is beautiful." He also argued for the use of what he felt was the more positive, celebratory term "gay" instead of "homosexual," and decried the fact that homosexuals were kept in their place at the three Bs: the bars, the beaches, and the baths. As the movement grew in size and power, debates on strategy and tactics occurred, most dramatically between those who wanted to withdraw into separate ghettos and those who wanted to enter mainstream society. The most extreme proposal was made in California by Don Jackson, who proposed establishing a gay territory in California's Alpine County, about 10 miles south of Lake Tahoe. It would have had a totally gay administration, civil service, university, museum—everything. The residents of Alpine County were not pleased with the proposal. But before the situation turned really ugly, Jackson's idea was abandoned because of lack of support in the gay community. In the end, the movement concentrated on integration and civil rights, not separatism. Gays would elect politicians who were sympathetic to their cause and celebrate their new identity by establishing National Gay Celebration Day and Gay Pride Week, the first of which was celebrated in June 1970, when 1,000 to 2,000 marched in New York, 1,000 in Los Angeles, and a few hundred in San Francisco.

By the mid-1970s, the gay community craved a more central role in city politics. Harvey Milk, owner of a camera store in the Castro, decided to run for the board of supervisors. He won, becoming the first openly gay person to hold a major public office. He and liberal Mayor George Moscone developed a gay rights agenda, but in 1978 both were killed by former Supervisor Dan White, who shot them after Moscone refused his request for reinstatement. White, a former police officer, had consistently opposed Milk's and Moscone's more liberal policies. At his trial, White successfully pleaded temporary insanity caused by additives in his fast-food diet. The media dubbed it the "Twinkie defense," but the murder charges against White were reduced to manslaughter. On that day, angry and grieving, the gay community rioted, overturning and burning police cars in a night of rage. To this day, a candlelight memorial parade is held on November 27. Milk's martyrdom was both a political and a practical inspiration to gay candidates across the country.

The emphasis in the gay movement shifted abruptly in the 1980s, when the AIDS epidemic struck the community. AIDS has had a dramatic impact on the Castro. While it's still a thriving and lively community, it's no longer the constant party it once was. The hedonistic lifestyle that had played out in the discos, bars, baths, and streets changed as the seriousness of the epidemic sunk in and the number of deaths increased. Political efforts have shifted away from enfranchisement and toward demanding money for social services and research money to deal with the AIDS crisis. The gay community has developed its own organizations, such as Project Inform and Gay Men's Health Crisis, to publicize information about the disease, available treatments, and safe sex. New cases of AIDS in the gay community are on the decline in San Francisco, but it remains a serious problem.

THE 1980S: THE BIG ONE, PART TWO

The 1980s may have arrived in San Francisco with a whimper (compared to previous generations), but they went out with quite a bang. At 5:04pm on Tuesday, October 17, 1989, as more than 62,000 fans filled Candlestick Park for the third game of the World Series—and the Bay Area commute moved into its heaviest flow—an earthquake of magnitude 7.1 struck. Within the next 20 seconds, 63 lives were lost, $10 billion in damage occurred, and the entire Bay Area community was reminded of its humble insignificance. Centered about 60 miles south of San Francisco in the Forest of Nisene Marks, the deadly temblor was felt as far away as San Diego and Nevada.

Although scientists had predicted an earthquake would hit on this section of the San Andreas Fault, certain structures built to withstand such an earthquake failed miserably. The most catastrophic event was the collapse of the elevated Cypress Street section of Interstate 880 in Oakland, where the upper level of the freeway pancaked the lower level, crushing everything with such force that cars were reduced to inches. Other heavily damaged structures included the San Francisco–Oakland Bay Bridge, shut down for months when a section of the roadbed collapsed; San Francisco's Marina District, where several multimillion-dollar homes collapsed on their weak, shifting bases of landfill and sand; and the Pacific Garden Mall in Santa Cruz, which was devastated.

President Bush declared the seven hardest-hit counties a disaster area; at least 3,700 people were reported injured and more than 12,000 were displaced. More than 18,000 homes were damaged and 963 others destroyed. Although fire raged in the city and water supply systems were damaged, the major fires in the Marina District were brought under control within 3 hours, mostly through the heroic efforts of San Francisco's firefighters.

After the rubble finally settled, it was unanimously agreed that San Francisco and the Bay Area had pulled through miraculously well—particularly compared with the more recent earthquake in Kobe, Japan, which killed thousands and displaced an entire city. After the quake, a feeling of esprit de corps swept the city as neighbors helped each other rebuild and donations poured in from all over the world. Although over a decade has passed, San Francisco is still feeling the effects of the quake, most noticeably during rush hour as commuters take a variety of detours to circumvent freeways that were damaged or destroyed and are still under construction.

During the early 1990s, nothing earth-shattering took place. The nationwide recession influenced the beginning of the decade, while the quiet rumblings of the new frontier in Silicon Valley escaped much notice. By the middle of the decade, San Francisco and the surrounding areas had discovered a new kind of gold rush—the Internet industry.

Not unlike the gold fever of the 1800s, people flocked to the western shores to strike it rich—and they did. In 1999, local media reported that every day 64 Bay Area residents were gaining millionaire status. Long before the last year of the millennium, real estate prices went into the stratosphere, and the city's gentrification financially squeezed out many of those who didn't mean big business. New business popped up everywhere—especially in the SoMa area, where startup companies jam warehouse spaces to the rafters.

As the most popular post-education destination for MBAs and the leader in the media of the future, San Francisco no longer opens its Golden Gate to everyone looking for the legendary alternative lifestyle—unless they can afford a $1,000 studio apartment.

It's impossible to guess what comes next. With fallout in the market and the stability of previously well-funded companies, the city is sure to get a dose of financial reality soon. Until then, we'll do as we always have: Let the good times roll.

Appendix B:
Useful Toll-Free Numbers & Web Sites

AIRLINES

Air Canada
☎ 888/247-2262
www.aircanada.ca

Alaska Airlines
☎ 800/426-0333
www.alaskaair.com

American Airlines
☎ 800/433-7300
www.americanair.com

America West Airlines
☎ 800/235-9292
www.americawest.com

British Airways
☎ 800/247-9297
☎ 0345/222-111 in Britain
www.british-airways.com

Canadian Airlines International
☎ 800/426-7000
www.cdnair.ca

Continental Airlines
☎ 800/525-0280
www.flycontinental.com

Delta Air Lines
☎ 800/221-1212
www.delta-air.com

Hawaiian Airlines
☎ 800/367-5320
www.hawaiianair.com

Kiwi International Air Lines
☎ 800/538-5494
www.jetkiwi.com

Northwest Airlines
☎ 800/225-2525
www.nwa.com

Southwest Airlines
☎ 800/435-9792
www.iflyswa.com

Trans World Airlines (TWA)
☎ 800/221-2000
www.twa.com

United Airlines
☎ 800/241-6522
www.united.com

US Airways
☎ 800/428-4322
www.usair.com

Virgin Atlantic Airways
☎ 800/862-8621 in U.S.
☎ 0293/747-747 in Britain
www.fly.virgin.com

CAR-RENTAL AGENCIES

Alamo
☎ 800/327-9633
www.goalamo.com

Avis
☎ 800/331-1212 in the U.S.
☎ 800/TRY-AVIS in Canada
www.avis.com

Budget
☎ 800/527-0700
www.drivebudget.com

Dollar
☎ 800/800-4000
www.dollar.com

Enterprise
☎ 800/325-8007
www.enterprise.com

Hertz
☎ 800/654-3131
www.hertz.com

National
☎ 800/CAR-RENT
www.nationalcar.com

Payless
☎ 800/PAYLESS
www.paylesscar.com

Rent-A-Wreck
☎ 800/535-1391
http://rent-a-wreck.com

Thrifty
☎ 800/367-2277
www.thrifty.com

MAJOR HOTEL & MOTEL CHAINS

Best Western International
☎ 800/528-1234
www.bestwestern.com

Clarion Hotels
☎ 800/CLARION
www.hotelchoice.com/
  cgi-bin/res/webres?clarion.html

Comfort Inns
☎ 800/228-5150
www.hotelchoice.com/
  cgi-bin/res/webres?comfort.html

Courtyard by Marriott
☎ 800/321-2211
www.courtyard.com

Days Inn
☎ 800/325-2525
www.daysinn.com

Doubletree Hotels
☎ 800/222-TREE
www.doubletree.com

Econo Lodges
☎ 800/55-ECONO
www.hotelchoice.com/
  cgi-bin/res/webres?econo.html

Hilton Hotels
☎ 800/HILTONS
www.hilton.com

Holiday Inn
☎ 800/HOLIDAY
www.basshotels.com

Howard Johnson
☎ 800/654-2000
www.hojo.com/hojo.html

Hyatt Hotels & Resorts
☎ 800/228-9000
www.hyatt.com

ITT Sheraton
☎ 800/325-3535
www.starwood.com

La Quinta Motor Inns
☎ 800/531-5900
www.laquinta.com

Marriott Hotels
☎ 800/228-9290
www.marriott.com

Motel 6
☎ 800/4-MOTEL6
(800/466-8536)
www.motel6.com

Quality Inns
☎ 800/228-5151
www.hotelchoice.com/cgi-bin/
  res/webres/quality.html

Radisson Hotels International
☎ 800/333-3333
www.radisson.com

Ramada Inns
☎ 800/2-RAMADA
www.ramada.com

Rodeway Inns
☎ 800/228-2000
www.hotelchoice.com/cgi-bin/res/
  webres/rodewayhome.html

Super 8 Motels
☎ 800/800-8000
www.super8.com

Travelodge
☎ 800/255-3050
www.travelodge.com

Vagabond Inns
☎ 800/522-1555
www.vagabondinns.com

Wyndham Hotels and Resorts
☎ 800/822-4200 in
  U.S. and Canada
www.wyndham.com

Toll-Free Numbers & Web Sites

Index

See also Accommodations and Restaurant indexes, below.

General Index

General Index

FROMMER'S® COMPLETE TRAVEL GUIDES

FROMMER'S® DOLLAR-A-DAY GUIDES

FROMMER'S® PORTABLE GUIDES

FROMMER'S® NATIONAL PARK GUIDES

Family Vacations in the
National Parks
Grand Canyon

National Parks of the
American West
Rocky Mountain

Yellowstone & Grand Teton
Yosemite & Sequoia/
Kings Canyon
Zion & Bryce Canyon

FROMMER'S® MEMORABLE WALKS

Chicago
London

New York
Paris

San Francisco
Washington, D.C.

FROMMER'S® GREAT OUTDOOR GUIDES

New England
Northern California

Southern California & Baja
Southern New England

Washington & Oregon

FROMMER'S® BORN TO SHOP GUIDES

Born to Shop: China
Born to Shop: France

Born to Shop: Italy
Born to Shop: London

Born to Shop: New York
Born to Shop: Paris

FROMMER'S® IRREVERENT GUIDES

Amsterdam
Boston
Chicago
Las Vegas

London
Los Angeles
Manhattan
New Orleans

Paris
San Francisco
Seattle & Portland
Vancouver

Walt Disney World
Washington, D.C.

FROMMER'S® BEST-LOVED DRIVING TOURS

America
Britain
California

Florida
France
Germany

Ireland
Italy
New England

Scotland
Spain
Western Europe

THE UNOFFICIAL GUIDES®

Bed & Breakfasts in
California
Bed & Breakfasts in
New England
Bed & Breakfasts in
the Northwest
Beyond Disney
Branson, Missouri
California with Kids
Chicago

Cruises
Disneyland
Florida with Kids
Golf Vacations in the
Eastern U.S.
The Great Smoky &
Blue Ridge
Mountains
Inside Disney

Hawaii
Las Vegas
London
Miami & the Keys
Mini Las Vegas
Mini-Mickey
New Orleans
New York City
Paris

Safaris
San Francisco
Skiing in the West
Walt Disney World
Walt Disney World
for Grown-ups
Walt Disney World
for Kids
Washington, D.C.

SPECIAL-INTEREST TITLES

Frommer's Britain's Best Bed & Breakfasts and
Country Inns
Frommer's Britain's Best Bike Rides
The Civil War Trust's Official Guide
to the Civil War Discovery Trail
Frommer's Caribbean Hideaways
Frommer's Food Lover's Companion to France
Frommer's Food Lover's Companion to Italy
Frommer's Gay & Lesbian Europe
Frommer's Exploring America by RV
Hanging Out in Europe
Israel Past & Present

Mad Monks' Guide to California
Mad Monks' Guide to New York City
Frommer's The Moon
Frommer's New York City with Kids
The New York Times' Unforgettable
Weekends
Places Rated Almanac
Retirement Places Rated
Frommer's Road Atlas Britain
Frommer's Road Atlas Europe
Frommer's Washington, D.C., with Kids
Frommer's What the Airlines Never Tell You